The
Dependent
City

The Dependent City
The Changing Political Economy of Urban America

Paul Kantor
Fordham University, New York

with Stephen David

Scott, Foresman/Little, Brown College Division
Scott, Foresman and Company
Glenview, Illinois   Boston   London

Library of Congress Cataloging-in-Publication Data

Kantor, Paul
    The dependent city.

    Includes index.
    1. Urban policy—United States—History.
2. Urban economics. I. David, Stephen M.,
1934–1985. II. Title.
HT123.K36 1988   307.7′6′0973   88-2808
ISBN 0-673-39782-3

1 2 3 4 5 6 7 8 9 10 — PAT — 94 93 92 91 90 89 88

Printed in the United States of America

For Anna
and
To my parents, Anthony and Pauline

In Memoriam Stephen David

Preface

SOMETIMES ideas spring from what is closest and most obvious. This book is surely such a case. It grew out of the utterly contradictory image that I saw during the late 1970s from my own university office window—the vague outlines of distant midtown Manhattan's proud skyscrapers appearing through a shroud of smoke from fires burning in abandoned buildings in the South Bronx. This vivid contrast of wealth and decay, pride and suffering, epitomized the vast changes sweeping through New York and other American cities; its magnitude also confirmed to me that such wrenching events were connected to powerful forces beyond New York City and its citizens. Yet the larger politics of this grand panorama of change were elusive. The practice of urban politics and its academic study were very much ensconced in the goings-on of the local scene, with its personalities, bureaucrats and power brokers. That the urban enigmas of our time ought to be examined through a more holistic perspective seemed as obvious as the smoke, the fires, and the skyscrapers.

This book constitutes such a perspective. Though these chapters do not offer a highly developed theory that can explain the dynamic of urban political and economic change, they attempt to move in this direction. *The Dependent City* is an eclectic response. It tries to provide original insight, but it also draws freely upon what I believe is the best social thought in order to probe the changes and frustrations of urban America. Though the scope of this study is necessarily broad, it does not attempt to be comprehensive—some important areas of urban policy, such as education, are hardly touched upon. *The Dependent City* seeks to understand the past, reveal the present, and suggest better future urban political alternatives.

I am indebted to many for helping to make this work possible. I am especially indebted to my dear friend and colleague, Stephen David. His contribution to the project was ended by his death in 1985. Steve drafted parts of Chapters 3, 4, 9, and 10. However, his understanding of the world of urban politics helped shape the conceptualization and planning of this book from the outset; his enthusiasm, even in illness, for what we set out to achieve carried through to me in my work on the project. Consequently, I am sure that Steve's contributions are also incorporated throughout this book in countless and subtle ways.

Through conversations or their reading of drafts connected with this project, many colleagues and friends provided invaluable encouragement and helpful criticism—even though they may not have realized it at the time. This includes Jewel Bellush, Bruce Berg, Janet David, Caryl and Joseph Feldmann, Martin Fergus, Richard Fleisher, Joyce Gelb, Conrad Kantor, Ira Katznelson, David Lawrence, Norton Long, Peter Lupsha, Dale R. Marshall, Dale Nelson, L. J. Sharpe, Martin Shefter, Clarence Stone, and David Tabb. Some people need to be singled out for special thanks. Paul E. Peterson's reading of an early rough draft of part of the manuscript reflected his fine professional generosity. Similarly, Dennis R. Judd provided invaluable criticism of some later drafts. Todd Swanstrom and two anonymous readers provided detailed and helpful comments on the final manuscript, making it a much better work than it would have been otherwise. John S. Covell proved to be more than a careful and competent editor at Little, Brown and Company. His encouragement of the project and his patient assistance to me throughout the creation of the book were crucial to it.

Further assistance in clarifying my ideas came from my students in my undergraduate urban politics courses and in my graduate courses in urban political economy. They graciously withstood reading early rough drafts of many chapters and made many useful comments. Their patience, interest, and enthusiasm in working out problems in the book's development helped sustain my own contribution.

Financial assistance was provided by the Mellon Foundation in a faculty development grant, a N.A.T.O. Post-Doctoral Fellowship from the National Science Foundation, a Faculty Fellowship from Fordham University, and several other grants that were given by the Fordham University Research Council. I thank the late Richard Doyle, S.J., and Deans Edward Dowling, S. J., and Dr. Mary Powers for their support and willingness to grant course reductions at critical times, permitting me to keep the research and writing moving along to conclusion.

Many people provided research assistance for me in small and in big ways. I especially wish to thank Barbara Carvalho, John Condon, William Conroy, Michael deBorja, Dorothy Krynicki, Caroline Kretz, and Shonna Mulkey. In various technical capacities, word processing assistance was provided by Terry Arroyo, Marie Conneely, Fran Koenig, and Diana Patulak.

Finally, greatest thanks go to my wife, Anna, whose loving support and words of encouragement were truly the foundation for my own effort; her patience in listening and talking about "the book" deserves more than words can convey. Gratitude also goes to my daughter, Elizabeth. Her cheerful quiet play when daddy was working was no small contribution. Though my debt to others is great, responsibility for this volume is mine alone.

Contents

BOOK TWO   THE CONTEMPORARY URBAN POLITICAL ECONOMY

CONCLUSION

The
Dependent
City

Introduction

CHAPTER ONE

Political Economy and City Dependency

N OT too many years ago, American cities stood prominently in the nation's political landscape. Racial turmoil, "white flight" from cities to suburbs, the "discovery" of poverty, fiscal crises, the ghetto, pollution, and other urban problems seemed to converge into a so-called urban crisis that won the attention of America's policymakers. There followed an outpouring of governmental programs targeted to ameliorate the urban condition, but more often than not these efforts did not succeed.

Since then, the distresses of the nation's urban areas have tended to meld into the apparent order of things. The race riots have abated, the sight of the poor has became ordinary, the disparity of suburb and ghetto is now taken more for granted, and talk of the fiscal crisis of cities has given way to routine calls for budget retrenchment. The urban problem has been displaced by other political issues in tune with more conservative times. Today the peculiar difficulties of cities are apt to be regarded as local matters that ought to be solved by making wiser community choices than in the past. "Better" local governance is the preferred remedy.

Yet these past views of the urban condition—as a special case that warrants a unique national effort, or as an ordinary circumstance that is best left to the cities—present a common danger: namely, further frustration of policy resulting from mistaken understanding of the nature of the city. Both echo the traditional Jeffersonian belief, founded on fear and antipathy, that cities are like "ulcers on the body politic" that can somehow be treated without disturbing the rest of the patient. This is implicit in the idea that one-shot crash programs can arrest urban evils or that the latter can be overcome by relying more upon locals to do what is best. Both ideas obscure the reality that the condition of cities is intimately connected to people, forces, and events beyond the locale and that any effective urban policy must contend with them.

This conclusion is best demonstrated by the experience of America's new black mayors, most of whom have been swept into power after years in the political wilderness. As big city populations grew darker and poorer, black political power in city halls also grew. The election of minority administrations

2

in traditionally white-run cities, such as Chicago, Detroit, Cleveland, or Los Angeles, symbolized a most hopeful transition, especially for those who had previously felt excluded from community power.

Once in office, however, black mayors bent on reform have discovered that their influence is often most limited on the issues that mean the most to them. For example, Detroit's mayor Coleman Young has managed to consolidate his political position to rank among the nation's major urban power brokers. As leader of a rusting central city whose high unemployment is closely tied to the fortunes of the auto industry, Young has made job creation one of his highest priorities. But he has discovered that getting business to provide more jobs is a matter over which he has little control. Plant closings in the city continue at a pace that defy the Young administration's booster efforts.

One of Mayor Young's more successful attempts to prevent a major auto plant shutdown during the early 1980s came after city officials scrambled to meet stringent demands laid down by General Motors executives as a condition for building a new Fisher Body and Cadillac plant within the city limits. The timing, planning, implementation, and even the governmental costs of this deal were not very much in the hands of the mayor or his officials. National and international competitive pressures within the auto industry during the late 1970s forced G.M. to achieve new cost efficiencies by seeking more modern plants and closing old ones. The city government had to act immediately or see the new plant operation go to some other suburb or town—an alternative that had been exercised by the automaker on previous occasions.

Yet the planning of the project, including the matter of selecting a neighborhood for the factory site, was dominated by G.M. staff who based their decisions on design and cost-effectiveness criteria. As a condition for building this project in Detroit, Mayor Young had to assemble for G.M. over $300 million in grants and loans from local, state, and federal government programs to match what other localities were offering in the way of similar inducements for the automaker's new factory. Finally, Young had to cope with the huge political repercussions of the land clearance the project required. Citywide acrimony and neighborhood protest arose from the bulldozing of the "Poletown" area in order to make way for the new plant; this involved the removal of 3,438 residents, 143 institutions or businesses (including the demolition of 16 churches, a hospital, and two schools), and the razing of 1,176 buildings (Jones, Bachelor, and Wilson, 1986; Fasenfest, 1986).

The story of external economic and political forces limiting what leaders like Mayor Young can and cannot do hardly ends with seeking jobs from corporate business in order to keep citizens working. The populations of poverty-ridden central cities are highly dependent upon government social service programs for food, cash income, housing, health care, and other necessities of life. For example, in Mayor Young's Detroit in 1983, 31 percent of city households had no earned income, 16 percent survived on welfare payments, and 29 percent received some form of social security (Hill, 1983:100). Yet resources and authority for responding to demands for these services mostly lie outside the city in the hands of federal and state agencies. For instance, cuts in federal housing programs have more or less called a halt to significant new low-income housing production in Detroit and other big cities even though they have experienced increasing homelessness during the 1980s. Similarly, public assistance (welfare) is administered locally, but resources for this program come mostly (and in many cities almost entirely) from federal and state governments. Yet it is local officials who must deal with the immediate political and social consequences of gaps in the safety net of the American welfare state.

Lest one suppose that better-off suburbs are very removed from the dependencies shared by the nation's old central cities, consider the following. Millions of families made the trek to suburbs during the last several decades, so that today America is a predominantly suburban nation. Yet suburbia does not exist as a matter of local choice. Without the huge federal and state governmental investments in highways and, to a lesser extent, mass transit that link suburbs with cities and each other, suburbia would probably have remained what it generally was in the early twentieth century—an area of isolated, poorly serviced hamlets that few bothered to visit.

Suburbia's foundations are also firmly set in other public and private institutions far removed from suburban communities. Federal authorities have long guaranteed and subsidized residential mortgages mostly for new suburban homes, fueling the flight of families from cities to the suburbs. Jobs that are now often located in suburban areas and underlie their prosperity—such as corporate headquarters and various service jobs—were once almost entirely confined to the downtowns of central cities. That these kinds of jobs moved from their original locations was much more a cause of suburbanization than a response to it. As we suggest later, the tremendous dispersal of business activity in our time reflects major changes in corporate America. The people of suburbia are caught in a web of economic and political dependencies over which they often have quite limited control.

All this is not to suggest that cities cannot do much about their problems. On the contrary, if the nature of our urban policy problems are heavily circumscribed by people and events beyond the city, then it is prudent to ask what local governments can do about them. This prompts a host of related questions. Are cities capable of tackling some urban ills better than other ones? Is local politics an appropriate political arena for those disadvantaged people who seek reforms that can substantially benefit them? Or is the dependency of cities on external institutions such that local politics is a waste of time for the poor?

Indeed, the very significance of local democratic institutions is at stake in answers to these questions. Truly democratic cities—where elected governmental leaders are responsive to the wishes of their citizens—can count for much only if the things that cities assert public control over are things that matter. Local democratic politics is reduced to a symbolic formality to the extent that exterior political and economic forces narrow urban policy issues to what is inconsequential.

The contention of this book is that the capability of city governments in the United States to control their policy problems has varied enormously across time and with respect to particular areas of public policy. Most important, this book explains why the contemporary American city faces an explosive dilemma that it cannot resolve on its own: namely, that while its political system has become progressively more open to community wishes, the city's enormous dependency on exterior economic forces seriously frustrates the ability of local political authorities to act responsively. That is, the modern city has become politically democratic, but economically dependent. While this situation has sometimes been ameliorated by the growing intervention of federal and state governments, in crucial respects the regulatory activities of higher levels of government have reinforced the city's dependent position. Any effort to address the serious urban problems of our time must take into account this dilemma of dependency if it is to succeed.

Approaches to Urban Political Economy

Answers to questions about the relevance of democracy and urban governmental capabilities depend on understanding the way localities are linked to the workings of the larger politico-economic order. If one is to assess local politics and make good prescriptions for achieving viable urban policies, it is essential to capture a sense of the economic and political *context* that shapes the policy choices cities have. This requires a holistic approach that explores the changing relationships between urban politics and economics. Such a political economy perspective can then signal the internal and external parameters that shape public problems and say something about the kinds of community choices (and the extent to which there are any local choices) that are possible in dealing with them.

The difficulty, however, is that extant social theories fall short of providing such an analytical tool kit. Three major perspectives provide some significant insights into the relationship between urban politics and economics, but each has important limitations in its capacity to integrate these two analytical "sides." These are the *community power*, the *public choice*, and the *neo-Marxist* approaches to viewing the urban political economy.

The Community Power Approach

Theorists working within the community power tradition are inclined to view city governance and policy in terms of the political coalitions—be they elite or broad-based—of interests that dominate the urban community. Consequently, they describe urban politics by way of theories that focus on the *internal pressures*, especially the competition for political power, which seem to drive governmental authorities to make policy choices. This approach has traditionally dominated the study of urban politics.

The major disagreement dividing these theorists has been whether or not the distribution of power and processes of governance are very open and democratic. The "pluralist" view (Dahl, 1961; Polsby, 1963) has stressed that in a society fragmented into large numbers of competing interests the governance of cities is bound to be very decentralized so long as the political system is organized along procedurally democratic lines. In particular, the system of competitive parties and elections together with widespread acceptance of the democratic creed ensures that virtually all groups having grievances will be heard, and can participate and gain some political influence over political authorities, if only indirectly. In contrast, "elitists" stress that American urban communities are more socially stratified than pluralists admit (Hunter, 1953; Jennings, 1964; Domhoff, 1978); the fact that a class of rich exists that possesses greater economic resources than others ensures that members of this stratum have political advantages which permit them to dominate political decisions regardless of democratic governmental institutions.

The valuable insight about political economy that this perspective provides, at least in its pluralist variant, is that there is a community political system where the struggle for power among groups and classes makes things happen. Cities do not, after all, automatically govern themselves. When there is any dispersal of political advantages and conflict among political activists within a democratically organized political setting, the internal intricacies of the system and the kinds of interests that compete for favor have much to do with the way issues are decided. Of course, this may not be true in all times and circumstances; even pluralists concede that where societies are rigidly stratified and democratic norms are weak, elitist rather than pluralist tendencies can be expected to prevail (Dahl, 1961:Chs. 2 and 3).

Nevertheless, the focus of these theorists on the competition among community political interests has limited their reach in understanding the impact of exogenous economic forces in urban politics. This fact was epitomized by the debate over the structure of community power noted above. To pluralists, "power" was conceived as the ability of an individual or group to veto or initiate a policy decision—that is, to get somebody to do something that they might not otherwise do. Thus, when New Haven mayor Edward Lee proposed an urban renewal project and eventually won the support of local business groups for this program, pluralists concluded that the mayor had power (Dahl, 1961).

However, critics pointed out that this measure of power could be illusory (Bachrach and Baratz, 1970; Lukes, 1974). How can one be sure that this mayor did not simply propose a project that he knew business would accept and systematically avoid other alternatives (like a public housing project)? Apart from being revealed by overt decision making, "power" can also be exercised covertly by "non-decision making"—the ability of some interests to keep issues from being voiced and getting on the political agenda. For instance, perhaps the mayor anticipated that if urban renewal plans were not proposed, downtown businesses would begin to leave for suburban locations or fail to expand their investment activities, leading to the kinds of things no public official wishes to be associated with—unemployment, derelict downtowns, falling city tax revenues, etc. The anticipated threat of various sanctions, such as harassment, terror, economic reprisals, or even the kinds of norms, values, and mores that powerful groups are able to propagate and get accepted as part of the prevailing "mobilization of bias" within a community can limit the kinds of political demands that are made (Bachrach and Baratz, 1970; Crenson, 1971). Non-decision making as a form of power also is neglected by elitists whose idea of political influence is characterized in terms of resourceful people (Castells, 1977:Ch. 11).

This flaw in the community power approach derives from the scope of the perspective. The focal concept of power does not systematically capture the impact of exogenous economic and political forces in shaping issues, demands, and other political relationships within the community. In respect to politics, the state is often viewed by these theorists as a kind of "cash register" that merely reflects, but does not itself influence, the preferences and demands of competing group interests.

However, the most glaring problem is the failure of the community power view to relate politics to economics. This perspective looks at city politics in terms of individuals—as aggregated into competing groups or as an exclusive stratum of elites. Consequently, the approach lacks the categories of analysis for relating broad, impersonal changes in the urban economic order to the political patterns within the local community. For example, a decline in a city's valuable manufacturing employment might cause local politicians to be more solicitous to the preferences (even if unexpressed in public) of business leaders for weaker air pollution ordinances. But this eventuality cannot be captured by community power theory (Crenson, 1971). Recent attempts to extend this perspective in ways that acknowledge the import of economic structures in indirectly shaping local political decisions are beginning to deal with this difficulty.[1]

The Public Choice Perspective

The approaches included in the public choice and the neo-Marxist traditions tend to emphasize the importance of economic forces on politics. Derived from orthodox market economic theory, the public choice theory stresses the logical application of such central economic concepts as competition, growth and profit-maximizing behavior, cost and benefit analysis, etc., to understanding political processes, chiefly in order to identify "rational" (that is, economically "efficient") forms of political behavior and public policy prescriptions (Buchanan and Tulloch, 1962; Frey, 1978; Downs, 1957; Froelich and Openheimer, 1978). With few exceptions (Tiebout, 1956; Bish, Ostrum, and Ostrum, 1973; Ostrum, 1976), this kind of approach had very limited application to urban politics until the publication of Paul E. Peterson's landmark work, *City Limits* (1981). Although Peterson's book is not entirely that of a public choice analyst, much of it is based on assumptions shared by these theorists.[2]

Peterson's most important insight—indeed, one that powerfully informs this study—is that city governments in a market economy are strongly inclined to promote the economic well-being of their communities. Capitalist cities are constrained by market forces to compete with other cities to attract people and jobs or they suffer the consequences of economic decline; it follows that local communities face very severe economic pressures in dealing with issues that pertain to urban economic development. He further concluded that cities must give priority to business expansion rather than to social programs for the poor. However, Peterson did not regard this circumstance as an entirely negative thing. He argued that city prosperity is presumably something that few dislike since it means jobs, tax revenues for public programs, and other benefits that to varying degrees trickle down to all residents in the locale.

Although this kind of analysis identifies an important source of economic constraint on city government (see also Molotch, 1980), it does not adequately consider the significance of political forces in shaping policy choices. To a large degree, this perspective relegates local political pressures to the periphery of analysis by assuming that there tends to be a consensus in cities to promote "rational" community economic goals.[3] Like economists who regard the firm as a unitary actor (Tiebout, 1956; Friedman, 1962) that seeks to maximize profits, Peterson is inclined to view the city almost as if it were actually sharing a unitary interest in promoting its economy. It is assumed that the advantages of city growth are so apparent and widely shared that only those who are mistaken or are very selfish oppose the objective of rationally enhancing the economic productivity of the city. The issues that do not have much to do with community economic well-being are the only ones that offer much room for local choice and so they are the focus of most political conflict.

Yet, as community power and neo-Marxist critics point out, this approach neglects important political forces in cities. The costs and benefits of promoting a city's economic well-being can be distributed in different ways among competing interests within a city, Indeed, even economic growth itself can be a contentious matter in many towns and suburbs (cf. Harvey, 1973; Stone, 1976; Harloe, 1977; Mollenkopf, 1983). Small shopkeepers who face going out of business to make way for a new shopping mall will pay heavily for town prosperity. Similarly, suburban homeowners who wish to preserve the serenity of their neighborhoods can usually be counted on to oppose nearby factories and retail strips even though the presence of these businesses might lower local residential tax burdens.

Defining the city's "economic interest" is apt to be as difficult as defining the so-called public interest, something that politicians and philosophers have fought over from time immemorial. Consequently, the matter of political bias in the process of promoting political support for public policies is an important aspect of the urban political economy. Public choice theory is not sensitive to this.

Neo-Marxist Approaches

Drawing upon the analytical traditions of Marx, contemporary neo-Marxists have utilized class models in order to relate urban politics and economics (Castells, 1977; Katznelson, 1981; Fainstein and Fainstein, 1982, 1983; Fainstein et al., 1983; Harloe, 1977; Tabb and Sawers, 1978). That is, they assume that class struggle over the material organization of society dominates political conflicts at all governmental levels in capitalist societies. The state, including the so-called "local state," predominantly serves the interests of the bourgeoisie in their struggle to control and repress the workers.

The state does this by acting to reproduce the capitalist class system via promoting capital accumulation (i.e., ensuring the profitability, growth, and stability of capitalism) and by stimulating the legitimation (acceptance of the idea that the capitalist system is "good") of the class order among the masses. Although early Marxists (Miliband, 1973) saw this process as very instrumental—where the ruling classes struggled to directly control state activities through political and economic pressures—more recent proponents of this perspective view the biases of the state as a much more indirect by-product of the structure (hence, the "structuralist" view) of capitalism (Poulantzas, 1972, 1978; Crouch, 1979). In fact, the latter argue that, in order for the state to function effectively to reproduce the capitalist class system and serve the general interests of the dominant class, it must be relatively autonomous from this class. For example, factions within the capitalist class may be too divided or selfish to support appropriate governmental programs for helping the capitalist class to prosper and maintain their economic dominance.

As a theoretical view that deliberately attempts to link economics and politics, neo-Marxism contributes much to our understanding of the urban political economy. Unlike community power theorists who neglect the process whereby economic forces shape political choices, neo-Marxist analysis provides a theory. Unlike the public choice perspective, neo-Marxism signals that no economic order is politically neutral and that social class is an important aspect of political conflicts. Further, this perspective points out that changes in the capitalist system during specific historical periods are likely to alter the role of the state (in promoting capitalism), redefining the ways in which the economic order limits public policy alternatives.

Despite these strengths, neo-Marxist theory leaves much to be desired as a means of understanding the links between urban politics and economics. It shares with the public choice perspective the incapacity to capture the importance of political forces in urban governance. Because neo-Marxism assumes the primacy of class economic forces in driving the activities of the state, it neglects the possibility that political power might emanate from other sources and reflect other divisions of interest (especially noneconomic ones). In particular, this view relegates the presence of democratic institutions to performing a process of legitimation that serves to mask the class system and to give the masses merely the appearance of political control.

Yet there is abundant historical evidence that business and other members of the so-called dominant class often have been divided in their expressed political interests and have been forced by popularly elected governments to accept laws that redistribute wealth and power in favor of have-nots. In addition to instances described in subsequent chapters, the most glaring cases of this kind have been in labor law, industrial regulation, taxation, and social welfare policy (Skocpol, 1980; Nordlinger, 1981).

Attempts by neo-Marxists to reconcile this evidence with their theories have been ambiguous at best. As they have recognized the import of social movements, public opinion, and the pressures of political competition in shaping state policy (Fainstein and Fainstein, 1974, 1983; Fainstein et al., 1983; Castells, 1977; Alford and Friedland, 1985:Parts III and IV; Balbus, 1981), the class theory has been stretched and redefined (such as assuming the "relative autonomy" of the state from the rich) to such a degree that all events—even those that appear to substantially favor the poor at the expense of the wealthy over the long run—are considered to be consistent with it. For example, trade union laws that measurably increased the bargaining power of workers with employers have been regarded by theorists as merely a means of imposing order on the work force, facilitating business power over the long run (Greenberg, 1985:Ch. 6). Thus, this theory is unlikely to be confirmed or rejected through empirical investigation (Balbus, 1981, 1982).

The Plan of This Book

Although we cannot formulate a theory of the urban political economy that overcomes all the limitations of past approaches, it is possible to build upon their best insights in order to probe urban economics and politics. This framework is described in the following chapter and serves to guide our analysis of the changing political economy of urban America since the founding of the Republic. Though this framework does not attempt to specify all aspects of the political and economic systems that shape urban communities, it does provide a scaffold for their investigation, and it reveals how the policy alternatives available to cities change over time.

This approach leads the reader to a most disturbing conclusion about the contemporary urban political economy in the United States—its perverse mixture of political democracy and economic dependency. These pages show why the capability of ordinary citizens to participate in democratic institutions has never been greater, but that the reality of local government economic dependency seriously frustrates public purposes on matters of crucial importance. This conundrum of democracy amid dependency explains why we face some of the most intractable urban policy problems of our time. Rooted in the urban past and often reinforced by the power and authority of higher level governments, we are compelled to fathom this dilemma in order to improve the well-being of American cities today.

Subsequent chapters convey this overarching theme as they examine the formation and evolution of America's urban political economy since 1787. These chapters show how three great urban politico-economic orders have emerged during our history as a liberal-democratic regime: *mercantile democracy*, *industrial democracy*, and, most recently, *postindustrial democracy*. Each of these urban political economies is described in respect to its form of economic organization, its popular control system, and in respect to the place of cities within the federal intergovernmental system. How these systems of control and constraint profoundly shaped the politics of local government in the developmental, redistributive, and distributive areas of public policy—and have led to the contemporary urban dilemma of dependency and democracy—is probed.

Last, the conclusion to this volume draws together these themes to consider the major public policy difficulties faced by the dependent cities of the United States. Some alternatives for expanding the political and economic choices of cities, towns, and suburbs are offered. The recommendations are oriented to utilizing the forces of urban dependency in order to liberate cities and enhance local democratic opportunities. Predictably, many of the more hopeful prescriptions are not matters of only local discretion—they, too, are contingent upon powers that lie beyond city borders.

Endnotes

1. But the difficulties inherent in this approach's attempt to conceptualize the politico-economic environment of cities in terms of individual and group categories remain. For instance, Stone (1980:980) refers to the notion of "systemic" power. This is ". . . that dimension of power in which durable features of the socio-economic system . . . confer advantages and disadvantages on groups . . . in ways predisposing public officials to favor some interests at the expense of others." The "durable features" remain ambiguous.
2. The ambitious scope and pathbreaking thesis of this work are among the things that distinguish it considerably from traditional public choice treatments of urban politics. Typically, the latter did not concern the broad issues of urban politics, economics, and public policy addressed by Peterson, who often draws upon diverse social and political theories in *City Limits*. Nevertheless, for reasons discussed above, Peterson's work reflects an attempt to extend public choice theory.
3. In fact, Peterson (1981:32) comes close to equating the interests of cities with the interests of their export industries.

CHAPTER TWO

The Liberal-Democratic Urban Political Economy

C ITIES in the United States may be conceived as forming part of a **liberal-democratic regime**, a kind of politico-economic order characterized by a division of labor between market and government.[1] Each provides a distinct but interdependent system for making decisions in the private and public sectors. In respect to the private sector, this regime is "liberal" in the broad original sense of the term that early political economists used to describe a capitalist society: one where individual competition and freedom of economic choice (especially regarding private property use) dominate economic relationships. This system of control follows a decisional logic (cf. Dahl and Lindblom, 1965:Chs. 6 and 7; Lindblom, 1977; Alford and Friedland, 1985:428) governed by market price mechanisms. That is, land, labor, and capital are allocated as though they were commodities that compete for sale in a market dominated by the laws of supply and demand.

For government, the workings of the market are of crucial import because some acceptable level of economic performance is required for the provision of public order, obtaining governmental revenues from which programs can be financed, and for generating political support. In a sense, "good economics is good politics" in this system—liberal government has a stake in promoting the productivity of the market system that provides jobs, tax revenues, and material well-being. Consequently, officials at all governmental levels are motivated to promote their economies by inducing business investment and performance.

The liberal-democratic state does not merely reflect the workings of the market, however. It exists separate from the market because it commands a monopoly of legitimate authority that is subject to a control system that is organized on a different basis than is the market (Nordlinger, 1981): namely, one in which the exercise of public power rests upon mass citizen approval, particularly through elections and interest group activities.[2]

Although this kind of state may be called "democratic," that term is much broader than the control system being referred to here.[3] More accurately, the state is constituted as a system of **popular control**. Popular control systems form the focal point of mass-authority relations in a democratic order. As such, decisions of government are tied to procedures whereby citizens are able to choose equally among competing leaders for public offices and to discipline them for their behavior in office (Lindblom, 1977; Schumpeter, 1942; Dahl, 1961, 1971). The extent to which this method of decision is realized in practice is a matter discussed below.

For business, the governmental sector is of importance for a variety of reasons. Most significantly, the state can offer inducements in order to enhance business growth and success, and it can limit business risks or help stabilize the environment for economic activity. This may be done through state intervention in the form of laws, regulations and assistance, and, more fundamentally, the protection of private property and basic economic freedoms that permit the market to function smoothly (Macpherson, 1965; Lindblom, 1977).

Thus, *in this type of regime public officials are constrained to reconcile their responsiveness to the citizenry (popular control) with the promotion of their economies (market control).* These dual control processes create a tension for government that is inherent in this type of political economy.

How government manages this tension is linked to a third dimension of liberal democracies, the **intergovernmental organization of the state**. Liberal democracies may organize the authority of the state along different lines. States may range from unitary systems that centralize governmental power to a considerable degree (as in Great Britain) to the U. S. federal system that apportions public authority and defines territorial jurisdictions among higher and lower level governments in a more decentralized fashion.

For cities, the organization of the state plays a powerful role in mediating the relationship between market performance and popular control. From the perspective of the urban political economy, federalism is more than a legal system of distributing political authority and defining governmental jurisdictions among national, state, and (via the states) local governments. In doing this, the federal governmental order also specifies the relevant market system and political constituencies to which each level of government must respond (David and Kantor, 1983).

Cities in the Liberal-Democratic Order

The **market system, popular control**, and the **intergovernmental organization of the state** constitute the main components of the political economy that constrain political authorities in managing regime tensions. Therefore, it is on the interaction of these dimensions of the liberal-democratic order that we focus our attention in respect to city governments.

The City and Capitalism: The Market Connection

The position of cities in a market economy is different from that of higher governmental units. Unlike the national government, cities cannot impose much control over the movement of people and wealth across their borders (Tiebout, 1956; Peterson, 1981). Although differences between the economic systems of cities and the national government should not be exaggerated, cities lack the ability to regulate capital movements, to control immigration by issuing passports and visas, to print currency or regulate its supply, to impose trade laws that control the import and export of commodities, or to influence other economies through military and foreign policy—powers that belong only to the national government.

For instance, the millions of families that left central cities for suburban living in recent decades were able to relocate freely and without the passports or visas required for international resettlement. That this suburban exodus seriously depleted the resident labor force and tax base of many cities was a consequence that city governments could not stop—as nation-states can do in parallel circumstances (as in South Africa, to take a recent example). Similarly, cities cannot effectively use tax and spending powers as a fiscal tool in order to influence employment levels and prices, as is the case with the national government, because the effects of city tax and expenditure policies spill over into neighboring jurisdictions. For example, those who receive tax benefits may not spend or reinvest them within the city's economy, defeating the effect of city policies on local employment levels or on prices in general (Thompson, 1965). Likewise, if city governments spend money to create jobs for their unemployed, this policy can fail because outsiders, rather than city residents, may take them.

To be sure, the national government must contend with forces imposed by the international economy. The ability of even giant industrial nations to influence their economies is subject to important limits. Nevertheless, it can be said that cities generally face a more competitive market environment than do the national and, to a lesser degree, the state governments. Economic rivalry among cities within the domestic market order disciplines urban communities to compete for capital investment and labor to a degree that is not usually found at the national level where economic development is subject to relatively greater political control. The permeability of city economies is perhaps best illustrated by the relatively large proportion of externally produced goods and services consumed by city residents as compared to the much smaller proportion of foreign goods and services purchased by American citizens (Oates, 1972)— something that can be confirmed simply by a casual inspection of goods in neighborhood shops.

Local governments are, therefore, highly vulnerable to economic penetration by the export activities of other cities and regions. In other words, they are economically dependent on market pressures to a degree that is not shared by higher-level governments within the federal system.

URBAN ECONOMIC GROWTH. This economic vulnerability has important implications for the economic development of cities and their governments. It means that the general prosperity of citizens within a city is ultimately tied to the city's market position—or competitive edge vis-à-vis other cities—in producing goods and services for *export* to other communities (Peterson, 1981).

The wealth of a city depends upon its capacity to produce goods and services for external workers. When goods are sold to a market outside of the city, labor and capital move into the city in order to increase the production of those goods. This continues until no more goods can be sold because the marginal (additional) cost of producing them exceeds the marginal value of the goods in the exterior market.

This is how cities grow (Thompson, 1965). As city export activities increase, those who are engaged in their production utilize the wealth derived from this (in the form of wages and salaries, for example) in order to consume other goods and services that other businesses supply. Further, ancillary businesses locate in the city to supply the export industries with goods or services that they need (such as hospital services needed by sales staffs) or because they can benefit from the exporter's presence or its by-products. This chain of economic activity has a multiplier effect on city incomes. Every marginal increase in export sales may eventually produce a four- or fivefold increase in economic activities within the community. Although economists disagree over the scope of economic activities that have export functions, it is this export process that is central to city economic growth.

This process of increasing city wealth is not present in the case of goods or services that are produced and consumed within the same local economy, however. The multiplier does not work because residents are merely exchanging value as producers and consumers without adding to the total wealth of the city. For instance, in New York City, Broadway theaters perform an important export function to the extent that their tickets are bought by out-of-towners (whose incomes originate from outside the city). As theater revenues are used to pay rents, salaries, or for equipment, etc., the multiplier is initiated, leading to city economic growth. In contrast, a neighborhood laundry whose services are purchased only by locals does not have this effect. These are but the crudest examples. Exactly which aspects of a city's network of private and public activities are significantly related to its export capability are not always clear, especially in large, complex urban areas that attract a diversity of export industries.

Just as expansion in export activities stimulates economic growth, a fall-off in these activities precipitates city economic decline. As a community exports less, the multiplier works in reverse to produce shrinking economic activity, often signified by unemployment lines, boarded-up shops, declining need for ancillary business functions, and a dwindling population. In effect, economic competition pressures all local governments to promote their communities' market position vis-à-vis other cities or suffer the penalties of decline or stagnation in community wealth.

PUBLIC POLICY AND THE URBAN ECONOMY. Consequently, the public policies of city governments can be understood in reference to the impact they have on the community's market position. It is difficult to rigidly differentiate public programs on the basis of their economic effects because virtually all policies probably have multiple consequences. Drawing upon Musgrave (1959) and Peterson (1981), however, we can roughly distinguish among **developmental**, **redistributive**, and **distributive** kinds of policies in order to see how a city government manages its market position.[4]

Developmental Policy. Developmental policies have a net positive effect on the economic base of a locality in that they enhance a city's competitive position within its market of cities. Even though cities have very limited ability to regulate the movement of capital or labor in their economy, it may be possible to induce or support changes in private sector economic activities in ways that enhance the local economy. As we elaborate in subsequent chapters, governmental resources may be used to alter land use, provide tax inducements to business, build housing or public facilities that are of use to businesses, and undertake a wide range of other programs that might help create a "favorable business environment." As such, developmental policies allocate governmental resources in accordance with the contributions of individuals to the production of wealth.

Redistributive Policy. In contrast, other public policies do not have this impact on the economic base of a community. Redistributive policies have a net negative impact on the economic base of a locality in that they diminish, if only in a small way, its market position as a production center vis-à-vis other cities. Today the classic case of a redistributive policy is public assistance (welfare). To the extent that it is funded by taxes imposed by local governments on its citizens and allocated to the needy who are not usually economically productive (owing to the lack of job skills, age, disabilities, etc.), city government is raising local production costs. The monies are being allocated to individuals in reverse proportion to their economic contributions to the city's productivity.

Many other policies, such as subsidized low-income housing, job creation programs, and most social services programs also are essentially redistributive because they tend to allocate resources "downward" in respect to productivity. It could be argued that some of these programs ought to be considered developmental because they are investments in "human capital." For example, providing decent housing and medical care to poor children will enable them to be productive later in life as adult workers. But this reasoning is more relevant at the national, rather than at the local, level. From the perspective of the local economy, there is no guarantee that paying for the health and well-being of children or the unemployed will ever redound to the city, for these people may move and their economic contributions would be captured by some other locale.

Distributive Policy. Finally, distributive policies are those that have highly diffuse consequences for the city's economic base; that is, they do not have very pronounced developmental or redistributive effects on the market position of the city. These policies are best exemplified by the housekeeping services, such as police and fire protection, garbage collection, street sweeping, and related activities that local governments generally undertake as a matter of routine. Although the political implications of these kinds of policies and their administration (who gets the jobs?) may be matters of political conflict and importance, their economic effects on the city as a producer are usually quite limited. While it may be the case that cities which fail to provide adequate policies and fire protection could have difficulty attracting business investment, these programs usually do not significantly promote developmental goals. The benefits of these services usually cannot be directed to those involved in export activities while being withheld from others (they have the character of what economists call "public goods"). Further, the provision of these services is unlikely to significantly affect business costs or provide many locational advantages as long as other localities also provide such services.

The City and the Political System: The Democratic Connection

In effect, cities in a market economy are driven by pressures of intercity economic competition to seek ways of promoting their economic base. Developmental policies are most relevant to this purpose. Whether cities choose to utilize public authority and resources to promote their economic productivity is, however, not an inevitable by-product of urban economic competition. Local governments and their citizens may wish to seek other community objectives even if this may mean sacrificing some economic growth. Cities are not only economic communities. Although economic theory treats them as such for the sake of analysis, in the real world they and their residents are not simply commodities in the marketplace. Cities are also social and political communities, and so local governments are constantly faced with choosing among alternative goals in allocating public power and resources.

URBAN POLITICS AND POPULAR CONTROL. The need to build political support for public initiatives is central to any governmental order. But in a liberal-democratic one, this must be done within a system of power that follows the logic of popular control of public decisions. At all levels of government, this requires that officials seek power and consent by attempting to increase their political followings among voters and by bargaining out differences among competing interests over issues and resources.

Federalism ensures that cities operate under rather different parameters than does the national government in building political support. At the national level, citizens who are dissatisfied with one or more decisions of government cannot easily leave its jurisdiction. As a result, political demands must be bargained out and all must accept the outcome. Although U.S. citizens and businesses historically have enjoyed relatively great freedom of mobility as a result of the nation's relatively superior (stable) domestic political environment and international trading position, this masks the very real power that is available to the national government to regulate the "flight" of people and business if it so chooses; this is best evidenced by the highly restrictive controls on the movement of citizens practiced by many weaker nation-states, particularly in Eastern Europe and the Third World.

But in the case of cities, if the process of bargaining over political differences should prove too costly or produce unfavorable outcomes, individuals and *directly yes. But income level say thro zoning requirements etc.*

groups may be able to choose the "exit" option—resolve the conflict by relocating to another political unit that is more sensitive to their demands (Hirschman, 1970; Cox, 1973). In effect, because cities cannot control citizenship, their ability to accommodate political demands is subject to special limits. In bargaining out conflicts and promoting political support, city political authorities must consider the consequences that these outcomes have on private sector relocation—particularly the "exit" or threat of disinvestment by businesses or others who belong to the revenue-providing segments of the population.

Although not all residents who are highly mobile belong to higher-income classes, it is certainly this segment that is most able to relocate, and it is their contributions to the city in the form of business investment, tax ratables, skilled labor, and general socio-economic resources that give them important economic leverage within this relocational process. In contrast, at the national level the political power of these advantaged population groups hinges more on the bargaining resources that they can muster in dealing with political authorities, such as their capacity to fund political campaigns or their ability to organize lobbies, etc. States tend to fall somewhere in between the national and local governments in respect to this relationship. But the inability of state governments to control citizenship and their limited territorial boundaries probably places them in a position similar to that of some large cities.

The Question of Political Privilege: Is There "Popular" Control? This aspect of the popular control process of cities might be considered a fatal flaw in the democratic order that invariably biases urban governance in favor of a single class, as Marxists are inclined to conclude. But that conclusion does not necessarily follow. For several reasons, the liberal–democratic state can achieve considerable autonomy from the market.

Most fundamentally, state autonomy springs from the authority inherent in being able to " . . . make and apply decisions that are binding upon any and all segments of society" (Nordlinger, 1981:11; cf. Weber, 1947). Business people do not make and administer the law. But office-holders of the state do. Separate from the market, the legitimate institutions, laws, and processes of the democratic state provide political authorities with a base for imposing their own preferences upon others and for regulating economic and political conduct (Krasner, 1984; Benjamin and Duvall, 1985; Lane, 1986). Therefore, just how tensions between market and popular control are managed is a matter subject to mediation by state authorities acting on their own.

This source of governmental autonomy is buttressed by other properties of the liberal-democratic order. Most important, democratic states follow a process of decision that is not identical to the market and does not have to reflect its logic. Office-holders are driven by a system of power that is ultimately dependent upon competition for mass political followings. Consequently, it may not be possible for political authorities to satisfy business or other resourceful groups (even if political leaders are so inclined) and, at the same time, secure political support. The politically relevant coalitions needed for supporting political authorities simply may not accept what the most mobile and economically advantaged demand (Polanyi, 1944:Chs. 12 and 13; Nordlinger, 1981:Chs. 5–7; Dahl, 1961).

This reality is best evidenced by the fact that business leaders so often grumble about what governments are doing. Government activities that are considered by business as "wasteful" or "intrusive" or "unnecessary" are more than likely to reflect perfectly rational political calculations by government leaders who seek their own specific goals, particularly that of political survival. For instance, in 1986 New York City and State officials decided to abandon a massive highway project that was to improve access to the city's lower Manhattan central business district and promise major redevelopment opportunities. Known as Westway, this project was strongly endorsed by New York real estate, financial and business leaders, as well as many city and state officials. But Westway's allegedly destructive consequences for adjacent neighborhoods, nearby fishing areas (owing to landfill in the Hudson river), and absorption of resources from the city's mass transit fund prompted years of protests, lawsuits, and public acrimony by citizens' groups, and it eventually divided local politicians. Their pressures and legal tactics defeated attempts to move the project along so often that the project's proponents halted further consideration of the plan. Although this case is by no means typical of how cities make development decisions (see Chapter 11), it does show how popular control institutions afford a power base for competing for political influence with economic institutions.

There are other characteristics of liberal-democratic politics that also work to enhance state autonomy from market institutions. The reality of issue areas in democratically organized political systems has been well documented; attempts to influence government tend to be specialized. Some issues may be capable of uniting a single class or group, but many others are not. Political demands are rarely broadly shared by an entire class (Dahl, 1961; Long, 1969). For instance, higher taxes are often opposed by some upper-income classes who wish to do without added public services. Yet this policy is also sometimes supported by other wealthy people who see important indirect benefits of better public services, such as enhanced property values or other business advantages. If political authorities cannot avoid making decisions that alienate some wealthy people, then the economic power of this class diminishes in political relevance.

Even when the well-off do share interests on particular issues, that fact alone may not provide the political leverage necessary to dominate government. For one thing, most political issues are not worth the cost of undertaking relocational activities (that is, leaving the local political system) even by those who are very mobile (Cox, 1973). It has been found, for example, that local business taxes generally are not highly consequential in attracting or discouraging actual business moves because labor costs and other locational advantages overshadow business taxes as factors in making industrial location decisions (see Chapter 10).

Further, the economic power that springs from the ability of the more resourceful interests to disinvest in (or move capital from) a community is not constant. As explained below, the market position of cities vis-à-vis other cities is a variable thing. City governments that have sufficiently powerful market positions may be able to tie many businesses to the community, undercutting their economic power as a means of political influence.

The upshot of this is that revenue-provider groups—especially business—are likely to have a privileged position within local popular control systems, but this does not mean that they can always dominate these systems. Because their position of privilege coexists within a political framework that otherwise disperses decisional control and ensures a separation of state and market, it is an inherent source of tension. But it is not necessarily the dominant system characteristic. It is part of what Lindblom (1977) terms an "uneasy relationship" between market and democracy that seems inherent in liberal-democratic orders. Federalism enables these privileged groups to more easily influence government policy at the local level than at the national level. Yet even this does not ensure their hegemony.

Cities and the Federal System

Federalism distributes authority and defines jurisdictions among governmental levels. In doing so, this intergovernmental system specifies the different markets and political systems to which national, state, and local governments must be responsive. Consequently, the politico-economic context at each governmental level has policy biases; some kinds of policies are easier for cities to promote than are others.

ECONOMIC DEPENDENCY AND FEDERALISM. Because cities face a more competitive economic environment than does the national government, their less secure market position impinges on governmental policy choices more severely than is the case with the national government (and, to a lesser degree, many states). All other things being equal, city governments can be expected to bias their policy choices in favor of developmental objectives because these programs enhance the competitive market position of the jurisdiction. Although local officials may favor programs that do not have substantial developmental payoffs for various reasons—such as the promotion of social stability or egalitarian ideals or to win political popularity—the competitive market environment of cities discourages such choices.

In contrast, the advantageous market position of the national government provides a relatively permissive policy context compared with that of local government (Peterson, 1981:Ch. 4; David and Kantor, 1983). In particular, policies that attempt to redistribute incomes more equitably or endeavor to achieve other egalitarian objectives, such as racial equality, are likely to find greater support at the national level because these policies involve less severe trade-offs with developmental objectives. Distributive policies at the national governmental level are less dependent on these market considerations, however; they do not have much effect on the market position of any level of government in the federal system.

States stand somewhat in between cities and the national government in respect to these economic effects of public policy. Although states vary enormously in size and economic diversity, their typically larger economic bases in comparison to most cities distinguishes them. To some extent, this can be a source of economic independence. But because they lack the capability to regulate the movement of capital and labor across their borders, they hold a very different position than does the national government. Therefore, one would generally expect the impact of their economic position on their policy biases to run a middle path between local and national government in respect to all three areas of public policy.

In effect, the general economic structure of federalism provides an economic context that favors developmental policy objectives at the local level and favors greater public choice on questions of policy at the national level. States fall somewhere in between local and national government in respect to economic constraints on public policy.

POPULAR CONTROL AND FEDERALISM. Since popular control systems promote responsiveness of political authorities to the masses, these institutions can serve to check governmental policy biases that derive from their market environment. At the local level, however, this capability is subject to an important countervailing influence. Local governments are sensitive to threats by revenue-provider interests to relocate away from or disinvest in the locale. Consequently, this reinforces the bias of local government in favor of developmental policy priorities. By the same token, local political demands for redistribution can be thwarted by such threats of relocation and disinvestment by economically important people and businesses. This feature of popular control is an inherent source of tension in local politics.

In contrast, the workings of popular control at the national governmental level reinforce the permissiveness in public policy that arises from the relative economic independence of this level of government. Since revenue-providers are not able to leave the governmental system as easily, their political power is more dependent upon their ability to bargain and to compete within the process of popular control. Compared to local government, their dependence on political struggle (rather than economic leverage) in national politics limits their ability to influence policy. Consequently, national politics is apt to be a more open, competitive forum for bargaining among diverse interests over a wide range of issues. In particular, national governmental authorities stand in a more potentially responsive relationship on redistributive policy matters.

In sum, the structure of federalism has some inherent public policy biases that political authorities may or may not choose to serve, but must work within. All other things being equal, the less advantageous market position of cities and the privileged position of business (and other revenue-providers) within their political systems favor developmental priorities in policy. The national government's less dependent market position and more competitive system of popular control afford a relatively permissive governmental environment in respect to policy choice. States fall somewhere in between these.

The Changing Political Economy of the City

These tensions and sources of policy bias that affect city governments do not influence their public policy choices in a static way. Each dimension of the urban political economy—the market order, popular control, and the inter-governmental system—can undergo change.

Urban Economic Change

First, the economic dependency of cities can vary over time as local, regional, national, and, indeed, even international changes in capitalism occur, forging particular kinds of urban economic systems that govern the competitive relationships among cities. As we indicate in subsequent chapters, the history of urban America has been one of periodic transformation in city economic systems, each system distinguished by different ways of utilizing land, labor, and capital in the process of production and exchange.

As new urban economic systems have emerged, the opportunities for particular cities to secure dominant market positions have also changed. This is most consequential. Cities that manage to obtain dominant market positions face limited competition from other cities, a relationship that increases their economic independence in the process of inducing capital investment. Potentially, at least, their more advantageous economic position within the urban order permits them to be more responsive to popular control pressures because of the diminished "exit" opportunities of economically important population groups. On the other hand, urban economic systems that disperse market power reverse these relationships, imposing more severe limits on policy decisions. In effect, the economic dependency of cities in a market order can vary enor-mously—and, therefore, so can the obstacles that this places on city governance.

Further, economic change can alter the character of public policy. Develop-mental, redistributive, and distributive forms of public policy are distinguished by their impact on the community economic base. But if the nature of the city economic base changes, then the relevance and meaning of particular kinds of public programs also change. For example, when city economic growth is contingent on the provision of certain supportive services, such as streets, water supply, and other physical infrastructure, those programs assume a develop-mental character. But if the system of production and exchange alters in ways that diminish the significance of a locality's physical plant for business growth, then city infrastructure programs are likely to assume a different economic impact—perhaps they can become more distributive.

Changes in Popular Control Systems

Second, the efficacy of popular control systems as a means of informing and checking city governmental authorities can change over time. Thus far, we have discussed popular control—that core of democratic governmental institu-tions—as though it were of one kind. But in fact the democratic state has undergone major developmental changes since the founding of the Republic, and it continues to do so in other liberal-democratic regimes elsewhere in the world. As an illustration, city political authorities during the first decades of the new United States typically faced an electorate that was essentially a select group (since only property-holders could usually vote) of Western European males who generally returned leading gentlemen of the community to office after relatively uncontested, disorganized, personal political appeals. It goes without saying that two centuries later city politics is colored by very different patterns.

Untangling all the complex changes that are possible in popular control systems (much less, explaining them) is well beyond our scope. But it is possible to identify some indicators of changes that are most likely to enhance popular control as a means of influencing political authorities. Popular control can best regulate governmental authorities when it is fully developed to support the general state of what Dahl (1971) calls **polyarchy**, a rough approximation of democracy. This is a condition in which " . . . top authority is assigned in response to a routinized indication of citizen wishes . . . in which any one citizen's vote is by some formula counted as equal to any others" (Lindblom, 1977:133).[5] Accordingly, the constraining influence of popular control systems on political authorities depends upon the opportunities they provide for the demands of the mass public to (1) *get voiced* and (2) *become issues* that are actually debated by governmental leaders who (3) can be *held accountable* for their behavior via mass electoral sanctions.

First, popular control systems must provide opportunities for making political demands. If governmental authorities can easily limit the kinds of demands coming to government from citizens to "safe" issues that conform to official predilections, popular control systems are left to deal only with a restricted universe of matters that are not very reflective of what citizens otherwise wish to voice. For instance, if prevailing political organizations are incapable of representing demands for the redistribution of wealth among social classes, this implicitly discourages the voicing of such grievances.[6]

Second, popular control systems must enable demands to become political issues. If demands that are voiced cannot become issues that are debated by state authorities, popular control systems fall far short of the polyarchal ideal. The ability to express grievances must be accompanied by private and public organizational capabilities to translate demands into matters of collective choice (that is, issues) that are the focus of consideration by political authorities. Intermediary associations, including political parties and interest groups, which are not under the tutelage of those in political authority, are usually important for achieving this. But less formal devices, such as the freedom and resources to form political coalitions, in the process of linking masses to governmental elites are also relevant.

Finally, the process of popular control must also ensure political accountability. In a polyarchal system, political authorities ought to be routinely held to account and easily sanctioned, usually via electoral systems, by the mass citizenry for their behavior in office. Unless the mass public is able to discern who is responsible for the way they have been governed and can "throw the

FIGURE 2-1   Three Dimensions of Popular Control Systems: Continuum from
Polyarchy to Social Control

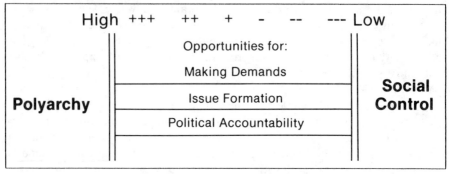

rascals out" in favor of alternative leaders, popular control hardly can be considered a very efficacious system of controlling the state.

Precisely what institutional arrangements are required to achieve this polyarchal condition are not always clear. For example, voters may function in a responsible (that is, effective) fashion in disciplining politicians even when alternative political programs are not clearly defined because voters are inclined to make broad retrospective judgments about how they have been treated (Key, 1966). Exactly how accountability is made possible—whether through internally democratic political parties, campaigns among personalities signaling competing sentiments, or even less organized, programatic processes—is less important than the result.[7] What matters most, suggests Schumpeter, is that there is some " . . . institutional arrangement for arriving at political decisions in which individuals acquire the power to decide by means of a competitive struggle for the people's vote" (1942:269).

Consequently, because popular control can vary in all three of these respects, its capability as a system of power over political authorities is subject to extensive change (see Figure 2-1). At one extreme, when political leaders can easily manipulate demands to what they regard as "safe" matters, when issues cannot form into program choices, and when political authorities cannot be routinely held accountable by mass participation, popular control is in reality an empty shell of procedural formalism. It is actually a means of social control of masses by elites who utilize it to legitimate their power, but in fact are only checked by the threat of mass unrest. At the other extreme of this continuum, when popular control conforms to something like a polyarchal system, it can be a channel through which masses may powerfully influence governmental authorities.

Changes in the Federal System

Finally, intergovernmental changes can mediate the relative impact of market and popular control structures in urban governance. As we document in the pages that follow, the federal order is highly capable of alteration in the way that it regulates market forces and popular control systems at the local level.

FIGURE 2-2   The Liberal-Democratic Political Economy.

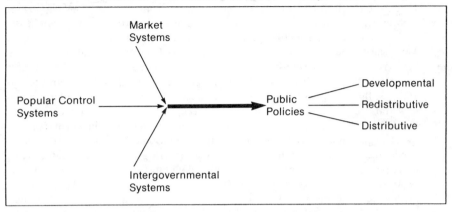

Historically, the activities of the national and state governments have expanded and contracted enormously in all three areas of public policy, especially within recent decades. For instance, because higher levels of government have been more economically advantaged and more open to political demands for redistributive programs than have local governments, the history of urban social welfare politics has been one of increasing intergovernmental intervention and resources.

Politics, Economics, and the Liberal-Democratic City

City politics in a liberal-democratic order can be viewed in respect to the constraints that market systems, popular control systems, and intergovernmental regulations impose upon local community political leaders and their citizens (see Figure 2-2). The remainder of this volume explores each of these aspects of the urban political economy in respect to the developmental, redistributive, and distributive areas of public policy. The fact that all these dimensions of the urban political economy have such tremendous capacity for change means that their actual consequences for local politics must be examined within specific historical contexts. It is to the great urban political economies of the old and new United States—the mercantile, industrial, and postindustrial democracies—that we turn.

Endnotes

1. Drawing from Elkin (1981, 1985), Lindblom (1977), and Macpherson (1965), this concept of "regime" denotes a politico-economic order that is defined by its dominant control systems for achieving public purposes. This contrasts with very different uses of the term elsewhere (cf. Easton, 1965:190–211 and Fainstein et al., 1983, for example). In addition to the above works, this approach to political economy is informed by some other especially pertinent literature. On the idea of control systems the earlier work of Dahl and Lindblom (1965) is also relevant. Loosely related perspectives are Polanyi (1944) and Schumpeter (1942), whose

works focus on the tensions of capitalism and democracy as separate, but related, systems. Explicit discussions of the democratic state and the problems that extant theoretical approaches present in comprehending it may be found in Benjamin and Elkin (1985), Nordlinger (1981), and Alford and Friedland (1985).

2. Thus, the democratic state has a separate existence from other social institutions in the sense that it plays a constitutive role of its own—a source of constraint on those who are within its orbit of power and authority. Although this is central to our analysis, this point is acknowledged to at least some degree by both pluralist and neo-Marxist writers. For instance, both recognize the importance of national defense as a parameter on the state's service to group demands in a democracy or the struggle among classes within the capitalism. Some Marxist writers, such as Poulantzas (1973), go considerably further and argue that state authority is exercised according to certain decision rules that oblige all to act in prescribed ways regardless of class background (a point discussed in Balbus, 1981:5).

3. Democracy is a much broader concept than what is suggested here as "popular control." The latter refers more to the method (or control process) of mass-public authority linkage in a democratic order. Although there is no consensus on the meaning of democracy, it most often is considered a type of political community— not only a method—whose institutions and practices stress values of liberty, equality, and fraternity. See the excellent discussion in Pennock (1979) and related points in note 7 below.

4. These policy types should be distinguished from those of Theodore J. Lowi (1964), who differentiates public policies on the basis of their impact on social groups.

5. The features of what Dahl and Lindblom call polyarchy in their joint and individual works have varied considerably (cf. Dahl and Lindblom, 1965; Dahl, 1956, 1971, 1982; Lindblom, 1977). For our purposes, the concept denotes a version of a democratic order that can actually be approximated in its essentials in the real world. As such, polyarchy places popular control institutions at its core and requires contestation for political office and very inclusive political participation by the masses. In addition, other characteristics commonly associated with the democratic political order are considered by Dahl and Lindblom to be part of polyarchy; these include freedom to form and join associations, alternative sources of political information, free and fair elections, and other rights and practices.

6. As noted in Chapter 1, it is possible to discourage grievances from being articulated by way of techniques of intimidation as well as by maintaining prevalent norms, mores, and cultural traditions (Bachrach and Baratz, 1970). It is impossible to identify all dimensions (that is, the sources of political bias in a society's dominant institutions) of this so-called non-decision making process (Frey, 1971). But it is possible to examine the extent to which the component parts of popular control systems, especially electoral systems and dominant political leaders, are disposed in favor of certain kinds of demands.

7. Nevertheless, political systems that (1) are highly inclusive of the citizenry in respect to voting and political participation and (2) provide organized contestation for office are probably the most likely to afford citizens greatest opportunities to discipline political authorities (Dahl, 1971; Downs, 1957). If political participation is discriminatory (and therefore limited) and/or costly in respect to monitoring political leaders and making vote choices (e.g., owing to such things as complex ballot choices, lack of party organizations, etc.), the capability of citizens to monitor, inform, and discipline political authorities tends to be weak. See Chapter 8 for a full discussion of this.

References for Introduction

Alford, Robert R. and Roger Friedland. 1985. *Powers of Theory*. New York: Cambridge University Press.

Bachrach, Peter and Morton Baratz. 1970. *Power and Poverty*. New York: Oxford University Press.

Balbus, Isaac D. 1982. *Marxism and Domination*. Princeton, N.J.: Princeton University Press.

Balbus, Isaac D. 1981. "The End of a Marxist Theory of Politics." *Paper Delivered to the 1981 Meeting of the American Political Science Association,* September 1981, in New York City.

Banfield, Edward C. 1960. *Political Influence*. New York: Free Press.

Banfield, Edward C. and James Q. Wilson. 1965. *City Politics*. Cambridge: Harvard University Press.

Benjamin, Roger and Raymond Duvall. 1985. "The Capitalist State in Context" in Roger Benjamin and Stephen L. Elkin, eds. 1985. *The Democratic State*. Lawrence: University of Kansas Press, Ch. 2.

Benjamin, Roger and Stephen L. Elkin, eds. 1985. *The Democratic State*. Lawrence: University of Kansas Press.

Bish, Robert L., Elinor Ostrum and Vincent Ostrum. 1973. *Understanding Urban Government*. Washington, D.C.: American Enterprise Institute.

Block, Fred. 1977. "The Ruling Class Does Not Rule." *Socialist Review*, Vol. 3 (May), 4-12.

Bowles, Samuel and Herbert Gintis. 1982. "The Crisis of Liberal Democratic Capitalism: The Case of the U.S." *Politics and Society*, Vol. 11, No. 1, 44-51.

Buchanan, James and Gordon Tulloch. 1962. *The Calculus of Consent*. Ann Arbor: University of Michigan Press.

Castells, Manuel. 1977. *The Urban Question*. Cambridge: MIT Press.

Cox, Kevin R. 1973. *Conflict, Power and Politics in the City*. New York: McGraw-Hill.

Crenson, Matthew. 1971. *The Un-Politics of Air Pollution*. Baltimore: Johns Hopkins University Press.

Crouch, Colin, ed. 1979. *State and Economy in Contemporary Capitalism*. New York: St. Martin's.

Dahl, Robert A. 1982. *Dilemmas of Pluralist Democracy*. New Haven: Yale University Press.

Dahl, Robert A. 1971. *Polyarchy*. New Haven: Yale University Press.

Dahl, Robert A. 1961. *Who Governs?* New Haven: Yale University Press.

Dahl, Robert A. 1956. *A Preface to Democratic Theory*. New Haven: Yale University Press.

Dahl, Robert A. and Charles Lindblom. 1965. *Politics, Economics and Welfare*. New York: Harper and Row.

David, Stephen and Paul Kantor. 1983. "Urban Policy in the Federal System: A Reconceptualization of Federalism." *Polity*, Vol. 16 (Winter), 283–304.

Domhoff, G. William. 1978. *Who Really Rules? New Haven and Community Power Re-Considered*. New Brunswick, N.J.: Transaction Books.

Downs, Anthony. 1957. *An Economic Theory of Democracy*. New York: Harper and Row.

Easton, David. 1965. *A Systems Analysis of Political Life*. New York: Wiley.

Elkin, Stephen L. 1985. "Pluralism in Its Place: State and Regime in Liberal Democracy" in Roger Benjamin and Stephen L. Elkin, eds. 1985. *The Democratic State*. Lawrence: University of Kansas Press, Ch. 5.

Elkin, Stephen L. 1981. "State and Regime in the American Republic." *Paper Delivered to the American Political Science Association*, in New York City.

Fainstein, Susan, et al. 1983. *Restructuring the City*. New York: Longman.

Fainstein, Norman I. and Susan Fainstein. 1983. "Regime Strategies, Communal Resistance and Economic Forces" in Susan Fainstein et al. 1983. *Restructuring the City*. New York: Longman, Ch. 7.

Fainstein, Norman I. and Susan Fainstein, eds. 1982. *Urban Policy under Capitalism*. Beverly Hills: Sage.

Fainstein, Norman I. and Susan Fainstein. 1974. *Urban Social Movements*. Englewood Cliffs, N.J.: Prentice-Hall.

Fasenfest, David. 1986. "Community Politics and Urban Redevelopment: Poletown, Detroit and General Motors." *Urban Affairs Quarterly*, Vol. 22 (September), 101–123.

Frey, Bruno. 1978. *Modern Political Economy*. New York: Wiley.

Frey, Fredrich. 1971. "Comment: On Issues and Non-Issues in the Study of Power." *American Political Science Review*, Vol. 65 (December), 1081–1088.

Friedman, Milton, 1962. *Capitalism and Freedom*. Chicago: University of Chicago Press.

Froelich, Norman and Joe Openhiemer. 1978. *Modern Political Economy*. Englewood Cliffs, N.J.: Prentice-Hall.

Gordon, David. 1977. "Class Struggle and the Stages of American Urban Development" in David C. Perry and Alfred Watkins. 1977. *The Rise of the Sunbelt Cities*. Beverly Hills: Sage, pp. 19–54.

Greenberg, Edward S. 1985. *Capitalism and the American Political Ideal*. Armonk, N.Y.: M. E. Sharpe.

Harloe, Michael, ed. 1977. *Captive Cities*. London: Wiley.

Harvey, David. 1973. *Social Justice and the City*. Baltimore: Johns Hopkins University Press.

Hill, Richard Child. 1983. "Crisis in the Motor City: The Politics of Economic Development in Detroit" in Susan Fainstein et al. 1983. *Restructuring the City*. New York: Longman, Ch. 3.

Hirschman, Albert O. 1970. *Exit, Voice and Loyalty*. Cambridge: Harvard University Press.

Hunter, Floyd. 1953. *Community Power Structure.* Chapel Hill: University of North Carolina Press.

Jennings, M. Kent. 1964. *Community Influentials.* New York: Free Press.

Jones, Bryan D., Lynn W. Bachelor with Carter Wilson. 1986. *The Sustaining Hand: Community Leadership and Corporate Power.* Lawrence: University of Kansas Press.

Katznelson, Ira. 1981. *City Trenches.* New York: Pantheon Books.

Key, V. O. 1966. *The Responsible Electorate.* New York: Vintage Books.

Krasner, Stephen D. 1984. "Approaches to the State: Alternative Conceptions and Historical Dynamics." *Comparative Politics,* Vol. 16 (January), 223–246.

Lane, Robert E. 1986. "Market Justice, Political Justice." *American Political Science Review,* Vol. 80 (June), 383–402.

Lindblom, Charles E. 1977. *Politics and Markets.* New York: Basic Books.

Long, Norton E. 1969. "The Local Community As an Ecology of Games" in Edward C. Banfield, ed. 1969. *Urban Government.* Revised edition. Glencoe: Free Press, pp. 465–489.

Lowi, Theodore J. 1964. "American Business, Public Policy, Case Studies and Political Theory." *World Politics,* Vol. 16 (September), 677–715.

Lukes, Steven. 1974. *Power: A Radical View.* London: Macmillan.

Macpherson, C. B. 1965. *The Real World of Democracy.* London: Oxford University Press.

Miliband, Ralph. 1973. *The State in Capitalist Society.* New York: Oxford University Press.

Mollenkopf, John. 1983. *The Contested City.* Princeton, N.J.: Princeton University Press.

Molotch, Harvey. 1980. "The City As a Growth Machine: Towards a Political Economy of Place" in Harlan Hahn and Charles Levine, eds. 1980. *Urban Politics.* New York: Longman, pp. 129–150.

Musgrave, Richard A. 1959. *A Theory of Public Finance.* New York: McGraw-Hill.

Nordlinger, Eric. 1981. *On the Autonomy of the Democratic State.* Cambridge: Harvard University Press.

Oates, Wallace E. 1972. *Fiscal Federalism.* New York: Harcourt, Brace Jovanovich.

Ostrum, Elinor. 1976. *The Delivery of Urban Services.* Beverly Hills: Sage.

Pennock, J. Roland. 1979. *Democratic Political Theory.* Princeton: Princeton University Press.

Peterson, Paul E. 1981. *City Limits.* Chicago: University of Chicago Press.

Polanyi, Karl. 1944. *The Great Transformation.* Boston: Beacon Press.

Polsby, Nelson. 1963. *Community Power and Political Theory.* New Haven: Yale University Press.

Poulantzas, Nicos. 1978. *State, Power and Socialism.* London: New Left Books.

Poulantzas, Nicos. 1973. *Political Power and Social Classes.* London: New Left Books.

Schultz, William. 1985. *Urban Politics: A Political Economy Approach.*

Englewood Cliffs: Prentice Hall.

Schumpeter, Joseph. 1942. *Capitalism, Socialism and Democracy*. New York: Harper and Row.

Skocpol, Theda. 1980. "Political Response to Capitalist Crisis: Neo-Marxist Theories of the State and the Case of the New Deal." *Politics and Society*, Vol. 10, No. 2, 155–201.

Stone, Clarence N. 1980. "Systemic Power in Community Decision Making: A Restatement of Stratification Theory." *American Political Science Review*, Vol. 74, No. 4 (December), 978–990.

Stone, Clarence N. 1976. *Economic Growth and Neighborhood Discontent*. Chapel Hill: University of North Carolina Press.

Tabb, William K. and Larry Sawers, eds. 1978. *Marxism and the Metropolis*. New York: Oxford University Press.

Thompson, W. R. 1965. *A Preface to Urban Economics*. Baltimore: Johns Hopkins University Press.

Tiebout, John. 1956. "A Pure Theory of Local Expenditures." *Journal of Political Economy*, Vol. 64, 416–424.

Weber, Max. 1947. *The Theory of Social and Economic Organization*. New York: Free Press.

BOOK

I

Historical Urban Political Economies in the United States

TWO urban political economies existed in the United States prior to the formation of the contemporary liberal-democratic city system. Mercantile democracy emerged during the seventy years following the American Revolution. Although cities at this time were subject to neither highly developed capitalist market systems nor well-institutionalized popular control mechanisms, their politics can be best understood as a response to the process of creating these dual control structures. Developing within a new federal state system, these liberal-democratic city governments undertook vigorous activities in all the major areas of public policy—development, distribution, and redistribution. By the Civil War, however, the passing of this governmental order was occasioned by changes that the urban mercantile democracies helped bring about.

Urban industrial democracy arose after the Civil War. In this political economy, cities assumed a central place in the nation's rapidly changing capitalist system, and urban political leaders confronted the new structures of mass democratic politics. It was a period of relative economic and intergovernmental independence for most larger cities of the United States; their politics focused on the struggle over the influence and meaning of popular control structures in local governance. This politico-economic order departed sharply from the mercantile era and from the contemporary urban political economy. Yet it illustrates the enormous scope for change in liberal democracies and reveals the political and economic origins of our time.

Mercantile Democracy: The Formation of a Liberal-Democratic Urban Order, 1787–1860

CHAPTER THREE

Mercantile Democracy

IT is tempting to look at city politics in the early decades of the Republic and see a world of simplicity and splendid isolation. Today's familiar urban problems, such as traffic congestion, industrial poverty, air pollution, soaring crime rates, and racial strife were virtually unknown. While citizens and political leaders faced woes of their own time and place, the scale of their difficulties at least matched the diminutive size of the cities. Even the largest of them were so compact that one could easily walk from one end of the city to another down their twisting pathways and roads. They had yet to experience the massive shock waves that industrialization and other social changes would later usher in during an era of dramatic urban growth. In a predominantly rural nation, the city had not yet become a truly important place to live; travel to cities along the nation's common roads was typically long, arduous, and painfully slow. The goings-on of Mainstreet generally began—and ended—on Mainstreet.

Nevertheless, the city of the new Republic was not a self-contained world where politics was bound to an insular and slowly changing urban community. Rather, the politics of these cities was decisively influenced by a torrent of exogenous political and economic forces in the years between the Revolution and the Civil War. Three features of the city's political economy were of decisive importance. First, a federal system of government developed from the nation's constitutional beginnings and defined a new political position for cities in America. Second, the nation's preindustrial economic order matured, circumscribing a growing role for cities in this economic system. These two politico-economic events coincided with the growth of democratic ideals and institutions within local politics. The interplay of these forces created urban America's first political economy: mercantile democracy.

Federalism: A New Governmental Order for Urban Politics

From the perspective of the nation's cities, the American Revolution and the new constitutional order that followed thrust them into a radically new political world. The colonial experience was one of considerable centralized control exercised by the Crown (or Parliament). Most major cities were chartered by the Crown. The charters for municipal corporations in England as well as in the New World were viewed as unalterable contracts that provided cities with a unique protected status within the British Empire.

Cities in the colonial order were intended to promote commerce for the mother country; their charters were designed to protect this particular economic role. Consequently, chartered cities were given powers to subsidize and regulate their local economies, such as extensive authority to regulate markets, provide bounties to attract skilled labor, regulate prices, and, most important, the power to admit "freemen" into the city, a status necessary before one could be accepted into a particular craft.

The city's protected status in this highly centralized system of government was shattered by the Revolution. In 1777, the Continental Congress approved the Articles of Confederation that accorded primacy to state governments. The states, in turn, acted to limit the economic independence of cities and democratize their governance by issuing numbers of new city charters and amending old ones.

The states, however, used their new authority to promote the same set of economic policies that the cities had been following: namely, the adoption of protectionist measures that impeded interstate commerce and trade. The weak national government, which was composed solely of a Congress (with no executive or judicial branch), had no authority to establish a uniform currency, to protect the enforcement of contracts, or to prevent state and local regulations that restricted commerce. Consequently, property, financial, and commercial groups led a movement to restructure America's intergovernmental organization (Redford, 1965:81–83).

What emerged from the Constitutional Convention was a novel federal system of government that cast cities into yet a different intergovernmental environment. This system was based on three principles. First, the Constitution divides governmental authority between the national government and the states; the distribution of powers owned by each level can be altered only by amending the Constitution itself (not unilaterally). Both levels establish their own governmental structures and can exercise power directly over individuals and businesses. Second, the national government has those powers specifically delegated to it and those that may be implied from their express powers. Within its scope of authority, the national government is supreme. The states have all the powers not delegated to the national government except those denied them by the Constitution. Last, the Constitution establishes the realm of concurrent jurisdiction wherein both state and national governments can tax and spend for the general welfare.

The Urban Impact of Federalism

The new federal order thrust cities into a far more competitive economic and political environment, ending their era of "protective independence." First, the Constitution created what was in effect a "free trade zone" throughout the nation for commerce, guaranteeing opportunities for the mobility of goods, capital, and labor. Among the express powers given the national government was the authority to regulate foreign and interstate commerce and to coin money and control its value. In addition, there were prohibitions against the states coining or issuing money, impairing the obligation of contracts, levying duties on goods from another state, or preventing migration from state to state.

No longer would states or cities, relying on their colonial prerogatives or rights under the Articles, be able to regulate their economies by interfering with interstate and foreign trade. Each would have to compete with one another in order to promote commerce within their respective jurisdictions. Only the national government was exempt from this, since it alone could impose tariff duties, issue passports, coin money, and otherwise control the movement of capital and people across its national borders.

Liberated from the tyranny of royal control, cities and states faced the uncertain prospects of greater competition with each other for the economic resources with which to govern themselves. Until the Civil War, the Supreme Court upheld and elaborated this distribution of power as it established itself as the arbiter of constitutional disputes. In *McCulloch v. Maryland* (1819) and in later cases, the court liberally interpreted the implied powers clause of the Constitution, giving Congress the right to choose any appropriate means of carrying out the powers of the national government and invalidating state laws that interfered with the exercise of this authority.

Second, federalism fostered a more competitive political environment for cities. It did so by carving out large areas of shared or overlapping jurisdiction among the national government, states, and cities; as a result, city interests seeking governmental aid would be able to "shop" for favorable forms of governmental assistance in dealing with their public problems. In the period up to the Civil War, governmental policies were adopted that involved two or more levels of government (see below), demonstrating the constitutional reality of concurrent powers in the federal system. Equally important, the practice of various groups pressuring local, state, and national government for assistance soon emerged on major policy issues of the day (Redford, 1965:119).

In creating a more pluralistic intergovernmental environment for cities, the new federal system also terminated their last vestiges of political independence. The Constitution reaffirmed the Articles by casting the city as a creature of the state. Consequently, the city charters, which were viewed before the Revolution as sacred compacts that could not be changed unilaterally, continued to come under attack by state legislatures. The essence of the state argument was that municipal charters were legislative statutes that could be changed at the will of the legislature " . . . as clay in a potter's hands" (Gluck and Meister, 1979:32). During political battles that continued into the first part of the nineteenth century, the position that municipal corporations were mere agents responsive and subordinate to the state tended to prevail. In 1819, Chief Justice John Marshall declared in the Dartmouth College case that incorporation was a grant of political power and thus could be modified by the state legislature. Thus began a long history of state involvement in the affairs of the city.

By forging a system of government that specified different jurisdictional responsibilities as well as areas of concurrent authority between states and the nation, a new liberal politico-economic environment for city politics was created. Stripped of their semifeudal protections in an empire commonwealth, America's cities entered into a governmental order that fostered greater political and economic competition.

The Preindustrial Economy and the City

The politics of America's early cities must also be looked at in reference to their economic setting. While the federal system defined important political constraints for cities, cities were also influenced by the prevalent economic system of the period, a preindustrial economic order. The early cities emerged out of an economy in which they remained overshadowed in economic importance by their agricultural surroundings. The nation was a largely self-sufficient rural economy where the business of most Americans was on the land, not in the city, in work undertaken on farms or in households, rather than in factories, warehouses, or offices located in urban areas. Only 5 percent of the nation's population lived in cities at the time of the first decennial census taken in 1790. Although the numbers of people who lived within urban areas grew throughout most of the decades up to the Civil War, the rural character of the nation's economy prevailed. Up to the first two decades of the nineteenth century, urbanization barely kept pace with the movement of thousands of settlers into the frontier. In 1860, only about one-fifth of all Americans were living in places where the population measured 2,500 or more (Glaab and Brown, 1967:26).

Few cities during this preindustrial age achieved imperial proportions. The typical cities had populations numbering no more than a few thousand or less. In 1820, the nation contained only twelve cities with populations greater than 10,000, and in them lived over two-thirds of America's total urban population. The country had only two cities of unusually large size, New York City and Philadelphia; in these two cities lived one-third of the total urban population. This pattern began to change in the two decades immediately preceding the Civil War. By 1860, the old walking cities of the preindustrial period came to characterize urban America much less; there were 101 cities of over 10,000 in population, including eight of over 100,000.

The Strategic Economic Function of the Mercantile City

Despite their diminutive presence, these cities played a strategic economic role in America's preindustrial order. Unlike the modern city, in which all roads lead to the central business area, in the preindustrial era "the streets of every large city led past the warehouse to the piers," (Glaab and Brown, 1967:27) in order to tap the resources of America's hinterland of land and sea. As such, the primary economic function of the city was commerce and trade. Through these mercantile cities, farmers in rural areas could exchange their agricultural surplus for goods shipped from abroad or produced by craftsmen located in the cities. In this way, the nation's preindustrial cities acted to convert what might otherwise have been a self-sufficient agricultural economy into a more commercialized system by organizing a market for domestic agricultural products.

Consequently, these mercantile centers were invariably located on waterways in order to promote the exchange of domestic and foreign goods. Initially, the major cities were located along the coast in order to function as ports within the colonial system. But with the expansion of the frontier and settlement of vast rural areas, these port cities developed important commercial functions: They housed the discounting, lending, wholesaling, retailing, and other entrepreneurial functions important for marketing the products of the hinterland and supplying rural populations with finished goods. As the population shifted westward with the development of interior lands, smaller cities appeared at strategic points on major inland waterways, such as the Mississippi and Ohio river systems or the Great Lakes; they supported the expanding penetration of the frontier by carrying on commercial and trading activities, much as the larger coastal cities did.

The prime mover in the cities' commercial and trading activities was the merchant capitalist, a sedentary entrepreneur whose business activities encompassed nearly every aspect of commercial trade (Taylor, 1951:11). Typically, these individuals bought and sold at retail and wholesale; they sometimes built and usually owned their own ships or other means of transport; in addition to trading on their own capital, they often acted as commission agents or factors for others, assumed insurance risks, and even performed various banking functions. As trade grew during the nineteenth century, greater specialization of commercial activities occurred as the merchant's role became more specialized. After 1815, the merchant community typically became more fragmented into retailers, jobbers, domestic wholesalers, manufacturer's representatives, auctioneers, marine insurance brokers, and the like. Prominent among these commercial capitalists were the ubiquitous factors or commission agents who traded goods for others by acting for principals in distant cities and arranging long-term credits upon which many planters and farmers were dependent (Taylor, 1951:11; Warner, 1968:79).

Manufacturing was of secondary importance in the mercantile city. As late as 1840, the ratio of investments in commercial activities as compared to industrial activities in eastern seaboard cities was about 7 to 1 (Pred, 1966:146–152). Typically, the mercantile city functioned as a craft center where artisans clustered to produce durable and luxury goods on a small scale and for limited markets. Artisans sewed shoes, built wagons, etc., with a helper or two and often with the aid of family or a servant. But workers did not labor under the close price and time disciplines of manufacture for large wholesale markets. Most craft workers were either independent contractors hiring out on a job-by-job basis or were shopkeepers retailing the products they produced by themselves. Although urban manufacturing grew in importance by midcentury, these industrial activities remained small scale and were intimately tied to the agrarian–commercial economy (Warner, 1972).

The Urban Consequences: Commercialization and City Growth

The workings of this preindustrial economy imposed important constraints on the development of the commercial city, a fact having far-reaching political consequences. As noted previously, the prosperity of a locality in a market economy is dependent on the city's ability to export goods and services. By expanding their export market, cities bring money into their environs in exchange for their services and products. This increased income then enters the local economy to create still more wealth. The individuals and businesses involved with export activity have "new" money to spend within the city, prompting new or expanded businesses to emerge in order to satisfy the increased demand that is created by this additional wealth.

In the mercantile era, the primary means by which a city expanded its export market was by increasing the supply of goods from rural areas. This was so because domestic trade (inland hinterland trade and goods received from other port cities) far outweighed foreign trade in importance and because manufacturing was of slight consequence for most cities until the later years of the period (Pred, 1966:146–148). As merchant capitalists broke down rural self-sufficiency by commercializing agriculture, a market system that centered in the cities was born. Those cities that were most successful at spearheading this change and gaining a competitive edge in developing an export sector were the ones that grew most in wealth and prosperity.

THE BARRIERS TO CITY GROWTH. The major obstacles to urban economic growth during the mercantile era were physical barriers that impeded the exchange of goods between rural and urban areas and among the commercial centers themselves. Neither high-value manufactured goods nor bulky agricultural products could be sold at a profit without overcoming the transportation problems of postrevolutionary America. While the United States possessed vast natural resources and potentially rich agricultural output, commercialization of these resources could not be exploited unless the physical barriers to hinterland trade could be overcome (Taylor, 1951; McKelvey, 1973; Gordon, 1968). At the close of the War of 1812, the only means of hauling bulky goods over significant distances on land was by way of heavy wagons drawn along common roads or turnpikes by four- and six-horse teams. This kind of transportation was so prohibitively expensive that it made it all but impossible to market these commodities.

A U.S. Senate committee reported in 1816 on the obstacles to the development of inland commerce:

> A coal mine may exist in the U.S. not more than ten miles from valuable ores of iron and other materials, and both of them will be useless until a canal is established between them, as the price of land carriage is too great to be born by either (Taylor, 1951:132).

The same report pointed out that a ton of goods could be shipped 3,000 miles from Europe to America for about $9 while for the same sum it could be moved only 30 miles overland in America on the primitive system of turnpikes and common roads. Little wonder that the early commercial centers were exclusively

America's port cities and major river towns. At the prevailing inland freight rates, none but the most valuable commodities could be carried very far; farmers were unable to market their bulky produce at a distance, and they lacked the ability to purchase even lighter manufactured products.

By the same token, the enormous time involved in transporting all kinds of goods was a further obstacle to commercialization. In 1817, the time required for freight shipments from Cincinnati to New York City was on average 52 days (Taylor, 1951:443). A lag of this duration between shipment and arrival not only discouraged regular commercial connections; it also meant that inland farmers and merchants could never be sure of the likely market prices for their commodities. In a period of two months, the market could become glutted and an entire crop sold for a loss. Unless the time lag between shipment and actual market sale were shortened, the risks were too great for commercialization of large agricultural areas (Watkins and Perry, 1977:29).

Consequently, these physical barriers to commerce meant that urban growth and prosperity would remain limited and would invariably be concentrated in those cities that were strategically located at break-in-bulk points along major waterways and established coastal seaports. In effect, nothing like a truly national economy could exist as long as the difficulties of regular commercial exchange bounded the commercial city. The cities would remain poor, small, and economically isolated appendages in an agricultural society.

Consequently, city development and prosperity were tied to important transportation improvements that permitted easier, faster, and cheaper commercial penetration of the sprawling new nation. Better roadways, fast river steamboats, and, most important, the construction of canals and railroads were the major transportation innovations that influenced the course of urban development. Each of these transportation improvements reduced the costs, time, and uncertainties involved in shipping the agricultural surplus to the cities, thereby expanding the regional trading base of particular cities located at the terminus of the newly enlarged trade routes. As a result, it was not sufficient for a city to be advantageously located along natural waterways, at natural coastal harbors, or established turnpikes in order to enjoy economic growth. It was also necessary that localities build on natural locational advantages by promoting transportation improvements into the hinterland that would enlarge their export markets.

THE POLITICAL SIGNIFICANCE OF COMMERCIALIZATION.   The political implications of this fact for city governments were enormous. Transportation innovations and the successes of their merchant capitalists in commercializing the city's hinterland could spell the difference between stagnation and prosperity for local communities. With the introduction of each transportation breakthrough, cities and their political leaders faced the prospect of fierce competition with other cities, old and new, to win economic dominion over their regions. Local politics could not remain isolated from this important transformation without neglecting the prosperity and well-being of the community itself. Conversely, cities entered into an era where their political decisions could not help but be influenced by the rise of these regional rivalries for economic growth.

Popular Control and the City: Incipient Democracy

Federalism and the nation's emerging economic system together fashioned a new external environment for cities. But the politics of the mercantile city must also be understood in reference to its internal political arrangements, which defined the processes by which local governmental choices would be reached. The ways in which city governments cope with their external environment is mediated by the views and preferences of those who can win local political power, define decisional alternatives, and formulate and execute public programs. The American Revolution sparked an intense awakening of democratic idealism and active building of governmental institutions based on the notion of popular control of political authorities. This kind of democratic awakening was also found at the local level of government where interest in democratic reform grew.

Initially, reformers at the state and local levels sought to change local governmental institutions that were established prior to the revolution in order to encourage greater opportunities for popular control. Most of the colonial charter arrangements had established corporations for city governments that were highly oligarchical. Many towns were chartered in accordance with English tradition wherein cities were ruled by "closed corporations" or self-perpetuating councils (where councilors themselves would select a successor on the death or resignation of one of the members). Elsewhere, more "open" forms of local government were used, including town meetings in New England where voters elected selectmen to conduct the day-to-day affairs of the community. Nevertheless, tight franchise requirements limited the right to vote. This, together with traditional inequalities in social status and wealth, assured power and leadership to the wealthy, particularly those gentlemen of high social standing in the community.

In the aftermath of the Revolution, over a score of towns were granted new charters by reformers in the newly independent states. One of their major aims was to encourage more popularly based local government. As a result, many closed corporate structures were eliminated, and new bodies of aldermen were elected by enlarged electorates for short terms. In a few cities, the franchise was even extended to all male taxpayers, and annual elections were held.

Merchant Oligarchy

Despite these reforms and the flood of democratic idealism unleashed by the Revolution, the governance of the mercantile city never became very egalitarian. The slow development of democratic practice and participation, together with the economic power of preindustrial elites, favored oligarchical rule in most cities for many decades. The colonial pattern of community leadership by patrician gentlemen of social standing in the locality continued until the era of Jacksonian democracy ushered in sweeping changes. The latter impacted all levels of government during the second quarter of the century, opening up opportunities for greater mass involvement in the political parties, the bureaucracy, and elective office.

In response to the spirit of Jacksonian democracy as well as purely local campaigns by the disenfranchised, a long series of reforms were adopted all across America to assure wider participation in local government (Bensen, 1961). The number of elected offices in cities were greatly expanded, wards were instituted in local elections, making campaigns cheaper and easier to conduct, compensation for officials was begun, and the use of secret ballots in local elections became widespread. Most important, property qualifications for voting were gradually eliminated for adult males.

Nevertheless, these and other reforms generally failed to overturn oligarchical politics in most cities during the commercial era. The realization of these reforms was felt only gradually at the local level. For example, in New Haven the secret ballot was introduced in 1826, and property qualifications were tacitly abandoned as a restriction on voting years before they were formally abolished in 1845 (Dahl, 1960:22–25). However, the increased participation did not lead to significant policy changes by city governments. The newly enlarged electorates chose to defer to new elites by supporting mercantile leaders who dominated the economic activities of the community. As organized party competition emerged in New Haven, the nominees of both major national parties were indistinguishable in social origins, occupations, and achievements; they reflected popular taste for government by urban America's "new rich"— the merchant and professional classes of the day (Dahl, 1960:28).

Similar patterns were repeated elsewhere. Merchant leaders, rather than worker–voters, almost invariably stepped into the positions of power abandoned by their patrician predecessors. Even in New York City, whose pace of political development may have been in advance of other urban communities, increasing mass participation in local party politics did not substantially displace traditional arrangements until near midcentury. As the old patrician–merchant elites began to leave political offices to more popular candidates, New York City notables continued to be prominent in party affairs as leaders, fundraisers, and other functionaries after 1845 (Bridges, 1984:71–73, 128–131). Even in the newly developing cities of the West, the leading merchants were the prime movers in town promotion and management well into the nineteenth century. "Throughout the West," describes Wade, "the pattern was everywhere the same, with city-council lists reading like the local business directory" (Wade, 1959:78).

The merchant communities whose members dominated the economic life of the city found that their power and position were easily transferred to the business of running local government. Public, professional, and philanthropic worlds in the mercantile city were virtually inseparable. Having strong roots in the community, these individuals typically worked alongside other notables of established prominence, such as honored and respected preachers, lawyers, and the occasional patrician gentleman to dominate the public affairs of the commercial city.

Incipient Popular Control Systems and Preindustrial Politics

Systems of local popular control during the ante-bellum era generally were procedurally democratic forms of party politics whose impact on the distribution of power were limited by the preindustrial socio-economic arrangements of the day. At a time when industrialization had yet to produce sharp, divisive social cleavages based on class, the major competing parties were quite inclusive socially, each striving to represent the "general interests" of all classes as articulated by traditional economic leaders. "Jackson, Commerce and Our Country," urged the New York City Republicans, who, like other party organizations, found that voter appeals based on national issues, ethnicity, religion, and related political cleavages dominated the political game (Bridges, 1984:69–70). Although these patterns began to manifestly change during the last ante-bellum decade or so, their effects on local political power, issues, and politics only became very salient after the Civil War.

In sum, democratic aspects of the American urban regime were put into motion during the commercial era, but these institutions had yet to constitute a system of constraint that was very independent of traditional political practices until the dawn of the industrial age. The procedures and organization of mass politics had developed in advance of transformations associated with industrialization that gave popular control a very different meaning. The policies and politics of America's early cities took place in a political setting where the values and perspective of the cities' merchant community could remain ascendant.

The Liberal-Democratic Urban Political Economy

In reviewing the forces that made up mercantile democracy, we see an urban environment of distinctive shape. Far from being isolated political entities, the nation's early cities formed part of a liberal-democratic political economy. Federalism broke down the semifeudal protections that had been built around America's cities; it constituted a new intergovernmental order where the allocation of powers and jurisdictions among governmental units created a more competitive environment for cities.

Cities also formed part of an economic order that promised greater competition and interdependence among them. The preindustrial economy of post-revolutionary America was maturing as cities, expanding their commercial and trading functions, were breaking down rural self-sufficiency in order to generate greater wealth and prosperity for their communities. By reaching into the hinterland to scoop up their regions' resources and divert them to their wharfs and warehouses, cities were extending their influence and building a commercial economy. With this arose the prospects of increasing economic competition among cities for growth and community resources.

Such diversity, competition, and pluralism in the external environment of the city was not, however, paralleled by similar patterns within the local communities. The democratic ideals of the Revolution had only begun to transform oligarchic traditions of urban leadership into political systems based on very effective popular control. How the interplay of these forces shaped public policy in the mercantile democracies is probed in the following chapters.

CHAPTER FOUR

The Politics of Development: Contest for Regional Economic Dominion

A LTHOUGH the role of cities in promoting their communities' economic growth was hardly novel even in the opening years of the Republic, the public policies and politics of city governments in this activity were distinctive. The politico-economic forces of the era made economic development the priority of local government and supported a politics dominated by merchant elites.[1]

Developmental Policy: Government Promotion of Transportation

Policies to promote the economic well-being of America's mercantile democracies were intimately bound up with the workings of the preindustrial economy. In an economic order where the resources for fueling the urban growth lay mainly outside of the city in the nation's vast hinterland, the priority of urban political leaders invariably focused on enhancing the city's position as a marketplace. Consequently, authorizations of public money for market houses and detailed regulations for the operation of the town's public markets were among the earliest ordinances and greatest responsibilities of local government. Measures to protect the public against adulterated food, false measurements, and rigged prices were important matters to local officials.

Policies for internal economic regulation of the city did not dominate policies for urban economic development, however. In fact, during the decades following the Revolution cities typically undertook less ambitious steps to monitor and regulate their marketplaces than in the period preceding (Teaford, 1975). Far more important were policies to promote *access* to the city's market itself. The major obstacles to city economic development existed outside the cities rather than within them. Commercial penetration of the hinterland by merchant capitalists in the cities depended on unchaining trade and commerce from the world of turnpikes, slow-moving riverboats, and coastal shipping. Consequent-

45

ly, developmental policies invariably focused on promoting transportation improvements to rural areas in order to enhance the city's economic position as a regional center for trade. The two most important development programs for the cities were the construction of canals and railroads. Along with other internal transportation improvements, such as steamboats, better turnpikes, and regular overseas packet service, these programs spearheaded a transportation revolution that eventually liberated the commercial cities of America from their limited territorial bonds.

Barriers to Commercialization: The Rise of Public Intervention

ECONOMIC OBSTACLES. How these programs for transportation improvements came to dominate city economic development strategies is a matter that goes beyond the politics of any particular city. In part, this choice of strategy was a function of the enormous obstacles that the underdeveloped American economy imposed on such ventures. Although the United States in the nineteenth century is often thought of as the golden age of laissez faire, the reality is that important economic barriers ensured that governmental assistance was inevitable for supporting the development of the merchant economy.

Most important, building pathbreaking transportation linkages through a largely undeveloped hinterland was a risky venture that promised at best late and uncertain returns on investment. Few canals or railroads could be built to exploit established channels of trade. Outside of limited areas along the Atlantic seaboard, most transportation improvements extended from an established urban center out into relatively undeveloped areas until very late in the nineteenth century (Goodrich, 1960:11). Since these undertakings had to depend for most of their revenue on the eventual settlement and the economic activity that the improvements themselves might generate, those who first put up the money could not expect early, direct returns from their investment. Even if the road, rail, or canal improvement proved successful, the original investors could not possibly capture all the economic benefits of the project; most benefits would be diffused throughout the community in the form of rising real estate values, more jobs, bigger markets and higher prices for commodities, and increased governmental revenues.

Another obstacle to development was the scarcity of private capital in the United States for financing transportation improvements. Whereas the capital needed for the largest turnpike could be calculated in hundreds of thousands of dollars, funds required for a canal of any significant size were rarely less than a million dollars and, more typically, were five or ten times that sum (Taylor, 1951:48). Outside New England, even capital for turnpike construction was difficult to raise from private sources. Most private savings were in the hands of small savers whose primary concern was security. Large pools of venture capital required for canals and even the early railroads were not available from private savers in the United States.

Finally, there was relatively little experience in the use of the corporate form, an institution that was necessary in order to mobilize and manage the resources for large transportation improvements. In the early days of internal improvements, private corporations were relatively rare. They required special legislative acts for their creation and were frequently viewed with suspicion as instruments of monopoly privilege. Outside the field of banking, few existed with much capital or business experience.

FEDERAL OBSTACLES TO COMMERCIALIZATION. All these economic barriers to development ensured that promoters of commercialization would have to seek governmental assistance for their endeavors. Such economic circumstances do not reveal how and why *city* governments came to play an important role in America's transportation revolution, however. As merchant communities turned to the nation's new federal system of government, they sought assistance for improvements from all three levels—cities, states, and the national government. But the workings of this intergovernmental system quickly revealed that all three levels of government could not play equal roles in the politics of urban development. The dominant role fell to cities and their state governments.

Sectional Politics. The story at the national level begins with Secretary of the Treasury Albert Gallatin's plan for a federal program of internal (that is, "internal" national) improvements, released in 1808. Congress requested Gallatin to propose a comprehensive plan for federal support of the construction of roads and canals. Gallatin proposed a federal transportation system linking the cities along the Atlantic seaboard and connecting eastern cities with the West. The linkage with the West would be done through the construction of a canal in the State of New York—where the only significant opening in the Appalachian mountain range existed—supplemented by four turnpikes through the mountains connecting eastern cities from Philadelphia to Savannah with rivers beyond the mountains.

The program foundered on this latter recommendation, however. Southern representatives saw the New York canal as linking the North and the West, while neglecting their region. The new turnpikes were not a very adequate means of connecting southeastern cities with the undeveloped areas beyond the Appalachian Mountains. Moreover, the most promising routes were outside the deep South through Pennsylvania and Maryland. Without the construction of a federal transportation system to breach the mountains, the West would have to continue to use inland waterways and remain linked with southern cities by transporting their goods via the Mississippi River (Goodrich, 1960:Ch. 2, especially 43–48). Southern opponents were joined by representatives from New England who viewed the Gallatin plan as one that would promote out-migration from their area to the West and aid the cities of New York, Philadelphia, and Baltimore to the disadvantage of Boston. Support for the program was limited to the West and the Middle Atlantic states—the areas that would most benefit from increased East–West trade (Taylor, 1951:21).

During the next several decades, sectional rivalries between the rural slave-holding South and the commercial and industrializing North intensified, making federal action even less likely. Southern opposition to Henry Clay's "American System"—which provided tariff protection for embryonic northern industries and internal improvements linking the North and West—is illustrative of the stalemate at the federal level. Further, representatives from the Middle Atlantic area eventually withdrew their support for federal involvement after their states had constructed transit improvements and it thus appeared that federal money would only aid less-developed sections of the country.

While federal assistance did eventually materialize when rival sectional interests could agree on particular railroad projects that simultaneously benefited northern, southern, and western states, sectional conflicts over internal improvements blocked significant federal aid until the decade prior to the Civil War. Consequently, urban mercantile groups were forced to resort to state and local governments in their drive to commercialize America's heartland. As a result of the national government's failure to exert leadership, what emerged was a diffuse struggle among cities and states in a game of intergovernmental warfare for economic growth.

The Politics of Canals

The landmark event that precipitated this struggle was the building of the Erie Canal in 1825. It catapulted New York City to a position of tremendous economic power far beyond the confines of its East Coast location and unleashed a wave of commercial rivalries among cities all over the United States. For New York and other eastern cities, the rural area having greatest potential for development was the West (today the Midwest), a farming region having extremely fertile soil and large numbers of widely scattered farmers engaged in subsistence agriculture. The West's great distance from eastern cities and the presence of the Appalachian Mountain barrier essentially closed off significant direct trade with the eastern seaboard cities.

Consequently, the prevailing trade route with the West utilized inland river systems leading to the Mississippi River and other major North–South waterways. During the earliest decades of this period, such cities as St. Louis, Cincinnati, Louisville, and Pittsburgh sprang up as a result of their strategic locations along the Ohio, Mississippi, and Missouri river systems; New Orleans, located at the mouth of the Mississippi, became the second busiest port in the nation by the 1820s. Commodities were shipped to these settlements where they were then loaded onto ships traveling to the Gulf of Mexico bound for East Coast cities and Europe. Although this trade route was time consuming and expensive, it was the only economic alternative to costly overland transportation. For example, it was cheaper to ship goods from Pittsburgh to Philadelphia via this long route than to ship the same commodities directly by wagon, a distance of only some 300 miles (Taylor, 1951:9,159).

If these trade patterns had gone unchecked throughout this entire period, southern cities—and the South as a region—would have been the beneficiary for opening up the market of the West. Economic growth in the eastern seaboard cities would have been limited to further development of their own region and to increased international trade (Goodrich, 1961:221). However, merchants in New York did not permit this development and sought to compete for the rich prize of the West by initiating a pathbreaking canal project.

Very few canals were constructed in America prior to New York's "experiment." In 1816, only about 100 miles of canals were built in all of the United States; these generally proved to be such financially unsuccessful ventures as to offer little encouragement to investors. Further, the building of canals required massive expenditures of capital and considerable engineering skill in their planning and execution, resources which were scant in America of the early 1800s. Nevertheless, the State of New York had an enormous geographic advantage. The state contained the one gap in the Appalachians between Maine and Georgia; the land between the Hudson River and Lake Erie (hence the Great Lakes) was relatively flat, thereby creating the opportunity for the construction of a water-level canal linking the two bodies of water. The canal could convert the West into an "island" for New York City that would have sole access to probably the richest underdeveloped area of the world. All this overcame doubts about the economic wisdom of the project and the reluctance of the federal government to provide financial aid for the canal. The State of New York authorized construction of the 364-mile waterway in 1817, and, even before its completion, the Erie Canal proved enormously successful. Traffic crowded its waters, and the revenues from tolls grew so rapidly that the state ordered the whole work to be enlarged in 1835.

THE IMPACT OF THE ERIE CANAL ON PUBLIC POLICY. The success of the Erie Canal dramatically altered the developmental politics of the mercantile city; it showed how cities could conquer the barriers that limited their development through a strategy which promised tremendous potential for commercial growth. For one thing, New York State's bold enterprise showed that large sums of money could be easily raised for public works by utilizing the state's credit. In a federal system, fledgling mercantile cities would not have to rely on their own resources or depend on uncertain assistance from the national government. When states shared interests in economic development similar to those of cities, the state could promote programs to aid urban development through the sale of state bonds.

Most important, the Canal's successful operation and low rates expanded the commercial opportunities of the cities tied into it, particularly New York City. Before construction of the Erie Canal, it cost about $100 a ton to transport commodities from Buffalo to New York City. But after the construction of this waterway, the rates fell sharply; by 1852, they ranged from $3.00 to $7.00 a ton (Taylor, 1951:137). This enabled the merchant capitalists of New York to gain a tremendous advantage over merchants in competing cities in the East as well as those as far west as New Orleans.

Prior to 1825, other eastern cities, such as Philadelphia and Baltimore, were much closer to the riches of the West than was New York City. Consequently, most direct commercial trade with the East flowed through these cities rather than through New York. The canal, however, offered a direct and inexpensive water route from the Atlantic Coast to the West. Running from Albany through the valley of the Mohawk to Buffalo on Lake Erie, it enabled New York City to penetrate the entire Great Lakes region. By the same token, New York merchants gained a huge advantage over their competitors located along the North–South trade axis. It was now often cheaper and quicker for the West to ship their bulk freight to the East rather than down the Mississippi and other inland waterways toward New Orleans. The growth in New York City's port activity and population reflected these developments; between 1800 and 1860, the City's share of total U. S. foreign trade climbed from 9 percent to 62 percent and its population, which was equivalent to that of Philadelphia, Boston, and Baltimore in 1800, was more than the total of the three cities in 1860 (Gordon, 1977:64).

THE NEW URBAN ECONOMIC STRUGGLE.   The lessons of the Erie Canal prompted a whole new pattern of interurban competition. Merchants in other cities fought back to reclaim the western trade that was being lost to New York City, leading to a canal-building boom all over the United States. Canals for crossing the Appalachian Mountains were attempted along four other routes in efforts to link rivers on each side of the mountains by the states of Pennsylvania, Maryland, Virginia, and the Carolinas. Merchants in Philadelphia began agitating for a rival waterway to the Erie Canal that was to extend from Philadelphia to Pittsburgh on the Ohio River.

In 1826, Pennsylvania proceeded to spend money lavishly on a system of artificial waterways all over the state. The most important of these was the Pennsylvania Mainline, which was to provide Philadelphia with access to the Great Lakes through a 395-mile route via Pittsburgh and enable the city to compete directly with New York City. Consisting of a system of canal and rail lines—cable cars designed to carry canal boats over mountainous terrain—the Mainline cost over $10,000,000 to build and opened its entire length in 1834. It never enabled Philadelphia to undercut New York's commercial superiority, however.

Similarly, Baltimore sought to contend with the challenges posed by the canal-building schemes of other cities, especially Philadelphia, by promoting internal improvements. The city established a governmental committee to implement a local transportation policy, and in the 1830s the city initiated a series of railroad-building efforts in order to undercut Philadelphia's commercial domination of the region (Livingood, 1947).

Generally, however, the initial wave of response by cities to the Erie Canal was to emulate it. With the economic benefits to be secured from artificial waterways apparently assured and the need for transportation improvements so great, a canal-building fury arose from West to East as cities sought to reap the advantages of this transportation breakthrough. By 1840, a total of 3,326 miles of canals were constructed in the United States, a distance greater than that across the continent from New York to Seattle (Taylor, 1951:52). Most of this mileage was completed between 1824 and 1840.

Urban proponents of canals almost invariably turned to their state governments to raise the massive capital needed for their construction. Private sources of capital, which eventually provided about 30 percent of the investment in these projects, was often unavailable for funding such costly and risky projects (Goodrich, 1960:266–271, 1961:5–6). Generally, the states made the major capital contributions, and they usually built and operated these waterways. Sixty percent of all public monies for canals were spent by several states in the fierce Appalachian competition (Goodrich, 1961:49). Where privately operated canals existed, they usually leaned heavily on state credit or were substantially subsidized by the states. Owing to almost continual political stalemate at the national level, the federal government's financial contribution was little more than 1–2 percent of total expenditure on canal construction.

The Politics of Railroads

Even more than canals, the promotion of railroads was a major developmental policy in the mercantile city. Canals, steamboats, and improved roads could not radically unchain the commercial cities from the physical bonds of their day—vast distances, virgin forests, unsettled plains, and huge mountain barriers. Only a mode of transportation that was fast, cheap, and flexible could do so, and in all these things the railroad proved unexcelled.

Railroads made it possible to transport heavy raw materials and finished products in bulk over long distances at great speed and at remarkably cheap cost. By 1860, steam railways were moving freight about five times as fast as was usual by wagon and canal boat. If transportation rates at the end of the mercantile city period are compared with those from 1815–1820, it is evident that the railroad had reduced rates for shipment by land of bulky products over appreciable distances by about 95 percent. Less than half of this decline mirrors a decline in the general level of prices; the remainder represents a real reduction in the cost of land transportation, a genuine revolution in domestic commerce (Taylor, 1951:135–139). Finally, railroads could be built where canals could not, and fixed waterway routes could be ignored as transportation obstacles. All these factors meant that the railroad could not help but become the merchant fleet of the city. Cities everywhere, big or small, new or old, could use the railroad to penetrate their hinterland in the expectation that they could gather up the trade of the back country and channel it into their own commercial streets. Consequently, the intercity rivalry that arose during the canal era became more widespread during the railway age.

RAILROAD POLITICS AND FEDERALISM. This heightened commercial rivalry was reinforced by the workings of federalism. Unlike European cities, American city governments seeking to use railroads to support their commercial expansion were not hampered by the political boundaries of nation-states, trade barriers, customs duties, or entrenched monopolies. Moreover, city efforts for development were not affected by significant direction by the national government until very late in this period.

Until 1850, the federal government's policy toward aiding railroad construction was similar to their policy toward internal improvement projects in general: namely, the national government generally refused to appropriate or loan money or provide land grants for this purpose, though there were some minor forms of indirect aid (Taylor, 1951:94; Goodrich, 1960:169–170). With few exceptions, the sectional alliance that opposed all federal action for developmental purposes—eastern and southern representatives—held firm and denied all requests for aid.

For these reasons, city policies for development during the railway era were closely linked to the expansion of intercity competition for commercial growth. The railways, unlike the state financed canals, were much more the products of cities themselves. "Whether," as Warner (1972:68) argues, "one thinks of giant projects like the Union Pacific and the Pennsylvania Railroad or of little coal runs like the Albany and West Stockbridge, we find behind them Kansas City, St. Louis, Pittsburgh, Philadelphia and Albany as prime movers as well as beneficiaries." Nowhere are the competitive forces that spurred cities to promote railways more evident than in the building of the first American railways. Three major commercial centers—Baltimore, Charleston, and Boston, each without important inland waterway connections—pioneered in railway development in a struggle to enlarge their markets to the West.

RAILROAD "WARS" OF THE CITIES. Baltimore's position in western trade became threatened by New York's success with the Erie Canal and by Philadelphia's plans to secure similar competitive advantages as soon as the massive state works of Pennsylvania came into operation. Baltimore business interests had little choice but to meet these challenges or accept uncertain losses to the other cities. "Whilst the Cities of Philadelphia and New York are making such great and efficient exertion to draw themselves the trade of the West . . . [a Baltimore newspaper warned], Baltimore must soon lose the comparatively small portion which remains to her . . . should she remain inactive" (Glaab and Brown, 1967:42). Several Baltimore merchants were impressed by the British experiment with the world's first commercial steam railroad line, the Stockton and Darlington. After a favorable eyewitness account of the British railroad, Baltimore leaders quickly decided against a canal and formed a committee to get a charter for a Baltimore and Ohio Railroad company—the first important railroad in America. Although the Baltimore and Ohio Railroad did not push Baltimore ahead of Philadelphia in its quest for a western market, it did narrow the gap between them. Baltimore won a third place position behind Philadelphia until after the Civil War when Chicago edged it out as a ranking commercial center.

Similar commercial pressures spurred railway building in New England. Bostonians, alarmed by New York's growing commercial prominence, began agitating for a railroad from Boston to Albany that would there connect with the Erie Canal. After numerous unsuccessful attempts to persuade the Massachusetts State Legislature to authorize a state railroad, during 1830–1831 three Boston companies were chartered to build several lines. In Charleston, citizens sought to gain a larger share of the inland trade by relying on the advantages of railway technology. They built a railway to Hamburg on the Savannah River. In this way, they hoped to capture the commerce from a rich cotton growing region that would otherwise have been exploited by Savannah at the mouth of the river.

The importance of intercity rivalry in promoting railroads for city commercial growth was strongly reflected in their financing. Unlike the building of turnpikes and canals, private capital played a greater role in funding railroad development; apart from the vast indirect public support (such as land grants), public sources probably provided a little more than 30 percent of the capital funds for railroad building during the commercial period while private sources invested about 70 percent of the total (Goodrich, 1960:266–271).

But private investments in railroads were generally unlike conventional investments undertaken to realize only personal gain. Generally, the funneling of private capital into railway building was generated by the struggles among cities to win rail connections. In the eastern seaport cities where most of the capital funds in private hands was to be found, merchant classes made the chief contributions of private capital. They banded together to pool funds for construction of rail lines for only their *own* cities. Though legally private, their investment activities were essentially public in character. Not until the 1840s did more than a small part of railroad capital come from the financial districts of Eastern cities; only a small proportion of railroad stocks were even listed before 1860 on the New York Stock Exchange (Taylor, 1951:98–100; Goodrich, 1960).

As plans for railroads extended west, rivalry among city promoters and real estate speculators to win railroads for their communities intensified. Since railroads could be built anywhere without being bound by natural trade patterns along rivers and lakes, railroad entrepreneurs were willing to bargain with competing towns in order to gain the best possible deal in stock subscriptions, bond issues, rights of way, and other subsidies upon which they were dependent for their ventures. Private capital combined with public resources provided by city, county, and state governments to be funneled into what were often bitter railway "wars."

Alongside the flow of private funds, cities themselves provided massive assistance for railroad promotion. In some cases, as in Cincinnati, cities built and operated railroads as municipal enterprises. Although precise figures for local government aid are difficult to estimate, such assistance probably totaled more than that of state assistance. By 1870, it equaled one-fifth of the construction costs of the railroads then in existence (Taylor, 1951:92). Particularly in states whose constitutions forbade or limited local government grants to private companies, local assistance to encourage railroad building was very large, imposing considerable debts on the citizenry and moving local governments to make gifts in the form of land grants for stations and yards as well as for materials, such as stone and timber.

State Politics, National Politics, and City Railway "Wars"

THE IMPACT OF STATE POLITICS. Railroad promotion was also important to state governments. However, state competition to promote these improvements was often frustrated by the fact that many states had committed their resources in canal projects. A number of state governments, such as Pennsylvania, had accumulated massive debts during the earlier decades of lavish canal building. Since new railways frequently directly competed with state-run canals and threatened to reduce revenues from these enterprises or even displace them, state legislatures and canal commissions sometimes refused to assist cities to obtain railway links.

In these cases, the most important form of state assistance to the railroads was usually indirect. Since most railroads were organized as corporations, charters had to be obtained from state legislatures. Although states sometimes imposed severe restrictions on railway companies as a result of popular fear of monopoly, their desire to encourage railroads was usually so great that most of the charters granted sweeping privileges and subsidies—freedom from restraints as to the form and amount of securities issued, powers of eminent domain, exemption from taxation in whole or in part, and, as in the case of private canals, lottery and banking privileges. All these amounted to very considerable subsidies to the railroads (Taylor, 1951:89).

Elsewhere direct state assistance was more important. Particularly in the early days of railroad promotion, state investment in private railroad companies was large. In New England, where private capital was most abundant, the state of Massachusetts provided about 70 percent of the funds needed to complete the western railroad to Albany in 1841. In the West, where the newer states had not weakened their credit by banking excesses and grandiose schemes for canal networks, state legislatures made particularly large grants to railroads linking their cities and in some cases even established state-run railroads when private enterprise was not directly forthcoming. State contributions to railroad building grew until after 1861 when the volume of private investment rose, federal grants to the western railroads came about, and local government assistance grew to very large proportions (Goodrich, 1960:271).

LIMITED NATIONAL INTERVENTION. Only after the development of the nation's rail network was well under way did federal government assistance become of much importance. The sectional stalemate that blocked the use of federal funds for internal improvements was broken in 1850 when federal land grants for a railroad extending from Chicago to Mobile was approved. The North–South rather than the East–West direction of the railroad was crucial in obtaining the necessary votes in Congress. As in past struggles for national aid, the representatives from western states supported this federal involvement. The West was the region that most lacked private capital and state resources for expensive internal improvements; hence, their political leaders saw the federal government as the best source of funds for promoting the region's development. Most important, southern support for grants was obtained from representatives of the Gulf states that would directly benefit from the line. In addition, merchants from New York and Boston pressured some eastern representatives into voting for the bill, since their rail lines were already connecting to Chicago and this new railroad would link the South to the windy city (Taylor, 1951:96). While most later bills proposing such aid did not pass Congress because of continuous sectional conflict, forty-five railroads in ten Western and Gulf states received similar subsidies during the ensuing decade.

The Cost of Urban Economic Warfare

The huge public investments in internal improvements laid the foundation for the development of a genuine national economy and a system of cities. But the urban economic development policies of the mercantile era were costly from a public perspective. Once Secretary Gallatin's Report failed to be adopted in Congress, so did the possibility of a national urban policy—a plan for a coherent national system of internal improvements. By default, then, government promotion of economic enterprise became a by-product of city and state rivalries in a mad scramble for growth. This kind of urban development policy produced appalling waste of very scarce public resources in what were relatively poverty-ridden cities and states.

By the 1840s, many states had acquired staggering debts for canal ventures that did not pay off, usually because of competing transportation projects in neighboring states and jurisdictions. After the Panic of 1837, bond defaults spread among state governments and public opposition to internal improvements became a groundswell in heavily indebted states. So ruinous was this experience to state governments that restrictions upon or prohibitions against further state aid for canals, railroads, and other internal improvements were written into many state constitutions during subsequent years.

Cities shared a similar experience. After state finances became hamstrung with debt, the burden of subsidizing railroads fell mostly upon local governments. Enormous numbers of cities and their citizens (and bondholders) were hurt badly in the ensuing urban railway wars. Railroads were often overbuilt or never completed as they zigzagged over the countryside in search of local government subsidies. The benefits of a railroad connection frequently turned out to be much less than expected. Other cities also had connections, and the eventual emergence of some large rail hub cities soon relegated other localities to economic whistle-stops. It was not uncommon for localities to find themselves heavily pressed with debt in payment for a totally useless or perhaps redundant roadbed. As in 1837, the financial Panic of 1873 precipitated massive defaults on railroad aid bonds by debt-ridden local governments. Probably one-fifth of all municipal debt was involved in railroad bond defaults in the 1870s. There followed state legislative action all over the United States to prohibit further local government aid to railroads and to regulate debt limits (Hillhouse, 1936:Ch. VII; Goodrich, 1960:Chs. 4, 7, and 8).

What urban and state governments discovered was that promoting their economies in a catch-as-catch-can economic order means shifting many of the risks of private enterprise onto the public sector. Such a system of urban economic competition produces public casualties.[1]

City Economic Development Politics

In pursuing their commercial development, city governments faced a host of difficult issues. They had to somehow take a long-range view of their commercial prospects and stake out promising trading areas. Once this was done, the matter of what, if anything, the city could do to promote the needed transportation projects had to be considered. If some program for internal improvements seemed appropriate, a strategy of action and a detailed program had to be formulated. This entailed important issues of financing, operating, and monitoring of the enterprises to protect both public and private interests in the community. Further, ways of seeking intergovernmental assistance and legislation for the city's projects often had to be considered. How these and related issues were decided would have far-reaching consequences for the economic well-being of the local community. As a result, city governments had to resolve differences within the community over these issues and organize support for their plans.

Consensus Politics

While the problem of organizing community support sometimes led to important conflicts over such issues, what characterized the politics of development more than anything else was its fundamentally consensual character almost everywhere. In city after city during the commercial period, the developmental arena revealed a tremendous capacity of local mercantile democracies to produce unity rather than division. Merchant elites nearly always seized the pivotal policymaking roles. Representing often diverse business and professional interests, they managed to put together progrowth coalitions in favor of programs of transportation improvements for their cities. Further, merchant politicians seemed routinely capable of stirring widespread public approval throughout their communities for their endeavors, producing almost a mania for city growth. The canal or railroad was touted as something desired not just by one group or another, or one segment of the business community or another, but by "Baltimore" or "Chicago" on the assumption that internal improvements were, by their nature, something nobody could possibly oppose.

This kind of city rivalry was to be repeated many times and in every part of the country; it always took the same forms and was expressed in the same sort of community personification. The community's general interest crystallized around a project conceived to stimulate growth, and the community's character was cast in terms of the success of its businessmen. Much of the pushing, aggressive spirit that attracted the attention of every observant foreign traveller in the United States during the nineteenth century stemmed from these efforts to foster city growth in thousands of places from New York to San Francisco (Glaab and Brown, 1967:45).

For example, in New York City the merchant community put together a remarkable campaign to secure state legislative approval for the Erie Canal. For years, sectional opponents within the state prevented passage. After again failing to gain legislative approval in 1815, merchants in the city decided to organize a mass-based campaign on behalf of the canal. With the support of the city's newspapers and financial contributions by city merchants, public meetings were sponsored in hamlets all along the route of the proposed canal and more than 100,000 signatures (one-tenth of the total state population) were gathered in a petition to the state legislature. The petition presented the reasons for the canal and claimed that it would make New York the "greatest commercial city of the world" (Rubin, 1961:54). The crucial vote change within the state legislature came when the state Democratic leader, Martin Van Buren, changed his position because "twelve thousand men of wealth and respectability in the city of New York last year petitioned for the canal" (Rubin, 1961:62).

Similarly, in Philadelphia the city's struggle with New York for regional expansion was decisively shaped by the Pennsylvania Society for the Promotion of Internal Improvements, a group of forty or fifty businessmen. After New York's canal posed a clear threat to Philadelphia's western connections, members of the society mustered all the city's resources and, through news-papers, public meetings, journals, and the city council, created a groundswell of support for the state to initiate massive canal projects (Glaab and Brown, 1967:40–41).

The Sources of Consensus Politics

Why city development politics was so highly consensual requires explanation. It might be argued that the economic benefits of progrowth policies were so widely shared that hardly anyone could oppose them (as public choice theorists suggest in Chapter 1). It is true that locally promoted programs for turnpikes, canals, and railroads were expected to bring and often did bring economic benefits to the sponsoring community as a whole; jobs, useful land, accessability to needed goods and services, together with lower consumer prices often resulted as the cost of transportation declined. Consequently, programs to assist city growth could be expected to attract the support of nearly all segments of the population in the mercantile city.

Nevertheless, this argument is an insufficient explanation for the dominant pattern of city politics. It does not account for the remarkable cohesion and activism with which merchant elites led their communities to promote what were really often risky, costly, and frequently massive programs of governmental intervention. Merchants whose own business practices might be cautious and fiscally conservative found themselves actively promoting steam railroads whose mechanics were little understood, bold canal experiments through unsettled lands, and the accumulation of massive state and local debts that strained the fiscal worthiness of the governments of the day. In short, what drove merchant oligarchies to cohere in support of radically interventionist and risk-ridden developmental schemes?

THE ECONOMICS OF CONSENSUS. The logic of the economic and political structures that composed the mercantile urban order provides an answer. The workings of the commercial economy tied the economic interests of merchant elites to the growth of their cities, a fact that powerfully drove them to close ranks and support the most ambitious plans for government-assisted community economic expansion which they could muster.

First, the explosion of urban economic competition during the mercantile era constrained merchant oligarchs to actively promote public intervention on a large scale or risk the survival of their business and communities. The pressures of commercial rivalry could not help but forge a close association of the interests of local business communities with city government programs for urban economic growth. Civic activism and unity within the merchant community as a whole were rarely matters of much choice in an economy where the resources of a vast hinterland were so open to development by enterprising elites in rival cities. The latter could be counted upon to profit by inaction elsewhere through improvement ventures of their own. Consequently, even the most conservative members of the business community often had little choice but to enter the urban sweepstakes for the largest prize available if only to eliminate the rise of competing trading centers.

The result was that issues concerning the wisdom of expanding governmental intervention in the local, regional, and even national economy—an important source of political division at all levels of government later during the nineteenth century—was remote from the urban political scene during the heyday of the mercantile city. In such an underdeveloped economy, nearly every substantial program of internal improvements was highly dependent on public participation in some form, and merchant leadership was rarely doubtful about the wisdom of shifting the risks of their ventures onto their only alternative, the government. Only after private capital became more abundant and local business communities established entrenched interests in secure patterns of commerce would business leadership find themselves opposing many forms of public works and enterprise.

Second, although the politics of economic growth indirectly opened economic opportunities for all, these spinoffs of urban development were dwarfed on an individual basis by the enormous benefits reaped by those who had or were in a position to soon have substantial fixed commercial investments in the city. With commercial development of the city, real estate values escalate, favorably located middlemen and bankers can expect higher profits, trading opportunities expand, and businesses get larger markets and higher prices.

Among the most gainful rewards of internal improvements were the rising land values they occasioned. For example, during Chicago's early growth merchant leadership aggressively promoted railroad building to found the city's commercial hegemony in the Midwest. At the same time, they capitalized on the speculative frenzy in real estate development that railroad building provided. Prominent citizens owned large tracts of land in or near Chicago and eagerly utilized their public and private positions to promote railways and other business projects that would enhance the value of their land holdings. The impact of their efforts caused a truly amazing boom in real estate values. In 1845, William B. Ogden, perhaps the city's leading citizen and railway promoter, bought property for $15,000 that was worth $10,000,000 twenty years later. In 1844, he paid $8,000 for property that he sold eight years later for $3,000,000 (Belcher, 1947:126).

These kinds of gains would be diminished if the group that reaped these benefits also were the investment group that sustained the risks of unlucky transportation improvements. But, as noted earlier, the merchant leadership by and large did not constitute such an investment group. The major risks and losses were more often than not borne by the public sector whose bond sales, revenues, subsidies, and charter privileges limited the losses sustained by merchant capital throughout the period, particularly in the turnpike and canal eras and in the early ventures in railroad building.

POLITICAL STRUCTURES AND CONSENSUS POLITICS. The economics of consensual politics was reinforced by the prevailing system of urban governance that excluded competing political demands. The mercantile city was but an incipient liberal-democratic regime whose institutions of popular control were more a means of supporting merchant elites than a system of power for checking them. Although differences between what merchant elites believed was "economically productive" for their communities and what the mass public might otherwise have favored undoubtedly existed, the political institutions simply did not exist to make this a major source of tension in developmental politics. As noted below, the presence of powerful groups demanding urban services, such as better sanitation, assistance to the poor, civic amenities, and other needs lay in the future. Further, such services were largely the responsibility of private philanthropy. Consequently, merchant leadership did not have to deal with many competing demands for scarce governmental resources.

Given the powerful forces that fostered political consensus within the merchant communities, the major sources of conflict were usually confined to the problems of overcoming local inertia and building support among these leaders in favor of a particular kind of civic venture. The problems of political leadership focused on convincing their peers through newspapers, public meetings, private conventions, city council debates, and the like that it was in everybody's interest to do all they could now to support and contribute to some specific public works, harbor improvement, railway venture, stock purchase, or whatever. Since no single internal improvement scheme could possibly enhance all trading and commercial interests equally, the major divisions within the community separated elites into those who stood to gain most from the proposed railway, canal, or other project from those who saw greater benefits from alternative developmental policies.

Merchant Elites and Urban Economic Management:
A Tale of Two Cities

The importance of these conflicts, though over matters of timing and means rather than objective, should not be underestimated. Their resolution by community elites had tremendous consequences for the city's economic future, sometimes making the difference between prosperity and regional dominion or decline and stagnation. One such case was St. Louis' economic rivalry with Chicago during the last several decades before the Civil War. The struggle between these two cities reveals how merchant elites made very different decisions to promote their cities' economic growth.

During the early nineteenth century, St. Louis seemed almost predestined to be the great metropolis of the Mississippi Valley. Owing to its strategic trading position on the Mississippi River, the city was the major break-in-bulk point for the flow of commerce between the interior and New Orleans. With the advent of stream riverboats and the development of New Orleans as a major shipping center for goods intended for the East Coast and Europe, the city of St. Louis quickly rose to become the premier river city of the interior.

The rise of Chicago as a railroad center challenged St. Louis as the major commercial center of the West. Although lakeside Chicago was not without its own natural locational advantages, it lacked good access to the interior. A little river extending barely 35 miles inland furnished the chief feeder for the inland trade of the city. Consequently, Chicago's merchant leadership began promoting internal improvements that would break the city's land-locked position. In 1848, a canal was constructed between Chicago and the Mississippi; this was soon followed by a determined bid for railway supremacy. The Chicago business community was led by William B. Ogden to build a number of major railway projects in the 1840s and 1850s. So successful were these that they cut the many economic ties binding much of the interior to St. Louis. With eleven main lines and their branch connections, Chicago became the nation's major rail city, shifting trade routes that had led to St. Louis over to Chicago and the East by the 1860s (Belcher, 1947).

Merchant leadership in St. Louis failed to react quickly to the threat posed by Chicago. They feared that their investments in riverboats, piers, waterfront property, roads, and the like might be placed at risk with the coming of faster, cheaper, and more convenient railroads, which paralleled important waterway routes. Further, existing trading opportunities were so substantial that leading businessmen were disposed to ignore distant commercial threats and look suspiciously at costly internal improvements.

The fact that St. Louis depended primarily on its own capital, which was tied up already in the substantial river trade, permitted bankers to occupy a dominant position in the city's civic affairs and to dictate to other business interests conservative practices that ruled out speculative ventures. Consequently, the city's many railway promotions usually foundered because of the unwillingness of the business community to provide local capital for these projects.

For example, when one of the more aggressive banking houses of St. Louis attempted to advance funds for the completion of the Ohio and Mississippi Railroad, the conservatism of the city's financial elite was decisive in crippling the enterprise. After this operation diverted large sums from the investment house's normal banking operations, the partners found that they had over-reached themselves financially. Because additional local capital was not forth-coming to save the company, this banking house failed, discouraging future interest in underwriting St. Louis railroad projects (Belcher, 1947). Ultimately, such stalemate within the city's merchant community doomed St. Louis to a declining economic pattern as interior trade shifted to Chicago and the fast-growing railway cities of the East.

Growth Politics and Mercantile Democracy

The development of a commercial economy within a new federal system of government precipitated a spirited contest among mercantile cities for regional economic dominion. The failure of the national government to assert policy leadership and the realities of capitalism's underdevelopment drove city and state governments to join ambitious and costly games of urban economic "warfare." In struggling to create a new urban political economy that joined market and democracy, America's first city political leaders—the merchant oligarchs—dominated the politics of growth.

Endnote

1. I am particularly indebted to Todd Swanstrom for calling my attention to several of these historical consequences of development policy.

CHAPTER FIVE

The Politics of Distribution and Redistribution: Containment of the Urban Public Sector

ALTHOUGH the struggle among cities for economic growth was the priority area of public policy from the perspective of the merchant elites who dominated urban affairs, city governments could not ignore other vital areas of the public policy. Distributive policies that provided housekeeping services were important to urban populations, and they grew with city wealth and populations during this period. At the same time, these fledgling mercantile democracies encountered new demands in respect to redistribution as the poor became a more prominent presence in the urban scene.

The Politics of Distribution

To say the least, most of America's commercial cities left much to be desired as a place to live. Since streets were paved in only a few sections of the larger cities before midcentury, mud was always present in rainy weather, causing wagons and coaches to sink and making life for pedestrians miserable, if not hazardous. Refuse and garbage could be found on streets nearly everywhere. Bands of hogs—usually protected as legitimate scavengers—roamed about towns and cities, normally arousing protest only when children were attacked. In Frances Trollope's famous account of life in nineteenth century Cincinnati, she found the herds of "unsavory animals" wholly unpleasant characters in the city's street scenes but admitted the importance of their "Herculean service" for without them the streets and gutters would have been clogged with mounds of decomposing filth and litter. Even in New York, often considered the showcase city of America, such conditions remained well into the century. Not until 1866, after the establishment of the New York Metropolitan Board of Health, was there a systematic clean-up of the city in a program that included the elimination of hogs from the city's streets (Glaab and Brown, 1967:86).

The absence of adequate sewage facilities also added to the unpleasantness and hazards of city life. Before 1850, the methods of removing waste remained mostly those of the country even in large cities. Privies emptied into cesspools, and the material soaked into the soil or was removed after vaults became filled. Kitchen waste ran directly into the street and was left to evaporate or run off by open drains into streams and rivers.

Not surprisingly, diseases were often epidemic in the congested districts of cities. Cholera, which spread largely through water contamination, broke out in waves throughout the United States in 1832, 1849, and 1866. Squalor, over-crowding, and urban filth paralleled a rising death rate in the larger cities. In New York City, the crude death rate rose from one death per 46.5 persons in 1810 to one in 27 in 1859 (Glaab and Brown, 1967:87). During periods of hot weather, the outbreak of diseases such as yellow fever and other contagion became most rampant; those who could afford it left the cities for healthier places in the country until the period of ravage was over.

It would be wrong to conclude that the residents of America's commercial cities did not care enough about these problems of convenience, amenity, and health to try to make life better for themselves. That they cared a great deal is attested by the voluminous grievances about filthy streets, political corruption, rampant crime, contaminated water, and other urban ills that filled the pages of city newspapers throughout the nineteenth century. The reality is that the unheavenly city was not a matter of choice.

Public Policy and Distribution: The Political Economy of Scarcity

Harsh economic realities of the commercial urban economy decisively limited what even the best-intentioned citizens could do about their environment. Until well into the nineteenth century, all but the largest port cities along the Atlantic seaboard lacked a very well developed revenue base from which many public resources could be derived. As their commercial activities expanded, the needs of their more rapidly growing populations quickly outstripped the ability of even these urban centers to raise revenues in order to deal with the more pressing community problems. For example, in 1810 relatively prosperous New York City had a population of 100,000 but spent on public services only about $100,000—a dollar per capita (Glaab and Brown, 1967:171). The rich economic base that the industrial revolution would eventually bring about for financing the growth of city government was well into the future. Little wonder that most community leaders believed they had little choice but to turn a blind eye to the discomfort and unpleasantness of the physical city and its emerging social problems in exchange for using their meager resources for a more pressing objective: namely, promoting the city itself as a center for trade and commerce.

Urban Housekeeping Policy

Consequently, policies for distribution mirrored the much higher priority placed on development in an economy of scarcity. What characterized urban housekeeping policy more than anything else was the poverty of the governmental programs for making cities better places to live. City policies almost invariably (1) were limited, (2) gave priority to protecting property rather than enhancing urban convenience and amenity, and (3) were notoriously inefficient.

First, throughout the era of the mercantile city the range of public services devoted to urban housekeeping was mainly limited to expanding those provided by towns in the eighteenth century. Typically, this included the maintenance and cleaning of roadways, police and fire protection, and, as cities grew larger, efforts at ensuring cleaner water and providing some kind of sewage system. But nowhere in the history of America's urban mercantile democracies were there programs of local initiative to improve the urban milieu that duplicated the bold efforts these cities often undertook in promoting turnpikes, canals, and railways. If aggressive urban enterprise and risk taking characterized city polices for economic development, their policies for regulating and improving the internal housekeeping services of cities reflected opposite tendencies.

Second, until almost midcentury the emphasis of nearly all cities, large or small, was on ensuring public order and protecting property. Matters of public health, sanitation, parks, libraries, and the like were relegated to secondary importance or were considered tasks for private philanthropy. Up against severely limited revenues for funding public initiatives, the priority for even the largest city governments was to devote their meager tax monies to activities that were basic to the goings-on of a commercial community.

Since commerce and trade could hardly carry on in an environment of threats to life and property, city political leaders had little alternative but to accord these concerns highest priority. Consequently, after street and roadway expenditures, the bulk of the budgets of cities was devoted to maintaining law and order and protecting the citizenry from fires. This was the era of the "private city" (Warner, 1968:4) when cities were expected to do little more than provide an environment for promoting individual enterprise in the hopes that trade and industry would flourish, eventually bringing the resources necessary to give cities the choices to do anything more.

Finally, measured by later historic standards the quality of urban services was almost universally low. Even when city governments made attempts to provide services that were important for maintaining an orderly and secure community, the results were usually quite appalling. City ordinances that prohibited the dumping of refuse and contaminated swill more often than not proved to be unenforceable in large cities, leaving an enormous job of street sanitation to unreliable private contractors, scavengers, and the free-roaming hogs. Attempts by cities to provide fire protection were usually so dilatory and haphazard that few people had much confidence in the city's ability to protect their homes and businesses from conflagration. As a result, city residents constantly feared that fires would break out on so large a scale that they could result in the destruction of entire neighborhoods and sometimes whole cities.

Police protection was often little better. Delinquency, corruption, and neglect of duty by appointed peace officers were rampant in many cities. Wade has found in his study of western cities that in 1815 there was no town where the police were strong enough to quell riots or major disorders or even to stop major waves of vandalism (1959:89). In larger cities, the threat of street crime was a constant problem. Groups of youths often roamed through neighborhoods, ruling the streets, and outbreaks of gang violence were common. Police often fled the site of disturbances in order to save themselves from beatings.

Such a sorry record of governmental services was sometimes due to the unexpectedly huge scale of urban problems local officials encountered and their lack of technical know-how in finding solutions for them. Nevertheless, the systematic failure of local governments to provide effective services was probably more directly related to the major economic constraint of the mercantile era—lack of resources for dealing with their problems. Despite the limited scope of city services, they always occasioned a heavy drain on the meager municipal budgets of the day. The reality was that the poverty of the public sector limited what any local community could do about providing anything like "efficient" responses even to their most simple problems. Public officials invariably had to provide basic services only through ways that permitted the close husbanding of scarce public resources.

Volunteer Government

Accordingly, the typical solution was to rely on an administrative approach used by local governments of the eighteenth century: volunteer government. In this system, even the most basic services relied extensively on volunteer efforts and private contributions. Until almost midcentury, even larger cities usually employed the type of law enforcement that had existed since colonial times—a combination of day policemen and night watchmen who were either hired part-time, often from the ranks of the unemployed, or groups of volunteers concerned with better community security. Almost invariably, the city provided little in the way of central organization, training, or discipline in service for these brigades, which often had the character of clubhouse or fraternal groups. This system cost the cities considerably in law and order on the street. For example, these groups of volunteers frequently resisted the wearing of uniforms because it was considered a sign of European servitude. As a result, policemen volunteers often fled serious street violence since they were not easily identifiable (Glaab and Brown, 1967:96).

As cities grew, pressure for upgrading urban law enforcement mounted. Native Americans complained of growing crime among new immigrant populations (Glaab and Brown, 1967:96); property owners were often distressed by street crime and rising vandalism from young people. Others wanted better control over slave populations (Wade, 1959:88). At first, these problems were met through laws that required all voters to serve in the night watch, increased the number of paid personnel, or imposed better methods of operation for the irregular police constabularies of the day.

Eventually, however, these highly informal systems fell in favor of the establishment of more professional police forces. Change came first in New York City where in 1844 the night watch and other duplicating law enforcement bodies were abolished and replaced by a single police organization of 800 men. Even here, this new force was hardly a major reform that brought about wholly improved security. It took nearly ten years for a board of police commissioners to be established and for the board to require the wearing of a uniform. By 1860, most large cities followed New York in "professionalizing" their security forces by creating departments of full-time officers.

Fire protection also reflected the volunteer approach to the urban community's resource constraint. Fires had always been considered a city emergency, and in the postrevolutionary years the entire community was expected to respond when they occurred. But eventually this sort of system proved clumsy, and most cities shifted the burden to volunteer fire companies. Though these organizations had existed for many years, their activity took on greater and greater importance as cities grew in population and size. As municipalities handed over increased power to these associations, the relationship between the public authority and the companies became quite ambiguous. Local governments provided these clubs with charters along with some funds and equipment; but the organizations usually made their own rules and determined admission requirements.

Though the volunteer approach undoubtedly saved much expense, it doomed fire protection to an exceedingly low level for the community. Firehouse gangs frequently fought with each other as much as they fought fires. Ill disciplined, independent, and hard drinking, they competed actively and often became a political force to be reckoned with in city elections. They earned a reputation in many cities for ignoring any kind of central professional direction and actively resisted the introduction of new equipment, such as steam fire engines.

Despite the fact that volunteer fire companies were an important cost-saving expedient, their independence, ineffectiveness, and unreliability usually proved to be more than it was worth as cities became larger and fires became more devastating to property and life. For instance, the resistance of Cincinnati's volunteer firemen to steam fire engines led the city to organize in 1853 one of the first paid municipal fire-fighting forces in the United States. Similar problems motivated other large cities, including Boston, New York, and Philadelphia, to follow suit.

Other services reflected an essentially similar pattern of extensive private participation. Water service is exemplary of this. Given the enormous capital costs of constructing a water system from scratch, very few cities attempted to build municipal systems until well after the 1840s despite the obvious benefits of clean and ample water for the health of the community. Although Philadelphia pioneered in building a publicly owned waterworks at the beginning of the nineteenth century, most other large cities depended on notoriously unreliable private companies. Even New York City was dependent on a shoddy private system from 1799 until 1835, when a public system began construction at tremendous expense to bring water by closed aqueduct from 40 miles north of the city. Most other cities were constrained to avoid such heavy public expenditures as long as they could; as late as 1861 there were eighty privately owned systems but only sixty-eight publicly owned waterworks in operation throughout the country.

Distribution and City Politics: Merchant Elites, Scarcity, and Crisis Management

Severely limited resources not only had a decisive influence on the character of distributive policies in the commercial city, they also had important consequences for decision making on these issues. Most of all, this meant that organized political interests that might mobilize in order to influence the allocation of city services were few. Particularly for less well off citizens who might have found jobs as municipal employees a very valued objective, participation in city politics was hardly a promising field of opportunity. Since most city services were at best limited and relatively dependent on voluntary participation and private efforts, there was little in the way of extensive patronage, official perquisites, or opportunities for providing favors.

For instance, in New York City during the late 1840s local politicians faced an electorate of about 40,000 with perhaps 2,000 jobs. If anything, patronage opportunities declined during the commercial era in New York City; in the 1790s, when the electorate numbered only about 4,000, the Federalist politicians had around 1,500 appointees (which they vigorously put to use). Partisan dominance in the city was mainly a means to state and federal governmental goals, including jobs: The state government controlled about 1,400 of New York City appointments as port wardens, judges, clerks, inspectors of commodities, etc. (Bridges, 1984:132).

Despite the fact that newspapers of the period are replete with citizen complaints about the inefficiencies, suspected corruption, and ineptitude of municipal government—not, perhaps, unlike today—it is doubtful that the failures of local government were closely linked to official exploitation of "riches and privileges" of public office. If cities of the mercantile period were badly run—and there is abundant evidence that they often were—it is because' of the meager resources available to do much better and the limited stake most citizens had in the goings-on of these feeble governmental units.

Merchant Elites and Political Decisions

Decisions over city services invariably fell into the hands of merchant elites whose social prominence and economic interests moved them to actively seek public offices and fashion local government to support their private undertakings. Like the volunteer-based public activities that they supervised, these leaders generally considered their own roles in city government to be part-time endeavors. Probably not until the late 1840s did many full-time professional politicians become prominent in cities. By then local services in larger cities started to require greater supervision and more full-time paid employees, and popular sentiment became less tolerant of a municipal corporation run by a self-perpetuating club of merchant oligarchs. The changing social and economic character of cities and the expansion of the voter franchise began to occasion different pressures on the new professional politicians. Further, by midcentury the intervention of state governments into the provision and administration of distributive services became a source of political conflict. As city services expanded, state party leaders began to take over more and more agencies, appointments, and functions from rival local party leaders, beginning a pattern of friction that later dominated city–state relations (Bridges, 1984:135–136).

During the heyday of the mercantile city, however, the decisions of the political elites were central to matters of distribution. Given the decrepit state of city services that they typically encountered, one might expect that city offices were frequently sought for the purposes of carrying out progams of "reform." There is no doubt that merchant leaders of the day usually saw unparalleled need for more and better police and fire protection, cleaner streets, pleasant parks, and many other services that decades later people in many cities would take for granted. Nevertheless, it was rare for many of these political authorities to seek public positions for promoting ambitious programs of social and economic improvement. Typically, political leaders regarded such proposals as well beyond the pale of the poor local governments of the day.

The Politics of Containing Public Expenditures

Much more important was their emphasis on running local government in order to minimize governmental expenditures—even at considerable cost to the capacity of their cities to solve problems of distribution. Faced with public sector poverty that checked all but the most basic public undertakings and motivated by powerful interests in promoting the commercial viability of their cities, the decisions of local politicians were dominated by finding ways of limiting municipal responsibilities. To achieve this, merchant elites perpetuated and extended the highly fragmented governmental organization founded in colonial times.

Their central governmental institution, on which they served on a part-time basis, was the City Council, which had to approve all appropriations and legislation. The locus of power within the Council was in its many committees, which were responsible for overseeing the various commissions, boards, and agencies that administered and carried out local governmental services. This highly decentralized system had one important advantage for the ruling mercantile elites: It enabled them to limit the expansion of services and give priority to controlling their cost. By dividing and subdividing powers in a proliferation of offices, local government became a poor vehicle for any coordinated attempt to solve public problems, diffusing public grievances. Equally important, the recruitment of large numbers of merchant volunteers to run the varied and semi-independent committees, commissions, and boards ensured close scrutiny of city expenditures.

Philadelphia is a good example of just such a system. After the Revolution, democratic reforms were enacted, enabling city taxpayers to elect a select and common council (bicameral legislature) to levy taxes, vote appropriations, and enact local ordinances. The mayor, not popularly elected but chosen by the council as in the colonial times, was the chief executive officer. His position, however, was for the most part honorific. When new municipal functions were added, such as for a city water system, the council created independent committees that did not report to the mayor, but to the councilmen themselves and the volunteers who served on the council committees (Warner, 1968:101). Such a system necessarily provided close financial control over city expenditures and checked the growth of municipal authority. At the same time, placing the administration of specific tasks in the hands of independent committees or commissions effectively ensured that there was no central direction of the city's affairs.[1]

Other cities followed similar patterns of governmental fragmentation and even extended it as growth in city services became inevitable and councils found themselves lurching from budget crisis to budget crisis during the period of urban expansion after the 1830s. By 1840, most American cities still modeled their governments along lines that tended to impede prompt action by city officials and to foster the containment of public expenditures. City councils were generally composed of two houses elected on a ward basis. By now, however, mayors were becoming more independent of the legislative branches and were usually elected at-large. Although the executive office in most places was acquiring greater strength by obtaining a veto power over city ordinances and wider appointive discretion, the mayors rarely accumulated enough power to curb the influence of the councilmen. In effect, local governance had evolved in a way that ensured limiting the scope and expenses of local services and preventing any central direction over service delivery.

The Politics of Expanding Public Services: Crisis Management

Despite the formidable internal barriers to the growth of city housekeeping services, throughout the first half of the nineteenth century the story everywhere was one of their inexorable expansion. By the Civil War, the "basic" housekeeping services were more than likely to include such things as a publicly or privately owned water system, perhaps a sanitary system of drains and sewers, a municipally chartered transit service of some kind, some publicly managed parks, and other services. Equally important, these services tended to become more professionally administered by more full-time appointees at the executive and at the street levels.

This pattern of growth in services was not usually a product of greater political movements in cities for civic improvement, however. In general, the decisions to expand public services were in response to conditions that immediately threatened public safety and social order. The political agendas of the maturing commercial city were set by urban population expansion that brought increasing crime and disorder, more devastating public health epidemics, more costly fires which leveled whole commercial and residential districts, and other urban problems. Since the cities' poverty-ridden political systems were essentially designed to limit governmental expenditures and had little capacity for planning the growth of public services to solve mounting problems, decisions about distribution were dominated by crisis politics over which merchant elites presided. Under the prod of grim necessity, city political leaders were forced to expand and improve the quality of public services as urban growth lurched them from crisis to crisis.

WATER POLITICS IN PHILADELPHIA AND NEW YORK CITY. The politics of water services in Philadelphia and New York City illustrate this pattern. The early development of Philadelphia's municipal waterworks in advance of the city's population growth is sometimes regarded as a tribute to the town's farsighted commercial leadership (Warner, 1968). Battling engineering difficulties, financial deficits, as well as considerable governmental and public apathy, merchant leaders on Philadelphia's water committee struggled to promote the ideal of better public health through clean water supplied by a city system. Nevertheless, it would be wrong to regard the civic activism of the city's fathers as essentially an outgrowth of public spiritedness. The expansion of water services and sewers was directly tied to the outbreak of epidemics that were greatly feared in all cities.

In Phildelphia, the ambitious waterworks schemes of city leaders were occasioned by the city's particularly severe public health crisis during the late eighteenth century. In the summer of 1783, 10 percent of Philadelphia's population died from yellow fever, the city's economy came to a standstill, and about one-third of its residents fled. In 1797, Philadelphia was hit again along with a dozen other cities; three-fourths of the city's population fled to the countryside, and 4,000 people died—about 7 percent of its population (Blake, 1956:4–6). City leaders had to act to contain Philadelphia's public health crisis or risk disorder and decline.

The initial stage of Philadelphia's waterworks was completed in 1801. However, the financing of the works was based on the assumption that many families would want direct water connections to their houses and that these private subscribers would carry the cost of building and operating the system. But by 1811, only 2,127 Philadelphians chose to subscribe for water out of a city population of 54,000. Consequently, until the 1840s the water committee struggled against heavy deficits while continuing to supply its water to the public at a loss in advance of popular usage because of grim public health reasons. Most of the city's population either could not afford to subscribe or chose to depend on street hydrants or private wells for their water (Warner, 1968:105).

Few other cities could afford such public spiritedness, and because of this their stories are much different. Given the harsh resource limits of the mercantile city and the urban economic competition that drove merchant politicians to utilize scarce public revenues for enhancing the city's commercial potential, most cities were unable to invest in waterworks or otherwise expand their public health services until local "disasters" and a growing revenue base provided the preconditions for change.

In the rapidly growing port of New York, tragic health epidemics similar to those of Philadelphia's moved city leaders to find a means of bringing more and better water to the city. But here the enormous costs of an ambitious municipal project dampened enthusiasm a great deal, and, after considerable controversy, it was decided to charter a private company to provide this essential service in 1799. The Manhattan Company proved to do poorly what public enterprise was unwilling to do at all, however. Unable to foresee much profit in providing the city with water, the Manhattan Company demanded and received substantial charter privileges, including the right to operate as a banking institution as well as a water company. Although its financial activities proved to be quite successful, the company had less enthusiasm for the water business, since the latter was more troublesome than profitable.

For decades, the city struggled along with notoriously unreliable and insufficient water service that was widely blamed for the city's periodic health epidemics and large fire losses. The company refused to invest sufficiently to provide adequate water for the growing city, and whole areas were not served at all; the company laid its pipes through the districts that promised the largest returns and left the poorer and more remote districts without a supply. Nevertheless, city leaders investigating the possibilities of building public works always drew back in view of the heavy expenses required.

Only after New York City's phenomenal growth permitted the raising of large capital during the 1830s and the twin scourges of disease and fire became intolerable did the city decide in 1835 to build an adequate water system no matter what the cost. In that year, one disastrous fire burned down twenty blocks of valuable buildings, including 529 stores, leaving 2,000 merchants out of business, 5,000–8,000 workers unemployed, and all the insurance companies of the city bankrupted from fire losses. Eventually, the Croton aqueduct was completed at the unheard-of cost of nearly $13,000,000 (Blake, 1956:Chs. 4, 6, 7, and 8).

Other areas of distributive policy follow a similar pattern. As urban growth brought both greater wealth and conditions that threatened public safety and order, even the most hard-pressed city governments were forced to begin providing more and better basic services.

The Politics of Redistribution

Until well into the nineteenth century, the problem of urban poverty was essentially of a preindustrial character. The social and economic forces associated with industrialization that would eventually make large-scale dependency a major political problem for cities lay well into the future. Massive immigration from rural areas and abroad and the social upheaval occasioned by rapid urbanization and industrial growth did not begin to significantly characterize America's larger cities until the 1840s and 1850s.

Despite recurrent periods of depression after 1815, the problems of the poor were not closely tied to the laying off of industrial workers during business depressions. Since only a small minority of the urban labor force was engaged in manufacturing before 1850, cyclical unemployment was far from widespread. During the ante-bellum period, it probably did not rise above 5 percent, and before 1840 it never exceeded 2 percent. These were preindustrial cities in an agricultural society; the major causes of poverty were to be found in low wages paid to farm help, seasonal layoffs, the lack of protection against sudden disasters, ill health or injury, and the inability of some to purchase and work land of their own (Rothman, 1971:160). Moreover, the opening up of the frontier to settlement and commerce further diminished the incidence of poverty. Generally, the number who received public relief in the early decades of the nineteenth century was quite small—rarely more than 1 percent of the population in major cities. Only after cities encountered the growth and upheavals of the industrial era was the scale of urban poverty to rise beyond these proportions.

Redistributive Policy in the Mercantile City: The Political Containment of the Poor

Intervention by local government to deal with problems of poverty and dependency was far from unknown during the mercantile era. During the colonial period, local responsibility for assisting the poor and destitute residents of the community became a well-established practice. This obligation was based on the English Poor Law system, which held the locality primarily responsible for raising funds and providing subsistence to qualified needy individuals and families within the community. In the years following the Revolution, this tradition continued to be the norm all over the United States, in effect giving established local residents a right to subsistence and making the locality unequivocally responsible for care of the needy. Neither the national government nor the various state governments provided significant programs to assist localities to meet their obligations.

While the Poor Law tradition of local responsibility was a clear legal duty, the actual policies and practices of mercantile democracies in providing assistance to the poor were quite restrictive and reflected the enormous obstacles that the political economy imposed on government aid to the disadvantaged. No city, least of all the resource-poor mercantile cities of the Republic, would open its doors to all of the unfortunate and care for them through public alms. To do so would force local communities to give up or severely limit their ability to achieve other objectives, such as basic public services like clean water and police protection, not to mention ambitious developmental programs. Further, the merchant oligarchies that imposed their own priorities on government hardly afforded the poor a base of power for making demands. Throughout the period, the policies for redistribution were geared to limit the allocation of scarce local resources for needy groups whose political ability to change this was feeble at best.

The Public Policy of Containment: The "Two" Poor

The workings of the traditional legal system of poor relief actually limited the burdens faced by local governments. In the mercantile city, this system distinguished two groups of "poor" who might be potential recipients of public assistance. One was the working class; it included the artisans, journeymen, and apprentices of the craft trades, together with other various individuals having roles in the commercial economy, such as laborers involved with transportation and, later, small numbers of factory workers. Under the Poor Law tradition, needy members of this group were able to claim public relief as a right after private means and charitable resources were exhausted. Generally, until the first three decades of the commercial period, the policy of local governments was to provide the eligible poor with outdoor relief, i.e., financial assistance at home rather than in an institution, such as a workhouse, almshouse, or other shelter. While the amount of aid usually provided the needy was little more than bare subsistence, this relief was obtained as a matter of right and was dispensed in a nonpunitive manner. The needy were rarely treated as outcasts or subject to investigations of their character and family life or dislocated from their homes.

The largest concentration of poverty in the commercial city lay outside, not within, them, however. On the city's outskirts, numbers of poor itinerant individuals and families—paupers, casual laborers, propertyless drifters, beggars, and the unlucky—lived in tents, shanties, and rooming houses. They lived dramatically apart from the life of the city. Unable to establish stable employment and become part of the city's social and economic life, they moved frequently from town to town. City policies harshly excluded these transient poor from relief. Settlement laws of seventeenth century England had been adopted during the colonial period and were continued for many decades into the nineteenth century by cities. These laws established a minimum period of residence before one could be considered a resident of the city and receive public aid if in need. Cities could deal with unwanted dependent strangers by forcing them to leave the city and preventing them from establishing legal residence.

POVERTY AND PUBLIC ORDER. Such an exclusionary system severely limited the actual burden of poor relief on city governments of the day. The settlement laws were essentially legal walls that spared cities from having to find funds in their meager budgets to assist itinerants who were unable to find a productive role in the commercial economy. At the same time, the traditional system helped promote social order and control within the city. The poverty that did exist within the city did not reveal itself in the presence of large numbers of poor families massed in particular districts and neighborhoods, posing a visible threat to public safety and political order. Poverty within the city was essentially individual in character, blending inconspicuously within the social organization of the city.

Concentrated around the wharfs, warehouses, and craft establishments of the city center, the resident populations lived and worked in a remarkably homogeneous social order. Unlike cities following the Industrial Revolution, the social geography of the mercantile city was characterized by the relative absence of residential segregation based on income and class. Typically, people of many and varied occupational backgrounds were scattered all around central city districts, making for a vibrant and heterogeneous street life. More often than not, city residents—rich and poor—lived and worked in the same neighborhood, enjoying a ". . . unity of everyday life, from tavern, to street, to workplace, to housing" (Warner, 1968:61).

The Disintegration of Town Walls

During the latter half of the commercial period, however, the traditional local government arrangements for dealing with the problem of poverty changed. Although localities continued to be the level of government primarily responsible for poor relief, the developing commercial economy unleashed changes that moved cities to begin making fundamental changes in their practices, abandoning the form and substance of the old policies. Most important, the more rapid growth of cities after the 1830s brought larger numbers of new residents and workers and hastened population mobility. As a result, the walls of the cities built on the foundations of ancient settlement laws crumbled; town officials found that they could no longer banish all needy strangers by relying on rigid and severe settlement laws. Not only did town officials find it more difficult to guard railway stations and highways as large numbers of migrants became a constant presence, but state regulations were passed that prevented local governments from maintaining their insularity by outlawing restrictions on intrastate movement of people (Rothman, 1971:204).

The weakening of the settlement laws is well illustrated by the case of New York State. In 1827, its revised statutes dropped property qualifications for residence and prohibited local communities from removing dependents from county to county or even from one town to another within the same county. Similar liberalization of resident and settlement regulations occurred in most other states. In Illinois, the state's twelve-month requirement for residence was shortened to six months in 1839 and to thirty days in 1841. Even where settlement laws remained on the books, practicality usually prevented local officials from enforcing them (Rothman, 1971:186).

THE PUNITIVE CONTAINMENT OF THE POOR.   Urban growth forced local officials almost everywhere to rely on some other strategem for poor relief or face increased costs for the larger numbers of dependent strangers settling in their midst. The typical solution was to establish a relief system that discouraged those eligible from seeking it. After 1830, local relief became more punitive as communities moved to replace outdoor relief for indoor relief in almshouses and workhouses that were maintained by the locality. The poor, no matter what their circumstances and difficulties, were placed in these institutions, which were notoriously harsh and custodial in character. The spirit of this was aptly captured by officials in Providence, Rhode Island, who, finding that it was ". . . in some cases utterly impossible to convey persons rejected by the said Town Council to the place of their last legal settlement," determined that they should be sent to a workhouse and there ". . . provided for and kept to labour" (Rothman, 1971:186).

Alongside this shift toward a more punitive system of relief was change in sentiment by political leaders who sought to justify the new arrangements. Although the old system and its recipients did not necessarily win public favor in earlier years, poverty was not necessarily considered a wholly personal failing on the part of the individual, and outdoor relief was not generally regarded as a reward for vice. Proponents of relief reform, however, denounced outdoor relief as a dole that sapped the energy and initiative of the poor, gave the idle means to indulge their vices, and discouraged them from seeking productive employment— in brief, it was mistaken benevolence that fed the moral deficiencies of the poor.

Political leaders also touted the financial benefits of resort to the poorhouse where assistance was dispensed "grudgingly, suspiciously and in very small amounts" (Rothman, 1971:185). By making conditions so unappealing, they hoped that dependents would most likely prefer to work outside these institutions and people would not willingly submit themselves to the workhouse unless they were in danger of starvation.

These changes in city policies were also reflected in the activities of voluntary charities. From the beginning, public relief efforts were almost always supplemented by those of private agencies, particularly in larger cities. Nationality groups, fraternal societies, churches, and other social organizations provided assistance for their members and often for others as well (Trattner, 1974:33–34). In particular, these organizations were important in assisting those who would not be helped by public means, such as itinerant strangers, needy seamen, and others. But as public policy became more punitive and treated poverty as solely a matter of personal failure, the voluntary agencies generally followed suit. A pattern emerged whereby private charities increasingly aimed not at giving assistance to the needy but at improving their moral character.

Most of these societies believed that since the nation offered unlimited natural resources, poverty resulted from moral failures of the individual— idleness, immorality, intemperance, and the like. They saw their role as one of countering these vices by helping the poor to develop opposing virtues, such as industry, frugality, and sobriety; they hoped that through their efforts the better nature of the needy would be reclaimed, thereby solving the problem of poverty. Probably the best known charity of this era and typical of many others was New York City's Association for Improving the Condition of the Poor. Founded in 1842–1843 to help cope with the city's growing problem of destitution, this charity utilized volunteer visitors to the poor to counsel them on how to become self-sufficient, rather than providing them with financial assistance (Trattner, 1974:63–64).

City Politics and Redistribution: Excluding Poverty As an Issue

The politics of the local redistributive arena reflected these shifts in policy. During the earlier decades of the commercial city era, decision making with respect to outdoor relief was simply a continuation of the processes and practices followed during the colonial period. There was little, if any, conflict over a relief system that protected the rights of the "worthy" poor and prevented the transient poor from becoming resident, and, hence, potential participants in the city's politics. The transplanted English Poor Law system was most appropriate for the poverty-stricken mercantile city; it enabled a locality's politicians to limit its expenditures by enforcement of the settlement laws while, simultaneously, preventing the growth and emergence of an under-class whose demands would have gone unheeded and whose presence would have presented a threat to social order. The social homogeneity that existed during the heyday of the commercial era was the underpinning for the redistributive policies followed during these earlier years.

When urban growth and the disintegration of the settlement laws prompted cities to begin containing the burden of relief through more restrictive and punitive measures, merchant communities faced greater potential for political conflict over redistribution. The implementation of these policies could create problems of maintaining social control and stability when applied to growing numbers of poor who were coming to participate more in city politics. The reforms of the Jacksonian era had extended greater opportunities for male suffrage, and party competition was mobilizing increasing numbers of workers to form parts of their political constituencies.

In confronting these challenges, mercantile city governments again gave priority to developmental and distributive objectives rather than to redistributive concerns. Lacking the resources for expanding local expenditures for relief, the merchant communities redefined the problem of poverty to smooth the way for more restrictive measures. Thus, local policies emphasized the moral weaknesses of the poor rather than their legal right to claim community assistance.

The local political and labor organizations that represented the poor did not oppose these changes in policy and outlook. The developing urban political parties, which were rarely led by representatives of the poor, were a feeble vehicle for responding to grievances among the laboring classes over problems of relief. Given the scant resources available to local government and the ascendant position of traditional elites within the preindustrial era party systems, local party organizations avoided class appeals that might stimulate demands which would not be easy to satisfy. Rather, they found ethnic, religious, and neighborhood appeals the most viable strategem for soliciting the votes of the underprivileged (Katznelson, 1981; Bridges, 1984).

Not only was party competition usually dominated by national and state issues (the governmental level where political power and resources were concentrated), but even the party organizations that did recruit large numbers of laboring class voters were hardly very inclusive or capable of promoting class-based appeals. The political categories that dominated debate and partisan rivalry in cities were of a preindustrial kind—emphasizing the need for commercial prosperity, jobs for all, sound government, responsible leadership, and other ideals that evoked the importance of government in the general interest. Consequently, the dominant local parties tended to have large, diverse mass followings. Even when working men's parties developed, as they did in a number of states by the early 1830s (and then to disappear), these parties were often as deeply divided as they were broadly inclusive. In New York City, the party's definition of "working man" was a broad one—it included artisans, laborers, farmers, grocers, merchants, and many others, excluding only those who made their wealth from "speculation" (Bridges, 1984:22). Moreover, early labor unions were more apt to focus their efforts to win concessions for workers at the workplace rather than at town halls (Katznelson, 1981).

Redistributive politics in the city was shaped by the leadership role of the merchant to solicit working-class votes. Confronted with a limited local revenue base and constrained to promote developmental priorities in a political economy of growing commercial competition, the mercantile leadership was able to secure minimalist redistributive policies. As a result, local politics involving the working class was ". . . defined in the main, not as a politics of capital and labor, but as a politics of competition between ethnic-territorial communities from which capital was absent" (Katznelson, 1981:65). It was not until the era of mercantile democracy had passed and industrial changes transformed local economies that city governments would give much greater attention to demands for redistribution.

The Passing of Mercantile Democracy

During the half century or so following the Revolution, a local politics emerged that broke with the patterns established during the colonial era. Fundamental changes in the external political economies of cities—the emergence of a capitalist mercantile economy and a novel federal system of government—were critical forces that shaped this transformation. At the same time, institutions of popular control were created during this age of democratic idealism that began to challenge traditional political practices within cities. What arose from this confluence of forces was an incipient liberal-democratic regime in which city politics was becoming shaped by markets and popular control systems. Neither fully capitalist nor highly democratic, this was America's first urban politico-economic order.

Led by the nation's ascendent mercantile classes, a politics arose to cope with the enlarged responsibilities of growing urban communities in the new nation. New policies for urban development, distribution, and redistribution were created. The commercial rivalries among cities to penetrate the hinterland, the expansion of public services in local communities, and harsher programs of relief evolved in response to the urban problems of the day. By midcentury, however, these responses by local government also brought about changes that signaled the end of the era of the mercantile city and its politics.

The Exhaustion of Mercantile Public Policy

In all three areas of urban policy, the political exhaustion of the mercantile regime became evident in the years leading up to the Civil War. It was in the struggle among cities for economic expansion that the most far-reaching urban changes took place, for the outcome of these commercial rivalries set the stage for a new urban market order based on industrial capitalism. First, the transportation revolution in which waterways and railroads joined distant interior cities and coastal ports was altering the economic foundations of urban America. A major impediment to the growth of manufacturing in urban areas was the lack of cheap and rapid transportation, particularly for the shipment of bulk materials. Without a means of distributing products cheaply over great distances, a national market could not exist and factories could not specialize in production. But the development of vast regional railroad networks removed this barrier during the two decades prior to the Civil War, laying the foundation for industrial cities whose factories, need for workers, and enterprising capitalists promised fundamental changes in the social and political life of cities.

Such a change portended a new politics of economic development. During the era of the commercial city, the game of interurban warfare for economic expansion almost always came down to a series of disjointed regional battles to extend the city's economic influence; regional centers emerged to penetrate their immediate hinterlands and develop trade that had not before existed (Riefler, 1979). With the exception of New York City, whose advantageous location and bold commercial ventures quickly assured it a national influence, it was possible for most cities to strive for growth by competing with rivals within quite limited geographical areas. But this network of disjointed city imperialisms was to pass as the rise of a national market broke down these regional barriers.

Second, the intercity rivalries of the commercial period produced patterns of uneven urban development that were to persist into the industrial age. Most important, the great eastern cities that so successfully promoted internal improvements became the dominant business centers of the United States. By 1860, the cities of the West were bound to those in the East by steel, steam, and canals that cut off the South from the maor commercial trade of the interior; the traditional North–South trade axis in the interior United States shifted to an East–West plane.

The policies of the commercial cities for distribution and redistribution achieved changes of almost equal magnitude, setting the stage for new issues as the industrial era approached. As cities grew in population and urban social conditions changed, the expansion of city services was inexorable. Merchant politicians turned their attention to solutions for rising crime and social tension, threats of fire and disease, and other urban ills. The expansion of city services could not help but evoke new political problems that would ultimately transform the politics of distribution. The volunteer solutions that cities relied upon to spare their meager budgets became inadequate. Government by committees of part-time politicians could not effectively organize and supervise the work of local government. Politics was becoming a full-time vocation, and the need for some direction in the city service delivery became inescapable.

Similarly, new political issues were bound to arise as more full-time public employees were hired to maintain the streets, fight fires, secure public order, and carry out other responsibilities because volunteers could either not be found or were not equal to the tasks. But what city political leaders failed to address was how these services should be administered. How employees should be hired, supervised, and disciplined were issues that cities were to resolve.

Finally, by the decade prior to the Civil War the commercial city encountered problems of social welfare that could no longer be coped with by traditional responses. Cyclical economic changes in production and employment were accompanying the arriving industrial age, testing the ability of local public and private efforts to cope with its attendant miseries. The workhouse, private charity, and moral exhortation, which were the initial solutions to emerging industrial poverty and its discontents, were politically precarious. Immigration from rural areas and from abroad to feed the needs of industrializing cities for factory labor was changing the social and economic complexion of cities. The presence of growing working-class residential enclaves and increasing ethnic diversity was coming to characterize the city. The massed presence of these groups, their growing participation in the political system of cities, and their social and economic problems in the new industrial order threatened a crisis of urban social control.

Endnote

1. On the relevance of this response to scarcity for contemporary urban budgeting and political theory, see David and Kantor (1979) and Chapter 16 of this volume.

References for Part One

Belcher, Wyatt Winton. 1947. *The Economic Rivalry between St. Louis and Chicago, 1850-1880.* New York: Columbia University Press.

Benson, Lee. 1961. *Concept of Jacksonian Democracy.* Princeton, N.J.: Princeton University Press.

Blake, Nelson, 1956. *Water for the Cities.* Syracuse: Syracuse University Press.

Bridges, Amy. 1984. *A City in the Republic: Antebellum New York and the Origins of Machine Politics.* Cambridge: Cambridge University Press.

Chudacoff, Howard P. 1981. *The Evolution of American Urban Society.* Englewood Cliffs, N. J.: Prentice Hall.

Coben, Stanley and Forest G. Hill. 1966. *American Economic History.* New York: J. B. Lippincott Co.

Dahl, Robert. 1960. *Who Governs?* New Haven: Yale University Press.

David, Stephen and Paul Kantor. 1979. "Political Theory and Transformations in Urban Budgetary Arenas: The Case of New York City" in Dale R. Marshall, ed. 1979. *Urban Policy Making.* Beverly Hills: Sage, Ch. 6.

Duffy, John. 1968. *A History of Public Health in New York City, 1625-1866.* New York: Russell Sage.

Glaab, Charles N. and A. Theodore Brown. 1967. *A History of Urban America.* London: Macmillan.

Gluck, Peter and Richard J. Meister. 1979. *Cities in Transition.* New York: New Viewpoints.

Goodrich, Carter, ed. 1961. *Canals and American Economic Development.* New York: Columbia University Press.

Goodrich, Carter. 1960. *Government Promotion of American Canals and Railroads, 1800-1890.* New York: Columbia University Press.

Gordon, David M. 1977. "Class Struggle and the Stages of American Urban Development" in David C. Perry and Alfred J. Watkins. 1977. *The Rise of the Sunbelt Cities.* Beverly Hills: Sage, pp. 19-54.

Gordon, David M. 1978. "Capitalist Development and the History of American Cities" in William K. Tabb and Larry Sawers. 1978. *Marxism and the Metropolis.* New York: Oxford University Press, pp. 25-63.

Hillhouse, A. M. 1936. *Municipal Bonds: A Century of Experience.* New York: Prentice Hall.

Katznelson, Ira. 1981. *City Trenches: Urban Politics and the Patterning of Class in the United States.* New York: Pantheon Books.

Livingood, James W. 1947. *The Philadelphia-Baltimore Trade Rivalry.* Harrisburg: Pennsylvania Historical and Museum Commission.

McKelvey, Bake. 1973. *American Urbanization: A Comparative History.* Glenview, Ill.: Scott, Foresman and Co.

Miller, Zane L. 1973. *The Urbanization of Modern America: A Brief History.* New York: Harcourt Brace.

Perry, David C. and Alfred J. Watkins. 1977. *The Rise of the Sunbelt Cities.* Beverly Hills: Sage.

Peterson, Paul E. 1981. *City Limits.* Chicago: Chicago University Press.

Pred, Allan R. 1980. *Urban Growth and City Systems in the U.S., 1840-1860.* Cambridge: Harvard University Press.

Pred, Allan R. 1966. *The Spatial Dynamics of U.S. Urban-Industrial Growth, 1800-1914: Interpretive and Theoretical Essays.* Cambridge, Mass.: MIT Press.

Redford, Ernest J. et al. 1965. *Politics and Government in the United States.* New York: Harcourt Brace.

Riefler, Roger R. 1979. "Nineteenth Century Urbanization Patterns in the United States." *Journal of Economic History,* Vol. XXXIX (December), 961-974.

Rothman, David J. 1971. *The Discovery of the Asylum: Social Order and Disorder in the New Republic.* Boston and Toronto: Little, Brown.

Rubin, Julius. 1961. "An Innovating Public Improvement: The Erie Canal" in Carter Goodrich, ed. 1961. *Canals and American Economic Development.* New York: Columbia University Press, pp. 15-66.

Taylor, George Rogers. 1967. "American Urban Growth Preceding the Railway Age." *Journal of Economic History,* Vol. XXVII (September), 309-339.

Taylor, George Rogers. 1951. *The Transportation Revolution, 1815-1860.* New York: Rinehart and Co.

Teaford, Jon C. 1975. *The Municipal Revolution in America.* Chicago: University of Chicago Press.

Trattner, Walter I. 1974. *From Poor Law to Welfare State: A History of Social Welfare in America.* New York: The Free Press.

Wade, Richard C. 1959. *The Urban Frontier.* Cambridge, Mass.: Harvard University Press.

Warner, Jr., Sam Bass. 1972. *The Urban Wilderness.* New York: Harper and Row.

Warner, Jr., Sam Bass. 1968. *The Private City.* Philadelphia: University of Pennsylvania Press.

Watkins, Alfred J. 1980. *The Practice of Urban Economics.* Beverly Hills: Sage.

Watkins, Alfred J. and David C. Perry. 1977. "Regional Change and the Impact of Uneven Development" in David C. Perry and Alfred J. Watkins. 1977. *The Rise of the Sunbelt Cities.* Beverly Hills: Sage, pp. 13-18.

PART TWO

Industrial Democracy: Markets, Machines, and Urban Political Struggle, 1860–1930

Industrial Democracy

D URING the sixty years following the Civil War, a well-developed liberal-
democratic political economy emerged that brought forth radically new
patterns of urban politics. To understand this period of revolutionary change in
city governance, we must begin by examining the economic system, popular
control institutions, and intergovernmental network, which together comprised
the new urban order—industrial democracy.

In this political economy, the local polity became subject to the forces of
industrial capitalism, a market system that altered the strategic economic
function of cities and fostered an era of remarkable economic independence for
many of them. At the same time, popular control underwent major development
as mass democratic politics became a powerful presence in cities. During this
period, national intervention in local affairs remained limited. The urban
industrial democracies formed a focal point for political struggle in the United
States.

The Economic Context: America's Industrial Transformation

During America's period of commercial development, an industrial revolution
was underway in Great Britain that eventually spread all over the Western
world. Following the publication of Adam Smith's *Wealth of Nations* in 1776,
England became the crucible for the creation of a new economic order based on
industrial production and far-ranging market exchange. Smith maintained that
enormous prosperity and wealth could be created by abandoning many past
governmental impediments to commerce and trade, permitting "the invisible
hand" of the market to determine the allocation of the main factors of
production. A new industrial order emerged in England, which was characterized by large-scale production in factories for national and international
markets. The new order seemed to behave very much as Smith and other liberal
political economists had described, making Britain Europe's leading economic
power.

When a similar industrial revolution actually began in the United States is a matter of some dispute, but it is clear that the period following the Civil War to the first quarter of the twentieth century was a time when the arrangements of the mercantile era were displaced by fundamental economic changes. Improvements in transportation were critical in bringing this about. In the post-Civil War period the completion of the nation's railroad network created the national and regional markets that enabled business to undertake large-scale production in a manufacturing economy. The rail system reduced the cost of long-haul transportation to a revolutionary degree (Pred, 1966:49). These were the years when almost all the nation's internal traffic moved by rail; in 1916, the network reached its peak with 254,000 miles of tracks, carrying 77 percent of intercity freight tonnage and 98 percent of intercity passengers (Warner, 1972:89).

Once this rail system was in place, businesses took advantage of economies of scale and established larger and larger factories to produce for a mass market. Further, the rail system freed many businesses from being tied to locations near sources of supply; the railroads could cheaply and efficiently transport the raw materials needed for production to the plants. Consequently, after the Civil War the old mercantile cities began to turn away from foreign commerce and local trading toward manufacturing and large-scale production (Pred, 1966:18–19).

The nation witnessed enormous growth of manufacturing activities carried out in more and more factories of increasingly large size. At midcentury, the United States was still a relatively unindustrialized nation, since only about 11.6 percent of the work force was engaged in manufacturing. But in the years following the Civil War, the situation altered dramatically. By 1869, the number of manufacturing workers had more than doubled. This record nearly repeated itself in subsequent years in a process of rapid industrialization. Between 1869 and 1929, the total number of manufacturing workers increased by 440 percent and the total value of manufacturing products climbed by 2,100 percent (Watkins, 1980:204). By 1900, the share of manufacturing in the nation's total ouput of commodities passed 50 percent, and in the following ten years manufacturing production grew nearly as much as in the previous thirty-year period (Pred, 1966:16). In essence, during the decades after 1860 the economy became transformed from an agricultural–mercantile order to an industrial–capitalist one.

Land, Labor, and Capital in Industrial Reorganization

The process of industrialization occasioned a fundamental reorganization of the factors of production. Once entrepreneurs broke out of their local trading hinterlands to serve a larger market, land values began to be determined by market forces arising from far beyond the borders of the locality. The market for labor underwent a most profound transformation. While the old mercantile economy, with its agricultural base, could function easily with limited numbers of workers in the craft and trading enterprises of the day, the new economic order required an ever larger pool of wage labor for the factories and mills of the industrial world. In 1849, the number of "gainful workers" totaled 7.7 million, but by 1889 the work force had grown to over 48,000,000 (Watkins, 1980:204). Employment in the wage labor market subjected the worker to a new discipline. Here the industrial capitalist acted to shatter the old labor organization of small craft enterprises and family shops in order to organize a larger scale of production in which establishments of a dozen, fifty, and even hundreds of workers became common.

Capital also underwent transformation in the course of industrialization. A national market for capital emerged as expanding national wealth led to the creation of numbers of financial and banking institutions to provide credit for businesses all over the United States, ending the days when merchant entrepreneurs were highly dependent on foreign and limited local sources of capital. By World War I, America no longer was a substantial importer of capital from Europe (Warner, 1972:189; O'Donnell, 1977:106).

Manufacturing concerns became progressively larger throughout the period, and capital became increasingly concentrated in them. Limited risk corpora-, tions, relatively rare before the Civil War, numbered 40,000 by the turn of the century. While they accounted for only about one-tenth of all business establishments, they produced over 60 percent of the value in manufacturing. In the 1890s, a number of giant corporations emerged, consolidating groups of railroads, metal firms, and other key industries. The giant corporations that formed between 1896 and 1905 included the U. S. Steel Corporation, International Harvester, General Electric, and American Telephone and Telegraph. Although a drive for the enforcement of antitrust laws occurred in the early years of the twentieth century, the internal economies of large-scale production and the advantages of owning enormous market power proved decisive, ending the free-swinging market of mercantile days (McKelvey, 1973:85).

The Industrial Revolution and the City

The Industrial Revolution fundamentally transformed the role of cities in capitalism and created a national urban system based on market competition. This new urban economy had enormous local political implications. Not least, it enabled some city governments to achieve powerful market positions and secure relative economic independence. This new reality would change the bargaining positions of local government and business.

The New Economic Function of the City

The nation's industrial transformation radically altered the primary economic function of cities. While cities of the commercial period survived by performing important transport node and marketing functions, they held a peripheral position in the predominantly agricultural economy. The industrial market system, however, placed cities at the very center of its workings. They became the central places where the factors of production could be efficiently organized for large-scale industrial production. The railroad directly stimulated economies (advantages) of agglomeration to such a degree that businesses were essentially tied to the terminals, docks, wharves, and central business districts of the large cities of the period. Freight cars were made into long trains at the terminals of major cities and then dispatched to other urban areas, permitting businesses and cities to specialize in mass production for distant markets.

Large-scale industrial production required the assembling of large numbers of skilled and unskilled workers; a developed transportation infrastructure to promote the efficient and reliable movement of freight and labor; and adequate sources of power for the large factories. Further, the risks associated with tying up large amounts of capital in massive plant and machinery necessitated continuous production. Only in cities, as opposed to isolated sites, could all these conditions be satisfied. With their pool of mass labor, capital infrastructure, and physical plant for moving, warehousing, and otherwise servicing industrial enterprise, the cities became central to the new economic order. The industrial development of cities created still other important economies that further enhanced their economic role. Cities became the host for allied services, including legal talent, banking and credit, repair facilities, raw material processors, medical facilities, and other kinds of goods and services directly related to undertaking large-scale business activity.

URBAN GROWTH. As a result of these kinds of economies, urbanization became linked with the process of industrialization during the post-Civil War period. Most striking was the dramatic growth of cities in number and in size. In the fifty years after 1860, when the total population grew from 31 million to 92 million, the number of people living in incorporated municipalities (of 2,500 or more) increased from 6 million to nearly 45 million—a percentage change in the urban population from almost 20 percent to more than 45 percent of the total. By the early 1920s, the United States had become a predominantly urban nation. Cities of all sizes grew very rapidly. During the period from 1860 to 1910, the number of cities of over 100,000 increased from nine to fifty while smaller urban places of 10,000 to 25,000 increased from 58 to 369 (Glaab and Brown, 1967:107–108).

This diffusion of urban places and populations was paralleled by the growth of giant metropolises. By 1898, New York, aided by the annexation of Brooklyn, tripled its population and surpassed all but London in the Western world in population. Chicago, Cleveland, Pittsburgh, and Detroit more than doubled their populations, while elsewhere Los Angeles and Seattle on the West Coast and Atlanta and Birmingham in the South more than doubled.

The pace of urban growth was furious. Chicago in 1860 had a population of 109,620 and was virtually destroyed by the famous 1871 fire, which leveled two-thirds of the city and left 100,000 people homeless. Ten years later, the city eclipsed its rival, St. Louis, in population, and by 1890 it surpassed the million mark as it became the nation's second largest city—from ashes to one of the nation's premier metropolises in twenty years! Many other cities demonstrated similar rapid growth (Glaab and Brown, 1967:111).

The industrial cities acted as a vacuum, pulling into them vast numbers of immigrants from rural areas and abroad. Most of the population growth came from foreign immigration. The flood of immigrants from abroad is generally considered to have occurred in two waves. One, beginning in the 1840s and peaking in the 1880s, mainly involved immigrants from Western Europe—Irish Catholics, German Catholics, German Protestants, and Scandinavian Protestants. The second mainly involved groups from Eastern Europe and Catholic parts of Western Europe. It began after 1880 and peaked between 1900 and 1910, declining in the 1920s when federal legislation closed the doors to unrestricted foreign settlement (McKelvey, 1963:104). Between 1880 and 1920, nearly 23.5 million people came to America's shores, and the bulk of these newcomers settled in cities. In 1920, 48 percent of the nation's total urban population came from abroad or descended from foreign parentage, and in cities over 100,000 the foreign born and their children amounted to 58 percent of the population (Miller, 1973:73).

The increase in urban population was also partially a result of migration from rural areas in America. The productivity of farm labor increased so much by the 1890s that a much smaller work force than that of the 1830s could produce even larger crops of the major agricultural commodities. Together with the pull of increased commercial and industrial demands for labor, these forces encouraged a massive rural to city movement. About 11 million of the 42 million city dwellers in 1910 had come from American farms after 1880. Probably about one-third of the total urban population of 1910 were American natives of rural origin (Glaab and Brown, 1967:136).

THE INTERNAL STRUCTURE OF THE CITY.   Fundamental changes in the economic function of the American city were reflected in its physical transformation. Not only did many cities grow far beyond boundaries established during the commercial period, but land use became much more segmented and specialized in ways that mirrored the city's new economic function. At the center, land typically rose in value, permitting only the most intense and profitable commercial, industrial, and residential uses. Businesses sought these central locations for the advantages they offered near markets, rail and port terminals, and intracity transit. Outside the center, a ring of constantly changing and mixed commercial, industrial, and residential land usually prevailed in which slum, factory, and commercial spaces competed with each other.

As land values declined from the center, residential areas became more prevalent. But, unlike the residential neighborhoods of the mercantile city, which were usually a jumble of rich and poor, immigrant and native, the neighborhoods of the industrial city revealed a more systematic pattern of socio-economic segregation. Areas of residential settlement usually followed the economics of land values and transportation. Workers and their families usually settled near the factory and tenement districts of the inner rings because of the cheaper housing costs and easier commuting to jobs and stores in that location. Further away, more affluent residential rings could be found filled with families who were able to afford the cost of commuting from the cities' fringe and the purchase of cheaper land for better, more spacious homes. So prevalent was this pattern of concentric zones of city growth that many social scientists believed that it was nearly universal for all industrial cities (Park, Burgess, and McKenzie, 1925).

The "Core and Periphery" Urban Economic System

While the city assumed a nuclear position within the industrial system, not all cities managed to win a leading place in this economic order. Uneven patterns of urban economic development emerged, creating a "core and periphery" system of cities; small numbers of major urban centers quickly established a dominant market position in relation to much larger numbers of other cities, which assumed a subordinate or peripheral place in the industrial order. Consequently, the widespread competition among cities and regions that characterized the commercial era declined in favor of a more hierarchical urban economy in which very limited numbers of large cities established secure dominion over their hinterlands.

THE "CORE" CITIES.   The "core" cities were mainly larger urban centers that had won prominence during the commercial period and were with few exceptions concentrated in the Northeast, Midwest, and Middle Atlantic states, a region which became the nation's industrial heartland. While the proportion of the labor force employed in manufacturing rose for every region of the country between 1870 and 1910, it tended to concentrate in the heartland cities. In 1910, the New England and Middle Atlantic regions had about 40 percent of their labor force engaged in manufacturing, followed by the Great Lakes states with over one-third; in contrast, other regions fell below the national average of 27.9 percent (Miller, 1973:69).

The tendency after 1870 was for manufacturing to concentrate in fewer and fewer large cities. For instance, manufacturing employment in New York, Philadelphia, and Chicago, the nation's three largest cities, grew by 245 percent between 1870 and 1900. In contrast, the number of industrial workers in cities ranked twenty-first through fiftieth in population grew by only 158 percent (Gordon, 1978:39). The ten most populous cities increased their share of national value-added in manufacturing from less than a quarter to almost two-fifths between 1860 and 1900 (Gordon, 1978:39; Pred, 1966:19–21). Consequently, the absolute population gains registered by these ten cities during the forty years after the Civil War were the largest in the country (Pred, 1966:23). Among all areas of the country, the region of commercial dominance, the Northeast, strengthened its position in the industrial era. By 1910, it contained 70 percent of the nation's urban population; it encompassed thirty-four of the country's fifty cities having populations over 100,000, and fourteen of the nineteen largest cities (over 250,000 inhabitants) in the United States (Miller, 1973:69).

In effect, the rapid emergence of dominant core cities capturing the lion's share of industry meant that opportunities for building new cities of much economic significance was foreclosed as early as 1890; by this date most cities that achieved even moderate size during the industrial era had been founded (Glaab and Brown, 1967:109). Table 6-1 is suggestive of the relative economic dominance that most of the nation's leading core cities displayed in this urban system. With some notable exceptions, the largest urban centers, especially those that eventually became the eleven most populous U.S. cities, had achieved a leading economic position at the outset of the industrial period and did not radically change their hegemonic positions. For instance, of the top twenty most populous cities in 1860, only two—Albany and Charleston—radically changed their urban rank by 1910, moving more than thirteen places (which is the next greatest move among cities in this group) and falling out of the top twenty. In contrast, large numbers of cities that were relatively smaller in 1860 generally exhibited much more erratic changes in urban rank. For example, among the eight cities ranked just outside the top twenty, five experienced changes in urban rank of more than (typically much more than) thirteen places. Despite the enormous changes wrought by the industrial system, its impact on the market positions of U.S. cities was a highly stabilizing one, creating hierarchy out of what had been a highly competitive urban economic order.

THE URBAN "PERIPHERY."   As the large core cities became the focal points of the industrial system, this left vast areas of urban America in a distinctly · peripheral economic position. "Towns remain," noted N. S. B. Gras in the 1930s, "but in economic subordination to the metropolis" (Glaab and Brown, 1967:273). Within the manufacturing belt, the growth of suburban enclaves and satellite towns beyond the borders of the central city were yet to become threats to the latter's economic hegemony. There was a tendency for populations and businesses to decentralize around the central city peripheries during the whole industrial period, a pattern that accelerated with each improvement in short-haul transportation. Nevertheless, these decentralist trends hardly began to check the economic dominance of the central city until the 1920s when the automobile precipitated a dramatic jump in suburban population (McKelvey, 1973:113). Even then, the suburban challenge lay in the future.

Outside the industrial heartland, cities in the various regions of the United States grew, most often in symbiotic relationship with the core metropolises. The South consistently lagged behind other regions in urbanization. Its biggest cities, such as New Orleans and Louisville, generally owed their preeminence to their traditional commercial ties with the cities of the Old Northwest, not to the economic development of the South. Even the more industrial cities of the new South remained small by northern standards. Atlanta, the South's dominant southeastern city, supported but 154,000 people, while the iron and steel town of Birmingham had only 132,000 in 1910 (Miller, 1973:71).

In the far West, urban centers boomed during the late nineteenth and early twentieth centuries with greater independence of the economic hegemony of the East than in the case of the South. The completion of the transcontinental

TABLE 6-1   Change in Rank of U.S. Cities with an 1860 Population of 25,000 or More, 1860–1910

	Rank in 1860	Rank in 1910	Net change in rank
New York	1	1	0
Philadelphia	2	3	−1
Baltimore	3	7	−4
Boston	4	5	−1
New Orleans	5	14	−9
Cincinnati	6	13	−7
St. Louis	7	4	+3
Chicago	8	2	+6
Buffalo	9	10	−1
Louisville	10	22	−12
Albany	11	44	−33
Washington, D.C.	12	16	−4
San Francisco	13	11	+2
Providence	14	21	−7
Pittsburgh	15	8	+7
Rochester	16	23	−7
Detroit	17	9	+8
Milwaukee	18	12	+6
Cleveland	19	6	+13
Charleston, S. C.	20	77	−57
New Haven	21	31	−10
Troy	22	63	−41
Richmond	23	35	−12
Lowell	24	41	−17
Mobile	25	90	−65
Syracuse	26	30	−4
Hartford	27	46	−19
Portland, Maine	28	78	−50

SOURCE: Adapted from Allan R. Pred, *The Spatial Dynamics of U.S. Urban-Industrial Growth, 1800–1914* (Cambridge, Mass.: MIT Press, 1966), p. 4.

railroad and branch feeders to these trunk lines produced numbers of challengers to the city of San Francisco, which had commercial ties to eastern cities. The rapid growth of Los Angeles, Seattle, Portland, and other communities pushed the total urban population of the far West to 56 percent in 1910, a level of urbanization second to that of the manufacturing belt (Miller, 1973:70).

The Driving Forces of the New Urban Economic System

The system of "core and periphery" cities emerged because the workings of the new industrial economy did not induce uniformities in urban development. The course of urban development tended to favor the growth of cities that had already achieved commercial prominence. The latter cities' initial advantages provided them with the inertia to become the dominant economic centers of the period, relegating other cities to subordinate economic positions.

First, among the most important of these forces were the railroads whose declining freight costs, particularly for long-haul traffic, favored the growth of larger centers. Large-scale production brought ton–mile or freight-volume economies to a firm and enabled still greater extension of its market area. In large heartland cities, these firms achieved lower freight tariffs on the major trunk lines. This acted to increase the attractiveness of these larger cities as centers for manufacturing, stimulated the expansion of existing production capacity, and, at the same time, diminished the importance of less favored and accessible points (Pred, 1966:50–52).

In theory, this advantage might have been depreciated by a number of factors that threatened core cities. Spiraling land values in the central city, land scarcity in their commercial districts, and the lengthening journey to work for urban commuters all loomed in core cities. But the significance of these problems was diminished by innovations that permitted the dispersal of commercial and industrial activities far around the central city core. For instance, steam power could be generated almost anywhere, and electrical power could be carried over large distances within large urban centers. Moreover, the revolution in short-haul transportation supported the constant expansion of cities. As long as horse-drawn omnibuses and freight wagons were the principal mode of urban transit, industrial establishments had limited opportunities for site location in cities—horse cars were so slow that two and a half miles was generally the maximum radius from which any plant could hope to attract workers. But as the electric street car and other forms of electric traction began to replace the horse car after the 1880s, much longer journeys to work were possible. Up to the 1920s, nearly all the transportation improvements of the period worked to the advantage of larger central cities and supported their meteoric rise as premier economic centers.

Second, capital-intensive innovations resulting in lower production costs tended to confer advantages on core cities. For example, the rapid evolution of larger and hotter blast furnaces, the introduction of the Bessemer process in 1867, and the spread of the open-hearth process in the 1890s revolutionized the iron and steel industry, causing productivity rates and the size of steel-making establishments to soar during this period. The capital requirements for building up-to-date iron and steel facilities became so great and the competitive position of small-scale plants deteriorated so much after 1880 that the industry as a whole underwent substantial concentration around Pittsburgh and other se-lected locations in the industrial heartland (Pred, 1966:66).

Third, the tendencies toward industrial concentration through the growth of trusts and mammoth corporations during the late nineteenth century also worked to the ascendancy of a few cities at the expense of others. The competitive strategies of a few industrial giants frequently hindered entry into the market by smaller firms in ways that worked to the advantage of major producing centers (Pred, 1966:66–77).

Perhaps the most notorious example of this involved the steel industry's Pittsburgh Plus pricing scheme that was instituted in order to concentrate steel production in northeast areas where plants in that region were not always as efficient as those in other regions. Pittsburgh Plus required that all steel products be sold in the United States at a price determined by the mill cost at Pittsburgh plus transportation charges from Pittsburgh to the point of consumption. This pricing scheme destroyed any cost advantages of mills located outside of Pittsburgh and encouraged steel producers to locate near Pittsburgh so they could minimize freight charges. As a result of this, the geographic market for steel products made in the South was very limited. This was a major factor in crippling the development of Birmingham's steel industry around the turn of the century. Birmingham remained an outpost of the national steel industry despite evidence that its mills were among the lowest cost operations in the country (Watkins and Perry, 1977:37–38).

Finally, the market for labor and capital operated in ways that provided initial advantages for existing industrial cities over other cities and regions. While skilled and unskilled labor might be found in many cities as immigration increased, the significance of the size of the city's labor pool became magnified as the size of the typical industrial establishment increased and technological advances demanded less skill, experience, and training. The big city, more than any place else, proved to satisfy with particular ease the voracious need of industry for cheap labor (Pred, 1966:79). Capital availability further provided initial advantages to large core cities. While the barriers to capital movements within the United States began to decline in the post-Civil War period, investment funds remained more readily available to manufacturing interests in established trading capitals. Significantly, banks here offered lower interest rates than most of their counterparts did in smaller competing cities within the same region as well as in other areas in the country (Pred, 1966:80). In the South, cities were not only encumbered with high local interest rates after the 1870s but the region's banks tended to be few, small, and often antagonistic toward manufacturing (Davis, 1965).

THE POLITICAL IMPLICATIONS OF AN URBAN-CENTERED MARKET ORDER. The Industrial Revolution created a market order that altered the traditional economic functions of cities, placing the central city at the center of its workings. This precipitated the development of a new core and periphery urban system in which the large industrial city achieved economic ascendancy vis-à-vis other urban areas. This fundamental transformation radically altered the possibilities of political choice for local governments. If city governments tie business and revenue-providers to its docks, rail terminals, warehouses, and factory districts, then the fundamental bargaining relationship between city governments and their business and investment communities must change. The more that the latter are captive of city economies, the less bargaining power they can muster by exploiting their economic power. Politics, not markets, becomes a focal point for public policymaking.

Popular Control and the Industrial City: The Emerging Tensions of Mass Democracy

The conspicuous economic surge of cities that liberated them from the catch-as-catch-can system of mercantile days was matched by an equally important political change: namely, the growth of mass popular control institutions. More than at any other previous time in America's urban development, the notion of popular control came to be tested in practice in the governance of cities. Until the industrial era, the development of mass democratic institutions tended to occur at a distance from the city. In the years following the Revolution, popular control underwent far greater development at the state and national levels of government than at the local level. The highly oligarchic features of city government during the commercial era contrasted sharply with the rapid evolution of more polyarchal patterns of governance in state and national politics during the same period.

With popular attention focused largely on the contests for major state and national offices and on issues of state, regional, and national importance, the nation gave birth to democratic mass political institutions. In particular, during the first half of the nineteenth century, a system of pragmatic, electorate-oriented, coalition-building parties had evolved, displacing the old politics based on elite personalities, factions, and cliques. During the Jacksonian revolution and its aftermath, the most enduring features of modern mass democratic politics emerged. Most important were the activities of the Democrats and the Whigs of the 1830s and 1840s in organizing a highly decentralized, but nationally focused, party system.

Consequently, this period witnessed sharply rising levels of voter participation in national elections, a race for new ways of mobilizing and managing masses of voters and party workers, and notable democratization of party organizations (Chambers and Burnham, 1967:11-12). The national convention system came to replace the congressional caucus, and in most states and counties more or less popularly chosen delegate conventions appeared as central features of the party structure. Concurrently, reforms were undertaken to expand the role of popular choice in government. These included the popular at-large election of presidential electors, the choice of congressmen by districts, the popular election of governors, printed ballots, the creation of small voting districts, and the consolidation of elections on a single day. Though the national political order crumbled with increasing sectional strife and the Civil War, these institutions of mass democracy were resurrected on their old foundations after 1865 as the Democrats and Republicans replaced the dying system of Whigs and Democrats.

Although ideas about political equality and popular governance were mainly forged in the struggle for national and state power, cities underwent some changes before the Civil War that followed the spirit of the national transition to mass democracy. By the end of the Jacksonian era, many cities had adopted the direct election of the mayor, and by midcentury many cities had entirely dropped the property qualification for voting. Similarly, the demand for popular government led to the electing, rather than the appointing, of hosts of officials with specialized functions. City charters had been altered to permit the election of officials responsible for services that had been previously controlled by city councils (Gluck and Meister, 1979:45).

The Urban Transformation of Popular Control: Mass Politics, Social Cleavages, and Political Tensions

Despite all these institutional changes that fostered the growth of popular government, their impact on local politics prior to the industrial era was always diminished by the fact that the politics of cities lacked the prizes of power and responsibility found at other governmental levels. Consequently, even though cities had sometimes adopted the forms and belatedly shared in the national transition to mass democracy, the ideals and institutions of popular government had yet to be tested in struggles for power as they had in the state and national arenas. But the industrial cities—with their growing populations and financial resources—provided richer prizes and greater potential for political conflict, infusing formal democratic mechanisms and egalitarian ideals with a new meaning.

First, the industrial city's quantum growth in voter populations coincided with the expansion of urban governmental services. This provided new incentives for political action by residents who increasingly saw local politics as a source of important patronage rewards. Alternatively, those classes who were less interested in jobs and other particularistic rewards also saw local politics as an important arena as city services and programs became important to the goings-on of the commercial and business communities. Consequently, the day of the political professional whose job it was to manage the newly enlarged electorates and represent the diverse interests that vied for attention arrived on the local scene. The arrival of the full-time professional almost invariably displaced the old political arrangements of government by mercantile and professional families (Warner, 1972, 1968).

Second, the coming of mass democracy to the cities coincided with social changes that invariably produced new, more intense political conflicts which tested the capacity of democratic arrangements to resolve differences and maintain political support for orderly governance. The growth of diverse urban populations characterized by important class, religious, ethnic, and cultural differences in an industrial–urban environment constituted a potentially explosive political situation (Katznelson, 1981). No less was at stake than the political cleavages that would be permitted to dominate the local community.

CLASS VS. PLURALIST POLITICAL CLEAVAGES. On one hand, forces were in place that could produce a politics based on class where politicians seek to win votes based on appeals to broad segments of the electorate sharing similar economic status. The advent of industrialization intensified these kinds of social conflicts as workers labored in factories rather than in their homes or in nearby shops and competed in a wage labor market that grew larger and more competitive. The new urban land-use patterns in which the central business district tapered off into segregated zones of lower-, middle-, and upper-class residential areas physically mirrored the importance of class social cleavages in the industrializing city. The separate and segregated city, where territorial differences based on class predominated, visibly contrasted with the political ideal of egalitarianism. These new conditions of life and labor invariably generated new demands among workers: demands for shorter working hours, better working conditions, higher wages, and social and economic security. At the same time, new economic power and social prestige were conferred upon business, professional, and managerial groups who could be expected to assert their claims for a political role in city government.

On the other hand, more pluralistic interests vied with class rivalries in the city. Throughout the commercial period, the artisan classes frequently shared similar religious, ethnic, and cultural characteristics as the economic elites of the city. But as cities grew, the social character of their enlarged electorates became more diverse. The impact of immigration swiftly reversed the homogeneous character of the city after midcentury (Warner, 1968; Bridges, 1984). These social differences gave birth to a new set of political interests based on neighborhood that overlayed those based on class differences. Just as the industrial city produced patterns of segregation related to class and income, it also created new interests related to residence and the life styles and cultural differences of groups found in city neighborhoods (Katznelson, 1981). The latter raised many highly emotional issues, such as those concerning temperance, the role of religion in schools, and the assimilation and recognition of ethnic groups in city politics.

The presence of these pluralist and class-based social cleavages within a context of mass democracy raised a central issue in city politics: On what social base would the popular majorities that were expected to govern the city be constituted? How this was resolved had far-reaching consequences for the liberal-democratic regime. Most important, it very much determined the extent to which the institutions of popular control could serve as a source of constraint on political leadership in the cities. The coming of mass democratic practices could remain a hollow shell of procedural formalism to legitimize the status quo and traditional leadership, as during the commercial era; or it could become a powerful check on the behavior and choices of political authorities. The outcome ultimately depended on the kinds of competing political demands that were permitted to become political issues, determine electoral outcomes, and define policy agendas. These matters, which previously had been a product of oligarchical settlement, became during the industrial age the focus of more widespread political struggle.

The Intergovernmental Context: Federalism and the Industrial City

How cities coped with their transition to industrial democracies was something that the national and state governments stood in positions to influence. The system of government based on divided powers and competing political jurisdictions constituted the fundamental rules of the game within which city governments acted to deal with the forces unleashed by the Industrial Revolution. Nevertheless, the industrial era witnessed a decline of federal activity in urban affairs and the ambivalent assertion of state power in the politics of cities.

The National Government and the Cities: Laissez Faire

The post-Civil War period saw a diminished presence of the federal government in urban affairs. The national government retreated to the sidelines and displayed little or no interest in initiating programs for cities. In Congress, the White House, and the Supreme Court, the political leadership of the country before 1900 almost unanimously supported laissez faire, the notion of private enterprise acting free of governmental interference, whether through financial aid or regulation.

While it is not possible to explain the emergence of this important theme, it is apparent that new forces arising from the national political economy were in accord with it. The sectional rivalries that drove the nation to civil war were diminished in importance with the victory of the Union and the political aftermath of Reconstruction, which left the South in political and economic subservience to the rest of the country. The northern Republican party, which dominated the national government, generally did not push for any expansion of federal power. Laissez faire effectively underwrote the political status quo, the hegemony of the Republican North.

At the same time, these political relationships were reinforced by the changing market position of the national government in the industrial transformation. As industrialization "took off" in the post-Civil War years and concentrated in the North, which happened to be the political power center of the nation, the economic need for federal intervention to promote national development abated, reinforcing the political views of those who dominated national government. From a jurisdictional standpoint, the major economic stake of the national government in the American economy had always been one of promoting national economic growth itself, not one of directing it and dealing with its urban consequences. Even during the commercial era, the limited federal assistance for canals, roads, and railroads had been justified essentially on the basis of promoting national growth, not regional need; political divisions over the latter usually worked to contain the federal role.

Although the federal government's stake in promoting economic growth did not change in the industrial era, the rapid development of the national economy permitted federal officials to assume a hands-off attitude toward the economy. Federal spending in general was substantially reduced and remained at a low level during the first thirty years of this period. Consequently, the federal program of grants to railroads, initiated during the ante-bellum period, ran into mounting opposition. No new federal grants to railroads were made after 1872, and in 1890 some of the earlier legislation granting land to the railroads was repealed in response to the ideals of laissez faire. As the maintenance of high tariff schedules and continuous sales of public lands generated high levels of government revenues, the national government was able to consistently run budget surpluses from the end of the Civil War until the mid-1890s, reduce or eliminate many taxes, and reduce the public debt from $2 billion to $0.5 billion (Poulson, 1981:353-354).

After the 1890s, however, a succession of Progressive era presidents— McKinley, Roosevelt, Taft, and Wilson—favored an expanded role for the federal government in the domestic economy. Nevertheless, the reassertion of federal power continued to reflect the federal government's limited role in promoting national growth itself rather than dealing with its urban implications. Roosevelt's trust-busting, the strengthening of the Interstate Commerce Commission, tariff revision, President Taft's promotion of a corporate income tax amendment, and Congress' creation of a central bank through the Federal Reserve System are illustrative of the growth of federal intervention with only the most indirect implications for the development of cities. Although these initiatives were accompanied by an upward trend in government spending—by 1914 federal spending was double that of 1890—few of these programs had much direct impact on city development. By the end of the 1920s, the two major federal efforts to assist cities were public works, such as harbors and flood control, and relatively small grants-in-aid made to the states for highway construction (Poulson, 1981:596).

The States and the Cities: The Ambivalent Assertion of State Power

The pattern of laissez faire between cities and the federal government was not duplicated in the case of states, however. As industrialization rippled through the nation, the economic and political constraints on state governments in dealing with their cities altered. Prior to the 1850s, state governments had solidly established their absolute legal and constitutional supremacy over cities, a fact that won final recognition in Dillon's Rule in 1868. In this and subsequent cases, cities were unmistakably mere creatures of the state legislature (Gere, 1982). Nevertheless, throughout most of the first half of the nineteenth century state officials adopted a policy of noninterference with the internal affairs of their cities, particularly because they found little interest in the "petty housekeeping of a few small communities which in the aggregate composed but an insignificant part of the entire population" (Gelfand, 1975:6).

THE POLITICAL ECONOMY OF STATE–CITY RELATIONS.   But the industrial transformation set into motion an assertion of state power over their cities. As urban populations mushroomed and wealth became increasingly centered in the urban industrial centers, state governments had to reassess their political and economic stakes in city jurisdictions. The growth of industrial cities entailed the increasing concentration of state wealth in such areas. These facts redefined the political and economic positions of states vis-à-vis their localities, particularly in the more populous regions of the industrial heartland, and initiated an era of far more widespread state intervention in the affairs of cities.

The growing political power of cities created greater political conflict and competition between state and local jurisdictions. First, as city government grew, politicians at the state level saw an opportunity to use local political systems in order to strengthen their power bases in partisan conflicts in state politics. Consequently, after midcentury, state legislatures initiated greater supervision and control over jobs and services delivered by localities.

Second, the increased political power of growing urban areas threatened rural political interests, whose representatives dominated most state governments. The emergence of larger urban populations threatened to upset the relative positions of state political parties and put voters in rural areas at the mercy of city voters. Unless states acted to check the numerical supremacy of voters in the cities, the careers of politicians and the survival of those parties whose power base lay in agricultural districts and small towns would be endangered. By the 1890s, the growth of large urban centers made the threat of urban domination of statehouses and legislatures a present reality rather than a distant danger. For instance, New York City and its environs had a population of 2.5 million, equal to about 45 percent of the state's population. Many of these people regularly voted for the entrenched Democratic machine, directly challenging Republican state chieftains whose voter strongholds were in rural upstate areas (Gelfand, 1975:10).

As a result, in New York and in many other states sharing similar imbalances in urban–rural political power, legislatures acted to deprive cities of equitable representation. Various devices for checking equal representation were used in almost every state in the industrial heartland. Probably the most widespread technique was to stop reapportioning even though the distribution and size of the state population changed. Though many state constitutions required a reallocation of legislative seats every decade in order to reflect population changes, these provisions were often ignored (Gelfand, 1975:12). In all, the changing political position of cities in state politics fostered greater partisan conflict and competition between state officials and many of their localities.

These tendencies toward greater political conflict between states and cities were counterbalanced by a very different pattern of economic relationship between these jurisdictions, however. In general, there emerged a tendency for the market positions of states and growing industrial cities to converge as the nation experienced the Industrial Revolution. During the mercantile period, state and city market positions were often quite different. The widespread and unstable economic competition among cities in the mercantile era constrained city governments to compete for state assistance. State governments retained an important and highly independent role as initiators of canal, roadway, and railroad projects that could spell the difference between economic life and death for particular cities. In the industrial era, however, the process of economic development tended to favor established, large, central city locations in ways suggested earlier. As a result, the economies of state governments became closely linked to the economic fortunes of their larger, most economically competitive cities; to promote the economic base of the industrial city was nearly identical to promoting the economic base of the state.

In summary, the developing federal system saw the emergence of new political and economic relationships between the national and state governments and localities. As political and economic developments at the national level fostered laissez faire, the national governmental presence in cities declined to a point where in 1904 a textbook on municipal government declared that "the city has no relations with the national government" (Gelfand, 1975:21).

In contrast, at the state level the growing political and economic power of the central city acted to redefine state–local relations within the federal framework. A pattern of greater political competition arose that was accompanied by convergence in the market positions of state and city governments. As subsequent chapters describe, this set of ambivalent forces colored intergovernmental relations throughout the period. As the growth of city political power and the movement of people from rural districts to cities challenged the stability of state political systems and the rural way of life, the economic power of the central city became the bedrock of state prosperity. Consequently, state and local relations ranged from active conflict and intervention to cooperation and autonomy in urban policy.

Industrial Democracy

The cities of post-Civil War America came to incorporate more of the features of a liberal-democratic regime in which markets and popular control decisively shape the activities of the state. Industrial capitalism forged a relatively hierarchical urban market order that diminished city economic competition, conferring an unprecedented degree of economic independence on most larger, rapidly growing cities that had won ascendance during the mercantile era. Simultaneously, the development of mass democratic politics became incorporated into local government. Federalism also underwent evolutionary changes, particularly the uneven development of relations between localities and their higher level governments.

How these characteristics of the urban political economy shaped local governance and public policy is the subject of the following chapters.

CHAPTER SEVEN

Development: Machines, Capitalists, and the Politics of Business Autonomy

Urban Development and the Industrial Political Economy

THE industrial political economy could not help but fundamentally transform the politics of local economic development. In almost every respect, the economic and political constraints on city development in the industrial era differed from those of the commercial period. First, the regional wars for city imperialism dissipated with industrialization and gave birth to a far less competitive core and periphery system of cities in which central cities were the prime locale of economic activity. With urban governments no longer absorbed in regional battles to overcome the physical barriers of the hinterland, policies for growth in the leading cities turned inward in order to promote themselves as sites for industrial enterprise.

In the industrial economy, the internal physical development of the city, rather than of the hinterland, became of primary importance for city growth. Beyond tightly bound commercial districts lay an essentially underdeveloped city having the most rudimentary urban services, hodge-podge patterns of land use, poor roads, rickety bridges, and scarce housing. All these things were barriers to community prosperity. Industrial development required an urban setting that fostered the efficient organization of land, labor, and capital for industrial enterprise. The primary developmental task facing leaders of the day was no less than the entire physical transformation of urban space.

Accompanying this change of direction was a dramatic loosening of the severe resource constraints of the past. Unlike the costly canal and railroad projects, which offered only the long-term prospect of prosperity for the community in intense competition with other cities, far less risky internal programs to accommodate industrial activities brought resources to city governments with speed and certainty.

Second, changes in local popular control systems created a new source of tension in city development. While the oligarchic government of the commercial era was nearly identical with the structure of economic power in local

101

communities, in the industrial cities mass democratic institutions provided a political framework distinct from the structure of the industrial capitalism. These institutions for determining public values were based on an entirely different logic than that of the market. Democratic government imposed on cities the mechanism of popular approval of governmental decisions affecting the community: Industrial capitalism worked to subject people, land, money, and even whole cities to private decisions under the discipline of the market.

In effect, the politics of urban economic development was thrown into an "uneasy relationship" between the calculus of democracy and the calculus of the market. The liberal-democratic characteristics of the regime assured that the division of labor (and control) between public vs. private power over community development loomed throughout the period. The issue constantly before city governments was this: How much economic autonomy could private economic enterprise be permitted in a political order that enabled other interests to voice political demands regarding urban development?

Finally, the evolving federal system ensured that this key issue was resolved with considerable political independence of higher levels of government. In an era of rapid industrial growth, the national government grew detached from the problems of city development. Because the processes of industrial growth favored established central city locations, the economies of state governments became closely intertwined with those of their cities. Even though city growth threatened to upset the political status quo in state governments, the prosperity of states was inextricably linked to the prosperity of their central cities. What followed from these new economic realities was a generally cooperative relationship between central cities and states on developmental policy. Accordingly, this relationship was enhanced by deliberate state policies that sought to ensure the economic self-reliance of cities. In effect, the federal system fostered local political and economic independence in shaping policies for urban development.

Developmental Policy: Promoting the Private City

As described earlier, developmental policy acts to enhance the economic base of the community. Given the ascendant market positions enjoyed by core city governments and the absence of much intergovernmental regulation in urban development, industrial cities turned inwards and provided mostly indirect inducements to the private sector in support of their investment activities. Generally, the thrust of public policy was to utilize governmental resources and regulatory powers to organize the internal physical infrastructure required for large-scale industrial production. Although this usually meant gradually increasing public intervention in the local economy, central cities limited their direction of developmental activities and extensively relegated this to the private sector. Overall, public policy tended to enhance and support the role of private market decisions as the dominant influence in city building.[1]

Three major policy strategies were employed by America's industrial cities to guide their physical growth: (1) policies to build the city's physical infrastructure, (2) policies to reorganize urban land in order to promote its rapid private development, and (3) policies to expand the political and economic boundaries of the city.

Building the City Infrastructure

First, cities undertook programs to provide public and private investment in their public infrastructure—roadways, bridges, tunnels, public buildings, wharves, port and transit facilities, sewage systems, water service, and other "public goods" which, though necessary for carrying out private economic activities, are not easily if at all provided by the market (Musgrave, 1943; Bish, 1971). While cities lacked the resources to develop a public infrastructure in the mercantile era, industrial cities had the wealth and knew it was central to the development of an urban industrial economy.

Large-scale industrial production could not occur unless an elaborate physical setting was in place that permitted easy and inexpensive commuter transportation by large numbers of workers, good roadways and bridges for moving both heavy and light goods and raw materials, massive sewers to carry off industrial wastes, and a voluminous water supply to satisfy the demands of industry and residents for clean water. One official explained, "Smooth and clean highways are a wise investment from every point of view . . . regardless of cost. No city should think itself rich enough to prosper without them, and no city is so poor that it can not afford them if it has any reason whatever for continued existence" (Kirkland, 1961:214).

Although municipal enterprise and ownership was sometimes viewed with suspicion by city business, even the most cautious supported massive public infrastructure investment by their city governments. Lacking assistance from other governmental sources, city after city borrowed to invest for this purpose on an unprecedented scale. Unlike operating expenditures, which went for current services, these public improvements were usually financed by long-term capital borrowing. Consequently, there occurred a dramatic increase in municipal debt. In 1860, net municipal debtedness in the United States was probably around $200,000,000, but by 1880 it grew to $725,000,000; in 1902, it approached nearly $1.5 billion. Interest on indebtedness accounted for an ever-increasing share of city expenses. For example, interest on the debt of Providence, Rhode Island, required the expenditure of 40 percent of its tax revenues in 1880. In New Jersey, cities' debt service ate up an average of 50 percent of revenues. In New York, cities' charges on debt exceeded the whole cost of running the state government (Glaab and Brown, 1967:180–181).

THE DOMINANCE OF THE PRIVATE SECTOR. Particularly during the first half of this period, political leaders generally permitted the private sector to dominate infrastructure development. This stance of city governments is most clearly illustrated in the case of public utilities and transportation services. To meet the demand for street lighting and street railways, most cities resorted to the use of franchises to private corporations, a contract in which the private company's performance is stipulated and its financial obligations to the city are specified, normally for a given number of years. These franchises were very valuable privileges that permitted a private corporation to acquire property through eminent domain and to use the streets to lay pipes, put down rails, string wires, and, in effect, enjoy a monopoly or semimonopoly position in operating a service.

Despite the fact that utility and electric traction companies that received these franchises could expect increasing business resulting from city growth as long as anyone could predict, the city councils tended to grant highly liberal contracts. Many early franchises were drawn up for periods of fifty to a hundred years and contained only the most vague obligations. New York City's early franchises had no terminal dates at all, while Albany granted one for a thousand years. Similar practices were followed elsewhere (Glaab and Brown, 1967:183; Kirkland, 1961).

Though these arrangements spared hard-pressed city governments from additional debt burdens that publicly funded enterprises would have required, the public paid for careless and liberal franchises through foregone taxes and often unreliable services. Nevertheless, tolerance of such abuses did often serve to rapidly promote industrial expansion in cities. Franchise "generosity" permitted cities to quickly leverage impressive amounts of long-term capital investment in their infrastructure. By the turn of the century, to consider only privately owned utilities, over $300,000,000 was invested in gas works, about $250,000,000 in electric lighting plants, and over $2 billion in street railway systems. Consequently, American cities got extensive street lighting and transportation systems much more rapidly than did most European cities that followed more cautious policies (Glaab and Brown, 1967:185).

PUBLIC REGULATION, PRIVATE CONTROL.   By the turn of the century, city governments became less reliant on private sector provision of major components of the urban infrastructure, however. As detailed below, major changes in the political economy of cities occurred, particularly the rise of big corporate business, which occasioned demands for more widespread local and state control over the city's physical plant. This began a trend toward greater public regulation and ownership.

In the case of the utilities, particularly the transportation and power companies, a reaction against franchise abuses set in once many utilities became consolidated by giant holding companies and began to impose a stranglehold over cities and their business communities. Numbers of cities initiated court actions, undertook franchise reform to curb the worst practices, and, through state governments, began to impose utility regulation, usually via independent commissions that often had the authority to disallow any grant or franchise. By the 1920s, regulatory commissions were functioning in most states. As the number of competing transit systems declined in the 1890s, larger cities, such as

Boston and New York, undertook public construction of subways and streetcar lines (McKelvey, 1973:Ch. II).

Coastal city governments responded in an even more interventionist fashion with respect to their strategic seaports. Prior to the turn of the century, private capital owned, developed, and operated port facilities in all but a few American harbors. Railroads were often the primary owners and had managed to establish private monopolies on valuable waterfront lands given to them by civic boosters seeking rail development for their cities. Eventually, many rail lines practiced monopoly abuses, such as discriminatory tariffs, inflated handling charges, and denial of port access, which discouraged city port development. Alternatively, other harbors under fragmented private ownership experienced overdevelopment as a result of intense competition; this led to underutilization of port facilities, high costs, and inability of groups of many small owners to amass sufficient capital for expansion of their terminals. Thus, private ownership of the ports could not keep pace with growing demand by shippers. Consequently, nearly all major ports came under public ownership within the first two decades of this century in response to local political movements that saw governmental ownership and operation as means of obtaining better service and cheaper rate schedules for users (Denning and Olson, 1981:30–31).

The expansion of public control over the city physical plant after the turn of the century did not necessarily occasion a decline in business influence over urban development, however. As detailed below, local political leaders were often willing to accommodate greater business involvement in the supervision and planning of the city's growth in the expectation that they could exploit city building ventures for jobs, patronage, and favors. For instance, Tammany politicians were willing to permit New York City's Chamber of Commerce to dominate the Rapid Transit Commission, which was established in 1894 to build the city's first subway (Hammack, 1982:Ch. 8). Similarly, once utility regulation was imposed on many cities by state legislatures, the utilities found regulation by friendly state commissions more open to their influence than was the case previously. Most important, as the reform movement grew after the turn of the century along with expansion of public authority in cities, the effect of most reform campaigns was one of restructuring local governments in ways that permitted business leaders and reformers to gain direct control of city and state agencies, commissions, and authorities in the developmental arena.

Land Use Policy: Laissez Faire "Planning"

Land use policies constituted the second component of central city development strategy. Apart from land, there is virtually no other economic resource over which city governments have such direct control; and because it is scarce, highly valued, and determinative of location in the production process, its allocation among competing uses could provide city authorities with decisive influence over economic development. The political control of vast but relatively empty urban open space afforded great opportunities for shaping the built environment at the outset.

City governments, however, generally adopted a laissez faire posture in regulating the development of their land. City commissioners typically permitted the decisions of private sector builders, developers, and businesses to dominate the allocation of urban open space in all but uncommon instances where public considerations for parks and educational and civic institutions displaced the free market.

This policy was most apparent during the nineteenth century in big cities where tenement districts were rapidly developed with few public restrictions, resulting in severe crowding and human misery. Here, the building and renting of what would be considered today the most substandard housing, such as cellars and poorly ventilated and lighted rooms in tenements, were left more or less to the laws of the market. As detailed below, proposals to proscribe the worst housing abuses were frequently debated, sometimes enacted, but rarely enforced.

Weak public control and the devolution of developmental decisions to the private sector were also reflected in the gridiron pattern of street layout that cities generally adopted throughout the period. Though this pattern left much to be desired from the standpoint of providing an attractive human environment, it served to spur rapid city development and private profit. The driving forces behind street design and layout were real estate speculation and quantitative efficiency in construction and sales of individual parcels, making the gridiron pattern the inevitable result.

For instance, during the 1860s the Central Park Commission in New York was entrusted to change the plan of the city's West Side, and the outcome, given the Commission's bias toward city growth, was predictable. Insisting on respecting established patterns of land ownership and individual property rights, the Commission planned a series of major avenues that conformed as closely as possible to the city's dominant gridiron. They avoided designing "new streets, avenues, squares, parks and terraces" because of "injury to existing subdivisions of property" which would be left "in unfit parcels to build upon, except by the tedious processes of exchange and sales between owners" (Mandelbaum, 1965:60; cf. Warner, 1972).

PUBLIC REGULATION, PRIVATE CONTROL.   Around the turn of the century, reform groups began a movement for city planning to provide an enlarged local governmental role in guiding the use of land in city development. But the history of this development is generally one of conspicuous failure at the local level because, as described below, the economic and governmental structures that drove the city governments to give priority to private sector regulation of land use remained unchanged. Consequently, programs to increase public regulation of urban development did little more than enhance private control of urban space.

Zoning practices reflect this outcome perhaps better than anything else. Although zoning regulations were applied in European cities around the turn of the century, they developed much more slowly in the United States. Their adoption in most cities tended to follow rather than precede their periods of dramatic industrial growth. Before 1916, only five American cities had zoning regulations, but in the following years many more cities adopted this land use policy so that by 1930 the number of zoned cities rose to 981 (Glaab and Brown, 1967:291).

While early ordinances were designed to do little more than keep residential areas free from business and industry and generally regulated land use only in selected areas of the city, later ordinances tended to be more comprehensive. They regulated not only land use, but also the height and bulk of buildings and progressively became more elaborate, requiring setbacks for tall buildings and so forth.

But the spread of zoning regulations usually had less to do with controlling growth than with enhancing and reinforcing through governmental power existing patterns of land use determined largely by private interests. For example, in New York City the adoption of a citywide zoning law in 1916 was supported by business interests hoping to enhance property values. Powerful support came from Fifth Avenue merchants who were distressed by the encroachment of garment industry operations into their exclusive shopping district (Makielski, 1966:140–141). The official rationale for this law echoed their sentiments:

> The natural result of a poor utilization of its land areas by a city is high rents for occupiers and low profits for investors. . . . It may seem paradoxical to hold that a policy of building restriction tends to a fuller utilization of land than a policy of no restriction, but such is undoubtedly the case. The reason lies in the greater safety and security to investment secured by definite restrictions (Glaab and Brown, 1967:292).

The development of the movement for urban planning exhibits a similar theme. Following the lead of European reformers and the indigenous success of isolated schemes in urban America, numbers of cities set up planning commissions after the turn of the century. The number of planning commissions and boards grew from seventeen in 1914 to over 735 in 1930, and, while they were invariably advisory agencies, their powers tended to increase. Nevertheless, compared to their European counterparts, the American planning movement never had a very substantial impact on urban land development.

Comprehensive plans for city development were almost universally utopian endeavors that brought together information about extant patterns of land use and development. Unlike America, planners in Europe typically had both municipal and national authority behind their endeavors, providing them with a powerful political base outside the local community. In contrast, in laissez faire America, reformers had little choice but to seek a political base in local business communities and governments, whose leaders were usually opposed to the extensive use of governmental powers that urban planning implied (Sutcliffe, 1982).

Consequently, the people who planned or who sat on planning commissions were usually downtown merchants, utility and transit executives, bank directors, real estate representatives, railroad bosses, and a sprinkling of professionals; their major interests were in issues related to improving the commercial environment of the city, bettering transit facilities, relieving downtown congestion, protecting property values, and undertaking occasional proposals to beautify public areas, rather than with ambitious plans to achieve larger public objectives (Warner, 1972:207; Lubove, 1970:324).

Annexation and Urban Development

Finally, the third prong of development policy was one of consolidating the central city's economic territory. As populations and economic activities spilled over into suburban and unincorporated areas, the city's limited political boundaries became an important obstacle to growth. Outside the city limits, residents and businesses were generally unable to obtain many important public services that only the central city, with its large tax base, could provide. Consequently, lack of essential public services in the economic territory of the central city threatened the ability of businesses, including those located within the city, to function or expand. Further, economic growth beyond the city's political jurisdiction meant that potential tax ratables were beyond the city's grasp.

Consequently, cities all over the United States undertook ambitious territorial expansion prior to 1920. Between 1870 and 1900, the nation's twenty most populous cities in 1940 won their greatest territorial conquests, expanding their combined legal territories around 18 percent every decade. Most other cities also underwent rapid expansion during this period. Although the total areas of the twenty major cities expanded less rapidly after 1900, the trend continued until the 1920s and then virtually ceased by 1930 (Teaford, 1979:75).

THE STATE POLITICAL ECONOMY AND ANNEXATION POLICY. Unlike other areas of development policy, the vigorous use of annexation by central cities was closely linked to the changing relationship of state governments with city economies. State policies became more permissive of central city political expansion as a result of changing state economic constraints. The incorporation of new municipalities and the consolidation of existing ones had always been a prerogative of the state governments that during the early part of the nineteenth century legislatures kept to themselves. However, this posture of central control dramatically waned during the last half of the nineteenth century. Though partly a result of increasing opposition to state interference in local affairs, changes in state policy were fostered more by the fact that they were compelled to support the rapid development of the central city because the prosperity of states became inextricably tied to the economic power of their large urban areas. The need to promote consolidation of growing industrial areas was as much in the interest of states as it was in the interest of the cities.

Thus, during the period from 1850 to 1910 state legislatures surrendered much of their central authority over annexation to localities in order to permit relatively easy expansion of central city boundaries. This was accomplished in most states by constitutional amendments that provided general legislation establishing procedures for annexation and municipal consolidation; usually these laws prescribed that such questions would be determined by voters in local referendums. Some states, particularly in the West, were more direct in their support of central city expansion. For example, in Kansas, Nebraska, Missouri, and Indiana most cities could annex unincorporated territory through passage of a simple ordinance without the consent of residents of the area to be annexed (Teaford, 1979:35, 50).

By devolving the decisions over annexation to the local level, these alterations in state law almost invariably made it easier for central cities to expand their limits into suburban areas. This was so because the central city, with its magnificent revenue base from which to fund city services, promised to satisfy the suburban desire for better public services following annexation. Few suburbs could equal the central cities in the provision of public services, and residents were often forced to pay high taxes and fees for the poor services they did have.

For example, water rates in suburban areas around major cities such as Chicago, New York, and Portland were often a third or more higher than the central cities, and most of these suburban localities lacked good police protection, professional fire companies, sewers, electric light franchises, or a piped water supply—things that were taken for granted by city residents. Law enforcement in suburbs was often wholly inadequate. As one Indianapolis police superintendent put it, "the toughs and roughs . . . have all gone out to the suburbs [where] they have a snap" (Teaford, 1979:51). Consequently, in suburb after suburb residents usually chose to unite with the central city.

State laws ensured that there was almost no alternative to annexation by the central city if a suburb wanted to enjoy better public services. Until well into the twentieth century, state laws did not permit existing township and county governments to provide many public services. No state during the nineteenth century authorized counties to build waterworks, lay sewer systems, construct gas or electric plants, or provide a range of public amenities; townships were authorized only to provide limited services appropriate for rural living (Teaford, 1979:25). Similarly, the use of special purpose districts to deliver services to numbers of scattered suburban localities was not permitted by most state legislatures until well into the twentieth century. In effect, by providing for "local determination" through general laws governing annexation, state legislatures enabled central cities to utilize their superior economic position to extend their political boundaries.

The fundamental unity of state and city interests in using annexation to spur urban economic growth is best illustrated by the creation of Greater New York in 1898. Because New York was one of the very few states whose lawmakers retained the power to legislate municipal boundaries, the state's direct cooperation with New York City vividly demonstrates their shared interests on matters of development. The state law consolidated old New York City, which consisted of only Manhattan and what is now the South Bronx, with Brooklyn, Staten Island, and what later became the modern boroughs of the Bronx and Queens to form Greater New York. For years, the city's business elites promoted the idea of extending the city's boundaries to knit the region's diverse municipalities into a coherent transportation system and a single, well-serviced real estate market. Most important, the Chamber of Commerce saw that a unified city could improve the all-important port better than could the disparate efforts of New York City, Brooklyn, and the petty municipalities of Queens and Staten Island acting independently (Hammack, 1982:194).

The city's business and political leaders ultimately put together a powerful and cohesive coalition during the 1890s to press the state legislature for action. Eventually, the harbor and its problems not only united five counties in an impressive proconsolidation coalition, it also guaranteed positive action by the Republican state legislature and party boss Thomas C. Platt, whose partisan interests were often opposed to New York City's Tammany Hall machine. Whipping Republican legislators into line to pass the consolidation measure, Platt easily overcame partisan rivalries in order to advance the most fundamental economic interests of the metropolis and of the state. He supported the city's merchant community in order to promote, as he put it, "the complete and rational development of the metropolis so as to protect its threatened . . . supremacy" (Hammack, 1982:216).

Developmental Politics: Spheres of Elite Influence

That the governments of central cities did not take a more directive role in managing their economies and, instead, promoted a "private city" approach to urban growth is a great irony of this period. This outcome cannot be explained by the economic power of business in local government affairs, a pattern that was more typical of local government during the mercantile era. In fact, the prevailing political and economic structures thrust city governments into a *potentially* powerful, if not commanding, position in development.

First, the coming of mass democracy all but shattered the tradition of elite government, ending the days when the city's commercial oligarchy selected the leading local officials. As the urban electorate expanded, merchant elites tended to leave city leadership positions. An era of mass politics emerged, compelling city political leaders to secure widespread political support in order to maintain their authority.

Second, the central city's favorable market position checked the economic power of business in city affairs. Because business opportunities in the industrial economy were tied to the central city, urban business lacked their most potent political resource: the threat of relocating or otherwise withholding their productive contributions from the locality. Given these important political and economic changes, business had no other choice but to compete with other groups for political power on a far more equal footing than before.

Finally, private sector interests in community development became more diverse and unstable compared with the mercantile era. As urban business turned to compete for economic opportunities within cities, tight-knit business oligarchies sharing easily identifiable interests in city development policy faded into the past. When the days of intergovernmental warfare abated and city policies for canals, railroads, and other improvements no longer unified merchant communities for the sake of their survival, urban business lost an important source of political cohesion.

These traditional sources of cohesion were not replaced during the industrial era by equally compelling ones. In industrial capitalism, the major shared interest of urban business in city government was that of autonomy, i.e., freedom to exploit and dominate the process of industrial growth (cf. McConnell, 1966; Kolko, 1967; Cochran and Miller, 1961). But this interest in autonomy could hardly serve as a very stable source of business unity in developmental politics because the process of industrialization was constantly forging new interests and political demands within urban business communities. Most important, industrial capitalism evolved new units of business enterprise, beginning with the rise of speculative entrepreneurs around midcentury and progressing to larger, more bureaucratic, and far less competitive forms with the rise of giant corporations tied to national markets.

Since these forms of business organization owned different scales of operation and shared different stakes in the urban economy, they could not help but promote different interests in the politics of development. As detailed below, during the upheavals of industrialization small entrepreneurs had an interest in preserving limited corrupt government willing to sell favors because capitalizing on speculative opportunities was essential to their growth and survival. But big business that owned a fixed stake in the prevailing urban economy could not be expected to share this interest; their ability to enhance their position depended more on order and certainty in the urban economy, and they saw bureaucratic government as a means of protecting their privileges and power. For the latter, the growth of urban governmental power was acceptable because it could serve as a conduit for business influence in city economic development. In effect, the demand for business autonomy took different forms as different types of businesses emerged and supported changing claims for the use of public power.

Consequently, the failure of city governments to utilize their potentially commanding influence to shape city economic development cannot be credited to the supposed economic power of urban business. This outcome is best understood as a by-product of a *political struggle* that took place within the developing liberal-democratic regime at the local level. The relative power of urban business in the developmental arena depended largely upon the bargaining advantages it could muster in competition with other groups via the process of popular control. This, in turn, depended on whether the party politics of the period—which defined the basic linkages between mass public and political authorities—could provide a viable system of mass influence over city political leadership.

As it turns out, the dominant pattern was the failure of popular control institutions to contain business' struggle for autonomy in urban development. City government's position of influence over the private sector was frittered away as party politicians capitalized on business' drive for autonomy in the course of building the political machine. What emerged was a politics characterized by spheres of interest between political party and economic elites seeking mutual exploitation of the city's growth; they accomplished this by insulating developmental issues from the discipline of popular control. Such a theme emerged during the three major periods of developmental politics: (1) disorganized politics, (2) machine politics, and (3) machine-reform politics.

Disorganized Politics and Economic Development

The disintegration of the old oligarchical politics of the cities was often followed by a transitional system of developmental decision making in which policies were largely by-products of highly disorganized political competition. The dominant characteristic of this political order was the weakness of city political organizations and the fluidity of local political alignments—a pattern of politics which resembled more that of an underdeveloped polity than the (later) highly organized politics of the machine era (Shefter, 1976).

During these years, the usual political divisions in major industrial cities involved unstable coalitions of politicians held together mostly by little more than a common desire for power. It produced a politics that tended to duplicate in the governmental order the upheaval, competition, and individualism of the new industrial economic system. Party and factional loyalties were so weak that political cooperation usually depended on personal payoffs in undertaking either electoral or governmental activities. Party officials, governmental leaders, as well as those seeking to influence governmental activities, all had to pay with cash, jobs, contracts, and the like in order to make the system work for them.

While it is not certain if all major industrial cities shared these characteristics during the transition from the mercantile era, such a pattern appears to typify many large cities prior to the rise of powerful party organizations. New York City during the years up to the fall of the Tweed Ring (1866–1871), a period that has been described as one of "rapacious individualism" (Shefter, 1976), illustrates this pattern. Though the Democratic party nominally dominated the city's politics, it was often divided by competing factions within the party's leading political club, the Tammany Society; the latter was in turn frequently challenged by anti-Tammany Democratic political clubs and factional groupings whose members were ". . . prepared to change their allegiance as their career interests dictated" (Shefter, 1976:22). The Tweed Ring merely extended this system rather than departed from it. Its members occupied positions in each of the major branches and boards of the city government. Since Tweed was unable to command the support of public officials in the Ring, he was forced to purchase it by creating a system of exchanging bribes and payoffs to win favorable legislation and electoral support from party leaders. The Tweed Ring was essentially an intragovernmental grouping held together by patterns of bribery and corruption.

Far from staunchly opposing this system of politics, there is considerable evidence that it found widespread business support. Although chaotic, disorganized politics provided many advantages to the kind of businesses that dominated the urban economy during the early years of industrialization—the speculative entrepreneurs. The latter's major interest was in seeking opportunities for new commercial ventures, capitalizing on the dramatic transformation of the city. Although this group included the numerous small business entrepreneurs—legitimate and illicit—who struggled to exploit petty investment opportunities, more politically important were the wealthier speculator-investors. This group included utility investors seeking lucrative franchise deals, real estate speculators whose fortunes were tied to rapidly rising land values, contractors looking for city contracts for roads and public buildings, and financiers such as the legendary entrepreneurs Jay Gould, Cornelius Vanderbilt, John Jacob Astor, and Jim Fisk, who made their personal fortunes in the commodity, stock, and bond markets (Shefter, 1976:29). To these entrepreneurs, the chaotic politics epitomized by Tweed offered immense advantage: It provided them with a political structure that was highly permeable to their demands and worked reliably to expand entrepreneurial opportunities in exchange for cash payments. This political "market" system shifted urban politics from its formal democratic foundation to an informal one based on the buying and selling of political power.

At the same time, this system of power expanded entrepreneurial opportunity by overcoming important governmental obstacles to city economic growth. Probably the most important of these was the chaotic and fragmented local governmental arrangements inherited from mercantile days that threatened to hamstring the rapid building of the city's physical infrastructure. In New York, as in other cities, public purposes were incessantly frustrated by the widespread dispersal of governmental authority in the hands of numerous officials, boards, commissions, and other legal authorities set up by charter and legislative provisions. In 1870 in New York, three different sets of officials controlled the streets; the metropolitan police were legally independent of local ordinances and supervision, and the mayor was a figurehead unable to control his subordinates. To overcome this dispersion of government authority, Tweed in 1870 paid $600,000 in bribes to have a new charter enacted that provided greater opportunities for centralizing control over governmental operations (Mandelbaum, 1965:71–72).

Elsewhere, entrepreneurial forces demonstrated similar support for disorganized politics. For example, in Republican Philadelphia speculative entrepreneurs and party bosses created a political system similar to New York's by directly joining the economic power of utility companies to the party machine. This produced an identity of interests that literally confounded any public–private distinction in the city's developmental politics. In the 1840s, the city bought out a private company that was supplying the city with gas and proceeded to run it as a municipal enterprise. This public enterprise had the power to contract for construction and repairs and could issue its own bonds; this meant that it could distribute favors to many contractors, and its control of over 2,000 employees gave it the largest block of patronage in the city. After the Civil War, the Gas Trust, a faction of entrepreneurial politicians, emerged under the leadership of James McManes. Through skillful distribution of contracts and jobs, he and his associates won control over most of the city's other utilities as well as the gas works. They soon acquired Philadelphia's largest street transportation company, adding to their patronage, and McManes gained considerable control over the city's Republican party (Glaab and Brown, 1967:206–207).

Machine Politics and Economic Development

Disorganized politics weakened almost at birth the popular control institutions that were created to assure public power in governmental policy. Such a system might well have been no more than a strange and short-lived aberration in democratic practices, as in many Third World nations where political leaders have responded along similar lines under parallel circumstances (Scott, 1972). Yet the demise of disorganized politics was followed by an attempt to systematically organize and entrench its essential political relationships in the form of a new political institution: the political machine.

CHANGING BUSINESS INTERESTS AND THE RISE OF THE MACHINE. As the machine became the dominant urban political institution, its emergence and survival was widely viewed as a product of the social groups that machine politicians organized by trading jobs and favors for votes (Banfield and Wilson, 1965). But such a view, which sees the corruption of machine politics as the choice of poor immigrants who traded their votes for petty personal gain, ignores the important political and economic constraints that limited the political alternatives (Shefter, 1976). Those alternatives were mostly shaped by those who saw major stakes in changing the developmental arena and struggled to reshape it to serve their interests—the urban business community.

While disorganized politics served the demands of many individual entrepreneurs during the chaotic early days of industrial urbanization, it soon proved threatening to newly emerging business interests. Although speculative entrepreneurs and small businesses may have found much value in a highly fragmented political system capable of smoothing the way to business opportunity, by the last quarter of the nineteenth century a different kind of businessman had begun to achieve a position of economic power in cities. This type valued a different kind of political environment. Unlike the speculative entrepreneur, the latter was more conscious of the need to enhance his established business activities. In New York, this group was composed of:

> corporation lawyers . . . entrepreneurs who managed as well as owned the firms with which they were associated . . . or traded in markets and exchanges whose maintenance depended upon the assumption of good faith among the parties to transactions. The entrepreneurs associated with Tweed and those . . . [who opposed

him] . . . prospered under two rather different modes of business competition, modes that rewarded different skills, fostered different values and were, in several respects, in fundamental conflict. If the former acquired their fortunes through great speculative ventures—by virtue of their willingness to assume risks—the latter did so through holding on to their enterprises and managing them well. If the former served their ends by bribing legislators to change, and judges to ignore the law, the latter did so by drafting and relying upon instruments whose value depended upon the predictability of the law. If the former sought to crush their competitors and to deceive those on the other side of the market, the business of the latter depended upon the preservation of the markets (Shefter, 1976:29–30).

In effect, once businesses became large and established, acquiring a fixed stake in the orderly operation of the city's economy, their developmental interests could not be served by a catch-as-catch-can political system. Disorganized politics not only was impermeable to these kinds of interest, it actually threatened them.

First, disorganized politics proved to be so prohibitively costly that it sometimes shook the very economic viability of the city and its businesses. So long as party politics remained a loose confederation of patronage-seeking politicians, the only feasible strategy for governance was an enormously inflationary one. Unable to command obedience, political leaders had to purchase it.

In New York City, the Tweed Ring's depredations were carried to such extremes to fuel this method of governance that the city's credit was threatened. To maintain his power, Tweed sponsored huge numbers of schemes and projects that were largely financed by the issue of city bonds. Municipal indebtedness in 1867 was a little under $30,000,000, but four years later it had climbed to $90,000,000. The size of the city's debt threatened to undermine the value of New York City municipal bonds, directly affecting the survival of many of the city's financial and business institutions. For instance, impairment of the city's credit in foreign capital markets crippled the ability of city financiers to place other securities abroad. In addition, the threat of heavy tax burdens on real estate acted to deflate real estate values and threaten corporate holders of mortgages. The interests of important segments of the business community had become inextricably intertwined with that of the city government (Mandelbaum, 1965:78).

Second, disorganized politics proved to be an ineffective means of imposing social control and order on the rapidly growing city, threatening the security of property and business. Three kinds of social conflict increased under this system. There was increasing tension between workers and employers, which periodically broke out in violent strikes. There were increasing confrontations between native-born Americans and immigrants whose growing presence was considered threatening to established ways and customs. Finally, general discontent arose from the immigrant wards of cities where overcrowding, ill health, poverty, poor housing, and crime were escalating. Virtually all big cities suffered major epidemics of violence arising from these causes. New York City alone experienced a succession of riots, eight major and at least ten minor, between 1834 and 1871. This climaxed in the fearful riot in the midst of the Civil War in 1863 when a protest against the draft exploded into a mixed class and race riot among the city's workingmen and the poor Irish.

Under these circumstances, business and financial leaders in major cities made dramatic moves to undermine disorganized politics in favor of a more organized, though equally corrupt, alternative: the political machine. Often this opportunity was afforded by the fiscal collapse of cities driven to financial excesses by their disorganized political systems. In New York, as Mandelbaum suggests, the "bond market was the Achilles Heel" of the Tweed Ring (1965:78). The city's bondholders staged what was essentially a coup by refusing to extend any more short-term credit to the city and demanded that they be given control over choosing individuals to supervise the city's financial management. In Philadelphia, similar events ended the days of the Gas Trust. The city's teetering debt motivated a reform coalition led by prominent businessmen to expel the McManes administration and put the government's finances in order (Glaab and Brown, 1967:207–208).

SPHERES OF INFLUENCE: BOSSES, BUSINESS, AND THE MACHINE.   Once in power, those who orchestrated the takeover of city government moved to set up a new and more disciplined political machine. In New York City, business leaders and reformers who overturned Tweed won a commanding position in Tammany Hall, and they managed to elevate John Kelly to a position of leadership to succeed Tweed. With business support, Kelly undertook to develop an organization capable of disciplining its members and centralizing power. Among Kelly's most important reforms was the setting up of machinery to control the admission and expulsion of members of the organization, authority to review decisions and membership of local units, and efforts to end personal bases of power and patronage within the party. In addition, public officials as well as party politicians became subject to the discipline and control of the organization. Although the party remained subject to factional challenges for some years, Kelly's efforts in centralization progressed until the late 1880s when Tammany eventually succeeded in crushing its rivals within the Democratic party (Shefter, 1976).

In other cities, the movement of business to support the machine appears to have been more gradual, particularly when precipitous fiscal collapse was avoided. For instance, in Cincinnati a period of crisis brought on by disorganized politics eventually led local businesses to support the rise of a Republican political machine. During the 1880s, Cincinnati witnessed growing social and economic disorder as its chaotic political system failed to cope with the city's industrial transition. The decade was permeated by rising crime, riots, and unprecedented outbursts of public disorder. In 1884, the total number of arrests came to 56,784 in a city with a total population of only 250,000—over one-fifth of its population. The political system was so fragmented into competing factions that throughout the 1880s no party could put together a decisive ruling majority on the city council. Consequently, the city government was regarded by hosts of citizens, especially the city's business leaders, as hopelessly ineffective. The relative decline of the city in regional economic importance heightened discontent and created an atmosphere of crisis late in the decade (Miller, 1968).

These events moved business to support the consolidation of governmental power in a political machine. During the 1880s, the Republican party under the leadership of George B. Cox emerged to impose political order. Cox worked his way into the party's leadership by garnering support from prominent business activists, particularly the gas and traction companies, the town's leading newspapers, merchants, and suburban reformers in the city's outer wards. His strategy was to explicitly build a party organization that could unite the city's inner "zone," comprising many poor, working-class, and ethnic voters, with the party's traditional power base in the better-off areas on the fringes of the city. As Miller describes it, ". . . the regime worked most earnestly toward those objectives of the new order deemed essential to the economic well-being of the city or the comfort or convenience of the party's supporters on the suburban fringe" (1968:100). While elements of this program also won votes in the "zone," the party's popularity there was more dependent on patronage, Christmas turkeys, private charity, personal loyalties, and Cox's charm and style, which appealed to workers, ethnics, and the poor who lived in these wards.

What emerged during the rise of the political machine was a new coincidence of interests between political and economic elites in the cities. The result was a liberal-democratic regime based on "spheres of influence"—or separation between market and polity—rather than tension between the private sector and popular control. On one hand, the machine provided urban party elites with a sphere of influence in which they could pursue personal enrichment by controlling things that capital did not deem important. By utilizing the distribution of jobs and favors and playing on ethnic and neighborhood rivalries in exchange for votes, the machine represented the individual demands of the immigrant, but not their demands as a class. In effect, the machine perverted popular control institutions into a system of elite social control of the masses.

On the other hand, the machine provided business with a sphere of influence: political autonomy in urban development policy. For several reasons, business found that the machine was unexcelled in delivering this. First, business found in the machine a political juggernaut of immense power to defuse and fragment the demands of disadvantaged groups who, because of their numerical preponderance, stood in a position to utilize city politics as a means of pressing their claims as a class. The machine boss not only shared business' interest in eliminating these demands in order to control the voter, he did so more reliably than business could hope to on its own. In New York, this fact was not lost on one business newspaper editor who observed, "Kelly has ruled the fierce Democracy in such a manner that life and property are comparatively safe. . . . It requires a great man to stand between the City Treasury and this most dangerous mass . . . dethrone Kelly, and where is the man to succeed him?" (Shefter, 1976:28).

Second, business found machine politicians to be highly supportive in limiting local government's role in developmental matters. Machine politicians did not usually seek governmental authority to operate services such as transit and utilities that could earn a profit; they were content with the illegal payoffs that accompanied the franchises offered private companies (Hammack, 1982:55–56, 169).

Third, the machine enabled business to achieve influence over urban economic affairs in an orderly and reliable way. Tied economically and, hence, politically, to the central city, business' potentially weak bargaining position in urban politics could in previous years only be overcome by capitalizing on periods of urban upheaval, political disorganization, and fiscal collapse. But these circumstances could never serve to provide business with a stable source of political power. Further, the devastating economic consequences of such events threatened business' interests in orderly urban development.

The machine overcame these problems, however. By centralizing power and corruption in the hands of party bosses, the machine acted to routinize and contain the system of exchanging bribes and other inducements that business could offer in return for political favors and support, be they forms of assistance for particular businesses or continuous support for more general goals of the business community. By making routine and orderly what under the old regime was transitory and chaotic, the machine conferred on business the capacity for political autonomy in promoting their developmental interests. The major struggles over developmental policy could take place within the business community. Once a consensus was achieved there, the centralized system of bribe-giving and favor-trading would assure the implementation of developmental decisions.

SPHERES OF INFLUENCE AT WORK. *Public Utility Politics.* This system of spheres of influence is most vividly illustrated in the case of utility companies that sought and received political support needed to dominate the growth of their industries. During the late nineteenth century, utility companies struggled to win monopoly positions in providing street railways, gas, electricity, water, and other services. With their considerable fixed assets and dependence on governmental intervention, the utilities were continually subject to the threat of extortionate demands from politicians in the old system of disorganized politics.

Consequently, the utilities in most cities actively supported the machine because it could strike long-term bargains and promote their monopoly objectives (Shefter, 1976:387; Thelen, 1972). Their demands met with favor from party politicians attempting to build a centralized machine because the presence of fragmented industries all competing to offer bribes was a disruptive force that subverted their ability to discipline subordinates. It was in the interests of both to promote consolidation. Thus, as New York City's street railway system underwent consolidation in the 1890s, the machine became a valuable ally to the monopoly objectives of this segment of the business community. For instance, under Richard Croker's leadership, the city government displayed considerable favoritism to the Metropolitan Street Railway Company and took a direct role in assuring the destruction of the Metropolitan's last remaining competitor, the Third Avenue Railway Company (Shefter, 1976:38).

The Politics of Annexation. When urban business communities could unite on progrowth policies that were considered important, the machine typically was willing to deliver its support or not obstruct their endeavors as long as the party's organizational interests were protected. In general, this relationship permitted a city's major developmental issues to be bargained out with considerable autonomy by city business elites.

The decision for the consolidation of Greater New York is illustrative of this pattern. As described earlier, proposals by business and political leaders to extend the city's boundaries were hotly debated for a number of years and were largely a response to the commercial community's feeling that hodge-podge political control of the metropolitan area discouraged investment and growth. But a remarkable aspect of the struggle by the city's economic elites to promote consolidation was the relative indifference of New York City's party power brokers to this issue. In the events leading up to the state legislation that created Greater New York in 1898, Tammany politicians generally took little interest. The machine permitted local business elites to maneuver and bargain out their differences with state Republican boss Richard Platt over the consolidation measure they wanted. Since the legislation offered the possibility of extending Tammany power and patronage, the major interest of machine leaders was to ensure that proposals that would deprive them of a large proportion of the patronage in New York and Brooklyn would be dropped. Once this was accomplished, Tammany support followed (Hammack, 1982:218).

BUSINESS, POLITICS, AND POPULAR CONTROL. The movement of urban business communities to the machine style of government was not inevitable under the social, economic, and political circumstances of the late nineteenth century; but the costs and uncertainties of reorganizing the mass politics of the industrial city along different lines was unacceptable to business reformers. A major alternative to machine government would have been for business to compete for power in cities by utilizing programmatic or ideological appeals that would attract mass followings, offering things that would have been valued by workers, immigrants, ethnics, and other nonproperty owners as a class. Electoral and governmental reforms that cleaned up the chaotic state of party politics and guaranteed greater political equality in running city government, policies for social reform that could have been delivered by the cities of the day, such as lower transit fares and cheaper utilities and other programs that would have broad electoral appeal, could have served and sometimes did serve (see below) as a means of garnering broad support for giving business candidates political power in cities. Much like the "Tory Democracy" of Disraeli's Britain, where the Conservative party of the nineteenth century successfully managed the nation's transition to democratic politics by associating the traditional ruling class with programs of social reform of appeal to new worker-voters (Beer, 1965), a similar strategy was open to America's urban business leaders.

Nevertheless, urban business leaders were usually reluctant to accept the uncertainties, compromises, and costs of such a political strategy. Whenever business reformers attempted to actually take on a more direct role in governing cities in the wake of periodic collapse of corrupt and disorganized boss government, they nearly always met with failure as a result of their unwillingness to compete with programs that would command sufficiently broad electoral appeal. For example, following Boss Tweed's downfall a reform commission appointed by Governor Samuel J. Tilden recommended that voting rights in municipal elections be limited to taxpaying property owners (Glaab and Brown, 1967:213). The major demand of these members of the city's business community was for programs of severe retrenchment unaccompanied by efforts to win popular confidence with social and economic reforms. In other cities, the story was very similar throughout the century, leading to a pattern in which early "reform" carried out by business-dominated civic committees became but a brief interlude between much longer periods of machine government.

Further, in the relatively few instances where broad-based reform efforts did occur and offered more popular alternatives to the machine, business leadership quickly found unacceptable disadvantages compared with their experience under the machine. Perhaps the most well known cases in which business made a deliberate bid for support through programs of social and economic reform are Hazen Pingree in Detroit, Samuel Jones in Toledo, and Thomas L. Johnson in Cleveland. All three were wealthy businessmen who were very successful in putting together reform administrations that won much popular support in the wake of corrupt, patronage-ridden governments around the turn of the century.

The three men resembled one another in that they won and held power through populist-style demagoguery, becoming outspoken "friends of the people"; at the same time, they put together ambitious reform programs that went well beyond the cost accounting and retrenchment appeals of earlier reform administrations. For example, Pingree, first elected mayor of Detroit in 1889 and successfully reelected until 1896 when he left to become governor of Michigan, gained great popularity by publicizing the corruption of Detroit's officials and its utility companies. He fought for carefully restricted franchises for the street railways and gas company and was a strong advocate of widespread municipal ownership, eventually creating a municipal lighting plant for the city.

The other two social reform mayors went even further than did Pingree. Samuel "Golden Rule" Jones, mayor of Toledo from 1897 to 1904, broke with the Republican party that first elected him, and he governed as an independent, advocating ambitious social welfare innovations, including an eight-hour day and minimum wage for city employees, free kindergartens, public playgrounds, and other social welfare reforms as well as municipal ownership of most public utilities. He was a self-proclaimed socialist. Tom Johnson, mayor of Cleveland from 1901 to 1909, was equally outspoken though more discrete than Jones. Advocating reforms very similar to those of Pingree and Jones, he also fought for public utility regulation, bringing the street railway fare down to three cents, instituted inspection of dairy and meat products, advocated municipal owner-ship, and promoted a wide range of social welfare projects for the city's disadvantaged.

Nevertheless, these reform mayors drew the vigorous opposition of most businesses, especially the utilities (Holli, 1969). Politics based on social and economic reform run by representatives of the business community opened up city politics to divisiveness on issues that went right to the heart of property ownership and city development. At a time when business was otherwise a relatively weak contender for urban political power owing to its dependent position in the urban economy, there were good reasons to fear that programs of social and economic reform could not easily be controlled by business. The machine, on the other hand, was poised to represent business interests without opening up such a possibility. Consequently, the Pingrees, Joneses, and Johnsons were few.

Machine-Reform Politics and Economic Development

So well did the machine serve to enhance the power of business in urban development that many early critics of the machine concluded that business was almost entirely responsible for this system of politics. Lincoln Steffens in his *Shame of the Cities* (1904) and *Autobiography* (1931) portrayed the machine order as a direct result of the dominance of politics by businessmen. Later, another reformer, Frederick C. Howe, wrote that it was "privilege of an industrial rather than of a personal sort that has given birth to the boss" (Weinstein, 1968). Yet almost as these criticisms were leveled at the city governments of the day, the alliance between urban business and the machine began to crumble. From the last decade of the nineteenth century onward, a fundamental change occurred in the developmental politics of cities: Major elements of business communities all over the United States dramatically broke this political partnership and eventually supported a powerful movement to destroy the machine.

Business support of the machine ultimately depended on the peculiar capability of this political institution to use governmental power to promote the general and individual interests of business in managing urban industrial growth. By the end of the nineteenth century, however, major changes in the industrial economy created new and powerful interests within big city business communities that the machine could not accommodate.

BIG BUSINESS AND THE MACHINE: DIVERGENCE OF INTEREST. Most important, the last decades of the nineteenth century saw the emergence of a new basic unit of industrial enterprise: the large, "vertical" corporation that carried out the major business activities—such as purchasing, production of parts and materials, manufacturing of finished products, marketing and finance—all within a consolidated organizational structure. Run by staffs of managers who were coordinated and supervised by a central office, these new enterprises frequently won an oligopolistic or monopolistic position in serving a national goods market. Although, outside of railroads, such organizations scarcely existed before the 1880s, by the 1890s they were rapidly coming to consolidate and centralize many producer and, later, consumer goods industries (Chandler, 1959:404).

This movement toward large oligopolistic enterprise radically altered the internal and external constraints on business decisions. In order to support their increased overhead costs and standardized production on a large scale, these new corporate organizations required very large national or international markets that could absorb their production. Their stake in preserving or enhancing a dominant position in these markets shifted profit-making activities away from competition and price cutting toward administering their markets via price leadership, advertising, brand names, and containing and rationalizing their costs. As a result, these large centralized organizations became far more bureaucratic and routinized in all phases of business activities, from finance and production to sales and distribution (Chandler, 1959:406).

Such a dramatic transformation could not help but alter the political interests of business in the developmental arena. Owners and managers of these large industrial enterprises seeking to expand into national markets came to regard cheaper, more reliable municipal government services and operations of large parts of the infrastructure as an important business priority. Hays (1965) notes that opposition to the machine appealed particularly to the more dynamic elements of the business and professional communities. In writing about New York City politics around the turn of the century, Hammack notes that the machine's alliance with "utilities magnates and their continuing commitment to laissez-faire prevented them from seeing that the economic interests represented in the Chamber of Commerce *now* [emphasis added] sought a municipal government that would actively pursue the city's interest in such matters as transportation, the water supply and public health" (1982:169).

The parochialism of the machine was for big business an obstacle to be overcome rather than a source of help. For example, one of the early big business organizers, Gustavus F. Swift, created a nationwide distributing and marketing organization during the 1880s in the meat packing business. Recognizing the potential of large herds of cattle on the western plains to supply the vast urban markets in the east for fresh meat, he connected this new source of supply to the cities by means of refrigerated railroad cars. However, in marketing the products Swift not only had to break down the prejudices of eating meat that was killed more than a thousand miles away, but also overcome the opposition of local slaughtering houses and butchers whose interests were defended by local machine politicians (Chandler, 1959:387).

The most dramatic effects of the growth of large corporations on the changing political interests of business were in the public utility industries. While the machine had initially aided these businesses by promoting the creation of utility franchises for the delivery of such services as gas, electricity, water, and transit, the machine became less useful as local utilities achieved a monopoly position and the industry as a whole became more oligopolist in character as many utilities underwent consolidation. By the early 1900s, holding companies located in the East controlled the street railway systems of most American cities of over 30,000 population. One syndicate even controlled companies in a hundred cities and had an aggregate capitalization of over $1 billion (Glaab and Brown, 1967:186–187). The parochial politics of the machine with its demands for bribes, favors, and boondoggles was a threat to utility combines once such a vast market was established.

Thus, at the turn of the century utility magnate Samuel Insull began leading an industry-wide movement to obtain state regulation almost explicitly to escape the ravages and raids of city political machines on urban utilities (Anderson, 1980). After 1900, financiers and utility company executives organizing large holding companies began to favor achieving public utility status subject to friendly state regulation; they preferred the predictability and support of state regulators to the favoritism and uncertainty of local political machines (Rose and Clark, 1982; Anderson, 1980).

At the same time, large business users also saw compelling reasons to forsake the machine in order to restrain the excesses of local utilities. Of all organized interests in the industrial city, none were as sensitive to unrestrained utility monopolies as the largest corporations, which used the most gas, water, and electricity and whose work forces were dependent on the mass transit systems of the day. The utilities comprised the central technological core of the city as a production site, and virtually every major business was tied to their quality, reliability, and cost. Once the consolidation movement had produced entrenched utility monopolies, however, business users became victims of price gouging, unreliable service, and low tax assessments granted as political favors by machine politicians.

Such was precisely the case in Wisconsin cities studied by Thelen (1972). He found that after the 1893 depression, utility monopolies in the cities used their position of political influence to cut services, impose higher rates, and press for further favors to help maintain their shaky positions; struggles broke out all over the state's major cities to bring the companies to heel. Many local political machines stuck by these monopolies, attempting to defend them from law suits, legislation, and public criticism. But city businesses, often led by chambers of commerce, broke ranks with utilities and machines in reform coalitions. Subsequently, city business communities went on to become permanent fixtures of the leadership of the state's Progressive movement (Thelen, 1972:Ch. 11).

Milwaukee's experience is illustrative of this transition. The city's trolley and lighting monopoly initially found defenders of its position within the business-dominated Municipal League, chambers of commerce, and other business organizations. But after the utility won exemptions from local taxes through judicial and legislative corruption at a time of falling city revenues during the 1893 depression, organized business in the city was infuriated. It led them to support municipal takeover of the utility, making them staunch allies in the Progressive cause (Thelen, 1972:258–260).

No doubt similar calculations of changing business interests occurred in other cities during fights with utility monopolies, for these struggles dramatically demonstrated the disadvantages of interlocking business monopolies and party politics to large businesses concerned with containing costs. While the machine served some business interests that were dependent on local favoritism, it was a menace to big businesses that were not. Among the latter, their interests were more likely to be served through adherence to the rule of law, rather than favoritism, and through city governments and their bureaucracies, rather than through parties and bosses.

CHANGING INTERESTS OF THE MACHINE. The machine was incapable of accommodating these changing interests on the part of the corporate business community. In fact, the interest of machine bosses was evolving in a direction opposite to what leading businesses wanted. Once party bosses consolidated their position in entrenched organizations, they acquired a stake in asserting their independence from the business community, not in compromising their position to suit business.

While party bosses were responsive to those who could buy their favor, they were hardly mere "errand boys" subservient to business demands. Machine power sprang from the organization's capacity to control urban electorates, to dominate recruitment to office, and to act as a broker trading governmental favors for cash. As such, party professionals shared interests that could not entirely coincide with those who bought their favor. They constituted a political group whose loyalties, skills in practicing their craft, and rewards arose from the organization itself—not from those who paid for their favors. District leaders, captains, and holders of high elective or appointive office typically were men with years of service to the party, specialists in their own right whose interests were separate from those who bought their favor (Yearly, 1970:126).

Machine bosses realized that it was in their interests as politicians to retain their independence from business. If they became mere puppets of business, they could not command privileges nor exact a high price for their favors; unless business remained subordinate and uncertain of cooperation, the demand for the favors that the machine could deliver would evaporate. As the machine matured, party chieftains were driven to operate in ways that would be hostile to business demands for sharing public office and obtaining predictable treatment before the law.

Consequently, this "professionalization" of politics usually was accompanied by the decline of business candidates in city political machines. In New York City, once Tammany discovered the means to bind ward heelers and voters to the party ticket, the business-dominated "Swallowtail" wing of the party was driven out of electoral politics by the bosses. From 1888 to the end of the century, Tammany's mayoral nominees were all professional politicians (Shefter, 1976:39). The story was similar elsewhere. "Except for occasions," says Yearly,

> when political tickets required hasty 'window dressing' or the unusual luster of
> some amateur's reputation or funds, bosses seldom permitted significant positions
> to come to men with less than a decade of party experience. There was little room
> for greenhorns from the business world and the pickings for them were slim unless
> they were broken to party operations and the specialization it required (1970:126).

Perhaps the most obvious parting of ways came about through the practice of extorting payments from corporations in return for immunity from hostile legislation. Thriving in an atmosphere of uncertainty and need for special favors from government, the machine created in the business community the demand for privileges through harassment. Strike bills, the manipulation of assessments, changes in corporate law that complicated business transactions, and scores of other methods were routine means to this end. In New York, the end of the 1892 legislative session saw 715 statutes spread over 2,500 pages, drawing tremendous fire from reformers and business groups who contended that many of the changes were purposely intended to throw the law into doubt in order to create opportunities for political deals (Yearly, 1970:130-131). Such instances of cavalier treatment of the law and arrogance brought many businessmen to the conclusion that they had created a Frankenstein's monster with an organizational life of its own and which could not be forced to accommodate business' new interests.

In response, large business enterprises gradually allied themselves with the reform movement in an attempt to change the rules of the game—overturn the system of party politics and invisible government that sustained the machine. This meant attacking partisanship itself and creating in its place a system of political competition that would not rely on material inducements, patronage, and favor giving in order to sustain political activity. Through the nonpartisan reform movement (see Chapter 8), large business could hope to tap the sense of moral outrage against the practices of the machine that was shared by members of the city's middle and professional classes and to undertake the reform of cities from the outside—through good government groups, charities, business associations, and other voluntary groups that had a base of political power independent of the party. In this way, business could hope to win an independent position of power in city politics and rely upon trained professional bureaucrats to serve business' interests. Through such reforms, business could manipulate the institutions of popular control in order to make a new bid for autonomy in urban development.

The Politics of Urban Industrial Development

As central cities became the focus of industrial economic activity, local governments turned inward to promote their communities' growth. Although increasingly interventionist, public policy remained geared to enhancing private sector decisions and participation in determining the course and pace of community economic development.

Power relations between the public and private sectors in the developmental arena became the focus of continuous political competition. At a time when urban economic independence and the growth of mass participation in local politics imposed limits on the economic influence of business in city affairs, developmental politics became dominated by political competition between those who controlled rival systems of power—political bosses and business leaders. Political machines emerged to provide urban business with its sphere of interest in dominating urban development. As the organizational interests of business and party machines diverged at the turn of the century, their partnership turned into a political struggle for control of city government.

Endnote

1. In other words, city building by urban governments was dominated by the objective of organizing urban space in accord with what Logan and Molotch term "exchange value," rather than "use value" (1987:Chs. 1 and 2).

CHAPTER EIGHT

Redistribution and Distribution: The Politics of Social and Political Control

Redistribution and the Industrial Political Economy

R EDISTRIBUTIVE governmental activities, those that allocate economic resources to population groups in ways that tax the productive capacity of a polity, assumed major political importance for America's urban industrial democracies.

Industrialization and Urban Poverty

For one thing, industrialization created new forms of deprivation among large segments of the population in the cities. Unlike the mercantile period, when urban poverty was limited, the workings of the industrial order systematically produced it and concentrated it in the cities. Industrialization drew millions of workers from farms and from abroad to work in factories; workers and their families became highly dependent on the capacity of the wage labor market to provide decent earnings and working conditions. These workers, as a result of periodic swings in the business cycle, suffered from widespread unemployment. Periods of healthy economic expansion were invariably counterbalanced by extended periods of depression that occurred with systematic regularity: Depressions occurred during 1873–1879, 1893–1897, 1907–1908, 1914–1915, and 1920–1922.

Even when the wage labor market provided stable employment, it did not operate to distribute the benefits of industrial growth very equitably, creating class divisions marked by wealth and want. Although there is little doubt that during the fifty years or so after 1865 the standard of living of all classes rose, low wages and poverty remained widespread (Cochran and Miller, 1961:261). One survey of studies of this period concluded that around the turn of the century "fully eighty percent of the people lived on the margin of existence while the wealth of the nation was owned by the remaining twenty percent"

(Glaab and Brown, 1967:224). While determining the extent of poverty is invariably hazardous (since much depends on one's definition of "poor"), it is clear that life for the vast majority of urban dwellers during most of the industrial period was hard and uncomfortable and fell far short of today's minimal standards of family well-being.

The logic of industrial capitalism ensured that problems of mass want and disadvantage achieved a particularly explosive configuration in the nation's cities. Unlike workers in rural areas, wage-workers in the cities lacked many of the resources that in earlier times enabled the poor to cushion themselves from periodic catastrophe and misfortune, particularly the ability to grow crops for subsistence and the presence of extended family networks for mutual self-help. Long work days under conditions of harsh industrial discipline and economic insecurity in a strange and anonymous urban community faced the migrant families seeking a better life.

Further, the industrial economy broke down many traditional forms of public control for coping with the political consequences of disadvantage. Massive migration to urban areas disintegrated the "walls" of legal restriction on the movement of labor and the poor that cities had employed for years during the mercantile era. Mass poverty became a phenomenon that cities could not limit by attempting to control population movement and residence. Similarly, the changing demographic character of poverty within cities ensured that the informal social mechanisms of the mercantile era for ameliorating class discontent and hostility were weakened. The jumbled neighborhood settlement patterns, which mixed rich and poor in work, leisure, and family life, gave way in the industrial era to pervasive patterns of residential segregation. Poor, middle-class, and rich families were separated into different residential clusters. Neighborhood, class, income, religion, and ethnicity often pushed in the same direction, dividing families into different social worlds. This could not help but constitute a potentially explosive configuration since it diminished even the appearance of a community of interests among disparate social groups in the locality.

In effect, the industrial economy imposed on cities a crisis of social welfare. Creating mass poverty, concentrating it in cities, and shaping it in ways that encouraged division and conflict within urban space, the new market order made the problem of economic equality an inescapable dilemma. American cities faced for the first time the matter of routinely dealing with the political consequences of mass industrial poverty.

City Government, Popular Control, and the Poor

Within the cities, local political leaders became major targets of social grievances by the poor. While claims of the disadvantaged for assistance fell upon both the private and public sectors, two factors tended to thrust city political leadership into pivotal positions of directly managing them.

First, the activities of the private sector in materially ameliorating the plight of the poor were extremely limited during the generations after the Civil War.

As urban poverty grew worse, the role of private charities grew only marginally in response. During the late nineteenth century, centralized institutions known as Charity Organization Societies were formed to coordinate private assistance to the poor. These charitable organizations were generally reluctant to help alleviate poverty by dispensing cash or material assistance, however. Dominated by Yankee middle-class reformers, the leading charity organizations espoused the notion of self-help and self-achievement in order to overcome distress on the assumption that poverty was most often a matter of individual failure or indolence (Trattner, 1974:90; Devine, 1939:42).

Consistent with this ethos, the various charities developed a number of strategies for dealing with urban poverty that eliminated or minimized reliance on material help. One leading approach began what is today standard social work practice: "friendly visits" to clients by trained personnel who help evaluate the problems of the poor family and offer advice. It was primarily during periods of severe economic distress that charities relented on their social Darwinist approach. When the private charities were faced with very large numbers of unemployed demanding relief, they did receive limited voluntary contributions and assistance from local governments. Most of this financial aid was supplied for a short period, such as a single winter season during a depression (Feder, 1936:34–37).

In all, the variety and kind of private assistance to the urban poor constituted a most limited response to the sea of human misery that existed in the cities of the industrial era. This default by private philanthropy left local officialdom to manage the problems of relieving urban poverty.

Second, popular control structures ensured that city governments would be a major target of political grievances by the poor. While private charitable institutions could uphold restrictive relief measures in the name of the prevailing morality of self-help, city governments and their political leaders could hardly command such independence. Unlike the private voluntary organizations, to whom the poor were merely clientele selected to enjoy the privileges of their charitable efforts, to city governments the poor were citizens with potential political power. The rise of mass electoral politics at a time of growing economic deprivation thrust upon city political systems the matter of relieving economic inequality. While lack of economic power may have deprived the industrial poor of leverage over the workplace, the system of elections and parties provided the poor and all other groups with a resource that grew with numbers.

Federalism and Redistribution

Federalism worked to make city governments the most important political targets of claims by disadvantaged groups. Throughout the industrial period, cities stood almost alone in managing the social consequences of rapid economic change owing to the reluctance of state and national governments to become involved in matters of redistribution. The laissez faire ideals of successive administrations limited or even drastically diminished federal involvement in virtually all areas of public policy. At best, federal attention to these problems was dominated by the hope that expanding economic opportunities in an industrializing nation would ultimately take care of most forms of deprivation. Although these ideas began to change somewhat under the influence of Progressive leadership after the turn of the century, the notions of limited government and defense of free enterprise all but removed federal officialdom from social problems of cities.

Throughout the nineteenth century, state governments generally followed the laissez faire posture of the federal government on matters of redistribution. While states wanted city economies to grow and did get involved in issues of distribution (see below), they were generally able to escape involvement in redistributive matters owing to the absence of significant political pressures on behalf of the poor at the state level. Only after the turn of the century, when the influence of the Progressive movement in state politics grew, did legislatures begin to evince some interest in utilizing state regulatory powers and resources to deal with urban disadvantage. At best, the influence of this movement was one of producing cautious experimentation with very limited programs of assistance to the poor.

The best known of these programs were workman's compensation laws and financial assistance for mothers with dependent children who had lost their husbands. Though innovative, these attempts to expand the role of state governments in accepting greater social welfare responsibilities were almost invariably limited by the overriding laissez faire posture of state governments. For instance, workman's compensation laws were often passed at the behest of business groups seeking to limit and regulate employer liability for industrial accidents, not as a result of support for broad-scale expansion of state social welfare legislation (Trattner, 1974:152). Widow's pension legislation was promoted as a cheaper alternative to maintaining workhouses or other forms of outdoor relief. In addition, funding for many of these programs was often minimal or sporadic, particularly in cases where pensions were dependent on local government for revenue (Leiby, 1978:213). In short, the Progressive movement proved to be a weak base on which to build political support for extensive state social welfare measures, leaving cities to cope almost alone with the political consequences of industrial poverty.

In essence, the industrial political economy placed cities in a crisis of social welfare. Industrialization generated new forms of mass deprivation that became concentrated in cities undergoing transition to mass democracy. While the federal system of government enabled national and state governments to avoid the problems of the disadvantaged, it left them to the localities where the poor constituted major political claimants and the city politician became a key target for managing their claims.

Redistributive Policy: Limited Government

America's industrial political economy created forces that limited the ability of cities to meet these political demands. Local redistributive efforts involved trade-offs with urban economic growth. In order to grow, cities needed, among other things, to ensure the availability of a large pool of low-wage labor hungry for the industrial jobs of the period; if cities were to undertake any kind of broad effort to help relieve the miseries of industrialization, these endeavors would be constrained by this developmental reality.

For instance, generous attempts to relieve the suffering of the poor via cash assistance programs were often justified on humanistic or other moral grounds, but laws to advance this purpose could be highly disruptive to rapid urban growth if the sums paid out to the poor were more than going wages, thereby pushing up wages in the private sector. It is possible that payments even as little as half the amount of going rates for workers could push private sector wages upward (Feder, 1936:180). Furthermore, relief payments had to be low enough to keep workers looking for jobs, many of which would be unattractive or even dangerous. Finally, public forms of assistance invariably diverted local resources from efforts to sustain industrial growth, particularly the costly public infrastructure projects, such as roads, bridges, sewers, and port and transit facilities.

Consequently, in an era when wages were notoriously low to begin with for most workers and when the demand for large-scale public outlays by cities for new capital investment pushed many near the brink of fiscal disaster and saddled their populations with tremendous debts, even modest relief efforts would conflict with these developmental constraints. For city governments to sustain ambitious programs to redistribute resources to the disadvantaged, the acceptance of such things as slower growth, higher taxes, and forsaken private-sector investment opportunities was necessary.

That most localities sought to minimize this kind of trade-off is evident throughout the period. Generally, public relief efforts were meager and tacitly paralleled the activities of private charities that endeavored to limit cash assistance to the needy whenever possible. When faced with hordes of unemployed during particularly severe depressions, most cities worked with private charities to provide small temporary relief for brief periods (Griffith, 1974:15). Outdoor relief or public assistance as a permanent program was gradually phased out around the turn of the century (Piven and Cloward, 1971:35–36).

How decisively the priority of growth limited local government in assisting the poor is best illustrated by the activities of those political leaders most motivated to do so—"radical" mayors who won political power for the explicit purpose of making local government more responsive to the underprivileged. Even in these cases, their success in creating a larger role for local government in the area of redistribution was very limited.

In Detroit, reform mayor Hazen S. Pingree, a highly popular and radical mayor who overcame machine and business opposition to carry out sweeping programs of political and economic reform, attempted to use city resources for relieving the misery of the 1890s depression. His most notable achievements included creating two shifts for public works projects and demechanization of certain tasks in order to provide more employment; establishing garden plots for the poor on vacant lots; and temporarily forcing the price of bread down in 1895 by threatening to build a municipal bakery (Holli, 1969:69–70). Though unusual, these limited accomplishments by a powerful figure most committed to helping the underprivileged are suggestive of the narrow options attainable by local governments of the day.

Efforts by early socialist political figures in cities suggest a similar pattern. Just after the turn of the century, the Socialist Party made inroads in numbers of cities and state capitals as the party's strength grew from 10,000 in 1901 to 120,000 in 1912; during the latter year, the party's high-water mark, some 1,200 Socialists held public office, mostly in cities, and managed to elect 79 mayors (Weinstein, 1968:315). Although the party precipitously declined in strength thereafter, during its heyday Socialist administrations in a number of cities sought to reorient local government in line with their highly progressive and often radical programs of reform. But time after time, Socialist city administrations were unable to find in local government a large base for carrying out many programs of redistribution. Most often they became known as "gas and water" socialists because of their focus on buying out and running local utilities as city enterprises, a reform sometimes even supported by business groups seeking cheaper, more reliable service.

Another redistributive policy area that suffered as a result of the same trade-offs with urban growth were programs to provide better housing for the poor. The major thrust of housing reformers was the enactment of regulations to improve the substandard tenements of the poor. Though cities passed numerous laws specifying minimal standards for slum housing, these laws went largely unenforced (Glaab and Brown, 1967:162). The most notable achievement of these reformers was the New York Tenement Law of 1901. While this law applied stringent building codes and was seriously enforced, its effect was limited because it only applied to new housing and could therefore not affect the numerous tenements that covered the city. Similarly, in other large cities the slums spread throughout this period despite the presence of fairly tough building codes. It was not until the 1930s, with the passage of federal slum clearance programs, that the growth of slums was somewhat checked.

The failure of cities and reformers to provide better low-income housing through code regulation flew directly in the face of the logic of achieving rapid urban industrial growth, a fact that always doomed these efforts from succeeding. "In order for the city to grow," suggests Banfield,

the city had to become a center of warehouses, shops and factories, which meant it had to have a plentiful supply of cheap labor, which meant it had to have a plentiful supply of housing that such labor could afford. If all the housing had been decent by the standards of the time, some of the labor required for the city's growth could not have afforded to live in the city at all (Banfield, 1974:49).

This fact was recognized by many housing reformers who were forced to base their case for housing regulation mainly on the public health hazards of spreading slums, not the social desirability of decent housing for the poor (Lubove, 1970:319).

Social Control Politics

The failure of local governments to effect more substantial sacrifices to urban growth in order to aid the disadvantaged was not inevitable, however. After all, the very rapid economic growth that so many industrial cities attained was not preordained. City governments could have accepted higher taxes and slower economic expansion in exchange for better programs in aid of their poor. In other policy areas, economic growth was quite deliberately sacrificed in order to attain other objectives. For instance, the tremendous waste, inefficiency, and corruption of the machine era were debits against urban growth in any strict economic sense. The costly corruption of local government during the machine era functioned as a second layer of "taxation," the impact of which was often quite inimical to business enterprise and city development (Yearly, 1970). While cities were often comparatively tolerant of corruption, despite the costs such practices imposed on city development, the "waste" of resources for assisting the poor was far less acceptable in city politics.

The key to understanding the limited efforts of local government in redistribution lies not in the economic constraints on the industrial city, but in the politics of cities that brought about widespread toleration of these policies, particularly by the disadvantaged themselves. More ambitious attempts to redistribute resources to assist the worst-off might well have materialized if those most likely to support relief from the miseries of poverty—the unemployed, the lowly paid immigrant, and the poor—had utilized their political power to demand it. The numerical preponderance of the urban working class in a formally democratic order provided them with a potentially pivotal position of political power. Yet what characterized local redistributive politics more than anything else was for have-not groups to participate in local politics without making strident demands for many programs to improve their lot as a disadvantaged class.

The Machine and Social Control

This failure to promote their interests as a class is best understood as resulting from the establishment of a political institution—namely, the political machine—that was biased against the representation of class interests. While one can never determine the "true" interests of any group or collectivity, one can examine the political institutions that represented them and ascertain which set of interests were systematically promoted and which were systematically thwarted. To the extent that prevailing political institutions frustrate or otherwise impede the ability of the poor or any other social grouping to promote their shared interests, we may consider this particular feature of political representation a process of social control (cf. Katznelson, 1981:Ch. 8). In the redistributive arena, the dominant politics throughout the industrial period was indeed one of social control for the urban poor.

The participation of disadvantaged groups in redistributive politics was dominated by the political machine, their primary political linkage to city governments. As outlined earlier, the machine found a social base of support within the immigrant community and evolved in response to powerful pro-growth forces, particularly urban business. The machine's strength among the working class resulted from its success in utilizing the social, rather than the economic, experience of the poor as the basis for its appeal. The American immigrant experience in cities was not only colored by the workplace (economic class identity) but also by those events related to residence and community, particularly ethnic, territorial, cultural, and religious affinities. The machine tended to exploit the latter rather than the former social cleavages in its bid for political support from the disadvantaged; it created a politics of social control on issues of redistribution by organizing out of politics competing economic class interests among its supporters in the electorate.[1]

THE TECHNIQUES OF SOCIAL CONTROL. *Representing Individual Interests.* The machine rewarded and represented the individual and neighborhood interests of the poor by exchanging jobs, favors, and other material incentives for their votes. At a time when the poor did not find particularly responsive allies elsewhere, such as from private charities or state and national governments, the political boss and his organization stood ready to help in exchange for votes, a commodity that the poor owned in large numbers and were willing to trade in order to improve their individual well-being. As one Chicago ward boss, Johnny Powers, was described,

> For him, winning votes was a year-round job: he was always on hand. When a death occurred in the neighborhood, Powers provided a stylish burial; he had a standing account at the undertakers. When a man lost his job, Powers provided him with work; he boasted that 2600 of the residents of the nineteenth ward were on the city's payroll. When a resident of the ward got into trouble, Powers would bail him out of jail and fix matters with the judge. If a citizen of the ward needed to travel out of the city, Powers got him a free pass on the railroad. At Christmas time the loyal voter could expect a turkey from the benevolent alderman, and when Powers made gifts it was with none of the restrictions of the charity organization society (Davis, 1967:156–157).

In contrast to the established charities that abhorred the "dole," the machine boss knew the value of material gifts to the needy, who had no one else to turn to when the meager assets of friends and relatives had been exhausted. The machine's largest material reward was the patronage it could deliver. Police, firefighter, teaching, and sundry skilled and unskilled positions were divided up among the various wards for distribution to the party faithful. The best jobs normally went to the party officials. Many of these positions required little work, sometimes not even the presence of the job-holder.

Once on the job, many positions offered opportunities to enrich oneself beyond just the salary attached to the position. In particular, "honest graft" (using position and inside information for personal gain) could often be exploited by an enterprising job-holder. The rewards of machine politics were not confined to government. In addition, private sector connections that political bosses established were sometimes utilized in order to create jobs for constituents. Since a franchise agreement was a monopoly granted by the machine, it afforded considerable leverage for future favors from the franchised businesses; ward leaders might name the laborers for the construction of gas, electric, and streetcar lines.

Patronage, Christmas turkeys, and other favors were the everyday currency of the machine in building support among the immigrant communities. At a time when other formal institutions provided relatively little help to the needy, the machine provided an informal "welfare" system that could not help but strike a responsive chord among those dependent groups who had little other alternative. One of the more important "latent" functions of the machine was that it humanized and personalized assistance-giving (Merton, 1957:72–82). The political boss, unlike the social reformer or charity worker, was unconcerned about moralizing and changing the personal character of the immigrant according to alien, Protestant middle-class norms. Help freely given with only the expectation of the family's vote was a powerful and attractive reward to most immigrants who viewed with suspicion the social reformers who sought minds and souls in return for what often proved to be little in the way of material help.

Further, the machine provided an avenue of social mobility for at least those immigrants who could master the art and craft of boss politics. At a time when many opportunities, particularly in employment, were closed to immigrants— signs such as "Irish need not apply" were not uncommon in the late nineteenth century—the party organization offered a chance for position and, at least in some cases, for wealth. A well-known study of twenty bosses found that thirteen were not educated beyond grammar school and that three-quarters of these were either first-generation immigrants or their progeny. Overwhelmingly, these bosses came from humble origins, most starting at the bottom of the organization and rising to the top after years of slow apprenticeship (Zink, 1968:3–12).

By utilizing a reward system that provided benefits to needy groups and individuals on a particularistic basis, the machine acted to convert the claims of the poor for assistance to matters of distribution, rather than redistribution. Personal help, individual cash assistance, jobs, and hosts of other petty favors were political responses that had the effect of encouraging individual claims and encouraging particularistic participation in city politics rather than promoting the socio-economic position of have-not groups in general.

Diffusing Class Interests. The machine also imposed social control by segregating and fragmenting the political participation of the poor along communal, residential, ethnic, and religious lines; this limited the opportunities for disadvantaged groups to mobilize as a class in order to make political demands. Perhaps the most prevalent technique of fragmenting political representation was by organizing the machine's vote-getting apparatus to reflect and encourage ethnic rivalries. In cities with ward and district systems of electoral organizations, machine leaders frequently took care to make this system coterminous with territorial patterns of ethnic and nationality segregation. Each nationality that owned significant numbers of voters would have its own ward.

Machine politics relied extensively on stirring up, bargaining out, and accommodating ethnic, religious, and other communal rivalries in tandem with the particularistic distribution of jobs and favors in exchange for political support. Ticket balancing (the handpicking of ethnic slates in primary and general elections to assure broad appeal) as well as the distribution of high party and governmental positions in "recognition" to various nationality groups in proportion to their voting strength became the art of machine politics. Consequently, the growth of ethnic diversity was of greater political salience in party politics than the disadvantaged status of these poor immigrant populations.

As the machine became a dominant political organization under relatively centralized leadership, its decentralization at the neighborhood level enabled it to capitalize on the city's changing social character. As Italian, Polish, and other "late" immigrant groups entered the political arena of the cities, "earlier" groups who had won positions of power and importance were often forced to yield some of their prerogatives. On other occasions, these older immigrant groups struggled—often successfully—to block these newer elements through time-honored strategies. Consequently, the major threat to machine leadership was not a broad-based coalition making political demands as a class, but internal divisions within the machine or in opposition parties comprised of groups seeking greater recognition in the distribution of patronage and power. Italians in particular rankled under Irish hegemony in numbers of northeastern cities where the Irish usually controlled the local Catholic parish church as well (Harrigan, 1976:61). As a result, in some of these cities Italians often joined and helped build rival Republican machines (Harrigan, 1976:62; Dahl, 1961:43–47).

As blacks began to migrate to northern cities near the end of the late nineteenth century, this group was incorporated into the machine on inferior terms compared with white ethnics. In New York City, black leaders were organized into a segregated citywide subsidiary of the Democratic party, the United Colored Democracy, in an attempt to loosen blacks from their predilection to vote Republican. This organization, led by black leaders handpicked by Tammany bosses, became the major channel for distributing patronage to black activists. It was ". . . a powerless segregated institution whose primary tasks were winning votes for Tammany and isolating blacks from positions of real political influence" (Katznelson, 1973:69).

ALTERNATIVES TO THE MACHINE. The machine's domination of working-class participation in city politics had far-reaching effects on the ability of the poor to promote demands for redistribution even through alternative political channels. In general, the presence of powerful urban political machines weakened two other political institutions that explicitly sought to represent the interests of workers independently of their communal, particularistic interests: trade unions and socialist political parties.

Trade Unions. The development of trade unions during the industrial period might have constituted an important challenge to the politics of social control imposed by the machine. Unions, unlike the party machines, attempted to organize workers on the basis of the workplace rather than residence, ethnicity, religion, or other social cleavages. In many European countries during the industrial period, unions often served as an important organizing base for the development of worker-oriented political parties at local and national levels. In Great Britain, for instance, the Labour Party grew out of a coalition of various political and social groups dominated by trade unions around the turn of the century.

The development of union organizations in America's cities never followed this pattern, however, at least partly because of the machine's dominance of urban politics. A politicized union movement with ties to immigrant political parties would have been highly disruptive to the particularistic organizational and reward structure on which party bosses relied in order to control the votes of the poor. Further, a union movement demanding machine political support for social and political reforms in order to assist union organization and workers in general would have disrupted the machine's ties to urban business communities.

Consequently, machine politicians not only often avoided incorporating organized labor within their electoral coalitions, but often suppressed, violently if necessary, labor organizing activities. For instance, in 1911 the Tammany-controlled New York police were ordered to put down a strike by garment workers. Pickets were systematically rounded up and sent to jail, most often after bloody confrontations. In Pittsburgh, the city's Republican machine used police to end a steel strike in 1919 by harassing workers (Judd, 1979:75). Foner's monumental histories of the labor movement suggest that machine governments were as likely to suppress union activities and strikes as were local governments dominated by reformers (Foner, 1947, 1955, 1964, 1965, 1980). The dominant trade union movement at the time, the American Federation of Labor (AFL), went so far as to deliberately pursue a policy of noninvolvement in politics—and to limit their efforts to collective bargaining at the workplace. From the AFL's perspective, government and party politics were viewed as dominated by business. Machine hostility to labor generally continued until the 1930s when some of the big city machines reached an accommodation with more moderate trade unions.

Socialist Political Parties. Finally, the control of urban working-class politics by the machine had a debilitating effect on the growth of third parties, particularly socialists, which sought to explicitly appeal to workers as a social class. Because they directly threatened the electoral base of the machine, socialist candidates were nearly always opposed by party bosses. For instance, in New York City's famous 1886 mayoral campaign, a coalition of unions and socialists supported Henry George, who proposed the radical idea that undeveloped land should be heavily taxed in order to capture the "unearned increment" of rising land values. Tammany did all it could to successfully defeat George, including attempting to bribe him to leave the Labor ticket or join the machine and smearing him as a political subversive (Judd, 1979:74).

Perhaps even more important than outright machine opposition to left-wing parties was the machine's hold on low-income voters through distributional politics, a fact that impeded attempts by socialist parties to attract immigrant votes through programs of reform. The presence of the political machine frustrated the Socialist Party's attempts to build a working-class constituency. Having to compete directly with machine organizations, Socialist candidates usually were forced to run on a good government ticket, promising clean, efficient government—in effect, campaigning on the same issues as Progressive reformers, thereby limiting their appeal to immigrants and workers (Weinstein, 1968:110).

Reform Politics and Redistribution

The Policies of the Reformers

The system of boss politics that underpinned the politics of social control found its most potent challenge in the reform movement that sought to overturn the machine's domination of city government. Particularly after the 1890s, when business' movement to the Progressive cause of municipal reform gave it great financial and electoral strength in cities, reform victories often led to the weakening of boss systems and, at least in many smaller cities, to their demolition.

In theory, the reformers who sought to challenge the machine could have done so by undermining the machine's social base of support through appeals and programs designed to attract have-not groups whose class interests were so poorly served by the boss system. But the bottom line in any such strategy surely would have been a willingness to reform local government in ways that facilitated the representation of working-class interests as such and, inevitably, to expand the social welfare functions of local government even at the cost of economic growth objectives. But the tendency was for Progressive reform to step back from the risks of such a strategy, which would have opened up local politics to political competition in the redistributive arena.

In reality, the dominant voices in the reform movement were those who feared the power of the masses and sought to limit or even reduce the responsibilities of local government in social welfare. Particularly in larger cities, where reformers faced large and often hostile immigrant populations, their leading figures tended to embrace what has been termed "structural reform." This emphasized introducing the system of the contemporary business corporation, especially its bureaucratic organization and methods, in an effort to lower taxes and to make local government more efficient (rather than taking on greater social welfare responsibilities) (Holli, 1969). Instead of building the political demands of the urban masses into their vision of reformed local government, they hoped to place power in the hands of men of substance, character, and integrity who would impose on the urban masses a governmental system geared to economy and impartiality through bureaucratization.

Consequently, this point of view all but precluded the movement's appeal to immigrant populations in cities. In New York City, Seth Low, a wealthy merchant, philanthropist, and university president who became mayor around the turn of the century, was a leading exponent of this view. Following a particularly flagrant period of corruption under Tammany rule, the city's reform-minded Citizens' Union induced Low to run as an independent candidate for mayor in 1901. Running on a platform of nonpartisanship, Low disowned the social welfare programs advocated by the Citizens' Union and advocated impartiality, honesty, economy, and responsibility during his campaign. Apparently winning mainly because of the public's reaction against the excesses of Tammany, rather than endorsement of his reforms, Low's major objective in office was one of imposing business-like efficiency and economy through tinkering with the machinery of government. Low imported experts to operate the various departments, eliminated some payroll padding, cut salaries while increasing the length of the workday for city employees, and reduced the city's budget substantially.

But these activities were not paralleled by other measures to broaden his coalition, particularly when governmental activities might have antagonized important business interests. He refused to investigate corrupt practices between businessmen and politicians or to press for low utility rates, and he balked at appointing a prominent housing reformer to head the tenement house commission for fear of disturbing conservative real estate interests (Holli, 1969:Ch. 8).

San Francisco's reform Mayor James D. Phelan, a wealthy banker who held office between 1897 and 1902, pursued a reform program similar to, if not more rigid than, Low's. Backed by the San Francisco Merchant's Association, whose goal was "scientific, systematic and responsible government," his administration was distinguished by sponsorship of a strong mayor, short ballot charter, rigid fiscal controls over expenditures, citywide elections, and civil service reform. Phelan pursued economy by supporting such a low tax rate that the city was forced to withhold teacher salaries, suspend some functions of the city health department, cut services at the city hospital, and turn off the street lights at midnight. He was ousted after his administration's strike-breaking activities led numbers of the city's unions to form their own political party to defeat the reformers in 1901 (Holli, 1969:167).

In effect, reform administration typically sought to consolidate and manage the limited social welfare responsibilities of local government. On a few occasions, especially where Progressive social reformers from the professions were a strong voice in reform coalitions, city services expanded, including social services for the poor, such as welfare agencies, public school bureaucracies, public libraries and museum establishments, public health clinics, and housing departments (Weinstein, 1968:11, 114–115). In particular, Progressive reformers undertook a massive drive to expand public education in cities (Bowles and Gintis, 1976:181). But in general, the influence of professional reformers was not one of fundamentally challenging the limited social service commitments promoted by the business wing of the municipal reform movement.

The expansion of governmental bureaucracies in the interest of "efficiency" was the price business reformers had to pay in order to accommodate the "claims by the new organized professions" (Katznelson, 1981:122). In other words, the expansion of urban bureaucracies in the interests of economy, efficiency, and scientific management reflected the internal dynamics of political accommodation between professionals and more conservative, avowedly pro-business, elements in the reform movement. The result was a larger bureaucracy that could employ and reward the new, growing class of professionals who administered the limited local social welfare programs acceptable to the more parsimonious business interests in the reform movement (Schiesl, 1977:126).

Reform Politics and the Dilemmas of Social Control

The stringent social welfare limits placed on municipal reformers as a result of coalitional politics that excluded the poor imposed a dilemma, however. Overturning the machine meant that reformers were dismembering an important agency of social control that had been a major barrier between the masses and the city treasury and replacing it with a bureaucratic order that could not easily duplicate this function. As long as the bureaucratization in social welfare was aimed mainly at institutionalizing the status quo in local responsibilities, reform governments remained vulnerable to the opposition of disadvantaged groups. Consequently, reformers sought to resolve this dilemma through the erection of new institutions that could break the power of the machine over low-income voters without opening up local government to political competition among organized class interests. Generally, this was attemped through governmental and electoral reforms that diffused the political power of income groups. In effect, this changed the politics of social control from one based on converting redistributive claims to distributional demands to one based on quasi disenfranchisement of the poor.

The most important method for achieving this was through electoral reforms that changed city elections in ways that undercut the control of the political machine over low-income voters and left the poor in a weak position to compete for power with reform candidates. Chagrined and troubled by the results of mass democracy since the mercantile era, many reformers called for restrictions on the suffrage as well as outright disenfranchisement in the decades following the Civil War (Holli, 1969:234; Weinstein, 1968:Ch. 4). But as the reform movement gathered strength toward the end of the century, these kinds of proposals were abandoned; at the very least, they would have made the reform drive into an obvious counterattack on a whole class, introducing the very political conflicts into local government that reformers sought to avoid.

In order to have much hope of success, reformers had to define issues of electoral reform in ways that would assure unity within their diverse coalitions while avoiding stirring up class antagonism. Initially, municipal reform drives did little more than concentrate on the regulation of elections in order to make them more accessible to public control and supervision. Much of the corruption in machine cities occurred because of weak or nonenforced election laws. Though these measures, which included setting up election boards, making it illegal to vote more than once, and regulating campaign funds, were widely adopted during the first two decades of the twentieth century, they were often unsuccessful because machines frequently controlled the prosecutors and courts who were to enforce these laws.

As Progressive coalitions made a determined bid for power, their programs of electoral reform did not remain targeted at merely cleaning up election abuses. The thrust of municipal electoral reform became one of fundamentally altering the rules of the political game in hopes of weakening the entire system of party politics in order to destroy the political machine and enhance the candidacies of reformers. The electoral reforms brought about by Progressives avoided any semblance of a frontal attack on the political power of the poor by the movement's powerful ideology. The latter sought to justify these reforms as attempts to make local elections more honest, to enable voters to act more rationally by separating local government from party politics, and to encourage a local politics based on "the public interest," rather than petty rivalries and individual self-interest.

One device was the nonpartisan ballot. Party machines had a major advantage in ethnic neighborhoods by relying on their supporters' ability to recognize the party label on the election ballot; they could be counted on to vote for machine candidates without knowing who they were, simplifying both the organization's and the voters' tasks in securing votes for the "right" candidates. The nonpartisan ballot undercut this advantage. By removing the party label as a vote cue for machine supporters, machine candidates would have much more difficulty in obtaining votes unless they had resources through which they could bring their name to the voters. In contrast, reform candidates could often rely on newspaper endorsements and their personal prominence for publicizing their name.

Another important reform innovation was the substitution of at-large for ward elections. The machine depended on small constituencies to enable precinct leaders and ward bosses to control voters. Ward lines could be drawn to be coterminous with particular ethnic and racial neighborhoods that would be "worked" by establishing close personal contacts, distributing jobs and favors, and otherwise courting the neighborhood vote for the machine. In particular, small wards made it easier for many minorities to gain representation in the machine. Abolishing the wards in favor of at-large elections meant that the city's council members were all elected by the entire city population. This change often had the effect of handicapping working-class and immigrant candidates who had to appeal to the whole city for support, not just to their neighborhood. Further, wealthy candidates and those sponsored by large organizations, such as voter leagues, business groups, or those endorsed by newspapers, had a decided advantage in citywide elections; they were more capable of raising the larger funds necessary to compete (Judd, 1979:95–96).

All these effects of nonpartisan and at-large elections were well understood by reformers and were important reasons for their widespread endorsement. They were endorsed by the Municipal League's model city charter in 1899 and in subsequent charters sponsored by the League. The League carefully gathered and evaluated statistics to ascertain the success of these reforms. In the first two decades of the twentieth century, nonpartisanship and at-large elections were successfully implemented in cities throughout the nation, though successes were most limited in many of the larger, heavily immigrant cities with entrenched political machines. Nevertheless, even here the closing decades of the industrial era saw reform programs succeed in whole or in part in some big cities. Nonpartisan, at-large elections were adopted in Los Angeles (1908), Boston (1909), Akron (1915), and Detroit (1918). Before 1910, nonpartisan elections were almost unknown, but by 1929 they were utilized in 57 percent of cities over 30,000 in population (Judd, 1979:96–97).

Particularly when these electoral changes were adopted with other governmental reforms that were intended to cripple the machine, such as civil service reform and other charter innovations (see below), their discriminatory effects on the participation of low-income groups in local politics became quite evident. In cities where working-class candidates, many of them socialists, had been elected to office before electoral "reform," citywide elections led to a precipitous decline in their numbers in office.

In Dayton, Ohio, Socialists managed to elect two aldermen and three assessors in the city's 1909 election where the party won only 25 percent of the total vote. Before the 1913 election, Dayton implemented citywide elections along with other reforms. Although the Socialists polled 35 percent of the popular vote in the 1913 contest and 44 percent in the 1917 election, in neither election were they able to elect any candidates (Weinstein, 1968:109–110). Similarly, after Pittsburgh changed to at-large elections in 1911, upper-class businessmen and professionals managed to replace lower- and middle-class candidates on the city council and school board (Hays, 1973).

Working-class parties could not muster the resources to run an effective citywide campaign after charter reforms diluted the strength of their supporters, who were usually concentrated in particular neighborhoods. Accordingly, machine politicians, socialists, trade unions, and other working-class organizations generally opposed reform programs, particularly electoral reform, because they perceived that these innovations would make it more difficult for them to win public office.

Consequently, the last years of the industrial era saw most large northern cities with powerful political machines fighting to keep the most threatening antiparty electoral reforms out of charters. Where reform was thorough-going and successful, it often led to administrations dominated by well-known and substantial businessmen. Once reform was accomplished, those key influentials who pushed for the changes in government were often unwilling to remain in the political trenches as candidates. "Satisfied that the machinery of the plan would eliminate lower class, ward-based representation, the elites left the actual office holding to small businessmen or acceptable politicians" (Rice, 1977:65). Reform governments had set into motion a politics of disenfranchisement.

Distribution: Machines, Reformers, and the Contest for Political Control of the City

The Industrial Political Economy and Distribution

The industrial transformation initiated a new era in public services. Unlike the earlier period, when city authorities had little choice but to carefully husband their scarce resources, public officials in the industrial era could view the problems of urban housekeeping with much more independence. The extensive areas of valuable real estate, commercial districts, factories, and port facilities of the central city were visible signs of a revenue base from which a whole host of programs, such as better fire and police protection, safer and improved streets, and higher standards of sanitation and public health, could be financed. At the same time, the demands for more and better city services increased as a result of their burgeoning populations.

These forces of supply and demand made the expansion of programs for urban housekeeping and amenity an inexorable trend. Regular police and fire departments staffed by trained full-time officers, a trend that only began around the time of the Civil War in larger cities, became the norm shortly afterwards. In 1900, cities with 30,000 or more people were paying for 28,000 uniformed policemen. The old volunteer fire brigades had yielded to regular paid forces supplied with expensive fire-fighting equipment (Glaab and Brown, 1967:177–178).

In the field of public health, there also was significant expansion of municipal activity. While earlier local boards of health usually had no regular staffs and did very little except in periods of epidemic, after the Civil War most larger cities undertook to create a permanent board of health with a force of inspectors and some authority to prescribe sanitary regulations. Similarly, cities took over control of sewage disposal by constructing public sewers and providing street cleaning on a regular basis. Finally, urban amenities were given a great boost by the willingness of city and state authorities to create more public parks. After Fredrick Law Olmstead's creation of New York City's Central Park, the idea of ambitious park schemes spread and became an important interest of the planning movement in America.

While the growth of city housekeeping activities was linked to the new economic position of the industrial city, other aspects of distribution were not, particularly the matter of how these services would be politically controlled. Unlike developmental and redistributive policies, the distributive endeavors of cities do not bear very directly on a city's market position; this permits those who run these public services to do so with relative independence of the city's economic base. In the urban industrial democracies, this reality had huge political consequences.

As public services expanded, their financing, staffing, and directing constituted a form of "currency" that was used to reward or sanction conduct in the city's political system. Neither those in state political positions, whose future was dependent upon city electorates, nor those who sought political power within the city could afford to ignore how this currency was spent. Consequently, the politics of distribution reflected the struggle among these interests for political control of city government.

Distributive Policy and the Machine

Since the machine was the dominant political institution in most larger cities, the control of distributive services reflected its organizational enhancement needs. The machine relied on an incentive system similar to that of a business (Banfield and Wilson, 1965:Ch. 9). Like a business that exchanges cash and other material inducements in order to secure production and profit, the political machine operated in a similar fashion, except that its "business" was securing political power. Accordingly, party workers cooperated to gain mass political support by trading jobs, favors, and other specific material rewards for votes. Consequently, machine politicians were not usually interested in policies for achieving ideological or moral ends. In fact, because disagreements over issues that had little or nothing to do with maintaining political support for the organization could be disruptive, party bosses were often capable of remarkable neutrality.

These organizational enhancement needs defined the major features of distributive policies in machine cities: (1) a vigorous "unplanned" promotion of all services, (2) a "market" approach to their administration, and (3) widespread corruption and inefficiency.

Promoting Public Sector Growth

First, as long as jobs, kickbacks, opportunities for "honest graft," and the like could be gained from expanding municipal responsibilities, it did not matter a great deal to machine politicians whether particular efforts to improve city services were well planned or judiciously chosen according to some larger scheme. What mattered most was that policies that might outrage any politically important group were avoided. Consequently, machine leaders worked to promote rapid, ad hoc, and essentially "unplanned" expansion of services in response to the claims of important groups of voters or those who were capable of buying political support for particular projects.

Ironically, this stance associated many urban political machines with periods of remarkable civic renaissance. Expanding police and fire departments meant more jobs for loyal party workers; better streets meant more contracts to contributors of the party; and new civic centers added cash to the party treasury through inflated building contracts and political kickbacks.

In the early years of Kansas City's Pendergast machine, James Pendergast vigorously supported bond issues for school improvement and other construction purposes, park and boulevard legislation, as well as major improvements in sanitation and garbage disposal services. The desirability of these things was widely recognized by anti-Pendergast forces in the city (Glaab and Brown, 1967:222). The machine became identified with the most impressive building programs in the city's history. In contrast to the mercantile era, where resources were carefully and meagerly funneled into only the most critical services having to do with the protection of property, the machine's internal dynamics functioned to promote a growth in services of all kinds.

The Political "Marketing" of City Services

Second, the workings of the political machine imposed an informal political "market" system of administering the delivery of public services. The distributional activities of local government were allocated by "selling" them in exchange for payments made to the members of the party organization. The result was a tacit system of political "taxation" that governed the provision of city housekeeping services. The police afford the best example of how this system worked. Their power to selectively enforce a vast body of formal laws and regulations in a polyglot community provided enormous opportunities for private gain.

Committees investigating police corruption in New York City from the 1870s to 1911 provide fascinating detail about law enforcement under the machine. The New York City police force was a great "tax assessing" arm of the Democratic Party. Throughout the last half of the nineteenth century to the early years of the twentieth, many police applicants customarily added from $250 to $500 cash to their qualifications in seeking to join the force. Once on the rolls, they were frequently assessed heavily, particularly for major promotions that could cost as much as $10,000 or more. These payments augmented the incomes of top police officials who were party favorites, while various amounts from the "take" at all levels of the department found their way to the party on a regular basis. In return, officers could exploit their positions of authority. For instance, information and recommendations for liquor licensing—necessary for saloon keepers and liquor dealers in the city—was gathered by the city's 7,000 policemen.

The political "tax" levied by the police was based on estimates of an establishment's likely income, ranging from $5 to $25 for ordinary liquor dealers, plus a subscription to the party newspaper; $100 to $250 a month was not uncommon for more fashionable places or those with notorious reputations. Generally, legitimate activities typically paid along with illegitimate ones for police protection. Bootblacks were often assessed 75 cents per week, while peanut vendors paid 5 cents and pushcart vendors 15 cents. Larger businesses paid considerably more. Steamship companies, for instance, paid monthly charges of $15 to $25 for the priority use of street space across from the wharves and for minor police services in connection with their operations (Yearly, 1970:114–115).

With the consolidation of party power in many large cities, the system of services mediated by payment became increasingly centralized in the hands of the organization leadership. Under Tammany boss Richard Croker, party finance via the market approach to public services became more hierarchical in New York City. Croker instituted "reforms" that placed party chieftains in more prominent positions as service providers *cum* party tax collectors. For instance, Croker began to draw levies directly from the Liquor Dealers Association rather than private establishments paying only police officials. The liquor interests alone probably paid Tammany between $2.5 and $10 million a year by the turn of the century (Yearly, 1970:116). "Voluntary" gifts to party headquarters from other large associations rather than from only individual members became widespread at this time—milk dealers, insurance companies, street railways, and various businesses and trade associations came to play a larger role in the quid pro quo system of urban policy.

The Inefficiencies of Service Delivery

Finally, the distribution of public services was characterized by widespread inefficiency. The market approach constituted an informal system of political control that paralleled the formal legal administrative system. These two systems of political control sometimes worked in tandem to produce substantial benefits from the standpoint of service delivery, particularly in instances where the private government of the machine managed to overcome the apathy or resistance of political groups by relying on the distribution of material payoffs. For instance, at a time when many municipal charters dispersed legal authority into the hands of numerous and often separately elected officials, the machine acted to secure their cooperation by offering private gain via bribes, rather than seeking to win political agreement on the basis of ideological or other (more uncertain) nonmaterial inducements.

More often than not, however, the market system of political control imposed tremendous costs in the form of waste, favoritism, and other compromises to economic efficiency in the city's distributional programs. Street cleaning offers one such example. Although the herds of swine that had been used in earlier days disappeared by the 1880s, the sanitation system that replaced them had its own severe limitations. In New York City, the task was entrusted in 1872 to a special bureau of the police department. In enforcing the antilitter ordinances or preventing householders from depositing garbage in the streets, the police spent much of their time squeezing contributions from householders (often to permit them to violate the codes) rather than in securing compliance with the sanitary code (Mandelbaum, 1965:167–168). Later, when the city set up a special street-cleaning department, it became rife with similar corruption and was manned by political appointees. Similar patterns could be found in most other larger cities (Melosi, 1981:46).

Distributive Politics and the Machine: Pluralist Bargaining

Unlike the other arenas of local decision, the politics of distribution was dominated by highly pluralistic competition and bargaining among diverse groups seeking to build a base of political power. Since decisions over local housekeeping services did not in themselves directly affect the city's economic position or directly deal with matters of redistribution, the distributive arena afforded enormous opportunities for playing out group rivalries, building coalitions, and otherwise seeking political support within the workings of the popular control institutions of the day. Consequently, virtually all successful political bosses made patronage in street, police, fire, and sanitation departments their primary currency in scrambling for political power.

This is revealed by the rise of James Pendergast of Kansas City in the late 1800s. A saloon keeper in a heavily Irish ward, he utilized his vast contacts with local immigrant residents and politicians to secure a seat as alderman in 1892. In his move up the organization ladder, he relied heavily on manipulating decisions over city distributive services to serve his drive for personal political power. In his first term as alderman, he successfully fought against salary reductions for firemen, promoted a city park in his ward, and opposed attempts to move a fire station out of his ward.

By 1900, Pendergast, in alliance with other politicians in the city, managed to dominate the Democratic convention and name the machine's mayoral nominee. Following the latter's successful election, he quickly raided the city's patronage-laden distributive agencies to further increase the size of his voter following by creating a loyal patronage army. Pendergast's brother became superintendent of streets, a department that employed over 200 men, as well as contracted out large orders for gravel and cement. Positions in the fire department also became available to Pendergast and his coalition. A loyal favorite was appointed as the city's deputy license inspector, a job that carried the authority to grant licenses to saloons and other business establishments. Two years later, he gained the city's largest plum by managing to name 123 men to the city's 173-man police force (Dorsett, 1968).

In effect, Pendergast worked almost exclusively within the rich, patronage-ridden distributive programs of the city to pyramid his political power and secure a stable army of workers. While not all successful machine politicians worked as single-mindedly in this arena as did Pendergast in their struggle for political power, his behavior is illustrative of the importance of these programs for building a power base in a machine system (Judd, 1979:48–49).

The State in Distributive Politics

The major external constraint on utilizing the distributive arena as a forum for building local political support was the state. While state government interference in the locality might often be limited because of shared interests with the locality on matters of city economic development, the distribution of patronage and the control of city housekeeping services did not significantly affect the state economy. These kinds of decisions did directly affect the political interests of state politicians, however. Particularly when state governments were run by politicians of a different party from that which controlled the cities, state–local interests over the control of city distributive services were obviously competitive, for the patronage these programs afforded could influence the outcome of elections at local, county, and state levels. Consequently, intervention by state party leaders and government officials in order to raid local patronage was a major feature of the local politics of distribution, a fact that reinforced the highly pluralistic character of this arena.

In the early decades of the period, before home rule legislation, the partisan nature of state intervention was baldly apparent. Many cities were grossly underrepresented in state legislatures. Throughout the 1860s and 1870s, Chicago, Boston, New York, St. Paul, St. Louis, and other large cities were controlled by one party while the state was controlled by another. State governments intervened to control city services without hesitation and, more often than not, the thrust of this interference in city affairs was explicitly partisan.

Among all distributive services of the city, the police department was the greatest political prize. Whoever controlled the police had a major source of jobs, could control entry into and out of illegal businesses subject to public regulation, such as taverns, and had a major advantage in elections. In Chicago, bitter state–local party rivalry focused on the police department. When Illinois Republicans emerged triumphant at the state level in 1861, they placed Chicago's police department under a board whose members were appointed by the governor for a six-year term. When the Democrats captured control of the state two years later, they enacted legislation reducing the term of the police board to three years. But by 1865, the Republicans came back into state office and acted aggressively to shore up their power in heavily Democratic Chicago. The party restored the six-year term, placed the fire department under the authority of the police board, and passed an act requiring the police commissioners to be elected by the voters of Cook County, who were less likely than those of Chicago to elect Democrats (Klebanow et al., 1977:113–114).

Later in the nineteenth century, legislative interference in city affairs ebbed, particularly because of the home rule movement and court decisions that prohibited special legislation. Support for home rule sometimes united both machine bosses and reformers who suffered equally from the political rampages on local services by state party bosses. Even after state constitutions were amended and laws were passed granting greater protection to most cities during the first few decades of the twentieth century, the distributive arena remained vulnerable to state intervention because of its obvious partisan significance.

Reform Politics and the Distributive Arena

Wherever political machines maintained their hold on political power, the distributive arena remained the city's biggest "market" for patronage, favors, and bribes. This kind of governance, however, was never acceptable to many. Not only did this aspect of machine politics offend middle-class moral sensibilities and seem terribly wasteful of public resources, but it also operated to limit decisively the power of these groups in local politics. As long as bosses and their organizations could exploit the public sector to secure power, the influence of those middle-class citizens who wanted government that was responsive to their brand of public morality would remain limited.

The Rise of the Reformers

Prior to the 1890s, the influence of middle-class activists hoping to build a reform movement for better city government proved to be notoriously fruitless. There were periods when exceptional circumstances, such as local fiscal crisis, outrageous political scandals, and fights within local political machines enabled reform administrations to attain power in machine cities. But these reform administrations nearly always lacked much staying power, especially because business communities soon found that their interests remained with the political machine once local government had its house put in order. Business often proved to be only a transient partner in any reform drive. Unable to compete with or break apart the machine–business alliance, many early reformers had concluded that business interests were an integral sustaining force in the system of corruption. Even as late as 1910, William J. Gaynor, mayor of New York, commented that the true corruptors were really the ". . . so called leading citizens . . . [who] get a million dollars out of the city dishonestly while the boss gets a thousand" (Weinstein, 1968:168).

By the 1890s, however, "reform" received a burst of energy and a new sense of direction as a result of events that made the Progressive movement a major force in city politics (Hofstadter, 1955). While it is hardly possible to describe the complex forces behind Progressivism as an ideology and a movement, two factors were important in shaping this reform coalition at the city level.

Most important, urban business communities became much more supportive of the reform cause and broke from the machine as a result of their changing interests on matters of urban economic development. As suggested in Chapter 7, established big business increasingly saw the machine as a threat to corporate expansion. At the same time, the machine had begun to outlive its usefulness as a means of social control in the nation's industrializing cities. The transition to mass democracy was accomplished without the rise of powerful working-class parties seeking to use city government to attack business or impose programs of radical redistribution.

The result was that urban business increasingly came to share the ideals of the growing Progressive cause that sought to achieve middle-class notions of good government and to break the power of the machine. Reform achieved a unity of purpose as well as the power to carry out a sustained program in cities as the demands of middle-class activists were joined to those of the urban business community.

Reform campaigns drew their support from a broad coalition which—though heavily weighted in favor of business, wealth, and the professions—remained quite diverse. Promoters of reform included good government groups, spokesmen for the business community, voluntary organizations such as local charities and civic groups, representatives of taxpayer associations, newspaper editors, and college professors (Hays, 1973; Hofstadter, 1955). While one side of municipal reform programs focused on altering the rules of the electoral game in order to disperse the power of low-income voters and weaken the machine (see above), the other side typically focused on changing the organization of government in order to centralize power in the hands of reformer elites. It was these reforms that were targeted at the distributive arena of local politics and were intended to deprive the machine of opportunities for their patronage, bribes, and favor-trading upon which it depended for survival.

Reformism and Distributive Policy

In their struggle for power, the reformers evolved a compelling ideology that reflected their middle-class notions of political morality, a view that saw government as a moralizing influence and politics as something that demanded constant disinterested activity on the part of the citizen (Hofstadter, 1955:75). The centerpiece of this ideology was a concept of "good government." First, the reformers held that there was a public interest that could be defined objectively and that could be implemented to serve all citizens equally. Second, they held that politics—meaning conflict in elections and through representation—could be separated from administration. Third, given their belief in the separation of politics from the business of city governments, they concluded that experts with training, experience, and ability should be able to make decisions in the public interest.

Finally, they assumed that government could be run scientifically. Drawing the parallel between the business corporation and the work of government, reformers contended that business principles could be and should be applied in the public sector in order to obtain efficiency and impartiality. This point of view was perhaps most succinctly put by Andrew D. White, who wrote in 1890:

> . . . the city is a corporation; that as a city it has nothing whatever to do with general political interests. . . . The questions in a city are not political questions. They have reference to the laying out of streets (and such matters). The work of a city being the creation and control of the city property, it should logically be managed as a piece of property by those who have created it, who have a title to it, or a real substantial part in it [and not by] a crowd of illiterate peasants, freshly raked in from the Irish bogs, or Bohemian mines, or Italian robber nests (Gluck and Meister, 1979:76).

Although no single program of municipal reform ever emerged to provide the prescriptions for implementing this notion of good government, the specific reform innovations that were promoted demonstrated a remarkable political coherence. They nearly all sought to weaken the machine and substitute a governmental order in which professionals could gain political influence and run cities in accordance with the ideals of the modern business corporation, with its emphasis on efficiency, impartiality, and centralization (Holli, 1969:Ch. 8).

Toward this end, reform measures spanned the whole range, from minor to wholesale alteration of governmental structures and administrative practices. Civil service reform, in order to end the practice of favoritism and spoils, became an important local innovation after it was adopted at the national level in the Pendelton Act of 1883. By 1903, one hundred cities in the United States had some form of civil service coverage for their employees by instituting regulations for hiring and prescribing merit criteria and classifications as the mechanism for personnel recruitment and advancement. This reform was particularly important because it removed the machine as the middleman in the public personnel system.

There also were attempts to impose greater accountability and more business-like efficiency in financial, personnel, and other practices, such as elaborate audit procedures and the use of watchdog organizations and municipal research bureaus to monitor local budgets and practices. Through these methods, it was hoped that more openness, regularity, and accountability could be imposed on city procedures governing purchases of equipment and supplies and in the awarding of city contracts.

Among the most ambitious of the reform efforts were the movements for commission and city manager government. These innovations drew directly on the business model of local government and explicitly attempted to separate politics from administration (Weinstein, 1968:166). The commission form of government was the first to reflect the integration of legislative and executive authority in the hands of professionals who were expected to run government in an impartial fashion. This reform concentrated nearly all local government authority in the hands of commissioners who were each responsible for the various services.

Though the commission idea spread very rapidly, some of the problems of commission government moved other reformers to propose an alternative. Since each of the commissioners was a separate executive heading his own department, this form of government fragmented leadership and responsibility, unlike the business model idea in which the board of directors separated policy making and administration. Consequently, reformers who were critical of the commission form on grounds that it obscured responsibility and leadership promoted the idea of city manager government. According to this plan, the city council would be policymakers only and place all administrative power in the hands of an appointed, trained administrator. More closely following the "pure" business model, the council manager alternative rivaled and later surpassed the commission plan as the leading reform. Widely supported by business, it was eventually endorsed by the National Municipal League that incorporated it into its model city charter in 1915 (Judd, 1979:108).

Machine-Reform Conflict: A Pluralist Struggle

Taken together with other reforms that were intended to place business and middle-class citizens in stronger electoral positions, these governmental innova-tions amounted to no less than an attempt to centralize and bureaucratize the distributive functions of local government. As such, they constituted a drive to end the system upon which the machine fed and to substitute in its place a bureaucratic order that would be supportive of government by business elites, professionals, and others who chafed for years under the political machine.

Consequently, the ensuing political struggle between the machine and the reform movement in the distributive arena was actually an extension of the competitive, pluralist struggle among groups to use the distribution of public services in order to enhance their base of political support. While the machine-reform conflict that was unleashed after the turn of the century has sometimes been viewed as a kind of grand class or ideological struggle (cf. Hays, 1973; Hofstadter, 1955; Weinstein, 1968; Banfield and Wilson, 1965), from the perspective of the distributive arena it was nothing of the sort. The class interpretation neglects all the fundamentally pluralist features of reform politics.

The struggle between political machines and reformers during the Progressive era was essentially a fight over the control of jobs and the ways of distributing local government services, not their redistribution between different social classes. In respect to the poor, the machine did not represent the class demands of immigrants for positive changes in the redistribution of local government resources. As suggested earlier, the machine secured its social base of support among have-not groups by representing their individual and particularistic group demands. By employing a market approach to public services, the machine actually acted to distribute patronage and favors in order to limit the demands of have-not groups for more redistributive responses.

Consequently, party bosses and their organizations sought to defend themselves from the reform movement in order to enhance their organizational power, not to defend the class interests of the immigrants. Even where reformers were successful, reform government could only diminish the opportunities for immigrant groups to pursue their particularistic interests in local government. Neither reform nor machine government was very responsive to their demands as a social class.

In respect to the well-off, the reform movement did not represent anything like an uprising of the wealthy as a class to win political influence in local affairs. That the middle-class professionals, clergymen, civic leaders, and others who supported the reform movement used it as a vehicle for ending their era of disenfranchisement under the machine is quite certain. But their goals probably involved cultural differences with the immigrant community; they sought to infuse the distributive arena with Protestant morality rather than permanently shackle the ethnic. They insisted that the immigrant become "Americanized" before securing rewards from the distributive arena.

The activities of the business community in reform politics hardly fits the notion of an uprising of a class either. Through years of active support and cooperation with the political machine, business had already secured a privileged position on matters of central concern to it, particularly city economic development. Only when changes within the business community led them to redefine their interests in machine politics did they adopt the reform movement as a vehicle for preserving their autonomy within an urban environment in which they were economically captive. The politics of distribution in the reform era centered on a competition for political resources by various groups for limited purposes—control of political offices and resources—not a clash of social class interests and ideologies.

City Government, Public Policy, and the Industrial Political Economy

The urban political systems of the industrial era were profoundly shaped by their distinctive politico-economic context: economic ascendancy for central cities, democratic development, and limited intergovernmental involvement with urban problems. As intercity economic competition declined during a period of emerging mass electoral politics, the economic power of business in cities waned. This forced business to vigorously compete for political power alongside other interests. When the machine emerged from this political struggle, the interests of economic and political elites coincided. The result was business autonomy in city development and limited mass participation in other arenas of local politics. What most decisively influenced the policies and power relationships in each of the arenas within this regime was the failure of popular control to evolve into a system of power in conformity with democratic ideas.

Consequently, city governments passed through an era of remarkable economic independence within the urban system to find that public choices were limited by political structures which were parochial, designed to render public authority incapable of changing the status quo, and biased in favor of the resourceful.

The machine limited the ability of have-not groups to utilize popular control as a vehicle for pressing demands for economic equality. This decisively limited governmental involvement in programs to aid the disadvantaged. Similarly, city growth produced continuous expansion of distributive programs for urban housekeeping, creating vast new sources of patronage and political reward. But these resources became the currency with which the political machine assembled power and maintained its dominance. When the reform movement gained strength, this pluralistic arena continued to be dominated by a protracted struggle to limit popular control. Reformers utilized the distributive policies of city government to serve the organizational needs of groups seeking political control via more bureaucratic-style government.

Political Change

These political responses to the industrial political economy could not survive, however. As early as the first few decades of the twentieth century, the policies and politics forged during the industrial era were threatened by changes in the urban politico-economic order. First, the developmental politics fashioned during America's rapid industrialization were challenged by major changes in the evolution of capitalism. Most important, after the turn of the century there were signs that the premier market position of the central city as a place of business was beginning to wane. Trends toward suburbanization, the decentralization of manufacturing outside of major cities, the growth of new service provider enterprises, and the evolution of large corporate businesses able to locate branch offices and plants in far-flung areas became discernible on the eve of the Great Depression. Urban congestion, escalating central city land values, and easier commuter transportation led numbers of residents and businesses to seek surburban locations during the 1920s and 1930s. Major cities countered by building soaring skyscrapers, larger central business districts, and extensive subway and other mass transit programs.

This trend toward business and industrial decentralization threatened to create dramatically different power relationships between business and city government. The increasing ability of business to relocate outside of major established central cities could force large and small cities to compete for capital and jobs, providing business with greater economic leverage in dealing with city governments. With growing economic independence on the part of business, the old politics of development in which business elites had to struggle with political elites in the internal politics of the city was not likely to persist.

Second, the redistributive politics that underpinned local government's neglect of claims by disadvantaged groups for social welfare improvements could hardly continue. The politics of social control that contained the redistributive demands of have-nots through the political machine was increasingly threatened by reform movements that could not effectively replace the machine's social control functions. Reforms that made it more difficult for disadvantaged groups to participate in local politics was an inferior means of social control because it relied on effective disenfranchisement of the poor, rather than providing a political reward structure to contain mass influence. A new crisis of social welfare was in the works with each reform success.

Finally, changes in the distributive arena that began toward the end of the industrial era were sure to evolve much further, creating new urban political conflicts. The trend toward increasing professionalization of city bureaucracies, the growth of a larger urban middle class, and the spread of municipal reform would weaken the machine. However, the eventual triumph of professionalization and bureaucratic governance could not end conflict over distribution. Rather, this trend would merely shift fights over distributive policies to a new set of political actors who would play according to new rules.

Endnote

1. Hence, "... a three-cornered relationship developed in which the machine could be viewed as a broker, who in return for financial assistance from wealthy elites, promoted their policy interests when in office, while passing along a portion of the gain to a particularized electorate from whom he 'rented' his authority" (Scott, 1969:1155).

References for Part Two

Abbot, Carl. 1981. *The New Urban America: Growth and Politics in Sunbelt Cities.* Chapel Hill: University of North Carolina Press.

Albion, Robert G. 1961. *The Rise of New York Port.* Hamden, Conn.: Archer Books.

Anderson, Douglas D. 1980. "State Regulation of Electric Utilities" in James Q. Wilson, ed. 1980. *The Politics of Regulation.* New York: Basic Books, Ch. I.

Banfield, Edward C. 1974. *The Unheavenly City Revisited.* Boston: Little, Brown.

Banfield, Edward C. and James Q. Wilson. 1965. *City Politics.* Cambridge, Mass.: Harvard University Press.

Beer, Samuel H. 1965. *Modern British Politics.* London: Faber and Faber.

Bell, Daniel. 1961. "The Three Faces of New York." *Dissent*, Vol. 8 (Summer), 62–73.

Bish, Robert L. 1971. *The Public Economy of Metropolitan Areas.* Chicago: Markham Publishing Co.

Bowles, Samuel and Herbert Gintis. 1976. *Schooling in Capitalist America: Educational Reform and the Contradictions of Economic Life.* New York: Basic Books.

Bridges, Amy. 1984. *A City in the Republic: Antebellum New York and the Origins of Machine Politics.* Cambridge; Cambridge University Press.

Brenner, Robert. 1956. *From the Depths: The Discovery of Poverty in the United States.* New York: New York University Press.

Brownell, Blaine A. and David Goldfield. 1977. *The City in Southern History.* Port Washington, N.Y.: Kennikat Press.

Brownell, Blaine A. and Warren E. Stickle, eds. 1973. *Bosses and Reformers: Urban Politics in America, 1880–1920.* Boston: Houghton Mifflin.

Bryce, Herrington J. 1979. *Revitalizing Cities.* Lexington, Mass: Lexington Books.

Cebola, R. J. 1974. "Local Government Policies and Migration: An Analysis for SMSA's in the U.S." *Public Choice*, Vol. 19, 85–93.

Chambers, William N. and Walter D. Burnham. 1967. *The American Party Systems.* New York: Oxford University Press.

Chandler, Jr., Alfred D. 1959. "The Beginnings of 'Big Business' in American History." *Business History Review*, Vol. 33 (Spring), 1–31.

Chudacoff, Howard. 1975. *The Evolution of American Urban Society*, Second Edition. Englewood Cliffs, N.J.: Prentice-Hall.

Coben, Stanley and Forest G. Hill, eds. 1966. *American Economic History: Essays in Interpretation.* Philadelphia: J. B. Lippincott.

Cochran, Thomas C. and William Miller. 1961. *The Age of Enterprise*, Revised Edition. New York: Harper and Brothers.

Dahl, Robert A. 1961. *Who Governs?* New Haven, Conn.: Yale University Press.

Davis, Allen F. 1967. *Spearheads for Reform: The Social Settlements and the Progressive Movement, 1890-1914*. New York: Oxford University Press.

Davis, Lance E. 1965. "The Investment Market, 1870-1914: The Evolution of a National Market." *Journal of Economic History*, Vol. 25, 355-399.

Denning, Michael and David J. Olson. 1981. "Public Enterprise and the Emerging Character of State Service Provision: Application to Public Ports." *Paper Delivered at the 1981 meeting of The American Political Science Association.*

Devine, Edward T. 1939. *When Social Work Was Young*. New York: MacMillan.

Dorsett, Lyle W. 1968. *The Pendergast Machine*. New York: Oxford University Press.

Ebner, Michael and Eugene Tobin, eds. 1977. *The Age of Urban Reform: New Perspectives on the Progressive Era*. Port Washington, N.Y.: Kennikat Press.

Falk, David and Herbert M. Franklin. 1976. *Equal Housing Opportunity: The Unfinished Agenda*. Washington, D.C.: The Potomac Institute.

Feder, Leah H. 1936. *Unemployment Relief in Periods of Depression: A Study of Measures Adopted in Certain American Cities, 1857-1922*. New York: Russell Sage.

Foner, Phillip. 1947, 1955, 1964, 1965, 1980. *History of the Labor Movement in the United States*, Vols. I, II, III, IV, V. New York: International Publishers.

Foster, Mark. 1979. "City Planners and Urban Transportations: The American Response, 1900-1940." *Journal of Urban History*, Vol. 5, No. 3, 365-396.

Gelfand, Mark I. 1975. *Anatomy of Cities: The Federal Government and Urban America, 1933-1965*. New York: Oxford University Press.

Gere, Edwin A., Jr. 1982. "Dillon's Rule and the Cooley Doctrine: Reflections of the Political Culture." *Journal of Urban History*, Vol. 8, No. 3 (May), 271-298.

Glaab, Charles N. 1963. *The American City: A Documentary History*. Homewood, Ill.: The Dorsey Press.

Glaab, Charles N. and Theodore A. Brown. 1967. *A History of Urban America*. New York: Macmillan Company.

Gluck, Peter R. and Richard J. Meister. 1979. *Social Changes and Institutional Responses in Urban Development: Cities in Transition*. New York: New Viewpoints.

Gordon, Daniel N. 1973. *Social Change and Urban Politics*. Englewood Cliffs, N.J.: Prentice-Hall.

Gordon, David M. 1978. "Capitalist Development and the History of American Cities" in William K. Tabb and Larry Sawers. 1968. *Marxism and the Metropolis*. New York: Oxford University Press, pp. 25-63.

Griffith, Ernest S. 1974. *A History of American City Government: The Conspicuous Failure, 1870-1900*. New York: Praeger.

Hammack, David C. 1982. *Power and Society: Greater New York at the Turn of the Century*. New York: Russell Sage.

Harrigan, John J. 1976. *Political Change in the Metropolis.* Boston: Little, Brown.

Hays, Samuel P. 1973. "The Politics of Reform in Municipal Government in the Progressive Era." Reprinted in Daniel N. Gordon, ed. 1973. *Social Change and Urban Politics: Readings.* Englewood Cliffs, N.J.: Prentice-Hall, pp. 107–127.

Hays, Samuel P. 1965. "The Social Analysis of American Political History, 1880–1920." *Political Science Quarterly,* Vol. 80 (September), 369–387.

Hays, Samuel P. 1957. *The Response to Industrialism. 1885–1914.* Chicago: University of Chicago Press.

Hofstadter, Richard. 1955. *The Age of Reform.* New York: Vintage.

Holli, Melvin G. 1969. *Reform in Detroit.* New York: Oxford University Press.

Judd, Dennis R. 1979. *The Politics of American Cities; Private Power and Public Policy.* Boston: Little, Brown.

Katznelson, Ira. 1981. *City Trenches: Urban Politics and the Patterning of Class in the United States.* New York: Pantheon Books.

Katznelson, Ira. 1976. "Other Ethnics and Citizen Participation" in *Urban Governance and Minorities.* New York: Praeger.

Katznelson, Ira. 1973. *Black Men, White Cities.* London: Oxford University Press, Inc.

Kirkland, Edward C. 1961. *Industry Comes of Age; Business, Labor and Public Policy, 1860–1897.* New York: Holt, Rinehart and Winston.

Klebanow, Diana, Franklin C. Jonas, and Ira M. Leonard. 1977. *Urban Legacy: The Story of America's Cities.* New York: New American Library.

Kolko, Gabriel. 1967. *The Triumph of Conservatism.* Chicago: University of Chicago Press.

Laslett, John and Seymour M. Lipset, eds. 1974. *Failure of a Dream?* Garden City, N.Y.: Doubleday Anchor.

Leiby, James. 1978. *A History of Social Welfare and Social Work in the United States.* New York: Columbia University Press.

Lindblom, Charles E. 1977. *Politics and Markets.* New York: Basic Books.

Logan, John R. and Harvey L. Molotch. 1987. *Urban Fortunes: The Political Economy of Place.* Berkeley: University of California Press.

Lowi, Theodore J. 1969. *At the Pleasure of the Mayor.* New York: Free Press.

Lubove, Roy. 1970. "The Roots of City Planning" in Allen M. Wakstein. 1970. *The Urbanization of America.* Boston: Houghton Mifflin, pp. 315–329.

Lubove, Roy. 1962. *The Progressives and the Slums: Tenement House Reform in New York City, 1890–1917.* Westport, Conn.: Greenwood Press.

Maisel, Louis and Joseph Cooper, eds. 1978. *The Development of Political Parties; Patterns of Evolution and Decay.* Beverly Hills: Sage.

Makielski, Stanislaw J. 1966. *The Politics of Zoning: The New York Experience.* New York: Columbia University Press.

Mandelbaum, Seymour J. 1965. *Boss Tweed's New York.* New York: John Wiley.

McConnell, Grant. 1966. *Private Power and American Democracy.* New York: Knopf.

McCormick, Richard P. 1967. "Political Development and the Second Party System" in William N. Chambers and Walter D. Burnham. 1967. *The American Party Systems*. New York: Oxford University Press, pp. 90–116.

McKelvey, Blake. 1973. *American Urbanization: A Comparative History.* Glenview, Ill: Scott, Foresman.

McKelvey, Blake. 1968. *The Emergence of Metropolitan America, 1915–1966.* New Brunswick, N.J.: Rutgers University Press.

McKelvey, Blake. 1963. *The Urbanization of America, 1860–1915.* New Brunswick, N.J.: Rutgers University Press.

McShane, Clay. 1979. "Transforming the Use of Urban Space: A Look at the Revolution in Street Pavements, 1880–1924." *Journal of Urban History*, Vol. 5, No. 3, 279–307.

Melosi, Martin V. 1981. *Garbage in the Cities.* College Station: Texas A&M University Press.

Merton, Robert. 1957. *Social Theory and Social Structure.* New York: Free Press.

Miller, Zane L. 1973. *The Urbanization of Modern America: A Brief History.* New York: Harcourt Brace and Jovanovich.

Miller, Zane L. 1968. *Boss Cox's Cincinnati: Urban Politics in the Progressive Era.* New York: Oxford University Press.

Mohl, Raymond A. and James F. Richardson, eds. 1973. *The Urban Experience: Themes in American History.* Belmont, Calif: Wadsworth.

Musgrave, Richard A. 1943. "The Voluntary Exchange Theory of Public Economy." *Quarterly Journal of Economics*, Vol. LIII (February), 213–237.

O'Donnell, Patrick. 1977. "Industrial Capitalism and the Rise of Modern American Cities." *Kapitalistate*, No. 6 (Fall), 91–127.

Park, Robert, Ernest W. Burgess and Roderick D. McKenzie, eds. 1925. *The City.* Chicago: University of Chicago Press.

Perloft, Harvey and Lowdon Wingo, eds. 1968. *Issues in Urban Economics.* Baltimore: Johns Hopkins University Press.

Piven, Francis Fox and Richard A. Cloward. 1971. *Regulating the Poor: The Functions of Public Welfare.* New York: Random House.

Polanyi, Karl. 1957. *The Great Transformation: The Political and Economic Origins of Our Time.* Boston: Beacon Press.

Poulson, Barry W. 1981. *Economic History of the United States.* New York: Macmillan.

Pred, Allen R. 1966. *The Spatial Dynamics of U.S. Urban-Industrial Growth, 1800–1914*, Cambridge, Mass.: MIT Press.

Rice, Bradley Robert. 1977. *Progressive Cities: The Commission Government Movement in America, 1901–1920.* Austin: University of Texas Press.

Richardson, James F. 1974. *Urban Police in the United States.* Port Washington, N.Y.: Kennikat Press.

Rose, Mark H. and John G. Clark. 1982. "Light, Heat and Power: Energy Choice in Kansas City, Wichita and Denver, 1900–1935." *Journal of Urban History*, Vol. 5, No. 3, 340–364.

Schiesl, Martin J. 1977. *The Politics of Efficiency: Municipal Administration and Reform in America, 1800–1970*. Berkeley: University of California Press.

Schlesinger, Arthur M. 1933. *The Rise of the City, 1878–1898*. New York: Macmillan.

Schnore, Leo F., ed. 1975. *The New Urban History*. Princeton, N.J.: Princeton University Press.

Scott, James C. 1972. *Comparative Political Corruption*. Englewood Cliffs, N.J.: Prentice-Hall.

Scott, James C. 1969. "Corruption, Machine Politics and Political Change." *American Political Science Review*, Vol. LXIII (December), 1142–1158.

Shefter, Martin. 1976. "The Emergence of the Machine: An Alternative View" in Willis D. Hawley et al. 1976. *Theoretical Perspectives on Urban Politics*. Englewood Cliffs, N.J.: Prentice-Hall, pp. 14–44.

Stave, Bruce M. 1975. *Socialism and the Cities*. Port Washington, N.Y.: Kennikat Press.

Stave, Bruce M. 1972. *Urban Bosses, Machines and Progressive Reformers*. Lexington, Mass.: D. C. Heath.

Sutcliffe, Anthony. 1982. *Toward the Planned City: Germany, Britain, the U.S. and France, 1788–1914*. New York: St. Martin's Press.

Tabb, William K. and Larry Sawers, eds. 1978. *Marxism and the Metropolis: New Perspectives in Urban Political Economy*. New York: Oxford University Press.

Teaford, Jon C. 1979. *City and Suburb: The Political Fragmentation of Metropolitan America, 1850–1970*. Baltimore: Johns Hopkins University Press.

Teaford, Jon C. 1975. *The Municipal Revolution in America, 1650–1825*. Chicago: University of Chicago Press.

Thelen, David P. 1972. *The New Citizenship: Origins of Progressivism in Wisconsin, 1885–1900*. Columbia: University of Missouri Press.

Trattner, Walter I. 1974. *From Poor Law to Welfare State: A History of Social Welfare in America*. New York: Free Press.

Wade, Richard C. 1959. *The Urban Frontier*. Chicago: University of Chicago Press.

Wakstein, Allen M., ed. 1970. *The Urbanization of America*. Boston: Houghton Mifflin.

Warner, Jr., Sam Bass. 1972. *The Urban Wilderness*. New York: Harper and Row.

Warner, Jr., Sam Bass. 1968. *The Private City*. Philadelphia: University of Pennsylvania Press.

Warner, Jr., Sam Bass. 1962. *Streetcar Suburbs: The Process of Growth in Boston, 1870–1900*. Cambridge, Mass.: Harvard University Press.

Watkins, Alfred J. 1980. *The Practice of Urban Economics*. Beverly Hills: Sage.

Watkins, Alfred J. and David C. Perry. 1977. "Regional Change and the Impact of Uneven Urban Development" in David C. Perry and Alfred J. Watkins. 1977. *The Rise of the Sunbelt Cities*. Beverly Hills: Sage, pp. 13–18.

Weber, Adna F. 1963. *The Growth of Cities in the 19th Century*. Ithaca, N.Y.: Cornell University Press.

Weinstein, James. 1968. *The Corporate Ideal in the Liberal State: 1900-1918*. Boston: Beacon Press.

Wiebe, Robert H. 1967. *The Search for Order, 1877-1920*. New York: Hill and Wang.

Wiebe, Robert H. 1962. *Businessmen and Reform*. Cambridge: Harvard University Press.

Winter, William O. 1969. *The Urban Polity*. New York: Dodd, Mead.

Yearley, C. K. 1970. *The Money Machines*. Albany: State University of New York Press.

Zink, Harold. 1968. *City Bosses in the United States: A Study of Twenty Municipal Bosses*. New York: A.M.S. Press.

BOOK

II

The Contemporary Urban Political Economy

D URING the Great Depression years of the 1930s, dramatic changes in all dimensions of the urban political economy began to occur. Major transformations in the capitalist economy of the United States eventually forged a new market environment for local governments. This change has cast cities into unprecedented positions of economic dependency and shattered the urban system of the industrial age. At the same time, cities, towns, and suburbs have undergone a veritable revolution in local popular control systems; their democratic character has been enhanced by important demographic, social, and political developments.

These changes have fundamentally altered the liberal-democratic order, resulting in a political economy of postindustrial democracy. In this new order, city governments must cope with unprecedented urban economic competition for growth while responding to powerful popular forces within their political systems. This management of economic dependency amid advanced democratization takes place within a new federal system that has afforded a major role for state and federal governments in urban politics.

In effect, capitalism, democracy, and federalism have all evolved to produce a mature liberal-democratic regime. The causes and character of this new urban regime are discussed in the following two chapters. The remainder of the book probes the major developmental, redistributive, and distributive policy dilemmas of city governments.

PART THREE

Postindustrial Democracy, 1930 to the Present

CHAPTER NINE

Economic Dependency and Popular Control: Postindustrial Democracy

---

T HE economic and political control systems of America's liberal-democratic cities underwent fundamental changes during the decades following 1930. The city-centered economy of the industrial period atrophied as giant multi-locational corporations arose, restructuring the economic order along decentralist lines. Cities now face a new economic dependency within the capitalist system. At the same time, however, urban communities have experienced a development that promotes greater citizen choice—the transformation of urban popular control systems along relatively polyarchal lines. So fundamental are these changes in market and government that they constitute a new urban political economy: postindustrial democracy.

The Economic Context: The Postindustrial Economy

In the past, American economic systems were best described by the dominant mode of wealth-producing activity that, in turn, shaped the economic functions of cities. Thus, the commercial cities were trading sites within a predominantly agricultural economy; industrial era cities functioned as centers for manufacturing activities. In the contemporary period, however, the national economy is best characterized by its dominant mode of organization—the multilocational corporation—because it is this that has profoundly transformed American capitalism and the economic functions of cities within this system.

The Multilocational Corporation

During the last generation or so, the rise of the large, multilocational corporation has assumed a commanding position, becoming the principal organizing force in the economy (Storper, 1981:19). These corporations are distinguished from ordinary business firms by their large size, their multiple administrative and operational units, and their location in scattered business sites. Today they control the movement of most goods, services, and capital throughout the United States. As they have extended their reach, they have decisively shaped the economic fortunes of communities ranging from the largest of American cities to rural outposts in Third World countries. The main economic function of cities in the United States is to afford a site for the varied operations of multilocational corporations.

The modern large corporation first emerged in America during the industrial era, but it was not until after World War II that these enterprises came to dominate the national economy and fundamentally change its organization (Noyelle and Stanback, 1984:36). This occurred because these huge companies were able to take advantage of dramatic technological advances that, by leading to new products or to changes in production and distribution systems, became the primary source of economic growth (Storper, 1981:20-21). During this period, manufacturing became revolutionized by almost countless innovations, such as automation, the computerized assembly line, the development of synthetics (e.g., plastics), and other advances. Greater efficiency in production and distribution processes occurred as a result of innovations in communications and information; advances such as the computer and electronic data processing enabled managers to know more about the flow of goods within the firm and in the market, thereby enabling more efficient use of personnel and facilities. The manifold development of new products—from VCRs to clothes made of synthetics—has been the result of related technological breakthroughs. The technological revolution has led to the proliferation of new products and services for a variety of national markets rather than the production of fewer kinds of goods for a more uniform national market.

Large businesses were in an advantageous position to capitalize on these new technologies during the postwar era. Compared to small firms, they have had far better access to large financial resources. With their capacity to generate substantial corporate savings and their ability to borrow large sums at favorable interest rates, large corporations could easily invest in critical technological advances and dominate their markets. Similarly, it has been the large corporation that has owned the organizational capability to develop, plan, and employ the new technologies via specialized research, development, finance, and marketing units within the corporation. This organizational capacity also has enabled the large corporation to coordinate the many operations involved in the introduction of a new product or a new system of production and distribution.

Consequently, the decades following World War II witnessed greater concentration of economic activities in fewer and larger corporations. The patterns among the Fortune 500 corporations—industrial companies, as distinguished from utilities, transportation, merchandising, and financial corporations—are generally regarded as representative of business trends. In 1955, this group accounted for 58 percent of sales, 64 percent of assets, 49 percent of employees, and 77 percent of net industrial income. By 1973, the Fortune 500 accounted for 66 percent of all industrial sales, 83 percent of industrial assets, 66 percent of all employees, and 79 percent of all industrial net income (Blumberg, 1975:25). The 1500 companies on the New York Stock Exchange in 1970 represented less than one-tenth of one percent of the approximately 1,700,000 corporations in the United States that year. Yet these 1500 firms earned 94 percent of the total net income of all corporations (Blumberg, 1975:16–17). Today, in the United States and in other advanced economies, a clear majority of private sector employment is directly associated with domestically headquartered multilocational firms (Pred, 1977:99).

THE RESTRUCTURING OF THE ECONOMY BY THE MULTILOCATIONAL CORPORATION. These changes in business and technology have brought about a fundamental restructuring of the national economic order that is centered on the multilocational corporation. All the major factors of production—land, capital, and labor—have been reorganized.

Land. First, the use of land in production has been radically altered. Production and distribution have become highly dispersed to multiple geographical locations. During the industrial era, goods were almost entirely produced in large factories in a single locale and then shipped along the rails to various consumer and producer markets. In the postindustrial economy, the opposite has become the norm. Component parts of finished products are increasingly produced in separate factories and then shipped to assembly locations that are usually near the point of consumption. Thus, a famous brand of St. Louis beer no longer travels by refrigerator car from the large brewery to scattered urban markets; instead, it is brewed in Tampa (Florida), Newark (New Jersey), Houston (Texas), and Los Angeles (California) and is distributed regionally from these points. Chevrolets may be designed in Detroit, but their parts are mostly manufactured in the suburbs, and the autos are assembled in places that include Arlington (Texas), Baltimore (Maryland), Doraville (Georgia), Janesville (Wisconsin), Leeds and St. Louis (Missouri), Lordstown (Ohio), South Gate and Van Nuys (California), North Tarrytown (New York), Willow Run (Michigan), and Wilmington (Delaware) (Warner, 1972:126–127).

One study documenting the decentralized operations of large enterprises examined employment patterns in large businesses located in seven western metropolitan areas in the early 1970s. The study found that only an average of 27 percent of their total employment was within the metropolitan area where the firm was headquartered; the remainder was scattered throughout the nation and the world (Pred, 1977:128).

Accordingly, these decentralist tendencies of business enterprise have altered urban land values. Heartland cities contained the most valuable land during the industrial era because they were the key business centers. But as firms have dispersed their facilities, land values have declined in the old northern cities compared with other areas of the country (Johnston, 1982:206–208).

Efficiency in production is now achieved through multiplant operations rather than through a plant of enormous size. Technological advances in such things as power, materials, communication, and transportation have brought this about. Electricity, which has replaced steam as the primary source of industrial power, can be transmitted over great distances without significant cost increases (as was the case in transporting coal to the factory). New materials used in manufacturing have also promoted industrial dispersal. Unlike steel, which had to be used in large plants to obtain efficiencies, plastics and other synthetics can be used in smaller plants. Weighing less, these new materials have reduced the importance of transportation costs and permitted the production of goods containing smaller portions of raw materials, enabling factories to be located far from the sources of supply.

The revolution in communications—from the telephone to the computer—has also promoted the dispersion of production and distribution by enabling management to obtain information and control over widely scattered operations. Perhaps most important, changes in the means of transportation of bulk products, finished goods, and labor have facilitated industrial deconcentration. With the advent of the truck, many factories are no longer required to locate along relatively inflexible railway lines in order to link materials, manufacturing, and markets. Similarly, the automobile has enabled workers to commute to their jobs over long distances from a variety of locations (Blair, 1972:98).

As a result, the restructuring of manufacturing and distribution has enabled particular corporate units to be located at their most economically advantageous location. For example, production processes involving low-wage work can be located in low-wage areas rather than in labor markets having a higher standard of living. This has proved to be more than merely a potential advantage to large corporations. Studies suggest that labor force requirements, rather than local economies generated by the proximity between units in production and marketing, are probably the most important factor in the locational choices of large firms (Storper, 1981:22–23).

Capital. Second, the multilocational economy has restructured capital, including the organization of the large corporation itself. As opportunities to decentralize production and distribution grew after World War II, most large corporations changed their internal organization in order to cope with the expansion and decentralization of their operations (Chandler, 1962:44, 393). Previously, they had been managed by a small top-level staff that had the dual responsibility of coordinating the activities of the entire enterprise and making daily operational decisions. The structure adopted by most firms during the postwar period separated these two functions and augmented their managerial and technical staffs.

The new corporate structure provided for a central headquarters staff and separate divisions for each major product line of the company. The central office became responsible for guiding the growth and operation of the entire enterprise, rather than the promotion of any particular division or unit. Its functions include allocating funds and resources within the organization, resolving conflicts among the various units, and developing new products and facilities for the enterprise. The operating level became headed by divisional staffs, who were responsible for the production, distribution, and marketing of one or a set of related products and were accountable for achieving a profitable operation. Their semiautonomy from the upper echelon enabled the divisions to operate the dispersed corporate facilities and to concentrate on making day-to-day decisions regarding production, sales, purchasing, and employment. In effect, this multidivisional structure insulates the central staff from daily management while providing the organizational capability that enables the enterprise to engage in highly enlarged and diversified business activities.

This reorganization of the corporation has decisively influenced capital investment patterns. The large corporation achieved an unprecedented degree of centralized financial control over the distribution of capital to cities and regions all over the nation and the world. Located in cities that are usually far removed from the sites of production, the investment decisions of corporate staffs establish production, distribution, and marketing systems and develop raw material sites in Western Europe, the United States, and the Third World.

Before 1945, these large firms had limited their investments abroad to obtaining raw materials needed for their finished products, which were then marketed domestically. After the war, however, many of these corporations added an international component to the product lines they were manufacturing for domestic markets and began servicing foreign consumer markets, particularly in Western Europe. During the 1970s, they expanded their international operations and began to locate facilities in low-wage areas that produced goods for both their domestic and foreign markets. These multinational corporations, as large American companies with subsidiaries or branches in more than one nation came to be known, were almost invariably among the largest U.S. corporate businesses; two hundred of them accounted for more than half of all direct investments made by U.S. companies abroad in 1970 (Chandler, 1977:480). As a result, the United States has become a major exporter of capital; not until the 1970s did foreign corporations begin to offer serious competition in the capital market and diminish American hegemony over Western economies (Bluestone and Harrison, 1982:141–142).

The primary type of corporate merger activity during this period has become known as conglomeration. The latter involves the purchase of totally unrelated businesses by a large parent corporation. It radically differs from the earlier processes that led to the growth of large businesses. Previously, large corporations usually grew by investing resources to industries similar to or related to their original line of products. Whether through mergers, by forming multinationals, or simply through internal expansions, the growth of large corporations built upon existing competitive skills. During the last several decades, however, huge companies took advantage of their access to capital resources and invested in a variety of companies producing very different and diversified products. Conglomeration became so rampant during these years that the number of conglomerate mergers far surpassed the horizontal and vertical mergers of earlier periods (Grey and Peterson, 1974:467).

In its way, conglomeration reflects the changed nature of the American economy during the postwar era. The conglomerate's organizational structure is similar to that of other large corporations (Chandler, 1977:481–483). What has become increasingly important, particularly since the 1970s, is for businesses to have the capacity to shift their investment capital in accordance with national and worldwide market trends. The large corporation, with its technological virtuosity, cost efficiencies, and managerial skills for operating worldwide businesses, has had the competitive edge in a growing and changing global market. With conglomeration it has even become irrelevant that the products of the various divisions be related; it is the capacity to move in whatever directions are "dictated" by a worldwide market dominated by corporate giants that is of greatest import.

Labor. Third, multiunit corporations have dramatically transformed the labor market during the postindustrial era. For one thing, the service sector of the economy has mushroomed at a rate that has far surpassed manufacturing employment, the key labor market during the industrial period. Although there has been no drop in the proportion of the GNP accounted for by the production of goods, during the postwar period there has been a decline in the proportion of the labor force working in blue-collar jobs. The proportion of Americans employed by the service sector increased from 56 percent in 1947 to more than two-thirds of the labor force by 1977 (Noyelle, 1982:119).

While some of this growth in service jobs has been due to government and nonprofit institutions (e.g., hospitals), large corporations have been responsible for most of the private sector growth. Remaining strongly tied to the manufacturing of goods rather than only services provided directly to consumers, corporate service jobs mainly have expanded from the enlargement of the managerial component in large corporations and the propensity of these giants to employ more people in office jobs compared with smaller firms (Friedland, 1983:61; Pred, 1977:104–105). In addition, there has been dramatic growth in firms providing specialized services to the large corporation, including finance, banking, law, insurance, public relations, accounting, and management; their numbers of employees have doubled largely owing to the demand for these services by large corporations (Noyelle, 1982:117–120).

The activities of multilocational firms have also acted to polarize and segment the labor market along class lines. Industrialization forged a class system where status was based on occupations. But one of the important social legacies of industrialization was the creation of a large class of skilled industrial workers who were relatively prosperous; their presence "softened" the social and economic disparities between the unskilled and those who held skilled technical, professional, and managerial jobs. This middle strata of the work force often became members of industrial unions and achieved substantial economic gains, job security, and upward mobility for themselves and their families (Noyelle, 1982:120–123).

However, as large U.S. corporations began to reorganize their division of labor and intensify their use of new labor-saving technologies, a greater polarization of the blue-collar and white-collar work force resulted. The large middle strata of blue-collar workers has shrunk. Between 1960 and 1975, the percentage of workers earning between 80 and 120 percent of the average worker declined from 36 percent of the workforce to less than 28 percent (Noyelle, 1982:122). Moreover, low-skill, low-wage jobs have become more separated from higher skilled occupations and are increasingly located in less-developed areas of the nation and world. The work of office clericals and assemblers in automated industries now often takes place in different geographical settings from that of managers, professionals, and technicians. In effect, the growth of dispersed corporate empires has contributed to a labor market characterized by a widening of social and economic class differences.

The Urban Consequences of the Postindustrial Economy: The Dependent City

The reorganization of the national economy by multilocational corporations has decisively redefined the economic functions of cities and unleashed wholly new patterns of urban development. As giant corporations have dispersed their administrative and production units to localities everywhere, few cities can "capture" any particular economic function as a business center. In contrast to earlier periods, when a city's geographical place, transportation, physical infrastructure, or other locational advantages were important factors that tied businesses to a specific urban community, the postindustrial city typically lacks this capability. The multilocational nature of the corporate economy has permitted such an enormously wide range of locational choices for most business activities that urban economies are now highly dependent on the investment decisions of these enterprises. The previously strategic economic function of the city has diminished to a point where they have largely become places where specialized functions that contribute to the operation of large corporate empires can be performed. *From the perspective of corporate managers, cities are usually interchangeable; from the perspective of those who live in the cities, they are economically dependent.*

Consequently, cities, surburbs, and even some rural areas have become captive of a highly competitive urban economic environment. Without substantial economies stemming from their geography, they have been compelled to engage in bitter competition over the capital investment decisions of large firms. This has reversed the historic bargaining relationship between cities and business. Today, cities are pitted against each other in a highly diffused system of urban competition for jobs and dollars, while large corporations may pick and choose in an investment process that gives them powerful bargaining advantages in determining the course of urban development.

The Wide Scope of Corporate Dispersal

Patterns of corporate location in the industrial and service sectors of the economy suggest the wide scope and form of the new urban economic dependency. In the industrial sector, large enterprises have almost invariably constructed their new factory systems outside the core industrial cities. Even those firms with large prewar plant investments in central cities have usually chosen to move from these facilities and construct new factories. Corporations involved in heavy industry, such as steel and automobiles, have located their new plants in suburban locales near their old central city sites; they moved their establishments only a comparatively short distance in order to retain most of their current workforce while building plants in urban fringe areas where land was cheaper and more plentiful. For example, of the nearly 300 bargaining units represented by the United Auto Workers in 1979, approximately 80 percent were located in northern suburban facilities and only 10 percent represented factories remaining in central city locations. Similarly, about four-fifths of raw steel plants are located in industrial suburbs in the Pittsburgh–Detroit belt (Mollenkopf, 1983:26).

On the other hand, light industries whose development is usually more recent, such as electronics and aerospace, have chosen to locate their production plants in the outlying areas of cities in the Sunbelt region. Closely linked to the defense industry, they emerged during the second World War when most government defense contracts were given to companies located in the Sunbelt. These industries developed sophisticated technologies and recruited a highly trained labor force; when they expanded into new nondefense work after the war, they chose to remain in the same area in order to draw upon the advantages of this high-tech environment (Johnston, 1982:145–146; Mollenkopf, 1983:27).[1]

Many large enterprises have also located their factories in nonmetropolitan settings as their technologies became highly automated and they required only a relatively unskilled workforce. During the decades right after the war, several such industries, including apparel, furniture, textiles, and tobacco, moved from the North to rural areas in the Southeast. In recent years, multilocational firms have been increasingly locating these industries in Third World sites and have even begun placing their more routinized production activities in other in-dustries—old and new—in rural settings. The current trend is one where an ever-larger proportion of American industry is leaving its urban locale with each new technological advance (Till, 1981:197).

The locational patterns of corporate service activities also suggest the wide net of localities competing for these economic functions. Three service activities can be distinguished—top management, skilled white-collar employees, and routine office work. The top corporate echelon has replaced the industrial worker of yesteryear as the occupational group most likely to be located in or near the central city, particularly the nation's largest cities. Two-thirds of the Fortune 500 have their headquarters located in the twenty-five largest metro-politan areas; 85 percent of the 800 largest corporations locate their top management in metropolitan areas of over 500,000 (Pred, 1977:113–114; Mollenkopf, 1983:30).[2]

The primary reason for this big city concentration of corporate headquarters is the top staff's need for face-to-face contacts with the suppliers of a bevy of specialized corporate services, such as banking, law, accounting, advertising, etc., and, to a lesser extent, with their counterparts in other large corporations. Consequently, corporate service firms have grown to become an industry in themselves and have located in the central city to service top management (Noyelle and Stanback, 1984:329). Yet even here, multilocational firms retain a significant degree of choice in that no single or small group of large cities can "capture" corporate headquarters. A study of the headquarters and regional office locations of the Fortune 500 and the 300 largest nonindustrial firms found that there was no relationship between the size of the metropolitan area and its usage as an office center. The study concluded that the locational choices were wholly asymmetrical; they only could be understood in terms of the individual inner logic of each corporation (Pred, 1977:111–116).

Other administrative units employing skilled white-collar staff, such as divisional headquarters, research and development laboratories, and regional sales offices, tend to be scattered among suburban sites throughout the country. Suburbia has provided the skilled labor pool needed by this middle level of corporate business. Otherwise, their locations appear to be based on factors that are peculiar to each specific unit. For example, corporate offices that mainly involve routine "back-office" clerical work, such as billing, payroll, and sales, are increasingly found in nonmetropolitan settings. Although they were initially located in suburbia during the early years of the postwar period, advances in informational technology have enabled many firms to move these functions beyond the environs of cities (Leven, 1979:25; Till, 1981:197).

In essence, there has occurred in the industrial and service sectors of the corporate economy a vast increase in the numbers of urban areas that serve as sites for particular units of the multilocational enterprise. As the scope for business location has widened, the interchangeability of many cities, suburbs, and even rural areas for performing particular business functions has precipitated new urban economic competition for corporate investment. What has emerged is an era of urban economic dependency.

The End of the Core and Periphery Urban System

Urban economic dependency has shattered the core and periphery system of cities. The latter system was an outgrowth of the industrial era that enabled a small number of large cities, mostly located in the nation's heartland, to achieve a relatively stable market position within a hierarchy of urban areas. By diffusing economic development in all regions of the nation, the postindustrial economy has impelled cities everywhere to compete with each other in response to the investment decisions of large corporations. A laissez faire-style urban system has replaced the core and periphery order.

This new urban system is reflected by the striking reversal of historic patterns of urbanization. The American population is no longer characterized by persistent agglomeration in relatively small numbers of large cities; rather, it has dispersed to increasing numbers of urban and nonmetropolitan areas. From 1930 to 1980, the proportion of the population living in cities increased from 45 percent to 75 percent. But this increase was primarily due to urbanization of all regions of the country and the population growth of suburbia; the number of metropolitan areas increased nearly fourfold—from 96 in 1930 to 279 in 1980 (Mollenkopf, 1983:36–37). During the 1970s, the population growth of rural areas actually outpaced that of cities by a ratio of three to one, as nonmetropolitan areas in all regions of the country experienced greater population increases than their urban counterparts. Accordingly, the job structure of rural areas has undergone fundamental change. Manufacturing and service employment has replaced agriculture as the dominant source of rural employment. In 1975, less than one out of ten rural workers were employed on farms while one out of four worked in factories (Till, 1981:196–197).

A close examination of regional population and economic development trends further reveals the collapse of the core and periphery urban system. Urban population growth has primarily occurred in the former "periphery" areas of the nation—southern and western cities and the outlying areas of all cities. During the 1960s, Sunbelt cities grew at more than twice the rate of cities in the heartland. During the next decade, with the burst of migration to rural areas, heartland metropolitan areas experienced no growth at all (and its larger cities actually declined in population); however, Sunbelt cities continued to grow at a rapid 10 percent rate (Sternlieb and Hughes, 1978:113). An analysis that compared the growth rate of cities with the national rate of urban growth found that 189 cities have grown faster than the national rate during one or more decades since 1940; almost all of these cities were in the southern rim of the nation (Watkins, 1980:Ch. 6).[3]

Underlying the growth of southern rim cities has been an enormous increase in blue-collar and white-collar employment in this region relative to the old heartland. Between 1960 and 1976, the Northeast–North Central region lost 10 percent of its industrial job base while blue-collar employment rose by 60 percent in the South (putting it ahead of the North in total industrial jobs) and 45 percent in the West. Newer industries, such as high technology, and the more routinized components of production processes in older industries have been largely locating in the Sunbelt region of the nation. Further, traditional northern heavy industries, such as steel, automobiles, and electrical machinery, have reduced their workforces because of absolute cuts in production or the construction of more efficient plants (Mollenkopf, 1983:25–26). Sunbelt cities have also shared in the expansion and dispersion of the administrative units of large firms, though they have not received a predominant portion of these service and office activities (Mollenkopf, 1983:232–235).

The core and periphery urban system has also been eroded by the explosive growth of suburbia. Population growth has dramatically shifted away from the central cities of the heartland to the outlying areas of cities throughout the nation. In 1950, three-fifths of the population in metropolitan areas lived in central cities; by 1980, three-fifths of these residents lived in suburbia (Department of Housing and Urban Development, 1980:1–10). This massive exodus resulted in the doubling of the land area designated as suburbia by the Census Bureau (Barabba, 1975:39–41). Suburban population growth reflects the movement of blue-collar and white-collar jobs to the fringe areas of cities. In 1930, central cities contained 75 percent of all industrial employment in metropolitan areas; by 1980, they contained 25 percent of these jobs. As multilocational firms closed many of their old plants in the core cities, they have tended to build new ones on the fringes of metropolitan areas. These firms have also located most of their administrative units in suburban locales (Pred, 1977:164).

The Changing Internal Structure of the City

Not only have the locational decisions of multiunit corporations transformed the urban network of cities, they have also reshaped the internal structure of urban communities. Variations in corporate economic activities performed within urban areas have acted to alter the social structures and even the built environments of cities. The most striking changes are between the old core cities of the industrial period and newly developed localities in suburbia and the Sunbelt.

Central cities in the heartland have undergone tremendous changes in the composition of their populations. The movement of jobs to other locations has resulted in these central cities becoming smaller, poorer, and more nonwhite. While their populations declined relative to other urban locales for several decades after World War II, during the 1970s most of these central cities began to experience absolute population declines. By 1980, one-third of the population in central cities was black or Hispanic; one-third of the members of these population groups were living in poverty (see below). In general, the older heartland cities have increasingly become home for minority groups and poorer whites working in declining sectors of the economy.

Despite their many similar features, divergent patterns of socio-economic development have characterized the old core cities. Some central cities of the heartland are undergoing a process of conversion as they have become the primary locale for the national headquarters of large corporations. These "converting" cities (Fainstein et al., 1983) have experienced an increase in service jobs while losing much of their manufacturing base. Among these cities, the nation's leading corporate headquarters center is New York City, where one out of six of the nation's 800 largest corporations places its top staff. Other heartland cities of this kind include Chicago, Philadelphia, Cleveland, and Boston. "Declining" cities have emerged in far greater numbers, however. Cities such as Buffalo, Youngstown, Gary, Newark, Toledo, Harrisburg, and many others have had to endure economic atrophy without replacement as administrative centers.

The greater social polarization and changing economic development of these former core cities has acted to transform their physical structure. In declining cities, the downtown shopping and entertainment districts have been undergoing a process of abandonment as large industrial plants close down, leaving only small, low-wage factories still operating. Empty lots are a common sight. The once-thriving downtown area is now primarily used by poor minorities, and thrift shops have replaced most of the older, more fashionable stores. In contrast, in converting cities other physical features are prominent. Skyscrapers for corporate offices and related service activities, highrise upper-income residents, and a network of expensive shops, restaurants, hotels, and thriving cultural institutions typically occupy the center. Neither large factories nor small plants involved in industrial production remain in any large numbers.

The prominence of residential areas segregated along relatively stable socio-economic lines—the pattern of the industrial city—has also passed as central cities have become polarized along racial lines. The exodus of white families, the in-migration of large numbers of minorities, and the large net population losses stemming from the core city's economic decline have destabilized residential settlement patterns, frequently producing a ravaging process of neighborhood racial succession that leaves in its wake housing abandonment and neighborhood decay.

The residents of the remaining blue-collar ethnic neighborhoods and the minority ghettos, confronted with an economy that has relegated them to a peripheral position, have found themselves in constant conflict over the limited resources available to them. The major exception to this pattern is in converting cities that are utilized for corporate headquarters activities. Even here, however, the process of economic transition has been a devastating threat to many residents. As the city job structure has changed in favor of highly skilled white-collar employment, the well-to-do have sought housing by "gentrifying" (or converting to high-income use) neighborhoods previously belonging to poor or low-skilled families.

The physical and social structures of newer localities in the Sunbelt and in suburbia contrast sharply with the patterns found in the old core cities. Unlike industrial cities, which usually grew in concentric rings of commercial, indus-trial, and residential areas emanating from the city center, newer cities were shaped in their early development by the decentralist forces of the postindustrial economy. The spatial organization of most cities of the Sunbelt have been determined by the contrasting principles of decentralization and deconcentra-tion. Instead of concentric zones, these newer cities simply scattered activities throughout the metropolitan area, with autos and trucks providing the connecting links. Instead of large downtown cores composed of office buildings, there are scattered islands of highrise offices of varying density housing the administrative operations of major corporations. Their typically clean and modern industries, such as electronics and aerospace, are generally located in sites in the outlying areas of the cities. Residential areas are also scattered about; while they are usually segmented along class and racial lines into neighborhoods, their populations are diffused into numerous residential areas rather than concentrated in huge continuous minority and working-class districts. In general, lower income and minority groups live in the central city along with upper-income groups, while suburban areas tend to be dominated by middle and working classes (Johnston, 1982:192).

The physical and social geography of suburban areas in the old heartland is characterized by similar patterns of dispersion. Suburban residential districts, industrial enclaves, and office centers sprawl as they appear to follow no particular pattern of land development. Residentially, these suburban communities tend to segment themselves along fairly rigid social class and racial lines. Despite the socio-economic diversity of suburbia as a whole, it tends to be far whiter and more affluent than the adjacent central city.

An Environment of Urban Economic Dependency

In summary, the multilocational character of the postindustrial economy has radically transformed the urban economic environment. Large corporate enterprises utilizing new technologies have virtually destroyed the core and periphery system of industrial age cities and restructured urban economies along decentralist lines. The uneven diffusion of economic development has affected the market positions of communities all over the United States and has decisively reshaped their internal social and physical organization. Most important, this economic transformation has redefined the relationship between business enterprise and the local community. Captive of an economic order that affords unprecedented territorial scope for business location and investment, cities and their governments are in an era of urban economic dependency.

Popular Control in the Postindustrial City

While economic dependency has imposed new external constraints on urban communities, the postindustrial city has also been affected by an internal change that works to expand the political choices and influence of citizens: democratization of urban popular control systems. This is not to say that some ideal state of political equality has become the norm. Lack of vigorous electoral competition, low voter turnout, and political systems that have biases against particular voter groups confound such a thing. Further, the postindustrial economy provides tremendous leverage to those owning great economic power in the locale, ensuring for them a position of privilege on many issues. Nevertheless, throughout urban America local government systems have undergone development in a polyarchal direction, providing a more formidable base for mass influence over political authorities than has existed previously.

While the impact of this development on local governance varies (see Parts Four–Six), it has decisively affected the general politics of the postindustrial city. Polyarchal development has mainly come about as a result of two interacting events: (1) changes in the internal political structure of cities, and (2) major alterations in the social character and distribution of urban populations.

The Structure of Postindustrial Urban Political Institutions

The vitality of local popular control systems has been most enhanced by the decline of the machine as the dominant urban political institution. As suggested previously, the machine effectively "organized" the demands of the immigrant and others who were responsive to its appeals of jobs, favors, and other particularistic inducements. Almost any procedurally democratic political system replacing the machine had the potential to promote greater popular control of city government.

In fact, however, extant institutional arrangements have gone comparatively far in providing a means of mass political control over urban government. Today, the machine has been largely cashiered in favor of various renderings of "reformed" local government. Many of these new urban political structures can be criticized for failing to provide a highly "democratic" alternative to the machine. As discussed in Chapter 8, many of the electoral and governmental innovations spawned by the reform movement have historically discriminated against lower-income groups and have enhanced the role of business, upper-income groups, and bureaucracies in city governance. These institutions of the reform era remain part of city governmental structures.

Nevertheless, the traditional shortcomings of reform government have substantially diminished over time. Important political and social changes have transformed reformed urban politics into a powerful, if imperfect, system of popular control that is, on balance, more supportive of polyarchal conditions than cities have generally experienced before. As described in Chapter 2, popular control systems are most supportive of polyarchal relationships between citizens and political authorities when they (1) provide opportunities for the *demands of the mass public to get voiced*, and (2) *become issues* debated by governmental leaders who (3) can be *held accountable* for their behavior. In respect to all three of these dimensions of structural linkage with the mass public—demand formation, issue formation, and political accountability—the political institutions of the postindustrial "reformed" city can be rated relatively high.

Demand Formation

First, demands and grievances of the citizenry that are directed at political authorities must be free of determination by the political authorities themselves. To the extent that governmental authorities can limit the kinds of issues coming to government by using political structures which restrict the wants of the public to "safe" matters, popular control suffers.

From the demand side, local government reform was over the long run a clear and radical departure toward more democratic politics. As suggested previously, the machine managed to organize the political demands of the mass electorate in such a way as to promote a circular linkage between local government and the immigrant. By exchanging jobs, favors, and other particularistic inducements for political support, the machine constituted a powerful structure of social control. By systematically avoiding or even repressing the voicing of certain kinds of popular grievances, it managed to influence the scope of political demands on the part of the mass electorate.

The reform movement not only helped destroy this process of social control—the major institutional forms it erected to replace boss politics did not

have the capability to decisively influence mass demands. Most reform innovations sought to disenfranchise, not control, the immigrant. At best, reformers
depended on good government groups, newspapers, social workers, and schools
to somehow help shape the values of the immigrant in accordance with their
political tastes (Fainstein and Fainstein, 1974:Ch. 1; Cremin, 1961; Katz, 1968;
Katznelson, 1981:Ch. 6). As a result, reform governments and their bureaucratic
institutions became confronted with far greater problems of social control
because it was less likely that masses and governmental elites would have
similar values and opinions. This became especially apparent during the social
turmoil of the 1960s (see Part Six) when reform governments had to contend
with widespread political upheaval and conflicting political demands emanating
from different racial communities. Unable to shape and organize mass demands
very effectively, reform governments have found that they must work hard to
solicit and anticipate shifts in popular opinion and the grievances of particular
groups in order to maintain political support.

Issue Formation

Second, if demands that are voiced cannot become issues that are debated by
political authorities, then popular control systems fall short of contributing to
very polyarchal (or "democratic") governance. At a minimum, the ability to
express grievances must be accompanied by private and governmental capabilities to translate demands into matters of collective choice (issues); political
organizations must not be systematically biased against representing salient
social cleavages and serving them through specific public programs. Popular
control is merely an empty shell of procedural formalisms if salient demands
can be neither seriously debated as matters of public decision nor served by
state authority (Sharpe, 1973).

Though the machine was certainly capable of centralizing power in the
hodge-podge local government of its day, its organizational structure was so
dominated by bribery, favoritism, and supreme inefficiency that this severely
limited the purposes for which this power could be employed. As described
earlier, the uncertainty of the machine's ability to deliver public services and
promote large undertakings literally drove business to the reform movement,
with its promises of universalism, bureaucratic efficiency, and rational organization. Further, the political bias of the machine in favor of only serving
individual political demands for the sake of preserving the political status quo
limited the range of issues to which it could respond.

While the solutions of the reformers initially served the mainly conservative
interests of their business and professional allies, in the long run they
constituted an organizational weapon that could also serve other interests,
including those of the poor. For one thing, the governmental innovations, such
as civil service reform, nonpartisanship, the direct primary, at-large elections,
and other reforms encouraged the dispersal of political influence. At least over
the long run, reform replaced the political monopoly of the machine with a

pluralism of public and private actors who are compelled to compete in order to assemble the power necessary to govern. As we discuss later, although this result sometimes poses problems of another kind, at least it precludes political monopoly.

For another, reform has created bureaucratic capability in local government that is basic to acting on wide-ranging issues, especially those that are likely to be considered important by the mass citizenry. Have-nots have found that postreform local government organization is capable of implementing many programs that matter most to them as a class or racial group. The implementation of programs of social justice, such as equal employment opportunity, public health care, subsidized housing, public assistance, compensatory education, and related programs of central interest to the poor, all require a powerful and resourceful bureaucracy committed to universalistic criteria in law and in practice. Although the interests of professional bureaucrats in defending their power and prerogatives can sometimes work to impede programs of importance to the disadvantaged (Rogers, 1968; Lowi, 1968; Pressman, 1972; Sayre and Kaufman, 1960), such bureaucratic power must exist in order to serve the poor. Unlike the political machine, professional bureaucracies at least have a stake in exploiting their clientele for what are often mutually beneficial ends; professional bureaucratic agencies are inclined to serve their own interests best by expanding services to their clientele—even when they are poor.

Political Accountability

Finally, political authorities must be held accountable for their behavior in office. This requires the existence of procedures whereby all citizens have the opportunity to be able to discipline authorities according to their responsiveness to citizen demands.

Historically, many of the reform innovations, particularly nonpartisanship and at-large elections, have discriminated against have-not groups by promoting the election of unrepresentative officialdom (Hawley, 1973). Without the party cue to guide voters and the availability of a ward-based party organization to get out the vote, worker candidates are at a disadvantage. Well-known "name" (often business) candidates backed by newspaper and civic group endorsements tend to be favored in citywide nonpartisan voting systems. Further, less resourceful candidates who can otherwise mobilize their neighborhood vote find it more difficult to win office when they must compete on a citywide basis in at-large electoral systems. Indeed, the most undemocratic aspects of urban reform may be found in the procedures for political accountability within many reform institutions.

However, these institutional deficiencies of reform have not had a lasting effect. The social context of urban government has undergone radical changes that have diminished many of the historic limitations of reform government. Since the heyday of the reform movement, major changes in the characteristics and distribution of populations have occurred in urban areas throughout the United States—in central cities, suburbia, and in the Sunbelt. The net effect has been to measurably enhance the process of political accountability. Let us look in detail at this important development.

POLITICAL ACCOUNTABILITY IN CENTRAL CITIES: THE POLARIZED CITY. During the reform era the populations of most major central cities of the heartland were distinctly *immigrant cities*. These cities were overwhelmingly white, foreign born, and poor by today's standards; the immigrant populations, whose presence and ethnic rivalries dominated the political character of these cities, were willing to accept very limited responsibility on the part of government for their condition. As Table 9-1 suggests, however, the immigrant city has vanished; a *polarized city* has replaced it.

The ethnic presence in cities has dramatically declined owing to the end of major white immigration many decades ago and because of the "Americanization" of traditional white immigrant groups. Although Hispanic immigration has been significant in some northern cities, such as New York and Chicago, this has not in any way regenerated the ethnic character of cities in the past. For example, three out of every four inhabitants of Chicago were foreign born at the turn of the century (Gutman, 1976). Today, fewer than two out of every ten Chicago residents were born abroad.

Race and class now divide the city more than anything else. On one hand, the traditional white immigrant groups are no longer very poor. Rising incomes and upward mobility among this component of city populations have created large numbers of relatively prosperous white blue- and white-collar families. Only relatively small numbers of whites living in large cities are found in government poverty statistics (even though this group as a whole is usually less well-off than its suburban counterpart). On the other hand, unprecedented numbers of predominantly poor black and Hispanic minorities now divide the city with the more prosperous white populations, creating a highly polarized social structure. This social polarization is further enhanced by the racial segregation in residential location that prevails in most cities of the heartland (Cox, 1973). Further, as indicated below, neither "end" of the population structure in the polarized city shares very limited expectations about their governments. Both have become politicized to a degree that dramatically breaks with urban tradition.

The Political Impact of Polarization. This social transformation has had far-reaching implications for popular control in the postreform era. In the immigrant city, reform government could play on politically fragmented and quiescent populations to limit public accountability of political authorities. However, the polarized city has broken down many of the traditional political biases of reform-style government.

Changes in Political Participation. As central city white populations have undergone a process of *embourgeoisement* that has weakened ethnic ties and lifted them into higher income classes, they have become more supportive of the reform ethos (Banfield and Wilson, 1961). This has also enabled the group to become skilled at manipulating the institutions of reform politics and win a pivotal position in city electoral coalitions. This reality is epitomized by the

TABLE 9-1 The Polarized City: Social and Economic Character of Populations in 7 Selected Cities, 1980 Census

City		Population characteristics						
	Foreign born (%)	Black (%)	Spanish (%)	Below 125% of poverty level (%)	Per capita median income ($)		Below 125% of poverty level (%)	
					whites	blacks	whites	blacks
Baltimore	3.1	54.8	1.0	28.9	7,619	4,493	17.4	38.0
Boston	15.5	22.5	6.5	27.2	7,448	4,620	21.8	37.3
Chicago	14.5	39.8	14.1	33.2	8,903	4,904	14.3	38.0
Cleveland	5.8	43.8	3.1	27.7	8,770	5,377	8.6	32.7
New York	23.6	25.3	19.9	25.9	8,902	5,014	17.8	36.8
Philadelphia	6.4	37.8	3.8	21.9	8,326	4,658	16.4	39.7
Pittsburgh	5.2	24.0	0.8	22.8	7,926	4,970	15.7	40.7

SOURCE: U.S. Bureau of the Census, *County and City Data Book* (1983), and 1980 Census of Population, *General Social and Economic Characteristics*, New York, Illinois, Maryland, Massachusetts, and Ohio, Tables 56, 57, 125, 130, 131, 136, and 137, Series PC 8.

prominence of relatively prosperous, white blue-collar homeowners in big city elections (Bellush and David, 1971). Another manifestation is the emergence of politically powerful public employee unions. As professional bureaucracies in city government arose when political machines crumbled, white and, to a lesser extent, minority groups have acted to build these unions into formidable power bases (Lowi, 1968).

Although far less upward social mobility has taken place within the minority community, the signal fact about this population has been the growth of its political presence in central cities. As Table 9-2 indicates, the postwar period was one of tremendous black migration to the central cities.

During the 1970s, the electoral presence of minorities achieved a critical mass that often forced their accommodation by urban party organizations and by city bureaucracies despite racial prejudice among white populations, despite the traditionally low turnout of minorities at the polls, and despite the relatively weak political resources owned by this disadvantaged group. In 1964, there were only 184 black state and local officials in the entire United States (there were only 280 black officials out of more than a half million officials at all governmental levels). But by 1978, there were 294 state senators, 170 mayors, 1,618 city councilors, and 1,086 school board members, as well as other local or state officials (such as judges) who were black—a tenfold increase (Karnig and Welch, 1980:viii). By 1983, the number of black officials at all levels of government rose to 5,606, including 248 black mayors, representing over 20 million citizens; further, another 47 cities had Hispanic mayors (Levitan, 1985:130). Most significantly, this huge increase in black representation mostly occurred in the central cities. Black administrations emerged for the first time in such major cities as Cleveland, Detroit, Chicago, Newark, Los Angeles, Gary, New Orleans, Atlanta, and elsewhere, while Hispanic mayors won power in Sunbelt cities such as San Antonio, Tampa, Denver, and Miami.

Politicization of Minorities. This phenomenal growth of central city minorities has been accompanied by their politicization. Two important events brought this about. First, the period since the 1930s has been one of almost uninterrupted expansion of social welfare programs of consequence to those have-not electoral groups whose participation in local politics was traditionally very limited. The poor, immigrants, and minorities became beneficiaries of welfare, health, and educational assistance programs that began with the Roosevelt "revolution." The creation of such a vast network of social welfare programs fundamentally altered political expectations, as Piven and Cloward (1982) have suggested. In particular, it ended the governmental tradition of laissez faire in regard to social welfare and forced local governments into becoming providers of a broad range of social services. This, in turn, created major stakes for the poor in the administration, staffing, and distribution of benefits in these programs; it also created a vast social welfare bureaucracy whose interests lay in promoting the expansion of the services they administered. The result has been that those who had been least likely to participate and compete in local politics now expect to do so with greater confidence, with formidable allies, and for important stakes.

TABLE 9-2   Percentage of Blacks in Central Cities in 12 Selected SMSAs, 1940–1980

	1940	1950	1960	1970	1980
New York	6.4	9.8	14.7	23.4	25.2
Los Angeles–Long Beach	6.0	9.8	15.3	21.2	16.4
Chicago	8.3	14.1	23.6	34.4	39.8
Philadelphia	13.1	18.3	26.7	34.4	37.8
Detroit	9.3	16.4	29.2	44.0	63.1
San Francisco–Oakland	4.9	11.8	21.1	32.7	24.1
Boston	3.3	12.3	9.8	18.2	22.4
Pittsburgh	9.3	9.3	18.0	27.0	24.0
St. Louis	13.4	5.3	28.8	41.3	45.6
Washington, D.C.	28.5	35.4	54.8	72.3	76.6
Cleveland	9.7	16.3	28.9	39.0	43.8
Baltimore	19.4	23.8	35.0	47.0	54.8
All 12 SMSAs	9.0	13.7	21.4	30.8	36.6

SOURCE: From Dennis R. Judd, *The Politics of American Cities: Private Power and Public Policy*, 2nd ed. Copyright © 1984 by Dennis R. Judd. Reprinted by permission of Scott, Foresman and Company. Data from Leo F. Schnore, Carolyn D. Andre, and Harry Sharp, "Black Suburbanization, 1930–1970" in Barry Schwartz, ed., *The Changing Face of the Suburbs* (Chicago: University of Chicago Press, 1976) and U.S. Bureau of the Census, *1980 Census of the Population*, Supplementary Reports, *Standard Metropolitan Statistical Areas and Standard Consolidated Statistical Areas* (Washington, D.C.: U.S. Government Printing Office, 1981).

Second, the urban experience of the 1960s further politicized these groups. Spurred on by the civil rights movement and new federal programs to combat poverty, urban minority communities during the 1960s became the scene of riots, rent strikes, and mass protest in an effort to overturn discriminatory practices in employment, housing, education, and other public services (see Chapter 17). While the widespread use of disruptive political techniques has ebbed in recent years, black and Hispanic populations have directed their energies into more conventional forms of political participation and have often become major elements in city electoral coalitions (Browning, Marshall, and Tabb, 1984).

The upshot of this is that social polarization and politicization within heartland central cities has come to overwhelm many of the traditional discriminatory features of reform government. As whites have become more politically active and influential owing to important social changes within this population group, minorities have achieved a similar political position, mostly for different reasons. The result is that local officials have become pressured by both population groupings in postreform governmental systems that have weak mechanisms for organizing and managing conflict. In a political community that is so bifurcated into stable electoral groupings which compete over many highly contentious issues, the historic class and ethnic biases of popular control institutions inherited from the reform era have declined as impediments to political accountability, especially in respect to the have-not groups.

The most direct evidence for this as a major factor in the surge of minority representation in cities comes from a study of all cities in the United States over 25,000 that were at least 10 percent black during the 1970s. It found that the key factor in promoting the election of black candidacies and electoral success in city council and mayoral contests was "black resources"—the relative proportion of blacks in city populations and their socio-economic characteristics. In respect to city councils, the most important factor in explaining black electoral success was simply the proportion of blacks in city populations (see Table 9-3)—the larger the black population, the larger the proportion of council seats won by blacks. The socio-economic resources of the black population was next in importance: Where they were better educated and had higher incomes, they were more likely to get black candidates into public office in competition with whites. Together these resources account for over half of the total explained variance. The overwhelming importance of these black resources was similar in the case of electing black mayors. In fact, demographic change favorable to minorities appears to be behind the success of black election victories even in very large contested cities like Chicago (Kleppner, 1985).

Significantly, the kind of political and electoral system had only a comparatively minor influence on the success of minority candidacies, especially in cities with very large black populations. Although district elections (rather than at-large elections) were found to be of some import in helping blacks win elections to city councils, nonpartisanship, partisanship, or the type of governmental system (council manager, mayor and council, commission, etc.) had little or no effect on either black mayoral or council representation. In district elections, blacks can campaign more cheaply, media attention is less critical, and the need for civic and newspaper endorsements is apparently less important than in citywide contests. But even this factor is of very limited significance in comparison to the more basic demographic ones (Karnig and Welch, 1980:Chs. 3 and 4). At-large elections seem capable of severely discriminating against minorities only when the latter cannot mobilize a substantial citywide vote and are divided by parochial group rivalries (Robinson and Dye, 1978). But this barrier diminishes in cities with very large black and Hispanic populations.

POLITICAL ACCOUNTABILITY IN SUBURBIA: POPULAR CONTROL AS NEIGHBORHOOD POLITICS.   While social polarization in central cities has precipitated greater political accountability in local government, an opposite pattern of population change has prompted a similar result in suburbia. Here the development of social homogeneity in political constituencies has forged a form of popular control where the governmental institutions that are supposed to organize a process of political accountability have been rendered relatively unimportant: A more informal process of neighborhood-style government takes its place.

Following decades of population dispersal from central cities, by 1970 a majority of those living in urban areas resided in suburban enclaves. By and

TABLE 9-3   Effects of Variable Clusters on Black Council Representation

Variable clusters	Total explained variance
Black resources (including percentage black)	52.0%
Percentage black (alone)	37.6
Political and election rules	11.7
White population and demographic factors	5.2
Federal antipoverty programs	2.7

SOURCE: From Alfred K. Karnig and Susan Welch, *Black Representation and Urban Policy*, p. 130. © 1980 by The University of Chicago. All rights reserved. Reprinted by permission of The University of Chicago Press.

large, those who participated in this great migration tended to bring with them to suburbia the ethos and institutions of reform government. Ironically, long after the heyday of the Progressive reformers and their struggles to change the governance of cities, the classic nonpartisan, business-like style of government they promoted for the cities found its greatest success where it was least intended—in suburbia where it is today the norm.

In general, suburbia provides a "natural" setting for reform government. The basic assumption of reformers was that all parties agreed (or should agree) on the core values that defined the public interest. Consequently, the governmental institutions they promoted were designed to insulate government from group rivalries and support governance conducted on the basis of problem solving rather than by conflict and bargaining.

Reform Government As Popular Control.   Despite the naiveté of this model of government, suburbia does tend to provide a social context where it comes close to working as a viable process of popular control. The suburbanization of urban populations has usually been accompanied by their political segregation along socio-economic and racial lines. Socio-economic homogeneity within large numbers of small suburban political systems that fragment the outer rings of most cities is the norm (see Chapter 13), particularly in the industrial heartland (Cox, 1973). Studies have indicated that social homogeneity in suburbia parallels the fairly rigid class and racial segregation found in central city neighborhoods (Fine et al., 1971; Cox, 1973); the difference in suburbia is that the "neighborhood" is usually a separate political jurisdiction with political authority.

The political consequence of suburban political fragmentation and social segregation has been to produce a low-key consensual style of politics that reform government appears to serve very well. Compared with politics found in many central cities, major conflicts over wide-ranging issues of local government are often absent. Rather than widespread community struggles among groups that seek to bargain with public officials over many well-publicized issues, community agreement on issues, such as schools, housing, land development, and other matters of intrinsic importance to residents, is the norm. Most conflicts that do emerge involve matters of problem solving, technique, and detail, and these are generally resolved without great controversy. Consequently, suburban local governments delegate considerable power in decision making to appointed officials, such as school superintendents and city managers, whose lead is often followed (Wood, 1958; Wirt et al., 1972). As one textbook has concluded, ". . . much urban community conflict can be attributed to differences over the appropriate means to agreed-upon ends" (Murphy and Rehfuss, 1976).

While the absence of active citizen participation in suburban politics can be criticized—for example, without much public debate citizens may be unaware of policy alternatives or implications—there are good reasons to suppose that the process of political accountability found in these reform governments is actually quite effective. In a system of fragmented, socially homogeneous local governments, the most important vote is "with one's feet" in locating to a jurisdiction that offers a package of public services and community life style that is appropriate to the core values of the individual and family. Consequently, actual participation in local politics will not be a very productive way of further enhancing the local political interests of most citizens. Not surprisingly, the general tendency for members of higher socio-economic groups to participate more actively in politics (Verba and Nie, 1972) compared with others seems to diminish in the case of voting turnout in higher income suburban communities (Alford and Lee, 1968). In fact, suburbanites participate in politics less than central city residents even when social status is ignored (Verba and Nie, 1972:229–248).

In this kind of political system, the accountability of public officials to the electorate poses few problems despite low turnout, limited conflict and debate over issues, and great tolerance of official autonomy in policy making. Widespread agreement among citizens on what government should and should not be doing imposes a powerful, if informal, influence on political leadership. With overwhelming numbers of citizens sharing similar life style values, sharing a major fixed financial stake in homeownership and property values and demanding roughly similar levels of public services, the electoral constraint becomes quite secondary to ensuring responsive government. In this context, reform government, with its emphasis on professional problem solving, efficiency, and "good government," is apt to reflect the popular will as well or better than any other governmental system.

POLITICAL ACCOUNTABILITY IN THE SUNBELT: REGIONAL POLITICIZATION.   Next to suburbia, reform government scored its greatest victories in the southern and western regions (or Sunbelt) of the United States. At-large elections, rather than ward systems, are used extensively throughout the South and West. Similarly, the council-manager form of government has proved to be most popular in cities outside of the old manufacturing belt of the nation, particularly in the West (Sanders, 1979).

The diverse socio-economic character and political traditions of particular cities in this region defy any sweeping generalizations about their politics. Nevertheless, many studies of local politics in the major Sunbelt cities suggest that the discriminatory effects of reform government have been widespread; a style of politics in which business and upper income groups assume a powerful and visible role in governance appears to have a long tradition. One study of Phoenix suggests that after a business-led Charter Government Committee secured a new reform-style charter for the city in the 1940s, many of the inherent biases of this type of government emerged:

> . . . The nomination process, and hence the selection process, were dominated by a small business elite; most council members . . . support the elite's basic philosophies. Most of the access to these policy makers is channeled through professional staff in city agencies. . . . Attendence at council meetings and turnout in general elections are generally low (Althiede and Hall, 1983:196).

Although it is uncertain just how much the pattern found in Phoenix was duplicated in other Sunbelt cities during the postwar period, studies of many other southwestern cities, such as San Antonio, Denver, Tucson, San Jose, and Houston, suggest parallel findings (Fleischmann, 1977; Judd, 1983a; Goodall, 1967; Betsalel, 1983; Abbott, 1981).

In many cities, Hispanic minorities, whose presence was often perceived as a threat to business-dominated local government, fared particularly poorly in gaining a role in local government. Most southwestern cities have barrio neighborhoods that house Mexican-Americans almost exclusively. Ward-based elections would give this group at least a minority presence on many local councils. But since at-large elections predominate in the Southwest, it has been a major factor in severely limiting or shutting out Mexican-Americans altogether from winning representation on local councils (de la Garza, 1979). For instance, in Tucson, where Chicanos constitute almost one-third of the population, only one Spanish-surnamed candidate had ever won election to the nonpartisan school board by the late 1970s (Garcia, 1979). Even in Los Angeles, where one million Chicanos live, hardly any Mexican-Americans have managed to win election to the city council (Garcia and de la Garza, 1977). Moreover, reform-style government has sometimes combined with the erection of still other political barriers in ways that discriminated against Hispanic minorities. Some Sunbelt states had English literacy requirements until the last decade; others had strict residency laws that often proved an obstacle to Mexican-American voting.

The Declining Barriers to Popular Control. Even though many Sunbelt cities have exhibited a history of considerable political bias in their political systems, this rapidly changing region of the country has not been immune from the forces that have acted to enhance popular control elsewhere. Consequently, since the 1970s political participation in the Sunbelt has shown signs of transformation. Several social and political forces have acted to break up traditional business-dominated electoral coalitions.

First, the rapid economic development of many of these cities has brought about larger electorates, primarily because of migration from other regions. During the 1970s, population growth in the West and South was twice the national rate (Department of Housing and Urban Development, 1980:1–2).

These new electorates have often been less willing to follow the lead of booster-oriented business elites (Fleischmann, 1977; Judd, 1983b). The traditional progrowth policies promoted by these elites have led to rising governmental expenditures, new environmental issues, and other matters relating to the quality of life in these communities—political issues that have prompted greater awareness and participation among professional and middle-income voters in city governance (*Economist*, 10 July 1982:23; see Chapter 13).

Second, the growing presence and political activism of Sunbelt minorities has begun to politically polarize numbers of cities in this region, much as is the case in older industrial cities. Legislative and court decisions over the last decade have abolished or weakened the most discriminatory electoral practices that kept many minorities from voting. The passage of the Voting Rights Act of 1965 and its subsequent reenactments have greatly expanded voter eligibility and protected the political rights of minorities in the most hostile of locales. This process of expansion of political rights has been reinforced by court decisions that have been generally unsympathetic to registration barriers (Crotty and Jacobson, 1980:18–22), districting arrangements, and even electoral systems that appear very discriminatory (*New York Times*, 30 May 1984:1).

Further, the proportion of urban Hispanic and black minorities in many western and southern cities has grown (see Table 9-4); this, together with the gains these groups have made in voter registration, has dramatically increased their political influence in recent years. This has sometimes resulted in the decline of traditional business-dominated electoral coalitions and brought about major governmental changes to enhance minority political influence. Several southern cities have witnessed the rise of black mayors, such as Atlanta's Maynard Jackson and Andrew Young, who have capitalized on their city's increasingly black electorates to secure a stable base of political power. Similarly, in the West, Hispanic voters have won new political influence, as in San Antonio with Mayor Henry Cisneros and even in predominantly Anglo Denver, with Mayor Federico Pena.

Political Change in San Antonio. San Antonio illustrates the dramatic impact that the power of a larger Hispanic electorate can have. Since 1951, when San Antonio adopted a council-manager form of government, members of the nine-member city council were elected at large. During subsequent years, the Good Government League (GGL), an organization of business and professional people, more or less ran the city government in response to the demands of downtown business interests. Endorsement by GGL was essential for victory in the citywide elections. But by 1970, San Antonio was 52 percent Mexican-American and 9 percent black, although these groups made up only around 46 percent of the city electorate. Even though GGL began to regularly slate a few minority candidates for council elections, minority groups became agitated and voted against GGL candidates. Nevertheless, they were unable to break the solid electoral front of Anglo voters supporting GGL candidates or match their higher voter participation rates.

In 1973, however, a GGL council member who was not slated as the organization's mayoralty candidate bolted and ran as an independent against

TABLE 9-4   Percentage of Black and Hispanic Population in Selected Central Cities, 1980

Central city	Black	Hispanic	Minorities
Los Angeles	17.0%	27.5%	44.5%
San Diego	8.8	14.9	23.7
Phoenix	4.9	15.1	20.0
Denver	12.1	18.7	30.8
Dallas	29.4	12.3	41.7
Houston	27.6	17.6	45.2
San Antonio	7.3	53.7	61.0
Miami	25.1	53.3	78.4
Mean for eight cities	17.5	24.8	42.3

SOURCE: Adapted from Dennis R. Judd, *The Politics of American Cities: Private Power and Public Policy*, 2nd ed. Copyright © 1984 by Dennis R. Judd. Reprinted by permission of Scott, Foresman and Company. Based on information from U.S. Bureau of Census, *1980 Census of Population*, Supplementary Reports, *Standard Metropolitan Statistical Areas and Standard Consolidated Statistical Areas* (Washington, D.C.: U.S. Government Printing Office, 1981).

the GGL nominee. Even though GGL endorsed a Mexican-American to head its ticket in hope of forging a coalition with the Hispanic community and loyal segments of the Anglo electorate, the independent won, and his backers also won a majority of the council. This broke the power of the GGL, and shortly after the election it folded as an organization. The new coalition of independents swiftly moved to raise a whole series of proposals that GGL had managed to keep off the civic agenda. Most important, a charter commission was formed that endorsed a number of governmental changes, including the use of single member districts for council elections. Although the charter reform narrowly lost the voter referendum in 1974, a similar plan was approved by 51 percent of the voters in a referendum three years later. Of the ten council members elected in 1977, four were Anglo, five were Hispanic, and one was black (Gibson and Tucker, 1978).

Finally, the proliferation of more popularly controlled Sunbelt political systems has been precipitated by the exit of important groups and interests from central city politics. On one hand, most large Sunbelt cities have witnessed the phenomenal growth of suburban enclaves within metropolitan areas, especially during recent years (Department of Housing and Development, 1980:1). Although the Sunbelt pattern has not exactly duplicated the population shifts of older cities elsewhere, Table 9-5 suggests that the dominant trend since 1949 has been toward formation of increasingly wealthy suburban rings surrounding poorer central cities. Like metropolitan areas in the North, as these suburbs age and grow, they too seem to be promoting opportunities for greater political accountability under reform-style government. The growth of more small, socially homogeneous suburban Sunbelt governments favors the kind of neighborhood politics for which suburbia elsewhere is well known. Further,

TABLE 9-5   Income Differentials between Central Cities and Their Metropolitan Areas

	Median family income Ratio of central city median to SMSA median			
	1949	1959	1969	1978
Six largest SMSAs in North and East				
New York	0.95	0.93	0.89	0.83
Chicago	0.97	0.92	0.86	0.72
Philadelphia, Pa.–N.J.	0.96	0.90	0.85	0.72
Detroit	0.99	0.89	0.83	0.79
Washington, D.C.–Md.–Va.	0.89	0.79	0.74	0.55
Boston	0.92	0.86	0.80	0.67
Average of Six SMSAs in North and East	0.95	0.88	0.83	0.71
Six largest SMSAs in South and West				
Los Angeles–Long Beach[a]	0.98	0.98	0.96	0.91
San Francisco–Oakland[b]	1.00	0.95	0.89	0.81
Houston	1.02	0.98	0.97	0.88
Dallas	1.03	1.01	0.96	0.95
Atlanta	0.91	0.87	0.79	0.63[b]
Anaheim–Santa Ana–Garden Grove, Calif.[a]	—	—	0.96	0.94
Average of Six SMSAs in South and West	0.99	0.96	0.92	0.85

[a]Except in 1978, ratio is for first-named central city only.
[b]Ratio is for 1977.

SOURCE: From James Heilbrun, *Urban Economics and Public Policy* (New York: St. Martin's Press, 1981), p. 279. Reprinted by permission.

where much of the suburban growth results from population movement from the central city, as in Atlanta and New Orleans, it can also create proportionately greater electoral importance for lower income and minority groups in central city elections (Smith and Keller, 1983; Stone, 1983), igniting greater political competition.

On the other hand, Sunbelt cities have witnessed the opening up of city politics because of the growing exit of business interests from involvement in civic affairs. Active business participation in local politics had usually been dominated by local business elites with fixed investments in the central business districts of Sunbelt cities. However, the growth of multilocational business within the Sunbelt has removed many traditional incentives for business dominance of local governance. Large corporate employers with headquarters in other cities have limited interests and stakes in the locale; their economic power assures them a privileged position in city affairs without the need to compete for electoral support. Consequently, traditional business-led governing coalitions have declined because local business communities could no longer remain united or attract the support of multilocational employers.

For instance, in San Jose during the 1970s the phenomena of the absentee corporate landlord grew in magnitude and business' traditional involvement in the city's political affairs waned, shifting more to matters of regional importance. By the late 1970s, one observer concluded that there was no longer any single dominant force in the city's politics. City elections began to assume renewed importance, including a dramatic increase in Hispanic political participation (Betsalel, 1983). Although the exit of important elements of the business community from active participation in governing coalitions by no means suggests that their economic power over Sunbelt cities has ebbed, it has permitted renewed importance of popularly controlled local government institutions.

Economic Dependency and Popular Control

The postindustrial urban political economy has developed in ways that place fundamentally new economic and political constraints on those who govern the localities. The development of popular control toward a more polyarchal system of politics has generated formidable mass pressures on city governments at a time when economic dependency imposes new limits on the capability of cities to respond to public preferences.

On one hand, postindustrial democracies are subject to widespread citizen pressures as a result of developments in their political systems and as a result of major social and demographic changes throughout urban America. On the other hand, new pressures are imposed on local governments by their highly dependent economic status. Because the multilocational character of American corporate capitalism has created unprecedented economic competition among local communities, the bargaining position of city governments with business has diminished.

The potential for tension between popular will and urban economics has never been greater in the American city. This character of the urban political economy is mediated by another set of forces, however: the changes within the federal system that have imposed a powerful intergovernmental dimension on urban politics, placing localities in a dependent relationship with higher level governments. To this we now turn.

Endnotes

1. The development of the electronics industry exemplifies this pattern. Defense applications of electronics gave birth to the industry and its primary location in "Silicon Valley" (an agricultural trading center before World War II), which is on the peninsula south of San Francisco in the San José metropolitan area. Nondefense applications of electronics developed rapidly after the war, and by 1980 half of the electronics market nationally was for civilian purposes. The geographical location of the industry has remained in the outlying areas of Sunbelt cities, with the Boston

metropolitan area the only significant exception. The aerospace industry has followed a similar location pattern, with most of its employment in suburban sites in the South and West (Mollenkopf, 1983:27).

2. While most of these headquarters are found in northern metropolitan areas, especially the central cities, a number of large Sunbelt cities also have attracted head offices.

3. A comparison of the 140 largest metropolitan areas found that only 10 percent of the heartland cities and 70 percent of the Sunbelt cities made up the top two growth quintiles among cities during the period between 1959 and 1976 (Noyelle and Stanback, 1984:107).

CHAPTER TEN

The New Intergovernmental Dependency: Federalism and the Postindustrial City

T HE limited involvement of the federal and state governments in city governance, which marked the industrial period, came to a dramatic end after 1930. The federal system underwent a revolution that brought about far greater national and state governmental presence in urban affairs. Most significantly, federal government activities expanded in all the areas of public policy—development, distribution, and redistribution—as national administrations evolved implicit national urban policies to regulate the urban environment in accordance with their policy priorities. A mature federal system has emerged in which the national government's expansion overturned the traditionally dominant roles played by states and localities in providing public services. What has accompanied this revolution in federalism is a new intergovernmental dependency of cities. More than ever before, localities must govern themselves in reference to the activities and grants-in-aid of higher level governments.

The National Government and Urban Policy

The Changing Political Economy of the National Government

As noted in Chapter 2, the economic position of the national government in a market economy provides a potentially wide choice for policy initiatives compared with state and local governments. Its greater ability to influence the movement of capital and labor within its domestic economy creates for it a potentially powerful role in inducing private investment and responding to political pressures to achieve public objectives. In the past, however, the laissez faire political tradition, rapid economic growth, and mass political quiescence limited national governmental activism—both in inducing private sector investment and in promoting public programs to cope with popular demands.

The broader scope of policy choice for national officials is of major import during the contemporary period, however.

Rejecting the laissez faire tradition, the national government assumed an important role in regulating the economy and aiding its human casualties after 1930. This new economic role stemmed from an acceptance by government and business that federal spending was required to supplement private investment in order to achieve a national economy performing at high productive capacity. The national government's new responsibilities for the disadvantaged reflected political pressures generated by the needy; this was later reinforced by a growing economy that provided increasing revenues to fund such programs.

Before the federal government could assume this activist role, it first had to gain the appropriate legal authority and financial resources. These hurdles were overcome during the first three decades of the twentieth century. The legal authority was achieved when the Supreme Court broadened its interpretation of the national government's authority under the Constitution. During the industrial era, the Court's restrictions on federal power and its grant of "reserve" powers to the states had given rise to the doctrine of dual federalism. Under this doctrine, the two levels of government were generally responsible for different functions, with the states having primary responsibility for most domestic matters, including city affairs. It was not until the constitutional revolution of 1937 that the Court completed the task of reversing its prior decisions and granted the national government broad powers to intervene in wide-ranging domestic matters under the implied powers clause. Even in the case of cities, the Supreme Court no longer considered city governments a "preserve" left to the states under the reserve power clause; cities were now subject to the jurisdiction of both levels of government, with the supremacy clause the arbiter in cases of conflict.

Federal activism also required a major infusion of financial resources at the national level. During the nineteenth century, the revenue base of the federal government was very limited. Its major revenue source was the sale of federal lands as new territories were added to the Union (Break, 1981:41). With the closing of the frontier around the turn of the century, the national government began to search for new sources of tax monies. This search was not completed until 1913 with the ratification of the income tax amendment (Sixteenth amendment) to the Constitution. The importance of the income tax to the federal revenue base was apparent from the outset; despite the very low tax rates initially enacted (in comparison to tax rates during this contemporary period), the income tax was already providing nearly 60 percent of federal revenues by 1922 (Break, 1981:44). By 1972, it accounted for nearly 60 percent of all tax monies collected by all governmental jurisdictions. The federal government has been the primary beneficiary, achieving a near monopoly of this most lucrative of revenue sources; in 1972, the national government collected over 90 percent of all income taxes.

What precipitated federal economic and social activism more than anything else was the Great Depression of the 1930s, when the private market failed to pull the national economy out of this disaster. This experience led federal policymakers and the business community to accept a far greater role for government in the management of the economy. The national government became responsible for ensuring the stability, growth, and orderly operation of the market system (Heilbroner, 1980:Ch. 8). The previous policy of laissez faire had assumed that, while there would be business cycles, the private market economy had its self-correcting devices and moved inexorably toward more prosperous equilibriums. But the events of the 1930s, together with their compelling interpretation in the writing of Lord Keynes, persuaded business and government to revise the fundamental principles governing their relationship. In addition, the Depression triggered civil unrest on a wide scale, unleashing popular demands for new social welfare programs.

THE POSTWAR PUBLIC POLICY CONSENSUS. The public policy consensus that emerged from the experiences of the New Deal and World War II contained three important components. First, the federal government became responsible for ensuring that there would be sufficient consumer demand for the products and services of the private sector. The primary government tool would be its expenditure policies; federal spending was expected to provide a steady stream of funds to stabilize the consumer market as well as shore up aggregate demand whenever there was a significant lag or fall-off in private sector activity. The depression was seen as resulting from the reluctance of the private sector to invest and expand when the economy was characterized by slack demand and high employment. Government spending was intended to remove these uncertainties associated with investment decisions and ensure the business community of stable aggregate demand for their goods. The growth in federal spending that resulted from this new federal role was reflected in a dramatic increase in the proportion of the GNP accounted for by federal expenditures. In 1929, federal spending accounted for little more than one percent; by 1979, total expenditures amounted to almost a quarter of GNP (Heilbroner, 1980:166–167).

Second, a large proportion of this increased federal spending went to' developmental programs intended to directly induce private sector investment, both at home and abroad. Keynesian expenditure policies to stabilize the consumer market and federal subsidies to business were not inconsistent. Thus, the federal government made huge ongoing expenditures to the defense industry for national security purposes, provided subsidies and tax credits to the construction and real estate industries, supplied farm subsidies to agribusiness and allowed infrastructure (roads, transit, etc.) subsidies to lower levels of government and private contractors. The federal government also promoted the competitive position of American business in the world market; there were tax policies that gave favored treatment to overseas investment, monetary-exchange policies to facilitate the same ends, and policies to promote freer trade among the nations of the West.

The third component of this policy consensus involved a set of redistributive programs that were initiated in legislation enacted during the New Deal. These measures included Social Security, unemployment insurance, public assistance for those unable to work, and legislation guaranteeing the right of workers to organize and bargain collectively. For the first time in the nation's history, the federal government had enacted a broad array of redistributive programs intended to aid workers, old people, the unemployed, and the poor. During the 1960s, there was further expansion of social welfare programs. New programs, such as Medicare, Medicaid, food stamps, and aid to education, were enacted, and old programs, such as Social Security, had their benefit structures vastly improved.

ECONOMIC CHALLENGES TO FEDERAL ACTIVISM. Since the early 1970s, however, the international market position of the United States has undergone a decline. During the decade 1973–1982, there was virtually no economic growth. The twin problems of chronic stagflation (the simultaneous occurrence of high unemployment and high inflation) at home and growing international competition abroad plagued the American economy. National policymakers found their ability to deploy Keynesian policies to "fine-tune" the economy undermined. The federal government has been unable to play its stabilizing and growth-promoting role with respect to the consumer market without incurring high rates of inflation. In the world economy, American firms have encountered much more severe competition from their European and Japanese counterparts. By the 1970s, these foreign corporations had rebuilt the productive capacity that had been destroyed by World War II and were gaining a greater share of the global market. As one indicator of this trend, American firms had averaged 61 percent of all foreign investment during 1961–1967; their share dropped to 30 percent by 1974–1978 (Bluestone and Harrison, 1982:142).

In order to restore business confidence and induce more private investment, federal officials have been driven to shift national policies to reflect a more developmental bias. To induce greater private investment in new plant and machinery, tax cuts have been enacted that disproportionately favor corporations and the wealthy. Government regulations in such areas as the environment, occupational safety, and consumer protection have been eased in an attempt to reduce the costs of production. The growth in federal spending has been slowed; and tight monetary policies have been imposed in order to reduce inflationary pressures. There have been cuts in the benefit levels of many of the redistributive measures passed in earlier years; these cuts have had the effect of increasing the numbers looking for work, reducing the power of labor unions, and providing management with leverage to impose greater discipline and productivity measures in the workplace. The declining proportion of federal funds spent for social welfare programs reflects this shift in national policy. Whereas the growth in social welfare spending had easily surpassed the growth in GNP during the decade of the sixties, it has been growing at a slower rate than the GNP since 1975 (David and Kantor, 1984:301–302).

The Federal Government's Urban Policies:
From the New Deal to the New Federalism

The consequence of the enlarged federal role in promoting national economic growth and political stability has been the emergence of national urban policies. These urban policies were by no means formal or even very coherent program plans. Yet they brought greater national involvement in urban affairs and embodied distinctive federal policy thrusts in development, redistribution, and distribution, thereby providing a particular framework for regulating cities. Four such periods can be identified: (1) President Roosevelt's first two administrations of the New Deal, 1933–1940; (2) the War and Postwar era, 1941–1960; (3) the New Frontier and Great Society period, 1961–1968; and (4) the New Federalism, 1969–present.

The New Deal, 1933–1940

Increased federal involvement with the cities began with the New Deal. Two levels of the federal system, which had been barely aware of each other's existence, began establishing relationships which, by the late thirties, were becoming patterned and fairly stable (Gelfand, 1975:65–66). The policy thrust of the national government's urban programs was primarily redistributive, though there were also significant developmental components in many of these programs.

The major New Deal programs affecting the cities were its relief efforts. From 1933 to 1940, there were national assistance programs for the unemployed. The Federal Emergency Relief Administration (FERA) provided cash allowances to the unemployed, and, beginning in 1935, the Works Progress Administration (WPA) provided work relief. The vast majority of the WPA's work projects were in the cities and were proposed by local governments; consequently, the WPA spent half of its monies in the fifty largest cities (Gelfand, 1975:42–45).

The other New Deal program that significantly affected the cities was the Public Works Administration (PWA). The PWA, along with the relief programs, constituted the two primary New Deal measures for dealing directly with urban economic distress. The PWA's objective, in addition to promoting job expansion, was to construct public works projects that would be of direct benefit to business. Whereas the WPA constructed projects that were labor-intensive and paid laborers the minimum wage, the PWA projects entailed massive, permanent improvements, and workers were paid the prevailing union wages. More than half of the PWA's expenditures were spent in cities on projects that aided the financially hard-pressed localities to cope with the deterioration of their physical plant (Mollenkopf, 1983:31).

Another urban-oriented program of the New Deal that had much less impact on cities was the establishment of a public housing program for the poor in 1937. While this program had symbolic importance, it had little effect on the housing stock of the cities because of legislative amendments that diminished funds for this program and limited the pool of eligible beneficiaries to the very poor.

These urban-oriented New Deal measures were no longer in effect by World War II, but their short-lived importance had transformed the federal system and placed urban issues on the agenda of federal policymakers. To understand the adoption of these programs that enabled the federal government to undertake massive aid to the disadvantaged, it is important to consider the political stakes of federal officials as well as their relations with the business community during the depression. On one hand, the New Deal sought to induce greater capital investment on the part of the private sector in order to promote economic recovery. The decision to adopt the PWA rather than allocate the federal monies solely to the WPA (which would have employed many more of the unemployed) is illustrative of the developmental priority of the New Deal. On the other hand, federal policymakers had to confront the political problems stemming from the depression. The massive numbers of unemployed in the cities constituted a potentially troublesome situation. During the Hoover years, city officials encountered this unrest and often became the targets of demonstrations, sometimes violent, when local and private relief funds had dried up and state and federal aid was unavailable.

In effect, the Roosevelt administration could not continue the federal government's policy of ignoring the plight of the unemployed without risking a crisis of political legitimacy and support. In addition, there were substantial electoral gains to be achieved by adopting a more sympathetic federal stance toward the cities and their economic difficulties. The programs of the New Deal helped the Democrats to achieve a political party realignment, becoming the national majority party by winning the support of important urban constituencies, such as working class ethnics, labor, minorities, and liberal reformers. At the same time, these New Deal programs were usually acceptable to a wide swath of the business community, which had little other alternative during the economic crisis of the period.

World War II and the Postwar Era, 1941–1960

The next two decades (1941–1960) were marked by fundamental changes in federal urban policy. While the social welfare commitments of the New Deal became a permanent obligation on the part of the national government, a tremendous expansion in federal development activities occurred. Developmental policies became the leading priority of federal policymakers, who also sought to target their aid more to newly emerging suburbs and Sunbelt cities than to the old heartland central cities. Consequently, the federal policies of this era had a dramatic and lasting effect on the postwar urban landscape.

The postwar growth of the cities in the Sunbelt region and in suburbia was aided by a number of federal programs enacted and/or implemented during this period. Probably the most important of these occurred during World War II, though it is usually not considered as a federal urban program. The decisions of the War Production Board (WPB), made in the name of the war mobilization effort, probably did more than any subsequent federal program to reshape urban America. The WPB did no less than reconstruct America's capital plant by investing enormous sums of federal monies to build new production facilities for American industry. In 1939, domestic manufacturing facilities were valued at $39.5 billion; within the next few years, the WPB provided American industries with almost two-thirds of that amount ($23.1 billion) for new manufacturing plants. By comparison, the PWA (the New Deal's development program) only spent $4.8 billion. In essence, there occurred an unparalleled expansion of the nation's productive capacity that was wholly financed by the federal government. It dwarfed the public works efforts of the New Deal and constituted a massive reindustrialization program (Mollenkopf, 1983:49–51).

The importance to cities of the WPB's reindustrialization efforts stems from its locational decisions with respect to new facilities. Unlike the New Deal agencies, the WPB was staffed and directed by executives of the largest industrial corporations—"dollar-a-year" men from industry staffed the Board while labor representatives only performed in an advisory capacity. Not surprisingly, the WPB chose to provide large manufacturing establishments rather than public agencies with the federal money. More important from the perspective of the city, WPB officials reflected the preferences of private firms in their locational choices and distributed new facilities disproportionately in Sunbelt cities and in the suburban regions of metropolitan areas to obtain cost advantages, such as cheap labor and land. Over the opposition of organized labor, business leaders used the WPB to have the federal government reconstruct the nation's industrial base in locales away from the core central cities (Mollenkopf, 1983:50–51).

Federal urban policy in the immediate postwar years—the fifteen years that spanned the Truman and Eisenhower administrations—reflected the same characteristics as the war mobilization effort. It emphasized developmental objectives, was biased in favor of Sunbelt cities and suburbia in comparison to the core central cities, provided subsidies to private sector institutions rather than public agencies, and strongly reflected the demands of business groups. The two best illustrations of this policy pattern were the federal interstate highway program and the Federal Housing Administration (FHA) mortgage insurance program.

The federal program that expended the most dollars and had the greatest impact in shaping urban land use patterns during these years was the interstate highway program. Enacted in 1956, this program spent $27 billion over the next decade; $15 billion of this was spent in urban areas, linking the various cities in a national highway system. Its impact was to promote the growth of new metropolitan areas by promoting long-haul truck traffic and to stimulate suburbanization by reducing the costs and time of road transit in metropolitan areas. The central city was far less advantaged by the program. Improved feeder routes to central business districts failed to appreciably solve the rush-hour commuting problem. Within four years after passage of the program, the nation's mayors, aware of the deleterious effects of the program on the central cities, persuaded the Senate to approve federal subsidies to commuter rail lines;

these subsidies were, however, blocked by the Eisenhower administration. In sum, the interstate highway program was based, as one observer has noted, "on dispersing population and physical investment away from the older central cities" (Mollenkopf, 1983:56).

Another program sharing similar characteristics was the mortgage insurance program of the Federal Housing Administration (FHA). Enacted in 1934 by the New Deal to aid the home-building sector, the intent of the program was to insure private bank mortgages issued for the purchase of new homes. FHA-insured mortgages provided home buyers with reduced down payments, lower interest rates, and longer payment terms. The full impact of the program was felt after World War II when postwar prosperity led to a mass migration from the central city. FHA policies discouraged giving mortgage guarantees on rental property and property potentially subject to blight. These practices virtually ensured that most FHA-insured properties would be in suburbia rather than in central cities.

While it is impossible to determine precisely how important FHA was in subsidizing the development of suburbia, changes in the location of new home construction sites provide a glimpse of its effect. In 1927, in the Chicago metropolitan area, 74 percent of all new home building was in the central city and 26 percent was in the surrounding suburbs. By 1954, the figures were reversed; 28 percent of new homes were built in Chicago and 72 percent in its suburban fringe (Gelfand, 1975:218).

Even the major programs directed more toward the central city during this period reflect the developmental, private sector orientation of federal urban policy. Two such programs were urban renewal and public housing. The former involved federal subsidies to private businesses for reconstructing the central business districts. The latter, a redistributive legacy from the New Deal, provided for construction of low-rent housing by local government authorities. Both programs were authorized in the 1949 Housing Act in a compromise piece of legislation intended to accommodate liberal reformers who wanted to eliminate slums and satisfy businesses seeking to restore central city property values. In subsequent years, however, the appropriations for public housing were kept far below the authorized limits while urban renewal gradually developed into a major national effort in rebuilding the central cities. On the other hand, the urban renewal program was gradually reshaped, via congressional amendments and administrative regulations, into a far more attractive package for private developers. The developer was provided with an increasingly wide range of choices for utilizing the cleared land, and local officials were given greater discretion in working out their arrangements with business interests. As a result, annual appropriations for urban renewal continuously increased and growing numbers of "downtown" areas began to reflect the impact of the program (see Chapter 12).

The highly developmental emphasis of federal urban policy during this period reflected the political relationships between federal officials and the dominant interests in their national party coalitions that had emerged after World War II. Federal spending programs were regarded by business as an essential component in sustaining sufficient consumer demand. Businesses most desired to see federal expenditures directed toward developmental objectives, thereby directly enhancing private sector economic expansion. Federal policymakers found themselves in the enviable position of being able to establish new federal programs without having to confront adverse public reaction.

These two decades were extremely prosperous, and both parties contended for the support of the rapidly growing middle class—composed of such groups as unionized blue-collar workers as well as white-collar professionals—whose interests and outlook had considerably changed from the Depression era as they came to enjoy a better standard of living. Many members of this emergent middle class had moved to the suburbs, and some had begun the move toward the Sunbelt. This population segment was not generally interested in new redistributive initiatives—though they supported the continuance of the measures passed during the New Deal. The politics of the era is best captured by the image of Dwight Eisenhower as President governing with a Democratic Congress. The two parties did not yet sharply diverge in policy or appeal to very different constituencies. Both ignored the urban, nonwhite poor, who were growing in numbers in the central cities, with consequences that would unfold during the next phase of federal policymaking toward the cities.

The New Frontier and Great Society, 1961–1968

The Kennedy and Johnson administrations were characterized by an enormous expansion of all kinds of federal programs for the cities. A few statistics graphically illustrate this expansion. In 1960, there were 44 federal grant programs for the cities spending $3.9 billion annually. By 1968, there were over 500 grant programs expending $14 billion in cities, a figure that grew to $26.8 billion by 1974 (Mollenkopf, 1983:45). Unlike the previous two decades when federal policy focused on the physical development of urban areas, most of these new programs sought to promote redistributive social reforms for the residents of the cities. This included the poverty program, aid for elementary and secondary education, Model Cities, community health facilities, manpower development and training, and rent supplements. In addition, these administrations expanded federal developmental programs by enlarging the urban renewal effort and by the enactment of aid to mass transit. Finally, new distributive programs were adopted.

The poverty program and new subsidized housing programs were exemplary of the redistributive priority that colored urban policy during this period. The Community Action component of the poverty program was the largest and most innovative aspect of the new redistributive endeavors. Unlike previous urban aid programs, the Community Action Program (and some other, smaller programs) by-passed local officials and directly funded (over $1 billion a year) neighborhood groups in poor areas of the cities. The program sought to overcome the opposition of big city officialdom to minority participation, and it provided cities with a mechanism for absorbing and directing the agitation and civil disorder brewing in the urban ghettos. By organizing these neighborhoods and providing training for a new group of nonwhite political leaders, the funding of local poverty groups constituted a very innovative extension of federal redistributive activities in the cities.

While the social welfare programs of the New Frontier/Great Society sought to bring funds and organizational skills to minority groups in the cities, it also employed redistributive programs to maintain the support of its traditional ethnic constituency. The various subsidized housing programs of these two administrations illustrate this thrust. There were four major housing bills passed in 1961, 1964, 1965, and 1968. This legislation reflected the ongoing commitment of both administrations for the construction of subsidized private housing for families with incomes below the median but above public housing eligibility limits.

The first housing act in 1961 initiated a new below-market mortgage interest rate subsidy program for private multifamily housing (Section 221(d)(3)). Subsequent legislation continued this drift in housing policy, culminating in the 1968 housing act. The latter established two new mortgage interest subsidy programs for privately constructed single-family and multifamily housing (Sections 235 and 236), which considerably enlarged the number of housing units built for this segment of the population. By the time President Nixon suspended the program in 1973, the federal government had subsidized the construction of 1.2 million units of housing for families with moderate incomes. The number of subsidized units constructed grew throughout these years; they averaged 60,000 units per year under Kennedy and grew to 430,000 annually by 1970 and 1971.

While redistributive programs were the priority of urban policy under Kennedy and Johnson, these administrations also enlarged the federal presence in cities with respect to the developmental and distributive policy arenas. Downtown development under urban renewal was greatly expanded as private developers were given greater latitude in their rebuilding on the cleared land. The federal funds spent for urban renewal during the first two years of the Kennedy administration equalled the total sums spent during the eight years of the Eisenhower administration. The sixties became the decade of the "downtown renaissance," though, by the end of the period, smoldering ghettos and new federal requirements for rehabilitating housing (rather than clearance) began to slow down the program. New developmental initiatives also included federal grants for mass transit in metropolitan areas. Authorized in 1964, eight years after the establishment of the interstate highway system and for much more limited funds, federal aid enabled the central cities to achieve an urban transit system that would benefit their downtown areas rather than fringe areas or new urban settlements.

Even local distributive policy was affected by the expanded federal urban role. The most noteworthy program in this respect was the Crime Control and Safe Streets Act of 1968; federal grants to local (and state) law enforcement agencies were authorized by the legislation. By 1976, some $5 billion had been expended by these agencies.

The redistributive priority of the New Frontier/Great Society urban programs is best explained by the economic circumstances and the political needs that constrained the Kennedy and Johnson administrations. On one hand, these eight years were the most prosperous of the entire postwar era. In fact, it was a period of sustained economic recovery without any significant declines in the level of business activity. As a result, the growth in federal spending did not cause any great apprehension within the business community; expansion in the federal government's activities was funded by the growing tax revenues generated by the economy. Nor did the redistributive spending thrust reduce business confidence. The business community had just as great a stake— perhaps even greater—as did the political authorities in finding ways to quell the disturbances arising from urban ghettos.

On the other hand, the Democratic administrations of Kennedy and Johnson were confronted with an important political dilemma. In order for the Democratic Party to continue domination of national politics, it had to retain the support and votes of two large population groupings that were growing progressively disenchanted with the party's record and whose interests were increasingly different and often antagonistic. The first group comprised blacks and other minorities; they had migrated in large numbers to northern cities, and their votes were now essential for Democrats to be able to capture the electorally important states of the heartland. While this group still retained their New Deal attachment to the Democratic Party, they were becoming dissatisfied with their exclusion from local Democratic politics and with their impoverished status in the big cities (see Chapter 16). The other group was the blue-collar and middle-class ethnics who had made the Democrats the majority coalition during the days of the New Deal. With larger numbers of them enjoying a better standard of living and often residing in suburbia, this group was becoming more concerned with the size of their tax bill rather than the benefits flowing from the federal government's largesse.

The Kennedy and Johnson administrations sought to devise a program that would appeal to both population segments. For blacks and other minorities, the two administrations followed the New Deal tradition of passing federal programs intended to provide them with more material assistance as well as greater political participation (as promoted by the Community Action Program). For the urban ethnics, federal "pump-priming" programs were enacted in order to enlarge the numbers benefiting from the nation's prosperity, while programs such as subsidized housing were also targeted to benefit this segment of the population.

The New Federalism, 1969–Present

While the New Frontier/Great Society programs sought to protect the Democratic Party's northern base of support, the nomination of Barry Goldwater in 1964 symbolized growing support for a new conservative alternative that would challenge the Democratic Party's electoral hegemony. This conservative coalition found its base of support among voters in the southern rim and in suburbia who were opposed to large-scale government programs seeking to achieve redistributive goals. During the past fifteen years, this conservative coalition has come to power in Washington and has dramatically reversed federal urban policies. Developmental rather than redistributive objectives have dominated national policy making.

The framework for the new policies emerged during the Nixon administration under the label of the "New Federalism." The New Federalism strongly tilted federal largesse away from redistributive activities in favor of developmental urban objectives by following two strategies. Both amounted to major departures from the "Old Federalism" of past administrations. First, Nixon relied on the workings of the intergovernmental system in order to bias federal programs in ways that promoted a more developmental urban policy. As discussed previously, the more competitive market environment of localities and states, together with the relatively privileged position of revenue-provider groups within their political systems, encourages these governments to give high priority to developmental objectives. Nixon capitalized on this bias in the organization of federalism by adopting the use of block grants to transfer authority over national urban programs from federal to state and local officials. Previous administrations had relied almost exclusively on categorical grants-in-aid to cities and states, providing federal funds only for very specific ("categorical") purposes and typically accompanied by considerable national oversight in their administration. In contrast, the New Federalism's approach collapsed many categorical grant programs into a single block grant for very broad or even general purposes, limiting federal oversight and increasing local discretion in determining the use of funds.

The General Revenue Sharing Act (1972) was the first block grant program to embody this decentralist thrust. Revenue sharing provided mayors and local chief executives with new federal monies without many expenditure restrictions. Later, two other block grant programs were enacted: The Comprehensive Employment and Training Act (1973) and the Housing and Community Development Act (1974). As we shall discuss in detail later, the policy effect of this devolution of federal authority in respect to all three programs was to encourage localities to pursue developmental and distributive goals, rather than redistributive programs. Further, the formulae used in distributing funds for these programs provided much more money for Sunbelt cities and suburban communities than they had received under the categorical programs of prior years (Mollenkopf, 1983:60–61, 63). Whereas the categorical programs of the Great Society favored the central cities of the heartland, the Nixon administration succeeded in shifting much federal urban aid toward the growing urban regions.

The other component of the Nixon administration's urban policy was an attempt to terminate or modify some of the redistributive policy initiatives established by the Great Society. The administration was far less successful in this attempt than with its programs to decentralize the administration of federal programs. Nixon made numerous attempts to reduce the funding of many of these programs, but with little success (Judd and Kopel, 1978:192–195). He was more successful in undermining the Great Society programs that endeavored to promote the political participation of minority communities. After a long battle with Congress, Nixon largely succeeded in dismembering the Community Action Program, limiting local community action agencies to providing services rather than mobilizing minority neighborhoods. Other programs having citizen participation mechanisms, such as urban renewal and Model Cities, were successfully folded into the new block grant system.

The administrations since Nixon have generally followed the New Federalism as an urban policy. The short tenure of Gerald Ford was marked by his successful vetoes of bills that attempted to increase federal spending in cities for redistributive purposes. Though a Democrat, Carter made no attempt to repeal the programs that provided local officials with broad discretion over federal expenditures, nor did he propose any significant expansion of redistributive programs for the cities. His most noteworthy policy departure involved developmental programs for older heartland central cities. The establishment of the Urban Development Action Grant Program (UDAG) and his support for changing the distribution formula of the Community Development program reflect the Carter administration's focus on subsidizing private investment in the distressed central cities of the North.

The Reagan administration's urban policies follow the framework initiated by Nixon. Reagan has continued to decentralize the administration of federal programs by combining numerous categorical grant programs into block grants, which are managed by state officials. Further, Reagan's budget cuts have drastically reduced funds for redistributive programs, such as the Legal Services Corporation and youth employment programs, while eliminating the remaining vestiges of the Community Action program and other Great Society programs.

In developmental policy, the Reagan administration has cut the budgets of programs that primarily aided the cities of the heartland. In their place, Reagan has vigorously promoted tax cuts for business and has increased defense spending—policies that are likely to disproportionately aid the cities of the Sunbelt. In sum, since 1968 no administration has supported an expansion of the federal government's redistributive role. Instead, the urban policies of all of the presidents have been to give priority to developmental objectives; the major differences between the parties have been regarding regional differences over which cities and which private interests should receive the bulk of the aid.

This pattern is linked to the weakened market position of the federal government in a declining national economy. Confronted with the problems of stagflation at home and greater competition from abroad, business confidence and capital investment sagged during the New Federalism years. Federal officials, in seeking to induce greater private investment in the national economy, have followed policies intended to restore American business to a more competitive position in the world economy. Their objective has been to make American businesses more productive—that is, to lower the costs of production—and hence become more competitive vis-à-vis their foreign counterparts. To help achieve this, federal policymakers have tried to reduce those costs to business that have resulted from governmental programs—i.e., tax cuts, easing of regulatory restrictions, and less government support for vulnerable (less productive) populations. As a result, the range of policy choice for federal officials has narrowed and will probably remain so as long as political coalitions opposing the developmental priorities of the national government fail to emerge as powerful forces and/or until the nation's market position changes substantially. The nature of the American regime requires that public officials induce sufficient private sector activity or suffer deleterious electoral and financial consequences.

The Changing Politics of National Urban Policy

A consistent objective of national urban policy throughout the postindustrial era has been to induce greater private sector investment in the national economy. While differences between the two parties over development policies have emerged, the dominant pattern is their joint support for national policies to promote private sector investment in urban areas. The major differences between the parties with respect to national urban policy have arisen over redistributive policies (see Table 10-1). Reflecting the divergent electoral bases of the parties, both the New Deal and the New Frontier/Great Society initiated bold social programs to aid the underprivileged while Republican administrations have often opposed such programs. Reflecting the federal government's strong market position relative to lower-level governments and its popular control system that accords greater influence to have-nots, major shifts of emphasis between developmental and redistributive priorities in urban policy have been evident.

Most recently, the New Federalism has aimed at reducing business costs and subsidizing business investment under comparatively severe national economic constraints that have discouraged political leaders favoring a larger redistributive role for the federal government in cities. Consequently, the major differences between the policies advocated by Republican and Democratic administrations have been over the particular cities and private interests they seek to advantage. The Republicans have sought to skew their aid to businesses in the Sunbelt and suburbia while Democrat Jimmy Carter focused his efforts on aiding the central cities of the North.

These differences are best understood in terms of the different constituent base of the two parties. The Republicans have developed "a conservative urban counterstrategy based on aid to the suburbs and newer metropolitan areas" (Mollenkopf, 1983:137). It has been the Republicans who have used federal urban policies to promote the economic growth of the urban locales that have developed since World War II; they have dropped their antiurban bias and have developed supportive constituencies in cities that are conservative and could not be included within the Democratic coalition. The base of urban support for the Democrats has been, since the New Deal, the central cities of the North. It is

TABLE 10-1   Changing Priorities in National Urban Policies, 1933–1987

| Period | Policy areas and relative priority | | |
	Development	Distribution	Redistribution
New Deal, 1933–1940	high	low	high
War/Postwar, 1941–1960	moderately high	low	moderate
New Frontier/Great Society, 1961–1968	moderately high	moderate	high
New Federalism, 1969–present	high	low	low

these cities that have been disadvantaged by the Republican "urban counter-strategy"; federal largesse has been used to promote private sector movement to strengthen the competitive position of these newer areas, thereby increasing the financial difficulties of the old central cities. The Democrats were the first of the two major parties to extensively use the federal government to develop a base of support in the cities. Learning from the Democrats, it has been the Republicans who have used federal urban policies to appeal to the areas of greatest urban growth.

States and Cities in the Federal Order: Intergovernmental Dependency

The growth of the national government during the postindustrial period has given birth to a mature federal system—one in which the traditional relationship held by states and localities in respect to the national government has been reversed. What has happened since 1929 is a dramatic reshuffling of positions among the three levels of government in a way that has increased the dependency of lower level governments, especially localities, on those higher.

In 1929, the localities and states were the dominant providers of public services within the federal governmental system. In fact, local government expenditures from their own sources of revenue dwarfed those of the national government and considerably overshadowed the states. Table 10-2 shows that in 1929, localities expended almost 54 percent of total public sector resources while states spent about a fifth and the national government claimed only around one-fourth (if defense is excluded, this drops to less than 15 percent). Since then, however, there has been a reversal of these positions no matter how governmental expenditure activities are compared. After years of gradual increases in federal domestic and defense spending, often at rates in excess of growth in local and state governmental spending, there occurred huge leaps in federal government expenditure relative to states and localities during the 1960s

TABLE 10-2 Government Expenditures, from Own Funds, Selected Years, 1929–1984

Calendar year	Total public sector	Federal Total	Federal Defense	Federal Domestic	State	Local
			Percentage distribution by level of government			
1929	100%	25.6%	7.8%	17.8%	20.8%	53.6%
1939	100	50.9	6.8	44.1	21.2	28.0
1949	100	69.7	22.2	47.5	14.9	15.4
1959	100	69.4	34.8	34.6	14.4	16.1
1969	100	65.7	26.6	39.1	18.0	16.3
1978	100	67.7	14.8	52.9	18.8	13.5
1984*	100	69.9	17.6	52.3	17.5	12.5
			Per capita in constant (1972) dollars			
1929	$ 258	$ 66	$ 20	$ 46	$ 54	$138
1939	472	240	33	207	100	132
1949	757	528	168	359	113	116
1959	1,090	757	379	378	157	176
1969	1,630	1,071	45	617	294	265
1978	2,034	1,377	299	1,078	382	275
1984*	2,380	1,665	420	1,245	417	299

*Estimated.
SOURCE: Adapted from Tables 1 and 6 in Advisory Commission on Intergovernmental Relations, *Significant Features of Fiscal Federalism*, 1984 Edition, M-141 (Washington, D.C.: U.S. Government Printing Office, 1985). For full notes on these data, see original.

and 1970s. By 1978, the federal share rose to just under 70 percent, while states dropped to 18.8 percent and local governments were reduced to 13.5 percent.

This revolution in intergovernmental provider roles was only partially affected by federal defense spending during the period. Even if defense and debt expenditures are excluded, the dominant federal position, the "middle" state position, and the very junior local government position are apparent when measured by the percentage of their own source expenditures in respect to GNP as well as in relation to per capita spending. During the 1980s, even the election of a president avowedly dedicated to paring down the size of all governments, especially the federal, has not affected the overall upward growth of governmental expenditures and the respective positions of local, state, and federal governments.

Policy Area Variation within the Federal System

This transformation of the federal system in the liberal democratic order has tended to create areas of public policy competency for local, state, and federal governments. Peterson (1981:Ch 4) has shown how the economics of modern federalism have tended to carve out fairly distinctive policy capabilities in this three-tiered system. Table 10-3 shows how each governmental level differs in the allocation of expenditures from own fiscal sources (i.e., excluding intergovernmental aid) among redistributive, distributive, and developmental kinds of policies. It is apparent that redistribution tends to be very much a federal expenditure function; more than 55 percent of the national government domestic budget was devoted to these social welfare programs in 1973, compared with less than 14 percent by local governments. The state allocation for these types of policies is somewhat in between.

As suggested previously, the powerful market position of the federal government, with its ability to impose much greater control over the movement of capital and labor, enables it to provide these kinds of policies without the severe consequences for development that local governments are apt to suffer. This economic capacity is further enhanced by the national government's greater political capability—i.e., it is more open and responsive to redistributive demands compared with local and state governments. Redistributive programs are less likely to win support at lower governmental levels because they can trigger relocational threats by business and other revenue-providers in the more permeable economic and political systems of localities and states. Even though the 1960s was a time of great expansion in redistribution in the United States (as a result of phenomenal national economic growth and unusual political pressures by civil rights and the poor at all governmental levels), the relative expenditure distributions among governmental levels changed very little between 1962 and 1973. The significance of redistribution as a form of local own-source expenditure changed less than a single percent, while proportionately larger increases took place at the state and national levels.

In contrast, distribution is a dominant area of local government expenditure because these types of policies generally do not influence the competitive market position of the community very much. Traditionally, distribution has been the dominant local government expenditure responsibility; it has remained so during the postindustrial period. In fact, these kinds of expenditures took claim to declining proportions of federal and state budgets over the period. The federal proportion shrank to under 4 percent, and the state allocation dropped from 12.4 percent to 8.4 percent while local government expenditures for this purpose increased from 26.8 to 28.5 percent.

Developmental expenditures tend to take up roughly similar proportions of the own-source expenditures of all three levels of government, although the federal role may be somewhat larger than localities and states to the extent that interest on the national debt is a result of federal activities in the regulation of the economy. The prominence of developmental expenditures throughout the federal governmental system can be best understood as something that is inherent in a capitalist system; it reflects the importance of the public sector in inducing private sector economic productivity. This is an activity that all levels of government share in a market system.[1]

TABLE 10-3 Governmental Expenditures from Own Fiscal Resources

| | Percentage distributions among functions | | | | | |
| | Local | | State | | Federal* | |
Function	1962	1973	1962	1973	1962	1973
Redistributive						
Welfare	2.5%	2.0%	6.2%	11.2%	12.2%	12.6%
Health and hospitals	6.1	8.4	7.4	6.2	3.3	3.5
Housing	2.4	0.9	0.2	0.4	1.5	3.4
Social insurance	1.9	2.3	14.4	17.0	29.7	35.6
Subtotal	12.9	13.8	28.2	34.8	46.7	55.1
Distributive						
Housekeeping	26.8	28.5	12.4	8.4	4.6	3.8
Developmental						
Utilities	13.2	11.1	—	—	—	—
Postal	—	—	—	—	7.0	5.1
Transportation	8.1	5.7	17.8	11.3	6.2	4.2
Natural resources	1.1	0.7	2.9	2.3	19.3	7.8
Subtotal	22.4	17.5	20.7	13.6	32.5	17.1
Interest	4.1	5.6	2.2	2.7	12.3	9.9
Education	33.4	34.2	33.6	38.4	3.2	8.2
Other	0.4	0.4	3.0	2.2	0.8	5.8
Total (%)	100.00	100.0	100.0	100.0	100.0	99.9
Total ($ m)	33,591	77,886	29,356	89,504	58,960	186,172

*Domestic only.

SOURCE: From Paul E. Peterson, City Limits. © 1981 by The University of Chicago. Reprinted by permission of The University of Chicago Press.

Variation in Revenue Sources among Governments

Federal dominance in redistributive activities and the more limited fiscal competency of lower-level governments are also reflected in their respective tax bases. Tax policy is linked to the capability of governments to extract revenues from sources in ways that avoid relocational threats or do not precipitate the movement of capital and labor to other jurisdictions. Consequently, the federal government is in the most independent position from which to impose taxes, such as income taxes, which have redistributive consequences and are more burdensome on revenue-producers because they are based on ability-to-pay principles. In contrast, local governments are least able to utilize this mode of taxation and are constrained (independently of state prohibitions) to employ tax sources that are not as likely to provoke either political opposition of revenue producers or their relocation to other jurisdictions (see related arguments in Peterson, 1981:Ch. 4).

Table 10-4 shows the reality of these forces within the intergovernmental system. Individual and corporate income taxes are the dominant form of federal taxation, providing over 80 percent of the national government's revenues during the period 1957 to 1982. Local governments have sometimes made use of this type of tax in recent years, but it still remains unimportant compared to the traditionally dominant source of local government tax revenues, the property tax. Localities continue to rely on property taxes despite the difficulties that this type of tax poses, especially in respect to its cumbersome administration, its regressive features (that is, its tendency to fall more heavily on those who are less well-off), and its general inequity owing to uneven implementation. Its major advantage, however, is that it extracts revenues from the only things that cannot move—land and the buildings upon the land. If only for this reason, the property tax is an invaluable revenue source more appropriate to local government than to any other government.

Consistent with this logic, states again stand somewhat in between the national and local governments in respect to their reliance on particular modes of taxation. They make significant use of income taxes, though far less than does the national government and invariably at lower tax rates than found in federal tax schedules. But the largest sources of state tax revenue are the excise and sales taxes, which the federal government has made declining use of in recent decades. Sales and excise taxes are usually quite regressive in their incidence among income groups and are often considered far less likely than the income tax to encourage relocational behavior (Kieschnick, 1981).

In effect, the market environments and the political systems that federalism creates powerfully affect the public policy capabilities of localities, states, and the national governments. The inferior market position and political system owned by cities in the federal governmental order make it difficult for them to undertake redistributive ventures, and it encourages more distributive or developmental uses for local resources. In contrast, the superior (independent) economic and political position of the national government has enhanced its capability to promote redistributive programs; states have been able to develop a middle position in respect to these areas of public policy.

TABLE 10-4   Tax Revenue by Major Source, by Level and Type of Government, Selected Years, 1957, 1972, 1983

		Percentage distribution by type of tax			
Fiscal year	Total taxes	Property taxes	Sales, gross receipts, and customs	Ind. and corp. income taxes	All other taxes
Federal government					
1957	100.0	0.0	15.9	81.3	2.7
1972	100.0	0.0	13.1	82.5	4.4
1983	100.0	0.0	11.7	85.5	2.8
State and local governments					
1957	100.0	44.6	32.9	9.5	13.0
1972	100.0	39.1	34.2	17.9	8.7
1983	100.0	31.4	35.2	24.4	9.0
State governments					
1957	100.0	3.3	58.1	17.5	21.1
1972	100.0	2.1	55.5	29.1	13.3
1983	100.0	1.9	48.9	36.7	12.4
Local governments					
1957	100.0	86.7	7.2	1.3	4.8
1972	100.0	83.7	8.6	4.5	3.3
1983	100.0	76.0	14.5	5.7	3.9

SOURCE: Advisory Commission on Intergovernmental Relations, *Significant Features of Fiscal Federalism*, 1984 Edition. M-141 (Washington, D.C.: U.S. Government Printing Office, 1985), Table 33.3. See original for notes on the data.

Intergovernmental Aid and Urban Dependency

Although these patterns of allocating revenues are suggestive of the fiscal capabilities of localities, states, and the national government, it would be wrong to conclude that modern federalism imposes separate functions on each governmental level. This is because the growth of intergovernmental grants-in-aid to localities has had a major countervailing effect on their policy capabilities. Expanding intergovernmental aid to local governments has established a powerful dependency relationship with higher level governments and brought about a massive state and federal presence in localities, especially in the redistributive policy area.

In aggregate, the growth of intergovernmental aid programs has been inexorable since 1930 (see Figure 10-1), and by 1980 it achieved staggering amounts. In that year alone, about $91 billion changed hands among governments, nearly all going "downward" in the form of revenues collected by the federal government and passed on to states and localities in the form of grants of various kinds or in monies transferred from states to localities (those from

FIGURE 10-1   Growing Fiscal Dependency of Lower Levels on Higher Levels
of Government

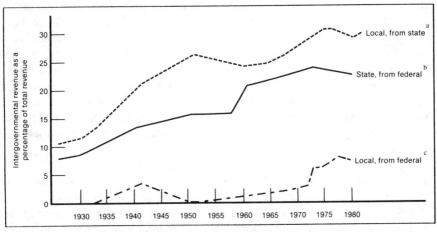

[a] Includes indirect federal aid passed through states to all local governments.
[b] Includes minuscule amounts of local transfers to states.
[c] Direct federal aid only.
SOURCE: From Virginia Gray, Herbert Jacob, and Kenneth N. Vines, *Politics in the American States*, 4th ed., p. 46. Copyright © 1983 by Virginia Gray, Herbert Jacob, and Kenneth N. Vines. Reprinted by permission of Scott, Foresman and Company. Based on information contained in *Significant Features of Fiscal Federalism, 1979–80* (ACIR, 1981): Table 108; in *Facts and Figures on Government Finance, 1979* (Tax Foundation, 1980): Tables 134, 135, and 196; and in *Governmental Finances in 1979–80* (U.S. Department of Commerce, 1981): Table 4.

lower to higher levels of government are insignificant).

State aid has always been the traditional major source of intergovernmental assistance to cities. During the postindustrial period, there have been strong economic, political, and intergovernmental forces favoring its expansion. The postindustrial economy's dispersal of population and industry in an era of widespread urbanization increased the need for greater state intervention, particularly because of the limited tax capability of local government and the much greater fiscal capacity of states. Further, state popular control systems underwent change. The traditional dominance of state legislatures by rural voters abated in response to the suburbanization of the electorate and because of court decisions, particularly a series of Supreme Court decisions beginning in 1962, which mandated "one man, one vote" reforms. This made state legislatures more responsive to urban populations, though often to those in suburbia and smaller towns, rather than in large cities (Caraley, 1977:71–76; O'Rourke, 1980). Finally, the growth of federal assistance for particular programs often required state contributions, such as in the case of public assistance, pulling state governments into new program commitments.

Although the expansion of state aid to local governments grew throughout this period, during the 1960s and 1970s an explosion in federal grants-in-aid occurred. Federal aid to state and local governments grew 1,500 percent, rising from $3.8 billion in 1957 to 61.4 billion in 1977. By comparison, state aid to local governments grew only a "modest" 750 percent, increasing from 7.3 billion in 1957 to over 62 billion in 1977. Of equal import was the phenomenal increase in federal aid given directly to cities without ever passing through the states. This grew by an astounding 4,892.7 percent during the two decades to 1977. This partly reflected a change in recipient emphasis by federal officials. While 86 percent of the increase in total federal aids went to the states between 1957 and 1972, only 63 percent did in the following years (Stephens and Olson, 1979:23–24). Although the upward expansion of federal assistance to cities and states reached their apogee during the late 1970s and has declined somewhat under the Reagan administration (see below), the tremendous state and federal fiscal presence in cities is firmly established and has not shrunk below levels of the early 1970s.

LOCAL FISCAL DEPENDENCY. One consequence of this expansion of intergovernmental aid has been a dramatic fiscal dependence of local governments on federal and state aid programs. Up until the 1980s, this dependency has increased steadily, as suggested by the federal government's own local government dependency index (Table 10-5). In 1980, state and federal sources of revenue made up about 40 percent of total local revenues (state governments received about one-fourth of their revenues from the federal level). It is apparent that lower levels of government, particularly local governments, are now highly dependent on higher levels of government and are not even close to being self-sustaining operations.

As a result of this intergovernmental aid, the local government revenue base has become more diverse. Because intergovernmental aid has increased, local government reliance on its own revenue sources has declined. In 1942, local taxes provided about 67 percent of local revenues, but dropped to only about 42 percent by 1977 (localities also collected 15 percent of their revenues from user charges and other miscellaneous sources, an insignificant source in 1942). Localities have become somewhat less reliant on the property tax. In 1942, the property tax provided around 82 percent of local own-source revenues and over 90 percent of tax receipts; by 1977, this tax still accounted for nearly 60 percent of own-source revenues and over 80 percent of total tax receipts (Break, 1980:224).

The extent of fiscal dependency for many local governments is actually concealed by these aggregate figures because of the great variation among cities in respect to reliance upon intergovernmental aid. There has been a strong tendency for many northern cities to be more dependent than others on intergovernmental revenue as a result of more ambitious state aid programs in that region and because of their more favorable treatment in urban aid programs by Congress during most of the postindustrial period. In 1984, federal and state aid to cities per $100 of their own revenues was $65 in the New England states, but only averaged $24 in the cities of the southwestern states; the cities in the Great Lakes states (Illinois, Indiana, Michigan, Ohio, and Wisconsin) approached the national average of $46 per $100 of own-source revenues (ACIR, 1985:66).

THE NEW INTERGOVERNMENTAL DEPENDENCY / 215

TABLE 10-5 Local Government Dependency Index, Fiscal Years 1962, 1975, 1978, 1980–1983

Unit of government	1983	1982	1981	1980	1978	1975	1962
Federal and state aid per $1 of own-source general revenue							
All local governments	$0.67	$0.71	$0.76	$0.79	$0.76	$0.73	$0.44
Counties	.63	.70	.77	.81	.80	.78	.60
Cities	.46	.50	.53	.56	.62	.63	.26
Townships	.40	.41	.40	.39	.41	.40	.28
School districts	1.13	1.15	1.23	1.25	1.01	.94	.65
Special districts	.36	.39	.47	.42	.44	.42	.15
Federal aid per $1 of own-source general revenue							
All local governments	$0.12	$0.13	$0.15	$0.16	$0.18	$0.13	$0.03
Counties	.09	.11	.14	.17	.19	.13	.01
Cities	.15	.18	.21	.23	.26	.19	.05
Townships	.09	.08	.09	.10	.13	.09	.01
School districts	.02	.02	.03	.03	.04	.03	.02
Special districts	.27	.29	.37	.33	.34	.28	.11
State aid per $1 of own-source general revenue							
All local governments	$0.55	$0.58	$0.61	$0.63	$0.58	$0.60	$0.41
Counties	.53	.59	.63	.64	.61	.65	.59
Cities	.31	.32	.32	.33	.37	.42	.21
Townships	.32	.33	.31	.29	.28	.31	.27
School districts	1.11	1.13	1.20	1.22	.97	.90	.63
Special districts	.08	.10	.10	.09	.10	.14	.04

SOURCE: Advisory Commission on Intergovernmental Relations, *Significant Features of Fiscal Federalism*, 1984 edition. M-141, Table 45.

Even within regions and states, there is often great disparity in the fiscal dependence of particular cities. For instance, in 1978 New York City derived more than 45 percent of its revenue from intergovernmental sources, while suburban New Rochelle, which lies a few miles beyond New York City's northern border, received only about 25 percent from higher governments. Similarly, while Sunbelt state governments generally have very limited local aid programs, particular cities within the region sometimes are highly dependent on federal assistance. In Texas, Houston receives little more than 15 percent of its revenues from intergovernmental aid, mostly federal, while El Paso and Corpus Christi depend much more heavily on such assistance—for about one-third of their budgets (Jones, 1983:272).

The particular urban policy consequences of the intergovernmental dependency of cities are very complex and far reaching. This matter is probed extensively in subsequent chapters. But the general impact is evident by simply looking at the policy emphasis of state and federal aid to cities.[2] As Table 10-6 suggests, redistributive programs dominate federal assistance to cities and also dominate, though to a lesser degree, state aid programs outside of education.

In 1973 over 40 percent of all federal assistance to cities was for redistributive purposes, and over one-fifth of all state aid monies to local governments were for these kinds of programs. Otherwise, education claimed the largest share of state assistance, making it the most heavily supported state function in intergovernmental aid programs. In contrast, distributive and developmental purposes are funded at much lower levels in intergovernmental aid programs to localities.

The importance of the federal role in supporting local programs of redistribution may even be understated by these rather rough calculations. In recent years, increasing amounts of federal aid to states have been directly passed through to local governments. By 1977, such "pass-through" monies constituted nearly one-third of all federal aid to the states and amounted to over 57 percent of state aid to localities for public welfare programs (Stephens and Olson, 1979:34–35). In effect, there has been a tremendous federalization of the redistributive functions performed by local governments. Federal and state largesse has brought a substantial intergovernmental presence in the area of public policy where localities are most constrained by their political and economic systems; it is therefore in this area of policy that intergovernmental forces are most likely to have an exceptionally powerful impact on local politics.

Federalism and Urban Dependency

The growth of federal and state governmental intervention in urban affairs has redefined the city's place in the intergovernmental order. The expansion of federal urban policies has touched on all three areas of public policy— redistributive, developmental, and distributive—during the postindustrial period. Although the policy emphasis of national political authorities has varied a great deal, the priority of all administrations has been to induce high levels of

TABLE 10-6 Intergovernmental Expenditures by State and Federal Governments (Percentage Distributions)

Function	State 1973	Federal 1973
Redistributive		
Welfare	18.4	29.0
Health and hospitals	2.1	4.2
Housing	.4	5.1
Social insurance	—	1.9
Subtotal	20.9	40.2
Distributive		
Housekeeping	—	2.1
Developmental		
Transportation	7.4	13.2
Natural resources	0.2	1.6
Subtotal	7.6	14.8
Education	57.1	20.1
Other and undesignated	14.4	22.0
Total (%)	100.0	100.0
Total ($ m)	40,822	41,666

SOURCE: From Paul E. Peterson, *City Limits.* © 1981 by The University of Chicago. Reprinted by permission of The University of Chicago Press.

private sector investment in cities in order to pursue national economic objectives and build political support for national party coalitions. Consequently, party differences over developmental policy have usually been limited to conflicts over which urban areas should receive the bulk of federal aid. The two parties have divided more sharply over the funding of redistributive programs for cities, with Democratic administrations generally more favorably disposed toward such programs than Republicans have been.

The monumental expansion in national governmental activities has been the primary force in creating an advanced federal system of government in which lower levels of government have become very dependent on those higher. The historic position of states and cities as dominant providers of services has been reversed in favor of the national government. Patterns of specialized capability by each level of government in particular policy areas have emerged, with redistributive activities concentrated at the national level, distributive functions more in the hands of local authorities, and developmental activities scattered throughout the intergovernmental system.

Yet the huge growth in grants-in-aid to local governments by national and state authorities has defied the possibility of any deep separation among the governmental levels. It has assured a massive intergovernmental presence in urban politics and made localities most dependent on higher levels of government in the area of policy where they are least economically capable—redistributive policy. Intergovernmental dependency is, with economic dependency, a hallmark of urban postindustrial democracy.

Endnotes

1. Education is not considered, but this function probably has both developmental and redistributive features. See the discussion in Peterson (1981:Chs. 3 and 5).
2. Not all governmental aid is of a categorical kind, and local governments vary considerably in the purposes to which they put general assistance. This may have some bearing on the kind and consequences of fiscal dependency. See the discussion in Fossett (1984).

References for Part Three

Abbot, Carl. 1981. *The New Urban America: Growth and Politics in Sunbelt Cities.* Chapel Hill: University of North Carolina Press.

Adrian, Charles R. 1952. "Some General Characteristics of Non-Partisan Elections." *American Political Science Review*, Vol. 46 (September), 766–776.

Advisory Commission on Intergovernmental Relations. 1985. *Significant Features of Fiscal Federalism*, 1985 Edition. M-141. Washington, D.C.: U.S. Government Printing Office.

Advisory Commission on Intergovernmental Relations. 1977. *The States and Intergovernmental Aids.* Washington, D.C.: U.S. Government Printing Office.

Alford, Robert and Eugene Lee. 1968. "Voting Turnout in American Cities." *American Political Science Review*, Vol. 62 (September), 796–813.

Altheide, David L. and John S. Hall. 1983. "Phoenix: Crime and Politics in a Federal City" in Anne Heinz, et al., eds. 1983. *Crime in City Politics.* New York: Longman, pp. 193–238

Banfield, Edward C. and James Q. Wilson. 1965. *City Politics.* Cambridge, Mass.: Harvard University Press.

Barabba, Vincent P. 1975. "The National Setting: Regional Shifts, Metropolitan Decline, and Urban Decay" in George Sternlieb and James Hughes, eds. 1975. *Post-Industrial America: Metropolitan Decline and Inter-Regional Job Shifts.* New Brunswick, N.J.: The Center for Urban Policy Research, Rutgers University.

Bellush, Jewel and Stephen David. 1971. *Race and Politics in New York City.* New York: Praeger.

Betsalel, Kenneth A. 1983. "San Jose: Crime and the Politics of Growth" in Anne Heinz, et al., eds. 1983. *Crime in City Politics.* New York: Longman, pp. 239–274.

Blair, John M. 1972. *Economic Concentration: Structure, Behavior and Public Policy.* New York: Harcourt Brace Jovanovich.

Bluestone, Barry and Bennett Harrison. 1982. *The Deindustrialization of America: Plant Closings, Community Abandonment and the Dismantling of Basic Industry.* New York: Basic Books.

Blumberg, Phillip. 1975. *The Megacorporation in American Society: The Scope of Corporate Power.* Englewood Cliffs, N.J.: Prentice-Hall.

Break, George F. 1981. "Fiscal Federalism in the United States: The First 200 Years, Evolution and Outlook" in Advisory Commission on Intergovernmental Relations. 1981. *The Federal Role in the Federal System: The*

Dynamics of Growth. Washington, D.C.: U.S. Government Printing Office, pp. 39–66.

Break, George F. 1980. *Financing Government in a Federal System*. Washington, D.C.: Brookings Institution.

Browning, Rufus P., Dale R. Marshall and David H. Tabb. 1984. *Protest Is Not Enough*. Berkeley: University of California Press.

Caraley, Demetrios. 1977. *City Governments and Urban Problems*. Englewood Cliffs, N.J.: Prentice-Hall.

Chandler, Jr., Alfred D. 1977. *The Visible Hand: The Managerial Revolution in American Business*. Cambridge, Mass.: Belknap Press.

Chandler, Jr., Alfred D. 1962. *Strategy and Structure: Chapters in the History of the Industrial Enterprise*. Cambridge, Mass.: MIT Press.

Committee on Political Parties. 1950. "Towards a More Responsible Two-Party System." *American Political Science Review*, Supplement, Vol. 44 (September).

Cox, Kevin R. 1973. *Conflict, Power and Politics in the City: A Geographic View*. New York: McGraw Hill.

Cremin, Lawrence. 1961. *The Transformation of the School*. New York: Knopf.

Crotty, William J. and Gary L. Jacobson. 1980. *American Parties in Decline*. Boston: Little, Brown.

Dahl, Robert. 1961. *Who Governs?* New Haven: Yale University Press.

Danielson, Michael N. 1976. *The Politics of Exclusion*. New York: Columbia University Press.

David, Stephen and Paul Kantor. 1983. "Urban Policy in the Federal System: A Reconceptualization of Federalism." *Polity*, Vol. 16 (Winter), 284–304.

de la Garza, Rudolph O. 1979. "The Politics of Mexican Americans" in Arnulfo d. Trejo, ed. 1979. *The Chicanos*. Tuscon: University of Arizona Press, pp. 107–118.

Department of Housing and Urban Development. 1980. *President's National Urban Policy Report*. Washington, D.C.: U.S. Government Printing Office.

Economist. 10 July 1982, p. 23.

Fainstein, Norman and Susan Fainstein. 1974. *Urban Social Movements*. Englewood Cliffs, N.J.: Prentice-Hall.

Fainstein, Susan, et al. 1983. *Restructuring the City*. New York: Longman.

Fine, John, et al. 1971. "The Residential Segregation of Occupational Groups in Central Cities and Suburbs." *Demography*, Vol. 8 (February), 91–101.

Fleischmann, Arnold. 1977. "Sunbelt Boosterism: The Politics of Postwar Growth and Annexation in San Antonio" in David C. Perry and Alfred J. Watkins, eds. 1977. *The Rise of the Sunbelt Cities*. Beverly Hills: Sage.

Fossett, James W. 1984. "The Politics of Dependence: Federal Aid to Big Cities" in Laurence D. Brown, James W. Fossett and Kenneth T. Palmer. 1984. *The Changing Politics of Federal Grants*. Washington, D.C.: Brookings Institution, pp. 108–165.

Friedland, Roger. 1983. *Power and Crisis in the City*. New York: Schocken Books.

Garcia, Chris F. and Rudolph O. de la Garza. 1977. *The Chicano Political*

Experience. North Scituate, Mass.: Duxbury Press.

Garcia, John A. 1979. "An Analysis of Chicano and Anglo Electoral Patterns in School Board Elections." *Ethnicity*, Vol. 6, 22–39.

Gelfand, Mark I. 1975. *A Nation of Cities: The Federal Government and Urban America, 1933-1965.* New York: Oxford University Press.

Gibson, Jr., L. Tucker. 1978. "Mayoralty Elections in San Antonio." *Paper Presented at the Annual Meeting of the American Political Science Association,* Houston, Texas.

Gilbert, Charles E. 1964. "National Political Alignments and the Politics of Large Cities." *Political Science Quarterly*, Vol. 74 (March), 25–51.

Goodall, Leonard E., ed. 1967. *Urban Politics in the Southwest.* Tempe: Arizona State University Press.

Gray, Ralph and John M. Peterson. 1974. *Economic Development of the United States*, Revised Edition. Homewood, Ill.: Richard D. Irwin.

Gutman, Herbert. 1976. *Work Culture and Society in Industrializing America.* New York: Funk and Wagnalls.

Harrigan, John J. 1981. *Political Change in the Metropolis.* Boston: Little, Brown.

Hawley, Willis D. 1973. *Non-Partisan Elections and the Case for Party Politics.* New York: John Wiley.

Heilbroner, Robert L. 1980. *The Making of Economic Society*, Sixth Edition. Englewood Cliffs, N.J.: Prentice-Hall.

Heilbrun, James. 1981. *Urban Economics and Public Policy.* New York: St. Martin's Press.

Hill, David B. and Norman Luttbeg. 1980. *Trends in American Voting Behavior.* New York: Peacock.

Johnston, Robert J. 1982. *The American Urban System: A Geographical Perspective.* New York: St. Martin's Press.

Jones, Bryan D. 1983. *Governing Urban America: A Policy Focus.* Boston: Little, Brown.

Judd, Dennis R. 1983a. *The Politics of American Cities: Private Power and Public Policy*, Second Edition. Boston: Little, Brown.

Judd, Dennis R. 1983b. "From Cowtown to Sunbelt, Boosterism and Economic Growth in Denver" in Susan Fainstein, et al., eds. 1983. *Restructuring the City.* New York: Longman, pp. 172–201.

Judd, Dennis R. 1979. *The Politics of American Cities: Private Power and Public Policy.* Boston: Little, Brown.

Judd, Dennis R. and Francis N. Kopel. 1978. "The Search for National Urban Policy: From Kennedy to Carter" in Theodore J. Lowi and Alan Stone, eds. 1978. *Nationalizing Government: Public Policies in America.* Beverly Hills: Sage, pp. 163–201.

Kantor, Paul. 1974. "The Governable City: Islands of Power and Political Parties in London." *Polity*, Vol. 7 (Fall), 3–31.

Karnig, Albert and Susan Welch. 1980. *Black Representation and Urban Policy.* Chicago: University of Chicago Press.

Katz, Michael. 1968. *The Irony of Early School Reform.* Boston: Beacon.

Katznelson, Ira. 1981. *City Trenches*. Chicago: University of Chicago Press.

Key, V. O. 1949. *Southern Politics*. New York: Vintage.

Kieschnick, Michael. 1981. *Taxes and Growth: Business Incentives and Economic Development*. Washington, D.C.: Council of State Planning Agencies.

Kleppner, Paul. 1985. *Chicago Divided: The Making of a Black Mayor*. DeKalb, Ill.: Northern Illinois University Press.

Ladd, Jr., Everett C. 1970. *American Political Parties*. New York: Norton.

Ladd, Jr., Everett C. and Charles D. Hadley. 1975. *Transformations of the American Party System*. New York: Norton.

Lee, Eugene C. 1960. *The Politics of Non-Partisanship*. Berkeley: University of California Press.

Leven, Charles. 1979. "Economic Maturity and the Metropolis' Evolving Physical Form" in Gary A. Tobin, ed. 1979. *The Changing Structure of the City: What Happened to the Urban Crisis*. Beverly Hills: Sage, pp. 21–45.

Levitan, Sar A. 1985. *Programs in Aid of the Poor*. Baltimore: Johns Hopkins University Press.

Lockard, Duane. 1959. *New England State Politics*. Chicago: Henry Regnery Co.

Lowi, Theodore. 1968. "Foreword" in Harold Gosnell. 1968. *Machine Politics: Chicago Model*. Chicago: University of Chicago Press.

McKay, David H. 1980. "The Rise of the Topocratic State: U.S. Governmental Relations in the 1970s" in Douglas E. Ashford, ed. 1980. *Financing Urban Government in the Welfare State*. New York: St. Martin's Press, Ch. 3.

Mollenkopf, John H. 1983. *The Contested City*. Princeton, N.J.: Princeton University Press.

Murphy, Thomas P. and John Rehfuss. 1976. *Urban Politics in the Suburban Era*. Homewood, Ill.: Dorsey Press.

Nie, Norman H., et al. 1976. *The Changing American Voter*. Cambridge, Mass.: Harvard University Press.

Noyelle, Thierry J. 1982. "The Implications of Industrial Restructuring for Spatial Organization in the United States" in Frank Moulaert and Pokius Wilson-Salimas, eds. 1982. *Regional Analysis and the New International Division of Labor*. Boston: Kluwer-Nijhoff Publishing, pp. 113–133.

Noyelle, Thierry J. and Thomas M. Stanback, Jr. 1984. *Economic Transformation in American Cities*. New York: Conservation of Human Resources, Columbia University.

O'Rourke, Timothy G. 1980. *The Impact of Reapportionment*. New Brunswick: Transaction Books.

Peterson, Paul E. 1981. *City Limits*. Chicago: University of Chicago Press.

Peterson, Paul E. and Paul Kantor. 1977. "Political Parties and Citizen Participation in English City Politics." *Comparative Politics* (January), 197–217.

Piven, Frances Fox and Richard A. Cloward. 1982. *The New Class War*. New York: Pantheon Books.

Pred, Allen. 1977. *City-Systems in Advanced Economies: Past Growth, Present*

Processes and Future Development Options. London: Hutchinson.

Pressman, Jeffrey L. 1972. "Preconditions for Mayoral Leadership." *American Political Science Review*, Vol. 66 (June), 511–524.

Reagan, Michael D. 1972. *The New Federalism*. New York: Oxford University Press.

Robinson, James and Thomas R. Dye. 1978. "Reformism and Black Representation on City Councils." *Social Science Quarterly*, Vol. 59 (June), 133–141.

Rogers, David. 1968. *110 Livingston Street*. New York: Random House.

Sanders, Haywood T. 1979. "Government Structure in American Cities." *Municipal Yearbook*. Washington, D.C.: International City Managers Association.

Sayre, Wallace and Herbert Kaufman. 1960. *Governing New York City*. New York: Russell Sage Foundation.

Schwartz, Barry, ed. 1976. *The Changing Face of the Suburbs*. Chicago: University of Chicago Press.

Sharpe, L. J. 1973. "American Democracy Reconsidered." *British Journal of Political Science*, Vol. 3, Parts 1 and 2 (January and April), 1–28, 129–167.

Smith, Michael D. and Marlene Keller. 1983. "Managed Growth and the Politics of Uneven Development in New Orleans" in Susan Fainstein, et al., eds. 1983. *Restructuring the City*. New York: Longman.

Sorauf, Frank. 1976. *Party Politics in America*, Third Edition. Boston: Little, Brown.

Stephens, G. Ross and Gerald W. Olson. 1977. *Pass-Through Federal Aid and Interlevel Finance in the American Federal System, 1957 to 1977*. A Report to the National Science Foundation. Kansas City: University of Missouri Press. Volume I.

Sternlieb, George and James W. Hughes. 1978. "The New Economic Geography of America" in George Sternlied and James W. Hughes, eds. 1978. *Revitalizing the Northeast: Prelude to an Agenda*. New Brunswick, N.J.: The Center for Urban Policy Research, Rutgers University, pp. 75–128.

Stone, Clarence N. 1983. "Race, Power and Political Change." *Paper delivered to the Annual Meeting of the American Political Science Association*, Chicago, September–4.

Storper, Michael. 1981. "Toward a Structural Theory of Industrial Location" in John Rees, et al., eds. 1981. *Industrial Location and Regional Systems*. Brooklyn: J. F. Bergin, pp. 17–41.

Till, Thomas E. 1981. "Manufacturing Industry: Trends and Impact" in Amos H. Hawley and Sara Mills Mazie, eds. 1981. *Nonmetropolitan American in Transition*. Chapel Hill: University of North Carolina Press, pp. 194–231.

Verba, Sidney and Norman H. Nie. 1972. *Participation in America: Political Democracy and Social Equality*. New York: Harper and Row.

Warner, Jr., Sam Bass. 1972. *The Urban Wilderness: A History of the American City*. New York: Harper and Row.

Watkins, Alfred J. 1980. *The Practice of Urban Economics*. Chicago: University of Chicago Press.

Williams, Oliver P. and Charles Adrian. 1959. "The Insulation of Local Politics under the Non-Partisan Ballot." *American Political Science Review*, Vol. 53 (December), 1058–1061.

Wirt, Frederick, et al. 1972. *On the City's Rim: Politics and Policy in Suburbia.* Lexington, Mass.: D. C. Heath.

Wood, Robert. 1958. *Suburbia.* Boston: Little, Brown.

PART FOUR

The Politics of Development

CHAPTER ELEVEN

The Mainstream of Community Development: The Politics of Economic Dependency

I N earlier eras, urban political leaders frequently launched bold governmental strategies to promote their communities' economic well-being. Yet these efforts were usually quite limited in purpose, scope, and time. They were driven by the expectation that governmental initiatives could secure long-term economic security for the locality within the system of cities. The early canals, the publicly assisted railroads, and even the more limited urban policies of the industrial period constituted such overarching strategies. Thus, massive one-time expenditures for rail links could place an isolated hamlet "on the map" to become an important regional center of commerce. The creation of a magnetic central business district could tie business to the large city during the industrial era.

Urban Entrepreneurship As Public Policy

What most differentiates urban development policy in the contemporary city is the passing of the idea that any "grand strategy" for community economic security is possible. Public intervention in the market has become dramatically open ended because few urban governments are driven by the expectation that any single program or series of one-time initiatives can assure a community's economic future in the old sense. Urban entrepreneurship has tended to replace the developmental strategies of the past. That is, local governments now compete to attract capital and labor by utilizing public policy in ways that assume many of the risks of private enterprise on a more or less continuous basis. They have gone into the "business" of entering fierce bidding wars with other localities by routinely "selling" public authority and resources to the private sector in hopes of attracting and keeping business investment in the locality.

Varieties of Urban Entrepreneurship

OLD CITIES, NEW AUTOS. The range and vigor of the new thrust in urban development policy is illustrated by events in the auto industry. Many of the old cities and states of the industrial heartland have witnessed widespread plant closings; intense competition has broken out among them in a struggle to lure new industries through governmental underwriting of new manufacturing investment. Cities and states in this region have put together expensive packages of development incentives for the auto industry.

For example, during the late 1970s the state of Pennsylvania and local governments succeeded in securing a deal with Volkswagen to move the company's first U.S. production plant to a southwestern site in the state where an incomplete and abandoned Chrysler auto plant was located. The new plant was expected to provide employment for 5,000 auto workers and 20,000 other jobs in an area plagued by high rates of unemployment. But the plant location decision was the culmination of nearly three years of bargaining and bidding between Volkswagen and state and local governments throughout the United States, including governors, mayors, and local officials in Maryland, Ohio, Puerto Rico, Tennessee, Arkansas, Mississippi, Michigan, and elsewhere, all of whom offered VW executives the most attractive packages of industrial development incentives that they could muster.

Pennsylvania's victory at the end of the three-year bidding war came at the cost of over $100 million in state and local government help. This included the building of a $10 million rail spur and a $15 million highway extension to the plant, a $40 million low-interest loan for plant completion, and a $3 million subsidy to train VW workers. VW received millions of dollars of tax abatements from local government. During 1978, when the East Huntington facility was to manufacture over 50,000 cars, VW was expected to pay local government less in taxes than the cost of a single new VW Rabbit. Together with wage cuts agreed to by United Auto Workers (UAW), which put the plant's workers 20 percent below that of other UAW plants, VW obtained what was in effect a massive public underwriting of its first American production venture (Goodman, 1979:Ch. 1). In the end, Pennsylvania officials made a bad gamble with the automaker. In November 1987, VW announced that it was closing its plant in response to poor sales, a decision that sent shocked local and state officials out looking for another corporate occupant for the East Huntington factory (*New York Times*, 22 November 1987:L31).

Ohio has done for Japanese auto makers what Pennsylvania localities did for VW. Competition over the estimated $50 to $60 billion new investment by U.S. auto companies with international operations has led to vigorous entrepreneurship between American and Canadian officials. In 1978, Ontario and Canadian government officials offered the Ford Motor Company $68 million to build a new plant in Ontario rather than in Ohio or Michigan, a decision that Canadian leaders defended on grounds that this was necessary in order to match what Ohio had offered Ford (ACIR, 1981:11). During the 1980s, such governmental rivalries have continued; they included lavish packages of favors and subsidies to Nissan and Toyota during their moves to set up American-based factories, and to lure domestic and foreign auto makers as they have dispersed their facilities. Detroit's struggle to retain existing auto plants has been particularly costly. As described in Chapter 1, its officials employed in excess of $300 million in subsidies and demolished an entire residential neighborhood in order to keep G.M. from building a new Cadillac facility elsewhere.

SMALL TOWN SURVIVAL. Such efforts by authorities to package their locations through business subsidies are so commonplace that even small and medium towns have embarked on costly economic revitalization programs. In western Massachusetts, where years of shrinking job opportunities and successions of plant closings among traditional New England industries have occurred, urban entrepreneurship is widespread. The dilapidated industrial town of Springfield, with its population of a little more than 500,000, managed to rejuvenate its downtown. Office buildings, new retail centers, parking garages, restaurants, and factory conversions mushroomed in the downtown over a brief five-year period, making it somewhat of a model of what middle-size cities can sometimes do to produce an economic turnaround. Yet such success is expensive from the standpoint of public resources. Springfield's downtown renewal required a massive combination of loans, tax subsidies, and new public facilities; governmental sources alone accounted for over a quarter of all new investment in the downtown area—about $200 million within a five-year period (*New York Times*, 9 June 1983:A14).

CITIES AND SPORTS. Urban entrepreneurship is particularly lavish in pursuit of the more footloose industries. With almost no fixed investment aside from fan loyalties, professional big league sports teams are able to employ this advantage to wring substantial deals from cities, including new stadiums, operating subsidies, shares in concessions and parking garages, etc., by threatening to or actually moving to localities offering more advantageous inducements.

For instance, New York City has spent enormous sums attempting to keep its home teams, often without great success. In 1971, the city committed itself to rebuilding Yankee Stadium at an estimated cost of $24 million in order to keep the Yankees from leaving town. But contract clauses, which required that the stadium be equal in all respects with the best new stadiums in other East Coast cities, forced New York to spend $100 million as well as to provide other subsidies to the Yankees (Goodman, 1979:16).

Yet the city has continued to be confounded by team departures to newer facilities and bigger subsidies in neighboring New Jersey. After years of playing in Yankee stadium, the Giants football team left to open their 1976 season in the nearby Meadowlands in a stadium built for them by the New Jersey Sports and Exposition Authority. In 1983, the Jersey Authority lured New York's last big league football team, the New York Jets, to this new $300 million sports complex. The Jets owner rejected the city's offer of a package of incentives valued at $43 million, which included costly renovations to aging Shea stadium, and accepted Jersey's offer of newer facilities and other incentives, such as 50 percent of concession revenues from the sale of hot dogs, beer, and other such items, as well as a portion of parking fees. The team's move later precipitated proposals by New York City officials for building a $200 million domed stadium to regain their competitive edge in the sports business (*New York Times*, 29 September 1983:B20).

Local authorities have been willing to take on such costly ventures not merely because fans look unkindly on politicians who do little to keep the home teams playing, but also because it is assumed that the economic benefits of even heavily subsidized professional sports can exceed public burdens. New York City Controller Harrison J. Golden estimated that when the New York Jets left the city for New Jersey, the city would lose $33.3 million a year. The $33.3 million includes direct losses to the city of $1.2 million in taxes, transit fares, fees, and rent, as well as indirect losses to businesses and individuals of much larger sums (*New York Times*, 29 September 1983:1).

Consequently, cities have come to share many of the financial costs and risks of team owners. Nearly all the stadiums built since 1960 and about 70 percent of all sports stadiums in America are publicly owned (Goodman, 1979:17). It is now quite debatable whether the sports facilities that were to provide a source of revenue for cities are instead a taxpayer burden. New Orleans' Superdome, completed at a cost of $163 million in 1976 in a city that ranks forty-fourth nationally in per pupil spending for education, lost money during the years following its opening; this fate was shared by numbers of other publicly financed sports facilities (Goodman, 1979:17). Intercity bidding wars to subsidize footloose sports teams have left behind such a trail of public debt, empty facilities, and angry fans that some cities have attempted legal action in order to keep teams from exploiting their bargaining advantages. In 1980, the city of Oakland, California, unsuccessfully tried to buy the Oakland Raiders football club by invoking their power of eminent domain before the team could move to Los Angeles. Baltimore sought to bring similar action in 1984 when the Colts football team decided to suddenly move their franchise to Indianapolis where a new stadium and financial incentives awaited them (*New York Times*, 2 April 1984:A14).

Urban Entrepreneurship and the Postindustrial Economy

The spread of public entrepreneurship is linked to the position of cities in the multilocational economy. The tremendous mobility of capital forms the major barrier to local economic development. So long as localities cannot firmly tie many business enterprises to the community's infrastructure and labor force, intergovernmental competition pressures city governments to provide business incentives. In fact, when these policies are targeted at large multilocational firms that hold a dominant position within their industries, the orthodox relationship between cities and business actually is reversed: Public authorities compete to assume many of the risks of business enterprise by offering better services and "prices" to consumer-firms that "buy" the best locations the market system of cities and states has to offer.

Consequently, the growth of public policy techniques for meeting the demands of capital has paralleled the growth of the multilocational firm. Though state and local tax and financial incentives to attract industry have been used since the earliest days of the Republic, they were never particularly important until after the 1930s and did not become very widespread until the 1950s. Then the number of states and localities using these policies took a sharp upswing between 1966 and 1970 and has continued to increase. For instance, the use of municipal revenue bonds to finance industrial projects as a low-cost tax-free source of capital began in 1936 but was not common practice until the 1950s. Now almost every state has authorized them. The first use of loan and loan guarantee programs for industry occurred in New Hampshire in 1955 and now has become a standard tool of public industrial finance authorities in all fifty states and in most major localities (prior to 1929 only a handful of state development authorities existed).

Tables 11-1 and 11-2 suggest the huge growth and scope of this trend in public intervention among localities and states. During the past twenty years or so, both state and local governments have steadily expanded their subsidy practices to a point where business tax incentives and financial assistance are routine matters of public policy. Certain types of subsidy programs have been perceived as so essential that the overwhelming majority of states make them available to new or expanding industry. Industrial development bond financing has become available at the state or local level almost everywhere, firmly locking the public sector into the business of promoting a "partnership" with capital (see also ACIR, 1981:24–27).

Along with the overall growth of governmental aid programs for industrial development has been a remarkable evolution in their scope and form. Ingenious packages of public subsidies to particular businesses can today include such things as publicly financed industrial parks, free or discounted land, full or partial tax abatement on materials, property, and sales, the training of the work force with local and state manpower or educational funds, rail hookups, new highways, sewer systems, and many other forms of direct governmental aid (Levy, 1981; Kieschnick, 1981).

More passive strategies to promote business expansion that do not involve direct subsidies have also grown in favor. Most often this takes the form of low taxes, particularly business-related taxes, in an effort to create a "positive business climate" for industry. The Sunbelt states as a group enjoy the advantages of fewer taxes and lower tax rates compared with other states (ACIR, 1981:14–15). Public officials in the region have tended to sustain this policy as a major development incentive. As one Houston official pointed out,

> Houston has not found the need to stimulate its economy . . . by the granting of special tax moratoriums on property taxes or the offering of industrial bonds through special economic development corporations. The major tax incentive is lack of a state or local income tax (ACIR, 1981:15).

This policy has not been characteristic of only traditional low tax jurisdictions, however. With the economic decline of many cities and states in the

TABLE 11-1 Number of States Employing State and Local Tax Incentives for Industry, Selected Years, 1966, 1978, 1983, 1986

	1966	1978	1983	1986
Corporate income tax exemption	11	21	27	33
Personal income tax exemption	15	19	21	26
Excise tax exemption	5	10	15	18
Tax exemption or moratorium on equipment, machinery	15	28	32	35
Inventory tax exemption on goods in transit (freeport)	32	41	45	47
Sales tax exemption on raw materials used in manufacturing	32	44	46	45
Sales/use tax exemption on new equipment	16	33	39	42
Accelerated depreciation on industrial equipment	9	25	33	34
Tax exemption or moratorium on land, capital improvements	10	23	33	34

SOURCE: "The Fifty Legislative Climates," an annual review published by Conway Research, Inc., of Atlanta in the November–December 1966, January–February 1978, 1984, and October 1986 issues of *Industrial Development*.

Frostbelt, officials in higher than average tax jurisdictions have moved to cap or reduce this disparity in order to better compete in the national scramble for capital. That this has tended to happen at a time of rising unemployment, urban decay, and overall rising demand for social services underscores the extent to which tax policy has become more and more a key development tool.

For instance, New York's state and local tax burden during the 1960s was about 30 percent higher than the rest of the nation, and it continued to mount as the state experienced sharp economic decline. During the 1970s, local and state officials launched a series of measures designed to appeal to business in response to what they perceived as New York's "unfavorable business environment." The maximum personal income tax rate was scaled down from 15 percent to 12 percent on wage income and to 14 percent on investment income. Corporate tax surcharges were abolished. Finally, the legislature did not act to change the level of welfare benefits for nearly ten years, despite rampant inflation during the decade. New York City undertook a parallel program of capping, lowering, or abolishing personal and business taxes following the fiscal crisis it encountered in 1975 (ACIR, 1981:57–58).

INDUSTRIAL LOCATION AND POLITICAL EXTRACTION. Given the tremendous variety of urban entrepreneurial policies, it is difficult to generalize about how effective they are in achieving their objectives. On one hand, numbers of economic studies have suggested that most types of tax and other business incentive programs are not particularly effective inducements to capital relocation. Though the evidence is not conclusive, other factors besides

TABLE 11-2   Number of States Employing State and Local Financial Assistance for Industry, Selected Years, 1966, 1978, 1983, 1986

	1966	1978	1983	1986
State programs				
State-sponsored industrial development authority	25	32	35	38
Privately sponsored development credit corporation	31	34	39	36
State revenue and/or general obligation bond financing	10	22	32	42
State loans for building construction	11	19	27	35
State loan guarantees for building construction	11	14	17	22
State financing aid for existing plant expansion	14	29	34	38
Local government programs (city and/or county)				
Revenue bond financing	28	45	50	49
General obligation bond financing	14	21	29	33
Loans for building construction	8	9	18	29
Loans for capital equipment, machinery	6	6	16	27
Incentive for establishing industrial plants in areas of high unemployment	*	10	25	29
Free land for industry	*	14	18	24
Publicly owned industrial park sites	28	49	49	49

*Not a reported category in report.
SOURCE: "The Fifty Legislative Climates," an annual survey published by Conway Research, Inc., of Atlanta in the November–December 1966, January–February 1978, 1984, and October 1986 issues of *Industrial Development*.

governmental incentives, such as labor, energy, space, and land costs, etc., seem to be of greater significance in capital location decisions under most conditions.[1] On the other hand, such economic analysis does not capture the political essence of urban entrepreneurship. It seems likely that this subsidy practice is not merely an economic process of inducing businesses to do what they might not otherwise do. It is also a *political* process in which a privileged group can *extract* rewards and subsidies for what they ordinarily do. In an economy undergoing major regional shifts of capital and declining locational advantages, these forms of movement and change generate uncertainty about business behavior, giving business in general a powerful political bargaining position with local communities. Local officials cannot easily resist demands for privileges on the part of corporate business as long as similar concessions are conferred by competing governmental jurisdictions.

Evidence for this conclusion is suggested by the fact that local and state governments all over the United States *do* act as if business incentive policies are of major importance to their economies. They vigorously promote their use regardless of economic evidence about their efficacy. The perception among governmental leaders and mass opinion that burdensome taxes and regulations drive out business from localities and that governmental inducements help stimulate economic expansion is well documented (Vaughan, 1979:83–84). Further evidence for the extraction process is the fact that the overwhelming number of governmental business incentive programs are targeted at *existing* industry in hopes that it will expand, not at luring new industries from outside the region (Vaughan, 1979; ACIR, 1981). For instance, New York City attempted during the late 1960s to impose a rise in the stock transfer tax. Threats of relocation and general grumbling by the city's important financial and brokerage community not only defeated the proposal but later led officials to offer tax subsidies in order to improve New York's position as a center of corporate finance (Danielson and Doig, 1982:280–282).

Urban Entrepreneurship and Federalism

The spread of urban entrepreneurship also springs from the growth of federal and state intervention in economic development. Federal policies have stimulated local government entrepreneurship by promoting the development of new regions and suburbs and by inducing localities to undertake entrepreneurial roles. As described earlier, federal outlays for defense, public works, and research and development, together with the national government's vast tax, regulatory, and spending policies, have strongly influenced urban growth. Federal intervention initiated disinvestment from the nation's older central cities while stimulating the development of the former urban periphery (the Sunbelt and suburbia).

Paralleling these indirect forms of federal activity in stimulating greater economic competition among states and localities have been the national programs to deal directly with the developmental problems faced by communities. As national coalition politics since the New Deal forced greater attention to local economic problems, federal intervention has provided little more than a hodge-podge framework of programs that reflected the lack of political consensus among national leaders regarding the regulation of urban development. Consequently, the aggregate impact of these programs has been to reinforce and support local economic competition and entrepreneurial activity, in effect leaving national urban development to be fought out by states and localities.[2]

THE OLD FEDERALISM. From the 1940s to the end of the 1960s, the Old Federalism dominated national activity in the cities. Congress created numbers of categorical grant-in-aid programs that enabled federal officials to induce states and localities to restructure their physical settings in order to cope with the restructuring of the national economy. On one hand, this federal effort stimulated greater urban economic competition by assisting the development of new towns and suburbs. The list of federal tax, regulatory, and expenditure programs that had this effect is almost endless (Solomon, 1980:Part V). Only a few of the more significant ones can be noted here. The massive funds allocated to urban transportation improvements since the 1950s flowed mostly to urban highway construction, rather than to mass transit, in effect subsidizing the opening up of new suburban areas for business and residential expansion (Small, 1985). Similar consequences were produced by the major federal housing programs that provided low-interest home mortgages or mortgage guarantees (see Chapter 10), subsidizing decades of explosive suburban residential growth.

On the other hand, when the federal government explicitly aided the economic development of the central cities, the thrust of policy was usually one of providing resources to enable cities to compete with the new economic communities that other federal policies had helped bring into being. In this regard, the most important initiative was the urban renewal program. This program linked federal resources to the developmental targets of the cities, rather than to national urban goals, and institutionalized entrepreneurship at the local level. As detailed in the next chapter, this program tied federal aid to the willingness of private developers to invest in the opportunities for new housing and commercial projects that city urban renewal authorities provided through their land clearance activities. Urban renewal became a framework for cities to subsidize the reconstruction of their central business districts.

Many other programs to subsidize community economic development that began in the Old Federalism days were less prominent than urban renewal but were highly consequential. Among the most important of these were the federal laws that permit localities to issue tax-exempt industrial bonds. By allowing a municipality to use its tax-exempt borrowing privilege to finance the construction of new industrial plant for private firms, federal tax policy helped support local government competition to attract industry. Though Congress acted to restrict the use of this public-private finance technique on a number of occasions, it has continuously tolerated its widespread practice (Peterson, 1980:410–413).

One of the few major urban aid programs that directed cities to achieve developmental goals that was not as contingent on securing private investment was the Model Cities program that Congress passed in the Demonstration Cities Act of 1966. This Act provided funds for cities to coordinate their physical and social redevelopment efforts away from downtown toward the rehabilitation and preservation of selected poor neighborhoods. But the developmental potential of this program was dissipated as more and more neighborhoods came to participate in it; further, it never grew in funding on a scale sufficient to counterbalance the direction of the other federal initiatives (Frieden and Kaplan, 1975).

In essence, the Old Federalism of categorical assistance to communities did not effectively substitute federal goals for urban development for those of the private sector. Rather, federal programs stimulated the creation of new economic communities and provided subsidy programs that promoted the growth of economic competition among governmental jurisdictions. This left cities dependent on their ability to accommodate the changing demands of capital.

THE NEW FEDERALISM: ENHANCING THE OLD POLICY.   Since the birth of the New Federalism in the early 1970s, federal policy has shifted more explicitly to reinforce urban entrepreneurship. This was accomplished by removing federal restrictions on urban aid programs or by creating new programs whose funding is contingent on loosely regulated private business participation. By relying on block grants or categorical programs that tie federal financial assistance to private sector participation, the use of federal funds is permitted to be decisively influenced by the pressures of urban and regional economic rivalry. Consequently, local governments are pressured by market forces to employ federal aid for entrepreneurial activities, often to the neglect of other social priorities.

Block Grants.   These results are evident in the two major New Federalism programs, General Revenue Sharing and the Community Development Block Grant (CDBG) programs. In both programs, the formulas for distributing funds tend to disperse federal assistance widely among localities rather than to deploy federal aid in ways that compensate only those areas with weak market positions; in fact, there is some evidence that the programs tend to shift funds more to newly developing areas (Fainstein and Fainstein, 1983:19). Most important, the decentralist structure of these programs has worked to facilitate urban entrepreneurship by permitting funds to be spent largely in accordance with the priorities of states and/or localities. Begun in 1972, the General Revenue Sharing Program (GRS) brought billions of dollars of federal aid to local and state governments with almost no strings attached. In probably the best known evaluation of the GRS, Michigan's Survey Research Center discovered that developmental and distributive programs were the local policy areas most heavily funded by local authorities; social services (redistributive programs) were at the very bottom of local government priorities (Juster, 1976:6).

The CDBG supplanted seven previous categorical programs, including Model Cities and urban renewal, with a block grant that has left local governments increasingly free to direct resources to promote their economies. The entitlement cities were subject to only minimal federal supervision under President Ford and moved strongly to use these federal funds to promote their revenue base instead of improving social and housing conditions in their most deteriorated neighborhoods (see Chapters 11 and 16). Between 1977 and 1980, federal regulations required targeting most assistance to low- and moderate-income neighborhoods, among other restrictions. These regulations of the Carter years were largely modified or eliminated under President Reagan, however, and the application and reporting requirements for cities were dramatically reduced (Fainstein and Fainstein, 1983:19; Struyk et al., 1983). As federal oversight has diminished, CDBG has become part of the tool kit of urban economic competition.

Categorical Programs.   Major categorical grant programs that have accompanied the New Federalism deliberately emphasize subsidizing private investment in redeveloping cities. Many cities that had relied on urban renewal funds to promote revitalization found that CDBG provided less federal help for this purpose. Consequently, since 1974 they have had to rely on two new programs aimed at inducing greater private investment to support projects via public subsidy.

The Urban Development Action Grant (UDAG) program, enacted in 1977 and operated by HUD, is similar to the old urban renewal program in that it provides funds on a discretionary basis, but only for economic development projects (which can include land clearance as well as commercial rehabilitation, as in the earlier program). Yet UDAG differs from urban renewal in that it provides funds for projects in economically distressed areas only when much larger private investment in a particular project is committed in advance. In effect, the program constitutes a subsidy for businesses moving to or remaining in distressed urban areas. Highly popular among cities, particularly for building new hotels, convention centers, and other industrial-commercial projects, the program has survived attempts to eliminate it under President Reagan.

The Economic Development Administration (EDA) of the Department of Commerce administers programs that parallel UDAG in that they subsidize economic growth in distress areas. But EDA programs differ in that they condition assistance on the job-creating potential of the project that can be privately or publicly operated. Since cities have often utilized this program to promote growth without creating many jobs for the poor, it functions in a similar fashion to UDAG in supporting entrepreneurship (David and Kantor, 1983).

Urban Enterprise Zones. The most recent turn in national policy proposes to formalize and extend urban entrepreneurship in a new area program structure, the so-called Urban Enterprise Zone (UEZ). The Urban Job and Enterprise Zone Act was sent to Congress in 1982 as the Reagan administration's major single urban initiative. It epitomizes the growing federal role in promoting urban entrepreneurship. The heart of the proposal involves the designation of depressed target areas; businesses in these zones will be provided with substantial packages of tax credits, relief from capital gains taxation, and the suspension of certain regulatory requirements, as well as with the possibility of making the zones free trade areas exempt from import duties. It is probable that the various major federal subsidies would permit a reduction of corporate income taxes in the range of 75 percent or more for businesses located in the zones (Walton, 1982:7).

Most important, the program will induce state and local governments to complement these federal subsidies to the zone businesses. In order to qualify for zone designation, local "contributions" in the form of state and local tax relief, improved public services, suspension of state and local regulations (such as zoning and professional licensing), and public financing of business endeavors are expected of localities by HUD, which would apply an elaborate point system to rank competing applications (Orlebeke, 1982:33). Although the program is expected to target aid to a small number of qualifying zones, the prospect is for a vast extension of the practice. When particular zones gain a competitive edge as a business location, adjacent neighborhoods and nonzone firms are likely to react by demanding an extension of zonal privileges. As the Wall Street Journal commented, ". . . we would like to see it [the federal government] bend its efforts . . . toward developing a set of tax and economic policies that would make the whole country an enterprise zone" (Walton, 1982:12). Already state governments have moved in this direction. Since the federal debate about UEZ, over twenty state legislatures have considered legislation for creating state versions of the federal UEZ model and several, including Kentucky, Connecticut, and Florida, have implemented such programs (Mier and Gelzer, 1982).

STATES AND URBAN ENTREPRENEURSHIP. State governmental activity tends to parallel that of the federal government in sponsoring urban entrepreneurship. Interstate economic rivalries have threatened the job bases of even the most wealthy and populous states and created new regional growth patterns, casting state governments into a struggle for growth similar to that of cities. In coping with these changes, state governments have had to deal with attendant internal economic and political changes. As noted in Chapter 9, the decentralization of business activity, the suburbanization of state populations, and the economic decline of many old central cities restructured the economies of most states. Except in certain areas of the Sunbelt, the state economic base is no longer very coterminous with their central cities (as was often the case during the industrial period).

Consequently, the market position of most states is not strongly tied to the prosperity of their central cities. Together with the heady political power of suburban and exurban jurisdictions, these changes in the state political economy have led to an explosion of demands for state intervention in urban development and have tilted state activities in favor of promoting newly developing areas, particularly suburbia. Legislatures have little choice but to enact programs to speed the restructuring of their economies.

State policies promoting dispersal have included: support for state and federal highway programs; the reversal of policies permitting easy annexation by cities of peripheral areas in favor of liberal authority to facilitate suburban incorporation; laws permitting local autonomy in the control of land use and housing; and state laws that have continued local government dependence on local (rather than state) revenue sources, such as property taxes, user charges, and sales taxes, for funding most local services, including expensive ones such as education. As economic rivalry among cities, towns, and suburbs has grown within states, the demands for state assistance to support local entrepreneurship commonly have proven to be irresistable. Nearly all major public entrepreneurial programs employed by local government are dependent upon state authorization; the pattern has been one of constant growth of their authorization (Shannon and McDowell, 1985).

Economic Conflict between States and Localities. While states generally are highly supportive of local entrepreneurship, they are far more directive in this endeavor than is the federal government—because states are constrained to promote the growth of the state economy as a whole. Consequently, state governments are quick to impose limits on local activities that threaten the smooth functioning of the state economy. Programs such as highway, seaport, mass transit, power generation, and other physical infrastructure projects that are crucial for the development of the whole state economy may well by-pass, disrupt, or even destroy particular localities. Highways do not lead everywhere, nuclear power facilities must be located somewhere, transit programs nearly always need heavy public subsidies to which localities may have to contribute, and so on; such state projects can provoke bitter resistance of localities impacted by them.

Consequently, state governments have erected a set of powerful institutions that are relatively independent of local control which promote the state's own entrepreneurial programs and limit those of the locality. The most widespread institutions of this kind are the state-run independent authorities that commonly are used to build, finance, and operate much of the state public infrastructure. For instance, in New York and New Jersey the Port Authority was created during the 1920s to control seaport and highway development in the New York region. It was deliberately created as a tool for guiding the port's growth independently of the local authorities in the two states and is under firm political control of the governors of New York and New Jersey.

State governments are quick to create new public authorities to capitalize on opportunities for growth that might be lost to feuding localities. As business rapidly underwent dispersal in the tristate New York metropolitan region during the 1950s and 1960s, the State of New Jersey moved to develop for business a vast swampland within a few miles of Manhattan by creating the Meadowlands Commission to plan, build, and finance a sports center and business complex. The commission's activities virtually doomed many older New Jersey towns, but permitted the state to attract large numbers of former New York business tenants (Danielson and Doig, 1982:345).

State highway agencies are undoubtedly the most vigorous promoters of state economic priorities over those of localities. Since highway programs are highly dependent on federal and state funds, state agencies have assumed the commanding role in planning and construction, assuring tremendous leverage over the local governments into whose backyards the highways run. Consequently, state highway planning agencies have established a long record of easy triumphs over local opposition to their projects, even in cases where powerful suburban opposition has attempted to stop or alter state plans (Danielson and Doig, 1982:114–119).

The Public Consequences

Caught in a world of unparalleled economic dependency and intergovernmental stimulation of urban economic competition, cities have become locked into a questionable "partnership" with business: They are promoters of entrepreneurial policies that provide open-ended support for private business activities. That such a developmental policy is illegitimate and wasteful from a public perspective seems beyond doubt.

The Illegitimacy of Policy

This urban development strategy lacks legitimacy in a liberal-democratic order because it shifts onto the public sector much of the risk and expense of ordinary private investment activity without generating public benefits. Unlike local developmental strategies of earlier eras, urban entrepreneurship constitutes a continuous commitment of public resources and authority for routine business purposes. Previously, the well-defined and limited-purpose infrastructure programs (for canals, railways, highways, ports, etc.) that once dominated local development policy had an explicit public objective—generally to supply things that capital could not by itself provide or to regulate private investment for community ends. In either case, public intervention into the market served to generate community benefits that might not otherwise be produced by the private sector left to its own. In contrast, urban entrepreneurship is more like a tribute payment that localities must make to footloose business as the price for community survival. It does not bring public control of the urban economy, nor does it provide things that the private sector cannot produce on its own. It is the socialization of business risk without legitimate public purpose.

The Waste of Public Resources

Urban entrepreneurship generates gross waste of national resources. For one thing, this subsidy practice does not create new wealth; it simply moves wealth. Its function is merely to induce capital investment to relocate or to keep it from leaving a particular jurisdiction. But this cannot add to the creation of net new national productive capacity. Public resources are squandered to attract jobs that would be located in some community anyway.

Urban entrepreneurship also is wasteful because it produces community casualties for whom the public sector ultimately must pay. This reality was evident even in the early nineteenth century when mercantile cities sometimes destroyed each other in canal and railway wars. This consequence is even more apparent in today's developed city system of widespread intercity rivalry. Public investment in schools, hospitals, highways, streets, housing, and other facilities is wasted when capital and labor flee to cities with "better" business climates where these same facilities again must be duplicated. Loser cities are stuck with empty schools, unneeded hospital beds, roadways that lead nowhere, and housing without families as jobs leave town. Their economic decline also sucks in the private sector, as real estate values fall, as customers are no longer there to patronize local shops, and when loans turn sour.

Citizens and businesses everywhere pay for this distress. They do so by having to contribute to national and state programs to aid the jobless and to provide welfare benefits and urban assistance programs, as well as by paying for the duplicate facilities that must be built in order to accommodate the movement of people and jobs into "new" areas.

Local Politics and Economic Dependency: The Tensions of Market and Democracy

Economic development in the contemporary city is marked by persistent tension between market and politics. Cities must promote their growth in a multilocational world where private sector locational decisions can exert unparalleled influence on policy. At the same time, the capability of local governments to generate political support for their economic programs has become more problematic than in the past. The decline of the machine, the spread of reform, and the growing participatory character of urban populations have created conditions favoring greater mass control of the machinery of local government. It is the management of this tension that conspicuously influences politics in the developmental arena.

The Politicization of Development

This relationship between market and politics has the potential to generate serious conflict in local developmental affairs. For one thing, managing the linkages between the locality and the urban economy is a highly politicized process. Urban entrepreneurship mandates continuous governmental intervention in the urban economy, bringing into the public sector issues over the local economy that were once left more to private sector decision making. This opens up many possibilities for communitywide political dispute. Equally important, this form of public policy levies heavy costs on the public in the form of higher taxes, foregone social programs, environmental quality, and public amenities. As community economic development becomes more governmentalized, successes and failures can be traced to urban renewal agencies, public development corporations, and other public authorities.

In addition, the multilocational economy offers multiple pathways to promoting the local economy via public policy. Urban economic competition constrains cities to promote private investment, but the range of alternatives for doing so is vast, opening up possibilities for public conflict. Even old industrial cities may formulate policies that go after various new markets, such as high technology, services, tourism, and the like or initiate programs to stimulate the expansion of existing industries. The creation of state and federal programs to assist job development also expands the field of public choice for cities.

Divisions among Class and Group Interests

For another thing, the impact of developmental policy on specific social interests within the community can trigger political conflict. Compared to other kinds of policies, development programs are capable of generating deep social divisions based on class and pluralist (group) interests (Logan and Molotch, 1987).

First, class conflicts can arise because programs to promote the city's market position ultimately must be directed to the demands of capital in order for public authorities to influence investment activity. This requirement does not mean that the expressed class interests of capital and the class interests of lower income groups must invariably clash—since programs that stimulate urban economic growth *can* benefit all income groups in the form of new jobs, better public services, lower taxes, etc. Nevertheless, because the economic logic of development policy is to reward producer (or revenue-provider) activity, the demands of nonprovider groups may be systematically ignored unless the political system works to take them into account (Swanstrum, 1985:Ch. 10).

In effect, the inherent economic bias of development policy in favor of rewarding capital investment is likely to threaten those social classes having a marginal economic role in the community. To the extent that capital investment in the locality can be increased by programs that diminish the presence or cost of these classes (e.g., through lower wages, demolition of housing for commercial redevelopment, cuts in social services to reduce taxes), class conflict is an endemic feature of the developmental arena.

SOURCES OF INTEREST FRAGMENTATION.   Class cleavage in the development arena overlays other important social divisions in local communities. Development politics cannot be reduced only to a battle between haves and have-nots because there is probably no single development program that can equally serve the interests of the diverse groups that have a stake in management of the local economy (Swanstrum, 1985; Logan and Molotch, 1987). This means that there are compelling pluralistic tendencies in the developmental arena.

City Officials.   City officialdom shares the most general interests in economic policy. The political future of all officials is intimately tied to the capability of the local economy to generate jobs, governmental revenues, and social order; these things, in turn, can enhance political support. Consequently, to some extent urban political authorities are inclined to support whatever economic strategy can promote business growth. Yet this is in itself an insufficient foundation for political cohesion among public officials on many specific issues. Because city government is comprised of officials serving different and often competing bureaucratic and political constituencies, it is unlikely to reflect any single interest. At best, city governmental authorities can be said to be more predisposed than many other interests to favor a broad range of progrowth policies.

The Urban Business Community.   Outside of city government, there are a wide range of potentially competitive interests in the developmental arena. The urban business community includes quite varied (and often rival) interests in city growth. Perhaps the most salient of these is the so-called *downtown business community*, comprised typically of banks, retail stores, newspapers, major corporations, real estate groups, and others, who own large fixed investments in the central business district. Given the immobility and size of their stakes in the CBD, they probably come closest to the city government in sharing an interest in promoting city growth per se (Cox, 1973:Ch 4); consequently, the executives of these businesses frequently participate in local politics (Friedland, 1983:Ch 2; Molotch, 1976; Banfield and Wilson, 1965).

Nevertheless, their capability to unite in favor of pro-CBD growth policies is limited. Unity sometimes proves elusive because city growth alone does not benefit all downtown business equally. For example, the real estate industry tends to see development in terms of promoting increasing property values, an objective that is sometimes perceived as injurious by businesses in high-rent locations or by marginal businesses threatened with physical upheaval occasioned by redevelopment. Moreover, specific CBD development programs can distribute costs in ways that can threaten particular businesses. For instance, between 1946 and 1969, businesses with a stake in New Orleans' French Quarter and tourist attractions formed the bulwark of a large coalition that opposed proposals for a bridge and elevated expressway along the city's historic waterfront. This strategy for promoting better access to the CBD was defeated so often that the business groups promoting the plan eventually gave up in favor of programs consistent with further development of the city's tourist-based economy (Smith and Keller, 1983:137). Conflicts between old vs. new businesses, small vs. large ones, and other patterns of cleavage are an endemic part of downtown business politics in major cities (Banfield, 1961).

Whereas many traditional central area businesses are often united by the immobility of their urban investments, these interests are not always shared by *large multilocational corporations* that are linked more to the world outside the city. Executives of these corporations are less likely to actively participate in the politics of the city (Friedland, 1983:49–50), and they may promote policies that threaten the survival of other businesses. For instance, Denver's spectacular growth into a booming Sunbelt city was stimulated during the 1950s and 1960s through downtown renewal schemes that brought in vast new investment, mainly from major out-of-state corporations seeking investment opportunities in high technology, tourism, insurance, real estate, and sundry other rapidly developing fields. By 1980, these outside business interests displaced local financial institutions from their dominant position in Denver; about half of the downtown business district belonged to outsiders, and nearly all the long-term financing for downtown office buildings was from out of state (Judd, 1983:180–181).

The interests of multilocational corporations in urban development are difficult to generalize about because they constitute far-flung economic empires that utilize particular localities for merely part of their mobile activities. The developmental programs that a multilocational business seeks in a particular urban setting depends on which part of the enterprise is located there. The corporate headquarters "end" of the enterprise may seek an environment of luxury housing, services, public amenities, and skilled labor upon which the corporate staff depends. But the production, distribution, and other "sides" of this corporate animal usually have a stake in supporting very different developmental environments because they do not depend as much on the kinds of governmental services and labor markets required by headquarters. For instance, manufacturing plants have a stake in reducing labor costs and environmental regulations or promoting public subsidies to industrial plant construction, policies that may have little to do with the headquarters activities of corporations in the downtowns of most cities.

Labor. In the case of labor, particular developmental policies may threaten or enhance the positions of workers much as is the case in regard to business. Labor's stake in urban development generally comes down to the bargaining power that organized and unorganized workers can expect to gain or lose as a result of city development strategies; programs that generate more jobs for the local workforce bring with it greater bargaining power in the labor market, in turn opening up opportunities for higher wages, better job security, and more amenable working conditions.

Consequently, the interests of workers in urban development can often parallel that of business, though for different reasons. Large downtown reconstruction projects have often generated considerable support from unions even when they have displaced low-income residents or threatened the jobs of other workers (Friedland, 1983:55-56; Hartman, 1974). By virtue of the same logic, cleavages within labor over development can often parallel divisions within the business community in response to policies that benefit or injure particular businesses; labor unions and their workers are tied to the fortunes of particular businesses within the locale.

One factor most distinguishes labor's interests in community development from that of business, however. While business' influence and benefits can be expected to increase with capital mobility, labor's shrinks. As long as the cost of labor constitutes a large—for many industries the largest (Vaughan, 1979)—and most negotiable component of business activity, the competitive position of local businesses and the city economy depends on minimizing this. Consequently, businesses seeking to enhance their competitive position and city governments attempting to promote their locational advantages can often do so by opposing labor demands and by exacting concessions from workers. For this reason, plant closings and threats of business relocation have frequently moved local governments to side with business demands for a docile, concession-ready work force willing to accept wage cuts (Bluestone and Harrison, 1982:79-80).

Ultimately, therefore, the interests of labor in urban development are far more narrowly defined than those of business and city governments, a fact that reinforces pluralistic tendencies in this arena of local politics. Labor unions seek to increase the demand for labor within the locale via developmental strategies that do not threaten their bargaining positions. Redevelopment of old residential neighborhoods, tax subsidies, government-sponsored loans, industrial parks, and other programs that shift the costs of promoting the community's market position to the taxpayers or isolated groups of residents are preferred to policies that impose costs on labor alone.

Neighborhood Interests.   Neighborhood residents are more likely than any other group within the city to have interests in development that compete with those of city officials, business, and labor. Unlike the other participants, neighborhood residents have political stakes in urban development that are almost wholly bound up in a single immovable resource—residential property and adjacent amenities (Cox, 1973:99). Efforts to promote the locality's economic base can often threaten the social and economic survival of these enclaves. The most frequent residential victims of urban development tend to be lower-income neighborhoods whose geographical location in many large cities (adjacent to commercial and industrial areas), low property values, less skilled workers, and weak political resources make them highly vulnerable to business expansion schemes, highway improvements, and other forms of economic "modernization." Although upper-income neighborhoods also are sometimes threatened by urban development programs (such as commercial construction in well-off residential areas), the rising property values and new housing opportunities that are often precipitated by governmental revitalization programs are likely to benefit these areas. Nevertheless, both low- and higher-income neighborhood residents own interests in urban development that are distinct from those promoted by other major participants, reinforcing the pluralistic tendencies of interests in this arena.

Elite Politics and Developmental Policy Making

Despite the competing class and pluralist interests affected by development policy, policy making in this arena is usually not overtly conflictual because the process of decision making often is not very open and participatory. The pressures of urban economic competition encourage political authorities to limit widespread participation and public influence in decision making. Local governmental leaders cannot effectively promote their community's market position unless their programs "work" in the private sector by inducing capital investment. Policies that do not elicit appropriate responses from private capital also threaten to bring failure to politicians in the form of lost jobs, declining governmental revenues, plant closings, neighborhood deterioration, and cuts in governmental services. This fact discourages public officials from leaving decisions about development to the uncertainties and preferences of popular opinion (or some politically influential segement of it). What particular groups—or even the majority of the citizenry—demand through the political system may well conflict with what is acceptable to the private sector as revealed in market decisions. Consequently, local government leaders are powerfully motivated to limit popular control and to provide business with a privileged position (i.e., granting them preferential access) in shaping developmental policies.

Granting business a privileged position does not necessarily mean local business domination of development policy, however, because local government leaders have a stake in maintaining their own independent policy influence.

First, their need to ensure political support requires that officials at least avoid policies that outrage segments of the public which keep them in power—or fashion them in ways that are politically palatable to groups threatened by the policies. Second, the ability of political authorities to utilize public resources in order to induce investment would dissipate if they became a mouthpiece for business; they would have no privileges or other inducements to trade with business in exchange for capital.

Finally, the locality's market environment constrains local political leaders to prevent entrenched segments of the business community from exploiting their position of power. Many large corporations that can potentially invest capital in the locality are not even likely to be aware of important developmental decisions until after they are taken. While traditional "downtown" business interests with local roots may be in a strong position to exploit their privileged position and make demands, large multilocational corporate business is often at a distance and usually lacks the local organization, personal contacts, and community ties of other members of urban business communities (Schultze, 1961; Friedland, 1983). Local political leaders must govern with an eye on the larger investment community, not just the local one, if they are to be successful.

The upshot is that there is a powerful tendency for urban governmental authorities to insulate the process of economic policy making from popular involvement while struggling against absorption by business. City government is neither a puppet for business nor is it very independent from it (cf. Lindblom, 1977; Elkin, 1981, 1987).[3] Rather, local government elites are constrained to sort out and reconcile conflicts over development with a highly limited universe of "relevant" (or privileged) revenue-producers in ways that avoid opening up matters of decision to widespread public involvement and scrutiny. In essence, they must manage the tension between business productivity and popular control.

Chicago's Convention Hall: An Illustration

The classic case was described by Banfield (1961) in his description of the way Chicago's Mayor Richard Daly sought to manage the economy of that machine city. When business groups, led by the city's leading booster newspaper, began promoting the idea of a new exhibition hall in order to promote Chicago's sagging convention and tourist industry, Mayor Daly avoided taking the lead despite his power at the head of perhaps the most powerful political organization in the country. The major downtown business interests worked quietly and informally during the 1950s to shape an agenda and formulate specific plans for designing, financing, siting, and building a new convention center that was eventually constructed just beyond the south side of the city's Loop (downtown). Virtually all their proposals were eventually approved by city hall and in the state capital with the assistance of the city's Democratic delegation.

The major public conflicts over the exhibition hall were few despite the large public costs of the project. Public conflict arose over the scenic lakefront site selected for the hall, an issue that mostly drew some opposition from downtown businesses who thought the site too remote and from environmental groups attempting to protect the city's parkland. Reluctant to visibly take sides for fear of expanding public debate and participation on the issue, the mayor waited until business and political sponsors privately sorted out their differences on the matter. Then he moved quickly to support and implement the scheme over the objectives of environmental groups who were accorded a single-day public hearing three months after all else had been officially approved (Banfield, 1961:Ch. 7).

Strategies for Limiting Citizen Participation

In seeking to minimize tension between business productivity and popular control, local governments have evolved a number of strategies for limiting public participation in the arena.

GATEKEEPER POLITICS. Undoubtedly the most effective strategy is "gate-keeper politics," i.e., limiting citizen access to the community itself. The demands of citizens and those of authorities promoting community development can become nearly identical if those who reside in the locality are screened to include only those likely to support prevailing developmental programs. In this case, the formal mechanisms of popular control are a meaningless constraint on development; public consensus is assured through controlling local "citizen-ship." Such is the pattern in many socially homogeneous suburban bedroom communities that afford a haven for higher income groups who seek the schools, housing, and other amenities these localities have to offer. As described in Chapter 13, the employment of land use, building, and other controls by these local governments can effectively exclude groups of potential residents whose demands for services and housing are likely to threaten the economic viability of this market strategy. Outside of such suburban areas, gatekeeper politics is more problematic. Nevertheless, elements of this practice are evident in virtually all cities where low expenditures for social services and discriminatory housing policies are utilized to discourage the presence of low-income groups.

INSTITUTIONAL BUFFERS. Another strategy for limiting popular control is the creation of institutional buffers that segregate decision making over issues of development from popularly controlled general-purpose local governments. This is most often accomplished by independent development authorities that are commonly authorized by state legislation to undertake the planning, construction, finance, and operation of ports, highways, bridges and tunnels, mass transit, redevelopment districts, and even more specialized projects, such as subsidized industrial parks, convention centers, and hotels. In most localities, they dominate the administration of developmental programs (Harrigan, 1981:199).

Independent authorities can provide a powerful political buffer because of their political and financial independence from the general-purpose local governments in whose jurisdictions they carry out their activities. Their political independence in part derives from the fact that most of these agencies' officials are appointed, often by state governors, rather than popularly elected (Bollens, 1961), and they tend to be staffed by leading members of the financial and business community with expertise in the projects undertaken by the authority. Where such special districts or agencies are elected, the low public visibility of their decisions, lack of public information about their activities, and the nonpartisan style of their politics discourage very effective public participation. Extremely low voter turnout in the elections of these agencies is the norm, often permitting incumbents to succeed themselves for years (Institute for Local Self Government, 1970; Scott and Corzine, 1963).

An equally important source of autonomy for these authorities is their tremendous financial independence. Rather than relying on resources provided by general local governments, these agencies almost always have the capacity to generate their own revenues, usually without voter approval, from the user charges (such as tolls, bus and subway fares, rents, and license fees) connected with their projects or from gasoline, property, and other taxes they may be empowered to levy. Further, the most common form of financing the activities of these agencies is by issuing revenue bonds, which are backed by the income of the projects (rather than general obligation bonds that are guaranteed by the full faith and credit of the government). Revenue bonds legally tie the user charges and other income of the authority to repayment of the bondholders and usually prohibit diverting the agency's revenues to other governmental purposes. Together with federal grants for which many development authorities qualify, these sources of funds provide a self-generating economic base that affords tremendous independence in developmental decisions.

The most vivid illustration of the power and independence of these authorities is New York's experience under Robert Moses. In the forty-four years in which Moses held public office (from 1924 to 1968), he planned, financed, and built highway, bridge, housing, and other infrastructure projects that transformed the economy of the New York region. Moses' activities displaced hundreds of thousands of people, particularly the poor, whose homes and neighborhoods lay in the path of his projects.

The key to this "power broker's" success was his skillful exploitation of the political potential of the independent authority. Although Moses held numerous (and often simultaneous) positions during his long career, the bedrock of his power was the tolls and other revenues generated by the Triborough Bridge and Tunnel Authority, which he controlled. The latter authority produced far more revenues than needed to meet its obligations to bondholders, permitting Moses to propose and run more and more expansive endeavors. As resources from his projects continued to expand and the demand for highways and other public improvements grew, Moses worked deftly to build a political network, including a long line of mayors and governors, that permitted him to virtually dominate New York City's developmental arena for many years (Caro, 1974).

Since the 1930s, localities have increasingly relied on independent authorities to finance and carry out developmental projects (ACIR, 1964:2–3, 1982:356–360) because this type of agency is a powerful economic tool and valuable political buffer. They are structured to assure responsiveness to the capital investment market by virtue of their specialized purpose, explicit accountability to investors, and their financial independence. This structure also precludes demands on city hall and state capitals from carrying off bit-by-bit those resources that might be allocated to economic development activities.

Particularly in hard-pressed central cities, the trend has been to create novel forms of institutions that can encapsulate development programs and resources. Special tax districts are sometimes used to segregate and plow back revenues generated in designated commercial areas in order to upgrade government services to business there. Tax increment financing allows the increased property tax revenues from a development project to be pledged to repay the costs of the project or to additional development in the project area. Alternatively, through lease financing a public agency leases a facility (such as a sports arena) to an operator who pledges a portion of the profits as rent. This arrangement requires no initial investment of public funds because the original funding comes from private lenders. But both forms of financing require that debts are borne by the public sector if profits fail to reach expected levels.

SOCIAL CONTROL STRATEGIES. When development policies are not segregated from mainstream local politics, governmental decision making can be insulated from mass political pressures through social control strategies. The latter diffuse or channel popular demands on developmental issues, permitting political and business elites considerable independence in decision making.

A most effective technique is to *convert developmental demands into distributive issues*, thereby channeling public involvement into matters that do not affect the substance of developmental policy (Peterson, 1981:Ch. 7). This is often accomplished through administrative mechanisms that fragment the implementation of developmental programs. Local governments commonly carry out large developmental projects through commissions and agencies that are organized on a district, rather than a citywide, basis; they are charged with formulating plans, working with the city to secure intergovernmental aid, and dealing with citizens and businesses within the target district.

While this kind of arrangement affords special access to neighborhood groups directly affected by agency plans, it also excludes others who are not, discouraging the mobilization of citywide coalitions seeking to influence development planning. Equally important, this structure enables developmental programs to be transformed into distributive policies by making the allocation of particularistic benefits, such as the rehabilitation of certain housing blocks, jobs with community agencies, paid work training, etc., contingent on cooperation with district planners. The more articulate leaders of the community can be coopted by being given advisory or even paid roles in the planning process, creating self-sustaining rivalries among neighborhood groups that confound any concerted attempt to mobilize neighborhood power around broad issues.

Such a pattern is evident in New York City's process of revitalizing the South Bronx, one of the poorest and most ill-housed urban districts in America. Since the 1970s, when housing abandonment, arson, physical decay, and the flight of jobs escalated wildly and the proportion of black and Puerto Rican residents grew to a majority of the borough's population, city efforts for coping with this transition have been concentrated in the South Bronx Development Office (SBDO). This special district office evolved elaborate plans for commercial, industrial, and residential revitalization of the area and established an elaborate network of political communication with community organizations and residents in the renewal district.

The thrust of SBDO's approach places commercial and industrial development of the South Bronx well ahead of expanding community social services and housing for residents, a strategy that unofficially forms part of New York City's general policy of opening up vacant land in the outer boroughs of the metropolis through "planned shrinkage" of services and population (Starr, 1976). Mayor Koch has been steadfast in opposing any attempts to increase SBDO's minuscule new housing commitments for the area and has defended the developmental priorities of the agency. "The fact is," declared Koch, "government just doesn't have as much control over economic development as it does over housing. We can build new housing, but we have a hard time persuading business to move there and invest their money" (Gannett Westchester Newspapers, 1979). Nevertheless, the promise of new jobs, the distribution of the limited housing renewal monies in selected areas, and spot neighborhood improvements have been instrumental in winning the broad acceptance of the South Bronx Plan by district residents who participated in elaborate consultative procedures with SBDO (SBDO, 1981).[4]

Apart from using such administrative techniques, popular control over urban development can be limited by *coalitional politics*. Groups that are most likely to oppose programs which enhance the city's market position may be isolated politically by forging an electoral coalition to limit their influence, permitting political and economic elites to shape developmental decisions with relative independence.

One means of accomplishing this is by promoting issues of race, ethnicity, and neighborhood rivalry in order to deflect voter attention from development in favor of other issues and conflicts. This political strategy was perfected during the 1950s and 1960s by Chicago's Richard Daly. His "booster" activities for the city's businesses and ethnic neighborhoods were combined with his segregationist policies in housing and education to win for his Democratic machine a stable broad-based voter following. This coalition included working-class whites, business, newspapers, community organizations, real estate interests, and others, leaving the machine as the only viable political alternative in minority wards in the city (Banfield, 1961). A somewhat similar strategy has been fashioned by Mayor Edward Koch in New York City. His cuts in social programs in combination with bold public entrepreneurial efforts have won wide support from a coalition much like Daly's and have politically isolated New York's minority community (Kantor and David, 1983; Shefter, 1985:Ch. 8).

Growth of minority participation in the electoral systems of many cities has made such traditional coalitional practices less viable, however. But because minority administrations in city hall face the same economic constraints as other cities, they too have taken steps to limit mass influence over development. In this case, however, their secure hold on the black electorate provides a political base for promoting development. As we demonstrate in the next chapter, the symbolic importance of minority control of city hall together with the use of distributive programs can build powerful political loyalties among constituents, enabling control over development to remain in the hands of political and business elites.

The Political Biases of Development Politics

Though developmental issues have the potential to trigger social division along class and pluralist lines, there is a powerful tendency on the part of governmental elites to find ways of limiting the emergence of such conflicts. Constrained to manage these tensions while seeking some control over the economic environment of the locality, city governments are under powerful pressure to resolve this dilemma by insulating developmental politics from widespread popular involvement. Although these efforts are not always success-ful—a matter elaborated in the next chapter—it is an inherent by-product of the tensions that arise from attempts by political authorities to reconcile their market management activities with building political support.

This conclusion raises troubling issues concerning the biases of policy making in the developmental arena. Even though popular control systems provide an indirect constraint on political authorities (citizens can inform and sanction political leaders) in respect to their economic management, other characteristics of this area of public policy discourage the consideration of nonbusiness, nonmaterial social considerations in making governmental choices (Logan and Molotch, 1987:Chs. 3 and 6; Swanstrum, 1985). Urban economic dependency assures business a position of privilege; and this limits developmental choices by the prospective threat of disinvestment. The insular political structure of the arena further reinforces this source of bias.

At worst, highly detached urban political leaders may take a slavish probusiness attitude toward public questions, if for no other reason than that they are inclined to respond most to those who are in a position to be heard and whose cooperation they must value highly in promoting the locality's market position. At best, governmental leaders seem likely to ignore important public considerations—such as getting the best deal possible from business, safeguard-ing the social quality of urban life, preserving valued neighborhoods, minimizing social upheaval, and protecting the vulnerable and disadvantaged. Indeed, whether economic growth itself is worth a possible trade-off in social costs or in foregone humanitarian achievements is a consideration that the politico-economic structure of this arena is currently not usually set up to debate very fairly.

The Politics of Urban Economic Dependency

Widespread urban economic competition, generally supported by federal and state policies, has prompted localities to seek capital investment through unprecedented business incentive programs. The local public sector has come to routinely absorb many of the risks of business activity, leading to costly "partnerships" between business and local governments that are of debatable public advantage. Thus, the politics of development takes place within a sphere of policy choices made narrow by the pressures of urban economic competition.

At the same time, economic dependency in an era of popular participation has made the management of tension between market and politics a central theme in the developmental arena. Faced with the dilemma of promoting their localities' market position while contending with the social divisions that are inherent in this area of policy, urban political leaders are pressured to insulate the shaping of development policy from widespread public involvement. There are strong tendencies for popular control of policy to be limited, indirect, and uncertain.

These mainstream tendencies in urban development should not obscure how the postindustrial political economy has created important differences among localities, however. The changing structure of the new economic order has created different market positions for particular cities, towns, and suburbs; intergovernmental programs powerfully assist some localities more than others and steer them along varied developmental pathways. Finally, differences in local political systems and in the social composition of communities are reflected in this area of local policy. While the complex impact of these forces defy sweeping generalization, their importance can be illustrated by examining some localities that share quite different politico-economic circumstances: the older central cities of heartland America, the suburbs that surround these metropolises, and the rapidly developing cities of the Sunbelt. To these we now turn.

Endnotes

1. Many economic studies have found most local and state business incentive programs ineffective (Schemenner, 1980:463-464; Bluestone and Harrison, 1982:185; Vaughan, 1979; Watkins, 1980:Ch. 2; ACIR, 1967) in meeting their avowed goals. In particular, most of these studies argue that such programs:
   a. Are likely to add little or nothing to growth of the overall economy and merely shift capital to different locations to the extent that they are all effective. Further, the supposed competitive advantages gained by localities in using business incentive programs diminish as they become widely adopted and cancel out their inducement effects.
   b. Are often ineffective because other locational factors are of greater importance to business decisions, particularly labor costs and quality, territorial proximity to markets, space needs, energy costs and requirements, etc.

c. Do not induce much capital movement because interregional and interstate movement of businesses, particularly manufacturing plants, is an uncommon experience. For example, one study by the Advisory Commission on Intergovernmental Relations of major manufacturing establishment moves among states between 1969 and 1976 found that the number of such decisions averaged about 5,000 per year, divided equally between new single establishment locations and new branches of existing firms. Since the universe of major manufacturing establishments in 1969 was about 140,000, the ACIR concluded that the interregional movement of such firms is extremely small (ACIR, 1981: Ch. 5; Vaughan, 1979:19).

On the other hand, there is evidence that differences in the rates of economic growth among states and localities are linked to state and local tax and expenditure policies (Joint Economic Committee, 1981; Armington, Harris, and Odle, 1984:108–143; Hicks, 1985). Also, certain types of governmental business incentive programs are more effective in inducing capital and population movement, particularly among neighboring states and localities. For example, there is some evidence that state differences in personal income tax may affect the movement of households among political jurisdictions, thereby affecting employment levels; further, governmental inducements to stimulate business seem to be of greater consequence in regard to intrastate and neighbor state development patterns (Vaughan, 1979:72–73).

One should be wary of the significance of findings on both sides of the issue, however. Assessing the effectiveness of any particular business incentive is problematic, a point conceded by virtually all students of the subject. Not only are the developmental effects of particular incentive programs difficult to isolate in economic studies—partly because it may take years or even decades for the direct and indirect payoffs to materialize—but also because the cumulative effects of numbers of business incentive efforts (the so-called positive business climate effect) are difficult, if not impossible, to ascertain (Soloman, 1980:463–464; Watkins, 1980:Ch. 2; Vaughan, 1979; ACIR, 1981).

2. The lack of an explicit national urban policy can be contrasted with the postwar British experience, which emphasized greater national restriction on urban population movement and business development as well as the use of compensatory expenditure and tax programs to assist needy localities (see Griffith, 1966; Cullingworth, 1972; Hall, 1973).

3. Public officials remain accountable to the indirect influence of public opinion even under these circumstances (Dahl, 1961). But this check is depreciated to the extent that economic constraints motivate governmental elites to minimize this influence and by the economic dependency of local governments that impose market sanctions which discourage some alternative policy choices.

4. The authors' participant observation during some of the meetings sponsored by SBDO in 1981 vividly confirmed this conclusion. At one meeting, a participant objected that the scale of housing that SBDO was planning ought to be increased in light of the growing need for housing in the borough; SBDO proposed to replace or rehabilitate only a tiny fraction of the deteriorating housing stock in the program area. He was shouted down by irritated residents who regarded the speaker as obstructive. They wanted city officials to elaborate their proposals and timetables for rehabilitating particular buildings and streets. To most residents, the meeting was an opportunity to bargain over the allocation of individual housing benefits, not a chance to influence the plan itself.

CHAPTER TWELVE

Central Cities: The Politics of Economic Decline and Conversion

D EVELOPMENTAL politics in the central cities of the nation's heartland has been shaped by three compelling transformations in their postwar political economies. First, the fundamental economic change with which most of these cities have coped has been the dispersal of jobs and population to alternative locations, together with the decline of older industries. For most of these localities, this has meant fairly steady relative decline in their market positions within the urban system, as suggested previously. This process of economic change has compelled these cities to undertake efforts to restructure their economies, mainly by promoting conversion from industrial to service-based activities. Such an effort has, in turn, required dramatic alterations in their physical structure, their employment mix, and their neighborhoods.

Second, central city governments have generally experienced increasingly severe tension between popular control and development policy as a result of changes within their political systems. As described earlier, in America's old core cities social polarization and mass political mobilization have grown to substantially revitalize the democratic features of urban politics. This has created greater political leverage then ever before for groups who are highly dependent on the process of popular control for obtaining. influence over governmental decisions.

At the same time, however, the capability of city governments to respond to mass demands on matters of development has become challenged by the economic power of revenue–provider groups, particularly urban business. Increasing capital mobility at a time of central city economic decline has strengthened their systemic power in local politics, affording them a strong position of influence over public policy independently of the process of popular control. Consequently, city governments have had to manage their economic decline and conversion in a process that centers on accommodating these dual sources of pressure.

Finally, these patterns of change in city development have been substantially reinforced by intergovernmental programs. Federal and state intervention in the economies of central cities has mainly supported tendencies toward economic conversion without measurably opening up the arena to greater popular control.

These three themes emerged during the two major periods of developmental politics since the end of World War II. The first extends from the 1940s to the late 1960s, when city governments initiated conversion by promoting the physical reconstruction of their central cores. The second period began after 1970, when changes in the political economies of many cities altered this political agenda and redirected the politics of conversion.

Urban Renewal and the Politics of Reconstruction, 1949–1969

During the decade following World War II, most old core city governments began their search for ways of responding to the adverse economic trends that challenged their traditionally secure economic positions. Growing suburbanization, business dispersal, and decline in manufacturing employment most seriously threatened their vital downtown central business districts. Aging commercial and industrial structures, lack of vacant land, crowded streets lined by numbers of small, marginal businesses, and dilapidated surrounding areas of mixed residential and commercial use typically dominated the profiles of these districts. Creatures of the industrial age, their physical obsolescence was usually compounded by their inaccessability from increasingly distant commuter populations. For central cities to diversify their economies and attract new capital investment, the revitalization of the strategic CBD was crucial.

The policy alternatives for pursuing downtown conversion were limited, however. Few, if any, cities were capable of undertaking the enormous costs of a very comprehensive effort. Even many businesses with large stakes in the central business districts of large cities, such as department stores, stood back from cooperating in locally funded efforts to clear and rebuild deteriorating central city areas, and they began to decentralize their own operations to suburban areas in pursuit of consumer markets. Endeavors by some city governments to revitalize their transportation infrastructures as a means of improving access to the central city began in the postwar years but eventually proved unsuccessful as a major urban development strategy. During the 1940s and 1950s, some large city governments, usually working through state and regional authorities, took over rapid transit systems from deficit-ridden private corporations. But the enormous cost of maintaining and improving these systems was almost always borne by the localities themselves, and efforts to "regionalize" this burden nearly always ran up against a wall of suburban opposition (Lupo et al., 1971:Ch. 16). Further, the lack of much federal support for mass transit, together with the expenditure of vast federal funds on urban and intraurban highways, virtually locked cities into a transit network that favored the dispersal of industry and population to the disadvantage of the downtowns of large cities.

Urban Renewal: The Federal Bulldozer

Consequently, the federally sponsored urban renewal program assumed major importance in supporting the postwar development efforts of cities during the several decades following its enactment in 1949. Although this program cannot be credited with shaping the goals of city development policy—since the decline of city economies left little choice other than to attempt conversion—it did provide funds and authority for cities to begin physical conversion of their downtown cores to serve as new service centers for the multilocational economy. City governments were empowered to purchase large areas of central city land through eminent domain in accordance with a federally approved plan. Once federal approval was secured (on a project-by-project basis), the local urban renewal agency would clear the land, provide appropriate public infrastructure, such as roads, street lighting, schools, etc., and then resell the land at a write-down (or discount) to private developers or, more rarely, to another public authority that could construct public housing on it. The federal government paid for up to two-thirds of the difference between the city's cost of the land aquisition and preparation and the revenues that the city received from the resale of land to developers.

URBAN RENEWAL AND CITY ECONOMIC DEPENDENCY. The federal program was structured to promote local development goals without imposing on cities many restrictions to regulate the social consequences of urban renewal. While urban renewal officially had certain housing objectives, these housing provisions did not check forces of economic dependency that worked to give the program a highly developmental thrust, to the neglect of other social considerations. Most important, the ability of urban renewal agencies to successfully redevelop land they cleared was tied to the private market for central city land development, not to publicly defined social priorities. Urban renewal agencies were expressly forbidden to redevelop the land parcels they cleared, and, unless developed by another public housing agency with resources of its own, new construction depended upon the willingness of private developers to invest in such construction. Given the prospects of most central city economies, however, even cleared land offered at a discount to private developers did not attract large numbers of buyers, particularly those who saw any profit in building low-income housing.

Accordingly, during the first years of urban renewal few projects were initiated, and throughout the history of the program urban renewal agencies in many cities were plagued by difficulties in finding developers. One result of this was that subsequent federal legislation consistently loosened up the residential requirements of the original 1949 Act, permitting larger and larger percentages of the federal capital grant to be used for nonresidential purposes (10 percent in 1954, 30 percent in 1959, and 35 percent in 1965).

Further, the developmental character of the program was reinforced by the reluctance or inability of local housing authorities to build low-income housing. Of the initial six-year public housing authorization, only one-quarter was ever built; in 1954, the authorized level of federal public housing was severely cut back and then increasingly replaced by other housing programs that were not legally tied to a city's urban renewal program and were generally ineffective in producing much new low-income housing (Friedland, 1983:81).

Finally, even the obligation of urban renewal agencies to provide adequate housing for those residents who were displaced by their slum clearance programs did not force the agencies to substantially deviate from developmental objectives. As cities implemented their slum clearance and reconstruction efforts, thousands of slum residents were forced to scatter to more overcrowded and often more expensive housing as relocation departments found that they were unable to find suitable alternative accommodation for them. Since urban renewal was not connected in tandem to a program of public housing construction, renewal agencies were compelled to ignore the devastating displacement problems that their land clearance schemes created or simply abandon their renewal efforts altogether. In the end, renewal agencies charged ahead, and in cities all across the country they earned an abysmal reputation for tenant relocation.

URBAN RENEWAL AND CITY ECONOMIC CONVERSION.   The process of conversion to a viable service economy required several physical changes in the central areas of the old heartland cities. It required assembling land for extensive new commercial development appropriate to an office economy; it required the demolition of deteriorating housing that typically surrounded downtown cores, blighting the possibility of commercial reuse; and it required the construction of more high-income housing in central locations for the skilled office workers on which a service economy is dependent. In general, urban renewal became directed to these objectives as cities, aided by federal funds, poured money into their projects. By 1971, local governments had invested $3.9 billion of their own resources (21 percent of total public and private investment in renewal) into public construction in renewal sites (Friedland, 1983:84).

First, city urban renewal agencies managed to take over and convert to new nonresidential use vast sections of their downtowns. Relying on powers of eminent domain, city governments were able to force individual owners of small, fragmented land parcels to sell out and permit the assembly of large parcels for clearance and redevelopment. For the majority of cities, residential reuse of the cleared land was not prominent, accounting for only about one-fifth of the planned use of central city urban renewal lands between 1949 and 1966; commercial, industrial, public-institutional, and public infrastructure (e.g., streets, public rights of way, etc.) accounted for the remainder (Friedland, 1983:81).

Second, the clearance projects opened up opportunities for new development while displacing economically "peripheral" businesses and populations. Most of the central city cores that were the major target of renewal tended to be disproportionately nonwhite, poor, and had aging, low-quality rental housing; small business proprietors had hung tenaciously to these central locations because of the low rents and ethnic clientele in the areas (Anderson, 1964; Zimmer, 1964; Friedland, 1983).

Finally, redevelopment enhanced the skilled labor market of cities by creating new higher income enclaves in the core areas while displacing those who were becoming redundant to the central city economy. Because redevelopment was so closely tied to the ability of the private sector to gain a high return from their investment and because local and federal officials were eager to maximize the productivity of their public investments, residential construction on urban renewal sites heavily favored luxury building at the expense of low-income housing (Bellush and Hausknecht, 1967). Typically, urban renewal destroyed large amounts of low-income housing and resulted in new housing that only the more affluent could afford. In the years through 1967, urban renewal demolished 404,000 dwelling units, mostly those that were inhabited by low-income residents. But these were replaced by only 41,580 housing units that could be afforded by low- or moderate-income families (and only 26 percent of these were in heavily subsidized public housing). In effect, 90 percent of the low-income housing stock demolished by the urban renewal bulldozer was not replaced. This emptied much of the central cores of cities of poor, nonwhite residents, forcing them to scatter to other areas of cities (Fried, 1971:88–89; Friedland, 1983:85).

The Philadelphia Story. Urban renewal in Philadelphia illustrates this pattern. Initiated in 1948, by 1965 it was heralded as one of the most successful downtown renewal programs in the country. After World War II, central Philadelphia was dominated by physical and social features characteristic of the industrial era. Old manufacturing lofts, warehouses, wholesaler and distributer outlets, and aging public infrastructure facilities dominated land use in the core; the space adjacent to the most prominent building in the city, city hall, was occupied by the terminal of the Pennsylvania Railroad. In and around the CBD of the city were areas of poor minority and white working-class residence.

Philadelphia's urban renewal transformed this core. By the 1960s, it stimulated a downtown building boom that replaced the old center with new office buildings, restaurants, tourist parks, hotels, specialty shops, university campus facilities, and thousands of luxury housing units. Land values in the central city increased as new building uses opened up and the deteriorating property in close proximity to the CBD was demolished. The transportation structure was changed as narrow streets, railroad tracks, and wharves were demolished to make room for parking lots, underground railway tunnels, and wider streets. The city's new physical pattern of concrete skyscrapers interspersed with plazas, malls, and historic districts was symbolized by the construction of a new complex called Penn Center, which occupied the space previously taken by the terminal of the Pennsylvania Railroad. The railroad, which previously was the bedrock of the Philadelphia economy, redeveloped the old terminal property for use by banks, insurance companies, and other office and commercial establishments that conformed to the new service character of the business district. Complete with a skating rink, Penn Center became known as the "Rockefeller Center" of Philadelphia (Kleniewski, 1984:207).

Urban renewal also changed the social character of the population in and around the central city from predominantly working-class, poor, and minority neighborhoods to enclaves of predominantly white, middle- to upper middle-class and professional residents. Within the central area, urban renewal eliminated extensive neighborhoods, such as the Triangle, skid row, and parts of Chinatown, with mostly poor, working-class populations, aging industrial buildings, and small shops. Although some public housing for low-income families was constructed, twice as much land was developed for private housing particularly suited for affluent groups, such as lawyers, business professionals, doctors, managers, and government workers. Besides the upper-income housing constructed on urban renewal land itself, the program stimulated a process of "gentrification" that lasted long after urban renewal had run its course. Many working-class neighborhoods near the CBD began to attract higher income residents. As the professional work force of the city increased, conveniently located housing for this group became scarce. Eventually, individuals, real estate speculators, and developers began to take over nearby working-class housing, forcing out the people who had been living there (Kleniewski, 1984:211).

In other cities with ambitious urban renewal programs, the results were very similar to those in Philadelphia. Most major cities used urban renewal to stimulate change to a service-based economy in their central districts, removing industrial era buildings, constructing new offices, and displacing segments of their low-income populations in favor of new, higher priced housing for skilled workers (Fainstein et al., 1983; Mollenkopf, 1983; Wilson, 1966; Caro, 1974).

Urban Renewal Politics

The dilemma for these city governments was that urban renewal offered the possibility of enhancing their community's market position at the cost of threatening important political interests. Within renewal areas, lower income residents stood to lose their homes while neighborhood shopkeepers and hosts of smaller businesses faced displacement.

Urban political leaders frequently feared the electoral uncertainties that urban renewal was bound to unleash. At a time when urban party machines were rapidly decaying and party bosses were being forced to broaden their base of electoral support, urban renewal promised to do no less than demolish many of the inner-city neighborhoods of their more reliable supporters and to initiate uncertain citywide patterns of population change. Similarly, liberal reform politicians and their "good government" allies in professional and civic groups who were struggling against traditional bosses to capture control of big city party organizations saw that urban renewal complicated their drive for power. Massive neighborhood displacement and upheaval in low-income communities could challenge the reality of their liberal ideological appeals for more "progressive" local government (Wilson, 1963). Finally, unions could not be unequivocal about the prospect of urban renewal because it threatened to displace unionized blue-collar jobs (Hartman, 1974:65). In effect, urban renewal could not help but precipitate powerful tension between economic growth and political support for city government.

THE RISE OF PROGROWTH COALITIONS. Nevertheless, the prospect of economic decline without redevelopment compelled city governments to find ways of defusing potential political upheaval and neighborhood opposition. Consequently, cities embarking on core area redevelopment typically underwent remarkable political change. Major power brokers closed ranks in order to build a broad coalition to support urban renewal and control its political repercussions. In cities where large redevelopment programs were launched, so-called progrowth coalitions emerged in support of urban renewal. Typically, they included large downtown business interests, particularly large corporations, department stores, and financial institutions, "progressive" reform mayors and political party leaders, "good government" groups and professional city planners, labor unions, and private development interests, including developers, real estate groups, lenders, and builders (Mollenkopf, 1983). This coalition not only comprised diverse groups whose constituencies were often quite hostile to each other on other issues; as suggested above, it also included many who saw serious political risks and losses from central area redevelopment.

Sometimes the lead in forging these coalitions was undertaken by corporate-sponsored policy organizations representing businesses with fairly unambiguous stakes in promoting reinvestment in the central areas of their cities. In San Francisco, urban renewal planning was launched by the Bay Area Council and its Blythe-Zellerbach Committee; in Los Angeles, the Downtown Businessman's Association; in Chicago, the Central Area Committee; in St. Louis, Civic Progress; in Philadelphia, the Greater Philadelphia Movement; in Pittsburgh, the Allegheny Conference; in Boston, the Civic Conference (Friedland, 1983:91).

Generally, these and similar business groups met privately, worked out more or less comprehensive development agendas and plans, consulted with public officials and then ". . . presented the plans to the press, the politicians and the public as their contribution to civic welfare" (Banfield and Wilson, 1965:267–268). Elsewhere, mayors and other prominent political figures were the instigating forces in launching urban renewal, as in New Haven where Mayor Edward Lee pulled local merchants and businesses into one of the nation's bolder schemes and, in New York City, where Robert Moses was a catalyst.

Exactly which sets of leaders—business or political—initiated renewal is less significant than the fact that a broad array of interests from both sectors supported it, signaling the similar economic constraints to which local business and political actors were subject. Harsh economic and political realities shared by nonbusiness members of urban renewal coalitions motivated their participation. First, the threat of central area economic decline prompted mayors, party leaders, reform leagues, planners, and trade unions to support some affordable program that had business support. Second, the forging of a broad-based coalition around the program permitted the containment of the adverse political repercussions of redevelopment by politically isolating those most likely to suffer the greatest costs of the program, particularly low-income residents and small businesses in and around renewal neighborhoods, as well as some blue-collar unionists.

To both traditional machine bosses struggling to hold on to power and to liberal reform mayors seeking to consolidate their positions of ascendancy, a political consensus on redevelopment diffused the issue of responsibility for the displacement of residents and businesses in renewal areas. This limited the political damage that a neighborhood backlash against city political leaders might cause. Further, both machine and reform politicians could associate themselves with the "progressive" cause of business and good government groups in the hopes of broadening their electoral followings among better-off voters supportive of community boosterism. Thus, urban renewal drew the vigorous support of old-style bosses like Mayor Richard Daly in machine Chicago (Banfield, 1961; Rossi and Dentler, 1961) as well as new-style reform mayors like New Haven's Edward Lee (Dahl, 1961).

To the unions, joining a broad-based coalition was also attractive because it enabled city labor movements to overcome the divisions between blue-collar unionists who stood to lose jobs and those unionists who expected to gain jobs from redevelopment. Given the prospect that urban renewal could prevent industrial relocation and perhaps increase employment, joining a citywide coalition would help isolate and overcome unionists who opposed labor support for the program. As a result, union support for urban renewal was obtained easily in most cities (Hartman, 1974; Edgar, 1970; Kaplan, 1963; Dahl, 1961; Williams and Adrian, 1963).

CONTAINING POLITICAL DISCONTENT. While the formation of broad-based coalitions supporting urban renewal worked to isolate political opposition to the program, city governments and urban renewal allies still faced the prospect of determined opposition from displaced residents and small businesses in the course of implementing the program. Once the devastating effects of bulldozing entire neighborhoods became apparent, neighborhood opposition was expected to mount. The renewal coalition could crack in response to disagreement over the social consequences of such large-scale redevelopment. City governments countered by organizing the political structures for implementing urban renewal plans to make it very difficult for political opposition to form, initiate alternatives, or otherwise block the program.

First, broad consensus in support of urban redevelopment enabled city governments to delegate tremendous power to urban renewal bureaucracies whose task it was to formulate specific projects and carry out land clearance. Eager to get on with the job, city governments usually provided local urban renewal staffs with the technical and administrative resources needed to internalize most of the planning, execution, and evaluation of their projects. This freed the agencies from dependence on local planning commissions, technical departments, and other city agencies that might compete to influence project planning, and it enabled them to fend off local criticism (Kaplan, 1963). In fact, in most large cities urban renewal and public housing were undertaken by different agencies. This separation meant that public housing authorities, whose responsibilities for providing low-income housing placed them in a position of having to deal with the political consequences of the displacement of low-income residents, had little authority over the renewal agencies (in fact, they were dependent on them for supplying public housing sites) and were in a weak position to represent this constituency. Moreover, the separation of urban renewal and public housing ensured that neighborhood opposition to clearance could not be easily fused with the mobilization of low-income groups for the provision of public housing (Friedland, 1983:101).

Second, the dependency of city governments on federal approval of their program and on the participation of the private sector in their projects worked to insulate redevelopment planners from scrutiny and challenge by neighborhood groups, other city bureaucracies, and even some public officials. Unless private sector investors were willing to redevelop urban renewal sites, the redevelopment agencies would be left with vacant land and plans left on the drawing boards. Similarly, federal funds would not be forthcoming unless renewal agencies gained federal approval, a process that invariably meant undertaking step-by-step negotiations with federal authorities, negotiating the labyrinth of federal regulations, and winning the confidence of the national and regional Housing and Urban Development (HUD) officialdom. In effect, the real "planning" of urban renewal centered on local redevelopment authorities undertaking negotiations to attract private developers and win the confidence of federal authorities.

These circumstances enabled renewal authorities to become highly independent in their activities. Extensive involvement in redevelopment planning by those outside of the renewal authorities, particularly by those whose neighborhoods were targeted for clearance, could create political uncertainty, cripple the authority's negotiating position, upset delicately forged deals, and drive away investors. This situation almost invariably enabled renewal planners to seize (with city hall backing) a dominant role in defining project priorities, securing developers, negotiating land prices, land uses, and most other issues before renewal plans were announced to targeted neighborhoods and even to some city officials. Once plans were announced, they were difficult to challenge and amend without unraveling the heap of complex agreements with private investors and federal officials upon which the city's program depended.

Urban Renewal Politics in Newark. The experience of Newark, New Jersey's urban renewal program during the 1950s under Louis Danzig exemplifies this process. Under Danzig's leadership, the Newark Housing Authority (NHA) undertook to clear massive tracts of slum housing with little more than random interference from other local interests, including those who were displaced from their neighborhoods. Danzig's NHA alone provided the initiative for the city's clearance projects. It was the city's sole representative in undertaking preliminary negotiations to attract private developers for Newark's program and to secure federal approval. Negotiations were rarely ever made public, and few, if any, people outside of the NHA had direct dealings with developers. Most local participants first learned of a new clearance project when they read about it in the local newspapers. NHA officials safeguarded the secrecy of their negotiations for fear that leaks would excite opposition in target neighborhoods and discourage investors who insisted on the privacy of their activities.

Once a plan was formulated, NHA formally announced it to the press for city council consideration, frequently on the eve of a federal deadline. By this time the pressure on the city council to approve most NHA proposals was overwhelming. Given the maze of carefully prepared understandings and agreements among developers, federal officials, and relevant city agencies, the city's urban renewal projects were effectively "frozen," leaving little more for the council than a "take it or leave it" choice—a choice that they almost always took rather than left (Kaplan, 1963:28–43).

While this style of operation in Newark was not always duplicated in other large cities, renewal agencies elsewhere were usually able to politically insulate redevelopment and overcome local opposition (Bellush and Hausknecht, 1967; Mollenkopf, 1983; Hartman, 1974; Fainstein and Fainstein, 1983; Caro, 1974; Hays, 1972). In cities where urban renewal started late and achieved less impressive results, this outcome seems to be related more to political disagreement at the elite level than to the influence of neighborhood opposition. For instance, in Oakland, city hall was unable to launch a program for years as a result of disagreement among governmental leaders in the city's fragmented, reformed governmental system (Hays, 1974:113–114).

The Development Arena Since 1970: Urban Entrepreneurship and Political Transition

The Exhaustion of Urban Renewal As a Public Policy

During the 1970s, the developmental arena in most large central cities underwent substantial transition because of the political and economic exhaustion of urban renewal as a form of urban entrepreneurship. For one thing, the local political relationships that supported urban renewal had weakened. After 1966, large numbers of cities began to experience civil disturbances and demands by the poor for greater participation in urban governance, particularly in the running of programs that were having the greatest impact on their neighborhoods. Almost uniformly, urban renewal was targeted by minority groups as a major source of discontent. The consequences of this included the slowdown of demolition progress in residential areas and attempts to include and consult with neighborhood opposition groups in renewal activities, as well as expanding housing rehabilitation and public housing construction in later stages of redevelopment. Another consequence was the weakening of progrowth coalitions. Big city party organizations and liberal Democratic mayors were forced to deal with upheavals in their political constituencies as civil disturbances mounted, criticisms of the social consequences of urban renewal grew, and the flight of businesses and white families to suburbia accelerated. City governments were forced to seek new means of achieving economic conversion that could accommodate increasing political and racial polarization.

Further, federal officialdom moved to limit the economic utility of urban renewal for cities. As political opposition grew at the local level and the Johnson administration made efforts to rebuild its urban political base, the Democratic Congress blocked efforts to continue to expand the size of nonresidential exceptions in project plans and required housing-oriented projects to specifically provide for low- and moderate-income families. For the first time since its inception, HUD issued guidelines that insisted that localities give the program a pronounced social focus. Subsequently, local renewal authorities were forced to pursue housing rehabilitation and preservation with more vigor, demolish less, and consult more with project area residents (Sanders, 1980).

Apart from urban renewal's growing political obsolescence, it was also becoming economically outworn. In cities that had fashioned large renewal programs, downtown redevelopment had largely fulfilled its mission of setting into motion the process of economic conversion. Vast slum areas had been demolished, new commercial and residential opportunities on vacant downtown land were in place, and the process of social "upgrading" in residential neighborhoods adjacent to renewal sites had begun. For example, in Boston's South End renewal area abandonment and private housing rehabilitation removed far more low-rent housing units from the city's stock than the Boston Redevelopment Authority itself did after 1965—even though the BRA's plans had not yet been completed (Mollenkopf, 1983:199).

Policy Change: Urban Entrepreneurship and Economic Conversion

Since the 1970s, these alterations in central city political economies have precipitated substantial changes in developmental programs. The major change has been a shift away from massive downtown redevelopment in favor of more varied and specialized urban entrepreneurial programs that serve to continue the process of economic conversion. The economic dilemma facing most older central cities is no longer one of physical restructuring of their cores. It is one of inducing continued conversion of their economies at a time of shrinking tax bases, cuts in intergovernmental aid, and increasing competition from urban jurisdictions in suburbia and the Sunbelt.

In general, this has meant that city governments must undertake more flexible, piecemeal strategies to induce capital investment in particular markets and businesses. Economic development policy mostly is one of accommodating the demands of individual revenue-provider groups and businesses through varied public entrepreneurial techniques that subsidize their activities or otherwise provide incentives for them to invest in the locale. The "packaging" of more or less tailor-made business incentive programs are now the major currency of development policy. As noted in Chapter 10, these packages can include such things as tax abatements, loans, discounted land sales, new industrial parks, housing rehabilitation grants, and other forms of business subsidy.

Changing intergovernmental policies have supported this redirection in policy. The birth of the "New Federalism" during the 1970s has increased local discretion in the use of federal grant-in-aid monies, enabling city governments to shift the use of grant revenues to serve developmental purposes. General Revenue Sharing and the Community Development Block Grant have been particularly important in opening up new opportunities for city governments to cash in older programs with federally sponsored redistributive objectives in favor of developmental activities. By the same token, certain categorical grant programs, such as the Urban Development Action Grant Program, were enacted in the 1970s in response to city demands for more flexible forms of federal assistance in promoting private sector investment. UDAG is specifically designed to help cities subsidize wide-ranging economic development projects that could attract new private sector employment.

The Restructuring of Development Politics

Changes in the political economies of central cities have also tended to restructure political participation and control in the developmental arena. Promoting central city conversion has become more politically difficult for urban governments. For one thing, city governments can no longer easily forge broad-based progrowth coalitions within the business community because the end of massive downtown renewal no longer serves as a source of business unity in city development. As cities are forced to utilize piecemeal efforts to induce private investment in the conversion process, rivalry and competition among business over who is indulged and who is deprived grows. Moreover, urban economic decline has made business support for developmental policy a more powerful constraint on city planners. Business power in the developmental arena does not depend very much on actual business participation in economic decision making; it is now more "systemic" in nature, i.e., it derives from the city's weak market position in the urban economic order.

At the same time, increasing social polarization in urban political systems has forced city governments to accommodate the demands of traditionally power poor groups in the developmental arena. It is not only the ability of these groups to create civil unrest that threatens viable development policy. It is also the fact that they have won a base of sustained, continuous power in the electoral systems of cities that interposes increased conflict between neighborhood and city government over the social costs of conversion.

The upshot of this is that city governments have become constrained to rebuild a base of political support for developmental programs while attempting to buffer these programs from very widespread popular control. Consequently, since the 1970s central cities have undergone profound electoral and administrative changes.

NEW POLITICAL COALITIONS. First, city political leaders have sought to organize new political coalitions within the mass electorate. No longer able to rely on stable progrowth coalitions and political quiescence among those most threatened by economic conversion, urban governmental leaders have struggled to forge new electoral bases that are permissive of increased governmental support for conversion. One strategy has been to build electoral coalitions that isolate those groups, particularly the poor and minorities, whose programs, jobs, and neighborhoods often stand as obstacles to continued economic change. As suggested in the previous chapter, this has been accomplished in cities, such as New York, by reaching out to a broad range of working class, ethnic, professional, and other groups via appeals to race rivalry, retrenchment in social services, and neighborhood interests to the disadvantage of minorities and the poor.

Alternatively, big city mayors have sought to build broad inclusive electoral coalitions. This has been done by utilizing neighborhood-oriented distributive programs to satisfy those groups hurt by central city conversion, while promoting developmental policies that attract the support of business, newspapers, white-collar professionals, and others. In Boston, Mayor Kevin White built a formidable "neighborhood-oriented" political coalition during the 1970s. This coalition supported the administrative decentralization of service delivery programs, the creation of Little City Halls to keep in better touch with neighborhood demands, and the sponsorship of numbers of neighborhood nonprofit corporations for delivering a range of social services (Mollenkopf, 1983:Ch. 5). At the same time, White promoted developmental programs that were tuned to stabilizing white ethnic neighborhoods and maintaining the momentum of Boston's renewal program.

This strategy for building electoral support for conversion is well supported by New Federalism programs that permit officials at the local level to use federal funds to pursue developmental objectives while accommodating neighborhood demands via distributive policy techniques. The CDBG has particularly functioned in this manner. Although federal regulations directed localities to use CDBG resources for assisting primarily low- and moderate-income citizens, lack of federal oversight and control permitted cities during the first several years of CDBG to move quickly to exploit the developmental possibilities of this program, particularly by utilizing it to help stabilize changing upper-income neighborhoods, extend the process of gentrification to areas around the central cores of their cities, and otherwise promote the residential conversion of the city for use by skilled white-collar workers. Local governments tended to disperse community development funds widely throughout the community rather than concentrate their renewal efforts on the poorest, most blighted areas.

Most localities expanded the number of census tracts receiving CDBG funds to new areas that were not predominantly low income and had not previously received assistance under the old categorical programs. Most of the funds were used for hardware-intensive projects, especially short term "spot" improvements designed to enhance neighborhood amenities and property values. Further, expenditures for housing rehabilitation were tilted away from areas of low income housing that needed demolition and replacement in favor of "marginal" neighborhoods where middle-income taxpayers are most likely to reside and which could be made more attractive through relatively low-cost rehabilitation schemes (David and Kantor, 1983).

The developmental thrust of CDBG generally has not met with great neighborhood opposition at least in part because the program has worked to channel citizen demands to matters of distribution, rather than development. For example, in New Haven representatives of low-income groups have had limited impact in planning the city's CDBG program. Many of these representatives were leaders of neighborhood corporations or other nonprofit groups having service delivery functions and were linked through jobs with various city agencies. Their main function has been to advise on the microtargeting of rehabilitation and infrastructure expenditures (i.e., which blocks to treat) and to compete for the allocation of public service money as quasi-governmental service delivery agencies (e.g., legal services, drug rehabilitation, etc.) (Fainstein et al., 1983:66–71). Divided by rivalries over such issues of distribution, neighborhood groups have not been much of a counterweight to city officials in using CDBG to revitalize New Haven.

Black Power, Old Politics. The stability of these coalition strategies is bound to be uncertain as cities cope with retrenchment during the 1980s and as the racial composition of big city electorates becomes darker and poorer. Yet there is little reason to expect that even the rise of minority administrations to power in city halls will substantially check this restructuring of the developmental arena.

As suggested in the previous chapter, minority officials face the same economic constraints as their white predecessors in managing the economic conversion process. But their task of assembling a stable base of political power for conversion may be easier. The symbolic importance of minority government combined with the use of distributive programs can enable black administrations to win stable support within their racial communities, while reaching out to business and other revenue-provider groups via developmental programs.

For instance, in Atlanta the 1973 electoral victory of Maynard Jackson, the city's first black mayor, and his succession by Andrew Young two terms later put the city's black majority firmly in control of city hall. Both administrations ambitiously concentrated on abolishing Jim Crow political traditions that kept blacks out of many city jobs, political offices, and city contracts, and they successfully assailed other remaining segregationist practices, particularly in education and public housing. However, threats of business disinvestment and "white flight" have moved both black administrations to abandon most programs to which the business community was hostile, such as minority employment targets in private sector businesses, and they have vigorously supported programs to revitalize the city's central business district, often at the expense of the neighborhoods. In fact, Maynard Jackson acted to visibly reassure the business and investment community that their position in the developmental arena was unchanged by abolishing the city's Office of Economic Development and replacing it with an independent Economic Development

Corporation that was located in offices near the Chamber of Commerce, rather than in city hall (Stone, 1983).

Atlanta's black power experience is by no means unique. Minority administrations in other cities have pursued similar strategies to assure business that their position of privilege would not be threatened by the new regime. Consider the remarkably strong parallel case in Detroit following Coleman Young's election as the city's first black mayor in 1973. He consolidated his power by adopting the same basic formula as Mayor Young of Atlanta. Gaining control over the city's predominantly white bureaucracies, he was steadfast in integrating them and carrying out the most extensive administrative reorganization in the city's postwar history. He eventually appointed blacks to 51 percent of positions heading city departments and agencies and to 41 percent of the top posts on municipal boards and commissions. Affirmative action programs were vigorously implemented throughout city departments. Between 1967 and 1978, the black percentage of the city's police force increased sixfold. In addition, the Young administration vastly expanded black business access to municipal purchasing and contracts and has insisted that firms which bid on city contracts meet strict affirmative action employment criteria.

This strategy for generating black jobs and business via municipal employment has enabled Young to avoid funding and creating neighborhood organizations and social programs that might form a rival base of political power within the black community. In fact, between 1966 and 1979, the percentage of Detroit's budget devoted to various social services (health and sanitation, etc.) remained stationary or declined. Yet at the same time, the mayor has been able to aggressively pursue economic development strategies (see below) that have been heralded by the business community (Hill, 1983).

POLITICAL BUFFERS AND CONVERSION.   Beyond the rebuilding of political coalitions to support economic conversion, city governments have acted to buffer their varied urban entrepreneurial programs in ways that limit popular control over them. It is in central cities—where internal tension between popular control and development is often severe—that the more innovative techniques of this kind are found. The use of independent development authorities that segregate decision making over development from the general-purpose local government is relied upon extensively there today.

For example, in Detroit a cluster of Economic Development Corporations plan and direct most public and private development in the city. Heavily weighted toward Detroit's business elites, they are empowered to control and develop land and issue industrial revenue and other bonds, as well as to establish industrial revenue districts; they can receive and administer grants and loans from higher levels of government and can offer public incentives, such as tax abatement and land banking, for private developments. One such authority administers a special tax district for the downtown area in a scheme whereby all new tax revenues produced in the tax district are given back to the authority for reinvestment in that area alone (Hill, 1983:103, 110). In effect, Detroit has separated the planning and finance of its conversion activities from mainstream local politics and placed it in the hands of interconnecting and overlapping business and governmental directorates.

While all other large core cities have not centralized development planning as much as Detroit has, virtually all make extensive use of mechanisms to segregate and insulate urban entrepreneurship from "politics." As noted in the previous chapter, this includes the use of independent authorities, control boards, special tax districts, lease financing, and related structures to promote the whole range of urban reinvestment—from ports, industrial parks, convention centers, sports arenas, and hotels to luxury housing projects and plant expansions and relocations.

Decline, Conversion, and the Tensions of Dependency in Cities

The cities of America's aging urban core have been pulled through wrenching social change during the postindustrial era. As this continues, developmental politics will remain a struggle over the control of the economic conversion process. City governments must manage their economic dependency in the face of uncertainty and agitation within their political systems. The relatively weak market position of many of the nation's older central cities forces local governmental leaders to place economic conversion programs high on their agendas. But the political tensions of this process may well create new political challenges from within in the future.

CHAPTER THIRTEEN

Suburbia and the Sunbelt:
The Contrasting Politics of Growth

THE disintegration of the nation's core and periphery urban system in favor of the new economic order precipitated a dash by communities to capitalize on this transition. The struggle on the part of the many localities of the old periphery to achieve ascendant market positions has varied considerably in form and consequence. But northern suburbia and the rising cities of the Sunbelt offer sharply contrasting patterns of postindustrial growth politics; these cases are suggestive of the problems of dependency that affect even the so-called winners in the contemporary urban political economy.

Suburbia: Development As Exclusion

In contrast to the central cities, governments in the suburban rings in the nation's heartland have been able to exploit the economic and political changes of postindustrial America to considerable local advantage. The growth of suburbia has transformed what were usually poor, thinly populated, and badly governed areas before 1930 into what are often prosperous jurisdictions that today are able to provide quality public services, low residential densities, moderate taxes, and other amenities that echo the stereotype of the "American dream." To be sure, not all suburbs fit this prototypical image. Crowded, working-class industrial suburbs are often found—usually at the edges of large cities—that seem to replicate in miniature the physical and social characteristics of the metropolis to which they are tied. Suburban poverty, though usually limited to particular areas, sometimes rivals that of the central city (Department of Housing and Urban Development, 1980:Ch. 7). The developmental problems of such enclaves are likely to parallel those of the nearby city. Nevertheless, these exceptions hardly overshadow the fact that suburbia has for the most part become a bastion of white, upper-income groups who have escaped the dilemmas of economic development faced by central cities today.

At the same time, suburban growth has imposed severe social costs on virtually everybody in metropolitan areas. The transformation of suburbia into a sprawling network of preponderantly low-density, white, prosperous communities has meant the creation of a veritable wall of separation between city and suburb based on class and race, visibly locking urban America into a segregated society. The central cities have come to house those left behind—the poor, minorities, and unemployed, and others—who cannot "qualify" for the "suburban dream." This has, in turn, created a mismatch of need and resources between city and suburb; hard-pressed central cities must cope with the greatest demands for public services while the governmental revenues for meeting them increasingly lay outside in the suburban rings (Cox, 1973; Department of Housing and Urban Development, 1980).

The suburban transformation has also imposed important costs on suburbanites themselves. Sprawling "sameness" of home and neighborhood often stretches for miles in almost uninterrupted development around major metropolitan areas, visually revealing the missed opportunities for social and environmental diversity and the preservation of valuable countryside that could complement suburban living. This pattern of development has also imposed long and expensive commuting costs to home and job on large numbers of suburbanites. By the same token, suburban exclusiveness has meant higher costs, particularly in housing, even for those who have managed to claim a place in suburbia. As suburbia was built to low densities with housing that had to be expensive in order to meet the mandate of the law, family budgets have been strained to meet huge home mortgages, and it has become more difficult for those who were raised in the suburbs to stay there. By 1972, 76 percent of the nation's white population and 89 percent of the black population were already priced out of the new housing market in suburbia (Danielson, 1976:78). Since then, rising housing costs and slow growth in personal incomes have eliminated even more families from the suburban housing markets (Department of Housing and Urban Development, 1980:7–14). Lack of suitable and affordable suburban housing has particularly discriminated against minorities, lower-income groups, young families, single individuals, and retirees.

Development Policy: Building Suburban Walls

This pattern of economic development was neither accidental nor inevitable. Rather, the suburban transformation was a result of deliberate governmental policy as localities scrambled to cope with the forces of dispersal in the postindustrial era. Changes in the urban economy, the federal system, and popular control of local government interacted to forge a policy of building social and economic walls around suburbia.

THE POSTINDUSTRIAL ECONOMY AND SUBURBAN EXCLUSION. As suggested previously, the nation's postindustrial economy unleashed people and jobs from their traditional central city locations in a pattern of inexorable dispersal during the decades following World War II. This massive movement was reinforced by federal policies that promoted suburban homeownership, highway construction, and new businesses. The suburbanization of America was unstoppable; previously isolated hamlets and unincorporated areas near central cities witnessed tremendous development pressures that continue even today (Tucker, 1984). The race to suburbia ignited a boom in suburban land values and the production of unprecedented numbers of new homes in the outer rings of most heartland cities.

If left to itself, however, the market governing this process would very likely have extended many of the familiar mixed patterns of residential development found in the central city. The huge demand for new suburban housing and the demands of businesses for cheaper land and more space put unprecedented pressure on suburban land development. Greater profits could be made by suburban land owners, real estate interests, and the construction industry by intensely developing suburban tracts for large numbers of housing units (rather than building fewer homes at large density).[1] In many older suburbs located at the fringes of larger cities, such a pattern was already in evidence during the 1940s. In short, the economic forces impacting the development of suburbia were poised to accommodate nearly everybody—except perhaps those with very low incomes who could not afford new housing of any kind—who might choose to move there.

FEDERALISM AND EXCLUSION.   That the history of suburbanization did not follow the logic of the market was a result of intergovernmental arrangements that permitted suburban local governments to regulate the development of their communities. State policies in respect to the governance of land use were most crucial. State governments ultimately have the authority to control land use through zoning, planning, and regulating standards of building construction. But it has been time-honored practice to delegate these responsibilities, together with extensive powers to tax, borrow, and provide most essential public services, to incorporated local governments (Babcock, 1980; Zimmer, 1976; Danielson, 1976:Ch. 2). The latter may be county, city, village, town, or other state-chartered corporations that state constitutions and laws designate as local government units having specific kinds of authority. Except for certain regional planning responsibilities in coastal zones, flood plains, and the like, state governments have generally delegated nearly complete authority to control land use to the lowest incorporated governmental units. In unincorporated areas, it is usually the county that owns this planning authority; otherwise, the county government's role in the planning of land use in incorporated areas is usually quite limited and is often only advisory.

Because state law in the twentieth century was altered to allow relatively easy incorporation in order to prevent further annexation by central cities of suburban areas, families and businesses moving to suburbia almost universally sought municipal incorporation in order to control the development of their communities. Incorporation not only cut the locality free of county control, where matters of land use might otherwise be subject to competing political interests from outside the locality, but it also gave the towns, villages, and similar governmental units the power to regulate their future residential and industrial development. Other state laws also encouraged local governmental incorporation, even by very small jurisdictions. State enabling laws were enacted to permit the creation of special districts for very expensive services, such as sewage treatment, schools, water supply, and other activities, which might be well beyond the fiscal capacity of many smaller localities to supply by themselves (Zimmer, 1976:180).

Most important, the practice of state governments to rely on the local property tax, rather than state assistance programs, to provide most of the funding for local government services made it essential for localities to incorporate in order to control their tax burdens. Over 80 percent of all local revenues in the suburbs are derived from property taxes; about 60 percent or more of all public expenditures are for education (Danielson, 1976:43). Since property tax yields depend mainly on the value of development within a jurisdiction and school costs are related to the density of residential settlement, the economic pressures to limit population while controlling development to pay the bills are overwhelming.

Consequently, it is no wonder that the development of suburbia was marked by small communities dashing to secure incorporation in order to achieve control over their fiscal and social destinies. As suburbia grew, metropolitan areas became fragmented into numbers of small hodge-podge jurisdictions, each struggling to guide their community development in competition with other jurisdictions. By 1972, there were more than 22,000 separate governmental units, excluding 517 dependent school systems, in 264 metropolitan areas (Zimmer, 1976:171). In the New York metropolitan area, there are over 2,000 separate governmental units, while most other heartland metro areas are fragmented into hundreds or at least scores of governmental jurisdictions (Danielson and Doig, 1982:3; Zimmer, 1975).

Given the pressures of population and industrial dispersal and the fragmented governmental framework for regulating these forces, suburban communities are motivated to utilize highly exclusionary development policies. The local community's market position as a "desirable" enclave of low taxes, fine residential amenities, and attractive public services can only be secured by making deliberate efforts to exclude a broad range of residential and industrial developments.

This generally has meant discouraging high-density residential developments that increase the demand for public services and can be expected to attract "undesirables"—meaning racial and ethnic groups—to the community. In communities that can afford it, it also has meant excluding commercial and industrial developments, particularly "dirty" industries, such as manufacturing plants that bring in large numbers of trucks and autos that congest local roads and are not harmonious with the quiet, residential life style of suburbia. In contrast, community prosperity is secured by encouraging net revenue-producing activities, particularly expensive residential developments, low population densities, attractive commercial tax ratables, and, if acceptable to community tastes, "clean" industries, such as office complexes, research labs, retail malls, and the like, which can lower tax burdens on residential property.

PLANNING FOR EXCLUSION: THE POLICY TECHNIQUES. The most important means of achieving this exclusionary objective is the control of residential development. Their small size and limited tax base often does not permit many suburban governments to utilize costly public investment strategies to lure business ratables (Danielson, 1976:69), and, more important, such development techniques are often unnecessary. In suburban areas that seek to include commercial and industrial tax ratables as a means of lowering property tax burdens on residents, achieving a low-density, low-tax, quality residential environment is important in luring attractive forms of business investment to the suburbs. Because the demand for quality industrial and commercial ratables exceeds supply, the competition to attract these kinds of businesses is often keen. More often than not, it is the wealthier, exclusive residential communities that are most successful in bringing them in. Business firms are as eager as suburban communities to avoid the tax burdens occasioned by large numbers of families with school-age populations; executives also seek "quality" residential environments for their families. Consequently, suburban jurisdictions that offer low taxes and residential quality have important advantages in the pursuit of industry and commerce (Danielson, 1976:45-48; Danielson and Doig, 1982:Ch. 3). Initial success in attracting industrial ratables helps to attract yet more industry owing to declining tax burdens (ACIR, 1967:78-79).

Accordingly, suburban governments have utilized numerous planning techniques dedicated to screening out the "undesirables" and bringing in the tax ratables. Severe restrictions on apartment construction have become the norm throughout suburbia, where most land is zoned for only single-family housing. In the New York metropolitan area, nearly 99 percent of all undeveloped land is restricted to single-family housing (Danielson, 1976:53). Although this practice sometimes reflects the suburban taste for a low-density residential environment, apartment restrictions usually have an important economic rationale. Apartments that have several bedrooms to accommodate families and are built to moderate-income standards tend to create considerable service demands (particularly on local schools) without generating high tax revenues. Furthermore, land set aside for apartment construction threatens the possibility of subsidized housing. Consequently, suburban governments seek to tap the higher tax revenues multifamily housing is capable of generating by limiting such construction to luxury developments that have only one or two bedrooms and are built to high-cost designs which sometimes include swimming pools, tennis courts, and other facilities.

Equally severe limitations are frequently imposed on single-family homes in suburbia. In order to achieve favorable tax-service demand ratios and an attractive neighborhood environment, suburban communities often prohibit all but costly single-family homes in low-density sites. One of the most important means of accomplishing this is through large lot zoning, i.e., requiring minimum size lots of up to one, two, or even more acres for single-family residents. Large lot sizes drive up the cost of housing, eliminating all but upper-income families from being able to buy into the community. Large lot zoning also yields low population densities, ensuring that there will be fewer children in the schools, fewer streets, and less demand for other public services, such as fire and police protection.

Other planning regulations are also used to limit or eliminate all but costly single-family homes. Minimum building size regulations, minimum lot widths, and related restrictions apply in many jurisdictions. Even more important are building code prohibitions, which in most states are specified by the local government. These often require very high standards of housing construction and prohibit many cost-saving forms of construction, such as prefabricated housing components and plastic plumbing; this drives up the price of housing to assure high property tax values and high-income residential ownership. Mobile homes are almost always excluded. Limits on residential growth even in wealthy, low-density suburbs are often imposed through yet other measures. Suburban planning boards in such areas sometimes zone considerable land for nonresidential purposes, such as parks and open space, in order to eliminate development pressure, or they impose moratoriums on all new building for periods of time.

Finally, exclusionary residential policies are almost invariably followed in respect to subsidized housing. Given the high cost of suburban housing in most governmental jurisdictions, only government subsidized housing could provide a route to the suburbs for most low-income groups. Yet very little low-income subsidized housing has been built in America's suburbs because of the development practices of suburban governments. For instance, in 1970 St. Louis had 10,000 units of public housing for its 662,000 residents, but suburban St. Louis County had only 50 units for its population of 956,000 (Danielson, 1976:102).

Prior to 1961, federal housing programs provided subsidized housing via local housing authorities, which had to be created in order to receive federal funds and build public housing by formulating a "workable plan." Typically, suburbs avoided participation in these programs by simply not creating a local housing authority or failing to provide a plan acceptable to federal officials. During the 1960s, new federal housing programs widened the range of sponsors of subsidized housing to include nonprofit organizations and other private agencies, eliminating the need for active local government participation by housing authorities. Further, Congress liberalized the income limits for residents of subsidized housing, opening up greater opportunities for larger numbers of people to live in publicly sponsored projects. Nevertheless, even under these circumstances, very little subsidized housing was built in the suburbs. Federal officials had no power to authorize housing unless local zoning and building regulations permitted it. Few suburbs did.

Much of the subsidized housing that was built in the suburbs was reserved for the elderly or built in older suburbs that already had substantial low-income populations (Danielson, 1976:Ch. 4). During the 1980s, retrenchment in federal housing monies has accompanied opposition by the Reagan administration to government-sponsored housing production programs. The federal government has favored providing very limited rent subsidies and housing rehabilitation grants rather than sponsoring many new building efforts. Since the basic problem that low-income groups face usually is the lack of much affordable suburban housing, federal policy reinforces the suburban status quo.

WHY PLANNING COUNTS: GROWTH CONTROL POLITICS IN SUBURBAN NEW YORK. That such exclusionary practices are a systematic by-product of the fragmented, competitive political economy of suburban development is illustrated by contrasting experiences of two counties in the New York metropolitan area, Westchester and Nassau. Located immediately north of New York City's Bronx, Westchester County was largely unsettled during the early decades of the century, and the county's political leaders made ambitious efforts to prevent "Bronxification." The county built parkways, rather than rapid transit or ordinary highways, that restricted commercial traffic and commercial strip development. Land use was vigorously controlled by localities that promoted expensive, low-density residential communities through regulatory techniques in advance of major development pressures.

As the county's growth boomed during the 1950s and 1960s, strict zoning and planning prevailed to preserve a rural ambience, low population densities, and high standards of housing and amenities in all but some of the older southern portions of the county. Large lot zoning was adopted extensively, and the residential capacity of the county fell from 3.2 million in 1950 to 1.8 million in 1969. Consequently, most Westchester suburbs have been able to provide high levels of services, such as extensive parks and lavish school programs, without severe burdens on taxpayers. Pressures to secure indiscriminate industrial and commercial development to relieve local tax burdens have been rare. Many of the more affluent communities want no industry, and other areas have been highly selective in those that are permitted.

On the other hand, Nassau County, which is located on New York City's eastern Long Island border, did not organize itself to pursue the highly exclusionary policies that Westchester did. Many of Nassau's residents and landowners were potato farmers, small property owners, and other less affluent groups. Residential development represented an opportunity for profit, rather than a threat to their rural way of life. Further, much of the county was, unlike rolling Westchester, flat and treeless and lent itself more for mass development than affluent, wooded sanctuaries that upper-income families often seek.

Accordingly, local residents sought profits in the postwar property boom, and these interests were well represented by local and county planning authorities. Except for a few communities, mostly located along the county's north shore, restrictive land use regulations were not imposed in advance of massive development pressures (Danielson and Doig, 1982:77–78). The result was that most of Nassau was given over to large numbers of relatively high density tract developments, including sprawling Levitown, a large community of homes built at a low cost by mass methods for working-class and moderate-income families.

With large numbers of pupils in the public schools, relatively great demand for most other public services, and a weak tax base to generate governmental revenues in most of the county's predominantly residential communities, Nassau's fiscal woes are substantial. Property taxes are high relative to Westchester, and services are usually much less comprehensive. Such consequences of nonrestrictive planning powerfully motivate suburban governments to develop more like Westchester if they can.

Gatekeeper Politics

The tensions between popular control and the exigencies of economic development that characterize central cities are not found in most suburbs. To the extent that suburban jurisdictions are able to control residential and industrial development in exclusionary ways, a "gatekeeper" process works to eliminate from the community the groups and businesses that are likely to challenge the status quo. Except in suburban communities that have failed to control their development, the relatively homogeneous, predominantly residential political constituencies of taxpayers and property owners are highly supportive of the discriminatory development policies that dominate suburbia. United by similar interests in enhancing property values, maintaining the status of home and family, keeping taxes low, and keeping people out, consensus among voters is the norm in regard to matters of economic development. In fact, exclusion provides so many benefits to all suburban residents (in the form of lower taxes, neighborhood amenities, and separation from the problems of the central cities) that even members of social groups who are usually victims of these exclusionary policies—such as suburban racial minorities and lower-income families who are residents of more wealthy enclaves—can often be counted on to support exclusion (Danielson, 1976:Ch. 6). The gatekeeper process ensures that the interests of the individual voter tend to be identical with the enhancement of the community's market position.

Most internal conflicts over development policy in suburbia tend to be minimal. They usually focus on the details of how to maintain the status quo in policy, i.e., whether to permit some industrial development to lower residential property taxes, allowing cluster housing, townhouses, or apartments rather than only single-family homes, permitting large retail stores in the village, and related issues. These issues have probably become more contentious in recent years as building costs have soared (making it more difficult even for very well off families to buy their single-family dream house) and the suburban tax bite has increased. Nevertheless, suburban political leaders can generally count on widespread consensus in the management of their community's economic development.

Why Political Change Is Difficult

The most significant conflicts over suburban development policy are generated by those outside of the local political arena who seek to overturn discriminatory housing and land use policies. Throughout the period of suburbia's dramatic growth, the most vigorous challenges to suburban autonomy have arisen from local, state, and national political leaders seeking to open up the suburbs to lower-income groups and from lawsuits brought in the courts on behalf of the excluded. In general, however, these efforts have largely failed to break down the walls of suburban separation owing to powerful economic and political constraints on reformers at all levels in the federal system.

POPULAR CONTROL AND POLITICAL COALITIONS. At the local level, there are many important groups within metropolitan areas that have significant "potential" interests (Truman, 1951) in limiting exclusionary development practices in suburbia (Downs, 1973). Taken together, these varied political interests could form a powerful political coalition to challenge suburban autonomy.

First, housing consumers located throughout metropolitan areas who are presently excluded from suburban living by discriminatory housing policies have a major stake in opening up the suburbs. This includes low-income groups and racial minorities who are concentrated in central cities and aging older suburbs. It also includes a host of others who are unable to find affordable housing, such as civil servants who cannot live in the communities where they work or young families and singles who cannot return to their old neighborhoods because of the lack of appropriate housing. Second, reform-minded voters and their organizations are scattered throughout metropolitan areas and have supported efforts to open up suburbia. Groups such as the NAACP, the Suburban Action Institute, religious groups, and individuals who are inclined to support housing rights have often initiated political action on behalf of those excluded from suburban communities.

Third, the political leaders of central cities often have been outspoken critics of suburban housing policies, not least because suburban exclusion has exacerbated their fiscal and social problems by concentrating low-income groups within their jurisdiction. Finally, suburban businesses could often gain something by less discriminatory land use and housing policies. Opening up the suburbs could ease problems of labor recruitment, particularly for clerical workers and less skilled labor, could reduce the journey to work time for those who commute to suburban jobs, and could help contain wage and salary demands in general by lowering the cost of suburban housing. In addition, the removal of the more restrictive zoning practices could work to the advantage of the suburban residential construction industry. By permitting more and cheaper housing units to be constructed, developers and construction unions would have greater opportunities for profits and jobs.

That these diverse groups have not acted on these interests to form a viable constituency for suburban housing reform must be credited to the structure of popular control and governmental organization in metropolitan areas (cf. Danielson, 1976:Ch. 6). First, as long as metropolitan areas are severely fragmented into large numbers of governmental jurisdictions, the political power of these widely scattered groups and individuals cannot be effectively combined to pressure individual suburban governments into adopting changes in zoning, apartment restrictions, and other policies. In fact, the political logic of gatekeeper politics is designed to prevent the emergence of such a political constituency in the first place. With political authority over housing and land use concentrated in the hands of individual suburban governments, the system of popular control enhances the ability of suburban communities to mobilize against all outsiders while depriving the latter of a political base from which to contest public policy.

Second, many groups that might gain by opening up the suburbs also enjoy competing benefits from the governmental status quo. Low-income housing consumers want low taxes as much as do others; consequently, suburban blacks have marched shoulder-to-shoulder with white homeowners to protest subsidized housing. Leaders of economically hard-pressed central cities wish to disperse their needy citizens to suburbia; but making suburbia more affordable would most likely prompt the flight from cities of more mobile working-class and lower middle-class families seeking to upgrade their housing, further destabilizing the central city economies.

Suburban business also has proved to be an unreliable ally in housing reform because of competing advantages conferred by the governmental status quo. Suburban businesses seek low-tax environments, and they are often permitted to locate in the most desirable suburban areas only if they do not threaten to change community character by bringing in workers' housing, raising housing densities, or taxing the capacity of local government services, particularly in education. Suburban business would face higher taxes and more restrictive locations in a more "open" metropolitan world—disadvantages that appear to outweigh difficulties faced by them in recruiting labor (Danielson, 1976:Ch. 6).

Even the construction industry has failed to unite in support of suburban housing reform (Lilley, 1980). Large national builders have frequently supported proposals to limit the ability of suburbs to keep out subsidized housing and restrict cheaper housing. However, smaller developers and construction trade unions that build most low-rise housing have not (Danielson, 1976:Ch. 6). Fragmented local governmental regulation of land use and building is an important barrier to mass-produced housing and the domination of suburban home building by giant national firms. Smaller suburban builders and construction trade unions survive by knowing local conditions and building codes and by having the flexibility to adapt to localized construction requirements.

FEDERALISM AND THE SUBURBAN STATUS QUO. While the system of fragmented popular control found in most metropolitan areas limits the prospect of any powerful urban reform coalition, the state and national governments provide what might appear to be a more promising arena for challenging suburban development practices. The larger and more diverse electoral arenas in state and national politics allow greater access to groups seeking housing reform, making governments at these levels more sensitive to their demands. Not surprisingly, most challenges to suburban autonomy have arisen from state and federal government efforts to build subsidized housing or limit restrictive housing practices. Nevertheless, formidable political and economic pressures have severely limited state and, to a lesser extent, federal responses.

The State Political Economy and the Suburbs. The political economy of state politics has decisively limited what even the most ardent suburban reformers can accomplish in this arena. As industry and populations have spread beyond central city borders throughout the postwar era, the political and economic base of state governments has moved in tandem. Metropolitan population dispersal has tipped the traditional rural–suburban political bias of state legislatures solidly in favor of suburbanites, making the suburbs a dominant voice in state elections in the more urbanized states of the heartland (Wirt et al., 1972). This has propelled state governments to support suburban political autonomy through permissive legislation regarding governmental incorporation, land use, and housing policies.

The place of suburbia in the economies of states has placed equally stringent limits on state government. Suburbanization has made state economic growth increasingly dependent on the capacity of suburban areas to attract capital and labor in competition with other states. Even where central cities have remained highly important in the state economy, the suburbs have also grown in importance as bedroom communities for the skilled white-collar work force that commutes to the cities or works outside of them (ACIR, 1981; Vaughan, 1979). Consequently, state governments are motivated to enhance the social and economic attractiveness of these areas for white-collar workers and their families in competition with suburban areas elsewhere. In effect, the economic stake of state governments in development has become tied to the perpetuation of exclusionary practices on the part of their upper-income suburbs.

By the same token, suburban exclusion also works to enhance the state economy by keeping declining central cities competitive in retaining older, smokestack industries and smaller businesses that depend on lower skilled labor. An inner city labor market of young people, minorities, and lower-income families locked into central city economies by suburban exclusion limits labor mobility and produces higher rates of unemployment, driving down industrial wages in these areas at a time of declining competitiveness for central cities (James, 1981; Sternlieb and Hughes, 1981; Peterson, 1979; Bluestone and Harrison, 1982:Ch. 3).

The Fate of the Reformer. The result is that even the most reform-minded governors and legislators are unable to build sufficient support for breaking through suburban walls on behalf of the excluded. A most dramatic illustration of this occurred in New York State during the late 1960s and early 1970s under Governor Nelson Rockefeller, a powerful Republican liberal committed to suburban reform. Rockefeller attempted to dramatically expand state power over suburban development. The prime vehicle for many of his initiatives was a novel authority, the Urban Development Corporation (UDC), which was created in 1968 with formidable resources to overcome suburban resistance to housing reform. The UDC was empowered to develop and finance housing of any kind on its own (rather than depending on outside developers to initiate proposals) and ample funds were voted for this purpose by the legislature. Most important, the agency was authorized to override local land use and development restrictions, removing from local governments their traditional veto power over subsidized housing and other state projects. Localities could not even modify UDC designs or plans. Finally, Rockefeller recruited one of the nation's most talented and aggressive development administrators, Edward Logue, formerly Boston and New Haven's urban renewal boss, to direct the agency.

Despite its sweeping authority and commanding resources, even the UDC did not manage to build much low-income housing in suburban areas or limit suburban autonomy. When the agency attempted to expand its programs to include upper-income suburban areas near New York City, a hailstorm of suburban and legislative opposition resulted, virtually ending the authority's suburban housing role. This occurred after the UDC proposed plans to build small amounts (merely 100 units) of subsidized housing in nine towns located in exclusive suburban Westchester County. Though local opposition to state projects, such as highways, was often ignored in the past by state representatives, suburban hostility on a matter that did not enhance strategic developmental objectives for the state easily moved the legislature to break with Rockefeller's support of the agency. In 1973, the governor's own party leaders in the legislature voted to repeal the UDC's power to override zoning and building codes in towns and villages and even gave local jurisdictions a veto over UDC residential projects in these areas. The agency was left with only the authority to build subsidized housing in the cities (Danielson, 1976:306–322). Since then, the economic crisis of New York State has engulfed the UDC and subsequent state governors. The UDC has shifted away from subsidized housing construction and has become a major economic development arm of the state government, constructing industrial parks, convention centers, luxury housing projects, and related programs in city and suburban areas (*New York Times*, 2 March 1983:C-6).

The Nation and the Suburbs. Compared with the states, the national political arena has been more open to demands for suburban reform, but even here federal officeholders have hardly been able to challenge suburbia's autonomy. While national administrations do not face the severe economic barriers in development faced by their state counterparts, neither Democratic nor Republican administrations have much stake in promoting programs to open up the suburbs. Not only does suburbia have a major voice in determining the political fortunes of presidential and congressional candidates, but the shifting political coalitions of the two parties in national politics have discouraged putting the issue of exclusion on the political agenda. Republican electoral strategies have focused on garnering the suburban vote and promoting the party's power in the Sunbelt. At the same time, Democrats have fought to increase their suburban political followings while maintaining their base of power in central cities; both objectives are more likely to be achieved by avoiding challenges to suburban autonomy and supporting urban aid programs to the cities.

Consequently, support for federal intervention in the social regulation of suburban development has been sporadic, marginal, and generally ineffective (Glazer, 1980; Ashton, 1984; Stone, 1980). During the whole of the postwar era of federal programs to promote suburbanization, neither Democratic nor Republican administrations have rigorously tied federal assistance to fair housing objectives—despite growing support in both parties for civil rights reforms, including bans on racial discrimination and prohibitions on the use of federal aid for such discriminatory objectives in the 1964 and 1968 civil rights acts.

Piecemeal attempts to deploy federal assistance to guide suburban development and to limit exclusion arose after the urban disorders of the late 1960s when national commissions and housing groups advocated that HUD use its authority to withhold federal funds for urban renewal, water and sewer projects, roads, and other capital improvements from communities that failed to provide housing for minorities and the poor. For example, in 1969 the Nixon administration permitted HUD secretary George W. Romney to utilize this resource in his Open Communities program, which was designed to discourage localities from employing restrictive land use and building regulations to prevent provision of federally subsidized housing. Unable to win broad support for this endeavor from the White House or Congress and anticipating suburban resistance, Romney attempted to maintain a low profile for the program by selectively targeting Open Communities at small numbers of suburban localities. Most of these were industrial suburbs with large working-class populations that were not integral to Republican electoral strategies. Some HUD aid was cut off from a few recalcitrant localities when they failed to accept Open Communities requirements. But when the program provoked intense suburban opposition, White House and Congressional pressure forced rewriting of the program to foster only voluntary compliance (Danielson, 1976:217–230).

Since the 1970s, the use of federal power in guiding suburban development has declined further. There has been a major decline in federal expenditures for building subsidized housing in favor of smaller programs to subsidize existing low-income housing—thus very little new government-sponsored housing is being made available in suburbia. Most important, the block grant approach embodied in the New Federalism has replaced many categorical forms of federal assistance to the suburbs, enabling localities to avoid much federal oversight in their allocation of program monies. The Community Development Block Grant program has since its inception in 1974 required qualifying localities to develop housing plans for both extant and new residents anticipated as a result of economic development. Most suburbs are not covered by this law. Only large suburban towns and counties are covered, and HUD has tended to approve their grant applications routinely.

State and federal permissiveness in the developmental politics of suburbia has left proponents of reform dependent on litigation brought in state and federal courts, usually under the due process clauses of state constitutions or under the equal protection provision of the national Constitution. Although occasional victories have been won, particularly in state courts, to limit restrictive development practices on the part of suburbs, court litigation has not made many breaches in suburbia's exclusionary walls.

The courts are subject to much the same limits that the political economy of state and nation impose on its other branches of government. Since the rise of suburban political power and changing national coalition politics severely discourage placing the issue on the federal agenda, the Supreme Court has tended to back off from intervening in suburban development practices in all but the most blatant instances where "intentional" racial discrimination can be proved. State courts have also faced stringent limits on their activity.[2] Suburban political power, increasing economic competition among states, and the decline of intergovernmental programs to build more affordable housing make state judges reluctant to enter thickets where there are neither sufficient governmental resources nor general governmental will to carry out verdicts.

Sunbelt Cities: The Changing Dilemmas of Growth Politics

Although the popular image of cities in America's Sunbelt is one of new-found prosperity and growth, in fact the diverse political economy of the region confounds simple generalization. The southern, southwestern, southeastern, and far western portions of the United States tend to differ considerably in respect to postwar economic growth and population change, making the matter of describing the Sunbelt as a single region a debatable proposition (Abbott, 1981:Chs. 1 and 2). For example, between 1950 and 1970 SMSAs of the relatively affluent Southwest and Pacific Coast generally were above the national level in educational attainment, white-collar employment, and median family income, while metropolitan areas of the Southeast were below, reflecting the relative poverty of this region (Abbott, 1981:48–49).

Moreover, within the states of the Sunbelt not all localities have shared equally in the general economic expansion of the region as a whole. Uneven economic development, variations in federal and state assistance, and demographic and other factors have promoted patterns of prosperity and hardship among cities of the Sunbelt that rival those found in the Frostbelt (Brownell and Goldfield, 1977:Ch. 6). There are poor large cities in the Sunbelt that probably have more in common with declining cities in the North than with many of their regional neighbors. For instance, New Orleans is hemmed in by a ring of relatively affluent suburbs, is heavily dependent on federal aid in running city government, and contains a large, poor minority population. After years of shrinking employment and flight of white middle-income families, the city has encountered fiscal difficulties similar to many old northern cities (Smith and Keller, 1983). By the same token, there are large older Sunbelt cities with aging downtowns that have been compelled to undertake economic revitalization efforts similar to those of large Frostbelt urban centers. For example, San Francisco's and Atlanta's urban renewal programs during the 1960s were designed to promote the conversion of their central business districts to service uses much as was the case in the North (Stone, 1976; Fainstein et al., 1983). In effect, there is no "typical" Sunbelt city.

Despite such diversity, large numbers of Sunbelt cities reflect the more prominent politico-economic changes that have transformed the region as a whole since the 1940s. Typically, they have moved during the postindustrial period from relative economic underdevelopment to achieving powerful market positions in the new urban order. Since it is in these urban enclaves where the most distinctive features of the region's development politics come into play, they serve as our focus.

The political economy of the Sunbelt is marked by several thematic changes that have shaped developmental politics in these cities. First, this region has moved during the past 40 years from relative economic underdevelopment as part of the nation's urban periphery to a region of rapid economic growth. Consequently, numbers of cities in the region have shed backward, slow-growth economies and have claimed powerful regional and national market positions. The West and the South together increased their share of personal income from 33 percent to 43 percent from 1940 to 1970. Their share of national population increased during this period from 42 percent to 48 percent and reached the 50 percent mark by 1976 (Abbott, 1981:15). Between 1940 and 1970, all southwestern and western SMSAs with populations of over 300,000 in 1970 grew more rapidly than the national average for all metropolitan areas; in the same period, only 13 of 47 large SMSAs in the North surpassed the same average (Abbott, 1981:244).

Second, the growth of these cities generally has been highly dependent upon federal and state assistance. As suggested earlier, the expansion of federal outlays for defense, research and development, and other programs since the 1940s, together with the tilt of federal urban aid programs in favor of the Sunbelt have played a major role in the region's economic transformation. More than in other regions of the United States, Sunbelt cities have been highly dependent on federal governmental activities and corporate contractors for the military as a source of economic growth. For instance, Ohio, which pays three times as much in federal taxes, has almost the same number of federal military and civilian employees as Alabama. Half of the Pentagon's research funding is spent in Sunbelt states. Payrolls in the Sunbelt's 140 military installations exceed those in the rest of the military bases in the United States combined. Between 1960 and 1975, almost a half million new federal civilian jobs were created; only 16,000 of these were in the Northeast, while 135,000 of them were in the West, and 270,000 were in the South (Tabb, 1984:6-8). Sunbelt state governments have also tended to be strongly supportive of central city growth compared with states in the North. For much of the postwar period, Sunbelt cities usually did not face economic strangulation by walls of incorporated suburban local governments because of state policies favoring easy annexation by central cities.

Finally, popular control has been a comparatively weak source of constraint on the politics of development in many Sunbelt cities, although this has been changing in recent years (see below). During the postindustrial era, systems of reform government came to dominate local government throughout the Sunbelt, imposing institutional barriers to organized political competition. This has often interacted with slow growth of minority political participation and the relative absence of ethnic cleavages and unions in the politics of Sunbelt cities to favor the election of business and other upper-income groups in local government.

Development Policy: Sunbelt Entrepreneurship and the Crisis of Growth

While regional political and economic forces have tended to produce a favorable environment for urban development, Sunbelt localities have rarely sat back in hopes that urban growth would simply come their way. Rather, Sunbelt cities have vigorously utilized local developmental policies designed to exploit the region's growth opportunities. In general, urban growth centers have undergone two phases in developmental planning. One extended from the 1940s to the 1960s when progrowth policies evolved in a context of highly supportive regional economic and political change. The other, which began during the last decade or so, has been characterized by the evolution of policies to contend with new obstacles to local government promotion of rapid growth.

POSTWAR URBAN PLANNING: THE POLICY TRIAD. During most of the postwar period, the major local developmental policies have been those characteristic of expanding communities quickly securing a favorable market position. In fact, in many ways they paralleled those used by growing central cities during the industrial era. Sunbelt entrepreneurship typically involved a triad of progrowth measures: major capital investment in physical infrastructure, promoting a laissez faire regulatory environment, and aggressive territorial annexation.

Capital Spending. First, after the 1940s many Sunbelt governments undertook large capital investment in order to construct new public facilities to support business expansion, including streets, water service, and bridges, as well as the physical renewal of downtowns, which were originally laid out for cities of much smaller size. The typical result of these capital spending programs was the creation of much larger and physically uniform downtown environments characterized by high-rise offices, convention centers, sports arenas, and freeways.

While building the urban infrastructure occasionally strained local resources, most Sunbelt governments did not encounter anything like the fiscal and political crises once faced by northern industrial cities in carrying through such programs. The availability of federal grants-in-aid for such things as highways, water and sewer facilities, mass transit, and other infrastructure limited the need to tap local revenues for these projects. Moreover, the importance of federal installations, such as military bases and research facilities, also limited the costs borne by local government. For example, after political leaders in

Texas managed to get the federal government to locate the Manned Space Center in Houston, the presence of this large federal installation helped establish Houston as a technological center of the Southwest without great expenditure of local and state resources (Fleischmann, 1977).

The federal urban renewal program also played a role in reconstructing aging, small downtown cores by tearing down blocks of small businesses, cheap hotels, and older housing that confined office expansion schemes. But because many Sunbelt cities did not have large built-up central business districts and surrounding slums, heavy reliance on massive urban renewal programs on the scale of postwar northern cities was not the norm. In fact, some major cities, such as Houston, Dallas, and Fort Worth in Texas, which could have qualified for urban renewal assistance during the 1950s and 1960s, chose not to seek this form of federal aid at all and relied on privately sponsored redevelopment in their modernization drives. Urban renewal projects were often little more than delayed responses to booms in downtown real estate that were already under way by the 1950s in many cities (Abbott, 1981:148)—booms that might well have continued independently of federal urban renewal.

Laissez Faire "Planning." Second, urban entrepreneurship to induce business investment has been an important feature of postwar development policy in the Sunbelt. Given the region's growing market position, state and local governments relied extensively on supporting a laissez faire environment to promote community growth—low taxes and limited expenditures for social welfare programs, as well as a policy of "privatism" in business regulation. As noted previously, low property and business taxes are characteristic of the region as a whole. This policy has worked in concert with low levels of local government spending, particularly for social welfare services, to induce business investment. Most Sunbelt cities do not provide money for higher education and welfare matching, and, as Table 13-1 indicates, they do not undertake large expenditures for other costly social services. For example, the table shows that in 1970, Worcester, Massachusetts, contributed nearly $50 per capita from local resources for public welfare programs, while Tucson, Arizona, spent only 16¢ per capita for this purpose.

As a result, Sunbelt prosperity has not brought about great income equality for groups who are dependent upon relatively "poor" public sectors for assistance. By the same token, low public expenditures for ordinary public services has sometimes required large private contributions on the part of other citizens. In some cities, such as Houston, many middle-class neighborhoods hire their own gardeners to care for nearby city parks and post private security guards on the streets because the city police force is undermanned; public libraries and recreational facilities for neighborhoods do not exist on the scale found in many northern cities (Mathias, 1979; Feagin, 1984).

Yet public sector poverty and a low-tax environment can function to promote business investment. Skilled middle-class workers and their families who do not depend on many social services and who demand low taxes are often attracted to these cities. Further, low levels of public assistance, public employment, and

TABLE 13-1   Local Government Revenue Per Capita in Selected SMSAs in the Sunbelt and in the Northern Tier in 1970

	Local government revenue per capita	Per capita local expenditures public health	Per capita local expenditures public welfare	Municipal employment per 1,000 population
U.S. average	$329.86	$2.96	$11.98	15.80
Sunbelt cities				
Population 500,000 plus				
Houston, Tx.	$256.75	$2.70	$ 1.16	8.00
San Diego, Ca.	425.37	4.40	42.41	7.30
Phoenix, Ar.	394.02	3.53	.05	9.10
San Antonio, Tx.	262.64	2.30	.45	10.70
Jacksonville, Fla.	330.59	3.29	.30	11.60
Population 200,000–500,000				
El Paso, Tx.	223.05	2.62	.88	8.20
Tucson, Ar.	313.27	3.32	.16	8.70
West Palm Beach, Fla.	402.19	1.49	6.85	14.60
Albuquerque, N.M.	287.17	1.70	.01	8.10
Population under 200,000				
Gainesville, Fla.	467.56	7.26	.32	14.90
Amarillo, Tx.	278.24	1.97	.63	10.20
Monroe, La.	250.31	1.74	.03	17.00
Tyler, Tx.	229.38	1.36	.89	9.00
Northern tier cities				
Population 500,000 plus				
Chicago, Ill.	340.32	2.51	9.09	12.40
Newark, N.J.	343.85	3.27	31.90	37.20
Columbus, Oh.	259.97	2.60	18.82	9.40
Cincinnati, Oh.	309.19	2.30	15.58	27.90
Rochester, N.Y.	426.09	8.23	32.50	33.40
Population 200,000–500,000				
Flint, Mich.	370.99	2.23	12.47	20.30
Bridgeport, Conn.	288.91	4.02	9.98	27.40
Worcester, Ma.	342.90	2.63	49.84	31.30
Trenton, N.J.	306.69	4.05	22.17	22.17
Population under 200,000				
Brockton, Ma.	325.87	2.10	50.25	23.90
Atlantic City, N.J.	337.60	3.49	46.15	46.30
Manchester, N.H.	194.62	1.64	2.96	21.40
Danbury, Conn.	506.90	5.60	37.29	21.60

SOURCE: From Peter A. Lupsha and William J. Siembieda, "The Poverty of Public Service in the Land of Plenty: An Analysis and Interpretation" in David C. Perry and Alfred J. Watkins, eds., *The Rise of the Sunbelt Cities.* Copyright © 1977 by Sage Publications, Inc. Reprinted by permission of Sage Publications, Inc.

social welfare services can discourage lower skilled workers from residing in communities where they cannot find employment and do not have much of a "safety net" of social services to fall back upon.

This laissez faire approach of local government has sometimes extended to other forms of business regulation. In contrast to most northern cities, land use controls, such as zoning, set back requirements, and rigorous building codes are not utilized very extensively in many Sunbelt cities. A most prominent case is Houston. Houston has had one of the weakest building codes among American cities. Until very recently, there has been no zoning regulation at all, preventing city agencies from exerting much control over even the largest commercial and residential developments. Although this laissez faire policy has resulted in hodge-podge patterns of land use, severe traffic congestion, and other problems (see below), it has undoubtedly facilitated the city's rapid development, a lesson of the industrial city era that has not been lost in Houston. Nonplanning has meant that developers can have shorter development times than in other cities where stricter zoning and planning controls might require a year or two to get a large project approved and finished. Further, lack of stringent requirements for public open spaces, streets, and building set backs lowers building costs. What controls development and land use is the private land market where decisions are based on narrow cost-profit criteria (Feagin, 1984:115–117).

Territorial Annexation. Finally, local governments have promoted economic growth through programs of vigorous territorial annexation. As populations and businesses expanded during the postwar years, Sunbelt city governments sought to contain suburban incorporation and to capture the economic benefits of urban growth through annexation of adjacent unincorporated areas. For instance, San Antonio grew phenomenally from 69 square miles in 1950 to 160.5 square miles in 1960, to 184.1 square miles in 1970, and to 253 square miles in 1974. Since the city also controls subdivisions and land use planning for 5 miles beyond its legal boundaries and is surrounded only by a weak county government and some scattered small suburban towns, San Antonio succeeded in controlling its metropolitan growth. Not all Sunbelt growth centers have annexed as extensively as has San Antonio. But most have made aggressive use of this development tool during the postwar period. Memphis, Oklahoma City, Tulsa, Houston, Dallas, Fort Worth, Phoenix, San Diego, and San Jose all added over 100 square miles between 1950 and 1970, while Atlanta, Mobile, and El Paso added over 90. During the 1970s, most important annexations continued to be in southern and southwestern cities (Abbott, 1981:48–51).

The Sunbelt's political economy strongly promoted this policy of the local governments. The region's growth in business and population threatened cities that failed to annex with suburban economic competition and the loss of future tax ratables. Since the economic and political bases of state governments were closely linked to the market positions of their cities, highly permissive state legislation and constitutional provisions were enacted to enable cities to easily extend their boundaries to large outlying areas, sometimes without the consent of people residing in the areas annexed (Fleischmann, 1977; Abbott, 1981:Chs. 2 and 3).

DEVELOPMENTAL POLICY SINCE THE 1970s: SHEDDING THE POLICY TRIAD.   Since the 1970s, the policy triad of infrastructure investment, laissez faire planning, and territorial annexation has become increasingly worn as a mode of urban entrepreneurship for many Sunbelt growth centers. New constraints on developmental policy have emerged. First, the rapid laissez faire growth of many of these cities has produced an accumulation of economic, environmental, and governmental problems that cannot be solved without abandoning many traditional policies in favor of increasing taxes and governmental regulations as well as undertaking costly public programs. In particular, highway congestion, air pollution, water shortages, overcrowded schools, understaffed city agencies, and accelerating real estate prices and housing shortages have become endemic to Sunbelt boom towns.

Houston, a growth juggernaut, is exemplary of this. Years of massive territorial annexations and rapid growth have challenged the city's ability to deliver essential services and maintain low taxes. About a quarter of the city's streets remained unlighted, and 400 miles were still unpaved in 1978. There is only one police officer for every 600 people, which is about one-third the police protection of Philadelphia; the average response time to an emergency call is 26 minutes, partly because only seven police stations serve the city's 556 square miles (Bluestone and Harrison, 1982:87). Yet Houston is a high-crime city. The city's homicide rate is one of the highest in the country—in fact, about two-thirds higher than that of New York City.

The costs of laissez faire development policy are coming due in Houston. Heavy reliance on autos, lack of investment in mass transit, and unregulated city growth have combined to create appalling day-long traffic jams in and around the city. For instance, years of unregulated development have made it difficult or impossible to extend or widen many streets because high-rise office buildings have been built almost up to the edge of street pavements or because long, unbroken blocks of development did not allow for streets to run through them, forcing traffic to funnel around them into small, overcrowded avenues. Consequently, in 1982 the city adopted controls on developers to stop them from hemming in highways with skyscrapers and cutting off streets with shopping centers (New York Times, 23 June 1982:A-12). Government and business leaders have moved to support a $12.35 billion bond issue for a modern urban rail system in order to diminish the city's heavy reliance on auto transportation (New York Times, 13 June 1983:A-11).

Houston's sewage and water problems also have become critical after years of rapid city growth. In 1981, three-quarters of the city was under a sewer moratorium because there was not enough sewage treatment plant capacity in many areas to permit more sewer connections, putting great pressure on the city to spend more for sewage facilities. The city's heavy use of underground water, together with oil and gas extraction, has created a major problem of subsidence, or gradual sinking of the city, which is only 50 feet above sea level. Most areas are sinking at a rate of one foot every five or six years, particularly in places that bear the weight of new development construction. Thus, serious flooding, construction, and structural problems have increased (Feagin, 1984:119–120). The city's general dilemma was dramatically signaled in 1983 when a revenue shortfall and budget deficit in the face of mounting development problems threatened the city government with a downgrading of its bond credit rating (*New York Times*, 20 February 1983:A-11).

Houston's kinds of problems are not unique within the Sunbelt. Denver, like most cities in the West that are highly dependent on the automobile and lack a well-developed mass transit system, has a serious air pollution problem that is directly linked to auto emissions. But alleviating this problem constitutes a potential threat to the metropolitan area's continued economic expansion. Further, the city and its suburbs have repeatedly faced chronic water shortages since the rapid population growth of the postwar years (Judd, 1983). Similarly, San Jose and its nearby "Silicon Valley" encountered like kinds of problems in the wake of its high-tech boom. Because housing production could not keep pace with the area's phenomenal job growth, housing prices soared to more than double the U.S. average. More than thirty years of sustained population growth and failure to invest in mass transit alternatives to the automobile have produced extraordinarily long commutes, chronic traffic congestion, and severe environmental pollution. Further, San Jose and nearby local governments face shortages of tax revenues and have been unable to provide improvements in sewers, roads, parks, and other basic public works to keep up with the demands of population growth and development (Saxenian, 1984).

These strangling economic changes have coincided during the 1970s with the growth of suburban belts around many Sunbelt cities that have limited or even halted further annexation as a developmental policy. Throughout the South and West, annexation could not keep pace with rapid suburbanization during and after the 1960s, leading to increased suburban resistance to annexation (Abbott, 1981:19–180). Metropolitan sprawl occasioned political and economic shifts in many parts of the Sunbelt that began to mirror the northern urban experience. Sunbelt state governments were compelled by suburban political and economic pressures to help localities resist annexation by central cities, leading to state regulations ending the era of easy city expansion (Abbott, 1981:Chs. 2 and 7; Fleischmann, 1977). For instance, Colorado voters in 1974 approved constitutional amendments that more or less effectively blocked further annexations by Denver; traditionally permissive Texas began to place restrictions on the rate and procedures for annexation (Abbott, 1981:50–51). Even without new state measures to promote suburban autonomy, the economic growth and incorporation of suburban enclaves around central cities has begun to doom territorial growth of many cities.

In effect, postwar policies to promote growth in Sunbelt cities have begun to give way in the face of changes in the urban and regional political economy that push these cities closer to the dilemmas which confound cities elsewhere in the United States. Along with cutbacks in federal assistance at a time of increasing fiscal need, spreading suburban economic rivalry and the costs of coping with the consequences of rapid growth are creating patterns of urban dependency that in the future seem unlikely to differ radically from other cities in the postindustrial economy.

Development Politics: From Business Government to Community Politics

As in the case of local governments elsewhere, Sunbelt governments have had to manage tensions between popular control and development policy. Mobilizing political support for progrowth programs favoring low taxes, limited social services, annexation, and other developmental initiatives raises many volatile and divisive issues that can threaten important community groups. Residents of unincorporated areas sometimes resist annexation; low taxes mean doing without valued public services; redevelopment always displaces someone; rapid economic growth can damage the environment and stretch the capacity of local government to provide essential services.

BUSINESS GOVERNMENT.   Until recent years, Sunbelt business elites have undertaken to play a direct role in managing these tensions. For most of the postwar period, business elites commonly have placed a high priority on dominating the electoral process in order to secure control of local government offices. From this position, most conflicts over development policy could be sorted out within progrowth coalitions of business elites and officials who are closely tied to the local business community.

Ironically, this pattern of business activism in the day-to-day politics of development appears to have been linked to the relatively disadvantaged position that local business held within postwar Sunbelt city governments whose economies experienced rapid growth. To be sure, business' political prominence in local Sunbelt politics is an old tradition, as many studies have suggested (Hunter, 1953; Stone, 1976; Key, 1949). But this tradition has probably been closely tied to the peripheral (weak) market positions of these cities in the city system, rather than to any prevailing cultural disposition on the part of citizens. Underdeveloped, dependent economic communities provide an environment broadly favorable to those who can produce jobs, revenues, and community wealth, regardless of whether or not business leaders actually control public office.

The sudden spurt of postwar economic growth in the region could not help but threaten local business' traditional position of power and status in community governance, however. As the market positions of many previously underdeveloped Sunbelt cities grew in response to massive federal spending and regional shifts in private business investment, the economic power of local business in community politics was shaken. Failure to invest in the local economy becomes an empty threat and a declining source of political power for business in cities that are already becoming boom towns. Consequently, business power in local affairs became highly dependent on securing direct governmental control and winning electoral influence.

Accordingly, during the 1940s and 1950s throughout the Sunbelt local business elites moved aggressively to capture positions of power in cities from city hall political machines and patronage-bound local governments. In cities as diverse as Tucson, Tulsa, Portland, Atlanta, Denver, Dallas, San Antonio, Norfolk, Phoenix, and elsewhere, the story of local politics after World War II is one of ambitious reform drives led by urban business groups and good government leagues to defeat entrenched local bosses who were considered obstacles to business growth (Bernard and Rice, 1983; Goodall, 1967; Abbott, 1981:Ch 5).

Business' drive for power was usually connected with the adoption of local government reforms that served to enhance the electoral fortunes of business candidates. The immediate postwar decades saw the widespread adoption of charter reforms that made it much easier for local business candidates to compete and win in local elections and to end sources of patronage that held traditional political machines together. This usually included the adoption of at-large elections, nonpartisanship and council manager government, and other reforms that laid new political ground rules for winning power in city politics. In the absence of widespread ethnic divisions among the electorate, strong unions and many well-organized challenges to reforms seeking to "modernize" local government, business leaders surged to positions of governmental power (Fainstein et al., 1983:212ff.; Abbott, 1981:Chs. 5 and 10).

Unlike many northern cities, where business power in development was almost invariably quite indirect and depended on building large, diverse, progrowth coalitions led by party leaders, in Sunbelt cities a close relationship between the public and private sectors was created once business consolidated its governmental power. In Dallas, the Citizen's Charter Association, a group of leading city businessmen, decisively ran the city; a similar group in Phoenix, the "Phoenix 40," controlled local politics and decided most matters of land use policy and development policy; in San Antonio, the Good Government League comprised the major business-dominated vehicle in dominating local elections and public policy. Similar patterns existed in Albuquerque, Memphis, Miami, Tucson, New Orleans, Atlanta, Houston, San Diego, and elsewhere (Johnson et al., 1983; Lupsha and Siembieda, 1977; Fainstein and Fainstein, 1983; Abbott, 1981; Stone, 1983; Feagin, 1984).

Consequently, the major conflicts that arose over development were usually settled within the governing coalitions of developers, real estate interests, lending institutions and large downtown businesses, and middle-class reformers who supported the progrowth impulse of local government. Up through the 1960s, the politics of city development generally centered on building a consensus among business leaders and professional bureaucrats to support the policy triad of capital improvements, laissez faire planning, and, where possible, ambitious annexation.

Business government not only permitted the containment of tensions arising from the implementation of these policies by making political opposition difficult, it also allowed local businesses with fixed investments in the cities to exercise some control over the consequences of surging private investment by outside corporate investors. Consequently, the story of many business-dominated governments during the 1950s and 1960s is one of fights to protect the position of local banks, department stores, real estate interests, and other local businesses in the face of the growing corporate dependency of the local economy (Abbot, 1981; Judd, 1983; Smith and Keller, 1983; Goodall, 1967).

COMMUNITY POLITICS AND THE DECLINE OF BUSINESS GOVERNMENT. Since the 1970s, changes in the political economies of Sunbelt cities have unleashed substantial alterations in the developmental arena of growth centers. On one hand, there are social, economic, and governmental changes that progrowth policies have fostered which have made business domination of the process of popular control increasingly tenuous.

For one thing, the spectacular growth of these cities has brought about larger, more socially diverse electorates that are less inclined to support business leadership and have grown more hostile to the progrowth programs because of their mounting social and economic costs. In particular, years of population growth have enlarged the numbers of middle-income professional and minority residents who have asserted their political independence from traditional governing coalitions.

Beginning in the 1970s, many Sunbelt cities witnessed the defection of middle-class urbanites from progrowth coalitions. These groups are commonly comprised of highly skilled workers who form the bulwark of local corporate service economies—scientists, government workers, corporate managers, educators, lawyers, and other professionals. Their defection has often been triggered by the social costs of growth programs that have affected the quality of life in their cities and neighborhoods. Dissatisfaction has stemmed from such things as the desire to protect established neighborhoods from encroachment by commercial uses, inadequacy of public services, such as police protection, reliable water supply, and educational facilities, and fear that continued development will exacerbate problems with air quality, traffic congestion, and lack of amenities, and will raise taxes (Booth, 1983; Bernard and Rice, 1983; Abbott, 1981:Ch. 9).

The 1970s also witnessed growth and activism of minority groups in the politics of many Sunbelt cities. During the heyday of business-style progrowth government, minority demands for participation in government decisions were frequently satisfied by consulting informally with community leaders, by slating single black or Hispanic candidates for at-large council elections, and by winning gains in legal treatment, city jobs, and public housing (Johnson et al., 1983; Abbott, 1981:214). But the slowing of annexation and greater minority in-migration has often increased the numbers of minorities in city electorates and has brought in more assertive neighborhood leaders who have sought a larger share of political power.

Because city employment growth tends to disproportionately benefit newcomers and highly skilled workers, rather than minority residents (Bluestone and Harrison, 1982:87–90), black and Hispanic residents have a stake in slowing growth in hopes of improving city services that serve them. One result has been the successful alteration of city charters in such cities as San Antonio, Fort Worth, Albuquerque, San Francisco, and elsewhere to provide for ward voting and other changes. This has increased the representation of minorities in city councils and enabled minority or white liberal mayors to achieve electoral victories.

These shifting electoral tides and new issues have seriously challenged the elitist character of development politics even in some of the most tightly controlled business-style governments. In Houston, the 1981 election of Mayor Kathy Whitmire with minority and liberal support, including that of the city's gay community, was a major departure from the conservative progrowth tradition of the city (*New York Times*, 17 June 1983:B-1). The city's voters have asserted opposition to continued business domination on major development issues. Led by middle-class reformers, Houston voters in 1983 rejected by a wide margin a $2.35 billion bond issue to finance the first segment of a new urban rail system. What led to this defeat was the well-publicized fact that the decision to build the costly, downtown-oriented rail system had been made unilaterally by the transit authority board and powerful downtown business and development interests who spent $114,000 promoting the scheme, while opponents spent only $12,000 (*New York Times*, 13 June 1983:A-11).

Similar voter opposition to progrowth business-dominated government has occurred in many other Sunbelt cities. For instance, in San Antonio the late 1970s witnessed several defeats of proposals to annex or permit development of new areas largely because of opposition by residents in established middle-class neighborhoods and minority districts; they saw further development delaying the provision of adequate city services to their areas, threatening the city water supply, and driving up local government debt and taxes (Johnson, 1983; Abbott, 1981:232–238).

Economic Dependency and Political Change. On the other hand, there have been changes in the Sunbelt political economy that have diminished the importance of popular control as a source of constraint in the developmental arena of cities. This has, in turn, diminished the importance of business activism in local government as a channel of political power. Since the 1970s, there have been marked suburbanization of Sunbelt populations, the diminution of annexation programs by central cities, and the spreading of economic growth to smaller Sunbelt SMSAs. Altogether, these changes have cast booming Sunbelt cities into much greater intraregional economic competition and threatened their previously ascendant market positions. The continuation of this trend seems likely to fundamentally alter the position of urban business in development politics even in cities that have experienced the political mobilization of neighborhood groups in the developmental arena.

First, greater suburban and regional economic competition is likely to enhance the systemic economic power of urban business because their locational choices are more extensive; business control over developmental policy is no longer as dependent upon their direct political participation in city decision making. Groups seeking to challenge progrowth policies by wresting political power from business-dominated city halls may be frustrated because business no longer will have much of a stake in preserving this vehicle for achieving influence over development decision making.

Second, the shift of economic and political power to suburbia and rural areas is likely to alter the traditional position of Sunbelt state governments in favoring central city development strategies. As Sunbelt state economies and populations decentralize, the role of state government in regulating central city economic growth will increase in response to suburban political and economic pressures. The future is likely to be one of greater political and economic dependency for Sunbelt cities.

This scenario is illustrated by the case of Denver. As a result of rapid suburban growth and business dispersal after the 1960s, Denver has today taken on many of the socio-economic characteristics of northern central cities. Over the past thirty years, the city's share of the SMSA population and economic growth has steadily declined so that the bulk of new economic activity is now located in the Denver suburbs. In 1958, the vast majority—in fact, two-thirds or more—of all SMSA jobs in retailing, manufacturing, and services were located in Denver City; but this has dramatically diminished so that by 1977 less than 38 percent of retailing jobs, 58 percent of service jobs, and probably less than half of all manufacturing employment remained in Denver. Similarly, after 1960 Denver residents had lower socio-economic status and incomes than those living in the city's suburbs. As in most other Sunbelt metropolitan areas, most of the suburban employment growth is due to new residents and industries moving to the suburbs, rather than to spillover from the central city. In 1980, only about 31 percent of the area residents lived in Denver City (Judd, 1983:187, 195–196).

Consequently, the 1970s saw city officials undertake large downtown revitalization programs, relying on tax increment financing, local revenues, and private capital when federal funding for urban renewal fell short of program needs. Through renewal programs that concentrated resources on reclaiming and extending the downtown in preference to housing rehabilitation in outlying neighborhoods, city hall has cooperated closely with private capital—mostly from Canadian and out-of-state corporations—to set the redevelopment agenda for the city. As in many northern cities, community opposition and participation in Denver's renewal efforts have been scattered and with few exceptions easily turned aside by vigorous renewal administrators and public officials dedicated to making Denver competitive (Judd, 1983).

At the same time, the mushrooming of suburbia has limited the possibility of state regulation of regional development in ways that might enhance Denver. Fights between Denver officials and suburban governments and developers that have drawn in the state government have usually wound up with Denver on the losing side since the 1970s. For instance, suburban and rural legislators have bitterly resisted substantial attempts to impose a regional solution for Denver's very serious air pollution problem because it would have required restricting suburban development and auto usage (Judd, 1983). In fact, proposals for state restrictions on suburban growth for social, environmental, or economic objectives met with continual defeat at the state level in the wake of outspoken opposition by developers and by business and political leaders outside of Denver seeking to develop their own economic bases.

Dependency and the Dilemma of Democracy in Urban Development

Differences in market positions and dependency on intergovernmental programs and in systems of popular control interact to promote divergent patterns of local development politics. The politics of decline and conversion in central cities, the exclusionary politics of fortress suburbia, and the growth planning of Sunbelt boom towns illustrate the range of this diversity. What also emerges in these varied contexts are the different ways in which the urban political economy tends to impede extensive popular control of urban development. While popular control systems generate important tensions in local economic management, our review suggests that opportunities for citizen influence on policy are greatest where it matters least.

In central cities, the politics of coping with decline has motivated political authorities to aggressively buffer and insulate developmental decision making from mass political pressures. The dual constraints of managing weak market positions while contending with relatively polyarchal governmental systems has motivated authorities to limit the conflicts that these circumstances trigger. More than elsewhere, achieving economic management targets while maintaining political support for programs forces Frostbelt city officials to walk a tightrope; to stay on it they are inclined to limit democratic procedures if for no other reason than that it facilitates reaching their economic objectives and serves their own needs for political survival.

Business-dominated government in Sunbelt cities has visibly given way in the face of social and economic changes that work to enliven popular control institutions. But as cities in this region are becoming more economically dependent, it is likely that tendencies toward democratization of developmental politics are only transitory. The political convergence of these cities with America's older central cities seems likely.

Only in suburbia do the political demands of local citizens and the economic and political structures for serving them seem to find easy accommodation. The interests that tend to dominate suburban popular control systems often coincide closely with the exclusionary policies that promote the market positions of these jurisdictions. However, even here the limits on popular control of development are substantial. Because suburban market management entails—in fact, it requires—gatekeeper politics to exclude groups that might make competing demands, the structures of popular control can serve only parochial demands. Suburban governmental systems cannot be responsive to the broad array of excluded groups found in metropolitan areas that have a major stake in suburban development. In its way, the diversity of urban development politics suggests a common feature of America's dependent cities—the uncertain and limited place of the mass citizenry in guiding their growth.

Endnotes

1. The effects of relatively "free market" suburbanization are aptly illustrated by one part of the New York region that grew without the usual public policies to restrict development, Staten Island. The opening of the Verrazano Narrows bridge in 1964 precipitated a building boom that led to the rapid "suburbanization" of this relatively isolated and underpopulated borough of New York City. The city had no master plan for the borough's sudden development, and it imposed few public constraints on building; even large tracts of city-owned land were sold off to private developers virtually without restrictions. Minimum lot sizes were so small—40 by 100 feet—as to constitute hardly any regulation. As a result, most of the housing built by the private sector on Staten Island was smaller, cheaper, and in greater residential densities than that built in the New York suburbs during the same period. Though the borough's relatively unfettered private development often outraged planners who criticized the "ticky-tacky" character of the housing and the lack of consideration given to services and amenities, few other areas offered so much space, privacy, and "country" at such affordable prices (Danielson and Doig, 1982:106–107).

2. New Jersey's experience in the wake of the state Supreme Court's famous Mount Laurel case in 1975 strongly supports this conclusion. The court held against towns using zoning powers to remain "enclaves of affluence or homogeneity," and it mandated more balanced residential development in order to meet regional housing needs. Though this decision was reaffirmed by the same court in 1983, the Mount Laurel doctrine has largely remained unfulfilled. Suburban, legislative, and gubernatorial resistance to plans for more low- and moderate-income suburban housing has undercut the court decision. By 1987, the housing agency created to enforce the law was emphasizing the rebuilding of inner city housing in an effort to respond to the state's housing needs (*New York Times*, 1 June 1987:B-1).

References for Part Four

Abbott, Carl. 1981. *The New Urban America: Growth and Politics in Sunbelt Cities*. Chapel Hill: University of North Carolina Press.

Advisory Commission on Intergovernmental Relations. 1982. *State and Local Roles in the Federal System*. Washington, D.C.: U.S. Governmental Printing Office.

Advisory Commission on Intergovernmental Relations. 1981. *Regional Growth: Interstate Tax Competition*. A-76. Washington, D.C.: U.S. Government Printing Office.

Advisory Commission on Intergovernmental Relations. 1967. *State–Local Taxation and Industrial Location*. Washington, D.C.: U.S. Government Printing Office.

Advisory Commission on Intergovernmental Relations. 1964. *The Problem of Special Districts in American Government*. Washington, D.C.: U.S. Government Printing Office.

Altschuler, Alan, et al. 1979. *The Urban Transportation System: Politics and Policy Innovation*. Cambridge, Mass.: MIT Press.

Anderson, Martin. 1964. *The Federal Bulldozer*. Cambridge, Mass.: MIT Press.

Armington, Catherine, Candee Harris and Marjorie Odle. 1984. "Formation and Growth in High Technology Firms: A Regional Assessment." Appendix B. Office of Technology Assessment. 1984. *Technology Innovation and Regional Economic Development*. Washington, D.C.: U.S. Government Printing Office, pp. 108–143.

Ashton, Patrick J. 1984. "Urbanization and the Dynamics of Suburban Development under Capitalism" in William K. Tabb and Larry Sawers, eds. 1984. *Marxism and the Metropolis*. New York: Oxford University Press, Ch. 3.

Babcock, Richard F. 1980. "The Spatial Impact of Land Use and Environmental Controls" in A. P. Solomon, ed. 1980. *The Prospective City*. Cambridge, Mass: MIT Press, pp. 264–287.

Babcock, Richard F. and Fred P. Bosselman. 1973. *Zoning: Land Use Regulation and Housing in the 1970s*. New York: Praeger.

Banfield, Edward C. 1961. *Political Influence*. New York: Free Press.

Banfield, Edward C. and James Q. Wilson. 1965. *City Politics*. Cambridge Mass.: Harvard University Press.

Bellush, Jewel and Stephen M. David. 1971. *Race and Politics in New York City*. New York: Praeger.

Bellush, Jewel and Murry Hausknecht. 1967. *Urban Renewal: People, Politics and Planning*. New York: Doubleday.

Bernard, Richard M. and Bradley R. Rice, eds. 1983. *Sunbelt Cities: Politics and Growth Since World War II*. Austin: University of Texas Press.

Bluestone, Barry and Bennett Harrison. 1982. *The Deindustrialization of America: Plant Closings, Community Abandonment and the Dismantling of Basic Industry*. New York: Basic Books.

Bollens, John C. 1961. *Special District Governments in the U.S.* Berkeley: University of California Press.

Booth, John A. 1983. "Political Changes in San Antonio, 1970–82: Toward Decay or Democracy?" in David R. Johnson et al. 1983. *The Politics of San Antonio*. Lincoln: University of Nebraska Press, Ch. 10.

Brownell, Blaine A. and David R. Goldfield. 1977. *The City in Southern History*. Port Washington, N.Y.: Kennikat Press.

Burchell, Robert W. and David Listokin, eds. 1981. *Cities under Stress*. New Brunswick, N.J.: Center for Urban Policy Research, Rutgers University.

Caro, Robert. 1974. *The Power Broker*. New York: Vintage Books.

Clavel, Pierre, John Forester and William Goldsmith, eds. 1980. *Urban and Regional Planning in an Age of Austerity*. New York: Pergamon Press.

Cox, Kevin R. 1973. *Conflict, Power and Politics in the City: A Geographic View*. New York: McGraw-Hill.

Cullingworth, J. B. 1972. *Problems of an Urban Society*, 2 Vols. London: Allen and Unwin.

Dahl, Robert A. 1961. *Who Governs?* New Haven, Conn.: Yale University Press.

Danielson, Michael N. 1976. *The Politics of Exclusion*. New York: Columbia University Press.

Danielson, Michael N. and Jameson W. Doig. 1982. *New York: The Politics of Urban and Regional Development*. Berkeley: University of California Press.

David, Stephen and Paul Kantor. 1983. "Urban Policy in the Federal System: A Reconceptualization of Federalism." *Polity*, Vol. XVI, No. 2, 284–304.

Department of Housing and Urban Development. 1980. *President's National Urban Policy Report*. Washington, D.C.: U.S. Government Printing Office.

Downs, Anthony. 1976. *Urban Problems and Prospects*. New York: Rand McNally.

Downs, Anthony. 1973. *Opening up the Suburbs*. New Haven, Conn.: Yale University Press.

Downs, Anthony. 1957. *An Economic Theory of Democracy*. New York: Harper and Brothers.

Edgar, Richard E. 1970. *Urban Power and Social Welfare*. Beverly Hills: Sage.

Elkin, Stephen L. 1987. *City and Regime in the American Republic*. Chicago: University of Chicago Press.

Elkin, Stephen L. 1981. "State and Regime in the American Republic." *Paper presented at the Annual Meeting of the American Political Science Association*, New York, September 3–6.

Fainstein, Norman I. and Susan S. Fainstein. 1983. "New Haven: The Limits of the Local State" in Susan Fainstein et al. 1983. *Restructuring the City: The Political Economy of Urban Redevelopment*. New York: Longman, Ch. 2.

Fainstein, Susan S., Norman Fainstein, Richard Child Hill, Dennis Judd and

Michael P. Smith. 1983. *Restructuring the City: The Political Economy of Urban Redevelopment*. New York: Longman.

Feagin, Joe R. 1984. "Sunbelt Metropolis and Development Capital: Houston in the Era of Late Capitalism" in Larry Sawers and William K. Tabb, eds. 1984. *Sunbelt, Snowbelt*. New York: Oxford University Press, Ch. 4.

Fleischmann, Arnold. 1977. "Sunbelt Boosterism: The Politics of Postwar Growth and Annexation in San Antonio" in David C. Perry and Alfred J. Watkins. 1977. *The Rise of the Sunbelt Cities*. Beverly Hills: Sage, Ch. 6.

Franklin, J. James. 1981. "New Dimensions of the Urban Crisis" in Robert W. Burchell and David Listokin, eds. 1981. *Cities under Stress*. New Brunswick, N.J.: Center for Urban Policy Research, Rutgers University, pp. 19–49.

Fried, Joseph. 1971. *Housing Crisis—U.S.A.* New York: Praeger.

Frieden, Bernard J. and Marshall Kaplan. 1975. *The Politics of Neglect: Urban Aid from Model Cities to Revenue Sharing*. Cambridge, Mass.: MIT Press.

Friedland, Roger. 1983. *Power and Crisis in the City*. New York: Macmillan.

Gannett Westchester Newspapers. 15 December 1979, A-15.

Goodall, Leonard E., ed. 1967. *Urban Politics in the Southwest*. Tempe: Arizona State University Press.

Goodman, Robert. 1979. *The Last Entrepreneurs*. Boston: South End Press.

Griffith, J. A. G. 1966. *Central Departments and Local Authorities*. London: Allen and Unwin.

Glazer, Nathan. 1980. "The Bias of American Housing Policy" in Jon Pynoos et al., eds. 1980. *Housing Urban America*. New York: Aldine, pp. 428–430.

Hall, Peter, et al. 1973. *The Containment of Urban England*, 2 Vols. London: Allen and Unwin.

Harrigan, John J. 1981. *Political Change in the Metropolis*, Second Edition. Boston: Little, Brown.

Harrison, Bennett and Sandra Kanter. 1978. "The Political Economy of State Job-Creation Incentives." *Journal of the American Institute of Planners*, Vol. 44, No. 4 (October), 424–435.

Hartman, Chester. 1974. *Yerba Buena: Land Grab and Community Resistance in San Francisco*. San Francisco: Glide Publications.

Hays, Edward C. 1972. *Power Structure and Urban Policy: Who Rules Oakland?* New York: McGraw-Hill.

Hicks, Donald A. 1985. *Advanced Industrial Development: Restructuring, Relocation and Renewal*. Boston: Oelgeschlager, Gunn, and Hain.

Hill, Richard C. 1983. "Crisis in the Motor City: The Politics of Economic Development in Detroit" in Susan Fainstein et al. 1983. *Restructuring the City: The Political Economy of Urban Redevelopment*. New York: Longman, Ch. 3.

Hunter, Floyd. 1953. *Community Power Structure*. Chapel Hill: University of North Carolina Press.

Institute for Local Self Government. 1970. *Special Districts or Special Dynasties? Democracy Denied*. Berkeley: By the Institute.

James, Franklin J. 1981. "Economic Distress in Central Cities" in Robert W. Burchell and David Listokin, eds. 1981. *Cities under Stress*. New Brunswick,

N.J.: Center for Urban Policy Research, Rutgers University, pp. 19–50.

Johnson, David R., John A. Booth and Richard J. Harris, eds. 1983. *The Politics of San Antonio*. Lincoln: University of Nebraska Press.

Joint Economic Committee, U.S. Congress. 1981. *State and Local Economic Development Strategy: A "Supply Side" Perspective*. Washington, D.C.: U.S. Government Printing Office.

Jones, Bryan D. and Lynn W. Bachelor with Carter Wilson. 1986. *The Sustaining Hand: Community Leadership and Corporate Power*. Lawrence: University of Kansas Press.

Judd, Dennis R. 1984. *The Politics of American Cities*, Second Edition. Boston: Little, Brown.

Judd, Dennis R. 1983. "From Cowtown to Sunbelt: Boosterism and Economic Growth in Denver" in Susan Fainstein et al. 1983. *Restructuring the City: The Political Economy of Urban Redevelopment*. New York: Longman, Ch. 5.

Juster, Thomas F. 1976. *The Economic and Political Impact of General Revenue Sharing*. Report Prepared by the Survey Research Center for the National Science Foundation. Washington, D.C.: U.S. Government Printing Office.

Kantor, Paul and Stephen David. 1983. "The Political Economy of Change in Urban Budgetary Politics: A Framework for Analysis and a Case Study." *British Journal of Political Science*, Vol. 13 (July), 251–274.

Kaplan, Harold. 1963. *Urban Renewal Politics*. New York: Columbia University Press.

Key, V. O. 1949. *Southern Politics*. New York: Vintage.

Kieschnick, Michael. 1981. *Taxes and Growth: Business Incentives and Economic Development*. Washington, D.C.: Council of State Planning Agencies.

Kieth, Nathaniel. 1973. *Politics and the Housing Crisis Since 1930*. New York: Universe.

Kleniewski, Nancy. 1984. "From Industrial to Corporate City: The Role of Urban Renewal" in William K. Tabb and Larry Sawers, eds. 1984. *Marxism and the Metropolis*. New York: Oxford University Press, Ch. 9.

Laska, Shirley and E. Spain, eds. 1980. *Back to the City*. Elmsford, N.Y.: Pergamon Press.

Levy, John M. 1981. *Economic Development Programs for Cities, Counties and Towns*. New York: Praeger.

Lilley, III, William. 1980. "The Homebuilders' Lobby" in Jon Pynoos et al., eds. 1980. *Housing Urban America*. New York: Aldine, pp. 32–50.

Lindblom, Charles E. 1977. *Politics and Markets*. New York: Basic Books.

Logan, John R. and Harvey L. Molotch. 1987. *Urban Fortunes: The Political Economy of Place*. Berkeley: University of California Press.

Lowi, Theodore J. 1968. *The End of Liberalism*. New York: Norton.

Lupo, Alan, Frank Colcord and Edmund P. Fowler. 1971. *Rites of Way: The Politics of Transportation in Boston and the U.S. City*. Boston: Little, Brown.

Lupsha, Peter A. and William Siembieda. 1977. "The Poverty of Public Services in the Land of Plenty" in David C. Perry and Alfred J. Watkins.

1977. *The Rise of the Sunbelt Cities.* Beverly Hills: Sage, Ch. 7.

Mandell, Lewis. 1975. *Industrial Location Decisions: Detroit Compared with Atlanta and Chicago.* New York: Praeger.

Mier, Robert. 1982. "Enterprise Zones: A Long Shot." *Planning,* Vol. 48 (April), 10–14.

Mier, Robert and Scott E. Gelzer. 1982. "State Enterprise Zones: The New Frontier." *Urban Affairs Quarterly,* Vol. 18, No. 1 (September), 39–52.

Mathais, Jr., Charles McC. 1979. "Contrasting Urban Problems: The Cases of Houston and New York" in Gary A. Tobin, ed. 1979. *The Changing Structure of the City.* Beverly Hills: Sage, Ch. 12.

Mollenkopf, John H. 1983. *The Contested City.* Princeton, N.J.: Princeton University Press.

Molotch, Harvey. 1976. "The City As a Growth Machine." *American Journal of Sociology,* Vol. 82 (September), 304–332.

Murphy, Thomas P. and John Rehfuss. 1976. *Urban Politics in the Suburban Era.* Homewood, Ill.: Dorsey Press.

National Commission on Neighborhoods. 1979. *People Building Neighborhoods.* Washington, D.C.: U.S. Government Printing Office.

New York Times. 9 June 1983, A-14.

New York Times. 29 September 1983, B-20.

New York Times. 2 April 1984, A-14.

New York Times. 22 November 1987:L-31.

Orlebeke, Charles J. 1982. "Administering Enterprise Zones: Some Initial Observations." *Urban Affairs Quarterly,* Vol. 18, No. 1 (September), 31–38.

Perry, David C. and Alfred J. Watkins. 1977. *The Rise of the Sunbelt Cities.* Beverly Hills: Sage.

Peterson, George E. 1980. "The Impact of Federal Policies on Urban Economic Development" in A. P. Solomon, ed. 1980. *The Prospective City.* Cambridge, Mass.: MIT Press, Ch. 13.

Peterson, James E. 1979. "The Role of the City in the Region's Economy" in Benjamin Chinitz, ed. 1979. *Central City Economic Development.* Cambridge, Mass.: AGT Books, Ch. 11.

Peterson, Paul E. 1981. *City Limits.* Chicago: University of Chicago Press.

Pynoos, Jon, Robert Schafer and Chester W. Hartman, eds. 1980. *Housing Urban America,* Updated Second Edition. New York: Aldine.

Rosenthal, Donald B., ed. 1980. *Urban Revitalization.* Beverly Hills: Sage.

Rossi, Peter and Robert A. Dentler. 1961. *The Politics of Urban Renewal: The Chicago Findings.* New York: Free Press.

Sanders, Heywood T. 1980. "Urban Renewal and the Revitalized City: A Reconsideration of Recent History" in Donald B. Rosenthal, ed. 1980. *Urban Revitalization.* Beverly Hills: Sage, Ch. 4.

Sawers, Larry and William K. Tabb, eds. 1984. *Sunbelt, Snowbelt.* New York: Oxford University Press.

Saxenian, Anna Lee. 1984. "The Urban Contradictions of Silicon Valley" in Larry Sawers and William K. Tabb, ed. 1984. *Sunbelt, Snowbelt.* New York: Oxford University Press, Ch. 7.

Schemenner, Roger. 1980. "Industrial Location and Urban Public Management" in A. P. Solomon, ed. 1980. *The Prospective City.* Cambridge, Mass.: MIT Press, pp. 446–468.

Schemenner, Roger. 1978. *The Manufacturing Location Decision: Evidence from Cincinnati and New England.* Report to the Economic Development Administration, U.S. Department of Commerce (March). Washington, D.C.: U.S. Government Printing Office.

Schulze, Robert O. 1961. "The Bifurcation of Power in a Satellite City" in Morris Janowitz, ed. 1961. *Community Political Systems.* Glencoe, Ill.: Free Press, pp. 19–80.

Schwartz, Barry, ed. 1976. *The Changing Face of the Suburbs.* Chicago: University of Chicago Press.

Scott, Stanley and John Corzine. 1963. *Special Districts in the San Francisco Bay Area: Some Problems and Issues.* Berkeley: Institute of Governmental Studies.

Shannon, John and Bruce McDowell. 1985. "Interstate Competition for Industry." *Paper delivered to the American Political Science Association,* September 1985 in New Orleans, La.

Shefter, Martin. 1985. *Political Crisis, Fiscal Crisis: The Collapse and Revitalization of New York City.* New York: Basic Books.

Small, Kenneth A. 1985. "Transportation and Urban Change" in Paul E. Peterson, ed. 1985. *The New Urban Reality.* Washington, D.C.: Brookings Institution, pp. 197–224.

Smith, Michael P. and Marlene Keller. 1983. "Managed Growth and the Politics of Uneven Development in New Orleans" in Susan Fainstein et al. 1983. *Restructuring the City: The Political Economy of Urban Redevelopment.* New York: Longman, Ch. 4.

Solomon, A. P., ed. 1980. *The Prospective City.* Cambridge, Mass.: MIT Press.

South Bronx Development Office, City of New York. 1981. *Policy Recommendations of the Draft Final Plan for the South Bronx.* June. New York: By SBDO.

Starr, Roger. 1976. "Making New York Smaller," *New York Times Magazine,* 14 November.

Sternlieb, George and James W. Hughes. 1981. "New Dimensions of the Urban Crisis" in Robert W. Burchell and David Listokin, eds. 1981. *Cities under Stress.* New Brunswick, N.J.: Center for Urban Policy Research, Rutgers University, pp. 51–76.

Stone, Clarence N. 1983. "Race, Power and Political Change." *Paper Delivered to the Annual Meeting of the American Political Science Association,* Chicago, Illinois.

Stone, Clarence N. 1976. *Economic Growth and Neighborhood Discontent.* Chapel Hill: University of North Carolina Press.

Stone, Michael E. 1980. "Federal Housing Policy: A Political-Economic Analysis" in Jon Pynoos et al., eds. 1980. *Housing Urban America.* New York: Aldine, pp. 448–458.

Struyk, Raymond, John Trucillo and Neil Mayer. 1983. *Federal Housing Policy at President Reagan's Mid-term*. Washington, D.C.: Urban Institute.

Swanstrom, Todd. 1985. *The Crisis of Growth Politics: Cleveland, Kucinich and the Challenge of Urban Populism*. Philadelphia: Temple University Press.

Tabb, William K. 1984. "Urban Development and Regional Restructuring" in Larry Sawers and William K. Tabb, eds. 1984. *Sunbelt, Snowbelt*. New York: Oxford University Press, Ch. 1.

Tabb, William K. and Larry Sawers, eds. 1984. *Marxism and the Metropolis*. New York: Oxford University Press.

Tobin, Gary A., ed. 1979. *The Changing Structure of the City*. Beverly Hills: Sage.

Truman, David B. 1951. *The Governmental Process*. New York: Knopf.

Tucker, C. Jack. 1984. "City-Suburban Population Redistribution: What the Data from the 1970s Reveal." *Urban Affairs Quarterly*, Vol. 19 (June), 539–549.

Vaughan, Roger J. 1980. "The Impact of Federal Policies on Urban Economic Development" in A. P. Solomon, ed. 1980. *The Prospective City*. Cambridge, Mass.: MIT Press, Ch. 12.

Vaughan, Roger J. 1979. *State Taxation and Economic Development*. Washington, D.C.: Council of State Planning Agencies.

Vaughan, Roger. 1977. "The Urban Impacts of Federal Policies." *Economic Development*, Vol. 2. Santa Monica, Calif.: Rand Corporation.

Walton, John. 1982. "Cities and Jobs and Politics." *Urban Affairs Quarterly*, Vol. 18, No. 1 (September), 5–18.

Watkins, Alfred J. 1980. *The Practice of Urban Economics*. Beverly Hills: Sage.

Watkins, Alfred J. and David C. Perry, eds. 1977. *The Rise of the Sunbelt Cities*. Beverly Hills: Sage.

Weiss, Marc. 1980. "The Origins and Legacy of Urban Renewal" in Pierre Clavel et al., eds. 1980. *Urban and Regional Planning in an Age of Austerity*. New York: Pergamon Press, Ch. 4.

Williams, Oliver P. and Charles R. Adrian. 1963. *Four Cities*. Philadelphia: University of Pennsylvania Press.

Wilson, James Q., ed. 1966. *Urban Renewal: The Record and the Controversy*. Cambridge, Mass.: MIT Press.

Wilson, James Q. 1963. "Planning and Politics: Citizen Participation in Urban Renewal." *Journal of the American Institute of Planners*, Vol. XXIX, No. 4 (November), 242–249.

Wirt, Fredrick M., Benjamin Walter, Francine Rabinovitz and Deborah R. Hensler. 1972. *On the City's Rim: Politics and Policy in Suburbia*. Boston: D.C. Heath.

Zimmer, Basil. 1976. "Suburbanization and Changing Political Structures" in Barry Schwartz, ed. 1976. *The Changing Face of the Suburbs*. Chicago: University of Chicago Press, pp. 165–202.

Zimmer, Basil. 1964. *Rebuilding Cities*. Chicago: Quadrangle Books.

PART FIVE

The Politics of Distribution

CHAPTER FOURTEEN

Politicos, Reformers, and Public Policy

THE postindustrial political economy has significantly altered the scope and content of local government's distributive public policies. Although economic and intergovernmental developments played a part in bringing this about, changes in urban governmental systems have been most decisive. Contemporary popular control systems have given rise to two competing approaches to distribution that dominate local governance—that of the *reformer* and that of the *politico*.

The Politico-Economic Context of Distribution

The Economics of Distributive Policy

As discussed previously, the distinctive characteristic of distributive policies is that they have very limited effects on the market position of a locality. Although it is difficult to gauge precisely the scope of such policy activities, it is apparent that in the postindustrial economic context the range of such policies is vast. For example, a local government can recruit and promote hundreds of job candidates on the basis of competitive "merit" examinations open to all, or selections can be based on party loyalty, ethnic identity, racial characteristics, or other particularistic criteria. Differences in competency among job-holders might result from use of one set of criteria or another (leading to greater or lesser "productivity" in the governmental work setting), but such differences generally are quite marginal. They are unlikely to become important costs or benefits to private sector operations (Peterson, 1981:Ch. 8).

Similarly, the traditional housekeeping programs of city governments, such as law enforcement, fire protection, and sanitation, have remained essentially distributive in function since the industrial era. Marginal differences in their provision usually do not significantly affect a locality's market position in respect to competing jurisdictions. In fact, even if housekeeping services are grossly underprovided by localities, the presence of other locational advantages, such as low taxes, and the ability of householders and businesses to purchase services from private sellers may cancel out any effects on a community's competitive position. It is probably the case that some city services which were of considerable developmental consequence during the industrial period, such as water supply and sewage, are today much more distributive in character. Although these services are of importance to industrial production, they are probably less integral to urban development in an economic world where nonmanufacturing enterprises sometimes find remote and "underserviced" suburban and rural governmental jurisdictions attractive business environments.

Personnel and housekeeping policies hardly exhaust the range of distributive activities in contemporary urban governance. Varied forms of symbolic and material benefits can be conferred by political authorities without much regard to economic consequences. Bus routes and schedules can be altered to please neighborhood preferences, streets can be named to honor the living and the dead, community boards and advisory committees can be set up to encourage local "participation," parades can be sponsored to promote ethnic pride, political appointments and ticket "balancing" at election time can reflect religious, racial, and ethnic "recognition." These things are the stuff over which local politics has often been fought, and the new economic order has not diminished them.

It is more than likely that postindustrial developments actually have increased the distributive activities of local government since the industrial period. Urban economic change has increased the demand for state and local services. The dispersal of population to larger numbers of jurisdictions and the expanded role of government as a regulator of the private sector and as a provider of goods and services have increased public employment, especially at the state and local levels (ACIR, 1982:22–25). Between 1954 and 1980, state and local government employment increased by 174 percent, while growth in the federal sector was only about 22 percent (Bahl, 1974:9). The state and local share of nonagricultural employment has increasingly dwarfed that of the federal government. During the 1950–1975 period, the government share of nonagricultural employment in the United States rose from 13 to 19 percent. While the federal share actually fell from 4.3 percent to 3.6 percent, state and local employment increased from 9 to 15 percent (Lewin et al., 1979:4). As noted below, the bulk of local government employment has been in distributive activities.

The Intergovernmental System and Distribution

Since 1930, there has been almost continuous expansion of federal and state programs that provide financial assistance or regulate the administration of local public services. This has imposed a large intergovernmental dimension on local distribution (Wirt, 1985). Whereas in 1929 virtually no federal grant-in-aid program to local governments for distributive purposes existed, today there are many. Until very recently, General Revenue Sharing provided funds that localities were free to use for nearly any legal purpose, and distributive expenditures for things such as new garbage trucks, police cars, and other housekeeping services were among the favorite choices of most local governments (David and Kantor, 1983). Similarly, the CETA program, although intended as a job-training and employment program, has provided personnel to help run local public services. During the 1960s, the federal government began providing funds for modernizing local police forces. Cities all across the country started to acquire flash bars for police cars, radio communication systems became standard, and many cities purchased helicopters, armored vehicles, and computers, and embarked on special training programs for law enforcement units (Jacob, 1984:5). With most new federal aid has also come new federal regulations in order to ensure that local practice adheres to national guidelines.

State programs have long played a major role in the local distributive arena, and this has continued to expand. As noted in Chapter 10, the postwar era has been one of tremendous growth in state aid programs to local governments, and new state laws governing taxation have significantly broadened the fiscal base upon which local service delivery depends. At the same time, state mandates and regulations for localities have affected the local administration of distributive services. For instance, a study of changes in state law in selected order maintenance offenses and serious crimes over a thirty-one year period suggests how continuously state governments have defined and redefined the obligations of local law enforcement agencies. The study found that state legislatures continuously altered the law in one or another category of offenses in all but one of the years since 1948 (Jacob, 1984:143).

Despite this surge of intergovernmental distributive activity, it does not mean that federal and state intervention now severely limit local policy choices in this arena. A major consequence of the enlargement of federal and state grant-in-aid programs to localities has been the expanded capability of local governments to provide distributive services. Intergovernmental funding today makes up about 40 percent of local government revenue sources; though much of this aid is targeted for essentially redistributive purposes, local programs for "basic" (mostly distributive) services rival the former in expenditure levels (see Chapter 10). This aid now comprises a major segment of the resource base for local distributional activities. In effect, many traditional distributive services can be provided by localities without relying as heavily as they once did upon locally generated revenues.

This impact is suggested by the fact that local governments have continued to dominate the provision of distributive services among the various levels of government despite increasing intergovernmental funding. As Table 14-1 indicates, governmental functions that are essentially distributive overwhelmingly are run by localities, rather than by states or the federal government. Aside from education, local government employees comprise from 69 to 100 percent of the staff for police, fire, sanitation, sewage, parks and recreation, libraries, and general services in 1967 and in 1977.

State and federal interest in dominating local distributive policy has not grown along with their program involvement. Greater local program linkages with higher-level governments could severely limit local policy choice if they

TABLE 14-1   Percentage of Full-Time Equivalent Employment, by Level of Government and Function: October 1967 and October 1977

| | October 1977 | | | October 1967 | | |
Function	Federal	State	Local	Federal	State	Local
Distributive:						
Police	9%	11%	80%	6%	12%	82%
Fire	—*	—	100	—	—	100
Sewerage	—	—	100	—	—	100
Other sanitation	—	—	100	—	—	100
Local parks and recreation	—	—	100	—	—	100
Libraries	—	—	100	—	—	100
General control	11	20	69	15	12	73
Correction	4	59	37	4	61	35
Redistribution:						
Public welfare	3	45	52	3	35	62
Hospitals	14	43	43	16	44	40
Health	27	33	40	30	28	43
Developmental:						
Highways	1	47	52	1	51	48
Natural resources	59	35	6	61	33	7
Airports	76	—	24	80	—	20
Water transport	56	19	25	69	9	22
Other:						
Education						
Local schools	—	—	99	—	—	99
Higher education	—	82	18	—	87	13
Other education	16	84	—	13	87	—
Housing and urban renewal	18	—	82	27	—	73
Financial administration	28	31	41	32	30	39
Total	20%	22%	58%	28%	19%	53%

*Represents zero or rounds to zero.
SOURCE: Adapted from Advisory Commission on Intergovernmental Relations, *State and Local Roles in the Federal System*, Report A-88 (Washington, D.C.: U.S. Government Printing Office, 1982), p. 24.

were accompanied by attempts by national and state officials to manipulate local policy in order to serve their own political interests. But, in fact, federal and state intervention in this arena has generally stopped well short of this. Officials in higher levels of government no longer have substantial partisan interests in the distribution of basic services within urban governmental jurisdictions. With the decline of the machine and spread of reform-style government, neither federal nor state political leaders are very inclined to "play politics" in this way.

Though state party officials routinely meddled in local distributive politics during the industrial era to reward their followers and gain partisan advantage, today this is not as necessary. With the dispersal of populations to suburbia and beyond, state policies governing the strategic use of special districts, municipal incorporation, and land use planning tend to segregate groups in ways that enable some to receive favored treatment in public services. From the perspective of state politics, this has replaced competition for favors from city hall as a means of dispensing favorable service packages to groups and neighborhoods in exchange for their political support (cf. Rich, 1980:243).

THE POLITICAL BIAS OF INTERGOVERNMENTAL ACTIVITY.   Consequently, on matters of implementing distributive programs, federal and state officials are mostly interested in matters of efficiency, honesty, and administrative rationality because there is not much else to divert them from these considerations. Most state and federal regulatory activities in local distribution work to prohibit favoritism and to encourage professionalism and economy in the administration of public services—the traditional ideals of urban reform.

For example, since the 1960s federal regulations have prohibited racial, religious, and sexual discrimination in public programs that receive federal aid. Moreover, state and federal laws prohibit discrimination by local governments in the delivery of basic public services, such as police and fire protection, sanitation, etc. Similarly, state legislatures typically put all local governments under a common statewide civil service law that regulates hiring, promotion, and discipline of public employees in accordance with merit criteria as enunciated by state and local civil service commissions (Horton, 1973:111; Stanley, 1972:11). Federal and state grants-in-aid almost uniformly require workable programs, planning requirements, and careful audits of expenditures to ensure accountability and "rationality" in carrying out even the more mundane programs, such as purchasing new street-sweeping equipment or police riot helmets.

The main constraint that state and federal intervention in this area of policy imposes on localities is one that cannot be easily manipulated—namely, support for reform-style governance. This is not of inconsiderable consequence for politics in this arena (see below). But it usually does not place state and federal actors in positions of power in local decision making. In effect, the expansion of state and federal involvement in local distributive activities has added a greater intergovernmental presence without displacing local government as the prime arena of policy decision. The major thrust of increased intergovernmental intervention has been to stimulate local provision of these services and to encourage greater conformity to the ideals of reform-style governance in their administration.

Popular Control and Distribution

Since distributive policies tend to have little influence on the market position of localities, and the policy preferences of intergovernmental actors usually do not loom large on these issues, political forces arising from within the city decisively shape the governance of this arena. In general, this means that the politics of distribution is strongly influenced by the extensive political decentralization and fragmentation of power that tends to characterize urban governmental systems today.

The restructuring of urban political systems during the last generation or so has unleashed ambivalent forces on local government. On one hand, as systems of popular control have moved closer to fulfilling polyarchal conditions, this has encouraged decentralization of power and enhanced the possibilities for responsiveness of rulers to the ruled. The decline of the political machine has opened up opportunities for urban political competition. The reform movement and its "good government" institutions have militated against partisan manipulation of elections. The socio-economic changes within urban populations have given rise to increased independence and assertiveness by groups that in earlier eras were under the tutelage of political bosses. All these events have worked to disperse political power and increase the opportunities for political competition in systems where demands are no longer easily "managed" by governmental authorities.

On the other hand, these polyarchal, decentralist tendencies have been accompanied by institutional changes that limit the ability of elected political authorities to respond to mass demands. Urban reformers sought to end political favoritism and partisan monopolies of political power by weakening partisanship itself and creating a larger role for bureaucratic experts in the running of cities. In particular, the reform ideal of relying upon expert professionals to make decisions on the basis of honesty and efficiency places bureaucratic organizations in positions of unprecedented independence and power. This has been reinforced by the expansion of intergovernmental programs which, as suggested above, are supportive of highly bureaucratic, reform-style governance.

Consequently, citizen demands now run a gauntlet of power within urban political systems that is likely to be procedurally quite democratic *and* politically fragmented. The industrial era system based on partisan monopoly of political control has been exchanged for one in which political leaders, bureaucrats, and citizen groups all must vigorously compete to achieve influence. A change of this magnitude and kind has major implications for the scope and purposes of local distributive policy. It also has profound consequences for the very governability of the city, a matter that is examined in the following chapter.

In sum, the postindustrial political economy has carved out a major place for local communities and their governments in matters of distribution. In this arena of public policy, local governments are most independent of economic discipline arising from their market positions and deal with fairly limited intergovernmental intervention in policy choice. Consequently, it is the workings of the decentralist, polyarchal urban governmental systems that we focus upon in order to understand public policy in this arena.

Reformer Vs. Politico Approaches to Public Policy

Because distributive policies in the contemporary city are so diverse, it is not easy to generalize about their political characteristics. Nevertheless, it is possible to identify the dominant political values that govern resource allocation and some salient patterns of bias in the content of these policies.

Recall that in the industrial era the market approach to public services was in its heyday. Then distributive policies mainly functioned to sustain political support for the machine. The allocation of jobs and services was governed by the use of particularistic criteria; whenever possible, material and symbolic benefits were used to reward the party faithful while being withheld from the opposition. Party organization chiefs "marketed" (or brokered) the administration of services in order to enhance their power and profit. As a by-product of this process, benefits were distributed in ways that were strongly biased in favor of satisfying the individual demands of groups whose contributions in votes, time, and money were valued by the machine.

In the postindustrial city, the decline of the machine weakened the use of distributive policies as a means of serving as *quid pro quo* for political support. Distributive policy now reflects the demands of a varied network of professional, partisan, bureaucratic, intergovernmental, neighborhood, and other interests that vie for power in the city. The result has been the emergence of two competing approaches to distribution—reformer and politico. Each differs in respect to the political values and functions of distribution.

Reformism: The Dominant Approach

To a large extent, the content of distributive policy has come into conformity with the traditional values espoused by the urban reform movement. Specifically, this has meant (1) the use of universalistic criteria as the standards of entitlement in allocating resources, (2) delegation of wide decision-making authority to public bureaucratic organizations, and (3) the insulation of distributive programs from the traditional function of political support-building.

REFORMISM AS LAW ENFORCEMENT. Local law enforcement has changed from a service dominated by political favoritism to an operation dedicated to making the police politically independent and bringing community behavior into conformity with the law. Today, civil service coverage has been extended to police officers nearly everywhere and removals from the force are precluded except in cases of corruption and extreme incompetence. Often appointments to all high-ranking positions, save perhaps only that of police commissioner, have to be made from within the organization in order to eliminate the appointment of party favorites to key positions.

In enforcing the law, the old connections between police officers and political bosses have declined enormously. Improved training, more centralized direction and supervision, and expectations that the law will be uniformly enforced are the norm; police officers are often routinely rotated among neighborhoods in order to discourage petty favoritism. Detailed reports are usually required of all significant incidents that police officers encounter in order to assure better supervision. Extensive division of labor is found in all large police departments, permitting specialization within the force, closer supervision of more sensitive tasks, and recruitment of highly qualified personnel for high-level positions.

These kinds of measures have undoubtedly reduced differential enforcement of the law among various racial, ethnic, and social groups and at least have eliminated the more blatant forms of political favoritism (Lineberry, 1983; Wilson, 1970; Richardson, 1974). For example, police interference with balloting on election day, once a widespread practice in inner city areas, now rarely occurs. Although the kinds of corruption and favoritism that reformers saw under the machine still sometimes plague police departments (see Chapter 15 and Jacob, 1984), at least they are no longer integral to the law enforcement operation.

REFORMISM AS HOUSEKEEPING. Studies of many other distributive policies overwhelmingly document how extensively the use of particularistic criteria in service delivery has given way to universalistic standards of entitlement. Studies of parks, libraries, streets, sanitation, fire and police protection, housing code enforcement, and other essentially distributive local public services virtually all fail to provide evidence that the pattern of service distribution is a product of rational political calculation to reward political supporters. These same studies also do not uncover any cumulative bias in service delivery in favor of particular income groups, racial groups, or neighborhoods (Levy et al., 1974; Lineberry, 1977; Jones et al., 1984, 1980; Mladenka and Hill, 1978; Rich, 1982A, 1982B). These findings tend to prevail in all kinds of cities, whether extensively reformed or traditional partisan governmental systems (Jones, 1984; Mladenka, 1980), in cities where elitist business-style governments have managed to centralize power (Lineberry, 1977), or in more fragmented, competitive political systems (Levy et al., 1974).

In probably the best examination of major fixed-site services, which included parks, libraries, fire protection, and water and sewers, Lineberry (1977) concluded that the placement and distribution of these resources were characterized by "unpatterned inequality." Neighborhoods marginally advantaged by some public services were usually marginally disadvantaged by other patterns of service distribution, precluding any cumulative inequality. In one investigation that did uncover some apparent bias in service delivery, the authors concluded that it was mostly against middle-income groups, while the rich and poor of the city were favored somewhat in the allocation of at least some of the services they studied (Levy et al., 1974:219).

The strong tendency of distributive policies to be dominated by reform-style approaches is not merely a historic legacy of the urban reform movement (cf. Banfield and Wilson, 1965). The growth of more polyarchal conditions in urban political systems has been crucial in providing political support for reformer-style policy values. Virtually all major groups that are able to compete for power in the city share interests which are to a large degree harmonious with this kind of policy approach. The spread of reform values among the general population has meant that political leaders who must compete to expand their voter followings now have a stake in promoting reformist policies. Mayors and other political leaders often find that efficient, honest, and professional public service delivery to citizens is good politics, too. For example, even in machine Chicago there is evidence that much voter support for machine-sponsored candidates derived from the public's perception that they were responsible for superior public services, such as faster snow removal and cleaner streets, than was the opposition (Fuchs and Shapero, 1983). Alternatively, in homogeneous communities such as well-off suburban enclaves where often there is little rivalry among voters over issues of distribution, not much can be gained and much can be lost by local government candidates challenging established bureaucratic practices (Wood, 1958).

Finally, even most neighborhood groups that enjoyed a favored position in the distributive arena under the machine—such as ethnics and the poor—are now inclined to support the reformer approach to policy because it confers on them other benefits that they highly value. Virtually all low-income groups now enjoy automatic entitlement to many distributive services such as nearby parks and recreational facilities, swimming pools, legal assistance, housing code enforcement, and environmental services. Under the machine, such benefits were usually given in an uncertain, discriminatory fashion and then only in exchange for obligation to the party. Job opportunities in city government are now more open to blacks than under the machine. Machine leaders usually exploited racial divisions and discriminated against blacks in order to win support in white ethnic communities (Katznelson, 1973).

The Politico Approach: Rewarding Political Supporters

Despite the primacy of reformer values in distribution, these policies still can often reflect the traditional politico approach, which emphasizes the allocation of resources in order to secure political cooperation. This approach favors the use of (1) particularistic criteria in the allocation of resources, (2) minimal delegation of decisional authority to professional bureaucrats, and (3) the use of rewards to increase voter followings and enhance electoral coalitions.

This form of distributive policy persists in even the most reformed local governments. This is because virtually all local political systems *supply* some opportunities for politicians to provide rewards on this basis and because the *demand* for these kinds of policy responses (among both governmental leaders and citizen masses) persists despite—and sometimes as a result of—the reform approach to policy.

THE SUPPLY SIDE: OPPORTUNITIES FOR THE POLITICO. Postindustrial governmental systems continue to provide a substantial supply of particularistic rewards to fight over. Some areas of distributive policy have remained subject to political manipulation and favoritism despite the adoption of charter reforms, civil service laws, electoral reforms, and other measures designed to end this.

The nomination process for candidates to local office is almost wholly political in the sense that ticket balancing (or coalition building and civic group endorsements) remains a time-honored art of political survival. At least in medium and large cities, top appointments to commissions, line agencies, and the like are nearly always at the pleasure of the chief executive.

Precisely how extensive these opportunities are is difficult to determine. Virtually all cities have some patronage appointments, and in some these are considerable, as a result of limitations in civil service coverage and the exclusion of certain high-level appointments (Wolfinger, 1984). For instance, until very recent years in Chicago the number of municipal jobs under the control of the mayor probably ran into the thousands. The city's civil service system traditionally has been a very narrow one. Job vacancies are not frequently posted and examinations are given only occasionally. Moreover, numerous jobs are filled by provisional appointees who actually have permanent positions as long as they serve the interests of the Democratic Party. In 1974, the city council approved a resolution increasing the number of patronage appointments (Lewin et al., 1979). Only during the last few years have attempts to reduce mayoral patronage been very successful.

On the other hand, Los Angeles is a highly reformed and politically fragmented local government system where the mayor is very weak. Since the City of Los Angeles has one of the strongest municipal civil service systems in the country, there are very few patronage appointments left to the mayor. All department and bureau heads are covered by civil service provisions. The mayor is empowered to appoint and remove commissioners of some non-independent city departments, but these must be confirmed by the city council (Lewin et al., 1979:40). In Los Angeles County, which bears little political relationship to the city government of Los Angeles, patronage appointments are also a rarity because of the absence of a strong, dominant party and the presence of a strong civil service system.

Most major cities tend to fall somewhere between these rather extreme cases. Obtaining precise data on various kinds of patronage is elusive because of the legal and political delicacy of the subject. But scattered evidence suggests it is alive and well even under ardent reform leaders. For instance, in New York City, "reform" Mayor John Lindsay added 24,000 more "noncompetitive" or exempt civil service jobs on top of the 50,000 that already existed in the city after he succeeded Mayor Robert Wagner in the 1960s. Lindsay also let much larger amounts of consulting contracts without competitive bidding than did Wagner, much of this probably a form of political patronage (Wolfinger, 1984:78).

Within reformed governmental structures, the allocation of resources in exchange for political support is not entirely foreclosed. Changes in civil service administration during the least few decades have opened up new opportunities for "playing politics." With the advent of civil service unions and collective bargaining, managing the merit system has often come down to bargaining over political support in exchange for job benefits between civil servants and political leaders in city hall (see Chapter 15). Many other kinds of resources for politico-style distribution are available even in highly reformed cities. The "political" targeting of special programs, such as Model Cities, the Community Action Program, the Community Development Block Grant, and other neighborhood assistance programs, has been permitted by the loose federal guidelines that govern the selection of areas, personnel, and project objectives (Frieden and Kaplan, 1975; Dommell et al., 1982). City contracts with private suppliers for materials and services are sometimes the source of "gravy" and political reward. Laws and ordinances regulate city contracting and usually require competitive bidding; but legal loopholes and uneven enforcement of regulations often afford some opportunities for favoritism to those who are bold enough to seize them. Finally, there is no end to the symbolic rewards that can be given to politically "important" groups and individuals as an act of "recognition," e.g., naming a street or park after a popular ethnic leader.

THE DEMAND SIDE: THE NEED FOR THE POLITICO. Opportunities for politico-type policy approaches are likely to be exploited because the demand for particularistic governmental responses remains a strong undercurrent in most local political systems. There are circumstances when political leaders as well as ordinary citizens actually prefer this form of public policy even though they may otherwise be quite supportive of reformist-style government.

Political Leadership. First, even though the machine has mostly withered away, the need to gain political support in winning elections and inducing political cooperation has not. Distributive policies offer political leaders the most appropriate resource for achieving these objectives because they can be used to secure political advantage without having much effect on the city's economy.

The prevailing structure of popular control in cities works to make elected political leaders far more uncertain about the stability of their electoral coalitions than in the past. As suggested previously, the postindustrial era is characterized by substantial urban political competition compared to the past— whether organized or disorganized—and by unprecedented opportunities for independent group participation in city politics. From the perspective of local policymakers, urban party reform has actually increased their *need* for specific material *quid pro quo* responses in electoral competition. The decline of partisan loyalty among the electorate and the fragmentation and atrophy of urban party organizations has made the search for incentives to secure political cooperation among party leaders and workers a grave problem in most cities.

For instance, in New York City the decline of Tammany has not been followed by the subjugation of old-line patronage-bound party politicians by reformers, but the decentralization and fragmentation of the city's old Democratic organization. The Democratic Party includes "regular" and "reform" clubs that regularly break up into factions fighting over nominations, candidates, and issues. Lack of party discipline weakens the ability of the organization to achieve much unity in electoral competition, much less in running the city government (Wilson, 1962), and puts a premium on finding some material or intangible bases for securing political agreement. In a loose and undisciplined system such as this, marginal amounts of patronage at the disposal of elected officials often become a key to achieving some measure of cooperation when other kinds of incentives fail. Specific material incentives like jobs, contracts, and petty favors that can reduce conflicts to dollar amounts are likely to facilitate bargaining and compromise.

Consequently, urban party leaders are often willing to forsake involvement with issues and substantive policies in preference to what Sayre and Kaufman call ". . . the discrete aspects of policy and its application rather than its range and content" (1960:474). For instance, during the 1950s in New Haven the Democratic Party's top two leaders were rarely present at meetings where decisions about city policy were made nor did they play much part in these matters. They apparently willingly absented themselves from these kinds of discussions out of lack of interest. But on strictly party topics, such as appointments, nominations, the distribution of city contracts, and the like, they formed a triumvirate with Mayor Edward Lee and negotiated these things among themselves and with an eye on the party's fortunes (Wolfinger, 1984:80).

Finally, urban political leaders require politico-style approaches to distribution because they must often implement programs that provoke intense political opposition at the neighborhood level. Without a "storehouse" of particularistic rewards to distribute in these situations, they face the prospect of program failure or political blacklash. For instance, big city redevelopment and renewal efforts typically are connected to programs that afford sponsored participation by neighborhood groups in carrying out nondevelopmental aspects of these activities. By the same token, the cooptation of particular groups and leaders via the distribution of jobs, the provision of special services, or grants to neighborhood organizations, etc., can serve to diffuse demands for more costly redistributive responses by city hall. In both the developmental and redistributive arenas, urban political leaders must frequently resort to providing distributive benefits, either symbolic or material, in order to secure political cooperation in carrying out major programs.

The Citizenry. Second, the mass citizenry often demand politico-style policy responses despite, and sometimes because of, the dominance of reform government. For one thing, the strong tilt of distributive policy toward bureaucratic solutions to urban problems limits political control of policy by particular clientele groups in the neighborhoods. Because public bureaucracies tend to adhere to professional, impersonal, and universalist criteria in delivering public services, the demands of particular clientele groups are often ignored, neglected, or considered illegitimate.

For instance, "professional" enforcement of the law has undoubtedly increased tensions between the police and the more powerless urban groups, such as blacks, chicanos, and young people, whose moral and social code often differs from that dominant in society. Family squabbles and teenage rowdyism, which police officers once ignored or bluntly took care of on the spot, now are more likely to lead to arrests and court proceedings. The extensive use of patrol cars in cities has sharply limited informal contacts between police and community, while the rotation of officers among districts and beats has made the officer often appear as a soldier in an army of occupation and less of a neighborhood "friend." Moreover, civil service examinations in the police and other city agencies have frequently made it difficult to recruit and promote minorities in numbers proportionate to their representation in the urban population (David and Peterson, 1976:264–265).

These patterns of hostility, mistrust, and conflict between professional bureaucrat and many citizens in the case of law enforcement are not unusual. Lipsky has described how the environment perceived by "street-level" bureaucrats who deal with the poor is often permeated by fear of and hostility toward their clientele; stereotyping, aggressive behavior, and routinization of tasks in ways that disadvantage the client often result (Lipsky, 1976). Even among more politically resourceful citizens, dependence upon highly insulated, rule-bound, bureaucratic organizations for everyday services can present frustration when, for instance, potholes in streets go unfilled because they are "off schedule."

Consequently, demands for greater community control and administrative decentralization of public service bureaucracies grew during the 1960s and 1970s (Altschuler, 1972). Numbers of riots were sparked by an incident between the police and a black suspect. Black leaders responded by demanding civilian review boards that would have the power to investigate allegations of police misconduct and brutality. Demands for greater community control of other services spread, making "reforming the reform" a major issue in most large cities. In effect, the bureaucratic character of the dominant reform approach to distribution has created a demand for its political mediation at the neighborhood level.

The Tensions of Reformers and Politicos

Since local distributive activities are only distantly related to the market position of the community and are relatively removed from the play of intergovernmental power compared to other policy areas, changes in the structure of urban governmental systems have been most decisive in shaping the content of local distributive policy. To a large extent, contemporary policy conforms to the reform-style governmental values of universalism, professionalism, and efficiency. This is mainly due to the transformation of local political systems along more polyarchal lines since the industrial era. In particular, the decline of the machine and the rise of professional bureaucracies have ensured that the allocation of distributive resources are no longer central to the process of building political support for governmental authorities.

Reformism has not entirely precluded politico-style approaches to policy, however. The dominance of reform values and institutions narrow the opportunities for using distributive policies in exchange for political support, but the demand by urban political leaders and citizens for particularistic governmental responses persists. This ensures that distributive policy still often displays many politico-like features. The rigidities of reform governance generate demands for deviations from it by practicing politicians and citizens alike. Most important, no other area of public policy provides so much scope for rewarding followers, punishing political enemies, and winning political cooperation.

CHAPTER FIFTEEN

City Governability: From Islands of Power to Pluralist Bargaining

H OW and when the streets are swept, whether a drug-crime task force is created, or how many city appointments should be "at the pleasure" of the mayor are among the matters that normally neither have much impact on city economic development nor significantly affect political actors at higher governmental levels. Distributive decisions such as these are apt to reflect community political tastes more than external politico-economic influences.

Nevertheless, even on these kinds of public policy issues the capability of local political authorities to serve their community's preferences is not without difficulties. Relative independence of forces in the external environment of the city does not ensure freedom of local political authorities from powerful *internal* challenges to what they may try to achieve. Distributive decision making is highly sensitive to the pulling and hauling among individuals and groups who vie for power in the locale. In this chapter, we examine the intricacies of local political systems and reveal how they afford tremendous variation in decision making on distributive issues. Compared with the other areas of public policy, distributive policy making is so pluralistic and fragmented that cities face serious problems of governability.

Policy Making in the Distributive Arena

More than in any other arena of public policy, distributive policies tend to be by-products of (1) the organizational enhancement needs of local groups that can penetrate the arena and (2) the political competition among these groups as they struggle to promote their interests.

The Multiplicity of Group Interests

The universe of group interests that manage to penetrate the distributive arena is generally quite extensive compared to the industrial era because of the growth of more polyarchal conditions in localities. Groups that were once objectives of social control by the machine, such as immigrants, commonly are no longer in such politically dependent relationships with political authorities. The party organization that once was a dominant governing institution in the distributive arena has weakened dramatically. No longer able to provide a cohesive and stable power base for elected political leaders, it has limited the ability of mayors to informally extend their influence over city government. The bureaucratization of public policy and the growth of intergovernmental programs independent of city hall control has fractured and fragmented the governing structures of cities along functional as well as "vertical" organizational lines. These factors have, among other things, opened up city politics to unprecedented opportunities for groups to actively enter the decisional system and make demands. Party leaders and public officials are but one interest among many in this area of policy.

Three kinds of political interests most frequently participate in this arena, each having fairly different organizational enhancement objectives. First, *public service bureaucracies* are in a position to capitalize on their role in implementing programs in order to command influence on distributive issues. Typically, their organizational enhancement depends upon acquiring autonomy on issues that interest them (Sayre and Kaufman, 1960:405). This is because independence from "political" interference enables public bureaucrats to shape the implementation of policy in accordance with standard operating procedures, professional objectives and practices that are tailored to their convenience and aggrandizement as organizations. These, in turn, enable bureacrats to achieve other valued objectives, especially certainty and stability in the environment of the members of the organization. Growth is usually a goal of most public agencies because it can often bring about greater political independence; large programs are hard to cut, huge agency staffs allow plenty of "fat," and a big constituency of clients helps to defend the agency from political attacks.

Second, *elected political leaders and their political organizations* constitute another set of interests in the arena. These interests obviously vary in the importance they attach to particular ideologies, in their commitment to favored programs, and even in their ambition to pursue political office (cf. Schlesinger, 1966; Eulau and Prewitt, 1973; Kantor and Lawrence, 1981). This makes generalization about their interests in matters of distribution difficult. Nonetheless, mayors, councilors, political appointees, party chieftains, and others like them are disciplined by systems of popular control that ultimately govern their ability to secure the legitimate power to act on their various beliefs. Consequently, their organizational enhancement on distributive matters generally comes down to utilizing public resources in order to build voter followings and otherwise secure public approval for their undertakings (Dahl, 1961).

While this organizational enhancement need may sometimes move elected politicians to support bureaucratic autonomy in certain political contexts (where "good government is good politics"), the narrow interests promoted by bureaucratic organizations often preclude this. All other things being equal, they have a stake in limiting bureaucratic power in order to assure the availability of distributive resources for their own enhancement needs. Elected politicians face severe limitations on political choice in the developmental and redistributive arenas and must contend with the increasingly participatory and polarized social character of many postindustrial cities. Therefore, they are strongly inclined to see distributive policies as bargaining resources that must be carefully husbanded and protected in order for them to secure some control over their political futures. As noted earlier, this reality has often compelled even dedicated reformers to uphold the value of politico-style approaches to public policy.

Finally, *citizen groups*, such as good government leagues, neighborhood betterment groups, taxpayer associations, tenant and homeowner groups, ad hoc protesters, and sundry others, are usually a substantial presence in the distributive arena. All of them represent voter-consumers whose organizational enhancement needs differ from those of public service bureaucracies and elected political leaders. Except for general interest citizen organizations, such as "good government" and other civic reform groups, what most distinguishes these groups is that they usually lack a very stable set of organizational interests on matters of distribution.

Their interest in seeking influence in this arena is almost always quite transitory and limited to winning concessions on particular issues. Typically, voter-consumer groups arise out of neighborhood, ethnic, or some other parochial interest that generally can be satisfied without obtaining stable power and access in city government. Moreover, these consumer groups may be well served by promoting bureaucratic autonomy or political bargaining, depending upon their particular demands. For instance, street cleaning operations that favor more frequent pickups in homeowner areas at the cost of less frequent service in other neighborhoods are likely to win the support of homeowners no matter who promotes this policy.

The major sources of power for these groups are their voter sanction that can discipline elected political leaders (Dahl, 1961; Eckstein, 1960), their ability to make public protests that can embarrass bureaucratic officialdom (Lipsky, 1970), and their ability to play off each of these interests against the other (Banfield, 1961). Since these political resources are by no means evenly distributed within urban populations (Schattschneider, 1960:Ch. II), organized consumer groups tend not to be particularly representative of voter-consumer populations. Lack of information, the costs and difficulties of organizing, leadership skill, and other requisites of group political participation tend to severely limit the ability of low-income and minority groups to use this channel, compared with more advantaged citizens (Verba and Nie, 1972). Even for those who are in a position to employ this means of influence, it is more often than not an uphill task because of the difficulties of organizing and their inability to speak for those whom they claim to represent. This limits the ability of these groups to secure stable allies among either elected elites or appointed officialdom.

Political Competition

In general, competition among these kinds of interests within a polyarchal political environment tends to create a pluralistic arena of policy making. Decisions are apt to be the outcome of group bargaining, coalition building, compromise, bureaucratic routine, or other patterns of group politics that change from issue to issue. Those who play influential roles on some kinds of distributive issues are unlikely to win similar power on many other issues, making the arena as a whole one in which power is dispersed and power relationships are frequently quite variable.

These pluralistic tendencies do not mean that policy making is necessarily governed closely by popular approval of results, although that outcome is often possible. City governmental leaders typically confront formidable internal obstacles to their exercise of authority even in the most well developed polyarchal local governmental systems. The fragmentation and dispersal of power to bureaucratic, professional, consumer, and other groups can undercut the ability of legitimate political authorities to respond to and implement what they think the public wants or needs. Local governmental authorities are constrained by these internal forces to share power. They must, therefore, struggle to control public policy.

Power, Pluralism, and City Governability

Consequently, the problem of governability (i.e., the ability of political authorities to impose their control over policy) confounds policy making in the distributive arena. Influence over policy hinges on the intricacies of the bargaining process in particular issue areas. This includes the stakes that various groups have in particular decisions; their authority to act; their willingness to mobilize in order to promote their interests; their bargaining resources, allies, and access to decision makers; and the negotiating skills they possess. The scope of political competition and influence over decisions can range from relatively open, where large numbers of actors vie for power and where compromise is the rule, to tightly closed processes of decision dominated by few participants. The extent to which these patterns of policy making make for city governability depends on whether elected political authorities have much say in deciding particular issues.

Varieties of Distributive Politics: From Islands of Power to Pluralist Bargaining

The variable patterns of pluralist power relations and the unstable governability of the distributive arena are suggested by an examination of major issue areas—city personnel policy, traditional urban housekeeping services, and local government budgeting. In none of these policy areas is a single pattern of group influence to be found. By the same token, in all these program areas city political authorities have found serious internal obstacles to their ability to extend their direction over policy very far.

The Politics of Jobs

The years of conflict between party politicians and reformers over patronage in local government are testament to the importance of this resource as a means of organizational enhancement. Civil service reform had the goal of substantially closing off the area of personnel policy from political bargaining and making it a matter of bureaucratic control.

To a large extent, reform succeeded in achieving this. Civil service systems are the norm virtually everywhere, limiting access to the public payrolls as a source of political rewards; "merit," as defined by supposedly "objective" tests of job competency, has become so widely expected as a qualification for civil service recruitment and promotion that it is generally considered to apply to all governmental positions, even to those jobs not covered by civil service laws.

In effect, the politics of jobs has become more than ever before an island of power where professional norms and bureaucratic routines dominate most individual decisions regarding recruitment, promotion, and discipline. Typically, merit systems are governed by complicated rules that specify in great detail matters of hiring, promotion, discipline, classification, etc. They usually are so intricate that they are often inscrutable to all but the most knowledgeable insiders. Civil service examinations are announced, administered, and graded; appointment lists are then posted from which appointments to or promotions from within the civil service are made. In cities that were once rife with patronage, such as New York City, studies have found that the civil service system is by and large conducted "by the book" (Horton, 1973:111). Manipulation of the system's day-to-day procedures in order to win political advantage is essentially a bureaucratic operation for narrow organizational goals. Insiders, such as budget bureaus attempting to save money or department heads seeking more staff, typically "play the system" (Thompson, 1975).

THE SCOPE AND PERSISTENCE OF PLURALIST BARGAINING.   Alongside these patterns of closed politics in day-to-day civil service administration, however, are far more open forms of pluralist bargaining politics regarding the management of the system's governing rules. The rules that define the meaning of "merit" in personnel policy and the standard operating procedures that govern hiring and promotion are quite capable of change in order to enhance particular interests without violating the "reform" rules of the game.

Jobs provide politicians with a desirable resource for their electoral enhancement because of the highly disaggregable nature of personnel decisions and policies (Lowi, 1964). They are likely to view rules governing merit systems in the light of the discretion afforded them in running public bureaucracies or the biases of particular rules for rewarding their political followers. Alternatively, bureaucrats and their unions are inclined to see the management of civil service policies in light of their demand for political autonomy.

Consequently, personnel management is a matter that is often open to political bargaining, particularly between elected politicians and bureaucrats. Typically, political leaders have struggled to expand their "managerial" discretion by advocating greater political control over job qualifications, more provisional appointments, a large role for performance evaluation, and open competition in promotions, etc. Public bureaucrats have usually resisted this by advocating unchanging recruitment practices, limitations on provisional appointments, and heavy reliance on seniority and closed career routes (Summers, 1974; Lewin et al., 1979:113).

For instance, most public employee unions tend to resist the lowering of job qualification requirements as well as attempts to change the nature of the entrance exams or the system by which exams are graded (Stanley, 1972:32–59). But as cities have changed in social composition, becoming blacker and poorer, city hall leaders have often found it politically advantageous to open up civil service jobs to racial minorities by reducing formal job qualifications, by limiting the import of written exams, or by providing minorities with "bonus" points on examination scores. When Mayor John V. Lindsay attempted this during the 1960s in New York City, he was met with considerable opposition and, often, defeat at the hands of the city's civil service unions (Horton, 1973:112).

When black administrations come to power in large cities, they have frequently been more successful in bargaining over and altering the rules of personnel systems to assist their supporters. One method is through vigorous promotion of federal and state laws requiring affirmative action programs in public employment. In a study of black public employment in forty-three cities, Eisinger found that the presence of a black mayor accounted for greater black recruitment than could be explained by the proportion of this group in the population of the cities or by other nonpolitical factors (Eisinger, 1984:251).

This change has usually been accomplished by aggressive recruitment of blacks and reevaluation of selection procedures, including deemphasis on written examinations. Another means has been the appointment of more blacks to head city hall agencies. Since department heads ultimately evaluate and promote employees under them, getting blacks into these key positions has led to increases in black employment opportunities. Finally, black mayors have succeeded in expanding minority employment in city agencies by imposing city residence requirements on municipal workers. This enables black job applicants living in increasingly minority central cities to face a more favorable structure of job competition that excludes much of the predominantly white metropolitan labor force. Although residency laws are not always passed to aid central city minority groups, they happen to often function in this way and city residency requirements almost invariably raise racial controversies (Eisinger, 1984:251–256).

Unions, Politicians, and Pluralist Bargaining. Job politics has become most open, pluralist, and unstable as a result of unionization and collective bargaining in the local public sector. Urban political leaders have sought to compensate for their declining patronage by capitalizing on the unionization of local government employees as a source of power and control. In recent decades, the tremendous growth of local government employment under civil service protection has been paralleled by the rapid spread of unionization among public employees. Unlike the private sector, where unionization has been on the decline since World War II, in local government unionization has skyrocketed since the 1960s (Stieber, 1973; Lewin et al., 1979:5–6).

There are a number of reasons for this phenomenal growth of public sector unionization. In 1961, President Kennedy legitimized union organization in the federal government, a fact that emboldened similar demands among local and state government employees. The sheer growth of local public employment under systems of personnel administration that protected them from becoming patronage arms of political parties were conditions favorable to the eventual assertion of power on the part of public employees. Nonetheless, a most compelling factor was the weakening of urban party organizations during the postwar years, a fact that left mayors and other political leaders looking for an alternative base of political support and organization. Unionization provided a channel through which local politicians could trade favors with public service bureaucracies via collective bargaining in exchange for political cooperation and support, particularly in the form of campaign contributions, endorsements, and union member support in getting out the vote.

For example, the rise of unions to power in New York City went hand in hand with the struggle among leaders of the city's faction-ridden Democratic Party to find a stable electoral coalition. Under attack from old-line Regulars and the factious Reform wing of the party during the late 1950s, Mayor Robert Wagner aggressively courted support from city employees by initiating measures to provide for union recognition, organization, and, eventually, collective bargaining. Wagner's success at changing the city's personnel system to his and the union's mutual advantage was revealed in his bid for reelection in 1961. When the regular Democratic organization dropped Wagner, city civil servants formed a crucial part of the new coalition Wagner fashioned, including a ticket and campaign organization studded with union leaders, to win the primary and general election. Mayor Lindsay, who succeeded Wagner, eventually demonstrated similar sensitivity to the city's unions in his bids for reelection. He used the collective bargaining process to trade concessions in personnel policy for union political support (Horton, 1973:27–28, 85–86; Chickering, 1976:186ff; Morris, 1980).

During the 1960s and 1970s, the growth of municipal unions and collective bargaining in other cities also appears to have been tied to the state of the local political party organizations. Where it was strong, political leaders resisted unionization in order to discourage the emergence of a rival power base; where partisanship was weak or disorganized, union organizers found fertile ground for growth. For example, in Chicago, where the powerful Democratic political machine dominated the city's political system until recent years, the party leaders stifled union growth and discouraged public sector collective bargaining. In contrast, in Los Angeles and other reformed cities, where politics is highly disorganized, public sector unionism moved strongly ahead as unions become recognized as a weighty factor in political campaigns and elections (Lewin et al., 1979:13–14; Boehm, 1982; Chickering, 1976; Spero and Capozzola, 1973). In effect, unionization is an issue that has been played out as a game of pluralist bargaining where the outcome has depended upon the organizational enhancement and coalition-building strategies of local politicians and city employees.

A NEW MACHINE? As Lowi (1968) has suggested, to some extent the organized public employees constitute a "New Machine" in city government. City hall politicians have found organized civil servants to be a formidable, however imperfect, alternative power base where parties are weak or absent. Public employees can exercise considerable electoral clout in local politics. In many cities, they can constitute a large proportion, sometimes as much as 20 percent, of the electorate (Peterson, 1981:162). In New York City in 1969, one out of every twenty-seven of the city's inhabitants was employed by the city, and union members constituted over 66 percent of the municipal work force (Spero and Capozzola, 1973:74). This power is often enhanced by the low voter turnout in most municipal elections—usually about half that of national elections, with their 60 percent turnout—and the absence of highly visible issues and personalities in many city campaigns. Unions can provide election-day troops, financial contributions to political campaigns, endorsements, and related political resources to politicians.

For instance, during Mayor John Lindsay's 1969 reelection in New York, the city's huge American Federation of State, County, and Municipal Employees (AFSCME) District 37 helped man street front headquarters, provided volunteers to ring doorbells, distributed campaign literature, and made thousands of phone calls to voters asking that they support Lindsay. Millions of pieces of campaign material were prepared and printed by the organization in support of the mayor. In addition to assisting with special registration efforts, the union arranged for the use of sound trucks and cars and provided drivers and poll watchers (Spero and Capozzola, 1973:94–95).

Union bargaining can serve as an important vehicle for public officials to build their political base because it enables them to trade favors on personnel matters in exchange for political cooperation, something that could not otherwise be done in most civil service systems. Typically, union policy has been to keep the protective features of the merit system, such as job tenure and rights to hearings, etc., but to transfer position classification, wage administration, and several other personnel functions to the bargaining table (Benjamin et al., 1979; Spero and Capozzola, 1973:208–210). Unionization permits bureaucratic power to be particularized and traded in exchange for recognition, material benefits, and other demands that bear upon the jobs of public employees. Pay, fringe benefits, working conditions, and union-sponsored political appointments can be meted out by public officials in recognition of union political contributions in elections and union cooperation in city governance. Concessions can be made in pay and working conditions without raising broader issues that might bear on election endorsements; sometimes costs can be hidden in budgets and disguised. Collective bargaining sometimes can be as great a boon to elected political authorities as it is to city unions.

In some ways, public sector unionism has brought back in highly organized fashion the old patronage politics because municipal unions often represent many of the different ethnic, racial, and status constituencies found in the electorate. For example, unions representing uniformed services (e.g., fire, police, etc.) often have higher pay, have greater status, and are more white and ethnic than is the case in other nonuniformed service unions, such as AFSCME, which tend to organize large numbers of lower-paid and minority workers in big cities. Conflicts over union "recognition" in pay, contract conditions, and political appointments sometimes parallel old-style ethnic, racial, and status politics during the days of the machine.

THE DILEMMAS OF NEW MACHINE POLITICS. In other ways, the new machine is very different from the old one, however. Most important, the new machine of public sector workers and their unions constitute a rival power bloc over which elected political leaders have only limited control. Particularly in the more disorganized reformed political systems, the power of organized civil servants is sufficiently strong that political leaders cannot harness and contain it to serve their own ends. These systems offer many opportunities for referenda campaigns to settle disputed issues, including pay and contract matters; in elections, union political activity is frequent and often determinative.

For instance, in many California cities municipal workers appear to be a formidable political force; their activity on behalf of Tom Bradley, a former police officer, in the 1973 Los Angeles mayoral election helped elect the city's first black mayor (Crouch, 1978:200–202). Uniformed services, particularly fire and police unions, have effectively defeated or obtained winning margins in proposition ballots of importance to them. In New York City, efforts by Mayor Lindsay to impose a civilian review board on the police led the police association to secure a referendum on the issue and to defeat the measure after a vigorous campaign among the voters (Bellush and David, 1971:Ch. 4). When the mayor of Seattle fired the city's fire chief, the firefighters' union retaliated with a recall petition (Chickering, 1976:Ch. 4). The use of referenda to introduce and to secure higher pay by police and firefighters has been successful in numbers of cities, including San Francisco, Detroit, St. Louis, and elsewhere (Spero and Capozzola, 1973:101).

The politics of jobs persists in the postindustrial city of "reformed" civil service systems as an island of bureaucratic power or as an open game of political bargaining. In either case, political authorities in city hall confront rival power brokers who stand ready to limit their reach in determining personnel policy.

The Politics of Housekeeping Services: The Dominance of Bureaucratic Power Islands

Fire protection, law enforcement, sanitation, street repairs, libraries, and related housekeeping services are also decisively shaped by competition among groups that govern, produce, and consume these services. But the extent of political rivalry and competition in this area of distribution is surely much more limited today than in the past. During the industrial era, the machine "marketed" these services in exchange for political support. But opportunities for this kind of favoritism and corruption were always limited by the "public goods" character of most of these kinds of services; i.e., they cannot be easily disaggregated and given to some while being withheld from others. These services were most important to party bosses as a source of jobs or contracts for party workers and contributors. Once reforms were adopted that limited opportunities for such political favoritism and corruption, the use of these local government activities to enhance the party organization dwindled. Partisan interest in controlling them in respect to policy also declined.

Consequently, in local government housekeeping services one frequently finds closed, bureaucratic politics as the dominant form of public policy making. Policy most often reflects the internal standard operating procedures and professional goals of local government bureaucrats, as expressed in service delivery rules that are adopted in order to allocate resources. Service delivery rules exist because participants in complex bureaucratic organizations (those that have a formal hierarchy and specialization of labor) seek to stabilize their environment and to avoid uncertainty. Precisely why this is so is the subject of long dispute (March and Simon, 1958; Weber, 1947, 1962; Crozier, 1964; Sayre and Kaufman, 1960). But making and adhering to general rules that are rationalized on professional or public interest grounds can serve to simplify bureaucratic tasks, reduce the need for information (Levy et al., 1974; Wildavsky, 1976; Simon, 1957), discourage inquiry by outsiders into the affairs of the organization, and enhance its legitimacy (Jones et al., 1980; Sayre and Kaufman, 1960).

As noted in Chapter 14, the use of such rules invariably has distributional consequences, and the rules are never "neutral" in the way they distribute services among groups, individuals, and neighborhoods. Such consequences are often unintended in the sense that they spring from the enhancement needs of the organization or their professionals and often are not consciously utilized to achieve particular patterns of reward and deprivation among clientele groups (Levy et al., 1974; Rich, 1982A, 1982B; Jones et al., 1980). The tendency is for professional public administrators to focus on services as products, rather than as scarce resources to be divided up by groups who disagree about their distribution. From the professional viewpoint, a rule is good if it is effective in contributing to the goal of the organization and, to some extent, if it is efficient in allocating services. Citizen input may play a role in the implementation of the rule but not in questioning or negotiating over the rule itself (which is "unprofessional" and illegitimate).

SOME BUREAUCRATIC "ISLANDS." What this kind of bureaucratic politics looks like has been described by Jones in respect to urban services in Detroit. The city's Environmental Enforcement Division (EED) polices violations of Detroit's environmental ordinances, such as debris, overgrowth, rodent infestation, etc., mostly by depending on citizen complaints or inspectors spotting violations in the field as they respond to citizen complaints. Because of this service delivery rule, areas that complain more often also tend to have more field "pickups" of violations; they therefore receive most enforcement activity by inspectors. Citizens do not have "power" over EED inspectors because they are able on their own to prod them into activity. Rather, inspectors come on call because they follow a set of performance rules (of their own making) that mandate a complaint-investigate system of response.

Other services in Detroit demonstrated more complex rule-oriented behavior. For instance, the sanitation division utilized what were in effect three delivery rules in distributing services: collect the garbage once a week, each week, but allocate somewhat more resources to heavy load areas and allocate more resources to the densely populated center city. All of these rules largely evolved in response to efficiency goals accepted by the department and its professional managers, rather than because of any kind of sustained political pressure on the part of the groups and neighborhoods served.

The politics of housekeeping services in other cities suggest similar patterns of bureaucratic, rule-bound behavior. The bureaucratic autonomy of local police departments even in large cities is legendary and many, such as New York's, are often beyond the routine policy control of the police commissioners (Sayre and Kaufman, 1960; Jacob, 1985; Richardson, 1974:124ff). Major changes in policy usually come about only in response to major scandals, riots, or other crises that undercut the professional legitimacy and independence of the department.

For example, in Philadelphia, findings of police corruption appear to follow a cyclical pattern every ten years or so. Newspaper exposures of police corruption are followed by reforms imposed after investigations by crime commissions and attempts to assert greater political control over departmental activities. But police autonomy quickly returns and political control lapses. The Pennsylvania Crime Commission, which headed an effort to upgrade the department and contain corruption in the wake of scandals in 1974, expressed the fear that "if another investigative body were called upon to examine the department ten years from now it would find little change." In 1985, Mayor Wilson Goode found precisely what the commission predicted as he launched a campaign against graft in the city's police force after newspapers reported its reappearance (New York Times, 22 September 1985:E-4). Variation in law enforcement behavior among cities appears to be related to a host of social, economic, and political variables that change slowly over time. "Deliberate community choices," suggests Wilson (1970:227), "rarely have more than a limited effect on police behavior, though they often may have a great effect on police personnel, budgets, pay levels, and organization."

Though sanitation, housing code enforcement, library, street maintenance, and other housekeeping services do not appear to exhibit the degree of political independence of many local police departments (whose almost inscrutable technical codes and powerful political organizations make them distinctive), they almost invariably tend to display very prominent rule-bound behavior in their distributional activities (Jones, 1980; Rich, 1982A; Levy et al., 1974; Lineberry, 1977). This led Sayre and Kaufman to conclude in their massive study of New York that the city's bureaucracies powerfully codetermine public policy because they influence ". . . what the city government does, for whom, how quickly, by what methods and at what cost" (1960:446).

The Narrow Scope of Pluralist Bargaining. The autonomy of housekeeping agencies is most commonly challenged on particular issues by consumer groups in the neighborhoods and by public officials. Typically, they both seek only to win concessions or marginal adjustments in an agency's distributional practices—rather than attempting to change the general bureaucratic rules and the division of resources among groups. As long as clientele groups do not challenge the basic legitimacy of the dominant rules and the authority of the agency to articulate them, line bureaucracies are often willing to bargain over particular decisions in service delivery if only to preserve their own professional legitimacy and autonomy. On these kinds of issues, a highly pluralistic game of bargaining can ensue among political leaders, neighborhood and civic groups, and public bureaucrats to resolve minor controversies (Yates, 1977; Lipsky, 1970, 1976).

Similarly, when neighborhood and other ordinarily quiescent groups of citizens suddenly mobilize to defend their interests, elected political leaders take notice and respond if only because of the publicity and potential votes that could be at stake (Dahl, 1961:192–199). A classic case is a bus route controversy that occurred some years ago in Manhattan. When a city-owned bus company in New York City decided to streamline its bus routes and simplify scheduling, it had the further effect of increasing the walking distance to the nearest bus stop for residents in several Manhattan neighborhoods. Many of these residents complained vigorously to city hall, moving local politicians and leaders of community organizations to gather testimony from residents about how far they had to walk and how long they had to wait for bus service. Eventually, numbers of residents descended on a Board of Estimate meeting that was reviewing bus route changes. After listening to community grievances, the mayor and other members of the Board eventually supported many of their claims and insisted that major adjustments be made in the routes; the bus scheduling and route plan was implemented, but in revised form (Yates, 1977:120–121).

Such patterns of minor controversy and political bargaining surely typify the politics of housekeeping policy (Rich, 1980:249). Issues of this kind intermittently arise out of the enhancement needs of neighborhood and other intermediary groups and are thrashed out in a politics of bargaining and compromise. But in these kinds of cases the groups (other than elected officials) are unlikely to seek or establish stable political power over the rules and routines of the service delivery agencies. They lack the interests and organizational resources for such an endeavor.

Even elected political leaders are not often likely to engage themselves in this level of service delivery politics for similar reasons. Unless political organizations are strong enough to insinuate themselves into the everyday operations of the line bureaucracies, elected politicians are not able to compete for power in this area of activity. There is evidence of this in Chicago, where the city's powerful Democratic organization appears to play a continuous role in the major phases of building code enforcement along with the line bureaucracy. It does this in order to win favor with voters in the neighborhoods, who generally are not yet able to use intermediary groups with much success to influence the practices of the agency (Jones, 1981). More often, however, sorting out the everyday issues of urban housekeeping is not likely to engage city hall leaders unless community controversies arise from complaints by particular voter groups.

Challenges to Bureaucratic Government. Despite the tremendous stability and routine that usually characterize this area of distributive politics, there have been increasing attempts by elected officials and community groups to challenge bureaucratic autonomy and influence the rules that govern their practices. As noted earlier, the insularity and professional values that dominate this area of policy have sometimes put these agencies at odds with the neighborhoods they serve, particularly low-income, minority neighborhoods in large cities. During the 1960s and 1970s, social polarization and the insularity of many bureaucrats from the neighborhoods sparked demands for greater community control over them. Racial strife and cases of alleged police brutality and discrimination prompted demands for limiting the autonomy of police departments and changing law enforcement styles. These kinds of demands could not be met by city hall without imposing greater political control over the agencies and seeking influence over their rules and rule-making processes.

Consequently, the momentum of bureaucratic government was broken as mayors saw the opportunity to win the favor of neighborhood groups and other critics of local government bureaucracies by supporting their demands for greater participation in service delivery. At the same time, municipal employee unions almost everywhere resisted this intrusion on their autonomy. This led to years of pluralistic bargaining over the organization of public services in large cities all over the United States (Kotler, 1969; Woshnic, 1975; Nordlinger, 1972). In no city was the objective of full community (neighborhood) financial and administrative control of any public service achieved. But the administrative decentralization of several public services and the creation of community liaison bodies, such as planning boards, "little city halls," and the like, were adopted in several large cities.

Apart from capitalizing on protest groups and attempting to restructure housekeeping agencies so they are more open to neighborhood demands, city political leaders usually lack substantial power to direct the activities of these agencies. As producers of governmental services, public bureaucracies can withhold their political cooperation and frustrate the implementation of programs; "blue flus," sickouts, and strikes are among the more notorious responses of organized civil servants when they wish to oppose policies they regard as threatening to their organizational well-being. Given the weak partisan political base of many mayors, the latter are often reduced to bargaining with their line agencies to shape the rules and routines of bureaucratic policy formation. Their influence over these bureaucracies typically hinges upon their bargaining resources and political skill, as well as the opportunities provided within the structure of local government for exchanging concessions of value to bureaucrats in return for their political cooperation.

In this respect, the collective bargaining process in a unionized local governmental system and the budgetary control elected officials have in allocating resources are major venues for this activity. As noted earlier, in union bargaining, concessions regarding pay, fringe benefits, and working conditions may be exchanged by city hall administrations for changes in bureaucratic rules that have important policy consequences (e.g., ending two-officer patrol cars in order to increase street protection). The budgetary process also provides some leverage for city officials over agency practices; the power of the purse enables local officials to allocate resources among and within city agencies in ways that could bring about greater bureaucratic cooperation in policy.

Nevertheless, both of these avenues for securing political control over housekeeping policy are usually very limited in practice. In fact, they can sometimes actually work to diminish the extent of political control by elected leaders and enhance bureaucratic autonomy. Today, collective bargaining in local government often includes matters that once were considered within the sphere of managerial prerogative prior to unionization (Spero and Capozzola, 1973:Ch. 8; Lewin et al., 1979:72–75). Presently, it is not unusual for police to negotiate regarding the number of officers assigned to a police car, for firefighters to bargain over the size of operating units, while other employee groups negotiate over case loads, work quotas, duty assignments, etc.

Is collective bargaining mainly a vehicle for expanding bureaucratic power, rather than a means by which officials can secure greater political control over bureaucratic behavior on matters of policy? The answer is hardly clear-cut. For instance, when New York City and its sanitation union disagreed over air pollution laws requiring the shutting down of incinerators because the union claimed it was not equipped to handle the additional garbage, the sanitationmen prevailed and the air pollution ordinances were changed. Generally, it is the unions, rather than local government management, who have sought to expand the scope of collective bargaining to include what have traditionally been regarded as policy matters (Stanley, 1971; Spero and Capozzola, 1973:173–187). That leaves the budgetary process as probably the most important means of exerting political control over city hall bureaucracies. While important, this, too, has its limitations. Most of a city's budget is not open to great change from year to year owing to committed and mandated expenditures. Most important, there are economic and political constraints on budgetmakers that severely limit the budget's use as a tool for dealing with bureaucrats. This we elaborate below.

Generally, the politics of housekeeping services tends to be so dominated by powerful bureaucratic organizations that usually only sporadic challenges to their power are possible. Politics focuses largely on a closed process of bureaucratic rule-making which, in turn, heavily influences patterns of distributing resources.

The Politics of Money: The Variable World of City Budgeting

The tax and spending activities of local governments entail program decisions about all three kinds of public policies—distributive, redistributive, and developmental. Nevertheless, bringing these activities together in a budget process often tends to produce a relatively closed politics with distributive features.[1] Unlike the national government, cities ordinarily are not inclined to undertake bold shifts in taxing and spending in order to achieve large economic and social targets. Scarce revenues, slowly changing (and state-controlled) authority to tax, spend, and borrow, and their inability to substantially regulate the movement of capital and labor across their borders limit the utility of the budget as a routine developmental tool. Similarly, cities are not apt to use their budget resources to achieve many redistributive goals. Such programs are costly for a government with a small revenue base and can discourage city economic development. Consequently, studies of urban budget politics have usually emphasized that local government budgeting tends to be a highly incremental activity where slowly changing decision rules and bureaucratic practices dominate policy making (Meltsner, 1971; Wildavsky, 1976; Crecine, 1969; Kantor and David, 1983).

SOURCES OF CHANGE IN BUDGET POLITICS.   Tendencies toward closed, bureaucratic budgetary policies are subject to important limits, however. All considered, the budget remains the largest resource city government has in order to cope with disturbances to its political system or to its economy. Consequently, substantial changes in (1) political support for city government and (2) a community's market position can have powerful influence on the policy and politics of city budgeting.

Distributive Budgeting: Closed and Open Politics.   When localities enjoy a strong market position, there is likely to be growth or at least stability in city revenues. This kind of economic base permits city policymakers to look inward and view budgetary decisions in terms of piecemeal concerns and particularistic goals. As long as the market position of the city can be taken for granted and is something that overall budget policy is unlikely to alter, budgeting tends to be most responsive to the presence or absence of internal political conflicts and the demands of competing groups.

On one hand, during periods of political consensus budget politics is apt to be highly closed, rule-bound, and directed largely toward political maintenance activity. Since demands upon budgetmakers for costly services, particularly those of a redistributive nature, are limited, they are likely to be satisfied by growth in future revenues. The primary focus of budgeting is on the management of individual or groups claims—be they from advantaged or disadvantaged segments of the population. Since there is widespread consensus among political actors about the basic pattern of resource distribution, there are few incentives for making major changes in public expenditure. In this context, budgeting tends to become yet another island of power among the distributive activities of local government. There is routinization of budget decisions, and this is expressed in the elaboration of widely accepted budgetary rules for dividing up resources, much as in most housekeeping services.

On the other hand, declining political support for local government authorities is likely to shatter such a power island of "incremental" budget politics. Upheaval in a community's political system (or major changes in political coalitions) means declining support for political authorities. This fact almost inescapably challenges existing patterns of resource distribution. Under these circumstances, political leaders are constrained to abandon many past budgetary commitments in order to use the budget as a means of knitting together new supportive alliances. Budgeting cannot remain an island of bureaucratic power held together by stable rules and routine political activity. Fiscal decisions become a by-product of a highly open, pluralistic process of group bargaining. Conflicts are resolved mostly by building winning group coalitions in a fluid game of negotiation and compromise. Budget outputs are unlikely to be very stable or predictable; in particular, the size of the budget is apt to grow as political leaders seek additional resources in order to reconcile group conflicts.

Developmental Budgeting. Neither of these two patterns of distributive politics can be sustained if a locality undergoes substantial economic deterioration, however. If this occurs, taxing and spending decisions cannot be as easily geared to satisfying competing interests. This is because the locality's weak market position pressures political leaders to use more of the city's resources in order to promote reinvestment by the private sector in the community—or face worsening economic distress, with all the political liabilities that can pose.

In this context, budgeting is very much a developmental matter. Budget politics acquires the characteristics generally associated with this type of policy. The city government becomes more dependent on external private sector and governmental investors who can minimize economic deterioration through their reinvestment activities. The bargaining power of revenue-provider groups within the city grows as their investment decisions (and relocational activities) become the prime counterpoint for budget decisions by government officials. At the same time, unavoidable cuts in programs produce conflicts that political authorities are unable to resolve by traditional coalition building and bargaining—because slack resources are not sufficiently available to distribute benefits very widely.

Political leaders are consumed with managing tensions between maintaining popular support and promoting community economic growth. In attempting this, they are strongly inclined to limit public involvement in budget decision making and to coordinate public policy with actors in the private and intergovernmental sectors.

Thus, budgeting is an area of policy that is susceptible to major changes as the politico-economic context of local governance undergoes alteration. Under conditions of economic growth, it tends to be a highly distributive activity. That is, it can be an island of power dominated by bureaucratic routine or an arena of pluralist group bargaining, depending on the state of political support in local governmental systems. But under conditions of economic decline, budgeting is apt to become more a developmental activity. The ability of urban political leaders to govern the budget process is quite variable. They may be cast into very different kinds of arenas of power—some over which they have substantial influence and others where their control is severely limited.

Budget Politics in New York City

These patterns of budget politics can be illustrated by the experience of New York City since 1945. That city's huge size and complexity distinguish it from other American cities, making it difficult to generalize about this case to all other localities. Nevertheless, most other major central cities experienced political and economic trends similar to New York's—periods of political stability and polarization, as well as periods of economic growth and decline (Sbragia, 1983). Many of the patterns found in New York are likely to have occurred elsewhere.

BUDGETING AS DISTRIBUTION: FROM A POWER ISLAND TO A PLURALIST BARGAINING ARENA. During the postwar decades up to 1962, the political economy of New York City was supportive of budgeting as an island of power. The city's more or less slow, but sustained, growth as a corporate headquarters center produced expanding employment and governmental revenues. At the same time, there were few coalitions of groups seeking major changes in city services; city employees had not yet gained major influence in determining salaries and wages, and the city's minority community, though large, had yet to enter the political arena as major contestants.

The Board of Estimate—a unique institution that represents the city's top elected executives—dominated budgetary affairs and adhered to a stable, rule-bound process of decision. The dominant alliance on the Board comprised the comptroller and the five borough presidents, whose combined voting power limited mayoral influence and almost invariably dampened attempts to increase spending for new programs. The prevailing bargains were most often struck by these six officials in a continuous log-rolling process that resulted in incremental budget increases designed to keep pace with inflation and contain growing union power through marginal improvements in wages and working conditions. The board invariably accepted existing revenue constraints as inviolate, kept the lid on taxes, and exercised tight controls over how money was spent (rather than with program management). Budget expenditures grew slowly and predictably, and decisions rarely occasioned major conflicts over the distribution of resources.

After 1962, this island of power gave way to a more open, contentious, and pluralistic budget politics that lasted until the mid-1970s. Although during the 1960s New York City did not depart sharply from its postwar pattern of slow but stable economic growth (particularly because growth in service sector employment compensated for declines in manufacturing), dramatic events disrupted the city's political system. The previously quiescent minority community became highly politicized and, through riots, protest, and increased political participation in general, they made a determined bid for political power. The city's civil servants matched the minority community as a major new power broker. Confronted by a mayor who sought to block their assertion of power, civil service unions fought against his attempts to mobilize public opinion, to stand fast against strikes, and, in one instance, to call for use of the national guard.

The impact of these two groups of claimants altered the basic pattern of political reckoning in the city's budgetary arena. The budget process turned into a forum for bargaining out differences among these contenders and those who sought to keep a lid on new programs. Budget decision making centered upon the mayor who began to use the city's money to deal with the management of group conflict. Mayors Wagner and Lindsay separated decisions that involved mandated or recurring expenditures from those associated with new programs; they seized control of the latter, increased their number, and then modified the budget to reflect the fiscal implications of their decisions. Budgeting became highly unstable and nonincremental. Major changes in spending patterns occurred for various services and programs as deals were struck to put out political fires and forge new voter coalitions. Because this necessitated dramatic growth in the size of the budget, the city abandoned its traditional revenue restraints and sought new sources of governmental money. This included major tax changes, intergovernmental aid, and a major new departure—public borrowing to pay for operating expenses that were then rolled over (or refinanced) from year to year.

THE COLLAPSE OF DISTRIBUTIVE POLITICS: BUDGETING AS DEVELOPMENTAL POLICY MAKING. Major changes in the city's political economy undercut the distributive features of budget politics after New York City's fiscal crisis. The city suffered precipitous economic decline, particularly in job growth and governmental revenues, after the 1969 recession. This, combined with the inability of the city's political leaders to cut spending or limit the growth of municipal debt, moved commercial banks in New York and across the country to dump billions of New York City bond holdings. This closed the credit market to New York and precipitated a fiscal crisis in 1975.

The distributive character of New York City budget politics evaporated. For several years, the real locus of power in the budgetary process shifted to financial and business elites who dominated new governmental institutions established at the state and national levels to control and monitor the city's fiscal affairs. A key institution was the Emergency Financial Control Board (EFCB), an agency appointed by the governor composed mostly of business and financial leaders. The EFCB had the power to approve the city's capital and expense budgets, to approve city contracts with unions and outside businesses, and to certify whether or not the city was taking appropriate steps to balance its budget and reenter the capital market.

The budget quickly developed into a program of long-term economic planning under which the mayor cooperated with business and other authorities (including the U.S. Treasury, which made loan guarantees available to the city) to make draconian cuts in services, limit growth in spending, impose debt reduction schemes, and otherwise orient the city's tax and spending programs strongly in the direction of rebuilding business confidence in the city. Not only were the old power brokers—the unions and minorities—displaced from the budget process, but they suffered most under the new regime. The city's minority community bore the brunt of city job layoffs and program cuts (last hired were first fired—social welfare programs were more drastically cut than "basic" services). The unions were forced to use their pension funds to purchase city debt while accepting pay, benefit, and job reductions—or face city bankruptcy, something that would have meant the total abrogation of union contracts and would have permitted courts to be city paymasters.

During the early 1980s, an upturn in the New York City economy began to provide renewed job growth and the expansion of tax revenues, an event that enabled the city's fiscal authorities to achieve many of their economic targets sooner than planned. In particular, the city achieved a balanced budget and began to sell its securities in the capital market. As New York's stringent fiscal position began to ease, the mid-1980s saw the city returning once again to distributive-style budget politics as groups scrambled to reclaim lost pay, positions, and programs. In time, a transition to wholly distributive patterns of budgeting may occur if New York City's economic resurgence and political stability continue.

The Dilemma of Governability

Since distributive policy is most sensitive to the internal political forces in local governmental systems, power relationships within this arena are broadly pluralistic. The decentralized, polyarchal features of city political systems ensure that policy making is a by-product of competition among groups seeking organizational and group enhancement. The intricacies of this process of decision making are such that the distribution of influence among actors can vary from issue to issue, ranging from closed, stable, islands of power to open, competitive games of pluralist bargaining. Only when major changes occur in the locality's economic environment that transform policies into matters of developmental consequence is the importance of internal political forces likely to diminish in public policy making.

Although it is in the politics of distribution that local political authorities are least dependent upon exterior economic and intergovernmental forces, this alone has not ensured their ability to govern. The distributive arena is characterized by substantial fragmentation of power and authority. Reform-style governance has placed bureaucratic officialdom in a position of considerable independence, while leaving elected political leaders with a less substantial power base (most often the party) from which to extend their influence over city affairs. Elected officials stand before powerful professional bureaucracies, civil service unions, party factions, citizen and neighborhood groups, and other power centers that challenge their direction of city services. Thus, the governability of this arena of policy has emerged as a major conundrum for city political authorities.

This poses a most important limit on the extent to which community-responsive policy choices can be achieved. Without the capability for effective direction by top political authorities, the government of city services becomes excessively driven by narrow, parochial interests. Matters that transcend the interests of particular groups get ignored or neglected; issues that provoke group rivalries get watered down, knocked down, or emasculated. Thus, the need for more or less public expenditure or whether parks are more deserving of attention than streets or sewers may not be considered because there often is no coalition of powerful groups to promote such issues. Cost-saving measures, such as substituting nonuniformed employees for routine police tasks or privatizing certain city services—transit and refuse collection, for example—via city contracting may not be undertaken because of the opposition of entrenched civil service unions. In a sense, popular control of the city has run up against its own internal limits. Without a balance-wheel of central authority, systems of democratic governance become consumed in their own inner logic, instead of serving the public.

Endnote

1. The following discussion of urban budgetary politics draws upon Kantor and David, 1983.

References for Part Five

Altshuler, Alan A. 1972. *Community Control.* New York: St. Martin's Press.

Antunnes, George E. and John Plumlee. 1977. "The Distribution of Urban Public Services." *Urban Affairs Quarterly*, Vol. 12 (March), 313–332.

Bahl, Roy. 1974. *Financing State and Local Government in the 1980's.* New York: Oxford University Press.

Banfield, Edward C. 1961. *Political Influence.* New York: Free Press.

Banfield, Edward C. and James Q. Wilson. 1965. *City Politics.* Cambridge, Mass.: Harvard University Press.

Bellush, Jewel and Stephen David. 1971. *Race and Politics in New York City.* New York: Praeger.

Benjamin, Aaron, et al., 1979. *Public Sector Bargaining.* Washington, D.C.: Bureau of National Affairs, Inc.

Boehm, Randolph H. 1982. *Public Employees, Unions and the Erosion of Civic Trust.* Fredrick, Md.: University Publications of America.

Boyle, John and David Jacobs. 1982. "The Intra-city Distribution of Services: A Multivariate Analysis." *American Political Science Review*, Vol. 76 (June), 371–379.

Chickering, Lawrence A., ed. 1976. *Public Employee Unions: A Study of the Crisis in Public Sector Labor Relations.* San Francisco: Institute for Contemporary Studies.

Crecine, John P. 1969. *Government Problem Solving: A Computer Simulation of Municipal Budgeting.* Chicago: Rand McNally.

Crouch, Winston W. 1978. *Organized Civil Servants.* Berkeley: University of California Press.

Crozier, Michael. 1964. *The Bureaucratic Phenomenon.* Chicago: University of Chicago Press.

Dahl, Robert A. 1961. *Who Governs?* New Haven: Yale University Press.

David, Stephen and Paul Kantor. 1983. "Urban Policy in the Federal System: A Reconceptualization of Federalism." *Polity*, Vol. XVI, No. 2, 284–304.

David, Stephen and Paul E. Peterson, eds. 1976. *Urban Politics and Public Policy*, Second Edition. New York: Praeger.

Dommel, Paul R. and Associates. 1982. *Decentralizing Urban Policy: Case Studies in Community Development.* Washington, D.C.: Brookings Institution.

Downs, Anthony. 1967. *Inside Bureaucracy.* Boston: Little, Brown.

Eckstein, Harry. 1960. *Pressure Group Politics: The Case of the British Medical Association.* London: Allen and Unwin.

Eisinger, Peter K. 1984. "Black Mayors and the Politics of Racial Economic Advancement" in Harlan Hahn and Charles H. Levine, eds. 1984. *Readings in Urban Politics*. New York: Longman, pp. 249–260.

Eulau, Heinze and Kenneth Prewitt. 1973. *Labyrinths of Democracy: Adaptations, Linkages, Representation, and Policies in Urban Politics*. Indianapolis: Bobbs-Merrill.

Fainstein, Susan S., et al. 1983. *Restructuring the City*. New York: Longman.

Freiden, Bernard J. and Marshall Kaplan. 1975. *The Politics of Neglect: Urban Aid from Model Cities to Revenue Sharing*. Cambridge, Mass.: MIT Press.

Fuchs, Ester and Robert A. Shapero, 1983. "Government Performance As a Basis for Machine Support." *Urban Affairs Quarterly*, Vol. 18, No. 4 (June), 537–550.

Hahn, Harlan and Charles H. Levine, eds. 1984. *Readings in Urban Politics*, Second Edition. New York: Longman.

Hawley, Willis D., et al. 1976. *Theoretical Perspectives on Urban Politics*. Englewood Cliffs, N.J.: Prentice-Hall.

Heinze, Anne, Herbert Jacob and Robert L. Lineberry, eds. 1983. *Crime in City Politics*. New York: Longman.

Horton, Raymond. 1973. *Municipal Labor Relations in New York City*. New York: Praeger.

Jacob, Herbert. 1985. "Policy Responses to Crime" in Paul E. Peterson, ed. 1985. *The New Urban Reality*. Washington, D.C.: Brookings Institution, pp. 225–252.

Jacob, Herbert. 1984. *The Frustration of Policy: Responses to Crime by American Cities*. Boston: Little, Brown.

Jones, Bryan D. 1981. "Party and Bureaucracy: The Influence of Intermediary Groups on Urban Service Delivery." *American Political Science Review*, Vol. XX (September), 688–700.

Jones, Bryan D., Saadia R. Greenberg, Clifford Kaufman and Joseph Drew. 1984. "Service Delivery Rules and the Distribution of Local Government Services: Three Detroit Bureaucracies" in Harlan Hahn and Charles H. Levine, eds. 1984. *Readings in Urban Politics: Past, Present and Future*, Second Edition. New York: Longman, pp. 224–248.

Jones, Bryan D., Saadia Greenberg and Joseph Drew. 1980. *Service Delivery in the City*. New York: Longman.

Kantor, Paul and Stephen David. 1983. "The Political Economy of Change in Urban Budgetary Politics: A Framework for Analysis and a Case Study." *British Journal of Political Science*, Vol. 13 (July), 251–274.

Kantor, Paul and David G. Lawrence. 1981. "Constituency Focus and Urban Policy Making: Local Politics in London." *Political Studies*, Vol. XXIX, No. 1, 151–172.

Katznelson, Ira. 1973. *Black Men, White Cities*. New York: Oxford University Press.

Kotler, Milton. 1969. *Neighborhood Government*. Indianapolis: Bobbs-Merrill.

Levy, Frank S., Arnold Meltsner and Aaron Wildavsky. 1974. *Urban Outcomes: Schools, Streets and Libraries*. Berkeley: University of California Press.

Lewin, David, Raymond D. Horton and James W. Kuhn. 1979. *Collective Bargaining and Manpower Utilization in Big City Governments*. Montclair, N.J.: Allenheld Osmun.

Lineberry, Robert L. 1983. *Crime and City Politics*. New York: Longman.

Lineberry, Robert L. 1977. *Equality and Urban Policy: The Distribution of Municipal Services*. Beverly Hills: Sage.

Lineberry, Robert L. 1974 "Mandating Urban Equality" in Harlan Hahn and Charles H. Levine, eds. 1984. *Readings in Urban Politics*. New York: Longman, pp. 184–211.

Lipsky, Michael. 1976. "Towards a Theory of Street Level Bureaucracy" in Willis D. Hawley et al. 1976. *Theoretical Perspectives on Urban Politics*. Englewood Cliffs, N.J.: Prentice-Hall, Ch. 11.

Lipsky, Michael. 1970. *Protest in City Politics*. Chicago: Rand McNally.

Love, Thomas M. and George T. Sulzner. 1975. "Political Implications of Public Employee Bargaining." *Industrial Relations*, Vol. 11 (February), 18–32.

Lowi, Theodore J. 1968. "Gosnell's Chicago Revisited via Lindsay's New York: Foreword to the Second Edition" in Harold F. Gosnell. 1968. *Machine Politics: Chicago Model*. Chicago: University of Chicago Press, pp. 7–16.

Lowi, Theodore J. 1964. *At the Pleasure of the Mayor*. New York: Free Press.

March, James C. and Herbert A. Simon. 1958. *Organizations*. New York: John Wiley.

Meltsner, Arnold. 1971. *The Politics of City Revenue*. Berkeley: University of California Press.

Mladenka, Kenneth. 1980. "The Urban Bureaucracy and the Chicago Political Machine; Who Gets What and the Limits to Political Control." *American Political Science Review*, Vol. 74 (December), 991–998.

Mladenka, Kenneth and Kim Hill. 1978. "Houston: The Distribution of Urban Police Services." *Journal of Politics*, Vol. 40 (February), 112–133.

Mladenka, Kenneth and Kim Hill. 1977. "The Distribution of Benefits in an Urban Environment: Parks and Libraries in Houston." *Urban Affairs Quarterly*, Vol. 13 (September), 73–94.

Mollenkopf, John H. 1983. *The Contested City*. Princeton, N.J.: Princeton University Press.

Morris, Charles R. 1980. *The Cost of Good Intentions: New York City and the Liberal Experiment, 1960–1975*. New York: McGraw-Hill.

Nordlinger, Eric. 1972. *Decentralizing the City: A Study of Boston's Little City Halls*. Cambridge, Mass.: MIT Press.

Peterson, Paul E. 1981. *City Limits*. Chicago: University of Chicago Press.

Rich, Richard C., ed. 1982A. *Analyzing Urban Service Distributions*. Lexington, Mass.: D.C. Heath.

Rich, Richard C., ed. 1982B. *The Politics of Urban Public Services*. Lexington, Mass.: D.C. Heath.

Rich, Richard C. 1980. "The Complex Web of Urban Governance." *American Behavioral Scientist*, Vol. 24, No. 2 (November), 277–298.

Richardson, James F. 1974. *Urban Police in the United States*. Port Washington, N.Y.: Kennikat Press.

Sayre, Wallace and Herbert Kaufman. 1960. *Governing New York City*. New York: Russell Sage.

Sbragia, Alberta. 1983. "The 1970s: A Decade of Change in Local Government" in Alberta Sbragia, ed. 1983. *The Municipal Money Chase: The Politics of Local Government Finance*. Boulder, Colo. Westview Press.

Schattschneider, E. E. 1960. *The Semi-Sovereign People*. New York: Holt, Reinhart and Winston.

Schlesinger, Joseph A. 1966. *Ambition and Politics*. Chicago: Rand McNally.

Simon, Herbert. 1957. *Administrative Behavior*, Second Edition. New York: Free Press.

Spero, Sterling and John M. Capozzola. 1973. *The Urban Community and Its Unionized Bureaucracies: Pressure Politics in Local Government Labor Relations*. New York: Dunellen Publishing Company.

Stanley, David T. 1972. *Managing Local Government under Union Pressure*. Washington, D.C.: Brookings Institution.

Stanley, David T. 1971. "The Effects of Unions on Local Government." *The Proceedings of the Academy of Political Science*, Vol. XXX, No. 2.

Stieber, Jack. 1973. *Public Employee Unionism: Structure, Growth, Policy*. Washington, D.C.: Brookings Institution.

Summers, Clyde W. 1974. "Public Employee Collective Bargaining: A Political Perspective." *Yale Law Journal*, Vol. 83 (May), 1156–1200.

Thompson, Frank J. 1975. *Personnel Policy in the City*. Berkeley: University of California Press.

United States Government, Advisory Commission on Intergovernmental Relations. 1982. *State and Local Roles in the Federal System*. A-88 (April). Washington, D.C.: U.S. Government Printing Office.

Verba, Sidney and Norman H. Nie. 1972. *Participation in America*. New York: Harper and Row.

Weber, Max. 1962. "Bureaucracy" in *From Max Weber*, translated by H. H. Gerth and C. Wright Mills. New York: Oxford University Press.

Weber, Max. 1947. *The Theory of Social and Economic Organization*, translated by A. M. Henderson and Talcott Parsons. Glencoe: Free Press.

Wildavsky, Aaron. 1976. *Budgeting*. Boston: Little, Brown.

Wilson, James Q. 1970. *Varieties of Police Behavior*. New York: Atheneum.

Wilson, James Q. 1962. *The Amateur Democrat*. Chicago: University of Chicago Press.

Wirt, Frederick M. 1985. "The Dependent City? External Influences upon Local Control." *Journal of Politics*, Vol. 47, 83–112.

Wolfinger, Raymond. 1984. "Why Political Machines Have Not Withered Away and Other Revisionist Thoughts" in Harlan Hahn and Charles H. Levine, eds. 1984. *Readings in Urban Politics: Past, Present and Future*, Second Edition. New York: Longman, pp. 74–97.

Wolfinger, Raymond. 1974. *The Politics of Progress*. Englewood Cliffs, N.J.:

Prentice-Hall.

Wood, Robert. 1958. *Suburbia*. Boston: Little, Brown.

Woshnic, George J. 1975. *Municipal Decentralization and Neighborhood Resources*. New York: Praeger.

Yates, Douglas. 1977. *The Ungovernable City*. Cambridge, Mass.: MIT Press.

PART SIX

The Politics of Redistribution

CHAPTER SIXTEEN

Urban Social Policy and Dependency: The Governmentalization of Inequality

C HANGES in the urban political economy have converged to make local governments focal points in the vast welfare state system of the United States. However, as urban poverty has become governmentalized, economic dependency has interacted with federalism to limit the ability of local and state governments to meet the claims of the disadvantaged for greater economic equality.

The Politico-Economic Context of Urban Redistribution

America's postindustrial economy has produced tremendous prosperity for the nation as a whole, but it has not been capable of overcoming persistent inequality in the distribution of income among citizens. Although all measures of poverty are subjective, about 15.2 percent of the American people were considered officially poor in 1983 by the U.S. government.[1] Without government assistance, the poverty situation would be far worse. Nearly 25 percent of all families and 37 percent of all unrelated individuals would live in poverty in absence of cash and benefits provided by government social service programs (Levitan, 1985:2–3).

The Urban Economy and Redistribution

The incidence of postindustrial poverty is linked to age, race, sex of family head, work status, educational attainment, and other factors. These are, in turn, related to forms of disadvantage that the market economy cannot ameliorate on its own. For instance, blacks are three times more likely than whites to be poor; this is because blacks are much more likely than whites to be poorly educated, unemployed, and suffer other disadvantages, including racial discrimination, which limit their job opportunities.[2]

Often the burdens of deprivation fall more heavily on some groups within the population than on others because these groups cannot "fit" within the employment structure of the economy. The elderly have traditionally been among poverty's most frequent victims because most cannot be employed; that their number among the poor has dropped in recent decades is mainly due to more generous pensions and government income transfer programs. Employment alone does not guarantee an adequate income, however. Almost half of the 7.6 million family heads who were poor in 1983 worked, but low wages, intermittent employment, or large families kept these persons and their families in poverty (Levitan, 1985:7-13).

CENTRAL CITY POVERTY: DISPARITY OF NEED AND RESOURCES.   From the perspective of the central cities, the postindustrial economy has distributed these problems of disadvantage in fundamentally perverse ways. The new economic order initiated patterns of fiscal disparity between need and resources among localities. As America's economy underwent industrial and population dispersal, more mobile, wealthier, and white families led the flight out of the older cities into suburbia and beyond, leaving behind disproportionate numbers of poor, particularly minority, families. This was paralleled by a massive movement of poor people, particularly blacks, from rural areas to central cities. As a result, blacks have become a predominantly urban population group. In 1940, only about one-half of all blacks lived in urban areas, but in 1965 over 80 percent did (Piven and Cloward, 1971:214-215).

During the postwar period, there has been growing poverty within the central cities of the United States. Between 1970 and 1982, metropolitan areas' share of the national poverty population increased from 56 to 61 percent. But in central cities, the percentage of the population below the official poverty level increased from 14.9 percent to 18 percent, while in the suburbs it rose from 8.1 to 8.9 percent. The greatest increase in poverty occurred in the central cities of large metropolitan areas. There the poverty rate rose from 14.8 to 19.6 percent.

Along with the growth of central city poor have been adverse changes in the composition of this population, enlarging the numbers of those whose incomes are most likely to lag behind. As a result of escalating rates of separation, divorce, and unmarried motherhood, households headed by women now constitute a large proportion of poverty households. In central cities, 5.5 percent of all white male and 10 percent of all black male family heads had incomes below the poverty level in 1982, compared with 22 percent of all white female and 50 percent of all black female family heads. The number of black female headed families with incomes below the poverty level in central cities actually more than doubled between 1970 and 1982 (Department of Housing and Urban Development, 1984:39-42). Major urban areas now are the national focal point of poverty and distress.

These changes in demography occurred at the same time that employment and investment have shifted away from central cities and manufacturing in favor of far-flung locations and service activities. This development has depleted the private and public sector resources from which cities can deal with problems of disadvantage. The loss of numbers of manufacturing jobs shrunk the employment opportunities and incomes for lesser-skilled workers in central cities. Manufacturing jobs were the traditional provider of employment for this group (Burchell and Listokin, 1981). Furthermore, city government's ability to generate resources for aiding the poor generally declined. Between 1970 and 1982, income differentials between central city and suburb continued to grow, as they did continuously during the postwar era (see Chapter 9). This decline in income has meant that central cities now have relatively less capacity to raise revenues or meet the demand for services that growing portions of their populations need.

POVERTY AND URBAN ECONOMIC DEPENDENCY. The restructuring of the urban economy also has indirectly limited the capability of cities to contend with problems of redistribution. The economic dependency of cities discourages city governments from promoting programs to combat urban poverty. As urban economic competition casts central cities into inferior market positions, this drives local governments to give high priority to policies that can enhance their market positions and avoid those public programs that detract from this objective.

This means that local political leaders and their citizens are typically faced wth a cruel choice—to promote community economic security or to trade this off from humanitarian efforts to help the disadvantaged. For instance, if cities are to promote better housing for low-income groups, it is likely to mean higher taxes and the use of scarce inner city real estate for low-income residents. If cities are to promote programs to end racial segregation in housing and schools, it probably will mean "white flight" of middle-income families. If cities are generous to the homeless, it probably will mean receiving even more homeless into the community, as these individuals move to find better conditions for themselves. All other things being equal, policies of redistribution have little or no "payoff" from the standpoint of enhancing the community economic base in an urban system that routinely disciplines city generosity with the penalty of foregone development and increasing economic insecurity for its citizens.

The Intergovernmental Order and Redistribution

Changes in the federal system have radically redefined the roles of the national, state, and local governments in coping with problems of redistribution. As suggested in previous chapters, federalism places higher governmental authorities in a more permissive position to promote redistributive activities compared with local government. Accordingly, the federal and, to a lesser extent, the state governments have become the dominant providers of funds for local social welfare activities. From the perspective of the cities, this growth in intergovernmental programs has been of enormous political and economic consequence. Not only has it created a national welfare state that at least touches nearly all forms of socio-economic deprivation; it has "federalized" the local politics of redistribution in the sense that local redistributive activities are highly dependent upon federal authority and programs.

THE GROWTH OF INTERGOVERNMENTAL PROGRAMS. During the Great Depression of the 1930s, the foundation of the American welfare state was created. By establishing federal programs to maintain incomes for various categories of need and through federally sponsored public housing and job programs, national responsibility for redistributing wealth to the disadvantaged was assumed. In addition to providing emergency relief to the able-bodied unemployed, Congress passed legislation in 1935 that made it a national policy to provide some federal support to any state that adopted a plan for old age assistance or for aid to dependent children or for aid to the blind. In later years, these so-called categories of assistance were extended by the addition of aid to the permanently and totally disabled, the medically indigent, children of unemployed parents, and certain others.

The postwar decades witnessed the continuation of the New Deal welfare programs (other than job creation efforts) and the expansion of federal housing responsibilities. There emerged a broad bipartisan consensus at the national level in support of a large and permanent federal responsibility for programs of redistribution, leaving state and local governments in clearly subordinate positions within the intergovernmental system—mainly as agents to implement and sometimes to share funding of federal programs (see below). These arrangements were extended and elaborated during the 1960s in a burst of federally sponsored antipoverty activity. As part of President Lyndon Johnson's Great Society, a War on Poverty was declared as Congress passed the Economic Opportunity Act of 1964 which, together with related welfare legislation, launched numbers of new federal programs intended to go beyond the alleviation of poverty and address its presumed root causes.

Targeted mostly at hard-core poverty areas within cities, the Great Society initiatives included manpower training programs, such as the Job Corps, youth employment programs, community mental health efforts, and the Community Action Programs, which sought to empower the urban poor to help fashion and run their own neighborhood-based antipoverty drives. At this time, the heavily Democratic Congress also undertook to expand non-area based programs that actually overshadowed in funding the administration's inner city initiatives. In 1965, Congress passed the Medicare program to provide hospital and medical insurance for aged Social Security pensioners, and it liberalized the program of comprehensive health care for the indigent poor (now Medicaid). Paralleling this were major new federal housing programs to stimulate greater low-income housing production and expand the range of eligibility for federal housing subsidies among the poor. Further, Congress approved other in-kind assistance for the poor, such as the food stamp program, which has since grown to become a permanent part of what is a very comprehensive, if somewhat hodge-podge, welfare system.

Although federal spending for social services began to slow during the 1970s (see Chapter 9) and the Nixon administration began to abandon most of the specifically inner city antipoverty endeavors, it was not until after the election of Ronald Reagan in 1980 that major cuts in federal social welfare spending occurred. Although President Nixon often verbalized opposition to the large federal role in programs of redistribution, in fact he presided over continued increases in such federal aid, as did Presidents Ford and Carter. Until 1979, real federal outlays for the poor had followed the upward trajectory that characterized the postindustrial era as a whole, increasing 275 percent above 1964 levels. After 1980, however, this trend reversed. Although total outlays in aid of the poor remained constant between 1981 and 1984, almost all of the nominal increases in current dollar spending went to programs that largely benefit the elderly, most of whom are not poor at all. If federal expenditures for these programs (mainly Social Security and health care for the elderly) are excluded, real federal outlays for the nonaged poor show a 9 percent decline (Levitan, 1985:21–23). Thus, the absolute slashes in federal funding for most federal programs in aid of the poor undertaken by President Reagan amount to a major break in the development of the American welfare state, although even his administration managed to make only marginal cuts and has actually abandoned few social welfare programs.

THE IMPACT OF NATIONAL WELFARE PROGRAMS.   Despite the so-called Reagan revolution, the overall growth in intergovernmental aid programs has had tremendous impact on the poor and the position of local governments in delivering assistance to them.

Federal Programs and the Reduction of Poverty.   First, in regard to the poor, the explosion of intergovernmental redistributive programs has actually reduced poverty a great deal and continues to do so. The impact of these various social welfare programs was very considerable by the mid-1960s and grew enormously during the following ten years. Cash payments alone were responsible for pulling about 33 percent of the pretransfer poor (5.1 million households)—that is, those below the official poverty line prior to calculation of government income transfer program benefits—out of poverty in 1965. This grew to 44 percent or 7.7 million households by 1972. If the value of in-kind benefits, such as food stamps and public housing, are added, about 60 percent of the pretransfer poor were removed from poverty.

A profile of the poor in 1974 dramatically underscores the importance of these redistributive programs. Without any such programs, about 20.2 million families, or more than one-quarter of the entire population, would have been poor by government standards. With social insurance and public assistance benefits added to their incomes, 9.1 million could be considered officially poor. Adding in-kind benefits makes this group shrink to 5.4 million or 6.9 percent of all families (Patterson, 1981:165–166). However, as a result of reductions in federal social welfare spending, inflation, and other factors, the number of poor has dramatically increased since to about 35.3 million in 1983. The national poverty rate went from 11.4 percent in 1978 to 15.2 percent in 1983—the highest poverty rate since 1965 (Levitan, 1985:138).

These figures should hardly be interpreted to mean that poverty essentially has been overcome through governmental largesse. Indeed, not only is it growing once again after decades of decline, but deprivation is taking on more vicious and demoralizing forms as it has become concentrated in urban ghettos. Moreover, the fact is that many programs in housing, health, food assistance, and income maintenance, etc., do not reach all who may be eligible, do not do enough to actually lift those who do qualify out of officially described poverty, or do not address all forms of deprivation (Levitan, 1985, 1986; Palley and Palley, 1981).

The Federalization of Local Redistribution. A second result of this expansion of intergovernmental activity has been to "federalize"—the term is meant in its broadest intergovernmental sense—the local politics of redistribution. The growth of federal and state programs of redistribution has created such a degree of intergovernmental dependency that there no longer is much of a purely "local" politics of redistribution. Table 16-1 gives a picture of the division of fiscal responsibility for funding redistributive activities among the different levels of government. It shows the percentage of each government's total resources (from own resources) devoted to the major kinds of redistributive programs between 1962 and 1973. The explosion in federal social welfare programs has made the national government the dominant provider for all programs in this area except for health and hospitals, by 1973 providing over 70 percent of all resources. At the same time, states have also become major contributors, providing around one-fifth or more of the funds among the three governmental jurisdictions. In contrast, the local government contribution from own resources for these major areas of redistribution was never much over 10 percent in total and has declined significantly, particularly as a provider of housing resources and funding for public welfare programs (Peterson, 1981:80). Even in the wake of the Reagan administration's welfare program cuts, the local contribution has remained small (see below).

The Local Political Implications of Federalization. From the perspective of local politics, this "federalization" of redistribution has converted an arena of policy that was once almost entirely a local community activity into a predominantly intergovernmental activity. This fact has several far-reaching implications. For one thing, it means that the local agendas of decision, the authority to make decisions, the structure of public programs, the power relations among those who compete for influence within the arena, and nearly all other features of the local politics of redistribution have an intergovernmental dimension. Most important, local decisions about social welfare are circumscribed not only by urban economic dependency, but also by extensive local dependency on state and federal programs and resources.

This intergovernmental dependency means that what was an area of public policy once dominated by community conflicts has since become an arena overlaid with major intergovernmental conflicts. This is so because the governmental jurisdictions that share responsibility for programs of redistribution do not share similar political economies and must respond to very different kinds of constraints in program administration. The federal government, with its

TABLE 16-1 Governmental Expenditures from Own Fiscal Resources (percentage distributions among governments)

Function	Local			State			Federal			Total		
	1962	1967	1973	1962	1967	1973	1962	1967	1973	1962	1967	1973
Redistributive												
Welfare	8.5	7.8	4.3	18.4	20.1	28.7	73.1	72.1	67.2	100.0	100.0	100.0
Health and												
hospitals	33.2	32.2	35.4	35.2	34.0	29.6	31.6	33.8	35.0	100.0	100.0	100.0
Housing	46.7	29.3	9.7	2.5	3.8	4.5	50.7	66.9	85.8	100.0	100.0	100.0
Social insurance	2.9	2.9	2.2	18.9	12.3	18.2	78.1	84.8	79.6	100.0	100.0	100.0
Subtotal	10.8	9.7	7.4	20.6	17.2	21.5	68.6	73.2	71.1	100.0	100.0	100.0

SOURCE: From Paul E. Peterson, *City Limits*. © 1981 by The University of Chicago. Reprinted by permission of The University of Chicago Press.

massive revenue base, comparatively secure market position, and highly permeable political system, has become the potentially most powerful promoter and producer of redistributive programs. In contrast, the generally weaker market position of local governments in the postindustrial economy disciplines them to limit their role in redistributive policies and focus on managing their intergovernmental dependency. In effect, each governmental level is inclined to accord different priorities to redistributive activities, making conflicts among federal, state, and local governments inherent in this area of public policy.

Popular Control and Redistribution

It is in the redistributive arena of local politics that the development of popular control linkages have most decisively altered traditional patterns of political calculation on the part of masses and elites. In the past, local governments were able to manage redistributive claims by manipulating the *input* side of local politics. That is, city governments dealt with problems of redistribution by arranging political institutions in ways that systematically relegated the poor to a peripheral position of political power and limited their demands. This traditional local government capability for undercutting mass-elite linkages via input management has declined during the postindustrial era. Although local political authorities may seek to employ public policy outputs in order to influence political demands of the poor, the development of popular control has ensured that the redistributive arena cannot be governed in ways that fail to incorporate the poor.

POLYARCHAL POLITICAL DEVELOPMENT AND THE URBAN POOR. The major changes that have pushed systems of urban governance in a polyarchal direction have brought this circumstance about.

Weakening of Traditional Social Control Institutions. First, the old social control politics based on substituting jobs, petty favors, ethnic recognition, and the like in order to satisfy redistributive demands no longer serves as the dominant nexus connecting political leaders and the poor because of the decline of the political machine. The trend in New York City's dominant Democratic Party organization conveys a sense of this dramatic transformation. During the period 1927 to 1933, one authoritative study counted 1,177 individual clubs within the city's boundaries, of which 703 were Democratic organizations. When that study was replicated during the early 1970s, the number of clubs had declined to 268, of which only 154 were Democratic (Peel, 1935).

Further, the activities of these remaining club organizations in providing individual rewards and control over party followers and the electorate were a pale shadow of what they once were. Most of the activity of the clubs involved maintaining the organization itself, such as publishing a newsletter, soliciting advertisements for an annual journal, and the like. Fewer than a third of the city's clubs held the traditional picnics, card and theater parties, and athletic outings. Most important, more than one-half of these clubs did not provide any kind of welfare, employment, or housing services, and only a small minority reported that they even provided "contact with the government." Patronage, particularly for any well-paid higher-level governmental positions, was scant. For instance, 66 percent of the clubs could claim no members in government appointments to positions of Deputy Commissioner or above in state or city government. Only 25 percent could claim at least five such members, and only 2 percent of the clubs had more than ten (Katznelson, 1981:127–128).

The rise of reform government and the growth of government social welfare programs has substituted for the machine a welfare bureaucracy that cannot entirely duplicate the machine as a means of social control. Bureaucratic organizations do not forge strong political loyalties with their clientele, and their political control over their constituencies is limited to their capability to manipulate policy outputs within limited spheres of authority. Further, service delivery bureaucracies are not politically reliable. In contrast to the party machine, the power of welfare bureaucracies is at least in part tied to expanding services to their clientele—rather than with undercutting demands for redistribution.

The Political Capability of the Poor. As local government's ability to manipulate political demands has declined, the capability of the poor to make redistributive demands has grown. For one thing, the poor have become a more potent political force within cities as a result of demographic and political changes described in Chapter 9. In the more socially polarized central cities, lower-income groups have managed to become empowered within the political systems. It is now commonplace for minority representatives in most large cities to at least have a crack at becoming part of governing coalitions—and in some cities to dominate local popular control systems.

Further, the poor are much more likely than in the past to exploit their positions of power in order to make redistributive demands on government. The sheer growth of welfare state programs has established a huge governmental presence within low-income communities that almost unavoidably influences the political calculations among the poor in the direction of greater expectations and bolder demands. The creation of widespread governmental social welfare programs shatters traditional notions of limited governmental responsibility and establishes professional and other political interests that have a stake in their expansion (Piven and Cloward, 1982:Ch. 4).

Because the structure of poverty has undergone a social polarization within cities, race and class now overlap to create the potential for greater political cohesion and shared expectations of entitlement on the part of the poor around specific redistributive programs. For example, a study of New York City's Washington Heights community during the 1970s showed how race, class, and dependency on particular kinds of social welfare programs tended to overlap. In 1972, about one in three residents in the neighborhood received some form of subsistence help from government. But the patterns of distribution of this cash assistance were not at all random. Of those who received some cash assistance from the state, 76 percent of the Irish, Jewish, and Greek residents were recipients of Social Security; only 11 percent of these white residents were on the welfare rolls or had been during the past year. In contrast, fewer than 2 percent of the Hispanic service recipients and only 22 percent of the blacks were receiving Social Security benefits. Yet 61 percent of both the blacks and the Hispanics getting some form of government aid were receiving or recently had received public assistance benefits (Katznelson, 1981:129).

In effect, the tremendous growth of government welfare programs, together with polarization among the recipients of this aid, has redefined the relationship between the poor and their local governments. Compared with times past, local governments now face a much more socially cohesive poor whose stake in ongoing programs and whose expectations of entitlement are very substantial. The input side of the redistributive arena has dramatically opened up in response to forces that enhance the significance of popular control in linking masses and governmental authorities. City governments must manage matters of redistribution by relying more than ever before on manipulating the output side of local politics.

Urban Social Welfare Policy and Politico-Economic Dependency

The dependency of local communities on exterior economic political forces has not meant that public policy in this arena has become highly centralized, uniform among jurisdictions, or removed from significant local political control. In fact, from the perspective of the federal system as a whole, an ironic result of economic dependency has been an opposite tendency; urban social policy has become subject to powerful local–regional influences, making for tremendous policy variation and intergovernmental conflict within the American welfare state.

It is true that the enormous growth of federal and state intervention has imposed control over the overarching objectives and content of local social welfare policy. For one thing, it has ended the traditional machine-style approach to the problem of redistribution. As noted previously, once federal and state laws were passed that provided assistance to the poor as a matter of legal entitlement, the traditional Christmas turkey or bucket of coal given by the political boss as *quid pro quo* for the recipient's vote became extinct. Machine-style favoritism in social welfare policy was replaced by bureaucrats whose professional values now dominate social welfare administration.

This governmental revolution has deeply transformed local government policy toward the poor. The doctrines and practices of professional casework have come to permeate relief giving, curtailing many of the harsh traditions of the industrial era. Though there is surely much continuity—for example, rather than finding moral defects among the poor, casework doctrine often traces causes of poverty to "psychological defects" of the poor—cash assistance and counseling have largely replaced the niggardly practices and moralizing of private philanthropy (Piven and Cloward, 1971:176–177; Banfield, 1974:Ch. 6).

In fact, the governmentalization of the poor has proceeded to a point where private charities, once the institutional core of local programs for the needy, now primarily serve higher-income groups in dealing with their problems; providing income assistance to the poor is no longer an important function of private philanthropy (Steiner, 1966:10).

Nevertheless, these centralist tendencies in policy do not overshadow the extent to which local politics and economics powerfully shape the content and bias of national redistributive programs. This is so because of interaction between federalism and the workings of the contemporary urban economy. Federal redistributive programs are usually structured to permit local and state governments a major role in their implementation. Money for these programs generally comes from the national and, to a lesser extent, state governments, while administration is largely a local function. Decentralization in program administration is not only typical of most past federal programs, it has dramatically increased within the last decade or so.

The delegation of administrative responsibilities to localities and states in carrying out federal programs would be of minor political significance were it not for the fact that these lower levels of government are more economically dependent than is the federal government. Localities and state governments must compete for capital investment, jobs, and labor in an economic system where high taxes and the presence of large dependent populations do not enhance their market position. Indeed, these things discourage business investment, and they discourage higher income families and skilled labor from residing in the community. In contrast, the federal government's more secure market position—its huge tax base and its much greater ability to control the movement of capital and labor—enables federal officials to enjoy far more economic independence in undertaking redistributive endeavors.

Intergovernmental Bias in Redistributive Policy: The Governmentalization of Inequality

These differences in governmental economic dependency within the federal system tend to facilitate divergent patterns of policy bias between higher and lower governmental levels. In general, the policy bias of the federal government is relatively permissive in respect to promoting redistributive policy objectives; local governments are inclined to avoid the costs of redistributive responsibilities in order to safeguard their weaker market positions. This has profoundly determined the structure of American urban social welfare policy: (1) As localities have struggled to limit their policy responsibilities, a checkerboard welfare system has developed that makes unequal local government treatment of the poor inevitable, and (2) intergovernmental conflict has become a major obstacle to assisting the poor.

These patterns of urban policy may be seen by surveying major programs of redistribution during the two periods of modern intergovernmental relations, the Old Federalism and the New Federalism years.

The Old Federalism and Urban Social Policy: The Politics of Inequality

During the Old Federalism period from the Great Depression to the early 1970s, federal–local relations were dominated by the use of categorical grants-in-aid. This type of program structure provided federal officials with a relatively directive role in social welfare policy. Nevertheless, even this type of intergovernmental aid approach usually left considerable local autonomy in the implementation of the programs. Consequently, states and localities struggled to adapt their program responsibilities to their regional and local economies. Conflict between federal and local governments tended to characterize program implementation when federal redistributive objectives clashed with the economic dependency of lower-level governments.

INTERGOVERNMENTAL POLICY DIVERGENCE: THE CASE OF AFDC. The classic case is the federal government's major public assistance program, Aid to Families with Dependent Children (AFDC). This program has always been a highly decentralized operation. Although the federal government generally provides about one-half or more of the cost of this program, state governments are responsible for the other half, and in several states the legislatures have required local government contributions. Moreover, even though the federal government has defined the various categories of eligibility for this and related public assistance programs, i.e., the blind, disabled, dependent families, etc., local and state governments are permitted to set the standards of eligibility (e.g., declare who is poor enough) and determine the level of cash assistance that will be provided to individuals in AFDC. As the following chapter describes, local government officials are inclined to exploit the discretionary role that is afforded by the structure of this program. Although cost sharing is not a consistent federal relief principle, it dominates programs specifically targeted at the poor and has always been a feature of federal relief efforts. This contrasts sharply with the Old Age and Survivors Insurance program (known as Social Security), which is administered directly and is funded entirely by the federal government via payroll contributions to assist the aged and other categories of individuals.

Restriction in State–Local Policy: The Dependency Connection. Within this decentralized program structure, localities and states have implemented AFDC in ways that reflect the reality of their economic dependency. That is, AFDC has been carried out in a restrictive fashion—often more restrictive than federal law mandates—in order to assure that AFDC does not disrupt regional low-wage labor markets or result in large tax burdens by making the locale attractive to the poor who might migrate there from out of state.[3]

In general, the bias of state and local government relief administration has been most restrictive in regard to the employable in order to ensure that public assistance does not discourage individuals from taking low-wage jobs. For many years, AFDC excluded giving aid to families with a working head, no matter how poor they were. The latter were generally neglected altogether or fell under the protection of state general assistance programs that usually provided only very low benefit levels. Until struck down by federal regulations and court decisions during the 1960s, state and local governments, especially in low-wage economies, utilized several notoriously harsh measures to discourage male-headed families from moving onto the welfare rolls. For example, "man in the house" rules, which held that a man living in an AFDC house was responsible for the children's support even if he was not legally liable, were adopted by many states to exclude families from the program. These regulations were sometimes reinforced by "midnight raids" of suspect households by welfare officials seeking to find the man.

Gearing welfare policy to regulate the employables also is reflected in other aspects of the AFDC program. State (and federal) levels of grant assistance under AFDC have always been less than the maximum grant payments for the aged, blind, and disabled (they are presumed not to be employable) who are funded through a separate program, Supplemental Security Income (SSI), which has been completely financed and administered by the federal government since 1974. When Congress amended the Social Security Act in 1961 to reimburse states for aid to families with unemployed fathers (AFDC-UP), most states eventually decided not to make use of the new option. By 1985, only twenty-four states elected to do so (Levitan, 1985:34), and their eligibility restrictions traditionally have been so severe that very few families with unemployed fathers actually managed to get on the rolls (Piven and Cloward, 1971:127).

More generally, states and localities have undertaken to adapt their relief-giving functions to their economies via practices that minimize the possibility that AFDC can disrupt low-wage labor markets or attract the interstate movement of poor. Until struck down by the Supreme Court in 1969, states and cities widely employed residency laws to restrict eligibility for public assistance. However, the most powerful regulatory technique that states use to adapt AFDC and related programs to their economies has been their control over benefit levels. Generally, states have followed the tradition of "less eligibility"— that relief payments should be less remunerative than wages (Piven and Cloward, 1971:130). Consequently, AFDC cash benefit levels vary enormously from state to state, as pictured in Figure 16-1. For example, in 1984 average monthly AFDC payments per family range (these figures exclude noncash and other forms of assistance) from as much as $466.00, $438.00, and $431.00 in Wisconsin, Michigan, and New York, respectively, to as low as $91.00, $139.00, and $184.00 in Mississippi, Texas, and Georgia, respectively.

Although direct causal connection between low-wage labor markets and AFDC benefit levels is difficult to establish, a broad relationship is certainly evident. Numerous studies have indicated that AFDC benefit levels, as well as related welfare programs that require state–local contributions, are strongly tied to state income (particularly median per capita income). The latter is roughly indicative of state market position, economic well-being (wealth and standard of living), and regional wage levels. State welfare benefit levels tend to display a strong regional bias: As Figure 16-1 suggests, lower wage economies

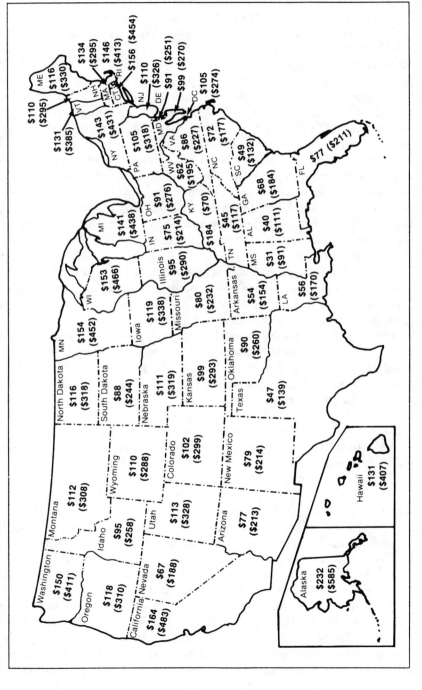

FIGURE 16-1   Average Monthly AFDC Payments per Person and Family, March 1984 (family payments in parentheses)

of the South and in most of the Sunbelt states outside of California rank low in welfare benefit levels. In contrast, northeastern and midwestern states tend to rank relatively high in this respect (Albritton, 1983; Piven and Cloward, 1971:Ch. 4).

The Scope of Intergovernmental Policy Bias.   Most other federal categorical redistributive programs that depend on state and local resource contributions exhibit patterns of variation that are similar to AFDC. For instance, the federal Medicaid program, the major comprehensive health care program for the very poor, is a case in point. The Medicaid program is a state program for which federal grants-in-aid are provided (the federal government's share of expenses ranged from 50 to 83 percent in 1984) to several specific categories of poor persons, including all AFDC recipients. State contributions to this program are, therefore, substantial, and in some states local jurisdictions are granted a measure of control over their Medicaid programs and are required to fund part of its cost. Eligibility is determined by state-administered means criteria, as is the package of medical benefits and coverage provided by the program. In general, variations in Medicaid services and eligibility are tied to the wealth of the jurisdiction. Broadest eligibility and widest service coverage tend to be sponsored in states that also make large general welfare efforts (Palley and Palley, 1981:224–225).

The amelioration of inequalities in cash and noncash welfare benefits among state and local jurisdictions has usually occurred when redistributive programs have been changed to increase federal governmental responsibility for their funding. For instance, since the federal government took over funding and broadened participation for the food stamp program in 1971, this program has gone a long way toward reducing variations in welfare benefits among jurisdictions (Steiner, 1971:209; Albritton, 1983). Similarly, when the federal government in 1974 nationalized assistance to the aged, blind, and disabled under SSI by removing them from state and local responsibility, the numbers of such recipients increased at a marked rate (Albritton 1983:398).

Because huge differences in such things as cash assistance, housing, medical services, food relief, rent subsidies, etc., combine together as matters of residence, this provides subnational governments with a powerful regulatory tool. These programs can be designed to ensure that state and local social welfare responsibilities do not excessively interfere with the promotion of their economic development (Peterson and Rom, 1987). This also defies the idea of anything like a national welfare system that can provide a safety net based on uniform standards of equity and need. Federalism combines viciously with state and local economic dependency to foreclose the possibility that any single standard of benefits can be set nationally that does not have a disruptive effect on the regional labor markets of some localities and states.

This reality became baldly apparent in 1969 when Congress became dead-locked and failed to pass President Nixon's Family Assistance Plan. This plan aimed to simplify relief giving, largely rid states of responsibility for its administration, and more or less set a national standard of benefit. A major reason the FAP failed was because representatives of high- and low-wage regions could not agree on a level of cash benefit. While northern congressional representatives feared that proposed welfare standards were so excessively low that they would trigger political unrest, the opposition of poorer southern states to the program was based on the fear that the proposal would disrupt their region's low-wage labor markets, particularly in agriculture (Piven and Clow-ard, 1979:340ff; Moynihan, 1973:Ch. V).

INTERGOVERNMENTAL CONFLICT. Restrictiveness on the part of local governments in implementing federal poverty programs has turned into active conflict when national governmental programs (1) threatened to impose significant developmental costs on local governments or (2) did not provide sufficient inducements to localities in order to "leverage" their cooperation (i.e., sufficiently compensate localities for the developmental trade-offs occasioned by the program). Old Federalism housing and antipoverty programs sharply reveal this pattern.

National Housing Policy and Local Resistance. Federal programs to promote racially integrated low-income housing have been repeatedly frustrated by intergovernmental conflicts arising from their developmental costs on localities. Since the 1949 Housing Act, the failure to achieve national subsidized housing production targets and the goal of racially mixed public housing can be traced in major part to the frequent opposition of local governments to these objectives. Old Federalism housing programs usually provided very substantial subsidies to localities for low-income housing construction; federal regulators traditionally have been major advocates of racially integrated housing in the approval process that governed these categorical aid programs. However, the programs have always been structured in ways that left local governments in a strategic position to defeat federal goals by refusing to implement national housing drives.

As noted in Chapters 12 and 13, local governments control the land-use regulation and site selection process through which virtually all federally sponsored housing plans have to pass. Since public housing and the minorities it often attracts are widely perceived as threats to the stability and property values in white blue- and white-collar neighborhoods, suburban and city governments typically have fought to contain these programs. Suburban governments defeated such proposals simply by failing to create public housing authorities, by failing to come up with housing plans acceptable to federal officials, or by using zoning, building, and other land use controls to make sites unavailable for government housing.

Similarly, city governments tend to restrict government-sponsored housing to already crowded inner city areas with large minority populations by controlling the selection of sites proposed by public and private housing sponsors. Federal sponsorship of racially integrated public housing is widely regarded as a threat that will trigger the flight of white, middle-income families from central city neighborhoods to suburbia and beyond. Consequently, even very liberal city governmental leaders are moved by these developmental considerations to cut back programs or, more often, to do little to avoid having housing plans knocked down by neighborhood groups that oppose public housing construction outside the ghetto (Bellush, 1971; Meyerson and Banfield, 1955).

Federal housing goals sometimes are not implemented because the incentives offered by federal authorities to cities for local cooperation are not adequate to compensate localities for the negative developmental consequences that the housing programs are likely to cause them.[4] President Johnson's "New Towns-in-Town" project was a case of this kind. Under this program, the national government offered cities surplus federal lands at very low cost, as well as grants and loans, if they would agree to use these sites for new residential development, mainly for the poor. The program proved to be a failure.

Local officials in the seven cities surveyed by Derthick (1972) almost invariably rejected the federal initiatives. The new towns program depended on inducing local officials to take advantage of the offer of cheap land in return for redistributing housing resources to the poor. But the cities found that the federal program was inconsistent with an important developmental constraint: Cheap land could not sufficiently compensate them for the costs associated with more housing for the poor. Moreover, in some cases local cooperation would foreclose important developmental opportunities.

City economic dependency discouraged local cooperation. "What defeated the surplus land projects locally," suggests Derthick, "was not different from what had defeated other attempts to build low income housing: the preference of local officials for types of development that will yield more tax revenue" (Derthick, 1972:85). Hence, in city after city federal officials' efforts to secure local cooperation foundered on indifference, procrastination, or hostility.

For example, in San Antonio local officials rejected a housing plan upon hearing from the commanding general of Fort Sam Houston that the surplus lands would be needed for future expansion of the army base, an installation that provided a large number of jobs for city residents. Only in Atlanta did the federal program meet with some sustained support. But here city leaders were conducting a massive urban renewal project in the city's central business district, and they needed more land in adjacent neighborhoods. The federal sites were to be used to rehouse displaced residents, facilitating the city's plans for commercialization.

The War on Poverty and Intergovernmental Conflict.   Conflict between city and federal governments over redistribution often became deep and protracted following the passage of the Economic Opportunity Act of 1964, which began the War on Poverty of President Johnson's Great Society. From the perspective of city governments, the 1964 Act and related federal legislation was most notable because it generally by-passed city halls in order to directly fund neighborhood and other community groups. The latter were empowered to administer federal job training, social service, rehabilitation, legal services, and other poverty programs targeted at the inner city poor (Sundquist, 1969:27). Along with the federal mandate for "maximum feasible participation" of the poor in the agencies running the programs, this program structure also facilitated the organization of the poor in order to pressure city halls and social welfare bureaucracies for service improvements.

City governments almost uniformly opposed participation of the poor in their poverty programs. The United States Conference of Mayors demanded that existing relief agencies be the local program authorities (Patterson, 1981:146–148). Although the local implementation of this program varied considerably from city to city, in general the mayors of most major cities resisted the devolution of power to the poor and their organizations. In fact, following the rise of social turmoil and attacks on city bureaucracies by groups of poor (including some federally sponsored poverty groups), city administrations succeeded in pressuring Congress to pass the Green Amendment in 1967. This amendment required that local poverty agencies be designated by state and local governments.

City governments also attempted to limit the potential of poverty organizations to pressure for increases in social services in other ways. The poverty war story in Oakland is suggestive of the thrust of city responses to the new federal program. Initially, "responsible" civil rights leaders in Oakland had the federal poverty monies given to "established" social agencies so they could increase their traditional casework services to the poor. But eventually the leadership in the city's minority community changed and demanded funding for indigenous poor people's organizations pressuring local agencies for redistributive programs. In effect, the poverty program moved away from a service orientation seeking better administration of existing services to a political orientation pressing for the expansion of local government welfare activities.

Subsequently, the city withdrew from the poverty program in an effort to curb its social welfare responsibilities. In effect, the city was receptive to federal poverty monies so long as they helped defray the cost of traditional social services; but it came into conflict with federal poverty objectives when it found that it meant devoting greater local resources for these purposes. When federal poverty policy changed during the Nixon era and funding terminated, no redistributive policies were being administered by the permanent government of Oakland (Pressman, 1975). Federal ambition to "wage war on poverty" is not as likely to be shared at the local level where economic dependency and pressing developmental priorities discourage intergovernmental cooperation, as Oakland's experience illustrates.[5]

The New Federalism and Urban Redistribution: Economic Dependency As Public Policy

Since the early 1970s, the New Federalism has reshaped the intergovernmental grant-in-aid system in ways that are most consequential for social welfare policy at the local level. As in other areas of urban policy, the New Federalism attempts to further decentralize authority from the national to the local level via the use of block grants. Unlike categorical grants-in-aid, block grants give localities wider discretion as to the purposes for which federal funds may be used. This form of assistance has not dominated most federal programs of redistribution for localities—the major public assistance programs, including AFDC, AFDC-UP, Food Stamps, Medicaid, Medicare, etc., are still essentially categorical grant programs. But it has grown to include more and more programs since 1972. By fiscal year 1984, general-purpose and broad-based grants constituted over one-fifth of the federal grants budget, and many of these grants have redistributive components (Palmer and Sawhill, 1984:229). Further, President Reagan has advocated the extension of the idea to several major categorical welfare programs, including the devolution of AFDC to the states.

While the New Federalism is often couched in terms of providing more freedom of local choice, this language obscures the substantive policy shift that it has brought to urban redistributive policy. A shift from categorical grants to the New Federalism in fact represents a change in the systemic forces that shape the purposes for which federal assistance is used. By altering the federal–local structure to afford greater local government discretion over the purposes of intergovernmental aid, New Federalism actually reinforces the pressures of local economic dependency, shifting urban social welfare policy away from redistributive objectives. Without federal regulation to contain the impact of local economic dependency on policy, the "freedom" that block grants afford to local governments actually makes it more likely that they will utilize federal grants-in-aid for developmental or distributive policy objectives, rather than for programs to assist the poor.

Experience under the major block grant programs, as well as recent developments in city–federal relations during the Reagan administration, are strongly suggestive of these realities. Surveys of the three major New Federalism programs—General Revenue Sharing (GRS), the Comprehensive Employment and Training Act (CETA), and the Community Development Block Grant (CBDG)—indicate that the decline of federal direction that accompanied the shift from categorical to block grant programs also facilitated a decline of redistributive activity on the part of local governments.

GENERAL REVENUE SHARING: FREEDOM TO NEGLECT THE POOR. The first of the New Federalism initiatives, General Revenue Sharing (GRS), arrived in 1972 as a response to the perceived failure of many past urban aid programs to deal with the urban crisis that had enveloped many cities and their state governments during the postwar decades. The proliferation of federal urban aid programs during the 1960s became a jumble of intergovernmental aid packages by the early 1970s, raising doubts about their sensitivity to specific local problems and changing conditions. General Revenue Sharing was expected to help simplify what had become complex and disorderly, while increasing yet again national governmental assistance to financially hard-pressed localities. Consequently, the program won broad support from city political leaders throughout the country.

The major opposition to the program came from the representatives of the poor and other liberal groups who rightly feared that such an open-ended grant of funds to localities and states would ultimately mean a diminution in aid to the disadvantaged (Judd, 1984:338). Examination of how local governments made use of GRS funding indicates an overwhelming tendency to allocate this assistance to distributive and developmental purposes, rather than to programs of redistribution. The University of Michigan's Survey Research Center discovered that housekeeping services, such as public safety, and developmental programs were the program areas most heavily funded by local governments. Redistributive services and functions were at the very bottom of local government priorities. The Survey Research Center concluded that "the picture that emerges from the data is one of financially hard-pressed large cities using revenue-sharing monies to maintain services perceived to be vital or to reduce what are perceived to be the heavy burden [sic] of local property taxation" (Juster, 1976:6).

Localities whose market position was considerably better also chose not to spend these federal dollars for redistributive purposes. Instead, they tended to spend heavily on small capital outlays for distributive housekeeping services (for example, police cars and fire engines). These localities were under less economic pressure to allocate federal funds for reducing local taxes or related developmental goals (Juster, 1976).

Other studies of the GRS program have indicated very similar findings—left to their own devices, local governments are strongly inclined to divert federal funds to nonredistributive purposes (Controller General of the U.S., 1974). This is true even of cities with large poor populations. For instance, in 1973 the five largest American cities—New York, Chicago, Los Angeles, Philadelphia, and Detroit—reported spending 97 percent of their revenue sharing funds for operations and maintenance (Judd, 1984:343–345). As state and local spending patterns developed during the 1970s, it became quite evident that GRS had little direct impact on serving the needs of the poor.[6]

CETA: FOR THE BEST AND THE BRIGHTEST. The Comprehensive Employment and Training Act was another attempt to consolidate a hodge-podge collection of federal programs that had mushroomed during the 1960s. Created in 1973 (and amended repeatedly in subsequent years), CETA became the major federal jobs and work training program for cities until President Reagan terminated it in favor of yet another, but much smaller, job training program that relied more on private sector participation (the Job Training Partnership Act, 1982). CETA transformed a patchwork of various categorical employment and job training programs into a block grant that transferred administrative responsibility from the federal government to local and state governments. President Nixon believed the new effort would streamline programs that he characterized as ". . . overcentralized, bureaucratic, remote from people they mean to serve, overguided and far less effective than they might be in helping the unskilled and disadvantaged" (Baumer and Van Horn, 1985:18). More than $60 billion was spent by the federal government to train millions of unemployed people and create millions of temporary jobs in the public sector; in ten years, more money was funneled into job creation than had been spent in the entire history of federal unemployment programs.

Because this block grant program was exclusively for upgrading the work skills of the poor and providing greater public and private employment opportunities to the jobless, local governments could hardly avoid carrying out the essential redistributive thrust of the program—for example, funds could not be used to build tennis courts in high-income neighborhoods, as had occurred on occasion with GRS funds. Nevertheless, lack of federal oversight in the local implementation of CETA and the broad mandates of the program allowed local governments to introduce their own priorities. Equally important, about 27 million people, or approximately 25 percent of the adult work force, were eligible for CETA. But because only a fraction of these people—not more than 2 million—could be enrolled in the program, local and state operatives had wide discretion over whom to serve (Baumer and Van Horn, 1985:62).

Local governments tended to pursue priorities that often contradicted CETA's overarching redistributive objective—to get jobs and training to those who needed it most. Studies of the local implementation of CETA have documented that during the first years following its enactment there was a strong tendency among local prime sponsors (nearly always local governments) to serve less economically disadvantaged persons compared with the pre-CETA programs. In particular, the most valuable services—jobs and training in public sector employment—tended to accrue to older, more experienced, and more educated individuals, while less valuable benefits, such as brief training programs, went disproportionately to the more economically needy.

Although evidence suggests that this pattern diminished somewhat after Congressional amendments forced sponsoring agencies to serve those considered most disadvantaged more vigorously, CETA sponsors continued to favor those who were most employable, better educated, and older until the Reagan administration terminated the program (Baumer and Van Horn, 1985; Franklin and Ripley, 1984). For instance, one study of selected programs indicated that during the (pre-CETA) fiscal year 1974, youths under the age of twenty-two comprised 63 percent of the clientele and that only about 34 percent of those served had a high school education. In contrast, by fiscal 1982 these proportions dramatically changed. Youths comprised only 33 percent of the program, and those with a high school education increased to 68 percent (Franklin and Ripley, 1984:195).

This pattern of localities blunting the redistributive features of the jobs and training program can be credited to a number of factors, including weak federal direction. But what stands out most clearly is the disposition of localities to exploit the greater freedom of block grant programs to promote developmental and distributive objectives. As one survey concluded:

> Elected officials were much more likely to take an interest in public jobs programs and were more concerned with providing good public services than with serving the poor. It is not surprising that elected officials sought the most highly qualified applicants to fill jobs in state, city and county governmental agencies (Baumer and Van Horn, 1985:83).

CDBG: COMMUNITY DEVELOPMENT FOR SOME.   The collapse of several categorical aid programs into the Community Development Block Grant (CDBG) in 1974 gave localities much broader discretion over the use of federal assistance for housing, redevelopment, and related community purposes. While

CDBG legislation specified that funds under this program were to primarily benefit low- and moderate-income families, these restrictions were never rigidly enforced. Federal oversight became routine in approving CDBG applications, and under the Reagan administration it has become almost perfunctory.

City governments generally took leave to implement this program in ways that tilted the distribution of funds and projects in favor of upper, rather than lower, income areas and populations. For example, during the first several years following the initiation of CDBG, HUD reported that the distribution of housing rehabilitation funds and other community development improvements tended to go disproportionately to moderate- and higher-income neighborhoods, by-passing the very poorest and most ill-housed. The percentage of funds spent for low- and moderate-income groups averaged 44.1 percent two years after the program was launched (Department of Housing and Urban Development, 1977:684). A Brookings study of the distribution of CDBG funds in sixty-two cities found that only about 29 percent of the monies were spent in city neighborhoods with below-average incomes (Judd, 1984:351). Further, few cities demonstrated willingness to spend the maximum portion of CDBG funds on social services rather than physical improvements and other developmental programs (see Chapter 11).

Although attempts were made during the Carter administration to force localities to spend more funds on serving their poorest areas, demands by cities to use CBDG monies to induce private investment in their more promising, "gentrifying" inner city areas limited the impact of these changes in federal oversight. Under the Reagan administration, program cutbacks and indifference to the redistributive objectives of this block grant program have permitted cities to continue to favor developmental projects (David and Kantor, 1983). As one observer stated before Congress, ". . . local priorities . . . articulated under the block grant program represent a pattern of divestment of federal resources from some of the most impoverished, low income areas of the city toward a favoring of investment in the less seriously, declining moderate-income areas" (Bach, 1977:630).

THE REAGAN ADMINISTRATION AND URBAN SOCIAL POLICY: THE FEDERAL PRISON OF CITY DEPENDENCY. Since the election of an administration dedicated to rolling back federal intervention, particularly in social services, the shift of urban social welfare policy in a less redistributive direction has continued. Although the Reagan administration has yet to enact any major new urban initiatives, there has been further withdrawal of federal participation from the local redistributive arena. This has effectively reinforced and federalized the regressive drift of local social welfare activities.

First, there has been severe retrenchment in federal assistance to urban aid programs in general and to programs in aid of the very poor in particular. Virtually all programs to assist the various categories of poor, except for the Social Security (OASI) program that serves large numbers of nonpoor, have been cut. Consequently, it has been up to lower-level governments to make up for federal retrenchment from their own resources or simply impose these cuts accordingly. Evidence is that neither states nor local governments have been able or willing to absorb most of these federal cuts in cases of making up lost funds to redistributive social programs (Peterson, 1984; Nathan et al., 1983).

For example, the Reagan administration's strategy of imposing new restrictions on AFDC eligibility were not usually offset by compensatory actions on the part of states and localities. States could have expanded their own general assistance programs to absorb families displaced from AFDC. But since this replacement carried a high cost, no state in a sample surveyed by the Urban Institute was found to have been willing to do this. In fact, two states— Michigan and New York—moved to cut back their general assistance eligibility because of fear that large numbers displaced from AFDC would move on to their relief rolls at state and local expense. Although there is some evidence that localities and states have not always taken advantage of the cuts (Peterson, 1984:235, 242), the general pattern of states and localities failing to fill in social services where the federal government has cut such assistance off is the norm. Constrained by their economic dependency, programs to promote development have proliferated while social service spending has not generally made up for federal aid cut-backs.

Second, President Reagan has attempted to move the New Federalism even further away from supporting redistributive objectives. In 1982, the President proposed a trade of programs with states under the flag of the New Federalism. He offered a ten-year program in which the nation's basic support programs, AFDC and Food Stamps, were to be turned over to the states in exchange for federal government assumption of full responsibility for Medicaid. In addition, sixty-one smaller intergovernmental programs were to be consolidated and returned to the states for their sole financing and administration in return for additional federal revenue to the states. If carried through, by 1991 the grant-in-aid share of the state and local budgets would shrink to 3 or 4 percent, the lowest level since the first year of the New Deal. Fearing the threat of huge cost increases in this "deal," most state governors and big city mayors opposed the idea, which has not yet found much of a constituency even at the federal level.

The Governmentalization of Inequality

Compared to previous periods of urban development, redistribution has assumed great importance in city politics. This has occurred by virtue of changes in the political economy that have converged to make local governments focal points in America's social welfare system, particularly in implementing national programs of redistribution. However, these same politico-economic forces have interacted to limit the ability of local governments and states to respond to problems of social disadvantage and meet the demands of the needy.

Economic dependency has promoted a bias in favor of restrictiveness in social policy on the part of local governments and states, making for wide regional variation in the implementation of social programs and creating tendencies for policy conflict with the national government. Although past national governments often have acted to counter local policy biases, their program endeavors have frequently been ill-designed or inadequate for the challenge.

Most recently, the national governmental effort in regulating local social welfare has moved in a less egalitarian direction. Rather than seeking to overcome local opposition to traditional national social welfare objectives, since the 1970s federal officials have changed grant programs to support resistance. Cities and their needy citizens are left as prisoners of their dependent economies.

Endnotes

1. This estimate includes as income government cash transfers, but it excludes the value of in-kind benefits, such as food stamps, Medicaid, and public housing.
2. Similarly, female-headed families are four and a half times more likely to be poor than families headed by males. Many female family heads cannot work or cannot work sufficiently to bring their incomes above the poverty level because of the responsibilities of raising children or because of related problems. When the head of a family has eight years of schooling or less, the family is five times more likely to be poor than families headed by a person with at least some college education. Poorly educated individuals are less likely to obtain steady, well-paid employment than those who are better educated (Levitan, 1985:7–13).
3. There is conflicting evidence over whether the poor migrate among states to obtain public assistance, although it seems likely that high welfare benefit states keep poor people from moving. See Steiner (1971:86–87), Patterson (1981:173–174), and Tilly (1968), who doubt the "migration" thesis. Contrasting views are found in Peterson and Rom (1987), (1974), and Clarke and Fergusen (1983:214–216). Nevertheless, that state and city public authorities act as though (and perceive) that their welfare policies have a major effect on the interstate migration of the poor is well documented in the literature noted throughout this chapter.
4. Parts of the following discussion draw upon David and Kantor (1983).
5. This conclusion is also shared by a study of intergovernmental programs in education, health, and housing in four urban areas. It notes the "propensity of (local) politicians to resist redistributive policies [but be] . . . effective implementors of developmental policy" (Peterson, Rabe, and Wong, 1986:214).
6. In fiscal 1977, only about 2.5 percent of total revenue sharing funds, or $165 million, was spent on social services by states and localities (U.S. Department of the Treasury, 1979:8).

CHAPTER SEVENTEEN

The City in the Politics of the Welfare State

GIVEN the powerful exogenous forces that tend to discourage the promotion of redistributive objectives by local government, are local political pressures very relevant to policy making in this arena? Is local government capable of being responsive to the demands of have-nots? Or are local communities and their poor simply forced to accommodate themselves to their economic dependency?

Although the obstacles to redistribution are certainly formidable at the local level, it would be wrong to underestimate the opportunities for change that do exist. For one thing, the policy revolution in the federal system that has made the national government the prime initiator and paymaster of programs of redistribution is a counterweight to local economic dependency; the growth of intergovernmental aid programs has ensured that local policy agendas, issues, resources, and programs are not exclusively—perhaps are not even predominantly—matters of control by local officialdom. The constant presence of federal and state authorities, monies, and regulations in nearly all significant local redistributive matters affects the kinds of demands that can be made, the life-chances of issues (Crenson, 1971) as they develop, the decisional strategies open to political actors, and the policy outcomes that are possible in local politics. While urban economic dependency has made the promotion of redistributive activities difficult for local government, the other side of the coin is that intergovernmental dependency has made local governmental responsibility for such programs inescapable.

For another thing, political developments within cities limit the extent to which local social welfare politics can be a process of conformity to economic pressures faced by cities. The political institutions (i.e., the machine) and the social setting that once made the politics of social control almost the exclusive relationship between the poor and local political authorities have largely vanished. Although social control politics has by no means lost its relevance in this arena, the revolution in popular control has limited it.

370

Local Politics and Redistributive Policy Change

The politics of redistribution is best viewed as a by-product of tensions arising from all three sources of constraint that can expand or contract the limits on local policy choice. Economic dependency disciplines local governments with market sanctions to avoid expanding redistributive activities, a theme suggested in the previous chapter. Consequently, fiscal capacity rather than need for welfare programs seems to be a very powerful predictor of state and local social service expenditures.[1] If this source of pressure is unchecked by other factors, demands for redistributive programs are very likely to be resisted by local political leaders and are unlikely to gain wide community political support. In these circumstances, the politics of redistribution is apt to become dominated by social control responses—local governments will attempt to play out costly demands for its resources via political techniques that diffuse, fragment, and isolate these pressures.

Expansion in local redistributive activities can occur as a result of forces in the urban political economy that resist the pressures of economic dependency. Specifically, these countervailing influences can arise from (1) officials at higher governmental levels who intervene in local politics to promote redistributive endeavors with their funds and authority and from (2) political activism by the poor and their allies who can exploit the machinery of popular control in order to promote their claims, forcing trade-offs in economic and social policy that might not otherwise be considered. The more that local political demands *and* intergovernmental program incentives work in the same direction, the less likely are local political authorities to resort to social control responses in order to deal with conflicts over redistribution. The redistributive arena becomes dominated by local expansion of material resources targeted at satisfying the claims of have-nots.

The Politics of Expansion

Conditions favoring a politics of expansion were met during the 1960s when there was convergence of local and intergovernmental forces favorable to social-welfare activism. At this time, the Old Federalism dominated national–city relations. The federal government shaped and fine-tuned assistance to cities in ways that targeted resources to the poor. The election of national Democratic and Republican administrations that were relatively favorably disposed—or at least not exceedingly hostile—to programs in aid of the poor characterized the period as a whole.

At the same time, changes in urban political systems occurred that simultaneously influenced local and national politics. In the wake of crumbling local political machines and national electoral realignment, minority groups and the urban poor made a determined bid for political power. They did so by seeking new allies, undertaking protest and voter registration drives, and, not least, by creating a national civil rights movement that had the effect of raising political expectations and activism among urban minorities. An examination of the two major urban-oriented social welfare programs of the period—public assistance and the War on Poverty initiatives—illustrates how city governments became dominated by these expansionary forces and were moved to enlarge their redistributive activities.

The Welfare Explosion and Urban Politics

During the nearly three decades after the creation of the major federal relief program, AFDC, the state and local governments that administered this program were generally highly restrictive in distributing benefits. A look at the local patterns of administration of this program around 1960 reveal a very parsimonious relationship between cities and their poor populations. First, large numbers of the urban poor who were eligible for benefits according to federal and state regulations were not receiving assistance under this program. Even though the immigration of huge numbers of needy families and individuals produced a large increase in the poverty populations of major northern cities during the 1950s (Piven and Cloward, 1971:Ch. 8), proportionate numbers were not able to claim or were too discouraged to claim public assistance from local relief offices. Perhaps only about 33 percent of those eligible for AFDC assistance were obtaining it in 1960 (Patterson, 1981:179). Second, localities and their state governments, particularly in southern and southwestern regions of the United States, were imposing welfare regulations that were regarded by the poor and welfare reformers as highly punitive and demeaning, the effect of which was to discourage applying for relief (Steiner, 1971:Ch V).

By 1970, however, the local administration of the AFDC program had undergone dramatic changes, particularly in America's large cities. Many of the more demeaning and restrictive state and local regulations in the administration of relief programs were swept away by court challenges and legislative changes. Congress allowed states to grant assistance to families that were dependent because of an unemployed parent (1961). Federal officials cracked down throughout the 1960s on abusive practices of local relief agencies, particularly use of "suitable home" grounds for disqualification from assistance. Between 1968 and 1971, the Supreme Court struck down the absent parent rule, residency requirements, and regulations that denied assistance to families with so-called employable mothers. Further, the Court also mandated welfare agencies to give fair hearings and proper notice to those threatened with termination of benefits (Piven and Cloward, 1971:Ch. 6; Levitan, 1985:34).

Most consequential, the decade of the 1960s witnessed an explosion in the relief rolls that happened to be concentrated in America's major cities (Piven and Cloward, 1971:184–186). The number of Americans on public assistance grew from 7.1 million in 1960 to 7.8 million in 1965 to 11.1 million in 1969 to 14.4 million in 1974. Virtually all of this phenomenal growth came in the numbers on AFDC, which increased from 3.1 million in 1960 to 10.8 million in 1974. A large part of this increase came as a result of a sharp rise in the percentage of eligible families who applied for and got aid (in addition to increases in the pool of eligibles as a result of regulatory changes). By 1971, probably about 90 percent of those eligible were getting assistance (compared with 33 percent 11 years earlier) (Patterson, 1981:171, 179).

THE POLITICAL ECONOMY OF POLICY CHANGE. What accounts for this tremendous liberalization of relief-giving was a remarkable convergence of local and intergovernmental forces that pushed back the boundaries of urban economic dependency. To some extent Piven and Cloward's (1971) well-known analysis of the period emphasizes the importance of urban civil disorder on the part of poor minorities in triggering new demands for relief and prompting governmental agencies to expand the distribution of resources for this program. To be sure, rioting and related forms of civil disorder became a hallmark of city politics during the 1960s. More than 329 important incidents in 257 cities occurred between 1964 and 1968 (Button, 1978:10). Several analysts have tested and confirmed to varying degrees a link between civil disorder and the expansion of the welfare rolls (Hicks and Swank, 1983; Isaac and Kelly, 1981; Patterson, 1981:Ch 11), although others are less convinced (Albritton, 1979, 1983; Trattner, 1983).

But the debate over Piven and Cloward's findings about urban riots during this period has usually obscured a much broader point upon which Piven and Cloward, their supporters, and, often, even their critics seem to agree: that more than civil disorder was responsible for the welfare explosion. Reanalysis of the history and literature of the period strongly suggests that interlocking politico-economic forces at the national and local levels worked in tandem to break down local obstacles to meeting demands for redistribution, forcing local political authorities to rely heavily on the relief system in order to meet these claims.

Popular Control and Intergovernmental Politics. Changes in the national and local systems of popular control were of central importance in providing a vehicle for mass political pressures. Rioting and related civil disorder in individual cities usually was not in itself sufficient to break through the intergovernmental and economic dependency that circumscribed local welfare policy. Rather, the simultaneous penetration of national and local electoral coalitions by the poor via orderly and disorderly political techniques eventually led to new patterns of federal intervention in social welfare policy. This then supported increased local political pressure by the poor on city halls to expand the welfare rolls. Consequently, particular cities did not need to become riot-torn before they became more solicitous to the welfare poor and expanded their welfare rolls (see especially Hicks and Swank, 1983; Button, 1978:Ch. V).

As Piven and Cloward (1971, 1979:Chs. 2 and 5, 1982) themselves contend, the story of the welfare explosion begins with the development of the civil rights movement. This movement slowly mobilized urban minorities, raised black political expectations, provided a national leadership, and, in city after city, spun off political drives to attack prevailing political coalitions during the early

1960s. The use of civil disobedience and protest forced national and, eventually, state and local authorities to place issues of racial discrimination, poverty, and powerlessness of blacks on political agendas. Eventually, these techniques and the later urban rioting that occurred in ghettos altered national and local political coalitions in ways that permitted greater incorporation of blacks in systems of popular control (Browning, Marshall, and Tabb, 1984; Piven and Cloward, 1979, 1982).

If only indirectly, electoral politics provided the fulcrum for making minority political agitation very efficacious. At the national level, the civil rights movement and the protest politics it helped spawn had a substantial influence on the Democratic Party, which was undergoing major changes in its traditional New Deal electoral base. As the Democratic Party was losing its traditional grip on the South, migration of blacks to the North created a major dilemma in that region. By 1960, more than one-third of all blacks were concentrated in nine key presidential election states (Button, 1978:26). With the movement of large numbers of minorities from the South to northern cities during the postwar decades and the development of political militancy among this group, Democratic political strategists under Presidents Kennedy and Johnson saw no alternative but to make a bid for black political support even if it threatened the party's traditional southern electoral base (Piven and Cloward, 1971:250–256).

The reluctance of local Democratic Party organizations to reach out to black voters and build broad multiracial political coalitions (particularly in large northern cities in key states that had a decisive impact on presidential elections) constituted a major obstacle to national Democratic Party revitalization. Consequently, during the last year of Kennedy's administration and throughout most of Johnson's, White House planners sought to respond to black civil rights demands and force big city Democratic organizations to extend their political coalitions by launching a host of new urban programs. Most of these programs became bundled in the War on Poverty drive and were targeted at the urban poor.

Aside from providing funds directly to poor minorities, the local administration of the poverty program was tooled to help urban blacks to organize politically and pressure city halls and local party organizations for a redistribution of power and resources. By requiring "maximum feasible participation" of the poor in the running and planning of most of the new urban aid programs, federal authorities created a power base from which the ghetto poor could attack city halls, initiate litigation to challenge local laws and regulations, and demand new services. At the same time, this activity tended to activate a new political leadership structure in the ghettos and organize masses of black poor to become a permanent, more powerful electoral presence in urban party politics.

This mobilization by the masses of poor minorities was reinforced by continuing activism of the civil rights movement and, especially during the later 1960s, by the urban riots. *In effect, what occurred during the 1960s was a drive for power by the urban poor that relied upon wide-ranging forms of political agitation which focused on electoral politics to federalize the poverty and race issues.* This then stimulated forms of federal assistance that helped support local political attempts to open up urban political systems to greater minority participation.

The Policy Response. The welfare explosion was the logical consequence of these political pressures. First, the role of new service program workers together with the organizational activities of the poor had a highly stimulative effect on new applications for public assistance. As social workers and community aids who were hired by community action agencies came into contact with the poor, they had to learn the welfare regulations and learn how to fight to obtain aid for them or face becoming irrelevant to their constituents. "Quite simply," suggests Piven and Cloward, "the poor needed money; the lack of money underlay most of the problems which families brought to antipoverty personnel in storefront centers and other . . . agencies" (1979:271). Antipoverty lawyers became active in bringing court cases when community action workers could not succeed in establishing a family's eligibility for assistance, challenging restrictive regulations. Further, antipoverty staff discovered thousands of potentially eligible families in the slums and ghettos, encouraged these people to apply for assistance, and otherwise contributed to a major change in expectations among the poor who became more willing to demand assistance (Rein, 1977; Gronbjerg, 1977:122–123; Piven and Cloward, 1979:272–273).

Second, given the intergovernmental program structure in the local redistributive arena, city governments found that enlarging the relief rolls was the path of least resistance in responding to minority claims. To have acceded to some black demands—such as terminating urban renewal, integrating schools and housing in white neighborhoods, building more public housing, or providing apprenticeships in white unions—would have imposed relatively great political or economic costs on cities compared with increasing the relief rolls.

Rising rolls are less objectionable to city governments than locating public housing projects in white neighborhoods, integrating schools, or enforcing fair housing and employment laws. Opening up the welfare rolls converts redistributive demands over changes in status and life style to a matter of monetary payments, facilitating political compromise. In contrast, stopping urban renewal meant stopping city economic revitalization, a top priority of local governments. Increasing relief rolls was not only less threatening to white political constituencies and city economic development, in most cities the cost was largely borne by the state and federal government. Perhaps most important, this satisfied a demand that the poor themselves generally considered to be their highest priority: higher income, *now*! (Piven and Cloward, 1971:242).

The War on Poverty

The political forces operating at the national and local levels that were tied to the welfare explosion were also instrumental in moving local governments to expand their redistributive activities in respect to the War on Poverty. In these cases, however, the actual redistribution of economic resources to the poor by local governments was less substantial than in the case of AFDC—in large part because federal assistance and authority was insufficient to overcome the local economic dependency that discouraged responsiveness to minority demands.

Despite the rhetoric of a "war" on poverty, the actual commitment of national governmental resources and power to the major urban aid programs launched in the 1960s was small. Funding for these programs never exceeded $2 billion a year. These explicitly urban programs were dwarfed by the federal government's creation or expansion of other more traditional antipoverty programs, such as AFDC, Medicaid, Food Stamps, and subsidized housing programs, which provided far more individual income assistance than did those directly tied to the War on Poverty agencies. The traditional antipoverty programs, many of which were also created or expanded at least in part because of the impact of minority political agitation (Button, 1978), undoubtedly did significantly improve the economic well-being of the American poor. It has been estimated that by the second half of the 1970s less than 8 percent of the American public remained below the poverty level compared with about 18 percent in 1960. This decline in poverty was overwhelmingly due to governmental programs, rather than to economic growth (Schwarz, 1983:Ch. 2).

Further, the major programs of the Great Society did little to attack many substantial community barriers to income and racial equality via the commitment of federal authority. Federal laws prohibiting housing discrimination were passed in 1968 but were not often enforced (*Economist*, 7 December 1985:22–25). Federal programs to build more subsidized low-income housing were usually hamstrung by suburban land use restrictions, fears of white flight, neighborhood resistance, and other obstacles that HUD officials were infrequently willing to challenge. As a result, most low-income housing for the urban poor remained concentrated in city ghettos. School desegregration efforts in northern cities sometimes succeeded, particularly under court-order mandates and propitious demographic circumstances (many whites, few blacks), but unwillingness of federal officials to withhold intergovernmental aid from uncooperative localities and bitter local resistance to school desegregation in many cities limited reform opportunities (Orfield, 1969; Peterson, 1981:Ch. 5).

Lacking major changes in the use of federal and state authority over such things as land use, educational decision making, and political boundaries, as well as intergovernmental funding, many federal antipoverty efforts were simply incapable of achieving their goals because they did not alter the basic parameters of urban policy. That is, they did not reduce local economic dependency and limit local political autonomy in the implementation of national programs—least of all by the programs of the Office of Economic Opportunity that formed the spearhead of the Great Society's poverty war.

REDISTRIBUTIVE EFFECTS OF THE POVERTY PROGRAM. *Changes in Political Power.* Nevertheless, the War on Poverty programs did combine with political activism on the part of the poor to prod local governments to expand local government activism on behalf of the poor in more subtle, yet very significant, ways. Most important, the federal poverty programs provided incentives and structures for enhancing the participation of the poor in city political systems—in effect bringing about a redistribution of political power. This provided the poor with a base from which they could often successfully press local governments for greater attention to their demands in carrying out a variety of other programs.

Although the political impact of the Community Action Program, the centerpiece of the War on Poverty, varied from city to city, the general pattern was for this program to generate much greater demands by poor minorities for participation in city political systems and in the administration of poverty-related programs in particular. In calling for maximum participation of the poor, the poverty program fundamentally altered the previously subordinate place of minorities in governing cities and forced local officialdom to begin bargaining with and incorporating them into urban political systems. As Greenstone and Peterson concluded:

> The content of the community action controversy involved a critical issue of political authority: namely which interests should participate in and be deferred to in the course of framing public policy. . . . One need not condone continuing economic inequalities to [recognize] that transformation of the black American's place in our political regime to which community participation in the war on poverty so clearly contributed (1976:xvi–xxii).

City governmental leaders and their bureaucracies generally resisted and sometimes defeated OEO's attempt to create and fund independent organizations to attack urban poverty. But in city after city, federally supported struggles broke out after 1964 as minority communities made claims for greater representation and influence in local political systems. New York City illustrates how successful these struggles could sometimes be in altering power relations.[2]

Initially New York City Mayor Robert Wagner and Paul Screvane, his hand-picked candidate for mayor in the forthcoming election, opposed demands by neighborhood and antipoverty groups that they be given a hand in directing the city's poverty programs. In a highly pluralistic city where the Democratic Party was already deeply divided and hosts of other interest groups vigorously competed for influence, these leaders felt threatened by any attempt that would encourage the formation of still more groups and deprive city officials of the right to direct the CAP.

Black and Hispanic electoral power had already grown to formidable proportions in the city, however. Appeals to these minorities were made by more liberal opponents of Screvane, including John V. Lindsay, who attacked his and Wagner's conservative politics. Under this pressure, Screvane modified his position and, like the other candidates, supported representation of the poor on the city poverty council and in the selection of these representatives by neighborhood organizations.

After his election, Mayor Lindsay made various changes that strengthened the influence of neighborhood groups at the citywide level in running New York City's poverty program. In addition, neighborhood poverty councils, which were chosen by community groups, obtained substantial authority over local poverty program policies and personnel practices, including the funds and support to undertake a wide range of community organization efforts.

As competing groups of poor emerged to seek power and influence in the program, their efforts to organize more and more poor widened; this, in turn, precipitated their making strident demands on city agencies for further community services and larger political influence. Shortly, these groups began demanding some control over a variety of city agencies, including the welfare and housing departments, as well as the school system. The poverty program prompted the community control movement that shook the New York City public school system and challenged the power of the school bureaucracy (Greenstone and Peterson, 1976:41–43; Rogers, 1968).

The extent to which minorities managed to secure a redistribution of political power in New York is not representative of all large cities. As described below, political leaders elsewhere were sometimes more able to contain demands for political participation. It is suggestive of the direction and rationale for the growth of black political power in cities during the 1960s and 1970s, however. In general, the War on Poverty helped urban minorities move from heavy reliance upon short-term, unstable protest strategies as a means of influence in redistributive politics during the 1960s to more stable electoral strategies during the 1970s and 1980s. The latter afforded the promise of a more formidable power base from which to promote sustained programs (Browning et al., 1984:211; Greenstone and Peterson, 1976).

Over the long run, there actually has occurred a growth in black political consciousness and organizational resources that at least partially derived from experience in the urban poverty "wars." Many minorities who cut their teeth, as it were, in neighborhood poverty politics gained experience, confidence, and constituencies that enabled them to go on to win elected office elsewhere. Eisinger's (1979) study of the CAP found that black officials with CAP experience accounted for nearly a quarter of all blacks elected to state legislative lower houses, city halls, and city councils since 1964. More generally, increasing minority political consciousness combined with demographic changes have produced a major increase in the presence of minorities in governmental leadership positions. The number of black elected officials at all levels of government rose from 1,472 in 1970 to 5,606 in 1983 (see Chapter 9). As more minorities have become incorporated as stable participants in governing coalitions (Browning, Marshall, and Tabb, 1984:20–24), the dominant debate within the nation's minority leadership councils no longer is dominated by how to gain an electoral foothold. The issue is how to best make use of their new electoral potential (Preston et al., 1982).

The Policy Impact of Minority Political Incorporation. It is difficult to gauge the extent to which the redistribution in political power supported by the poverty programs of the 1960s later occasioned any significant redistribution of resources to the poor by local governments. Given the failure of subsequent federal programs to substantially alter the economic constraints that have discouraged local government cooperation in redistributive endeavors, one can only expect fairly limited outcomes. Attempts to systematically probe this matter on any large scale have been problematic. Studies that rely on expenditure data to ascertain local governmental responses to minority political influence are usually confounded by problems of comparability among jurisdictions and other methodological problems (Clarke and Ferguson, 1983:Ch. 5; Karnig and Welch, 1980; Browning, Marshall, and Tabb, 1984:199; Peterson, 1981:Ch. 2).

However, an analysis of ten California cities during and since the political upheavals of the 1960s does suggest that when minorities have managed to become incorporated into city political systems they can make a difference in certain policies. Browning, Marshall, and Tabb (1984) found that when minorities became partners in the dominant political coalitions within cities (particularly those coalitions with powerful liberal allies), their policy influence was substantial. In these cases, minority interests were notably successful compared to other cities in obtaining a civilian review board, getting minority appointments to governmental boards and commissions, allocating city contracts to minority firms, and promoting greater minority employment via public programs. In effect, minorities managed to convert many pedestrian distributive programs into ones having significant redistributive features. In addition, minorities were more successful than elsewhere in achieving important political reforms, such as district elections, which were likely to enhance the further growth of their political power.

This evidence of minority influence also must be considered in light of findings that indicate the somewhat limited redistributive impact of these gains, however. Nearly all of the programs that provided substantial material benefits to minorities from city resources still were either essentially distributive programs, e.g., the civilian review board, municipal employment, etc., or they relied on federal and state funds, such as Model Cities and federal manpower training programs, etc. Further, of all the California cities, only in Berkeley, where minority groups were most powerful, did substantial social service expenditures demanded by minorities penetrate the local fund budget. When social services were expanded elsewhere, cities were careful to use only intergovernmental revenues for providing them (Browning et al., 1984:150).

Finally, when local governments were willing to respond to minority demands for governmental appointments, minorities were least likely to get these appointments in agencies dealing with economic development matters (Browning et al., 1984:158). Thus, even where the political power of the poor has been formidable and rewards have been won, the redistributive policy payoff has continued to be blunted by economic dependency and intergovernmental limitations.

The Politics of Social Control

Given their dependent economies and the limits to which intergovernmental programs support redistributive activities, local political authorities are driven to seek ways of minimizing the allocation of community resources for social welfare purposes. Yet the need to secure political support in popular control systems compels city governments to be responsive to these claims. As a result, local governments constantly face the dilemma that their capacity to meet redistributive demands will be inadequate to maintain secure political coalitions or that they will be forced to sacrifice desired developmental programs.

To some extent, this dilemma is minimized because political actors often do not make redistributive demands on local government, recognizing the formidable political and economic barriers at that governmental level. The poor frequently do not even bother to raise issues that require substantial redistributive policy responses on the part of cities unless doing so locally will contribute to involving state and national officialdom in meeting their demands. For example, Button found that most of the politically motivated urban racial violence during the 1960s was directed at the national, not the local, government. A national survey undertaken after the major riot period of 1967–1968 indicated that 77 percent of black respondents felt that they should target their demands specifically at federal authorities in order to compensate for a perceived decrease in assistance from the white community in their localities. Not surprisingly, this view was also shared by local officials (Button, 1978:10). There can be very little doubt that the obstacles to using local government as a vehicle for achieving redistributive goals diminish the range and scope of issues that do eventually get on to local government social welfare agendas (Bachrach and Baratz, 1970).

Nevertheless, local political authorities can hardly count on groups to project their grievances over matters of redistribution onto higher governmental levels or drop them altogether. As suggested previously, with the decline of the machine, local governments no longer have great control over the input side of redistributive politics. At best, they must rely upon the manipulation of political outputs in responding to demands. Further, the contemporary urban economy has imposed on central cities a most perverse situation in respect to needs and resources. City governments must manage the political consequences of welfare problems that they alone cannot solve.

Consequently, social control politics looms large as a means of minimizing local government welfare responsibilities. As Gamson has suggested, modern techniques of social control generally involve authorities responding via ". . . some modification of the content of the decision and some effort to control the potential [claimant]" (Gamson, 1968:113). That is, when faced with demands that public officials are unwilling to satisfy, they can attempt to remove these pressures by yielding some ground in policy or by regulating the claimant in order to maintain the status quo in public policy.

Generally, these two aspects of social control are folded into a repertoire of techniques that rely on manipulating the outputs of policy. Although their variety is probably countless (cf. Peterson, 1981:Ch. 9; Katznelson, 1981:Ch. 8; Gamson, 1968, 1975; Trattner, 1983; Fainstein and Fainstein, 1974), the following techniques are common:

Symbolic responses

Cooptation of leadership

Isolating redistributive demands

Transforming redistributive demands into distributive issues

Symbolic Responses

One time-honored strategy is to substitute symbolic policy responses for the material redistribution of resources. This can be accomplished by manipulating political symbols in such a way that they (1) provide positive satisfaction to discontented groups or (2) provide negative images that diffuse group grievances.

PROVIDING POSITIVE SYMBOLS. The utilization of positive symbols in policy responses involves allocating low-cost or costless benefits that provide satisfaction and reassurance to political interests in order to gain their political quiescence (Edelman, 1964; Elder and Cobb, 1983). Lipsky's (1970) study of a 1964 rent strike in New York City's Harlem described how the use of symbolic policy outputs served to provide partial satisfaction to groups that attempted nonviolent but highly disruptive protest techniques, while undercutting their ability to continue this activity.[3] A rent strike involving several hundred participants organized under the leadership of Jesse Grey attacked the housing conditions in New York City's largest ghetto. The participants demanded tremendous expansion of New York City's role in redistributing housing resources, insisting that the city rehouse the poor in public housing or rehabilitate existing housing in the private sector via massive subsidies, stricter code enforcement, and other measures.

The city government could not meet the rent strikers' demands without a huge commitment of public resources that far outstripped local fiscal capacity and intergovernmental assistance possibilities. If code standards were enforced without public rent subsidies, private landlords would abandon their properties because housing values and rent rolls were so low that they would lose money on such improvements. Consequently, only massive rent subsidies or other forms of assistance to the private rental sector could produce housing improvements. Attempts to do othewise would simply lead to housing shortages (and loss of property tax revenues) as landlords abandoned their buildings. The only other alternative was public housing construction. But this was an even more expensive solution as long as state and federal funds were not sufficiently available for finance. City officials had reason to believe that even if the demands of the rent strikers were met, demands for similar programs would escalate; the organizers of the movement sought to sustain a publicity campaign intended to reach hundreds of thousands of poor people living in substandard housing.

Jesse Grey's strategy was to appeal to powerful groups outside of the poor neighborhoods participating in the rent strike, particularly newspapers, good government and planning groups, and candidates for mayor and other city offices who were searching for issues in the forthcoming elections. The protesters hoped to win concessions by taking advantage of free media publicity, dramatizing the legitimacy of their case, and mobilizing the pressures of more powerful allies in the city's political system.

However, Lipsky's description of events suggests how very fragile such a protest strategy is in the face of skillful use of symbolic resources by political authorities bent on not taking on anything like the housing programs that were being demanded. As the media gave publicity to horror stories involving some of the very worst buildings and most hard-pressed families, the city countered by giving some of these cases special treatment and ensuring that they received publicity from the press. Searching for "news" and wishing to appear even-handed in their treatment of events, the media were quite willing to oblige by covering and reporting these cases.

City officials also created small programs that, while they were incapable of substantially redistributing housing resources, did provide symbolic reassurance that the city was responding to the poor's complaints. For instance, an emergency heating program was established with federal funds in order to aid tenants whose buildings were without heat on cold winter days. In the wake of well-publicized stories of small children having been bitten by rats, other federal funds were employed to set up a rodent extermination program. Housing officials, who cooperated with higher political leaders in order to minimize public criticism, supported "reforms" that were supposed to provide better housing for the poor. These included a city commission to investigate reorganizing the various departments responsible for housing and announcing with much publicity plans for new federal public housing in low-income neighborhoods.

Although these responses by the city probably did not alone cause the protest movement to collapse—for protest strategies are inherently hard to sustain for long periods without major economic inducements to the protesters—they permitted officials to turn aside all the major demands of the rent strikers. In addition, these symbolic assurances worked particularly well in splitting off more powerful white supporters from the movement; the latter were inclined to interpret city actions as conciliatory and regard the protesters as unreasonable.

Black Power As Symbolic Politics. More general positive symbols may function to reassure the discontented without substantively responding to their redistributive claims. This has undoubtedly been important in cities where black administrations have come to power in recent years. Most black urban political leaders face unenviable political tasks. Typically, they have been elected to local political offices in cities with large poor minority populations whose need for social services is large, but which lack many governmental resources. Most important, because black administrations face the same economic and intergovernmental dependency relationships as do white political leaders, their capacity to make policy changes that provide greater redistributive services to their populations is limited.

There is little evidence that minority governments generally have a more redistributive effect than other governments. One of the most comprehensive studies of the policy consequences of black political leadership during the 1970s in southern and northern cities concluded that the election of a black mayor had no more than a minor positive effect on city social welfare programs compared with cities with white administrations. Further, black council representation made virtually no consistent difference in this regard (Karnig and Welch, 1980:Ch. 7). Studies of individual cities where black administrations have come to power have tended to reach similar conclusions (Preston et al., 1982; Cole, 1976; Fainstein et al., 1983).

Black political leaders can capitalize on their symbolic importance in representing minority interests in local government affairs in order to maintain their popularity and win reelection without providing any major expansion of redistributive programs by their administrations. In fact, most black city administrations appear to be marked by a reluctance to declare their own wars on poverty and have been sensitive to the need to reassure white voters and businesses that they will not have to pay for any radical new social programs (Preston et al., 1982:Part III; Hill, 1983; Smith and Keller, 1983). For instance, Ernest N. Morial, New Orleans' first black mayor, won two terms with widespread black support while advocating a "trickle down" social welfare approach that also won favor within the city's business community:

> The basic premise underlying the New Orleans Economic Development Strategy is that the expansion of the private sector employment opportunities for central city residents, particularly for residents of the city's low and moderate income neighborhoods, is a necessary, though perhaps not sufficient prerequisite for reducing both the incidents of the effects [sic] of poverty, unemployment and subemployment (Schexnider, 1982:235).

NEGATIVE POLITICAL SYMBOLS. In contrast, negative political symbols may be used to thwart the voicing of redistributive claims—though presumably without promoting loyalty to the regime, as is the case with employing positive symbols. Due to their pivotal position in implementing public policy, local government bureaucracies stand in a strategic position to discourage the poor from making demands through the bureaucratic manipulation of symbols. Since social service agencies must accommodate groups outside of the relief system in order to maintain their bureaucratic independence, harsh treatment of the poor via political symbols is one strategy for organizational enhancement (Piven and Cloward, 1971:147).

Welfare agencies can employ procedures and practices that have the effect of discouraging the poor from applying for aid to which they may be legally entitled (Piven and Cloward, 1971:174). The use of degrading questions about one's sex life and family relationships, attacks on personal honesty, abusive interviews, long waits in dingy offices, and campaigns by city agencies to find welfare chiselers are among the more familiar devices that are sufficiently degrading to convey highly negative images and feelings among the poor, turning individuals away from claiming assistance. One survey found that during the 1960s over one-half of New York City's AFDC mothers agreed that "getting money from welfare makes a person feel ashamed" (Steiner, 1966:4).

Cooptation of Leadership

Political leaders who make claims for major changes in the status quo are likely to see things differently when they become part of the status quo. This time-honored political wisdom is the foundation for cooptation as a mode of social control. When particular leaders become prominent advocates for groups who demand costly redistributive measures, it is possible to nip off these highly visible figures from their groups and get them to moderate or even drop their demands. This may be done by giving such leaders a stake in administering governmental or quasi-governmental operations that would be threatened if their earlier demands were to continue (Gamson, 1968:135–142).

THE WELFARE RIGHTS ORGANIZATION EXPERIENCE. The response of city governments in dealing with local branches of the National Welfare Rights Organization (NWRO) during the 1960s was characterized by cooptive relationships. Beginning in New York City and then spreading to several other northern cities during the urban turmoil of the early 1960s, this movement to organize the poor for the purpose of attacking restrictive practices emerged. Although this organization was probably not considered more than a distant threat by officials at either the national or local levels—in fact the "movement" probably recruited no more than 25,000 members before it died out in the 1970s—NWRO's tactics and pressures were a different story. Led by skillful and militant organizers and backed to some extent by white liberal groups, including some trade unions, NWRO groups sought to win concessions and build membership by utilizing highly disruptive protests. This included lengthy sit-ins at relief centers, disrupting agency routines, picketing city hall offices, and challenging administrative decisions. The short-term politics of this group presented an immediate challenge to the authority of local governments in carrying out their relief operations. Accordingly, local officials sought to limit the impact of these groups.

The best-known study of NWRO has described how cooptation of local organizational leaders easily blunted their demands and eventually undercut the growth of the movement (Piven and Cloward, 1979:Ch. 5). As disruptive tactics were employed, local officials and relief agency heads usually initiated procedures for the negotiation of grievances. This was often followed by the creation of special advisory councils of relief recipients to welfare departments; sometimes recipients were even appointed to agency policy-making boards. Where local WROs were wary of participating in these arrangements, welfare officials sometimes formed independent recipient organizations to which they tried to attract the leaders of the WROs. For instance, in New York City the department of welfare established a "Community Relations" Division staffed by "community coordinators" (who were usually young minority graduates of schools of social work). The latter went into the ghettos to organize "client advisory committees" that met periodically to discuss grievances and advise on policy changes.

The impact of these arrangements on WRO leaders was one of moderating their demands and increasing their loyalty to the welfare bureaucracies of which they formed a part:

> Each such "victory" was the occasion for self-congratulations among recipient leaders who, upon reading in the press of their appointments to advisory committees or upon receiving written invitations to negotiating sessions or upon being invited to testify at legislative hearings, envisaged the emergence of a new period of justice for the poor (Piven and Cloward, 1979:329).

Ultimately, the effect of these cooptive linkages was organizational decline of the movement. Groups that were given access to welfare offices and the right to negotiate with officials were expected to do nothing to disrupt office routines or to interfere with agency dealings with individual clients. As WRO leaders became enmeshed in these arrangements, they soon abandoned the demonstrations, picketing, and sit-ins that once were of strategic importance to sustaining membership. WRO leaders become increasingly dependent upon external recognition and resources as a substitute for a mass base. As urban unrest subsided during the 1970s, the WRO movement collapsed.

THE SCOPE OF COOPTATION AS A SOCIAL CONTROL RESPONSE. Cooptation by urban bureaucracies of group leaders making redistributive claims has hardly been limited to dealing with unusual protest movements seeking major changes. The strategy is so relatively inexpensive and so easily carried out even by bureaucratic actors who lack many political skills that it has become a pervasive and routine "face" of local government in the redistributive arena. Since the 1960s, government-sponsored community groups have multiplied and become permanent fixtures in education, planning, social services, and community development activities. This appears to have had the effect of limiting protest and advocacy activities on the part of the poor.

One study that sought to survey the most active school-issue organizations representing the poor in three cities (Los Angeles, Boston, and Atlanta) uncovered evidence that strongly suggests the cooptive impact of these programs (Gittell, 1980). The study found that there were very few such organizations to investigate because there was a strong trend since the 1960s for groups to undergo a change from advocacy (self-initiated, issue-oriented groups) to becoming government-sponsored advisory committees or service delivery organizations. The advisory organizations were often mandated by law and received funding for their activities. Those carrying out service delivery roles almost always served multiple purposes—such as school dropout programs, tenant services, community development planning, and supplementary social and educational services (e.g., bilingual education).

This change was directly due to the expansion of federal and state programs to sponsor such groups. It was found that neither type of organization could maintain its advocacy and protest efforts after it had become dependent on outside funds and became responsible for implementing public or quasi-public supplementary programs. Generally, the organization's agenda became defined by officials. Paid staff tended to dominate organizational activities. Little time was spent on contacting and involving membership, and their involvement in policy issues (as opposed to providing services) declined (Gittell, 1980:242–243).

Isolating Redistributive Demands

Demands for the expansion of redistributive programs may be minimized by policy responses that prevent them from becoming widespread. Programs of redistribution may be designed to segregate the most outspoken groups in the assistance-giving process by creating a special arena with its own rules, institutions, funding sources, and conflicts—in effect channeling the participation of low-income groups to a limited part of the redistributive arena where they become consumed by the "games" it has to offer.

COMMUNITY ACTION AS COMMUNITY ISOLATION. Although the politics surrounding the Community Action Program (CAP) of the War on Poverty days often had the effect of stimulating more widespread participation of the poor in city politics, nearly all city governments fought to contain this effect. In some cities, this was done very successfully by using the CAP to isolate the poor from having much to do with the rest of city political affairs, including the running of important redistributive programs. One example of this form of political linkage between local government and the poor was in St. Louis. According to investigators of the city's CAP, poverty area residents managed to gain a great deal of influence within the program during its lifetime, but the program failed to serve as a significant vehicle for influence in the larger redistributive arena of the city's political system (Kerstin and Judd, 1980).

In the early Great Society years, the city government and its civic leaders responded to the federal antipoverty drive by organizing a Human Development Corporation (HDC), St. Louis' CAP. Dominated by whites, it had very limited representation of inner city poor residents and relied mostly on traditional city social agencies in order to carry out its programs (rather than by HDC itself). This organization generally avoided controversy. Its conservative stance in respect to support for protest activities drew widespread criticism from civil rights leaders.

For several years, the major fights in the city's poverty war took place within the program as civil rights and neighborhood activists fought to gain greater representation on the HDC governing board and prod the agency to undertake more direct political action. Eventually, major changes were made in the administration of the program. The private agencies receiving contracts from the program left the War on Poverty, and HDC gradually took direct control over their programs. HDC became an overwhelmingly black organization with few ties to either the social welfare community or the business and political activists of the city. It also became dominated by competition among specific black organizations and neighborhood groups that fought over how money would be divided among programs funded by the HDC and over the allocation of appointments within the agency. Consumed by the politics of keeping outsiders out, the "new" HDC also soon moved away from undertaking overt political activities for fear that demonstrations, voter registration drives, and other political activities would breed new challengers (Kerstin and Judd, 1980:215).

The isolation of redistributive demands via the creation of a special institutional arena within the governmental structure was probably not the norm during the War on Poverty (though there are no systematic investigations of this proposition), since local poverty agencies were often militant advocates for the poor. Nevertheless, it appears that local governments displayed a tendency to utilize the CAP program in this fashion most successfully where entrenched political party organizations existed, where political authorities were highly unsympathetic to the demands of the poor, and when minorities were not highly militant in pressing their claims (Greenstone and Peterson, 1976; Bellush and David, 1971; Austin, 1972; Bachrach and Baratz, 1970; Hallman, 1968).

Transforming Redistributive Demands into Distributive Issues

Finally, one of the more common modes of social control politics is to convert redistributive demands into distributive issues. If class and racial conflicts that breed costly redistributive demands (such as for new housing programs or for neighborhood and school desegregation) are transformed into distributive issues, they can be "managed" more easily by local governments. Distributive demands usually can be satisfied by means of limited material resources or even by symbolic responses.

Although the decline of the machine has undercut city government's ability to control the "input" side of the redistributive arena in the traditional manner, programs to assist disadvantaged groups and their neighborhoods can be structured in a way that enables local governments to deflect political pressures by the poor into matters of distribution. This social control strategy became prominent in the wake of the inner city social turbulence of the 1960s when city halls almost everywhere initiated schemes to decentralize parts of their service delivery operations in education, social services, neighborhood services, and related fields (see Chapter 14).

COMMUNITY CONTROL AS SOCIAL CONTROL. The history of these decentralist responses in New York City's Washington Heights–Inwood neighborhood is suggestive of the issue conversion politics that seemed to dominate the programs. Although New York City experimented with the use of community boards for planning purposes prior to the 1960s, it was not until after rioting and social disturbances broke out there that public officials became advocates of greater political linkages to the city's diverse neighborhoods:

> The holistic view of black nationalism produced demands that in two respects were radically different from the usual articulation of urban issues. First, it did not respect traditional boundaries between issues. School, welfare, police, and housing issues were treated together, as aspects of a total condition. As a result authorities had to manage conflict that was much more intense and less susceptible to

piecemeal solutions than they had been accustomed to. Second, these policy areas were the objects of demands for a radical redistribution of resources and opportunities (Katznelson, 1981:122).

One of Mayor John Lindsay's initial responses was the use of Neighborhood City Halls and Task Forces to tap street-level activists, engage them in discussing their grievances, and enmesh them in problem-solving projects funded by the city. Although the schools had probably become the central issue of local protest, school issues were explicitly excluded from consideration because they were not within the province of the mayor. The neighborhood's City Hall-Task Force units mostly collected information, permitted irate group leaders to talk directly with city officials, and provided a forum to address a narrow and specific agenda, such as the placement of litter baskets, the removal of abandoned cars, block cleanup campaigns, etc.

This task force unit was eventually replaced by a pilot program that was to lead to the establishment of a system of neighborhood government which the mayor hoped would cover all communities within the city. Entitled the Neighborhood Action Program (NAP), it merged the old task force with the Community Planning Board that had been set up by city charter years before and provided $500,000 a year in capital funds that could be spent by the neighborhood on projects that would require little or no maintenance by the city.

The NAP quickly became a focus for community groups and their leaders who participated actively in the monthly meetings held to consider budget proposals and to question service bureaucracy representatives. An elaborate paid and voluntary staff and committee structure evolved that incorporated neighborhood leaders who specialized in working on specific problems within the community, such as parks, narcotics, health, housing, and so forth. However, since there was not much that this agency could do about these complex community problems with $500,000, the emphasis in NAP activities was on funding small-scale projects, such as new street lighting, athletic equipment for the local high school, wall murals, additional police, and sanitation hardware, etc. which were objects of competition among neighborhood groups.

These arrangements were later formalized and extended by Lindsay's creation of a central Office of Neighborhood Government. But after urban unrest subsided during the 1970s and a traditional party Democrat, Abraham Beame, took office in 1974, Beame swiftly dismantled the Lindsay programs of neighborhood government. He sought to reinvigorate local party organizations while instituting a more "orthodox" system of administrative decentralization (Katznelson, 1981:Ch. 6). Yet Lindsay's neighborhood approach was successful in transforming redistributive issues into more humdrum matters of distribution. The New York model was endorsed by the Kerner Commission as a means of diffusing civil disturbances and was copied in other major cities (National Advisory Commission of Civil Disorders, 1968:290).

More recently, the New Federalism block grant structure for providing aid to poor neighborhoods has permitted local governments to extend this approach. As noted previously, the Community Development Block Grant has enabled local governments to diffuse most of this program's resources out of reach of the poor while incorporating them into its consultative mechanisms.

Community groups that might otherwise have rallied against this kind of program have often become consumed by petty conflicts over the distribution of funds allotted for their blocks, clubs, and pet projects. The block grant structure does not afford much of a base for independent organization of the poor around redistributive issues (Browning, Marshall, and Tabb, 1984:Ch. 6; Dommel et al., 1982).

ISSUE CONVERSION AND POLITICAL LEADERSHIP. City governments need not rely entirely upon bureaucratic measures in order to convert redistributive conflicts into issues of distribution. Issues that involve the redistribution of wealth and status can be redefined by political authorities in ways that provoke competition among ethnic, territorial, and other particularistic interests. As conflicts build around the latter, pressure for redistributive responses is diffused. For instance, big city governments have usually failed to achieve much neighborhood racial integration via the building of subsidized low-income housing in predominantly white areas. City hall political leaders have been fearful that such projects would not only threaten their white neighborhood constituencies, but could also precipitate "white flight" of working-class and middle-income families to nearby suburbs.

Accordingly, city officials have struggled to avoid confronting this issue except when it has been thrust upon them by federal officials, court judgments, or militant demands by the minority communities. When pushed to face this matter, it is possible for political leaders to stimulate, rather than to minimize, rancorous racial and neighborhood rivalries over specific housing programs. The protracted conflicts that have resulted generally have blocked the implementation of housing plans, discouraging minorities from making future demands for such programs.

The classic case of this sort of conflict was described by Meyerson and Banfield (1955) in Chicago during the late 1940s. In order to build badly needed public housing and achieve more racial integration in the city's projects, Chicago Housing Authority planners sought to utilize vacant land located outside the black ghetto in their postwar plans. However, powerful machine bosses who controlled the city council rejected most of the CHA housing sites in favor of locations chosen to deliberately provoke neighborhood opposition and racial backlash (e.g., in prime, upper-class lakeshore neighborhoods, on a university's tennis courts, and in ethnic single-family homeowner areas). The resulting groundswell of opposition by ethnic, real estate, and neighborhood groups to these proposals forced the CHA to drop its plans and confine nearly all postwar housing projects to locations in the ghetto. Parallel events elsewhere have produced similar results (Bellush, 1971).

Urban Dependency and the Dilemma of Social Welfare

The local politics of redistribution is one of relatively narrow public choice and unstable power relationships. Local government's dependent economic position severely constrains its capability to resolve most pressing social welfare problems. Yet, popular control systems at the national and local governmental levels provide a formidable power base from which the poor and their allies can influence social policy. Consequently, local political authorities confront a chronic social welfare dilemma. They tread a narrow pathway where the pressures of their economic dependency discourage redistributive achievements, while forces within their political and intergovernmental constituencies often counsel otherwise and reward opposite behavior. At best, local governments are unreliable agents of social justice in America's welfare system.

Expansion of local redistributive programs is most likely to arise when intergovernmental forces and local political mobilization link to promote this goal. Otherwise economic dependency discourages governmental activism and motivates authorities to favor social control responses in order to limit redistributive claims. Thus, the politics of redistribution veers from expansion to contraction as local communities cope with their problems of disadvantage. The changing boundaries of local choice and social justice are powerfully tied to the politico-economic forces beyond the locale itself. Local conflicts over inequality have become highly captive of the politics of the whole American welfare state.

Endnotes

1. Numerous studies have indicated that spending on welfare programs by state and local governments is linked to state–local fiscal capacity, particularly as indicated by such things as median per capita income. Thus state–local (combined) wealth (which somewhat corresponds to market position) tends to be a good predictor of welfare spending levels. For an excellent survey and critique of this literature, see Peterson (1981:Ch. 3). Nevertheless, attempts by these typically quantitative studies to assess the impact of political pressures, especially on the part of low-income groups, on state or local redistributive expenditures have been flawed by formidable methodological obstacles. In particular, the quantitative indicators of so-called political inputs in these studies have been very formalistic and, therefore, relatively insensitive to the complex, intergovernmental impact of popular control processes. See a critique in Kantor and David (1983).
2. The following discussion draws upon Greenstone and Peterson (1976:Ch. 1).
3. For a somewhat similar interpretation see Peterson (1981:175–180).

References for Part Six

Albritton, Robert B. 1983. "Subsidies: Welfare and Transportation" in Virginia Grey, Herbert Jacob and Kenneth Vines, eds. 1983. *Politics in the American States*. Boston: Little, Brown.

Albritton, Robert B. 1979. "Social Amelioration Through Mass Insurgency? A Reexamination of the Piven and Cloward Thesis." *American Political Science Review*, Vol. 73 (December), 1003–1011.

Austin, David M. 1972. "Resident Participation: Political Mobilization or Organizational Cooptation?" *Public Administration Review*, Vol. 32 (September), 400–420.

Bach, Victor. 1977. "Prepared Statement." Presented to the U.S. Congress, House Committee on Banking, Finance and Urban Affairs. Housing and Community Development Act of 1977. Hearings before the sub-committee on Housing and Urban Development, 95th Cong. 1st sess., 1 March 1977.

Bachrach, Peter and Morton Baratz. 1970. *Power and Poverty*. New York: Oxford University Press.

Banfield, Edward C. 1974. *The Unheavenly City Revisited*. Boston: Little, Brown.

Banfield, Edward C. and James Q. Wilson. 1963. *City Politics*. New York: Vintage.

Baumer, Donald C. and Carl E. Van Horn. 1985. *The Politics of Unemployment*. Washington, D.C.: Congressional Quarterly Press.

Bellush, Jewel. 1971. "The Scattered-site Housing Controversy" in Jewel Bellush and Stephen David, 1971. *Race and Politics in New York City: Five Case Studies*. New York: Praeger, Ch. 6.

Bellush, Jewel and Stephen David. 1971. *Race and Politics in New York City*. New York: Praeger.

Browning, Rufus, Dale R. Marshall and David H. Tabb. 1984. *Protest Is Not Enough: The Struggle of Blacks and Hispanics for Equality in Urban Politics*. Berkeley: University of California Press.

Burchell, Robert W. and David Listokin, eds. 1981. *Cities under Stress*. New Brunswick, N.J.: Center for Urban Policy Research, Rutgers University.

Button, James. 1978. *Black Violence: The Political Impact of the 1960s Riots*. Princeton, N.J.: Princeton University Press.

Cebula, R. J. 1974. "Local Government Policies and Migration: An Analysis for SMSAs in the U.S." *Public Choice*, Vol. 19, 85–93.

Clarke, Terry N. and Lorna C. Ferguson. 1983. *City Money: Political Processes, Fiscal Strain and Retrenchment*. New York: Columbia University Press.

Cole, Leonard. 1976. *Blacks in Power: A Comparative Study of Black and White Elected Officials*. Princeton, N.J.: Princeton University Press.

Controller General of the United States, General Accounting Office. 1974. "Controller General's Report to Congress: Revenue Sharing—Its Use and Impact on Local Governments." Washington, D.C.: U.S. Government Printing Office.

Crain, Robert L. 1968. *The Politics of School Desegregation*. Chicago: Aldine.

Crenson, Matthew. 1971. *The Un-politics of Air Pollution*. Baltimore: Johns Hopkins University Press.

Dahl, Robert. 1961. *Who Governs?* New Haven: Yale University Press.

David, Stephen and Paul Kantor. 1983. "Urban Policy in the Federal System: A Reconceptualization of Federalism." *Polity*, Vol. XVI, No. 2, 284–304.

Department of Housing and Urban Development. 1984. "The President's National Urban Policy Report." Washington, D.C.: U.S. Government Printing Office.

Derthick, Martha. 1972. *New Towns-In-Town*. Washington, D.C.: Urban Institute.

Dommel, Paul R. and Associates. 1982. *Decentralization and Urban Policy*. Washington, D.C.: Brookings Institution.

Dye, Thomas R. 1966. *Politics, Economics and the Public*. Chicago: Rand McNally.

Economist, 7 December 1985, 22–25.

Edelman, Murray. 1971. *Politics As Symbolic Action*. New Haven: Yale University Press.

Edelman, Murray. 1964. *The Symbolic Uses of Politics*. Urbana: University of Illinois Press.

Eisinger, Peter K. 1979. "The Community Action Program and the Development of Black Political Leadership" in Dale R. Marshall, ed. 1979. *Urban Policy Making*. Beverly Hills: Sage, Ch. 4.

Eisinger, Peter K. 1973. "The Conditions of Protest Behavior in American Cities." *American Political Science Review*, Vol. 67 (March), 11–28.

Elder, Charles and R. W. Cobb. 1983. *The Political Uses of Symbols*. New York: Longman.

Fainstein, Norman I. and Susan S. Fainstein. 1974. *Urban Political Movements: The Search for Power by Minority Groups in American Cities*. Englewood Cliffs, N.J.: Prentice-Hall.

Fainstein, Susan, Norman Fainstein, Richard Child Hill, Dennis Judd and Michael P. Smith. 1983. *Restructuring the City: The Political Economy of Urban Redevelopment*. New York: Longman.

Franklin, Grace A. and Randal B. Ripley. 1984. *CETA: Politics and Policy, 1973–1982*. Knoxville: University of Tennessee Press.

Gamson, William A. 1975. *The Strategy of Social Protest*. Homewood, Ill.: Dorsey Press.

Gamson, William A. 1968. *Power and Discontent*. Homewood, Ill.: Dorsey Press.

Ganz, Alexander. 1985. "Where the Urban Crisis Has Gone." *Urban Affairs*

Quarterly, Vol. 20, No. 4 (June), 449–468.

Gittell, Marylin. 1980. *Limits to Citizen Participation: The Decline of Community Organizations*. Beverly Hills: Sage.

Greenstone, J. David and Paul E. Peterson. 1973. *Race and Authority in Urban Politics: Community Participation in the War on Poverty*. New York: Russell Sage.

Gronbjerg, Kirsten A. 1977. *Mass Society and the Extension of Welfare*. Chicago: University of Chicago Press.

Hallman, Howard. 1968. "The Community Action Program: An Interpretive Analysis" in Warner Bloomberg, Jr. and H. J. Schmandt, eds. 1968. *Power, Poverty and Urban Policy*. Beverly Hills: Sage.

Harrigan, John J. 1981. *Political Change in the Metropolis*, Second Edition. Boston: Little, Brown.

Hicks, Alexander and Duane H. Swank. 1983. "Civil Disorder, Relief, Mobilization and AFDC Caseloads: A Reexamination of the Piven and Cloward Thesis." *American Journal of Political Science*, Vol. 27 (November), 695–716.

Hill, Richard C. 1983. "Crisis in the Motor City" in Susan Fainstein, et al. 1983. *Restructuring the City: The Political Economy of Urban Redevelopment*. New York: Longman, Ch. 3.

Hopkins, Ellen. 1985. "The Dispossessed." *New York Magazine*, 13 May 1985, 49–52.

Isaac, Larry and William R. Kelly. 1981. "Racial Insurgency, the State and Welfare Expansion: Local and National Evidence from the Post-war U.S." *American Journal of Sociology*, Vol. 86 (May), 1348–1386.

Jennings, Edward T. "Urban Riots and the Growth of State Welfare Expenditures." *Policy Studies Journal*, Vol. 9, No. 1 (Autumn), 34–40.

Judd, Dennis R. 1984. *The Politics of American Cities*, Second Edition. Boston: Little, Brown.

Juster, Thomas F. 1976. *The Economic and Political Impact of General Revenue Sharing*. Report Prepared by the Survey Research Center for the National Science Foundation. Washington, D.C.: U.S. Government Printing Office.

Karnig, Albert and Susan Welch. 1980. *Black Representation and Urban Policy*. Chicago: University of Chicago Press.

Katznelson, Ira. 1981. *City Trenches*. New York: Pantheon Books.

Katznelson, Ira. 1973. *Black Men, White Cities*. New York: Oxford University Press.

Kerstin, Robert J. and Dennis R. Judd. 1980. "Achieving Less Influence with More Democracy: The Permanent Legacy of the War on Poverty." *Social Science Quarterly*, Vol. 61, No. 2 (September), 208–220.

Levitan, Sar A. 1986. *Programs in Aid of the Poor*, Sixth Edition. Baltimore: Johns Hopkins University Press.

Levitan, Sar A. 1985. *Programs in Aid of the Poor*, Fifth Edition. Baltimore: Johns Hopkins University Press.

Levy, Frank. 1980. *The Logic of Welfare Reform*. Washington, D.C.: Urban Institute Press.

Lipsky, Michael. 1970. *Protest in City Politics: Rent Strikes, Housing and the Power of the Poor*. Chicago: Rand McNally.

Lowi, Theodore J. 1964. *At the Pleasure of the Mayor*. New York: Macmillan.

Marris, Peter and Martin Rein. 1969. *Dilemmas of Social Reform*. New York: Atherton.

McConnell, Grant. 1966. *Private Power and American Democracy*. New York: Knopf.

Meyerson, Martin and Edward C. Banfield. 1955. *Politics, Planning and the Public Interest*. Glencoe: Free Press.

Mollenkopf, John. 1983. *The Contested City*. Princeton, N.J.: Princeton University Press.

Moynihan, Daniel P. 1973. *The Politics of a Guaranteed Income*. New York: Vintage.

Nathan, Richard P. and Fred C. Doolittle. 1983. *The Consequences of the Cuts; The Effects of the Reagan Domestic Program on State and Local Governments*. Princeton, N.J.: Princeton Urban and Regional Center.

National Advisory Commission on Civil Disorders. 1968. New York: Bantam Books.

Oates, W. E. 1972. *Fiscal Federalism*. New York: Harcourt, Brace and Jovanovich.

Orfield, Gary. 1969. *The Reconstruction of Southern Education*. New York: John Wiley.

Palley, Marian L. and Howard A. Palley. 1981. *Urban America and Public Policies*, Second Edition. Boston: D.C. Heath.

Palley, Marian L. and Howard A. Palley. 1975. "National Income and Services Policy in the U.S." in Dorathy B. James, ed. 1975. *Analyzing Poverty Policy*. Lexington, Mass.: Lexington Books.

Palmer, John and Isabel V. Sawhill, eds. 1984. *The Reagan Record*. Cambridge, Mass.: Ballinger.

Patterson, James T. 1981. *America's Struggle against Poverty, 1900-1980*. Cambridge, Mass.: Harvard University Press.

Peel, Roy V. 1935. *The Political Clubs of New York City*.

Peterson, George E. 1984. "Federalism and the States: An Experiment in Decentralization" in John Palmer and Isabel V. Sawhill, eds. 1984. *The Reagan Record*. Cambridge, Mass.: Ballinger.

Peterson, Paul E. 1981. *City Limits*. Chicago: University of Chicago Press.

Peterson, Paul E. and Mark C. Rom. 1987. "Federalism and Welfare Reform: The Determinants of Interstate Differences in Poverty Rates and Benefit Levels." *Paper Delivered to the Annual Meeting of the American Political Science Association,* Chicago, September 3-6.

Peterson, Paul E., Barry G. Rabe and Kenneth K. Wong, 1986. *When Federalism Works*. Washington, D.C.: Brookings Institution.

Piven, Francis F. and Richard A. Cloward. 1983. "Humanitarianism in History" in W. I. Trattner, ed. 1983. *Social Welfare or Social Control?* Knoxville: University of Tennessee Press.

Piven, Francis F. and Richard A. Cloward. 1982. *The New Class War*. New

York: Pantheon.

Piven, Francis F. and Richard A. Cloward. 1979. *Poor People's Movements: Why They Succeed, How They Fail.* New York: Vintage.

Piven, Francis F. and Richard A. Cloward. 1971. *Regulating the Poor: The Functions of Public Welfare.* New York: Vintage.

Pressman, Jeffrey L. 1975. *Federal Programs and City Politics.* Berkeley: University of California Press.

Pressman, Jeffrey L. and Aaron Wildavsky. 1979. *Implementation.* Berkeley: University of California Press.

Preston, Michael, et al., eds. 1982. *The New Black Politics.* New York: Longman.

Rein, Martin. 1977. "Equality and Social Policy." *Social Service Review*, Vol. 51 (December), 565–587.

Rodgers, Harrell R., Jr. 1979. *Poverty amid Plenty: A Political and Economic Analysis.* Reading, Mass.: Addison-Wesley.

Rogers, David. 1968. *110 Livingston Street.* New York: Random House.

Rubin, Irene S. 1985. "Structural Theories and Urban Fiscal Stress." *Urban Affairs Quarterly*, Vol. 20, No. 4 (June), 469–486.

Schexnider, Alvin J. 1982. "Political Mobilization in the South: The Election of a Black Mayor in New Orleans" in Michael B. Preston, Lenneal J. Henderson, Jr., and Paul Puryear, eds. 1982. *The New Black Politics: The Search for Political Power.* New York: Longman, Ch. 10.

Schneider, Mark and John Logan. 1985. "Suburban Municipalities: The Changing System of Intergovernmental Relations in the Mid-1970s." *Urban Affairs Quarterly*, September, 87–105.

Schwarz, John E. 1983. *America's Hidden Success: A Reassessment of Twenty Years of Public Policy.* New York: Norton.

Smith, Michael P. and Marlene Keller. 1983. "Managed Growth and the Politics of Uneven Development in New Orleans" in Susan Fainstein et al. 1983. *Restructuring the City: The Political Economy of Urban Redevelopment.* New York: Longman, Ch. 4.

Steiner, Gilbert Y. 1971. *The State of Welfare.* Washington, D.C.: Brookings Institution.

Steiner, Gilbert Y. 1966. *Social Insecurity: The Politics of Welfare.* Chicago: Rand McNally.

Sundquist, James L. 1969. "Origins of the War on Poverty" in J. L. Sundquist, ed. 1969. *On Fighting Poverty.* New York: Basic Books.

Tilly, Charles. 1978. *From Mobilization to Revolution.* Reading, Mass.: Addison-Wesley.

Tilly, Charles. 1968. "Race and Migration to the American City" in James Q. Wilson, ed. 1968. *The Metropolitan Enigma.* Cambridge, Mass: Harvard University Press, pp. 135–158.

Trattner, W. I., ed. 1983. *Social Welfare or Social Control?* Knoxville: University of Tennessee Press.

U.S. Department of the Treasury. 1979. *Sixth Annual Report of the Office of Revenue Sharing.* Washington, D.C.: U.S. Government Printing Office.

United States Government. 1980, *President's Commission for a National Agenda for the Eighties.* Washington, D.C.: U.S. Government Printing Office.

Welch, Susan and Albert K. Karnig. 1979. "The Impact of Black Elected Officials on Urban Social Expenditures." *Policy Studies Journal*, Vol. 7, No. 4 (Summer), 707–714.

Conclusion

CHAPTER EIGHTEEN

The Future of the Dependent City

M ARKET and polity have evolved during the history of urban America to compose a mature liberal-democratic urban political economy. Popular control institutions gradually have become differentiated from their former identity with dominant economic institutions, as in the days of mercantile democracy, to form a rival system of power through which the mass citizenry can inform and discipline local political authorities. The place of cities in the capitalist economy has also undergone fundamental transformation. The contemporary structure of urban economic competition has created a highly dependent position for cities within the market order. At the same time, federalism has been marked by radical changes, having acquired an enlarged presence of national and state authorities in local affairs and creating unprecedented intergovernmental dependency. In a sense, the American city has fulfilled the logic of liberal-democratic development—it has achieved a remarkable degree of governmental democratization amid severe economic dependency on exterior forces.

The Public Policy Dilemmas of the City

These characteristics of the urban political economy are also the sources of the major public policy dilemmas of cities. First, communities face a *dilemma of economic development*. The economic dependency imposed by the postindustrial urban system limits citizen control of community development decisions and it biases local government in favor of many wasteful public policies that enhance the privileged position of business and other revenue providers to the neglect of others. In particular, severe urban economic rivalry to induce capital investment narrows local policy choices in ways that often sacrifice the interests of the disadvantaged and those seeking to promote social values that require limited growth.

398

Second, in respect to redistributive policy, cities confront a *dilemma of social welfare justice*. The postindustrial economy has concentrated problems of want and disadvantage within urban communities while imposing upon their governments an economic dependency that discourages them from fulfilling their social responsibilities. The urban economic rivalry that pits jurisdiction against jurisdiction in a struggle for survival strongly disciplines localities to avoid allocating local resources, be they cash, land, capital, staff, amenities, or even intergovernmental resources to assist the disadvantaged. Only the emergence of the federal and, to a lesser degree, the state governments as dominant influences in welfare state activities has compelled local governments to cooperate in enlarging their social policy roles.

Yet even the latter event has not resolved the problem of urban social justice. Federal program structures and resources often do not sufficiently counter the pressures of urban economic dependency. Localities remain in a strong position to water down, knock down, or otherwise obstruct the implementation of national or state efforts at redistribution. Further, as have-nots achieve greater political influence within urban political systems, they are finding that winning local political power often does not bring much control over the social policies that matter most to them. Control over the programs and revenue sources for promoting redistributive goals are mainly in the hands of other governments in the suburbs or at higher governmental levels. The weak market positions of their city governments discourage them from redistributing the things over which they do have more control, such as school desegregation, neighborhood improvements, housing renewal, etc. Such disparity between local government capability and the openness of city political systems to demands for redistributive responses forms an explosive situation.

Finally, in the area of distribution, cities contend with a *dilemma of governability*. The growth of popular control as a potent system of power has not been without costs for local government. The reform of local government institutions has been bought at the price of fragmenting political power, weakening party systems, and enlarging the role of bureaucratic professionals in making public policy. Consequently, on matters of distribution, where neither economic nor intergovernmental constraints are especially limiting, urban governmental systems display powerful centrifugal tendencies, limiting the ability of elected political authorities to provide central direction in dealing with public problems.

While lack of central direction in city governments is not always a grave problem when there exists a wide consensus on policy—such as about how to sweep the streets—not all distributive issues are of this kind. Effective and responsible law enforcement, fair salaries for civil servants, public service recruitment and promotion procedures, budgetary allotments for competing "basic" public services, etc., are among the more obvious matters over which there may not be much political agreement. In these cases, the danger is that narrow entrenched bureaucratic interests can easily triumph over those interests that are more diffuse, general, and unorganized. Such ungovernable politics can produce related governmental failures: the inability of political authorities to deal at all with problems that do not command a powerful bureaucratic constituency, unfairness and capriciousness in day-to-day administration, cynicism about government, and even corruption.

What Can Be Done?

Given the very different kinds of policy dilemmas that cities face, it is doubtful if there is any single solution that is relevant to resolving all of them. Moreover, in these concluding pages it would be impossible to survey the whole range of complex possibilities, much less evaluate their political and economic feasibility. Nevertheless, it is possible to consider the strategic alternatives that are relevant to the public problems of our contemporary cities and identify the most feasible and effective choices in light of what we know about the urban political economy. In this regard, it is useful to look at strategic changes that might be made in respect to all three dimensions of the urban politico-economic order.

Enhancing Popular Control Systems

First, changes in local popular control systems that enhance the polyarchal quality of local governance can probably have a positive influence on all three urban policy dilemmas. Most of all, however, the reform of popular control systems could have the greatest impact on the problem of city governability. Strengthening the political positions of the cities' highest officials could help counter tendencies for political influence to fragment into bureaucratic power islands in the formation of distributive policy. Rebuilding urban party systems to provide a base of power for mayors that is independent of city bureaucracies, charter reforms to strengthen mayoral powers of appointment and budgetary control, and related reforms are among the possible pathways to enable mayors to assert greater central direction over city governmental systems (Lowi, 1968; Yates, 1977).

No doubt rebuilding urban party systems in an age of declining partisanship is an uphill task. But the payoff for doing so is strong. Achieving such a goal could greatly extend the reach of mayors and other elected officials over city government and provide voters with more accountable leadership and clearer electoral choices. Particularly because central cities are likely to become less polarized in socio-economic character as their minority populations expand and their white populations continue to shrink, voter choices are likely to be clearer if politics is organized around parties, rather than around passing personalities, vague symbolic appeals, and other extraneous features that seem to be found in no-party politics (Key, 1947; Peterson and Kantor, 1977).

The reform of popular control institutions can also positively affect the redistributive problems of cities. The political influence of those who lack many economic resources is highly dependent upon their ability to use popular control institutions to their best advantage. Promoting voter registration and high voter turnout in elections, grooming minority candidates for public office, and organizing the poor to demand what the American welfare state can and ought to provide can be consequential in the allocation of urban and intergovernmental resources. Though local politics provides a limited venue for accommodating redistributive demands, the political power of the poor and their allies in state and federal popular control systems is not unrelated to their ability to organize themselves into formidable local power brokers, as our earlier discussion documents.

The developmental politics of cities would also be enhanced by infusing it with greater popular control. The insularity of decision-making structures for urban development, such as independent development authorities, special tax and service districts, and related agencies, undercuts public awareness and control over the economic planning of the locale. The financial and organizational independence of these institutions frees the public officials who run or monitor them from close public scrutiny and accountability. Consequently, these officials are too easily pressured to trade off socially desirable objectives— such as decent housing for all, the preservation of old neighborhoods, and small business prosperity—in order to promote local economic growth. The more indirect and remote is public involvement in developmental decisions, the more likely it is that public officials become consumed by their market management activities and the pressures of business.

Reforming local government to stimulate public accountability in this area of public policy would therefore be a valuable check on the biases of decision makers. In addition to reforms that could strengthen the party system and the role of the mayor, there are administrative changes that could do so. Independent development authorities could become fewer in number in order to help focus public attention on them; they could be restructured to become more representative of nonbusiness opinion; and they could be made more publicly accountable via requirements for referenda and by giving general-purpose governments a greater role in developing their programs.

Perhaps even more desirable is the alternative of separating the raising of capital investment from the public agencies that plan and operate development projects. Higher-level government agencies could approve, market, and guarantee bonding for local government development agencies as is the case in Great Britain and other Western industrial nations. This would free development authority officials somewhat from the narrow investor perspective for which they are famous, yet still provide financial accountability for their activities (U.S. Congress, 1979). It would also remove a major reason why there are so many authorities in the first place—to get around local government debt limits.

Restructuring the Exterior of the Dependent City

Changes in urban popular control systems can enhance the political accountability of city governance. But such internal governmental reforms do not alter the exogenous forces that limit the public policy alternatives of cities. Outside the distributive arena, the dilemmas of urban politics can mainly be traced to urban America's economic dependency and to the programs and structures of the federal governmental system that are supportive of this dependency. Consequently, opening up opportunities for greater community choice on matters of development and redistribution rests very much on finding ways of diminishing city economic dependency or on regulating its social consequences. This means that private or public sector changes must be undertaken to either reduce the rivalry among local governments for jobs and dollars or to compensate the "loser" communities for the social and economic problems they incur when businesses leave town for greener urban pastures. Local politics would become less biased in favor of revenue-producer interests, more open to the demands of ordinary people, and more likely to be supportive of diverse community values.

Two Radical Alternatives: The Empty Choices

Restructuring the Private Sector: Urban Corporatism

One alternative is to get the private corporate sector, which today owns an ascendant economic position within the urban economy, to assume more responsibility for regulating the social costs of their investment and disinvestment activities in cities, towns, and suburbs. For instance, there are already voluntary industry programs that pool capital for "urban reinvestment" in neighborhoods and cities that have been "redlined" by financial institutions which are unwilling to extend credit to them for residential and commercial mortgages, business loans, and even governmental purposes. Such a program has been operated on a small scale by the insurance industry as a means of redirecting some capital back into inner city neighborhoods faced with economic decay (Orren, 1974). This kind of reinvestment activity is presently promoted by federal legislation that requires financial disclosure on the part of lending institutions, permitting advocates of this approach to identify urban disinvestment patterns and to prod corporate America into a more activist role in rebuilding the inner cities.

It might be possible to expand this kind of endeavor. Such an approach could include having business conduct job creation schemes, venture capital programs for smaller businesses, work training, and related social and business activities in order to help boost the market positions and clean up the social problems of declining urban areas. Already, larger businesses often participate in summer job programs for youth, and they donate funds to various inner city causes, from drug rehabilitation centers to neighborhood improvement projects (like "adopting" a tree, park, or even a school). Why not let America's "corporate statesmen" do more in planning urban development and helping the losers?

Perhaps the strongest argument for such "urban corporatism" is that it could be the path of least resistance. In an age when relatively small numbers of giant corporations have control over so much domestic investment, one can make the case that we should simply acknowledge the reality of their economic power and rely upon business leadership to take more of a community view of their activities and recognize their social responsibilities.

There are very serious objectives to this stratagem, however. Urban corporatism means shifting responsibility for urban planning and governance onto individuals and institutions that are not and cannot be made politically accountable. After nearly two centuries of developing popular control systems into a powerful means of disciplining governmental leaders, the corporatist model would have us remove the most important urban questions of our time from their reach. In fact, urban corporatism is merely a form of economic dependency of the worst sort—one that leaves local communities and their governments as cap-in-hand petitioners to economic institutions over which they have no political control at all. At the same time, this arrangement would place on business an impossible social responsibility that is inappropriate in a liberal-democratic political economy; it means no less than effectively making civil servants out of business leaders and trusting them to govern well (cf. Friedman, 1962:133–135; Lowi, 1979). As such, it is more in keeping with fascism than with either capitalism or democracy.

The Socialist City: Trading Dilemmas?

A socialist nation-state is an alternative radical means of dealing with America's urban frustrations. Given the economic rivalry that drives cities to scramble for growth and people while avoiding social welfare responsibilities, it could be argued that terminating the market economic order is the obvious prerequisite to making better, more independent cities. By placing the means of production in the hands of national governmental planners, local governments would be reduced to administering mandates regarding social services and carrying out minor roles in respect to matters of production, distribution, and consumption. The privileged position of business would no longer impinge on the economic and political systems of cities. Such a vision fits into the Marxist notion of the appropriate role of the state that was described in Chapter 2.

Although incorporating city governments into a socialist nation-state could well end their developmental and redistributive dilemmas as we now know them, one must entertain grave doubts about this "solution." Even if a socialist alternative were politically feasible in the United States, such a wholesale exchange of one politico-economic system for another could never rest only or even mainly upon its urban effects. The political debate over capitalism vs. socialism has always focused upon matters of productivity, efficiency, equity, liberty, freedom, and social justice that go far beyond the urban-related dilemmas described in this volume (cf. Friedman, 1962; Hayek, 1944; Miliband, 1969; Lindblom, 1977; Gordon, 1977). Unless these general issues regarding the overall social implications of a socialist political economy are resolved in favor of this type of order—a job that goes well beyond what is possible here—it is hardly appropriate to entertain this as a desirable solution to today's urban dilemmas of dependency.

Nevertheless, even if one could experiment with replacing one type of political economy for another, there are reasons to believe that socialist cities would face dilemmas of economic dependency that rival those of liberal-democratic systems. Economic competition within markets would be in all probability supplanted by political competition within a huge bureaucratic labyrinth of planning controls that would be determinative of urban development. Though matters of redistribution probably would be much less of an issue (because they would not be subject to much community control at all), there seems little reason to expect that cities and their populations would be treated alike by central planners whose dominant priorities are likely to be linked to national productivity goals and the rigidities of their politico-bureaucratic environment (Szelenyi, 1983; Lindblom, 1977:Part VI).

Socialist systems have created their own serious urban dilemmas. In centrally planned nation-states today, booming, relatively prosperous cultural centers (like Moscow in the Soviet Union) can exist alongside economically backward localities capable of offering their captive labor pools little more than dead-end or makework jobs (Szelenyi, 1983; Morton and Stewart, 1984; Harris, 1970; Sawers, 1978). Further, state-owned enterprises in socialist systems can assume a dominating influence over cities and their governments which overshadows that of corporate America—a type of economic dependency about which, for example, citizens and politicians in Soviet cities bitterly complain (Morton, 1984).

Liberal-Democratic Reforms

Whatever the merits of one politico-economic system over another, real-world policy alternatives hardly ever boil down to such choices. The liberal-democratic order is a complex mixture of political and economic control systems. The powerful federal role as a regulator of the capitalist economy and as a provider of welfare state services is only the most obvious illustration of this truth. Public and private control structures are separate, but highly interdependent, in the modern liberal-democratic state. The possibilities for combining and mixing these systems of decision and power to achieve desirable social objectives are almost endless (Dahl and Lindblom, 1953:Part I). A liberal-democratic political economy is capable of dramatic change in regard to the respective roles of state and market, a fact that the mercantile, industrial, and postindustrial urban experiences vividly illustrate.

By reconstituting the functions of market and state and by reallocating public authority for specific programs among the levels of government within the federal governmental system, it is possible to restructure the liberal-democratic system to deal more effectively with its dependent cities. The task is to identify proposals that can recast this system to promote constructive changes that favorably address the urban condition. To this end, it is necessary to think strategically about how any specific kind of reform will work within the dynamics of the prevailing politico-economic order.

The Urban Development Dilemma and Liberal-Democratic Politics

Key reforms for liberal-democratic cities must focus upon the process of urban development and seek to reduce their severe economic dependency.

The Role of the States

Attempts to limit urban economic competition by expanding the scope of state regulation in local development policy constitute one such strategy. For instance, state plant closing legislation already exists in some states (Leary, 1985); typically, it requires that businesses inform workers and communities in advance of their decision to relocate. Some laws require that compensation to workers and communities be paid by businesses in order to help finance the social costs of disinvestment (e.g., job training, school closures, etc.). Similarly, states could do more to discourage public entrepreneurship as a means of bidding for and subsidizing capital. The uses of industrial revenue bonds by local governments could be restricted, the "public" purposes of local government expenditures could be more narrowly defined than they have been, and the authorization of independent development authorities could be curtailed. As creatures of states, the authority of local governments could be changed in countless ways in order to drastically limit the use of public resources for stimulating the interurban economic rivalry that produces little or no net gain in the nation's wealth and productivity.

The difficulty with this strategy is that state governments are unlikely to be very effective vehicles for such self-denying reforms. State governments are, like local governments, very economically dependent—indeed, poor, slow-growth states are as desperate for new capital investment as are many cities. Efforts by a particular state government to regulate the movement of capital and labor is likely to diminish its market position vis-à-vis other states that do not, not to mention in respect to jurisdictions outside of the domestic economy that fail to follow suit.

For this reason, most attempts by state governments to impose significant penalties and regulations on business relocation have been relatively feeble. Plant closing legislation has almost always been tailored to have more symbolic value than regulatory "teeth." In fact, even the more benign requirements of such legislation, such as "early warning" of plant closures, are often opposed by public officials because of the negative image they are perceived to give the state's business climate (Harrison and Bluestone, 1984:235-243).

If all other things remain equal, there is every reason to expect that state governments will become progressively less responsive and move in the opposite direction in respect to regulating urban development. As urban and regional economic rivalry spreads, states are likely to further stimulate new urban entrepreneurial programs, authorize more remote and powerful development agencies, and encourage bolder forms of capital subsidy.[1] This has been the historic trend in postindustrial America, and there is little reason to believe it will not continue. Economically competitive localities mean economically competitive states.

National Urban Policy and the Liberation of Cities

The most likely pathway to liberating urban communities from their dependency is to expand the federal governmental role in regulating urban development. The kinds of measures cited above in respect to states, together with related programs noted below, are most likely to work if they are part of a national governmental urban program. Only if urban development legislation is imposed uniformly on all states and localities can the social costs of business investment and disinvestment be controlled without bringing about devastating effects on the market positions of individual jurisdictions. The strategic developmental aim of such a national policy should be to more equitably regulate the social costs of urban development than the market system does presently and to ensure that "loser" communities are compensated and, if possible, "recycled" in the process of economic change.

Such a policy could take a variety of forms. Specific programs would probably be very wide ranging. For instance, in addition to the above proposals, the federal tax system could be used in order to reflect the urban effects (costs) of business activity. That is, "loser" communities that undergo disinvestment could be compensated for this via federal tax formulas that spread the burdens onto business, "winner" communities, or even the general public. Specific tax changes could build into the capital investment process tax surcharges on new and old business to pay off undepreciated public infrastructure and to fund such things as job training, worker relocation, and economic revitalization programs for specific urban areas (cf. Peterson, 1980; Vaughan, 1977; and Luger, 1984).

Reliance on local revenue sources (especially the property tax) could be diminished in favor of intergovernmental aid programs based on need and related compensatory criteria. Such national grant-in-aid programs have been used for years in Great Britain and Western Europe. In Britain, central government grants to local authorities provide compensatory support to poorer jurisdictions to provide a national standard of basic public services and amenities (Boaden, 1971; Griffith, 1966).

Urban enterprise zones could be designated for distressed areas while—unlike the recent proposal for them—checking competing efforts by growing communities to attract still more capital investment. Restraining competing localities would be no easy task. But the federal government possesses the capabilities for such an endeavor. For example, federal enterprise zones could be run in concert with laws that eliminate or severely restrict tax-exempt industrial revenue bonds by states and localities. Federal grant-in-aid monies might be apportioned by formulas that automatically penalize local governments which apply their tax revenues for business subsidy purposes.

These proposals are barely a beginning for what is, in effect, a national urban policy. The creative possibilities are enormous once federal authority is committed to the task.

Why a National Urban Policy Makes Sense

A strong case can be made for this relatively centralist strategy if the most likely objections to it are considered. Most criticisms would undoubtedly focus on the political feasibility of this idea or would challenge its effectiveness in achieving solutions to the problem of urban dependency. Below are five such criticisms followed by my answers to each.

Any such national urban policy is politically unfeasible because of potentially widespread business opposition to it.

Given business' privileged position in the liberal-democratic system, it could be argued that greater federal regulation of private investment activity, especially legislation that forces business to shoulder more of the social costs occasioned by their activities, would meet with unmitigated corporate opposition. Why should business pay for "urban equity" when the existing system permits them to escape from such burdens?

This perception of business' interests is naive, however. It misinterprets the interests of many businesses and is based on a false sense of actual business history in respect to governmental regulation. First, the present urban economy continually imposes important costs on business, particularly those caught in "loser" localities; falling real estate values, shrunken markets, declining labor supply and labor quality, undepreciated capital plant, relocational costs and uncertainties, not to mention the morale problems of executives and workers faced with undiminishing workplace upheaval, are among the problems of businesses left behind in the process of urban disinvestment. This does not even consider the political costs to business in the form of threats to their economic freedoms. Socially blind corporate investment practice is simply bad politics for businesses wishing to preserve a large degree of relative autonomy from state control.

Further, the corporate sector historically has not been uniformly adverse to public programs that have the effect of eliminating business uncertainty. In addition to the urban policies of the industrial period, the history of national governmental regulation of particular industries and the growth of national monetary and fiscal policies to assure sufficient aggregate demand and stabilize prices has been widely supported by big capital. They have often favored government programs that can reduce business risks and uncertainties (Galbraith, 1979; Kolko, 1967; Weinstein, 1968; Greenberg, 1985). By the same token, business has largely accepted welfare state programs that compensate individuals, groups, and even communities which have been displaced by economic changes (e.g., unemployment insurance, pensions, and public assistance in its various forms) (O'Conner, 1973).

A national urban program that is essentially good for business and good for the public is not beyond possibility. In particular, a national urban policy that could spread the costs of the process of urban change might very well attract business support and also provide considerable public benefits in the form of reduced economic dependency. For instance, there may be a case for a system of federal compensation that socializes some or even most of the costs of community disinvestment brought about by capital movement and innovation.

These costs need not be imposed only on the businesses that precipitate them or be left to be picked up by the "loser" communities (which include segments of the business sector, as suggested above). Greater federal governmental responsibility for compensating "loser" communities makes sense on grounds of both economics and equity. Industrial disinvestment in particular areas often (some economists would claim almost always) is economically "good" for the nation as a whole in the sense that it signifies the reallocation of land, labor, and capital to more productive uses, enhancing the competitive position of the United States in world markets and bringing cheaper and better products to American consumers. Thus, there are benefits to ensuring considerable freedom of capital location. A national urban policy could permit this freedom while more fairly allocating its social costs among citizens and businesses.

National urban policy is unfeasible because there is no broad national constituency supportive of national urban planning.

It is true that presently there does not exist wide consensus on enlarging the national government's role in urban policy to achieve more equitable developmental objectives. The shifting regional political coalitions driving national governmental policy in respect to urban development have generally supported efforts to promote some urban areas rather than others, a pattern described in Chapter 10. Political competition of this kind remains a divisive factor, making difficult any explicit, enlarged national urban planning attempt.

But building a national urban development policy is possible if appeals are made to political interests among urban communities that are likely to grow more intense in the future. Urban and regional job shifts, disinvestment, and attendant social upheaval touch virtually all communities in almost all regions, demonstrating that even "winner" localities can only achieve transient economic security. As this grows, then the reality of economic dependency is likely to become a foundation for supporting national efforts to regulate urban changes more equitably. Economic stress that threatens to envelop urban America is a powerful generator of new interests and new political coalitions that favor containing the consequences of city economic dependency.

Recent experiences of high-growth "winner" areas in the United States should sober the most enthusiastic of urban "boosters."[2] During the mid-1980s, the once meteoric economic growth of many parts of the Sunbelt region of the nation precipitously diminished and even underwent reversal as a result of declining oil and gas prices, agricultural depression, and the movement of large numbers of jobs in high-technology industries, textiles, sporting goods, assembly, and other sectors to lower-cost areas, mostly in the Third World. The failure of numbers of Sunbelt cities to diversify their economic bases and provide competitive advantages on par with other lower-cost regions made them vulnerable to business downturns and capital flight.

For instance, southeastern states, which were once big gainers of garment and textile industry job shifts away from New England and other northern cities, found that their low-cost, nonunion, cheap tax business environment could not prevent many companies in this industry from hopscotching to even cheaper, less regulated, underdeveloped countries. In 1984, pay for apparel workers was about 33¢ per hour in Haiti (about $2.65 per day). Hourly rates in this industry were 56.5¢ in Costa Rica, 60¢ in Panama, 68¢ in Taiwan, 97¢ in Hong Kong, and $1.20 in South Korea (*New York Times*, 17 June 1984:F-4). American workers cannot compete in this low-wage labor market, rendering hopeless local and state governmental attempts to persuade these kinds of businesses to stay put.

The federal government does not have the capability to regulate urban development. It is "dependent" on the world economy.

Although the national government cannot regulate urban development without consideration of the effects of its public policies on the United States' international market position, the size, diversity, and productive power of the national economy and the power of the national government to control the movement of capital and labor sharply distinguish it from lower-level governments. Far from a mere theoretical difference, this book is filled with evidence of the consequences of this historical reality. The relative economic independence of the national government compared with lower-level jurisdictions has enabled it to fund major redistributive programs and to tax business and the rich to a degree that other governments do not dare. This capability also can be directed to promoting more humane urban development.

A national urban policy would merely substitute political competition for urban growth in place of market competition. The result will be the same— "winner" and "loser" localities.

That national urban policy is "political" and is likely to be tilted in favor of some interests, cities, and regions more than others is undeniable. Any role the national government plays (or fails to play) in respect to urban and regional development will render advantages for some areas and disadvantages for others. But the relevant question is whether greater national control over urban development is likely to yield superior (more fair) results compared to the system we now have in which so much is governed by private sector decisions.

Having the national government expand its regulatory responsibilities in this area of policy is tantamount to shifting decisions about urban change to be settled more by national popular control processes than by private market decisions. Given the postindustrial economy's waste of national resources, socially destructive consequences for all communities, and the lopsided bargaining relationships that it creates between localities and business, it is difficult to believe that allowing national popular control processes to play a greater role in urban development would be worse.

In fact, a substantial case can be made that it would be considerably better. A well-developed process of popular control permits matters of equity, social costs, and other broad political values to be publicly considered and bargained out by all interests (something that the "invisible hand" of market control does not permit). It places considerations of political fairness and rationality ahead of considerations of microeconomic efficiency. Unlike a market control process, popular control also provides for political accountability of results. Finally, the American political process is more capable of being responsive and accountable to the demands of have-nots in urban development than are the private sector's market institutions. The latter are not organized to take care of the losers—be they individuals or localities—in the economic order. Simply put, making urban development more of a democratic process by the most appropriate level of government would afford greater possibilities for public choice and provide a much more substantial safety net for the disadvantaged than does the present system.

This argument need not and ought not to be stretched to conclude that all social decisions should be dominated by the logic of popular control. It only suggests that a politico-economic system that egregiously neglects the kinds of values and interests which popular control promotes ought to have more of the latter. The advantage of a liberal-democratic political economy over other systems is that it affords great flexibility for dealing with public problems by changing the "mix" of private and public control forces. The old mixture is outworn and the direction of change seems obvious.

A national urban policy will threaten local freedom and initiative in community affairs.

That greater federal regulation of urban planning would involve greater legal restrictions on local communities is certainly true, particularly if some of the proposals for limiting urban entrepreneurship are made into law. But the present urban order is also a "planning" system that restricts local policy choice and initiative by imposing on all communities an economic prison constructed of intercity market rivalry and business dependency. Further, this "urban planning system" already has a huge national governmental component; as earlier chapters describe, de facto federal urban policy has been to act in a hodge-podge and often contradictory fashion to substantially support urban dependency, rather than effectively counterbalance it for other objectives.

The relevant issue is whether this de facto urban policy should be traded for one that is coherent, explicit, and directed toward different national and community development goals. Our conclusion is that if the reality of federal planning power in urban development is acknowledged and employed to diminish local economic dependency, then neighborhoods, cities, and states have a chance to enjoy new freedoms in community development, particularly in considering a broader, more balanced range of community values other than maximizing growth to assure their survival.

National Urban Policy and Redistribution

These considerations in respect to urban economic development policy are also relevant to the dilemma of redistribution in urban politics. As the chapters throughout this book suggest, the redistributive impulse that is present in urban communities runs right up against the limitations of their economic dependency. The great expansion in governmental social welfare activity during the post-industrial era is linked closely to the growth of national governmental programs for the disadvantaged; local government responsiveness to the needs of these individuals will in all likelihood continue to depend on the intervention of higher-level governments.

There are instances where local governments can take the initiative to expand their responsibilities in this area of policy, but they are few and limited in a political economy of dependent cities. City governments (and states) with strong market positions can expand their redistributive roles to some degree. For instance, New York City, with its huge, relatively diverse postwar revenue base, managed to provide a package of social services, including free university tuition at its city university, a sprawling municipal health care network, low transit fares, and comparatively generous public assistance contributions. Its position as a world corporate headquarters city facilitated a dramatic expansion of this municipal welfare system during the 1960s.

Similarly, in recent years some cities that have undergone economic booms have created new housing programs for low-income families by capitalizing on their surging market positions. One way this has been done is by requiring private developers to contribute to building low- and moderate-income housing in exchange for permission to build commercial or luxury residential projects in desirable inner city locations (Marcuse, 1987; Walker, 1986). In 1981, such a "linkage" plan was adopted in San Francisco and won the agreement of developers who were hungry to participate in the city's commercial real estate explosion (Fainstein et al., 1983:234). With Boston's downtown renaissance in the mid-1980s, populist Mayor Raymond Flynn has followed suit with a similar scheme. In a somewhat different twist, New York's Governor Mario Cuomo provided the state's chartered banks with new regulations that allowed them to invest in real estate development—a power they long sought—in exchange for their agreement to expand by $1 billion their investments in poor neighborhoods (*New York Times*, 20 September 1984:A-1).

Though such redistributive efforts signify the direction that local and state public policy can sometimes take, they do not suggest a solution to the social welfare dilemma of cities. Even a city with a strong market position is a weak foundation upon which to build very significant programs of redistribution. Few local economies are as ascendant in their market positions as are New York City, San Francisco, or Boston; most states do not have the economic base that New York owns. Even in large cities, most efforts at redistribution are inevitably small-scale operations relative to the demand for such programs from their large poor populations. Perhaps most important, cities like Boston, New York, and San Francisco are unlikely to sustain many significant programs of redistribution from their own resources because their market positions are precarious in today's multilocational economy. All three of these cities encountered severe economic doldrums for many years during the postwar decades and their recent surge in economic growth is unlikely to be sustained. Indeed, the fiscal woes of these cities forced their governments to undertake major cutbacks in public services during the 1970s. New York City narrowly averted municipal bankruptcy in 1975, forcing its liberal leaders to dismantle or severely reduce many of the programs founded during the preceding decade to serve the poor.

Given the reality of city economic dependency, getting cities to participate in and promote redistributive efforts is strongly linked to changes in national governmental policy. Indeed, the entire history of building America's welfare state since the 1930s has been dominated by the initiative of the federal government. Particularly under political leaders most responsive to the poor, but also under less enthusiastic leaders, federal authorities have been the major paymasters and drovers for the herds of local authorities and states that serve the disadvantaged.

The appropriate means of enhancing the redistributive functions of local government is by utilizing national urban policy to challenge city economic dependency in ways outlined above. If local communities are not as threatened by urban and regional economic rivalries, then the humanitarian impulses of local governments and their citizens are likely to get freer play; more cooperative relationships are apt to characterize their participation in national social welfare programs.

Enlarging the federal role in financing programs of redistribution would also be necessary to motivate local communities to fulfill their obligations to the needy. Federalization of the costs of most major social welfare services, such as public assistance, Medicaid, and other expensive programs, would lift the financial burden of caring for the poor from those governmental jurisdictions that disproportionately shoulder it (Peterson, 1981:Ch. 11). A first step in this direction could be made by terminating the New Federalism approach to national-local relations. Illusory in the "freedom" it affords states and localities, this open-ended and decentralist way of managing urban problems does little more than leave citizens free to choose within their cells of economic dependency. Enlarging the federal direction of intergovernmental programs within a national urban policy that has clear developmental *and* redistributive objectives would avoid the pitfalls of the old hodge-podge categorical program approach, while directly challenging the socio-economic plight of the nation's cities.

Local political action to meet America's urban problems is not enough. What will count is whether resources and policies are employed in ways that recognize the politico-economic dependencies of the nation's cities.

Endnotes

1. For example, during 1985–1986 federal legislation was enacted that curtailed the use of tax-free industrial revenue bonds; this tax reform drew vigorous objections from state and local officials all over the United States. Unable to practice self-denial as long as competing jurisdictions continued to offer revenue bonding inducements to businesses, local and state authorities raced to beat statutory deadlines and 1987 saw a surge in such bonds (*Gannett Westchester Newspapers*, 1987).
2. Thus the reality and character of interurban economic rivalry casts doubt upon the proposal of Logan and Molotch (1984) for enhancing local control of community development. They suggest that "more strategically placed" cities in the "urban hierarchy" can utilize their advantageous bargaining positions vis-à-vis business to make greater demands on capital in the urban investment process:

By squeezing capital's locational options from the top, residents can force firms to move down the place hierarchy in their search for satisfactory sites. This will strengthen the bargaining position of each place below. . . . All places will gain through this process, even places at the bottom (p. 295).

The difficulty with this well-reasoned idea is that it assumes that there actually is a well-stratified urban economic system where cities "at the top" are sufficiently secure in their economic positions to drive a hard bargain with business on developmental issues. As our previous analysis suggests, however, the postindustrial urban system lacks such economic stratification in the capital investment process; even large boomtowns are inclined to compete with smaller, less-developed localities owing to the relative ease of capital mobility.

References for Conclusion

Boaden, Noel. 1971. *Urban Policy Making*. Cambridge, U.K.: Cambridge University Press.

Dahl, Robert A. and Charles E. Lindblom. 1953. *Politics, Economics and Welfare*. New York: Harper.

Fainstein, Susan, Norman Fainstein and P. Jefferson Armistead. 1983. "San Francisco: Urban Transformation and the Local State" in Susan Fainstein et al. 1983. *Restructuring the City: The Political Economy of Urban Redevelopment*. New York: Longman, Ch. 6.

Friedman, Milton. 1962. *Capitalism and Freedom*. Chicago: University of Chicago Press.

Galbraith, John K. 1979. *The New Industrial State*, Third Edition, Revised. Boston: Houghton Mifflin.

Gannett Westchester Newspapers. 23 November 1987:B-1.

Gordon, David G., ed. 1977. *Problems in Political Economy*. Lexington, Mass.: D.C. Heath.

Greenberg, Edward S. 1985. *Capitalism and the American Political Ideal*. Elmsford, N.Y.: M. E. Sharpe.

Griffith, J. A. G. 1966. *Central Departments and Local Authorities*. London: Allen and Unwin.

Harris, Chauncy D. 1970. *Cities of the Soviet Union*. Chicago: Rand McNally.

Harrison, Bennett and Barry Bluestone. 1984. "The Incidence and Regulation of Plant Closings" in Larry Sawers and William K. Tabb. 1984. *Sunbelt, Snowbelt*. New York: Oxford University Press, Ch. 15.

Hayek, Fredrick A. 1944. *The Road to Serfdom*. Chicago: University of Chicago Press.

Key, Jr., V. O. 1947. *Southern Politics*. New York: Vintage.

Kolko, Gabriel. 1967. *The Triumph of Conservatism*. Chicago: University of Chicago Press.

Leary, Thomas J. 1985. "Deindustrialization, Plant Closing Laws, and the States." *State Government*, Vol. 58 (Fall), 113–118.

Lindblom, Charles E. 1977. *Politics and Markets*. New Haven: Yale University Press.

Logan, John R. and Harvey L. Molotch. 1987. *Urban Fortunes: The Political Economy of Place*. Berkeley: University of California Press.

Lowi, Theodore J. 1979. *The End of Liberalism*. New York: Norton.

Lowi, Theodore J. 1968. "Foreword" in Harold E. Gosnel. 1968. *Machine Politics: Chicago Model*, Second Edition. Chicago: University of Chicago Press.

Luger, Michael I. 1984. "Federal Tax Incentives As Industrial and Urban Policy" in Larry Sawers and William K. Tabb. *Sunbelt, Snowbelt: Urban Development and Regional Restructuring*. New York: Oxford University Press, Ch. 8.

Marcuse, Peter. 1987. "Who Will Pay the Piper? Zoning for Justice in New York City." *City Limits*, February, 12–15.

Miliband, Ralph. 1969. *The State in Capitalist Society*. New York: Harper.

Morton, Henry W. 1984. "The Contemporary Soviet City" in Henry W. Morton and Robert C. Steward, eds. 1984. *The Contemporary Soviet City*. Armonk, N.Y.: M. E. Sharpe, Inc.

Morton, Henry W. and Robert C. Stewart, eds. 1984. *The Contemporary Soviet City*. Armonk, N.Y.: M. E. Sharpe, Inc.

New York Times. 17 June 1984, F-4.

New York Times. 20 September 1984, A-1.

O'Conner, James. 1973. *The Fiscal Crisis of the State*. New York: St. Martin's Press.

Orren, Karen. 1974. *Corporate Power and Social Change: The Politics of the Life Insurance Industry*. Baltimore: Johns Hopkins University Press.

Peterson, George E. 1980. "Federal Tax Policy and the Shaping of Urban Development" in Arthur D. Solomon, ed. 1980. *The Prospective City*, Ch. 13.

Peterson, Paul E. 1981. *City Limits*. Chicago: University of Chicago Press.

Peterson, Paul E. and Paul Kantor. 1977. "Political Parties and Citizen Participation in English City Politics." *Comparative Politics*, Vol. 9 (January), 51–72.

Sawers, Larry. 1978. "Cities and the Countryside in the Soviet Union and China" in William Tabb and Larry Sawers, ed. 1978. *Marxism and the Metropolis*. New York: Oxford University Press, pp. 338–364.

Szelenyi, Ivan. 1983. *Urban Inequalities under State Socialism*. New York: Oxford University Press.

U.S. Congress, Committee on Banking, Finance and Urban Affairs. 1979. *Summary of Requests for Comments on a Proposed National Development Bank*. Staff Study Prepared by the Subcommittee on Economic Stabilization, 96th Cong. 1st sess.

Vaughan, Roger J. 1977. *The Urban Impacts of Federal Policies*: Volume II, *Economic Development*. Santa Monica, Calif.: Rand.

Walker, Jeffrey. 1986. "Privatization of Housing Programs: Policies and Implications." *Journal of Housing*. Vol. 43, No. 6 (November), 241–253.

Weinstein, James. 1968. *The Corporate Ideal and the Liberal State: 1900–1918*. Boston: Beacon.

Yates, Douglas. 1977. *The Ungovernable City*. New Haven: Yale University Press.

Index